LIBERTY, RETRENCHMENT AND REFORM

In common with republicanism or socialism in continental Europe, Liberalism in nineteenth-century Britain was a mass movement. By focussing on the period between the 1860s and the 1880s, this book sets out to explain why and how that happened, and to examine the people who supported it, their beliefs, and the way in which the latter related to one another and to reality.

Popular support for the Liberal party was not irrational in either its objectives or its motivations: on the contrary, its dissemination was due to the fact that the programme of reforms proposed by the party leaders offered convincing solutions to some of the problems perceived as being the most urgent at the time. Part 1 examines popular Liberal attitudes towards issues of economic and social reform, starting from an analysis of what ordinary people thought and the way they expressed it – 'the language' of popular Liberalism. As one labour leader put it in 1878, the mainstays of popular Liberalism could be summarised 'in the old watch-word of the Whigs of "Civil and Religious Liberty, Retrenchment and Reform"'. 'Liberty' and 'Retrenchment' are discussed in Part 1, which concentrates on questions of content and rational argument, while 'Reform' – democracy as the hoped-for panacea – is at the core of Part 11. The latter gradually switches the focus on communication, and the means wherby the activists managed to involve those of a less developed political consciousness. Here rational arguments and emotional factors are studied as they affected one another, leading to a climax in the last chapter: an investigation of Gladstone's 'rational-charismatic' leadership.

This is a revealing, innovative synthesis of the history of popular support for the Liberal party, which emphasises the extent to which Liberalism stood in a relationship of continuity with British radical traditions, and shared in the common heritage of European and American democracy.

LIBERTY, RETRENCHMENT AND REFORM

Popular Liberalism in the Age of Gladstone,
1860–1880

EUGENIO F. BIAGINI

Sir James Knott Research Fellow,
University of Newcastle upon Tyne

CAMBRIDGE UNIVERSITY PRESS

Cambridge
New York   Port Chester
Melbourne   Sydney

To my mother, Federica,
and to the memory of my father, Mario

Published by the Press Syndicate of the University of Cambridge
The Pitt Building, Trumpington Street, Cambridge CB2 1RP
40 West 20th Street, New York, NY 10011-4211, USA
10 Stamford Road, Oakleigh, Victoria 3166, Australia

© Cambridge University Press 1992

First published 1992

Printed in Great Britain at the University Press, Cambridge

A catalogue record for this book is available from the British Library

Library of Congress cataloguing in publication data
Biagini, Eugenio F.
Liberty, retrenchment, and reform: popular liberalism in the Age
of Gladstone, 1860–1880 / Eugenio F. Biagini.
p.   cm.
Includes bibliographical references and index.
ISBN 0521403154 (hard)
1. Great Britain – Politics and government – 1837–1901.
2. Liberalism – Great Britain – History – 19th century.   3. Gladstone,
W. E. (William Ewart), 1809–1898.   4. Liberal Party (Great Britain)
I Title.
DA560. B53 1992
941.081 – dc20   91–19673   CIP

ISBN 0 521 403154 hardback

CC

Contents

Illustrations (between pages 254 and 255)

Illustrations 1 (a–b) and 6 (a–e) are from the George Howell Collection, Bishopsgate Institute, London. Illustration 2 is from the J. Cowen Collection, Tyne and Wear Archives, Newcastle upon Tyne. Illustration 3 is from a photograph in the possession of Dr N. Scotland, who has kindly agreed to its reproduction here. Illustration 4 is from A. Howkins *Poor Labouring Men* (London, 1985) and Illustration 5 is reproduced from R. Groves *Sharpen the Sickle!* (London, 1949).

Acknowledgements

The debts of gratitude that I have accumulated during the years leading to the completion of this book are many and considerable. I wish to thank Mr R. C. Webb, the Librarian of the Reference Library, Bishopsgate Institute, London, both for letting me quote from George Howell's Papers and the printed materials preserved in the Howell's Collection and those of nineteenth-century popular radical movements, and for the wealth of apparently inexhaustible personal erudition that he placed at my disposal on my every visit to the Institute. I also wish to thank the Librarian of the Tyne and Wear Archives for letting me quote from the Joseph Cowen Papers and Collection, and the Sub-Librarian of the Birmingham Library for letting me quote from the J. Chamberlain Papers. Always precious has been the help of the staff of the Cambridge University Library, and the unique borrowing facilities there have rendered my work much easier. I am greatly indebted to the courtesy, efficiency and competence of the staff responsible for: the Marshall Library, Cambridge; the Archives Centre of Churchill College, Cambridge; the archives of Nuffield College, Oxford; the British Library, Newspaper Division (Colindale), and Main Reading Room and Manuscript Room (Great Russell Street). I also owe a debt of gratitude to the Librarian of the Newcastle Central Reference Library, to the Archivist of the Durham Miners Association (Redhill, Durham), to the staffs of Durham County Record Office, the National Museum of Labour History, Manchester, St Deinol's Library, Hawarden, and the Archives of the 'Fondazione Feltrinelli' in Milan, and – in Florence – to Dr P. Pirovano of the 'Istituto E. Ragionieri', Dr M. Bossi of the 'Gabinetto G. P. Vieusseux', and the staff of the National Library.

I am very grateful to the Direttore, and Preside of the Classe di Lettere of the Scuola Normale Superiore di Pisa for the extraordinary facilities for research provided when I was a Perfezionando; to the Master and Fellows of Sidney Sussex College, Cambridge, for electing me a Visiting Scholar for the academic year 1985–6, and welcoming me amongst them with such cordiality and warmth that excelled even the highest expectations generated by the well-deserved reputation of British hospitality; and to the Rotary Foundation, for generously funding that period of research with one of their Fellowships. I am also very grateful to the Master and Fellows of Churchill College, who – electing me one of their number from 1987 – enabled me to complete this work in the best possible environment by providing much encouragement and support; to the Nuffield Foundation for funding my travels, and to the British Academy, for electing me to one of their 'Thanks-Offering to Britain Research Fellowships' for 1990–1, as this work was being completed and a new one – conceived to be its logical and chronological successor – was begun.

It is a particular pleasure to thank Professors Luciano Cafagna, Eric Hobsbawm, Norman McCord, Paolo Pombeni, Giorgio Spini, Roberto Vivarelli; and the scholars and doctors Richard Brent, John Burrow, John Coffey, Pietro Corsi, Mark Curthoys, John Dunbabin, Sheridan Gilley, Paul Ginsborg, Graham Goodlad, Richard Grove, Boyd Hilton, Jon Lawrence, Ross McKibbin, Rohan McWilliam, Jonathan Parry, Floyd Parsons, Henry Pelling, Raphael Samuel, John Shepherd, Jonathan Spain, Gareth Stedman Jones, Jonathan Steinberg, Duncan Tanner, Miles Taylor, Pat Thane, Frank Wilkinson, Stephen and Eileen Yeo, who in various ways have helped me with their valued advice. Special thanks go to to Franco Andreucci, Peter Clarke, Colin Matthew, Alastair Reid, Raffaele Romanelli, Massimo Rubboli, and Paolo Viola, for their teaching – which has been particularly influential – and also for their friendship, well-demonstrated in their readiness to discuss early versions of parts of this book.

But my greatest debt of gratitude is to Professor Derek Beales, who – during four crucial years – has been my informal supervisor, offering continual encouragement and always showing great patience, tolerance and a sense of humour which rendered my work not only more profitable, but also much more enjoyable. It is difficult to imagine what this book would have been like without his sensitive, prompt, obliging, and indefatigable guidance.

Finally, I would also like to express my gratitude to to Mr

Umberto Parrini, co-ordinator for the computer service of the Scuola Normale Superiore, for the courtesy with which he makes his rare competence in word processing available to laymen like myself. And I am very grateful to my friend Ian Wilson, who has shared many long hours of work (and jokes) to improve the somehow Italianized Dickensian English of this book.

Churchill College Cambridge   E.F.B.
March 1991

Abbreviations

[l.a.]	leading article
[n.t.]	no title
[rep.]	report
DNB	*Dictionary of National Biography, and Supplements,* Oxford, Oxford University Press, 1917–
DLB	*Dictionary of Labour Biography*, ed. by J. E. Bellamy and J. Saville, London, Macmillan, 1972–
PP	*Parliamentary Papers*
Hansard PD	*Hansard Parliamentary Debates*
BH	*Bee-Hive*
DC	*Durham Chronicle*
DN	*Daily News*
LM	*Leeds Mercury*
LW	*Lloyd's Weekly*
MG	*Manchester Guardian*
NC	*Newcastle Daily Chronicle*
NR	*National Reformer*
NW	*Newcastle Weekly Chronicle*
RN	*Reynolds's Newspaper*
TI	*The Times*
WT	*Weekly Times*

Note on the text

Capitals are used for nouns and adjectives descriptive of political opinions (such as Liberal, Radical, Labour, Socialist, Liberalism, Radicalism, etc.) only when there is a reference to membership of, or close association with, a formal political party organization or parliamentary group. In all other cases – i.e., when such nouns and adjectives have been used to refer to general opinions or tendencies, independent of formal party organizations – lower case is used. Thus, 'popular Liberals' is used as a synonym for 'Liberal party rank-and-file' or for supporters of the official Liberal party candidates while 'popular liberals' is used to refer to a wider group which included those hostile to local Liberal party organizations, e.g. the supporters of Joseph Cowen in Newcastle in the 1880s (see below, chapter 6). Likewise, 'labour' is used to describe trade unions and other working-class organizations while 'Labour' is reserved for organizations or persons affiliated to the Independent Labour party or the Labour Representation Committee.

Introduction

My sentiments are well expressed in the old watch-word of the Whigs of 'Civil and Religious Liberty, Retrenchment and Reform'. If they have in any way deserted their colours the fault is theirs and not mine.[1]

I believe in civil and religious liberty, for all men and for all countries, and consequently I am opposed to the dominant Anglican church in Catholic Ireland.

I believe in the virtues of justice on all occasions to effect a reconciliation of contending parties . . .

I believe that a volunteer force is far better for individual and national liberty than an array of red coats, whose duty is to obey any order issued by its commander, however tyrannical; and that the money spent on a standing army is much better in the pockets of the people . . .

I believe that every parish in the kingdom is much better able to manage its local affairs . . . than any centralized board sitting in London and appointed by the Crown or by Parliament.

I believe that [sic] the constitution of the metropolitan police to be defective and to be dangerous to the liberties of the people . . .

I believe it to be the duty of the State to insist that the elements of education are taught to all children under thirteen years of age . . . [2]

THEMES AND PROBLEMS

'Every boy and every gal, / That's born into the world alive / Is either a little Liberal, / Or else a little Conservative' – W. S. Gilbert wrote quite realistically in 1882. The fact that the two traditional parties managed to satisfy popular needs for political and parliamentary representation even after the enlargement of the

[1] G. Howell, 'Religious beliefs as a test question at elections', n.d. [but Spring 1878], in *Howell Collection*, ix, Letter Book, 230, No. 14.
[2] T. M. Webb, 'The Liberal's Creed', *BH*, 5 Sept. 1868, p. 1.

I

franchise has always fascinated political scientists and historians. In particular, it is remarkable that the radical reformers among the subaltern classes, the 'extreme left', who in France, Germany or Italy would have supported republican, socialist or anarchist politics, in Great Britain were loyal activists of the Liberal party. This book sets out to explain why and how that happened, focussing on the period between the mid-1860s and the mid-1880s.

As with any other, this work has methodological and interpretative presuppositions. I have followed an established trend in both Italian and British historiography[3] by assuming that ideas matter and that they have a social and political influence, since people's behaviour is deeply influenced by what they think, and especially by what they believe firmly. Moreover, I share Peter Clarke's understanding of Victorian politics as based on status and culture, rather than class, and consider his model to be of particular use in assessing the appeal of the Liberal party to the subaltern classes: what held the rank-and-file together were the values shared by activists, electors and supporters in general,[4] rather than the material interests of the social groups to which they belonged. Politics then did not have the function of providing favourable legislative changes for class-conscious groups: rather it supplied a collective identity to groups whose social and material interests did not in themselves lead to a politically relevant class consciousness.[5] I regard this approach as the only one offering workable hypotheses to explain the evidence that I have collected.

But the debate on these issues is very extensive. Two main problems need discussion here: the first is the nature of Gladstonian Liberalism in general, and the second is the nature of popular liberalism in particular. Since the publication of Shannon's work on the Bulgarian Agitation,[6] many historians have tended to stress the importance of religion in contrast to that of the more traditional 'secular' and economic components of liberalism. This interpretation has provided a useful corrective to the debate, which for too long had been excessively influenced by reductionist forms of

[3] See Chabod, *Storia della politica estera italiana* pp. 10, 14; Parry, *Democracy and Religion*, pp. 2–3.
[4] Clarke 'Electoral Sociology of Modern Britain', pp. 44–5.
[5] Harvie, *Lights of Liberalism*, p. 274.
[6] Shannon, *Bulgarian Agitation*; Parry, *Democracy and Religion*; Hilton, 'Gladstone's Theological Politics', in Bentley and Stevenson (eds.), *High and Low Politics in Modern Britain*, pp. 28–57; and Brent, *Liberal Anglican Politics*.

historical materialism. Nowadays, however, the danger is that we will go too far in the opposite direction, and replace historical materialism with a sort of 'historical mysticism', dismissing the role of rational motivation in politics.[7] This trend has been evident since the 1960s, when John Vincent wrote that

coherent thought among Liberal leaders was as rarefied as the atmosphere on the moon . . . Whatever the merits of all theories, no politician could gain from them any addition to his information about the world he had to deal with, or learn to pick out the great issues of policy and place them in relation to a vision of history.[8]

This approach has since been further popularized by D. A. Hamer, whose work is based on the assumption that

Liberal politics in the late nineteenth century were not controlled by any single and generally accepted system of thought, any set of ideas, creed or philosophy relevant to contemporary needs and situations and capable of guiding political practice. Liberals were not held together by any strong sense of common purpose. There was not seen to exist any central core of principle and belief to which were related and in which were cohered all the particular things that Liberals did and all the particular reforms in which they were interested.[9]

In other words, there was no such a thing as 'Liberalism', and the party held together only because its leaders managed periodically to raise 'some single issue or cause around which the diverse elements in Liberal politics could be induced to rally by being persuaded that it was of such overriding importance that their own various interests ought to be subordinated to it'.[10] In these difficult acrobatics the great mediator was Gladstone who, almost miraculously, invented unity and imposed it on backbenchers and rank-and-file alike.[11] No wonder that Hamer thinks that Liberalism outside Westminister was just 'faddism', with each pressure group pursuing in a sectarian way its own specific 'cause', and only occasionally being ready to co-operate with the others.[12]

---

[7] See Shannon, *Gladstone*; Cowling, *Religion and Public Doctrine*; Parry, 'Religion and the Collapse of Gladstone's First Government', pp. 71–101.

[8] Vincent, *Formation of the British Liberal Party*, pp. 68–9. See Goldman's effective criticism in 'The Social Science Association', pp. 123–4.

[9] Hamer, *Liberal Politics in the Age of Gladstone and Rosebery*, p. xi.

[10] *Ibid.*, p. 42; the thesis that liberalism was basically an invention has recently been suggested by Bentley, *Liberal Mind* and *Politics without Democracy*.

[11] Hamer, *Liberal Politics in the Age of Gladstone and Rosebery*, pp. 57–78.

[12] Hamer, *The Politics of Electoral Pressure*.

But this interpretation has a number of flaws, in that it under-values both the cultural unity of the Liberal movement at all levels, and the influence of intellectuals at a time when many politicians were themselves intellectuals. Moreover, even the 'faddists' were not so 'disintegrated' as Hamer maintains: in spite of the seeming anarchy, their aims had a remarkable cohesion and complementarity, to the extent that those who supported one radical cause also tended to uphold many of the others, as shown by the fact that the membership of these associations tended to overlap.[13] These facts can be explained only if we accept the existence of a global and articulated vision of politics and its goals.

In the present work I therefore maintain that Gladstonian Liberalism[14] had a remarkable 'ideological' cohesion, greater than that of any continental Socialism. This cohesion was founded not only on a Reformed religious culture and the Whig constitutional consensus, but also on the pervasive influence of the social and economic thought of the political economists, and J. S. Mill in particular. Cobden was important, as Vincent stresses, but his contribution consisted in clothing free trade with a moral cloak, not in elaborating a 'philosophy of history' (which was already there, having been articulated in the classical works of Macaulay). As for Gladstone's contribution, it was surely crucial, but it was not the alchemy of a 'magician of compromises': rather it was the work of a great executive politician who expressed 'with ideal adequacy both the whole civilization and the needs of the time', and 'translated a social, political, and economic vision, which was comprehensive as well as historically correct, into the clauses of a set of co-ordinated fiscal measures'.[15] Moreover, as a great charismatic leader, Gladstone was able to square the circle of making classical liberalism viable in a mass democracy.[16]

This leads us to consider popular liberalism more closely. When Vincent pointed to the existence of a specific working-class dimen-

---

[13] Harrison, 'State Intervention', in Hollis (ed.). *Pressure from Without*, p. 319.

[14] Both in Britain and elsewhere in Europe there were people and movements who shared in one or more of the main traditions of historical 'liberalism' without being connected with a political party called 'Liberal'. With this in mind I have reserved the terms 'Liberal' and 'Liberalism' (capital initials) for the Liberal party, its ideology, or the rank-and-file support for it. See Note on the Text, p. xvi.

[15] Schumpeter, *History of Economic Analysis*, p. 403; see Matthew, *Gladstone 1809–1874*.

[16] See Matthew, 'Rhetoric and Politics', in Waller (ed.), *Politics and Social Change*, pp. 34–58.

sion in rank-and-file Liberalism,[17] he thought that this phenomenon – which in those days seemed 'strange' – required a special explanation, different from that used to assess the participation of the subaltern classes in Chartism or the Labour party. Partly because of his devaluation of 'official' Liberalism, and partly because he could find no plausible reasons why the poor voted Liberal, Vincent maintained that for the working classes liberalism had a purely symbolic and psychological meaning,[18] and that the Gladstone they admired and followed was a product of their own imagination.[19] More recently a similarly irrationalistic approach has also been accepted by other scholars who – like D. C. Moore and P. Joyce – have tried to demonstrate that popular electoral behaviour was basically regulated by 'tribal' or 'feudal' loyalty to landlords, squires, or industrial entrepreneurs:[20] in this way politics were not 'a matter of reasoning, opinion, understanding, but perhaps of discipline exacted or, more often, of identification with a "community"'.[21] Derek Beales, however, has pointed out three weaknesses in this approach.[22] First, Moore and Joyce try to generalize from conclusions reached in the analysis of constituencies which were not representative of the national situation, as other historians have shown.[23] Second, the evidence offered by Moore and Joyce illustrates not only that many electors voted *for* the candidates of their patrons, but also that many others voted *against* – the latter constituting a large minority whose existence requires an explanation.[24] Finally, Moore and Joyce underestimate the effectiveness with which religion could generate 'independent' attitudes in popular politics, at least so far as the influence of the notables was disregarded when it contrasted with the politics of

---

[17] Vincent, *Formation of the British Liberal Party*, pp. 76–82.

[18] *Ibid.*, p. 113.

[19] *Ibid.*, p. 265.

[20] See Moore, *Politics of Deference*; Joyce, *Work, Society and Politics*. However, Joyce has subsequently modified his interpretation of popular politics (*Visions of the People*, pp. 27–141).

[21] Beales, 'Victorian Politics Observed', p. 702.

[22] Actually Beales deals only with Moore, but his observations apply to Joyce as well: *ibid.*, pp. 702–4.

[23] See Fraser, *Urban Politics in Victorian England*; Nossiter, *Influence, Opinion, and Political Idioms*; but also Waller, *Democracy and Sectarianism*, and Smith, *Conflict and Compromise*.

[24] Beales, 'Victorian Politics Observed', p. 702; McClelland, 'Patrick Joyce, Work, Society and Politics', p. 173.

the religious groups locally predominant.[25] The credibility of Moore's and Joyce's works as general interpretations (rather than as explanations of particular cases) is also limited because the best histories of popular radicalism during the second half of the century provide a very different insight into the politics of the subaltern classes. Tholfsen and Crossick[26] have demonstrated the importance and diffusion of 'independence' in popular politics, and Royle has studied the extent to which plebeian radicals could go on the basis of a consistent loyalty to this notion.[27] Royle's secularists and republicans were few, though influential, but working-class Dissent had a similar effect on a much larger scale, as has been shown by J. P. D. Dunbabin, R. Moore, N. Scotland, A. Howkins,[28] and others.

In this work I maintain that popular support for the Liberal party was not irrational in either its objectives or its motivations, but that – on the contrary – its dissemination was due to the fact that the programme of reforms proposed by the party leaders offered convincing solutions to some of the problems perceived to be real and urgent at the time. In this sense I also part company with Vincent, whose views on the irrationality of popular liberalism are in my opinion reductionist, and rather than helping to explain the existing problems only tend to generate new ones.

Moreover, I develop the hypothesis that working-class liberalism was not the fruit of the ideological success of bourgeois ideas during the mid-Victorian decades, but rather the continuation of older and genuinely popular plebeian traditions. Thus it is striking that most of the ingredients of Gladstonian Liberalism were already present in previously existing movements: independence, anti-State attitudes, free trade, anti-clericalism, had all been energetically supported by plebeian radicals since the days of Thomas Paine.[29] In this interpretation I also disagree with Marxist historians – though nowadays it is difficult to define who they are and what they stand for, since several of them have abandoned the materialist interpretation of history and have begun to argue that

[25] See Waller, *Democracy and Sectarianism*, pp. 1–81; Beales, 'Victorian Politics Observed', p. 703.
[26] Tholfsen, *Working Class Radicalism*; Crossick, *An Artisan Elite*.
[27] Royle, *Victorian Infidels*; and *Radicals, Republicans and Secularists*.
[28] Dunbabin, 'The "Revolt of the Field"'; Moore, *Pit-men, Preachers and Politics*; Scotland, *Methodism and the Revolt of the Fields*; Howkins, *Poor Labouring Men*.
[29] Prothero, *Artisans and Politics*.

the key to understanding the political behaviour of the subaltern classes is rather to be found in their culture. Many have pointed to the continuities between early nineteenth-century plebeian radicalism and Chartism; some even appreciate the 'Liberal phase' in working-class politics, and rather than rejecting it as a 'bourgeois' deviation, stress its reforming tendencies which 'prefigured' the Labour party.[30]

But historians who have not abandoned Marxism are still struggling to explain the 'anomaly' of an organized labour movement which was solidly Liberal. Among the interpretations proposed by them, the most extreme and least credible is that of Foster,[31] while one of the most convincing has been advanced by Hobsbawm. The latter has focussed on the 'spontaneous' development of the British labour movement,[32] and the frustration of 'revolutionary ideologists' as a result of its early acceptance and legalization. These factors, operating in a cultural climate dominated by liberal constitutionalism, 'enmeshed' the labour movement 'in the web of conciliation and collaboration more deeply, and far longer, than anywhere else'.[33] In other words – as Ralf Dahrendorf would put it – these legal and constitutional developments made it possible for the popular desire for political transformation to find satisfaction through institutional channels, while political conflicts were institutionalized and 'isolated'[34] from the complex of other conflicts. These phenomena meant the dissociation of the social subordination of the subaltern classes from their political subordination.

In this situation, a crucial role was played by the law and the ideology of 'neutrality' of the State. Again, this was not a completely new development in Victorian Britain, as in both the eighteenth century and the early nineteenth the law had been an instrument of social mediation.[35] However, in the second half of the nineteenth century the scale and effectiveness of this mediation changed in a significant way: after factory legislation, free trade,

---

[30] Samuel, 'Liberalism', pp. 1–2; Smith, 'Labour Tradition in Glasgow and Liverpool', pp. 32–56.
[31] See Foster, *Class Struggle and the Industrial Revolution*.
[32] Hobsbawm, *Labouring Men*, pp. 334 ff.
[33] *Ibid.*, p. 336.
[34] See Dahrendorf, *Class and Class Conflict*, pp. 269 ff.
[35] Thompson, *Whigs and Hunters*, pp. 258–69; Harvie, 'Revolutions and the Rule of Law', in Morgan (ed.), *Illustrated History of Britain*, pp. 421–60.

and fiscal reforms had reduced the bitterness of political and economic conflicts, the law became a terrain on which radicals and labour leaders could realistically hope to achieve significant gains,[36] as illustrated by two particularly significant examples, the debate on taxation and the struggle for the reform of the labour laws.[37]

This helps to explain why the tradition of revolutionary socialism was so weak in Great Britain.[38] McKibbin has shown that during the second half of the century a change took place in the mediation of class interests, since the reforms passed by both Liberals and Conservatives sanctioned the withdrawal of the State from the labour market. Once the ruling elites had placed politics on the level of the social contract,[39] the stress on the rule of law, which was a central tenet of classical liberalism,[40] also became crucial to the ideology and strategy of the organized labour movement: a fact important in itself for the understanding of popular liberalism, which was based not on empty rhetoric but on concrete results.

WHO WERE THE POPULAR LIBERALS?

But let us now focus on the social composition of the movement. For a long time the theory of the 'labour aristocracy' seemed to supply an answer to any question: it singled out a privileged social group within the working class – almost a sort of 'sub-class'[41] – which on account of its superior living standards and security of employment was ready to provide political support for the ruling classes.[42] But during the 1980s this interpretation has entered into an apparently irreversible crisis.[43] As a theory it had several weaknesses, including the difficulty of showing that the best paid and most 'respectable' workers formed a coherent stratum,[44] and that they were politically more moderate than the other sections of

---

[36] McKibbin, 'Why was there no Marxism in Great Britain?', pp. 322–4; see also Matthew, 'Politics of Mid-Victorian Budgets', p. 616.

[37] See *infra* chapters 2 and 3.

[38] McKibbin, 'Why was there no Marxism in Great Britain?', pp. 305–26.

[39] *Ibid.*, p. 319.

[40] Vivarelli, *Il fallimento del liberalismo*, p. 289.

[41] Hobsbawm, *Labouring Men*, pp. 272–3.

[42] Hobsbawm, *Age of Capital*, p. 225; and *Labouring Men*, p. 325.

[43] See Gray, *The Aristocracy of Labour in Nineteenth-Century Britain*, pp. 63–5; Hobsbawm, *Worlds of Labour*, pp. 215–19.

[44] See Hobsbawm, *Labouring Men*, pp. 276, 279–80, 295.

the working classes.[45] More recently Hobsbawm has even admitted that the very use of the word 'aristocracy' in this connection can be misleading, since the 'better-off' among the working classes included about 40 per cent (rather than 10 per cent, as previously assumed) of the workers.[46]

But the doctrine is not simply untenable: it is also superfluous, as Stedman Jones has written.[47] One of the questions which the theory of the 'labour aristocracy' tried to explain was the change in popular politics between the 'revolutionary' first half of the century, and the 'bourgeois' second half: but in the light of recent research this alleged shift appears much less important than the elements of continuity characterizing popular radicalism throughout the century.[48] Important changes did take place during the second half of the century, but they primarily concerned not the attitude of the subaltern classes, but that of the ruling classes, as I have suggested in the previous section: a change which is well symbolized by the fact that a man like Joseph Arch, who in the 1830s would have been transported like the 'Tolpuddle Martyrs', was by the 1880s accepted as a personification of the 'respectable' working man. As for the shift in the tone and rhetoric of popular radicalism, this can easily be accounted for once the role of generational changes is considered, as A. J. Reid has demonstrated in his important essay on Thomas Wright.[49]

Historians are now revising their interpretations along these lines. Dorothy Thompson has conceded that Chartism differed from previous radical movements more because of its dimensions and dissemination throughout the country, than because of its programme.[50] In a more energetic and consistent way Stedman Jones has argued for an interpretation of Chartism as alien to industrial society, and based on a strong continuity with eighteenth-century radicalism:[51] Chartist ideology was in general that

[45] Pelling, *Social Geography*, pp. 424–5; and *Popular Politics*, pp. 56 ff.; this interpretation has eventually been accepted by Hobsbawm (*Worlds of Labour*, p. 223).
[46] Hobsbawm, *Worlds of Labour*, pp. 182–3, 218, 226, 245–6; again, it is remarkable that only in 1979 did Hobsbawm accept this point, which was originally made by Pelling in 1968 (*Popular Politics*, pp. 53–4).
[47] Stedman Jones, *Languages of Class*, p. 107.
[48] See in particular Stedman Jones, 'Rethinking Chartism', in *Languages of Class*; and editors' introduction to Biagini and Reid (eds.), *Currents of Radicalism*.
[49] Reid, 'Essays of Thomas Wright', in Winter (ed.), *The Working Class*, pp. 171–86.
[50] Thompson, *The Chartists*, p. 47.
[51] Stedman Jones, *Languages of Class*, pp. 18, 171, 173.

of 'Locke and Adam Smith, viewed through the eyes of Godwin',[52] based on 'natural rights' and including 'the natural right of the producer to his *property*, the fruit of his labour'.[53] Only landed property was criticized since 'the works of God's creation' could not be 'bought and sold in the market, the same as if they were the works of human hands': it was the very principle of the right to property which forbade it.[54]

But if there is continuity between Chartism and pre-Chartist movements, there is also continuity between Chartism and popular Liberalism as proposed by Brian Harrison and Patricia Hollis in their work on Lowery,[55] and confirmed by a number of other historians with fresh evidence from local case-studies on Oldham,[56] Halifax,[57] Leeds and West Yorkshire.[58] This has been further illustrated by T. C. Smout, who has placed Scottish Chartism in its proper context by emphasizing the influence of the American and French Revolutions filtered by a deep faith in the virtue of moderation, 'the power of reasoned argument', the reluctance to condone violence 'as a means to a good end', and 'a belief that cooperation with the middle classes could still ultimately pay higher dividends than class struggle'.[59] Like Stedman Jones, Smout has also contributed towards dismissing historiographical superstitions about popular desire for 'State socialism' and has made it clear that 'the early Victorian world was still far from thinking in terms of any sort of government intervention as being a good thing, except in exceptional circumstances. Chartism was about liberty, and about the political self-help of the people acting collectively':[60] exactly the same can be said of later popular liberalism. Nowadays, even Dorothy Thompson and Hobsbawm admit that in the second half of the century it was 'Chartist democracy which still prevailed amid the sober suits of Liberal

---

[52] *Ibid.*, p. 135.
[53] *Ibid.*, p. 156.
[54] *Ibid.*
[55] See Harrison and Hollis, *Robert Lowery*, p. 19.
[56] Weaver, *John Fielden*, pp. 272–3.
[57] Tiller, 'Halifax 1847–1858', in Thompson and Epstein, *Chartist Experience*, pp. 312–15, 338–40.
[58] Layburn and Reynolds, *Liberalism and the Rise of Labour*, pp. 20–1. See also, on Northumberland, the evidence offered by Muris, *Thesis*.
[59] Smout, *A Century of the Scottish People*, p. 234.
[60] *Ibid.*, p. 239.

Radicalism'.[61] There is nothing surprising in these acknowledgements, save the fact that it has taken almost a century for historians to return to the common wisdom of the Victorians.[62]

One of the last doubts entertained by some scholars derives from the growing emphasis on self-help after 1850, which could indicate the existence of introspective tendencies within radicalism after the defeats and frustrations of the 1840s.[63] But in fact even the radicals of the 1830s and the Chartists 'stressed the importance of collective self-help and "moral" improvement',[64] while all three generational 'schools' of working-class radicals of Thomas Wright's essays prided themselves on the 'virtue of independence'.[65] The latter appears to have been the most typical value of artisan and peasant culture throughout the 'European world',[66] so that if the original traditions of the British left appear to have been closer to Paine's decentralized democracy than to any socialist model, this was not one of the famous 'peculiarities of the English'.

In fact, urban popular liberalism was made up of social groups similar to those which in revolutionary France had formed the backbone of the *sans-culotterie*, or in America the rank-and-file of Jeffersonian and Jacksonian radicalism: a mixture of independent artisans, small employers and tradesmen, and organized workers.[67] They did not consider themselves to be a class, but 'the People',[68] a group to which there belonged (potentially) all those who were excluded from privilege and aristocratic 'monopoly'.[69] It has been

---

[61] Hobsbawm, *Worlds of Labour*, p. 267; Thompson, *The Chartists*, pp. 301, 307. The same point was made by Clarke in 1971: *Lancashire and the New Liberalism*, pp. 33–4.

[62] For a Victorian interpretation of Chartism as a precursor to Gladstonian Liberalism see [lett. by] B. Wilson, 'The Independent Labour Party and Mr Ernest Jones', *Halifax Courier*, 23 Mar. 1895, p. 2.

[63] Morris, 'Samuel Smiles and the Genesis of Self-Help', pp. 89–109.

[64] Epstein, 'Chartist Movement in Nottingham', in Thompson and Epstein, *Chartist Experience*, p. 222; see Johnson, 'Really Useful Knowledge', in Clarke *et al.* (eds.), *Working Class Culture*, p. 77.

[65] Reid, 'Thomas Wright', p. 180. See Crossick, *An Artisan Elite*, pp. 196–7; Tholfsen, *Working Class Radicalism*, p. 246.

[66] See for an American example Zahler, *Eastern Working Men and the National Land Policy*, pp. 36–7; and for an Italian example Sarti, *Long Live the Strong*, pp. 39, 101.

[67] Williams, 'Druids and Democrats', in Samuel and Stedman Jones (eds.), *Culture, Ideology and Politics*, p. 253. See Soboul, *Les sans-culottes parisiens*, pp. 451–2, 473; Palmer, 'Popular Democracy in the French Revolution', p. 453; Peterson, *The Jefferson Mind in the American Image*, pp. 81–2.

[68] See for an example J. A. Partridge, 'House of Lords', *BH*, 4 Nov. 1871, p. 1.

[69] Kirk, *Working Class Reformism*, p. 61; See Cobb, *Les armées revolutionaires*, p. 51; Soboul, *Les sans-culottes parisiens*, p. 473.

said that this situation had changed by 1848,[70] and certainly the role of organized labour became more prominent from the 1860s. Yet, there are many examples that the expression 'the people' continued to be used in the all-inclusive sense of the 1830s.[71] Indeed, not only in Britain, but also in America, France[72] and Italy,[73] plebeian radicals preferred to speak of 'the people' rather than of 'the working class' for a large part of the century. In Britain, this tendency lasted for longer and was reinforced by the fact that – as a perplexed German miner reported after visiting Newcastle in the 1890s – 'the middle and working classes [were] on very familiar terms . . . because they [were] brought together in clubs and religious organizations', and Dissenting denominations 'strive[d] to outdo each other in the exercise of practical Christianity'.[74] In such circumstances, the old notion of the town forming a 'community' was preserved or recreated. The ultimate ideal was the spirit of village politics, the direct democracy of the town meetings, a sort of British *landesgemeinde* – a fact reminding us of the common heritage of European democracy, stretching from New England to the Swiss cantons, and back to the Italian republics of the Middle Ages.[75]

Plebeian radicals were consequently ready to accept political messages which centred on 'a democratic crusade against the privileged orders',[76] like the one contained in Bright's Liberalism, though neither they nor their middle-class leaders were ready as yet to assume the direct responsibilities of government. Therefore,

---

[70] Crossick, 'Shopkeepers, Master Artisans, and the Historian', p. 15; and 'The Petite Bourgeoisie in Nineteenth Century Britain', pp. 73–4; both in Crossick and Haupt (eds.), *Shopkeepers and Master Artisans.*

[71] [L.a.], 'Politics for "common people"', *LW*, 26 Jan. 1868, p. 6; see Roe, *Kenealy and Tichborne*, pp. 164–73; McWilliam, 'Radicalism and popular culture', in Biagini and Reid (eds.), *Currents of Radicalism*, pp. 44–64. Thomas Wright offered a different interpretation when he wrote: '"The People" – 'the phrase being used as a synonym for the working classes' (Wright, *Our New Masters*, p. 62). A similar usage can be found in an article by Thomas Burt ('Working men and reform', *NW*, 28 Jan. 1867, p. 4), where 'people' and 'working men' were used almost synonymously. However the identification was meant as an absolutization of the working classes as the 'people', not as a relativization of the concept of 'people' to mean the working class: working men were 'the nation', and consequently Burt praised the 'few noble-minded men in the middle and upper ranks of life who are standing forth to fight what is emphatically your battle'.

[72] Magraw, *France 1815–1914*, p. 105.

[73] See Soldani, 'Contadini, operai e "popolo"', pp. 557–613.

[74] Harrison, *Drink and the Victorians*, p. 366.

[75] Fisher, *The Republican Tradition in Europe.*

[76] Trevelyan, *John Bright*, pp. 267–8; Fraser, *Trade Unions and Society*, p. 148.

the adjective 'plebeian' – with its allusion to 'simultaneous resistance and insurgency', but also 'dependence upon the ruling orders and classes'[77] – is well suited to describing this political culture: a culture somehow appropriately symbolized by the imagery of the 'ass', common in Bright's speeches as well as in the popular press,[78] later adopted by Bradlaugh,[79] and significantly also by the Independent Labour party (ILP).[80]

What is particularly interesting, though, is that Gladstone's party did not limit itself to unifying and re-vitalizing popular urban radicalism: it also evoked a rural radicalism, which by 1885 may even have become the backbone of popular Liberalism. In the West Country, in Wales, in the Midlands, in East Anglia, in the north-east of England (including Yorkshire), and in the whole of Scotland, miners, shepherds, organized labourers, small farmers and crofters became increasingly politicized from the early 1870s. In some cases, such as the Northumberland miners, this revival had a long tradition of radical and Nonconformist militancy,[81] but in general it was quite a new phenomenon.

In rural constituencies the electoral fortunes of the Liberal party depended on a variety of factors, among which the most important were the structure of landed property, the tolerance of landlords, and the local strength of Methodism, 'Old Dissent' or Calvinism – the last ones being the stabilizing factors in popular Liberalism from Cornwall to Sutherland. The regions where stock-raising predominated allowed a greater independence to working-class electors, and in some instances historians have even spoke of an English version of 'Frontier conditions'.[82] There was a similar situation

[77] Medick, 'Plebeian Culture in the Transition to Capitalism', in Samuel and Stedman Jones (eds.), *Culture, Ideology and Politics*, p. 86.

[78] 'Issacchar is a strong ass, crouching between two burdens' (Bright cit. in [l.a.], 'The Political Ass and Its Burdens', *NW*, 24 Nov. 1866, p. 4).

[79] 'The Englishman, like Issacchar, is a patient beast of burden, crouching down between its two grievous loads, Toryism and Whiggism; but even the long-enduring ass is dangerous when it turns and uses teeth and feet alike against its persecutors' (C. Bradlaugh, 'To the Right Hon. W. E. Gladstone, MP', *NR*, 31 Oct. 1869, p. 274).

[80] See the cartoon showing 'Labour' as an ass with a Phrygian cap, which is about to unsaddle 'Capitalism' after having unsaddled 'Landlordism': *Special May Day Number of 'Justice'*, London, May 1895, in *John Johnson Coll.*, 'First Numbers Political, 2'. The imagery was recurrent also in continental Socialist movements: see Andreucci, 'Il mondo dell "Asino"', in *Il marxismo collettivo*, pp. 141–83.

[81] See Briggs, 'The Local Background of Chartism', in Briggs (ed.), *Chartist Studies*, p. 2; Dickinson, *Radical Politics in the North-east of England*, pp. 12–20; Muris, *Thesis*, pp. 22, 32–3.

[82] Pelling, *Social Geography*, p. 320.

among peasant farming communities in vigorously Calvinistic and/
or Nonconformist environments like Wales, the West Country and
Scotland – the 'Celtic fringe' where Liberal seats were generally
safe.[83] Another preserve of Liberal votes was the mining village in
predominantly Nonconformist regions. There, Liberalism was a
community creed embracing the whole of the local population: as
Hobsbawm has written, ' "Everyone" was for Gladstone'.[84] The
cases of Durham and Northumberland – where the Liberals
preserved their hegemony even in difficult years like 1874[85] – are
well known,[86] but similar patterns can also be found elsewhere,
like the Forest of Dean[87] and the Staffordshire Potteries.[88] Finally,
there was a comparable situation in the purely agricultural villages
of a number of regions, and particularly the Midlands and East
Anglia: there, Nonconformity and closely-knit community life were
the ingredients of the rural democracy of Joseph Arch,[89] and the
labourers were still attached to the lifestyles and mentality of the
independent peasant.[90]

The diversity of these examples and the further variations which
can be listed by comparing them with the urban cases, make it
impossible to reduce popular liberals to a specific social category
or group.[91] But one of the effects of this irreducible lack of
homogeneity is, by contrast, to further enhance their remarkable
homogeneity at the cultural level. It is difficult to escape the
conclusion that throughout the country there was a correlation
between popular liberalism and the geography and strength of the
Reformation (rather than simply of Nonconformity). The alliance
between Christianity and Liberalism was one of the reasons for
the latter's success, while the separatist zeal of congregational

[83] *Ibid.*, p. 158–73, 380–81. Though the concept of the 'Celtic Fringe' is debatable (see
   Robbins, *Nineteenth Century Britain*, pp. 97–130), more important than ethnic differences
   was the compactly Calvinistic culture of the Scots, Welsh, and West Countrymen (see
   Biagini, 'Rappresentanza virtuale e democrazia di massa', pp. 810–11 and n. 7, 823 and
   n. 83).
[84] Hobsbawm, *Worlds of Labour*, p. 248.
[85] See [l.a.], 'The Toryless County', *NW*, 14 Feb. 1874, p. 4.
[86] See Moore, *Pit-men, Preachers and Politics*.
[87] Pelling, *Social Geography*, p. 156.
[88] *Ibid.*, pp. 272–4; Anderton, *Thesis*, p. 104.
[89] Pelling, *Social Geography*, pp. 104–5, 426–7. See Charlesworth (ed.), *An Atlas of Rural
   Protest*, pp. 172–3.
[90] Obelkevich, *Religion and Rural Society*, pp. 24, 27.
[91] Hobsbawm, *Worlds of Labour*, p. 248.

polity prevented the development of any 'Christian democratic' party.

Thus, working-class liberals provide a good illustration of E. P. Thompson's thesis on the 'peculiarities of the English', and more particularly of his assertion that a large part of the history of the labour movement and the left in Great Britain should be read with the centrality of Nonconformity in mind.[92] So close was the correlation between Nonconformity and popular liberalism that prototypes of the Thompsonian model of the Nonconformist radical worker abounded wherever the Liberal party was electorally strong. All plebeian Dissenters – including not only Methodists, but also Congregationalists, Baptists, Presbyterians[93], and even organized atheists – shared a Puritan cultural background[94] requiring high moral standards[95] and stimulating political radicalism. Their conflict with the Anglican Church was mainly political and social and was rationally motivated, being the struggle of subordinate groups to achieve self-determination,[96] both of individual and of the community to which he belonged, against religious and political 'orthodoxy'. As Deborah Valenze has written, the faith of plebeian Dissenters 'was simple in theory and free in style. The sects derived ideas concerning self-expression, sexual equality, self-government, and the priesthood of all believers from seventeenth-century Quakerism and early Methodism'.[97] As in the days of

---

[92] Thompson, 'The Peculiarities of the English' in *The Poverty of Theory*, p. 58; also see 'An Open Letter to Leszeck Kolakowski, in *The Poverty of Theory*, p. 106; see also Samuel, 'British Marxist Historians, 1880–1980', p. 50. Indeed, this tradition was continued well into the twentieth century: if in 1906 60 per cent of Labour MPs had a Nonconformist background, in 1962 this proportion was still as high as 50 per cent (Hobsbawm, *Worlds of Labour*, p. 181; Alexander and Hobbs, 'What influences Labour MPs?', in Rose (ed.), *Studies in British Politics*, pp. 111–21). K. D. Brown has qualified these figures by showing that a Nonconformist background does not necessarily entail personal membership of a church ('Nonconformity and the British labour movement', pp. 113–20): but Scotland, and possibly Wales and the English mining communities, do not fit in with his revision (Knox, 'Religion and the Scottish Labour Movement', pp. 609–30).

[93] Reid, 'Robert Knight', in Biagini and Reid (eds.), *Currents of Radicalism*, pp. 214–43; Lancaster, *Radicalism, Cooperation and Socialism*, p. 66; Knox, 'Religion and the Scottish Labour Movement, 1900–39', p. 610. In late nineteenth-century Bethnal Green, manual workers represented 55 per cent of married men among Baptists, 52 per cent among Wesleyans, and 38 per cent among Congregationalists (McLeod, *Class and Religion in the Late Victorian City*, p. 33).

[94] Hobsbawm, *Labouring Men*, pp. 372–3.

[95] Hobsbawm, *Rebels*, pp. 145–6; and *Labouring Men*, p. 372.

[96] Pelling, *Popular Politics*, p. 21.

[97] Valenze, 'Pilgrims and Progress in Nineteenth Century England', in Samuel and Stedman Jones (eds.), *Culture Ideology, and Politics*, p. 144.

Cromwell, radical Dissent constituted not simply a popular religion, but also an example of democracy, a whole frame of mind, indeed an 'alternative culture',[98] which stood up against the aristocratic institutions and values of the day.[99] The programme of plebeian liberalism was to a large extent the *political* projection of the Dissenting experience of its activists.

Yet, I am unable to agree with Jonathan Parry's thesis that 'it was *only* religious issues that *were* able to link the world with which the politically interested public was concerned to the high political world'.[100] Not only were fiscal questions paramount – as he concedes – but there were a variety of other crucial issues, like electoral reform, which were ultimately related to the question of democracy. The latter was the really all-embracing issue for popular liberals. To them religion, far from ruling politics, was a battle-ground only in so far as it affected democracy and liberty: Anglican ascendancy in Ireland and Roman Catholic despotism in Italy, for example, were opposed not for the religious principles they propounded, but because they were 'tyrannical' and politically incompatible with liberalism, let alone popular radicalism. These were conflicts about church power, not religious principles. Likewise, Dissent's democratic polity and separatist attitude in its relationship with the State offered a political model which had acquired further prestige as a result of its adoption by the greatly admired United States. But as far as theology was concerned, the differences between Church and Dissent, Auld Kirk and Free Kirk were politically uninspiring. Indeed, when only the preaching of the gospel was at stake, there was scope for wide-ranging co-operation between denominations: this is particularly well illustrated by the 'ecumenical' spirit of the Moody and Sankey campaigns – a mass phenomenon, involving from three to four million people between 1873–5. Nonconformists, Anglicans and Kirkmen heartily joined in a common effort, and even in Catholic Dublin Moody the Congregationalist and Sankey the Methodist attracted an audience of more than 20,000.[101]

Thus, the title of this book well summarizes the mainstays of popular liberalism, as well as the kind of struggles in which its

[98] Howkins, *Poor Labouring Men*, p. 56.
[99] Springall, *Labouring Life in Norfolk Villages*, p. 77.
[100] Parry, *Democracy and Religion*, p. 53, the first italics are mine.
[101] See Coffey, *Thesis*, p. 6.

supporters were involved. 'Liberty' – 'civil and religious' – included both the Nonconformist and Secularist crusades for equality before the law, and the trade union struggles for a more equal law, as well as the other radical campaigns described mainly in chapters, 1, 3 and 4. 'Retrenchment', the central theme in anti-State radicalism – an old artisan creed[102] – constituted the ground on which the Liberals could always be confident of meeting with unanimous support in all sections of the party, both in the House and the country; via free trade, it involved redistribution of taxation from the mass of consumers to those better able to pay. And 'Reform', which first and foremost meant reform of the franchise and the representative system, and ultimately the democ-ratization – or, as some said, the 'Americanization' – of the whole society; but which also implied a whole frame of mind, an opting for a gradualist – though determined and systematic – approach to the amendment of the social and political evils of the world.

In the following chapters I have tried to look at these themes from different angles, exploring them in their change, reciprocal interdependence, and in relation to the question of democracy. Chapter 1 analyses 'the language' of popular liberalism, and the influence of the heritage of the Reformation and of the two British Revolutions (Puritan and Whig) on popular radical views of contemporary phenomena – such as the Italian Risorgimento, the American Civil War and the Paris Commune. Then chapter 2 studies the way in which this political idiom was reflected in plebeian liberal ideals of social organization and government. I point out some strong parallels with the politics and ideology of the American Jeffersonians and Jacksonians, with their emphasis on the model citizen as a yeoman or artisan 'independent' of patronage, State subsidy and upper-class control alike. Such a frame of mind lay at the root of popular support for free trade as the policy of 'no burdens on the striving poor', also implying, in fact, no State control on the labour market. This was the system which best suited not only the popular liberal project of a self-governing society of independent producers, but also the reality of every-day life for the common people – be they labouring con-sumers, members of co-operative societies, or trade union activists. Such correspondence of means and ends, and of opportunity and

---

[102] Stedman Jones, *Language of Chartism*, p. 168.

ideals is typical of the ideology of popular liberalism, and contributes towards explaining its prolonged success.

Yet there was little complacency in its rhetoric; in spite of the praises lavished on Gladstone's achievements, the emphasis was always on further reforms, freer trade, lower taxation, central government 'minimized' even further – and, simultaneously, greater popular control of whatever public intervention was enacted. The problems of economic reform were thus identified with those of political control, an aspect also illustrated in chapter 3 on the 'social question'. Here the main point is that all the remedies envisaged implied that the workers were to be given – individually or collectively – management of their own life and work, as well as of the life of the whole community *via* representative local government. Still, theirs would not be a sort of 'dictatorship of the independent working men', but a democracy under the 'rule of law', as in the Puritan tradition. Once more the comparison is appropriate, since labour reformers maintained that the law whose rule should be enforced was not only – nor even necessarily – the law of the country, but first and foremost the law of God, the Bible being their supreme *Code Civil*. This was one of the factors which opened the gate to the 'exceptions to the rule' of *laissez-faire*, including factory legislation, public health, drink control and poor relief. However, popular plans for solving the 'social question' culminated not in the various proposals for community self-policing, but in land reform, aimed at re-establishing the dispossessed yeomanry and restoring the lost balance between country and town. This also meant that, since the land was still largely controlled by the ruling aristocracy, no final solution to the 'social question' would be feasible until full democracy had been achieved. Thus – as in the days of the Chartists – social reform had to be preceded by political reform.

Chapter 4 deals with two other aspects of this struggle for popular control of society: the intellectual and spiritual sides, involving education and anti-clericalism. The latter two issues were closely linked – both in Britain and elsewhere in Europe – as the established Church's influence on the minds of future generations was disputed by religious and irreligious 'dissenters' alike. In Victorian Britain this aspect of the anti-clerical conflict became institutionalized through the electoral procedure of the comparatively democratic school boards, which extended the ethos of the anti-clerical Dissenting polity far beyond the chapels' direct range of action. While the case was more complicated with the 'upas tree' of the established Churches, especially that of sacerdotal Anglicanism, democracy – this time at a national level – once again was to be the cure; the Reform Act of 1867 had brought Disestablishment to Ireland; the expectation in the 1880s was that greater democracy would 'liberate' the Church from 'State control and patronage' in the rest of the Kingdom as well.

This leads on to the discussion of franchise reform in chapter 5, the representative system as community politics in chapter 6 and the 'nationalization' of community politics in chapter 7. Together these three chapters form part II, which deals with 'democracy' in its various spheres as the hoped-for solution to the problems outlined in part I. While the latter focuses on questions of content and rational argument, part II increasingly includes the way in which that content was communicated, and the means whereby the activists managed to involve those of a less developed political consciousness. Here rational arguments and emotional factors are studied as they affected one another; the climax is reached in the last chapter, an investigation of Gladstone's 'rational-charismatic' leadership. While the chronological limit of 1880 has generally been respected in part I, in part II I have felt free to pursue my argument into the mid-1880s or even later, when the question of democracy received a satisfactory settlement; no similar attempt could have been made in part I, as the questions examined there were not answered within the decade, and indeed entered into a new and more complex phase.

The basic theme in part II is community: in contrast to the Thatcherite panegyrics of Victorian individualism, nineteenth-century liberalism – and especially its *popular* manifestation – was a 'community ideology'. As the reader will discover, this involved important restrictions and qualifications of individual liberty. In the case of the franchise, for example, even 'manhood suffrage' was still contained within modified theories of 'virtual representation'; the very concept of representation did not involve individuals, but groups – including households – with a collective, corporate identity. The last section of chapter 6 shows that the only successful Lib-lab MPs were those leaders who could identify with the idiosyncrasies of local working-class communities, for which they also provided some sort of charismatic leadership.

The last chapter (7) translates these concepts of representation from the local/regional level, to the national one. Gladstone provided the focus necessary both for the full deployment of the energies of popular liberalism, and for the co-ordination of its various organizations. The 'Grand Old Man' allowed the Liberal party to reach its maximum effectiveness not only in mobilizing the people whose political consciousness was already articulate – both electors and non-electors – but also in reaching out to the great numbers of those who were not committed to any political idea. Some of the latter were generally uninterested in politics, but tended to react and become more active when well-argued programmes were displayed and advertised with spectacular propaganda and emotional appeals. Chapter 7 is designed to provide a conclusion to this book by completing the reply to the initial question regarding the success of the Liberal party as a mass movement. But it also represents a link between the present book and the next one – on which I am currently working – which will deal with popular attitudes to issues of foreign politics, the Empire and Ireland: basically, the themes of the Midlothian campaigns.

A final warning. This book does not attempt to demonstrate – nor does it imply – that all working men were Liberals. It is not about working-class politics or culture in general, or about the working classes as such. It is about popular *liberalism*: it describes what beliefs the latter entailed, how they related to one another and to reality; it offers an assessment of the reasons why for such a long period so many working men were basically satisfied with the solutions to the questions of domestic politics proposed by Gladstone's party.

A NOTE ON THE SOURCES

The sources used for this research are largely the traditional ones of political history, and in particular of the history of popular politics: papers of politicians and trade union leaders, Parliamentary Papers and Debates, contemporary printed works, biographies and newspapers. The latter deserve a short discussion here because their reliability and value has been questioned more than once in recent years.[103]

[103] See in particular Ellegård, 'Darwin and the General Reader', pp. 7–394, and particularly pp. 18ff.; and Pickering's criticism of Stedman Jones' use of newspaper evidence in 'Class without Words', pp. 144–5.

A summary examination of footnotes in books on Victorian Britain shows that the works based mainly on the evidence contained in the newspaper press are much more numerous than one would expect on the basis of what the authors are ready to admit.[104] This arises from the fact that newspapers, unlike other sources, are really 'containers' of sources of various kinds. But first of all it is useful to recapitulate the reasons why the newspaper press – both daily and weekly – is particularly relevant for the study of the politics of the subaltern classes in nineteenth-century Britain.

The first point to make is that from the 1850s and 60s there was a series of newspapers which enjoyed a really mass circulation: in particular, between 1866 and 1886 *Reynolds's Newspaper*, the *Weekly Times*, and *Lloyd's Weekly* sold respectively *c.* 350,000, 300,000 and 600,000 copies per issue.[105] The newspapers published in the industrial regions had a circulation which was smaller, but geographically more concentrated, and therefore as influential at a local level: this is the case with the *Newcastle Weekly Chronicle*, one of the newspapers of the north-eastern workers,[106] which in 1875 sold 57,000 copies in Northumberland and Durham.[107]

Moreover, popular newspapers in general had a very pronounced political identity. Not only was the percentage of the content devoted to political news extremely high,[108] but also the other news – even 'police news' – often had a markedly political character (in the sense of being strongly anti-aristocratic):[109] indeed, it was not possible to read *Reynolds's* without assuming a political stance, and the very fact of buying a copy was a political act, as much as – on the continent – reading official Socialist papers like *Vorwärts!* or *L'Avanti!*.

Virginia Berridge has demonstrated that in the case of the mass-

---

[104] A remarkable case is Fraser, *Urban Politics in Victorian England*, which is almost completely based on newspaper evidence. But a similar case is that of another fundamental work, often quoted in these pages: Stedman Jones' 'Rethinking Chartism'.

[105] See Berridge, 'Popular Sunday Papers', in Boyce *et al.*, (eds.), *Newspaper History*, p. 263; and Berridge, *Thesis*, pp. 40–3. The figure published in *LW*, 15 Jun. 1879, p. 6, spoke of 612,902 copies 'on average'.

[106] See G. Howell to the Editor of the Newcastle Chronicle, 7 Nov. 1872, in *G. Howell Coll.*, *Letter Book ix*, p. 145; W. Crawford, 'Newcastle Weekly Chronicle', in *Durham Miners Association, Monthly Circular*, 1884, p. 6, in Durham Co. Rec. Office, D/DMA 8.

[107] Figures published in 'Circulation of *Newcastle Weekly Chronicle*', *NW*, 1 Jan. 1876, p. 4.

[108] Berridge, *Thesis*, pp. 257–8.

[109] *Ibid.*, p. 257.

circulation weeklies the identification between the newspaper and
the reader was as close in the 1870s as it had been for the
unstamped papers in the 1830s.[110] In particular, she has pointed
out that the percentage of advertisements was low in comparison
with the late nineteenth century. This implies that the profits of
these newspapers depended mainly on sales, and therefore on their
appeal to their readership. But there were two alternative strategies
which editors could follow to 'cultivate' this special relationship
with their readers. One was what a contributor to the *Bee-Hive*
described as the orthodox approach of the mid-Victorian press:

> Everyone is agreed that an ordinary leading article must faithfully reflect,
> or, at least, not go far beyond, the prevailing popular sentiments. At the
> same time it . . . should seek to represent, so far as practicable, the highest
> aspirations, the nobler aims and purposes of the average readers.[111]

Such an approach could be followed to the extent of periodically
modifying the newspaper's line in order to adapt it to the swings
in the readership's opinion – a strategy well-illustrated by *Lloyd's
Weekly*. This was a London newspaper owned by Edward Lloyd
(1815–90) – an enterprising journalist and businessman, son of a
shopkeeper[112] – who shared the editing with the radical-liberal
journalists Blanchard Jerrold (1826–84)[113] and Thomas Catling
(b. 1838).[114] Though on the whole it remained within the liberal
fold, *Lloyd's* regularly changed its politics, following, or even
anticipating, the changing mood of public opinion with a surprising
sense of timing: it was aggressively radical in 1866–7, it became
more moderate after 1868, anti-Gladstonian after 1873, supported
Hartington and Beaconsfield in 1876–8, and went back to Gladstonianism in 1879. Then, after supporting the Liberal governments between 1880 and 1886, it became Unionist before the
general election of that year on the basis of opportunistic considerations. As Lloyd and Catling admitted, they had to guess which
political line would be more popular, and to support it.[115] This
does not mean that the editors had no consistency at all, but that

---

[110] *Ibid.*, pp. 32–4.
[111] J. T. Hoskins, 'Federal Home Rule', *BH*, 6 Dec. 1873, p. 3.
[112] DNB, vol. XXXIII, *sub voce*.
[113] A professional writer of some renown: DNB, vol. XXIX, *sub voce*.
[114] Son of a gardener, he became editor of *Lloyd's* in 1884 following Jerrold's death: see
Catling, *My Life's Pilgrimage*, pp. 160 ff.
[115] Catling, *My Life's Pilgrimage*, pp. 168–9.

they tried to formulate the newspapers' line in terms sufficiently general to allow some flexibility. In fact Catling shared the creed of post-Chartist liberalism, which involved – as he maintained – the abatement of 'class monopoly', and 'free trade, a free press, the free expression of opinion, and all our social and religious liberties';[116] his were the politics of the southern-English centre-left – rather nationalist, and usually unmoved by, or even positively opposed to, crusading Nonconformist radicalism. Inevitably, *Lloyd's* was disliked by many of the most extreme radicals,[117] but attracted many southern liberal-minded working- and lower middle-class people. In commercial terms this strategy was very successful: by the end of the century *Lloyd's* boasted a circulation of about 1,000,000 copies, then apparently the largest in the world.[118]

An alternative approach was to try to 'make', rather than to reflect, public opinion: this was the traditional approach of the popular political press, the tradition of the 'unstamped' radical papers, and in practice implied concentrating on a readership with a strongly defined political identity. Such a strategy allowed – indeed required – that a newspaper had a well-defined political platform, to which it adhered under all circumstances with the greatest consistency, as if it were a party organ: indeed, in some cases there were feelings like those of 'party' loyalty between readers and newspapers.[119] The disadvantage was that circulation would remain substantially static, being limited to the 'militants', and would increase only in exceptional cases, such as when 'great causes' boosted a revival of plebeian radicalism. This was the strategy of *Reynolds's Newspaper*, owned and edited by the ex-Chartist and extreme radical G. W. M. Reynolds (1814–79). Son of a Naval officer and trained for a military career, Reynolds served not in the British forces, but in the National Guard of Paris, where he lived for many years. He was greatly influenced by the revolutions of 1830 and 1848 and by continental radicalism in general (two of his sons were named Ledru Rollin and Kossuth

---

[116] T. Catling's contribution to Reid (ed.), *Why I am a Liberal* (1885), pp. 38–9.
[117] See the remarks by the shipwright Abbot in [rep.], 'Assassination of President Lincoln. – Great Meeting of Working Men', *BH*, 6 May 1865, p. 6.
[118] Berridge, *Thesis*, p. 41.
[119] Berridge, 'Popular Sunday Papers', pp. 250–2.

Mazzini).[120] In 1850 he started his famous and successful weekly, in which he wrote regularly, together with his brother Edward (who used the significant pseudonym of 'Gracchus'), and various occasional correspondents. Though published in London, from the start *Reynolds's Newspaper* was widely circulated and 'avidly' read in the industrial districts of the Midlands and the north of England, amongst the most radical, democratic, and insolently 'plebeian' manual workers.[121]

Politically akin to *Reynolds's* were the *Newcastle Weekly Chronicle* and *Newcastle Daily Chronicle*, two of the most interesting popular newspapers of the time. Owned by Joseph Cowen, they were edited by the ex-Chartist and republican William Edwin Adams ('Iron-side', 1832–1906),[122] and by the Gladstonian radical James Annand,[123] and published contributions from many radicals and labour leaders, such as Thomas Burt, and even revolutionaries such as Prince Kropotkin. The two *Chronicles* were exceedingly successful and influential, and though their politics were really advanced, their rhetoric was never insolent and vulgar like that of *Reynolds's* while the quality and quantity of news reported placed them in the category of the best 'provincial' papers.

At that time there was a great number of small, locally-circulated working-class newspapers, modelled on the old unstamped press, and appealing only to manual workers in certain districts or trades: such was the case, for instance, with the *Forest of Dean Examiner* and the *Potteries Examiner*. In various respects the latter was typical of the category: funded by trade unions – the pressers, potters, miners and ironworkers of the region[124] – it was edited by William Owen (1844–1912), a Wesleyan and staunch Liberal.[125] With the expansion of labour organizations, this kind of periodical thrived during the 1870s – the most successful and widely-circulated being the farm workers' newspapers, which at one and the same time

---

[120] DNB, vol. XLVIII, *sub voce*; DNB, vol. III, *sub voce*; Baylen and Gossman, *Biographical Dictionary of Modern British Radicals*, vol. II, *sub voce*; Humphrey 'Reynolds', pp. 79–89.

[121] Grant, *The Metropolitan Weekly and Provincial Press*, pp. 97–9. The enthusiastic empathy between *Reynolds's Newspaper* and its readers is effectively conveyed by some of the letters, like the one by 'A Working Man', entitled 'The starving classes', *RN*, 17 Oct. 1869, p. 2.

[122] Adams, *Memoirs of a Social Atom*, p. 1; see DLB, vol. VIII, p. 1.

[123] Milne, *Newspapers of Northumberland and Durham*, pp. 102ff.

[124] Anderton, *Thesis*, p. 106.

[125] Anderton, *Thesis*, pp. 250–60.

were the unions' 'official' organs and their readers' main source of information and political education.

Finally there was the famous *Bee-Hive*, which should be placed in a category of its own, since it was anomalous in every respect: it was more 'intellectual', and also more 'official' than the other workers' weeklies, without being linked to any trade union in particular, or to a mass readership; one of its peculiarities was that for many years it represented an open forum for the British labour movement and its allies.[126] The *Bee-Hive* was not mass-circulated, but its few thousand copies reached labour leaders throughout the country, and were likely to be taken regularly by the better-educated workers from whose ranks trade union leaders sprang.[127]

Rather different was the case of the dailies. They did not have a predominantly working-class readership (though at least some artisans used to read them regularly).[128] Their interest for the historian of labour politics derives from the fact that some, like the *Daily News*, were often very interested in the vicissitudes of labour and radical movements, while others, like *The Times*, tried to offer a careful and complete coverage of most important events, both national and local. It is well-known that these papers played an important political role in that they extended the influence of the main political leaders by publishing detailed reports of their speeches.[129] But the historian of popular movements finds them especially valuable for their reports of working-class meetings. It is through these reports that rank-and-file participants in demonstrations were occasionally allowed a public voice: they were people who in many cases have remained completely anonymous, and who would be buried in total obscurity were it not for a single word shouted in the heat of the moment. Their active participation, their collective approval of, or hostility to, politicians and spokes-

---

[126] See Coltham, 'George Potter, the Junta and the "Bee-Hive"', *International Review of Social History*, IX (1964), pp. 390–432, and X (1965), pp. 23–65.

[127] These 'educated workers' did not form a 'labour aristocracy', but rather represented an extremely influential minority in most workshops: they were looked up to as 'scholards' by their fellow workers, and 'constantly in demand to read or write letters, settle disputes, draw up petitions or addresses and act as a spokesman in putting forward demands or grievances to the employer' (McCann, 'Artisans and the Education Act', p. 135).

[128] In the case of the *Leeds Mercury*, see the explicit declaration in [rep.], 'Death of Mr John Snowden', *Halifax Courier*, 6 Sept. 1884, p. 7.

[129] See Matthew, 'Rhetoric and Politics', in Waller (ed.), *Politics and Social Change*, 34–58; Koss, *Rise and Fall of the Political Press*, I, p. 215.

men of the official parties provide us with a way of testing whether the opinions which can be collected from other sections of the press were really representative.

There are good reasons, therefore, for thinking of each newspaper as a *group* of sources rather than as a single source. Leading articles, reports, letters to the editor, and advertisements, can all be utilized, but we need to be aware of their differing value and usefulness. The case of leading articles, which have been extensively utilized in the present work, deserves special attention.

Berridge has maintained that political comment material is not representative of the opinions of the readers, but indicates only what the journalists themselves believed.[130] I think that this hypothesis is open to several objections. The main problem is that the evidence which she offers in support is very slight: only a few declarations by contemporary observers, against which many more statements of the opposite point of view may be found. In particular, reports of meetings of working men's clubs show that leading articles in newspapers like *Reynolds's*, *Lloyd's*, and the *Newcastle Chronicle* were often publicly read aloud, commented on and discussed,[131] as much as were the speeches of Liberal and radical MPs.[132] It is also significant that in the advertisements published by *Reynolds's* to boost its own circulation, leading articles were mentioned among the newspaper's 'General Features' of greatest interest, being listed first among the characteristics which

---

[130] Berridge, *Thesis*, pp. 36–7.

[131] See [rep.], 'Holborn Branch Reform League', *NR*, 19 Mar. 1871, p. 190: 'On Saturday last, Mr Osborne, who occupied the chair, commenced by reading the leader from *Reynolds's Newspaper* . . .'; see also [letter by] 'A Bristol Joiner', 'The Income Tax and the Working Man', *BH*, 28 Feb. 1874, p. 8: 'Lloyds's weekly newspaper had a leader advocating the working man's view of the question last Saturday . . .'. See the advice given by W. Crawford to his miners in 'Newcastle Weekly Chronicle', *Durham Miners Association, Monthly Circular*, 1884, p. 6: 'The articles of Mr Jones are every week worth the money it costs . . . The leaders alone are worth more than the twopence per week'; see also letter by J. Lucas, 'Education', *NW*, 17 Jul. 1875, p. 4. On the *Chronicle*, see 'Cowen, Joseph', in *DLB*, vol. II. See for other examples: [rep.], 'Nottingham Secular Society', *NR*, 6 Jul. 1873, p. 13; [rep.], 'Progressive Club, Notting Hill Gate', *NR*, 17 Sept. 1876, p. 189 (both about *Reynolds's*); letter by G. Howell to 'Littlejohn' of the *Weekly Times*, 4 Nov. 1867, in *G. Howell Coll., Letter Book* IX, 78 (thanking for a leading article).

[132] See for a few examples: [rep.], 'Plymouth, Devenport and Stonehouse Secular Society', *NR*, 16 Apr. 1876, p. 254; Lee, *Jack Lawson*, p. 29. See also Berridge, 'The Language of Popular Radical Journalism', p. 6.

were expected to attract readers.[133] Moreover, it is certain that
Conservative electoral agents took the editorials much more
seriously than Berridge does, and in fact were 'obsessed' by the
'pernicious doctrines which such papers as the *Lloyd's* and the
Reynolds's spread on Saturday nights through the length and
breadth of the country'.[134] Indeed, Berridge's own thesis about the
complete ideological identification between working-class newspapers and their readers makes sense only if leading articles were
actually read, because the newspapers' political opinions were
expressed mainly in the editorials.

This interpretation is corroborated by the external evidence
pointing to the existence of a lively interest in politics among the
subaltern classes (such as, for instance, the high turn-out at general
elections, which suggests that the electorate at least was highly
politicized).[135] The same is also implied by the unparalleled
proliferation of political clubs and debating societies – which also
involved working men[136] – and by the popularity of knick-knacks
and political souvenirs, inspired especially by Gladstone and
Disraeli. All these are elements which further suggest that politics
was a pervasive presence in the daily life of a considerable number
of people at every social level, in the same way that sport is
nowadays: and in fact it is significant that up to the 1880s mass
periodicals had only a small sporting-news section, but a much
larger proportion devoted to the parliamentary debates.

For all these reasons leading articles and political commentaries
have been methodically examined in this study. The criterion
adopted has been to pick up themes recurring frequently over a
period of several years: the hypothesis being that consistent,
prolonged advocacy of a politically relevant cause would not have
been feasible without some substantial degree of support among

---

[133] See the advertisement 'The Best Weekly Newspaper for Sunday Reading' on the back of
the pamphlet *The Minority Report of the Royal Commission on Labour*, London, 1894 (in *John
Johnson Collection*, 'Employment 14').

[134] Koss, *Rise and Fall of the Political Press*, i, p. 184.

[135] It should be remembered here that a high degree of politicization of the pre-1918
electorate is the hypothesis accepted by the great majority of the scholars (see Matthew
et al., 'The Franchise Factor in the Rise of the Labour Party', pp. 723–52).

[136] Hodge, *Workman's Cottage to Windsor Castle* (n.d.), pp. 21–2. The Newcastle debating
society had 'more than' 1,000 members in 1882: *The Debater, A Weekly Record of the
Parliamentary Debating Society*, 23 Feb. 1882, p. 4 (in Tyne-and-Wear Archives, Newcastle).
Seventy-five Parliamentary Debating Societies were represented at the 1882 Liverpool
Conference: *ibid.*, 20 Apr. 1882, p. 3.

the readership, lest the newspaper's circulation were negatively affected – as happened to the *Daily News* in 1886.[137] A check on this hypothesis is provided by a comparison of the developments in editorial policy of newspapers of similar political attitudes, of readers' comments as expressed in the correspondence sections and in reports of meetings, and the evidence collected from working-class biographies, autobiographies, memoirs and diaries.

[137] Berridge, *Thesis*, p. 33.

PART I

Liberty and Retrenchment

CHAPTER I

The language of popular liberalism

All men are equal in His sight –
The bond, the free, the black, the white:
He made them all – them freedom gave;
God made the man – Man made the slave.[1]

Some of my Warwickshire forbears fought with Cromwell at Edgehill, and in other battles of the Civil War,
against tyranny and oppression and for the liberty of the
people. I expect that it is where I get my fighting
propensities from: fighting was in the blood, and I just
harked back to those old Roundhead ancestors of mine,
who struck many a brave and sturdy blow on the right
side.[2]

THE BIBLE AND THE PHRYGIAN CAP

'"The carpenter of Nazareth" came not only to take us from earth
to Heaven, but to make this earth a Heaven begun below'.[3] These
words – of a Welsh Baptist minister at the time of the 1873 miners'
strike – provide an indication of perhaps the most basic attitudes
reflected in the experience of popular liberalism, as in earlier and
later popular radical movements. They also show the centrality of
Biblical language and culture. Within the Protestant world, from
as early as the sixteenth century,[4] the Bible had been a source of
intellectual and moral independence for the common people.[5]

---

[1] Chartist hymn, cit. in Mathews, *Methodism and the Education of the People.* p. 102.
[2] Arch, *Story of His Life* (1898), pp. 3–4.
[3] T. D. Matthias, 'The working classes', *BH*, 15 Mar. 1873, p. 6.
[4] See, for example, Blickle, *Die Revolution von 1525*, chapter 6.
[5] See Williams, *Quarryman's Champion*, p. 10; and Williams, 'Intellectuals and the First
Welsh Radicalism', in Samuel and Stedman Jones (eds.), *Culture, Ideology and Politics*,
p. 255; Valenze, 'Pilgrims and Progress', *ibid.*, pp. 113–25.

Through the right to free enquiry and private examination, ordinary artisans and yeomen had been given direct and immediate access to 'the Book', or 'the Truth': this opportunity had encouraged a disposition towards enquiry and reflection which could easily be extended from the theological sphere to more secular contexts. Even the humblest working man or woman knew that in the Bible – without the mediation of middle-class intellectuals or sacerdotal figures – he or she had access to the ultimate criteria of right and wrong in any moral, political or social question. Victorian plebeian Nonconformists – like their sixteenth- and seventeenth-century predecessors – were strengthened by 'the notion of a democratic God'[6] who liked the poor and talked to them through 'that most radical text, the Authorised Version'.[7] With this God they felt themselves to be in a personally close and intimate relationship: indeed, as the Anti-Corn Law League lecturer John Buckmaster wrote about a popular religious meeting in the 1840s, 'They talked familiarly about Jesus Christ, as if He were a farm labourer keeping a family on nine shillings a week'.[8]

The workers who underwent a conversion experience within one of the 'sects' tended to develop a heightened political awareness,[9] as can be seen from the biographies of the majority of the labour leaders. The first of the psychological effects of conversion was something like the famous 'innerworldly' asceticism described by Max Weber.[10] This was based on a new attitude to life which encouraged the believers to engage in social and political, as well as religious, activities on behalf of their community; it also gave them the energy and courage to do things that, before their conversion, they would not even have dared to contemplate, like learning to read and write in order to become teachers and organizers of the education of fellow-workers in their chapel's Sunday school.[11] True to the Puritan tradition, popular Nonconformists emphasized the practical application of their theology: to them life became service to a God who loved their fellow-labourers; they emphasized the prescriptions of Christian ethics, 'the Christi-

---

[6] Howkins, *Poor Labouring Men*, p. 56.
[7] *Ibid.*, p. 49.
[8] Buckmaster, *A Village Politician* (1897), p. 39.
[9] For an interesting collection of testimonies of the conversion of Durham miners, see Salisbury (ed.), *Me and Jake* (1916).
[10] Bendix, *Weber*, p. 202.
[11] Cox, *The English Churches in a Secular Society*, p. 137.

anity of Christ, of the Sermon on the Mount, a Christianity under which brotherly love would abound, and the spirit of which would be visible in the life of the week-day, work-day world'.[12] Thus, for example, the farm-labourer George Edwards wrote about his conversion: 'The faith I then embraced created within me new ideals of life, and, although an illiterate and uneducated youth, I became very thoughtful and most strict in my habits, thinking I had to give up everything I had indulged in.'[13] The abandonment of drinking, betting, and other expensive habits helped to make ends meet,[14] and the greater availability of free time allowed more scope for other activities. As the miner John Wilson wrote in his memoirs, 'This change made, I began seriously to consider how I could be useful in life. And I felt how foolish I had been to waste the chances of youth, and to find myself unfit to take a proper part in the public affairs of the nation.'[15] Encouraged by his wife, Wilson studied grammar, logic, history, poetry, etymology, stenography and theology, and eventually acquired the educational qualifications necessary for teaching in the Primitive Methodist Sunday school, and preaching from the pulpit of the village chapel.[16] 'Proficiency in the pulpit', he said, 'was my chief aim. With it there came proficiency on the platform.'[17] Edwards' career was even more dramatic, and his case too illustrates the influence of women in the working-class family and in the making of early labour leaders: before his conversion he was completely illiterate, but, with the help of his wife, he became a lay preacher, and eventually learnt to read and write.[18] In this way, some self-taught

---

[12] Wright, *Our New Masters*, pp. 104–5. Interestingly enough, a similar attitude characterized continental secular anti-clericals: see Gadille, 'French Anticlericalism', pp. 127, 137ff.; Lyttleton, 'Italian Anticlericalism', p. 236; Giovannini, *La cultura della 'Plebe'*, pp. 46–8.

[13] Edwards, *Crow Scaring to Westminster* (1922), p. 30.

[14] In some parts of the East End of London, this saving was assessed as 5 s. per week at the end of the century: Cox, *The English Churches*, p. 140.

[15] Wilson, *Memories of a Labour Leader* (1910), p. 207.

[16] *Ibid.*, pp. 208–14; see *Autobiography of a Cornish Miner*, pp. 16–17, cit. in Mathews, *Methodism and the Education of the People*, p. 76. For examples of illiterate workers becoming Sunday school teachers as a result of their commitment to self-education, see Cox, *The English Churches*, p. 137.

[17] J. Wilson, quoted in 'Trade Unionism Sprang from the Primitive Methodist Chapel', *Advertiser*, 10 Dec. 1954, [newspaper cutting in] *J. Wilson Papers*. D/X 188, 15.

[18] His first sermons were prepared by learning by heart the relevant parts of the Bible: Edwards, *Crow-Scaring to Westminister* (1923), p. 32; Lawson, *A Man's Life*, (1932), p. 111. On the role of working-class wives in this process of education, see Hobsbawm, *Worlds of Labour*, p. 189.

working-class Dissenters acquired a remarkably wide culture: the miner Jack Lawson recalled that

One, who had only been taught by his wife to read when he was in his thirties, used to wait for me when I was putting and he was hewing at the same flat [in the pit]. As we went 'out bye' . . . we would talk books while we walked, bent double in the dark roadway. I remember when this elderly man first struck Nietzsche. That was a 'find' . . . This man read the New Testament in Greek, and oratorios were as easy to him as the latest song is to the man in the street.[19]

The next step was commitment to political and social causes, seen as 'applied Christianity': 'With my study of theology'. Edwards wrote, 'I soon began to realize that the social conditions of the people were not as God intended they should be.'[20] But, in true Puritan fashion, before devoting himself to trade unionism Edwards wanted to make sure that

I was doing the right thing from a religious point of view, and again by the assistance of my dear wife I searched the Scripture and soon was able to satisfy myself I was doing the right thing. Then, as now, to me the labour movement was a most sacred thing, and . . . one cannot divorce labour from religion.[21]

The conviction he then reached gave him a 'Jacobin' – or rather a 'Leveller' – zeal and self-confidence which otherwise would have been quite difficult to acquire by a man born and brought up in extreme poverty. Thus, Dissent exercised the classically Weberian function of 'compensating' for the social and political disadvantages which characterized the mass of the poor: 'All, even the most ordinary – or, if you like, ignorant as far as education goes – all of them were "something". Methodism took the "nobodies", and made the most humble and hopeless "somebody".'[22] In fact, Edwards no longer considered himself an oppressed, exploited country proletarian, feeling rather that he had been called and 'predestined' to a mission whose final triumphal end had already been sealed and settled by God's will since the foundation of the

---

[19] Lawson, *A Man's Life*, (1932), p. 112.
[20] Edwards, *Crow-Scaring to Westminster*, (1922), p. 36.
[21] *Ibid.*, p. 43. For another example, see 'Miners' Camp Meeting at Silverdale', *Potteries Examiner*, 16 Sept. 1871, p. 5. For the link between plebeian Nonconformity and industrial relations, see Reid, 'Robert Knight', in Biagini and Reid, (eds.), *Currents of Radicalism*, pp. 220–8.
[22] Lawson, *A Man's Life* (1932), p. 112. On this 'compensatory' effect, see Scotland, *Methodism*, p. 33; Obelkevich, *Religion and Rural Society*, p. 247.

world. Evans, the farmworkers' journalist, expressed this conviction well when he wrote: 'I believe firmly that in politics as well as
religion God has his own elect chosen out from the rest of the
world to be the pioneers of progress'.[23] The 'call' was specific and
personal, and the certainty of salvation implied the certainty that
– though insignificant and helpless by human standards – each of
the 'saints' had an immense value in the sight of the Lord
Almighty, whose will was the guarantee of their ultimate success.[24]
Joseph Arch declared that his career as an apostle of trade unionism began when he became convinced that he was one of the 'elect':

> I know that it was the hand of the Lord of Hosts which led me that day;
> that the Almighty Maker of heaven and earth raised me up to do this
> particular thing; that in the counsel of His wisdom He singled me out
> and set me on my feet in His sight, and breathed of the breath of the Spirit
> into me, and sent me forth as a messenger of the Lord God of Battles. So I
> girded up my loins and went forth. It was from the Lord God of Battles I
> came, that there might one day be peace in the land. Only through warfare
> could we attain to freedom and peace and prosperity; only through the
> storm and stress of battle could we reach the haven where we would be: I
> was but a humble instrument in the Lord's hands . . .[25]

It was of great political importance that his conviction was also
shared by the members of his trade union, who interpreted the
growth of the movement and Arch's personal victories as evidence
of the 'call' received by him.[26] Indeed, many farmworkers seemed
to think that Arch's great ability as an orator and readiness as a
controversialist was the fulfilment of the prophecy contained in
Matthew 10:19: 'when they deliver you up, take no thought how
or what ye shall speak: for it shall be given you in that same hour
what ye shall speak'. Whatever the case, his gifts were to some
extent shared by hundreds of other labour leaders, who, like Arch,
had had much practice in public speaking from the pulpit.[27]

---

[23] H. Evans, 'The Franchise – Local and Imperial', *English Laborers Chronicle*, 20 Apr. 1878,
p. 1.
[24] Moore, *Pit-men, Preachers, and Politics*, p. 24.
[25] Arch, *The Story of His Life* (1898), p. 402.
[26] Sage, *The Memoirs of Josiah Sage* (1951), p. 49. A recent study (Colls. *The Pitmen of the
Northern Coalfield*, p. 176), has emphasized the Arminianism of working-class Methodists:
however, in spite of the official doctrines of the denominations, testimonies like this one
of Arch are not infrequent and seem to suggest the existence of a Calvinist sub-culture
among rank-and-file Primitive Methodists.
[27] A. Richardson, 'Character Sketches. – 1. The Labour Party and the Books that Helped to
Make It', *Review of Reviews* (1906), p. 579.

Popular Nonconformity was not only 'charismatic', but also millenarianist, the latter tendency being stimulated by difficult conditions of life and precarious employment.[28] One of the poems published by the artisan J. B. Leno in 1868 was entitled 'The Last Battle (AD 2000)', and celebrated Armageddon as God's final triumph over his enemies:[29] it would be the apocalyptic event *par excellence*, the final liberation of the 'poor in Christ' from all oppression and suffering. According to R. Moore – who has studied 435 sermons delivered in a group of Primitive Methodist mining communities in Durham between 1874 and 1923 – working-class theology emphasized themes like 'regeneration', 'new life', the 'kingdom of God' and focussed on passages containing 'the promises', which gave reassurance: especially Psalms 23 ('The Lord is my shepherd; I shall not want') and 84 ('For the LORD God is a sun and shield . . . no good thing will he withhold from them that walk uprightly').[30] Apocalyptic and liberation themes, figures and language were also quite common, with a preference for Revelation,[31] Exodus,[32] Ezekiel 37 (the resurrection of the dry bones of Israel's slain army),[33] and Daniel.[34] Exodus and Ezekiel were especially inspiring because they contained a 'call' and a regeneration which concerned not only individuals, but the whole of 'God's chosen people' – allegedly identifiable with the Victorian working-class 'saints'.[35] The drawing of a parallel between the Israel of old and the modern labour movement was quite a common feature of plebeian Dissent: the farmworker George Nicholls wrote that 'the Old Testament stories of the godly men of past times became so real to me that I have long been convinced that the history of Joseph, Daniel, David, and many others is being repeated today'.[36] And the navvy John Ward declared: 'When I was first taught to read, the Bible was my chief source of inspiration. The struggles of the shepherd communities in the Old Testament I have worked out in my imagination on the hills of

[28] See Harrison, *Popular Millenarianism*; Oliver, *Prophets and Millennialists*; Yeo, 'Christianity and Chartist Struggle, 1838–1842', pp. 109–39.
[29] Leno, *The Aftermath* (1892), 12–14.
[30] Moore, *Pit-men, Preachers and Politics*, pp. 97–8.
[31] Arch, *The Story of His Life* (1898), pp. 68, 265–8.
[32] *Ibid.*, p. 73.
[33] *Ibid.*, pp. 78–9.
[34] Edwards, *Crow-Scaring to Westminster* (1922), p. 81.
[35] Warwick, 'Preface' to Arch, *The Story of His Life* (1898), p. xi; Scotland, *Methodism*, p. 153.
[36] 'Character Sketches', *Review of Reviews* (1906), p. 577.

Hampshire when driving the plough.'[37] The comparatively egalitarian nature of the Jewish society of the early Biblical period assumed a normative character:

They were on the side of the Prophets, rather than of the Kings, the institutions. The ground for self-respect their fathers had lost in England they found afresh in Palestine. There were not two nations of the ancient Jews and there should be no great cleavage among Englishmen. They had heard the injunction to the King of the Jews that 'his heart be not lifted up above his brethren'.[38]

The political teaching of Bunyan's *Pilgrim's Progress* was similar. Christian, the tinker's hero, was a man of small means but great faith; he was oppressed and persecuted by wicked judges and gentry-like giants living in castles – in short, by the powerful and wealthy of this world;[39] nevertheless he had been chosen and elected by the Lord. His 'exodus' from the city of Destruction was reminiscent of the vicissitudes of many emigrant labourers and tramping artisans, in the sense that he had left his home because 'the *wages* of sin' were 'too low'. As Christopher Hill has pointed out, *Pilgrim's Progress* was not only a classic of Puritan devotion: it also told the story of 'a man with a burden on his back . . . the product of centuries of unequal society', and contained the promise of deliverance, and an encouragement to endure evil, fight for a better world, and be true to one's ideals to the very last.[40] Not surprisingly, the influence of this little book among the subaltern classes was extraordinary, comparable only to that of the Bible: as Will Crooks exclaimed, 'Bunyan is the ideal of our working people!'[41]

From the 'ideological' point of view, in spite of Bunting's theology of submission to 'the powers that be', the prevailing doctrine seemed quite close in spirit to that of the Covenanter Samuel Rutherford: working-class Nonconformists tended to be socially non-deferential and sometimes even 'subversive'. In particular, from the beginning of the nineteenth century Dissent

---

[37] *Ibid.*, p. 571.
[38] Ashby, *Joseph Ashby* (1961), p. 114.
[39] Hill, *Bunyan and His Church*, pp. 212–21.
[40] *Ibid.*, p. 377.
[41] 'Character Sketches', *Review of Reviews*, (1906), p. 573.

supplied labour with many of its leaders,[42] with viable organizational models, and with a style of mass communication. The latter
included politicized 'camp meetings', which remained very popular
throughout the century[43] with their choirs, songs and hymns as a
necessary preliminary to collective action.[44]

Dissent also provided popular radicalism with a language, that
of the Authorised Version.[45] It was difficult to start any radical
popular movement without arguments involving a political interpretation of the Bible: when John Buckmaster began his campaign
to convert the agricultural labourers and artisans of country
villages to the cause of free trade, he focussed on 'the anti-
Scriptural character of the Corn-Laws', maintaining that 'if the
Corn-Laws had been in existence when Jesus Christ was on earth
He would have preached against them'.[46] Buckmaster's opponents,
the Chartists, spoke a similar language, Biblical in style, wording
and often content: indeed, they set up their own chapels, which
preached Jesus Christ as 'a teacher of democratic politics'.[47] Later,
on the eve of the 1867 Reform Act, an observer wrote that 'All our
political questions are, in fact, daily running more and more into
religious questions. All our politics are every day becoming more
religious, and religion more political.'[48] The householders' democ-

---

[42] See the famous case of Thomas Hepburn, the organizer of the Pitmen's Union of the
Tyne and Wear in 1831 and leader of the great strike of that year: he was a Primitive
Methodist preacher, just like Benjamin Embleton, John Richardson and 'most of the
other leaders' of that strike (DLB III, p. 100; Richardson, 'Primitive Methodism: Its
Influence on the Working Classes', *Primitive Methodist Quarterly Review*, 5 (1883),
pp. 261–73).

[43] From the days of the Chartists to those of the ILP. For the similarities between Chartist
and Primitive Methodist methods of mass communication, compare 'Chartist Camp
Meeting' (1842), in Mather (ed.), *Chartism and Society*, pp. 301–2, with 'The Mow Cop
Camp Meeting, 1807', in Thompson (ed.), *Nonconformity*, pp. 25–6.

[44] Kent, *Holding the Fort*, p. 35.

[45] W. Brace, 'Character Sketches', *Review of Reviews*, (1906), p. 572; see Edwards, *Crow-
Scaring to Westminster* (1922), pp. 81–2; Morgan, *Keir Hardie*, pp. 8–9.

[46] Buckmaster, *A Village Politician* (1897), p. 190.

[47] Norman, *Church and Society in England*, p. 507; Tiller, 'Late Chartism', in Epstein and
Thompson (eds.), *Chartist Experience*, p. 313; see Epstein, 'Some Organizational and
Cultural Aspects', *ibid*, pp. 250–1; Yeo, 'Christianity and Chartist Struggle 1833–1842',
ibid, pp. 109–39; Thompson, *The Chartists*, pp. 116, 227. See Faulkner, *Chartism and the
Churches*, pp. 123–34. For the persistence of this language well into the twentieth century,
see Howkins, *Poor Labouring Men*, p. 56. It is remarkable that out of 73 Chartists
imprisoned in 1840–41, as many as 32 belonged to one or other of the Nonconformist
denominations. For the rest, 26 declared themselves to belong to the Church of England,
9 declared that they had no religion, and 6 were Roman Catholic (Thompson, *The
Chartists*, p. 116).

[48] Rev. J. Ritchie, 'The Politics of the New Testament, No. 1', *NW*, 20 Apr. 1867, p. 4.

racy did not change things: popular meetings in the run-up to the 1885 general elections followed the old Chartist model of a politicized Nonconformity: a reporter who was present at one of them described how the new electors congregated in the evening, at the end of a long working day: pitmen, ironworkers, and 'women from the chain and spike shops' 'came in hundreds'. 'The men walked in as if wearily, sat down, put their hands into their pockets, and stared into space. The women, some with their shawls on their heads, took their seats with the air of visitors coming not for politics but for prayers'.[49] When the hall was full

An old man stood up and made an address, but not to the workman who filled the chair. 'Oh, Lord, we are a downtrodden people; we are wretched, we are miserable; we cannot help ourselves. Bless what is about to be said this night for the guidance of our rulers and for the good of the poor of the land.'[50]

Often working-class radicals discussed social and political questions in the guise of Bible studies or lectures on Israel in the days of the prophets.[51] In this way the Bible helped to articulate the workers' point of view on social conflicts:[52] though the language of class struggle was unfamiliar to them, the Authorized Version provided a good substitute, as exemplified by the card circulated among the agricultural labourers during the 1874 lock out.[53] Even the mottoes embroidered on trade union banners were often

---

[49] [Rep.], 'The New Democracy – The Message of the Black Country', *DN*, 20 Nov. 1885, p. 2.

[50] *Ibid.*

[51] 'Nehemiah: His Patriotism and Piety. Lecture in the Town Hall, Bilston', *Miner and Workmen's Examiner*, 14 Apr. 1876, p. 5.

[52] Buckmaster, *A Village Politician* (1897), p. 40. See Dunbabin, 'The "Revolt of the Field"', p. 69.

[53] From the farm labourers of Christian England to their arch-enemies, Elliot, Strdbroke, Rutland, Bristol, Walsingham North, Salisbury and company . . .
  'Behold the hire of the labourers who have reaped down your fields which is of you kept back by fraud, crieth: and the cries of them who have reaped are entered into the ears of the Lord Sabaoth.' 'Ye have lived in pleasure on the earth and have been wanton, ye have condemned and killed the just.' 'I will come near to you to judgement, and I will be a swift witness against those who oppress the hireling in his wages, saith the Lord.' 'Hear, O ye heads of Jacob, and ye princes of the house of Israel. Is it not for you to know judgement, who hate the good and love the evil?' 'Hear this, O ye that swallow up the needy, even to make the poor of the land to fail, that ye may buy the poor for silver, and the needy for a pair of shoes.' 'Forasmuch, therefore, as your trading is upon the poor, and ye shall take from him burdens of wheat, ye have built houses of hewn stone, but ye shall not dwell in them; ye have planted pleasant vineyards, but ye shall not drink of them. For I know your manifold trangressions, and your mighty sins, afflicting the just, taking bribes, and turning aside the poor from their right.' 'Woe unto him that buildeth his house by unrighteousness and his chambers by wrong, that useth his neighbour's services without wages, and giveth him not for his work.' . . . 'Moreover the profit of earth is for all.' (Cit. in Scotland, *Methodism*, p. 93).

appropriate Biblical passages, such as 'Bear Ye One Another's Burdens', 'Go and Do Likewise', and 'Faith can Remove Mountains'.[54] And in the 1880s Henry George's 'socialism' spread rapidly and successfully because it too was worded in the familiar language of the Authorized Version.[55] This symbiosis was also encouraged by the fact that in some regions – notably Wales – the rights of labour and the cause of religious freedom seemed closely intertwined.[56] Moreover, in general the Nonconformists were seriously concerned with social problems,[57] and to some of them democracy and equality were almost religious dogmas.[58] Small wonder that there prospered a sort of Puritan 'liberation theology', whose principles were eloquently expressed by the Reverend J. Ritchie in a series of articles in the *Newcastle Weekly Chronicle*:

Christianity consecrates the principle of appealing directly to the common people on the very highest and deepest questions of human interests. The gospel treats the popular intellect with respect and friendliness. There is nothing esoteric in its doctrines and spirit . . . It recognises no aristocracy of caste or class, of birth or office – no aristocracy of intellect even. It 'honours all men' by addressing itself to faculties and feelings which all men in common possess.[59]

But the Gospel went even further, according to Ritchie, teaching an authentic respect for the poor, the model recipients of the Messiah's 'good news':

This preaching of the gospel to the poor assumes that the poor have faculties for appreciation of the profoundest of moral truths; that there is nothing too good to be given to them . . . The gospel is, then, an appeal to the many, the millions, the common people; assumes a capacity in the common people receptive of the deepest and weightiest of moral truths. It is more than this. It is an appeal to the many against the few – to the people against their rulers.[60]

---

[54] Moyes, *The Banner Book*, p. 98.

[55] *The Bible and the Land Question*, n.d., in *John Johnson Collection*, 'Land and the People', p. 2.

[56] Williams, *Quarryman's Champion*, pp. 71–2. See Brown, 'Nonconformity and Trade Unions', in Biagini and Reid (eds.), *Currents of Radicalism*, pp. 86–105.

[57] Cox, *The English Churches*, p. 157; Thompson, *Socialists, Liberals and Labour*, p. 24; Wald, *Crosses on the Ballot*, p. 167.

[58] H. Evans, 'The Franchise – Local and Imperial', *English Labourers' Chronicle*, 20 Apr. 1878, p. 1; Buckmaster, *A Village Politician* (1897), p. 41. See Valenze, 'Pilgrims and Progress', in Samuel and Stedman Jones (eds.), *Culture, Ideology and Politics*, p. 144.

[59] Rev. J. Ritchie, *NW*, 20 Apr. 1867, p. 4. Ritchie, a Scottish minister, had been a Chartist and was 'a fearless Radical and platform speaker' (Todd, *Cowen*, p.26).

[60] Ritchie, *NW*, 20 Apr. 1867, p. 4.

Hence 'the politics of the New Testament', as the practical implications of this intellectual attitude, were that

The gospel consecrates the principle of moral-force agitation. It recognizes the right and duty of insurrection – the insurrection, that is, of the heart and understanding against hypocrisy and falsehood – though hypocrisy and falsehood seat in the very seat of Moses and are environed with the prestige of antiquity and legitimacy . . . The politics of the New Testament are anti-hierarchical. The whole book is an emphatic proclamation of religious equality . . . By its doctrine of human equality and brotherhood it ignores all social distinctions, except the immutable natural distinctions between wisdom and folly, righteousness and iniquity. It denounces all mammon-worship and title-worship. Its social spirit is that of a republican simplicity, equality, and self-respect . . . It is a very levelling gospel.[61]

FROM THE REFORMATION TO THE RISORGIMENTO

The centrality of the culture of Dissent was reflected in the renewal of popular interest in the political significance of the Reformation. For example, the *Newcastle Chronicle*, pointing out that John Knox had sprung up from the people, maintained that he had become 'the representative of the Third Estate' and the leader of 'the Constitutional Opposition of his age'.[62] Likewise the Covenanters – whose deeds and sufferings were celebrated in the then popular *Scottish Worthies* – were seen as freedom-fighters and much admired by people such as Keir Hardie.[63]

But it was the Puritan Revolutionaries, and Oliver Cromwell in particular, who became the most important source of inspiration

---

[61] *Ibid.* As a Sheffield artisan put it in 1874:

> I have for 40 years taken a great interest in political matters . . . & if I may be allowed to confess it I will say that the principles of my political creed have been drawn from the *New Testament* – when I was a young man in my teens . . . I read it over & over again untill [sic] its facts, truths and principles became has [sic, sc. as] it were a part of myself. & I have no hesitation in pronouncing that book to be the most democratic book in the world & lays the basis for the noblest political superstructure in the universe. – Equality, Liberty, Fraternity has [sic, sc. as] therein taught are the only proper things we should aim at . . . (Robert Sykes to J. Chamberlain, Feb. 1874, in J. Chamberlain Papers, 6/5/58).

> The New Testament had made him 'a dissenter thorough', 'a Chartist', and eventually a Liberal (*ibid.*).

[62] [L.a.], 'The Political Principles of John Knox', *NW*, 30 Nov. 1872, p. 4.
[63] 'Character Sketches', *Review of Reviews* (1906), p. 570.

for the radicals.[64] The re-evaluation of the Puritan Revolution first took place between the age of the French Revolution and the days of Peterloo. Although in the 1790s 'Levellers' and 'Commonwealth Republicans' were still terms of abuse applied to the radicals by their enemies,[65] only a few decades later the radicals themselves were proudly adopting these Civil War labels.[66] At least from the beginning of the 1830s Cromwell became an established radical symbol, and in some regions the phrase 'Oliver's days' was used to mean a period of unusual prosperity.[67] Between 1841 and 1845 Carlyle published his influential revision of the life and work of the Lord Protector, and from the 1850s W. J. Linton began to popularize Carlyle's 'new' Cromwell,[68] helped by many other radicals of different inclinations, including the 'physical force' republican G. J. Harney,[69] the 'moral force' Liberal Henry Vincent,[70] and the Nonconformist journalist Edward Miall.[71]

Later, various radical MPs including Cowen, made a great deal of their own Cromwellian heritage.[72] Both Cobden[73] and Bradlaugh were sometimes called 'the coming Cromwell',[74] and even Gladstone was likened to the great Puritan hero by his plebeian

---

[64] On the Victorian revival of Cromwell, see Anderson, 'The Political Uses of History in Mid Nineteenth-Century England', pp. 87–105; Smith, 'The Image of Cromwell in Folklore and Tradition'; Mason, 'Nineteenth century Cromwell', pp. 187–91; Dunbabin, 'Oliver Cromwell's Popular Image', in Bromley and Kossmann, *Britain and the Netherlands*, v, pp. 141–63; Howell, 'Cromwell and the Imagery of Nineteenth-Century Radicalism', pp. 193–9.

[65] Godwin, *The Friends of Liberty*, p. 92.

[66] At least from 1818: Belchem, *'Orator' Hunt*, pp. 89, 93.

[67] Dunbabin, 'Oliver Cromwell's Popular Image', p. 143; see Mason, 'Nineteenth-Century Cromwell', p. 188.

[68] W. J. Linton, 'Britain's Worthies: Oliver Cromwell', *The Northern Tribune*, Dec. 1854, pp. 409–14; in *J. Cowen Collection*, D. 161; this series on 'Britain's Worthies' – which took its name from the more famous *Scots Worthies* – also included an issue devoted to John Milton (*ibid.*, D 87).

[69] Schoyen, *George Julian Harney*, p. 236.

[70] Solly, *These Eighty Years* (1893), i, pp. 417–18; DLB, i, p. 331.

[71] Dunbabin, 'Oliver Cromwell's Popular Image', p. 151.

[72] [Rep.], 'Mr Leatham on Working Men's Clubs' [lecture on 'Oliver Cromwell'], *LM*, 29 Jan. 1869, p. 3; C. Bradlaugh, 'To Edward Vaughan Kenealy, MP for the Borough of Stoke', *NR*, 27 Jun. 1875, p. 402; [rep.], 'Mr Bradlaugh in Newcastle', *NW*, 19 Jun. 1875, p. 5; C. Bradlaugh, 'Cromwell and Washington' (this was one of a long series of lectures published under this title), *NR*, 24 Jan. 1875, pp. 50–1; [rep.], 'Newcastle Election . . . Mr Cowen's Speeches . . . Shieldfield', *NW*, 17 Jan. 1874, p. 2.

[73] 'Cobden sprung of a sturdy yeoman stock, like Cromwell one of the "common people" of the great land of which he was a son' [l.a., n.t.], *LM*, 14 Jul. 1874, p. 4.

[74] Harrison, *Before the Socialists*, p. 233.

admirers.[75] Part of Bright's popularity was allegedly due to certain Cromwellian traits in his personality, such as his incorruptible honesty,[76] his style and rhetoric. Some alleged that even the

Tribune's physique, his resolute carriage ... resembled some of the Friends of the seventeenth century ... His 'strength of chest and limb' suggested other leaders of men.
'So sturdy Cromwell pushed broad-shuldered on,
So burly Luther breasted Babylon.'[77]

Cromwell and Bright were two of the four politicians whose portraits adorned the membership card of the National Liberal League,[78] a radical artisan group organized by Howell, Broadhurst and William Morris in 1877. The Lord Protector was the subject of many lectures in working men's clubs during the 1860s and 70s,[79] and there existed republican clubs which bore his name.[80] In the 1860s Liberal electoral songs and hymns mentioned Milton, Cromwell, Sydney and William of Orange as the founders of the tradition of British radicalism.[81] Then, on the eve of the 1868 general elections, Cromwell and Milton were finally 'enrolled' as Liberal electoral agents:

Can any man of dispassionate mind doubt as to how Milton would vote were he alive in England next week, or Cromwell, or almost any other of our forefathers who were devoted to freedom and progress, and whose memories we are proud of? We cannot conceive Milton voting against

[75] Bebbington, *The Nonconformist Conscience*, p. 12.
[76] 'This is rare, as rare as Daniel unhurt in the lion's den, the three Hebrews unsinged in the fiery furnace, or the Apostle Paul unstung by the viper which came out of the heat and fastened on his hand. We are proud of this fine example of incorruptible integrity and steadfastness not to be shaken' ([l.a.], 'John Bright', *BH*, 4 Feb. 1871, p. 9).
[77] Mrs Boyce, *Memoirs of a Quaker Family*, cit. in Trevelyan, *Bright*, p. 104; see pp. 19, 342 for other 'Cromwellian' parallels. For examples of 'Cromwellian' rhetoric in Bright's speeches, see the quotation from John Milton in his speech to 4,000 workers in the Edinburgh Stock Exchange in November 1868: [rep.], 'Working Men's Meeting', *MG*, 6 Nov. 1868, p. 3.
[78] One of these cards has been preserved in *G. Howell Collection*, 'Political Parties' (see illustration 1b below); the other three figures were another (unidentified) seventeenth-century Puritan, R. Cobden and J. S. Mill.
[79] [Rep.], 'Meetings of Branches', [Bloomsbury Branch: G. Howell lecturing on 'Oliver Cromwell'], *BH*, 30 Mar. 1867, p. 1: [rep.], 'Leeds Branch of the National Secular Society' [Mr Symes lecturing on: 'Cromwell: the Friend of Man, the Terror of Kings'], *NR*, 14 Apr. 1878, p. 1116.
[80] [Rep.], 'Cromwell Patriotic Club and Institute', *NR*, 9 Jan. 1881, p. 29.
[81] Like 'With Gladstone and with Bright', in Bishopsgate Institute, *Political Parties Folder*.

Mr. Gladstone and for the unscrupulous politician whom fate has ironically made Premier of England for the time being.[82]

This was the period when one of the main contributors to the radical *Newcastle Weekly Chronicle*, the ex-Chartist W. E. Adams, signed his articles as 'Ironside', referring to Cromwell's 'New Model' soldiers. In the early 1870s, with the wave of republicanism, working-class newspapers throughout the country published letters criticizing the Court and signed with pseudonyms like 'Cromwell'[83] and 'Roundhead'.[84] The 'Revolt of the Field' further rekindled interest in the Civil War, 'when the Puritan preacher was the soul of the army of the Commonwealth',[85] just as the Primitive Methodist preachers were the soul of the labourers' union. In 1875 the 230th anniversary of the Parliamentarians' victory at Naseby was solemnly commemorated by the agricultural labourers, who celebrated Cromwell in one of their hymns:

> An army fought in years long gone
> While Cromwell led the way;
> In freedom's cause they nobly stood
> While victory crowned the day.[86]

History, besides stimulating politics and inspiring popular poetry, also occasioned fiction: serials set in Civil War England were published in the working-class press, with Cromwell playing the role of the fearless reformer;[87] readers followed these serials with such interest, that some of them even wrote to the editors to discuss the various episodes.[88] The following notice, published in the republican *National Reformer* in 1873, is also interesting:

Parties in London having an evening to spare may profitably employ it in witnessing the play of 'Cromwell' now being represented at the Queen's

---

[82] [L.a.], 'Next Week', *BH*, 14 Nov. 1868, p. 4. For Milton's popularity as a radical and republican symbol, see also G. W. Foote, *NR*, 18 May 1873, p. 318: 'John Milton was the sternest Republican that the country had ever produced'.

[83] Cromwell [lett.], *RN*, 3 Oct. 1875, p. 3.

[84] Roundhead [lett.], 'The Advance and Objects of Republicanism', *RN*, 28 Jan. 1872, p. 3.

[85] Warwick, 'Introduction' to Arch, *The Story of His Life*, (1898), p. xii.

[86] 'The Fight for Freedom', cit. in Horn, *Arch*, pp. 126–7. The agricultural unionists' awareness of the Puritan heritage must have been strengthened by the fact that the New Model Army had been raised in East Anglia and Cromwell himself came from Cambridgeshire.

[87] Cf. [rep.], 'Cromwell and the Commonwealth', *RN*, 21 Nov. 1875, p. 1; W. W. Robson, 'The Battle of the Stuarts. Falkirk', *NW* 12 Dec. 1874, p. 3; 'No Quarter – A Romance of the Parliamentary Wars – By Captain Mayne Reid', *NW*, 28 Aug. 1880, p. 6.

[88] Mr Williams [lett.], 'Cavaliers and Conservatives', *NW*, 21 Aug. 1880, p. 5; 'A Yorkshireman' [lett.], 'Cavaliers and Conservatives', *NW*, 28 Aug. 1880, p. 5.

Theatre. It is a capital production in favour of republican views, and has some excellent hits at the folly of despotism of kings. I was delighted, when present one night last week, to find the audience take up the democratic point so enthusiastically. When Cromwell said, 'We will have no more kings', the cheering was deafening, and extended throughout the house. So general was it, that a gentleman behind me exclaimed, 'There is a good lot of Bradlaugh's party here!'[89]

Oliver Cromwell was seen as the personification of the Puritan Commonwealth, whose traditions were cherished as the first victory of 'the People' against 'Privilege'. When Charles 'the tyrant' tried to rule without Parliament and ignore the will of the nation, the latter demonstrated that it was able to rule itself without need for a king. The ancient Puritans, strong in the democratic culture of Dissent, had successfully fought the battle for political liberty and social equality, by pulling down the monarchy and its appendages. The bicentenary of the 1662 'Great Ejectment', in 1862, greatly stimulated this cultural revival,[90] which went on to provide a title for the ultra-radical newspaper, *The Commonwealth*, edited by Leno and others.[91]

The link between Puritanism and radicalism was so strong that some plebeian liberals were apparently unable to conceive a radical movement which was not in some sense also a 'puritan' one. An example is provided by plebeian liberal comments on the Franco-Prussian war of 1870–1 and its aftermath. According to 'Littlejohn', France had been routed because it had been made so 'corrupt, frivolous, and licentious, that it might easily be ruled by an immoral chief', and even 'the Zouaves – made cowards and knaves by Bonapartism – fled from the enemy in disgraceful confusion'. In contrast, the victorious Germans – who then seemed to be fighting just for the independence of their country – were commendable for their Protestant virtues, being 'the highest class of troops that Europe has seen since Cromwell's Ironsides put down the Cavaliers'.[92] Later, as the Germans' aggressive nationalism became evident, they lost their reputation for holiness, though the French – by then republican – were still disparaged as morally hopeless:

[89] C. Watts, 'Extra Notes by the Way', *NR*, 5 Jan. 1873, pp. 2–3.
[90] Vincent, *Formation of the British Liberal Party*, pp. 28–9.
[91] Leno, *The Aftermath* (1868), p. 62.
[92] Littlejohn, 'English Workmen and the French Republic', *WT*, 2 Oct. 1870, p. 6.

That the French have great qualities no one will deny; but in addition to
the canker of vanity they have – as a people – no sense of duty. The
notion of Duty is, that a man owes something and makes up his mind to
pay it. A little while ago I pointed out to your readers that France wanted
a grand Puritan reaction. They who can lead such a movement will put
the revolutionary devil in his right place.[93]

In the hands of Puritan leaders revolutions never degenerated into
anarchy. 'Littlejohn' had precise models in mind:

William the Silent, Luther, John Knox, the Regent Murray, Coligny,
Cromwell, Milton, Bunyan . . . These men made revolutions, but they
were not revolutionists; and this is the distinction I wish to draw attention
to. They formed in their own mind a notion of God's law. To that above
all things they acknowledged obedience. They never went about the
world whining and canting for their own salvation. They left all consequences to the Deity, and all they asked was, to be doers of His will. . . .
Revolutionary France is made of quite other stuff. It has courage,
devotion, sentiment, but not Duty; and there it fails. Egotism and equality
run mad are the characteristics of the Revolution. Puritanism was the
exact contrary of French Revolution. It worked logically with facts at its
disposal. Confusion and anarchy could not consist with obedience to God's
law; they belonged to the Devil's law, and were to be trodden under foot . . .
[The Puritans] did their best to choose good leaders and secure good rulers,
and so long as leaders and rulers went in what they thought the Lord's way,
there was no limit to their obedience and support.[94]

In contrast to the 'corrupt' French revolutionaries, their neighbours, the Italian republicans, were 'virtuous'. 'Mazzini's famous
war-cry against despotism, "God and the People", gave the right
tone to the Italian movement', as it translated into effective
political language the Protestant notion of a direct relationship,
without intermediaries, between the Deity and believers. Mazzini
also gave the Italians 'the Puritan idea – the grandest man can
attain to – . . . that of duty',[95] with the characteristic stress on
personal responsibility, and the idea of politics as a call to a
'mission field'. A delighted Thomas Burt observed that 'Mazzini
declared that we, none of us, have any business to speak of our
rights, unless, and until, we have performed our duties. "The sole

[93] Littlejohn, 'Revolution the Enemy of Liberty', *WT*, 26 Mar. 1871, p. 6.
[94] *Ibid.*
[95] Littlejohn, 'The Great Conspiracy of Priestcraft', *WT*, 17 Jun. 1875, p. 6. Cf. Ashton,
    Adams, pp. 49–50. 'Duty' had been celebrated aslo by S. Smiles.

origin of every right is in a duty fulfilled".[96] Consequently Mazzini's definition of liberty was 'the right . . . to exercise without obstacles or restrictions one's faculties in the fulfilment of one's special mission'.[97] John Wilson, quoting a favourite Mazzinian passage, considered that the Italian patriot had put his priorities right when he wrote:

From the idea of God, I descended to the conception of progress; from the conception of progress to a true conception of life, to faith in a mission and its logical consequences – duty, the supreme rule of life; and having reached that faith, I swore to myself that nothing in this world should again make me doubt or forsake it.'[98]

This attitude had a familiar ring to people influenced by Evangelical Christianity. In one of his sermons Wilson asked:

How would the world be saved? It would be saved when every man saw his duty in the welfare and well-being of others; it would be saved when they realised that they were not for themselves designed, but to please and help mankind . . . That was what the Cross taught them – it was their duty to give themselves in order to save others. The Cross of Christ was an example for all of them to do their duty as He did His.[99]

It was Mazzini's personal 'holiness' that most contributed towards generating an interest in him, because he consistently 'lived' his philosophy even when this involved paying a high personal price: in this he was likened to John Bunyan, as a man 'marked from childhood to make his pilgrimage through life on the plane of high ideals'.[100] Romantic style, Puritan content, and a martyr-like life were at the basis of the fascination with Mazzini: his works – bits and pieces of which were also published in working-class

---

[96] Burt, *Lecture on the Life and Work of the late Joseph Cowen, M.P., 14 October 1911, Armstrong College*, Newcastle upon Tyne, 1911, p. 13 (in Newcastle Reference Library). This passage may have been one of Burt's favourites, as he quoted it on one other public occasion at least: see Watson, *A Great Labour Leader* (1908), p. 189.

[97] Mazzini, *Note autobiografiche* (1866), p. 253. This affinity between Mazzinianism and Protestant Nonconformity found expression in Italy too, especially after 1860, with the establishment of 'free' Evangelical Churches whose leaders were Mazzinians and Garibaldians: Spini, *L'evangelo e il berretto frigio*, pp. 7–31.

[98] Armstrong, *Pilgrimage from Nenthead* (1938), p. 135.

[99] 'Mr John Wilson, M.P., at Stalwell [Presbyterian Church]', *The Consett Guardian*, 13 Sept. 1901, [newspaper cutting in] J. Wilson Papers. See the case of John Snowden: 'In his speeches he used to speak of rights being dependent on duties – that when the latter cease to be performed, the former have no existence.' ('Death of Mr. Snowden', *Halifax Courier*, 6 Sept. 1884, p. 7.

[100] Armstrong, *Pilgrimage from Nenthead* (1938), p. 134.

newspapers[101] – were often quoted with the reverence due to a modern 'revelation' whenever an authoritative condemnation of anti-democratic social and political systems was required.[102] Mazzini was 'the . . . prophet of democracy'.[103]

Thus the extent of Mazzini's popularity was quite extraordinary,[104] and was reflected in the popular press: throughout Britain, he always found apologists and poets ready to celebrate his work and thought.[105] His supporters included radical leaders like Charles Bradlaugh,[106] P. A. Taylor, and J. Stansfeld.[107] In many respects William Lovett, the Chartist, was so influenced by the Italian patriot that he looked like an English Mazzinian,[108] and the many labour leaders who mentioned Mazzini's writings as a relevant influence on their political and cultural formation included G. Howell,[109] W. R. Cremer,[110] John Wilson,[111] C. Fenwick,[112] J. Johnson,[113] H. Vivian,[114] J. Havelock Wilson,[115] and W. Johnson.[116] One of the leaders of the 'New Unionism' of the 1880s, F. Maddison, declared: 'if I had to name a single writer to whom I owe most it would have to be Joseph Mazzini, especially his essay on "The Duties of Man". He has shaped my political, economic, and religious thinking, and no one has gained so entirely my agreement.'[117] When in 1862 the London Trades' Council answered the greetings of one of Naples' friendly societies, two 'Italian worthies' were mentioned: 'your great Poet – Dante' and

[101] *BH*, 7 Sept. 1872, pp. 2–3.
[102] Ironside, 'Caste', *Nw*, 15 Jan. 1870, p. 4.
[103] Armstrong, *Pilgrimage from Nenthead* (1938), p. 137.
[104] See also Claeys, 'Mazzini, Kossuth, and British Radicalism, 1848–54', pp. 225–62. For a different interpretation, see Beales, *England and Italy*, pp. 31–3.
[105] Ironside, 'Joseph Mazzini', *NW*, 29 May 1869, p. 4; [l.a.], 'Giuseppe Mazzini: a Patriot', *LW*, 17 Mar. 1872, p. 1; see G., 'A Tribute to Mazzini' [poem], *BH*, 22 Feb. 1868, p. 3. To 'Ironside' Mazzini was 'the greatest leader since Christ' (Ashton, *Adams*, p. 3).
[106] Bradlaugh Bonner, *Charles Bradlaugh* (1895), pp. 152–3.
[107] See Fraser, *Trade Unions and Society*, p. 152. P. A. Taylor owned a beautiful cameo representing Mazzini (now in the Fitzwilliam Museum, Cambridge).
[108] Wiener, *Lovett*, pp. 47, 108–11.
[109] Collins and Abramsky, *Karl Marx and the British Labour Movement*, p. 18.
[110] *Ibid.*
[111] Wilson, *Memories of a Labour Leader* (1910), pp. 319–20.
[112] 'Fenwick, Charles' in DLB, 1. Books by Mazzini in his library included *European Democracy* and *Faith in the Future*.
[113] 'Character Sketches', *Review of Reviews* (1906), p. 576.
[114] *Ibid.*, p. 580.   [115] *Ibid.*, p. 582.
[116] *Ibid.*, p. 576.   [117] *Ibid.*, p. 577.

'your noble martyr, Mazzini'.[118] A few years later Howell wrote to Luigi Wolff:

I have at last been able to obtain a copy of the address I wrote while Secretary of the London Trades' Council, will you kindly give it to Mazzini. How his name has been cherished by us this humble address will show to some little extent, but how much he has aided our cause in England we can never tell. His example has kept many of us to our work when all seemed dead around.[119]

But perhaps the most enthusiastic of the British Mazzinians was the miner Chester Armstrong, to whom 'Mazzini . . . was a divine revelation, worthy to be placed among the few immortals who have lived and suffered to redeem the world'.[120] Armstrong had first come across the Italian patriot through a biography which also contained two of his writings,[121] but that had been just the beginning of a life-long interest: 'I sprang to Mazzini hungry for spiritual insight. I did not rest content until I had sifted the whole of his literary work. This work is compiled in six volumes under the title of *The Life and Writings of Joseph Mazzini*. It was to me a spiritual feast.'[122] His thought 'was simplicity itself. It was pitched on a high note of religious fervour. His whole political plan rested on the broad basis of God and humanity.'[123]

Mazzini – together with Garibaldi – was thus credited with having started the 'Italian Reformation'.[124] At the root of his popularity in Britain there was that same Leveller zeal, Puritan moralism, and reformed religiosity which had formed the basis of Cromwell's success as a radical symbol: not surprisingly the most fervent of the Protector's admirers – such as Henry Vincent, W. J. Linton and Joseph Cowen – were also passionate supporters of

---

[118] 'The London Trades' Council to The General Neapolitan Society of the Working Men of the Sections of Mutual Help', n.d. [but early 1862], in *G. Howell Collection*, I, *Autobiography Materials*, Chapter v, pp. 65–6.

[119] G. Howell to Major Wolff, 14 Mar. 1867, in *G. Howell Collection*, Letter Bks, 342.

[120] Armstrong, *Pilgrimage from Nenthead* (1838), p. 137.

[121] *Ibid.*, p. 134. These writings were 'Thoughts on Democracy in Europe' and 'Duties of Man'.

[122] *Ibid.*, p. 136.

[123] *Ibid.*, p. 135.

[124] [L.a.], 'Mazzini and His Career', *WT*, 17 Mar. 1872, p. 1. On Mazzini's puritan-like religiosity, see Bolton King, *Mazzini*, pp. 222–48; and Passerin D'Entreves, 'Il vangelo politico-religioso di Giuseppe Mazzini', pp. 248–68, 354–8.

Mazzini.[125] The latter, like Luther, Knox and the other great Christian leaders, was a symbol of 'liberation by faith': 'Mazzini and Garibaldi with only justice and truth on their side have been more powerful than kings with armies and politicians with state papers'.[126] When the patriot died in 1872, *Reynolds's* wrote: 'A great prophet has fallen . . . It was the lot of Joseph Mazzini to be born in an age of royal tyranny and ecclesiastical corruption and he was called to the work of deliverance. There lay before him, as before all great teachers, a mission of forty years in the wilderness . . .'[127] – in other words, a mission like that of Moses, the founder of Israel as a nation.

THE 'PEOPLE' AGAINST 'PRIVILEGE'

The Nonconformist – indeed, more generally, the Protestant – frame of mind was also politically relevant in another context: it accounted for the anthropological pessimism peculiar to the tradition of British popular liberalism, in contrast, for instance, to the French Jacobin-Republican tradition. Victorian plebeian radicals believed that the moral nature of man was sinful and – despite Darwin, Comte and the ideology of progress – basically non-evolutionary: 'What man is here and there, man is everywhere – a creature of impulse, of liability to temptation'.[128] Such pessimism provided the background to some important affinities between 'official' and popular liberalism, and was of course a major component of one of the progenitors of both, namely Locke's constitutionalism.[129] Since evil was built into human nature, the greater the power and wealth of individuals and classes, the greater their power to do evil, unless their sinful inclinations were 'checked and balanced' through the working of democracy. Thus, progress depended on the success of the latter; in this sense it was politically conditioned. However, while the wealthy needed institutional

---

[125] See 'Vincent, Henry', in DLB, 1, pp. 331–2. 'Cowen, Joseph', in DLB, 1; Howell, 'Cromwell and the Imagery of Nineteenth Century Radicalism', pp. 193, 196. Linton was a Mazzinian in the proper, 'Italian' sense of the word: see his *English Republic, God and the People* (1851), pp. xvi, 216, in which the influence of both Mazzini's thought and style is evident.

[126] Robin Goodfellow, 'The Gossip Bowl', *NW*, 19 Oct. 1867, p. 4.

[127] [L.a.], 'The Death of Joseph Mazzini', *RN*, 17 Mar. 1872, p. 1.

[128] Northumbrian, 'Labour, Lawlessness, and Lechery', *RN*, 18 Feb. 1883, p. 3.

[129] Locke's works were widely read among plebeian radicals (Prothero, *Artisans and Politics*, p. 98; Stedman Jones, *Languages of Class*, p. 138 and note; Dunn, *Locke*, p. 7 n.).

checks and balances, the poor had their wicked tendencies 'balanced' by their lack of power, 'checked' by their humble social standing, and disciplined by 'Adam's curse', hard work. Hence the democratic belief that 'the people are less selfish and more open to conviction than interested sections of the Community, whether squires, farmers, parsons, manufacturers or any other select class'[130] – a belief shared even by Gladstone, as exemplified by his famous appeal to the 'masses' against the 'classes'.

This frame of mind was also to be found behind the doctrine of the irreconcilable conflict between the 'People' and 'Privilege', already mentioned above in the introduction.[131] The radicals regarded the landed aristocracy as the section of society most hopelessly corrupted by unchecked power, excessive authority and influence, and the lack of exertion and daily labour. This 'theological' criticism of the aristocracy went hand in hand with the traditional democratic emphasis on the evils of monopoly in landed property, and contributes to the explanation of the pre-eminence of rural themes in the ideology of popular radicalism.[132] As in the days of Chartism, the struggle against the aristocracy was perceived as a political and social struggle at one and the same time, a struggle for the control of legitimate authority, from which 'the People' had hitherto been excluded. This was the closest to the Marxist idea of 'class struggle' that Victorian working-class radicals went. However, *their* 'class struggle' was not the war of the 'proletariat' against the 'capitalists', but rather the struggle of the 'Nation' of the producers – the 'industrial orders' which included both employers and workers – against the landed aristocracy. By contrast, between the 'industrial orders' there was no 'class struggle', only competition, as their fundamental interests were supposed to coincide.[133] This interpretation was shared by the spokesmen for parliamentary and intellectual radicalism, including John Bright, Richard Cobden, J. S. Mill and Joseph Chamberlain. Bright was closest to the popular sensitivity on this as on other points;[134] indeed, it was his concern

[130] A. J. Mundella wrote to a friend, cit. in Hamer, *Liberal Politics*, p. 17. For Gladstone's case, see Parry, *Democracy and Religion*, pp. 150, 167, 170–4, 451–2.
[131] See above, pp. 11–13.
[132] Thompson, *Making of the English Working Class*, p. 105.
[133] Cf. Biagini, 'British Trade Unions and Popular Political Economy', pp. 811–40.
[134] Vincent, *Formation of the British Liberal Party*, p. 203.

for land reform and the ending of 'Privilege' which became the basis of the middle- and the working-class 'progressive alliance' on which late-nineteenth-century Liberalism prospered as a party for the masses.[135]

It may seem odd that the ideology of working-class radicalism in industrialized Britain contained such an emphasis on the land question and such hostility towards the nobility. But, as Rubinstein and Thompson have shown,[136] contemporary observers were not deluding themselves with anachronistic visions: on the contrary, they were quite realistic in their assessment of the distribution of wealth and influence within Victorian society. Moreover, they were also reacting to the evident contrast between the liberal-democratic ethos of urban radicalism and the aristocratic political and social system still intact in the countryside. In the rural districts working men still lacked – as late as the 1860s – trades unions, electoral rights, elective local government, popular primary education, and apparently, even a political consciousness. Farm workers were looked down on by urban artisans as 'land's serfs'[137] or indeed 'white slaves',[138] and even farmers were disparaged as servilely deferential to their titled masters. Indeed, 'independent' farmers were supposed to be so rare that – as evidence of the bondage shared by both farmers and their labourers – the mass-circulation press exploited sensational cases of unyielding farmers evicted for voting against their squire's wishes.[139]

The political and social disadvantages which still characterized the situation of the rural producers accounted for the bitterness of the radicals' attitude to social conflicts in the countryside. The democratization of social relationships in the rural districts was still seen almost as a revolutionary measure, just like borough franchise before 1867: it was expected that the introduction of 'urban' institutions and attitudes to social relations would drastically alter not only the relationship between labourers and farmers

---

[135] Briggs, *Victorian People*, pp. 216–17.
[136] See Rubinstein, 'The End of "Old Corruption" in Britian', pp. 55–86; and 'New Men of Wealth'; Thompson, *Landed Society*; Arnstein, 'The Survival of the Victorian Aristocracy', in Jaher (ed.), *The Rich, the Well-born, and the Powerful*.
[137] [L.a.], 'Land's Serfs', *RN*, 28 Feb. 1875, p. 1.
[138] 'Gracchus', 'Landlords and Land-Serfs', *RN*, 17 Mar. 1872, p. 3; Lloyd Jones, 'The Agricultural Labourers', *BH*, 13 Jan. 1872.
[139] [L.a., n.t.], *LM*, 9 Sept. 1868, p. 2.; [l.a.], 'Landlord Influence in Wales', *NW*, 10 Jul. 1869, p. 4; [l.a.], 'The Breconshire Election', *LW*, 30 May 1875, p. 1.

or farmers and landlords, but also those between the 'People' as a whole and 'Old Corruption', whose hold on society would be undermined in its very stronghold.[140]

Thus, it was not simply the fact that agricultural labourers were rewarded so poorly that filled urban radicals with indignation; what really aroused their anger was the peculiarity of social conflict in the countryside, in a context in which the 'market' had not yet been 'isolated' and separated from politics. Landed property was political power: it was desired not so much for the riches it produced, but because it was accompanied by authority, influence, privilege, and access to political office. Aristocratic landed property implied a whole *system* of power that many still described as 'feudalism',[141] the *bête noire* of radicalism, the ultimate target of the whole anti-aristocratic polemic.[142]

But what did Victorian radicals mean by 'feudalism'? They maintained that the decisive battle against the *ancien régime* was still to be fought. The *ancien régime* had been defeated and dislodged from the towns between 1832 and 1846: substantial religious liberty for Dissenters, industrialization, the expansion of trade, the emancipation of entrepreneurial groups and the organization of workers' trade unions had contributed towards breaking up the aristocratic monopoly both in politics and in economics. But none of these changes had reached the countryside yet, nor was it evident that they would reach it in the near future: indeed, for a long time after 1867 the main radical newspapers continued to describe the cause of democracy as an essentially urban one, with little scope outside the industrial towns and the great commercial cities.[143] The most extreme illustration was Ireland, an almost totally rural part of the kingdom which seemed to stand at the antipodes of the British urban-liberal model: there, wealth and power were monopolized by the landlords, while the starving tenants seemed totally unable to defend their interests and needed special parliamentary legisla-

---

[140] Northumbrian, 'The Ruling Minority', *RN*, 25 Aug. 1872, p. 3.

[141] *Ibid.* 'Northumbrian' concluded: 'We have lost the yeomen who were once the pride and glory of England, and the miserable, spiritless farmer is a poor substitute for the sturdy yeoman'. In this case, too, plebeian liberalism was closely parallel to American Jacksonian radicalism: 'It is the feudal past, perpetuated by corrupt, repressive institutions, that accounts for the evil economic and military depredations of Europe.' (Marx, *The Machine in the Garden*, p. 138).

[142] See Northumbrian, 'The Abolition of Feudalism', *RN*, 13 Mar. 1870, p. 3; [l.a.], 'Our Landed System and How to Mend It', *WT*, 22 Sept. 1867, p. 1.

[143] This issue is discussed in detail below, chapter 5, pp. 257–88.

tion just to survive. The analysis of plebeian radicals was that, unchecked by any equivalent of British urban radicalism, the power of the aristocracy was exercised to the detriment of the whole society. The results had been disastrous: Ireland had been reduced to chronically desperate conditions, a classical example of the destructive power of 'feudalism',[144] and one of the 'scandals' of Europe, comparable to Tzarist Russia.[145] Thus, by 'feudalism' plebeian liberals meant the monopoly of all positions of power and authority by one social group, causing the overlapping of political, social, economic, and religious conflicts, in each of which the people who controlled legitimate authority were the same as those who controlled it in all the others.[146]

Typical of this stress on 'feudalism' was the survival of archaic ideological forms, like the doctrine of the 'Norman Yoke' and the lost 'Saxon democracy'. Both theories had an extraordinary influence and continuity from the seventeenth century,[147] and in Victorian Britain they were still being taken seriously enough to be quoted by such politicians as John Bright,[148] Joseph Cowen,[149] and even Gladstone.[150] Working-class radicals had used these doctrines especially during the campaigns for the reform of the electoral system.[151] The Saxon mythology provided the people with something like the laurels of a 'republican nobility' of virtue, honesty, and hard work.[152] On the other hand, the economic and social hegemony of the aristocracy drew its origins from robbery, when the 'ruthless bandits' led by 'the Norman butcher' William I invaded Britain. Thus, the typical aristocrat was originally a man like William de Warenne, whose crimes were rewarded with the gift of

---

[144] Gracchus, *RN*, 23 May 1869, p. 3; and 'Republican and Monarchical Statesmen', *RN*, 28 Jan. 1872, p. 3.
[145] Mill, *England and Ireland*, (1868), p. 11.
[146] [L.a.], 'The Evils of Hereditary Aristocracy', *RN*, 11 Sept. 1869, p. 1.
[147] Hill, 'The Norman Yoke', in Saville (ed.), *Democracy and the Labour Movement*, pp. 15 ff.; Godwin, *The Friends of the People*, p. 21; Briggs, 'Saxons, Normans and Victorians', in *Collected Essays*, II, p. 217.
[148] Trevelyan, *Bright*, p. 24.
[149] [Rep.], 'Newcastle Election ... Mr Cowen's Speeches ... Shieldfield', *NW*, 17 Jan. 1874, p. 2.
[150] Hill, 'The Norman Yoke', in Saville (ed.), *Democracy and the Labour Movement*, p. 57.
[151] See below, chapter 5, pp. 257–75.
[152] Plain Dealer, 'The Working Men's Meeting in the Guildhall', *BH*, 11 Aug. 1866, p. 4.

28 villages in Yorkshire alone. This William de Warenne was ancestor of the famous William de Warenne, renowned for his exploits in the reigns of Henry the Third and Edward the First, and still more celebrated for his answer on being required to show a title to his estate. Drawing his sword he exclaimed, 'William, the bastard, did not conquer the kingdom for himself alone; my ancestor was a joint adventurer in the enterprise; what he gained by the sword, by the sword I will maintain'.[153]

This interpretation of the origins of the aristocratic system – sometimes accompanied by anti-clerical details[154] – was quite common in the popular press,[155] especially in republican and secularist circles.[156] Probably its largest-scale application took place during the famous agitation on behalf of the 'Claimant' to the Tichborne estates – seen as the 'man of the people' victimized, like the Saxons of old, by 'Government oppression, legal corruption, and Romish machinations'.[157] Not surprisingly, in 1875 the 'Claimant's' lawyer, Kenealy, who stood successfully as a candidate for the radical borough of Stoke-on-Trent, was enthusiastically supported by the most anti-aristocratic organs of popular liberalism.[158]

In spite of the naive character of many of these attitudes, the 'Norman Yoke' could still be quite useful as an ideology: with its

---

[153] J. Frearson, 'The Land and the People', *BH*, 14 May 1870, p. 204.

[154] The Normans were supported by a band of French priests, and the Pope himself had blessed their enterprise: [l.a.], 'The Evil of an Hereditary Aristocracy', *RN*, 11 Sept. 1869; Littlejohn, 'The Primogeniture Folly – Mr Locke King's Bill', *WT*, 25 Jul. 1869, p. 6.

[155] Gracchus, 'The Robbery of the Land by the Aristocracy', *RN*, 10 Jan. 1869, p. 3 (which included a celebration of Robin Hood as leader of the anti-Norman resistence); [l.a.], 'Hold Fast to the Land', *LW*, 23 Apr. 1871, p. 6.

[156] [Rep.], 'Central British Democratic Convention', [address by the chairman, Mr Weston, and address by Mr Mooney, 'Who Owns the Land?'], *NR*, 9 Mar. 1873, p. 156.

[157] [L.a.], 'The Startling Elections', *NW*, 20 Feb. 1875, p. 4. For a detailed discussion of the 'Tichborne agitation', see McWilliam, 'The Tichborne Case', in Biagini and Reid (eds.), *Currents of Radicalism*, pp. 44–64.

[158] Gracchus, *RN*, 4 Apr. 1875, p. 3; [l.a.], 'The Election of Dr Kenealy', *Labourers' Union Chronicle*, 20 Feb. 1875, p. 1:

Dr Kenealy goes the 'whole hog' in politics, and is a root and branch reformer of the most decisive and thorough-going school. Talk of the grievances of agricultural labourers, of land reform, of State Church abolition, of reconstitution of a legal system, of rational Sabbath observance, of absurd pretensions of priestism, of the destruction of privilege, or of any of the numerous evils, obsoletism, and anomalies which fetter the liberty of the people and obstruct the national growth; and Dr Kenealy is the man to reduce your talk into a form of practical action.

However, a majority of the working-class newspapers criticized the Stoke electors for returning such a controversial and eccentric man, rather than the much more respectable 'working man's candidate' A. A. Walton. In 1880, Kenealy was defeated by the Lib-lab Henry Broadhurst (see the comment in [l.a., n.t.], *NW*, 17 Apr. 1880, p. 4).

celebration of the Saxon 'ancient' democracy, it provided a social
and political model – the egalitarian 'peasant democracy' – which
represented one of those 'collective dreams' that, as Theodor
Shanin writes, 'matter politically'.[159] Moreover, it undermined the
legitimacy of the aristocracy, and helped to spread a radical
critique of landed property, thus preparing the ground for Henry
George's later campaigns:

It is not likely – *Reynolds's* wrote in 1874 – the present state of things will
endure for ever. Some day or another a revolutionary cloud must burst
over the nation, and then the uppermost question amongst the masses
will be that concerning the ownership of land. The other day, when Mr
Arch questioned the right of many great landowners to possess the estates
they hold, the Marquis of Bristol indignantly asked what better title to
land can be shown than that which was conferred by sovereign and by
Act of Parliament? But Mr Arch's logical rejoinder, that if one parliament
had the right to give, another assuredly had the right of taking away,
must have 'shut up' his lordship . . . by teaching the masses of the people
how they have been defrauded, pillaged, and wronged by those who hold
them subjugate, Mr Arch and his followers are preparing the mind of the
country for the time when the great question shall arise, Who gave you
the land, and by what right or title have you taken it from us?[160]

As far as Britain was concerned, this verbal violence was not
accompanied by a corresponding intensity in social conflict in the
rural districts. There were, however, two kinds of events which
contributed towards rekindling the traditional radical zeal for land
reform. On the one hand there was the old struggle between
poachers and keepers, made fiercer by the Game Laws, and
occasionally accompanied by loss of life; on the other there were
the endless land crises in Ireland, which generated periodical
eruptions of violence followed by coercion.

The Game Laws – with the limits they imposed on the farmers'
control of the land they cultivated, and the personal liberty of all
the rural folk[161] – had always been a symbol of aristocratic
privilege, 'a badge of serfdom and slavery for farmer and peas-

---

[159] Shanin, 'The Peasant Dream', in Samuel and Stedman Jones (eds.), *Culture, Ideology and Politics*, p. 227.

[160] Gracchus, 'Labourers and Landlords – Toilers and Despoilers', *RN*, 26 Jul. 1874, 3.

[161] 'The day that the Poaching Prevention Act of 1862 became law was a black day for the labourer; from that time onwards he might at any hour be subjected to the indignity of being assailed and searched by the police officer' (Arch, *Life* (1898), p. 148).

ant',[162] and their repeal was one of the oldest radical requests.[163] They also represented a good illustration of the 'feudalism' radicals attacked because of the lack of guarantee of a fair trial for arrested poachers: as *Reynolds's* put it, 'no mockery of justice can be conceived greater than that of game-preserving squires sitting to convict a poacher on the evidence of a gamekeeper'.[164]

Working-class and artisan radicals were not alone in their protest, as many parliamentary leaders shared their concern and were ready to give them full support.[165] Yet few politicians, if any, would have had the courage to endorse the concept – then quite widespread among the rural common people – that the poacher was a kind of freedom fighter.[166] This line was taken only by the most extreme of the working-class newspapers, and in particular by *Reynolds's*. The latter claimed that the landlords

> could not open their text book, the Bible, and point to any passage in the Book of Genesis containing the account of God's creation of the world which says He made the fishes of the sea and the birds of the air for the special behoof of the privileged few. On the contrary it distinctly declares that they were created for the good of all. And the circumstances of our flying in the face of this decree leads to bloodshed and other direful calamities.[167]

This emphasis on poaching as a battle for the 'God-given rights' of 'free-born' Britons was not just archaic plebeian-radical rhetoric, since what was at stake was in fact one of the most politically delicate questions of the time, that of the limits of the rights to landed property: if game was to be declared the common endowment of all Britons, or of the local community, arguably land itself would follow suit. Thus, this campaign against the 'old shackles of semi-feudalism'[168] could easily lead towards 'confiscation' of property rights and even republicanism, the only logical option left to

---

[162] Littlejohn, 'Scotch Game-Preserving: A National Wrong', *WT*, 16 Jul. 1878, p. 6; see [l.a.], 'The Iniquitous Game Laws', *RN*, 23 May 1869, p. 1; Hawker, *Journal* (1979), p. 109.

[163] Robbins, *Eighteenth-Century Commonwealthmen*, p. 353.

[164] [L.a.], 'The Diabolical Game Laws', *RN*, 12 Jun. 1870, p. 3.

[165] Trevelyan, *Bright*, pp. 125–6.

[166] Jones, 'The Poacher: A Study in Victorian Crime and Protest', pp. 825–60; poachers were also seen as Robin Hood figures by the French peasants: see Magraw, *France 1815–1914*, p. 149.

[167] [L.a.], 'Bird-butchers and Man-butchers', *RN*, 3 Dec. 1876; see 'King of Norfolk Poachers', *Life* (1982), p. 182.

[168] Littlejohn, 'The Last Days of Squirearchy', *WT*, 22 Aug. 1880, p. 6.

those who did not hesitate 'to tear away the tinsel rags that cover royalty and nobility, unmask them to the world, and let their hideous nakedness be seen by all'.[169] The logical conclusion of the anti-aristocratic polemic was thus the request for a complete reform of the constitutional and social edifice.

If land reform in Britain was only potentially explosive, the situation in Ireland was much more immediately threatening. British plebeian radicals showed considerable sympathy for the Irish tenants, in spite of the violent methods used by some of the latter to resist the imposition of rents and the eviction of those who would not or could not pay. In their zeal to reform Irish land British plebeian liberals reached the climax of their radicalism, which occasionally could sound almost like socialism:

You talk of nothing else but the 'rights of property', and when they are infringed you try, by the help of gaols, gibbets and fetters, to make them respected. But you cannot, because they are so vilely iniquitous, so accursedly unjust, so diabolically mischievous, that they must ultimately succumb to the laws of right, of humanity, and of justice.[170]

Since the lives of millions of people were endangered by the selfishness of a few, even moonlight terrorism was justified as an expression of the Lockian right to resist tyranny:

Is it a good thing that a nation shall perish in order that some three or four thousand persons should fatten upon its soil? . . . Thus, therefore, when an Irish peasant drills a hole in the backbone of an evicting landlord, the former is only dealing in a somewhat unceremonious manner with an oppressive and despotic squatter.[171]

Between the case of Ireland and that of rural Britain there were many differences, but also some affinities, as the fundamental problem in both cases was that of making the structure and working of the rural society approximate more closely to that of the urban one. The solution to both the 'social' and the 'political question' seemed to centre on the elimination of the aristocracy as a system of power. By contrast, entrepreneurial rural capitalists did not attract any comparable amount of hostility. As *Reynolds's* wrote in 1869,

---

[169] Gracchus, *RN*, 19 Nov. 1871, p. 3.
[170] Gracchus, 'The "Rights of Property" and the Wrongs of Community', *RN*, 28 Nov. 1869, p. 3.
[171] *Ibid.*

For the landowner who throws open every acre of his estate to industry, and for the enterprising manufacturer who boldly embarks his fortune in an enterprise founded upon productive labour, distributing the highest wages which can be earned, after satisfaction for the charges for redemption of capital and of a fair proportion of the profit earned as the difference between cost and price, the English working man can regard with profound respect. The men they need to dread are the landlords, who, in the possession of their estates, for political and social objects, deliberately exclude the people from thousands of acres allowed to lie waste or unemployed, in the form of parks and moors, upon which game is much more cared for than human life.[172]

If only the rentier's stranglehold on land was broken, emancipation of rural labour could be achieved – as it had been in the towns – through trade unionism; then farmers and farmworkers would be left to sort out their differences on their own, through the well-tested mechanism of collective bargaining which mediated conflicts and prevented the growth of extreme social tensions.[173]

Yet, by the 1870s, without any major land reform, the urban model of industrial relations, with peaceful trade unionism, was being extended to the country districts.[174] Game Laws incidents still attracted public attention, especially as they were so clearly at odds with the prevailing trends of the time: in Britain (though not in Ireland) the rural rebel exchanging shots with the keeper was rapidly becoming the last romantic symbol of a world which was fading away. Land reform was more necessary than ever, but with the aim of emancipating capital as much as labour:

the farmer of the future will be an independent capitalist, claiming full liberty to cultivate how he finds best, to make what improvements he thinks will be profitable, and to hold them as property for which the landlord must pay the full market value when a lease expires. The old sort of vassal farmer is used up and turned out.[175]

It was in this frame of mind that at the beginning of the 1870s working-class journalists began to describe a new human type, hitherto virtually unknown: the 'independent' agricultural

---

[172] [L.a.], 'The Division of Profit', *RN*, 29 Sept. 1869, p. 1. The similarity with the *sans-culotte* ideology of the 1790s is remarkable: Soboul, *Les sans-culottes parisienes*, pp. 412–13. Moreover, even in this respect the continuity in radical ideology seems complete: see Godwin, *The Friends of Liberty*, p. 370; Stedman Jones, *Languages of Class*, p. 136.

[173] Lloyd Jones, 'Agricultural Labourers', *BH*, 13 Jan. 1872.

[174] [L.a.], 'A Significant Sign of the Times', *RN*, 24 Mar. 1872, p. 4.

[175] Littlejohn, 'The Control of the Land', *WT*, 4 Mar. 1883, p. 6.

labourer. The newspaper prototype of the 'new model' farm worker was Joseph Arch. He was presented as a man with an active, inquiring mind, eloquent to the extent of being worthy to sit in the Commons, dignified, self-controlled, Methodist, teetotal, attached to his family. But first and foremost he was a trade unionist with a very clear mind about his rights and interests, and determined to bring to an end the tradition of social paternalism. As he declared, he and his men were fighting 'for the recognition of the fact that there was no compliment as between employer and employed, if the latter gave honest labour for a fair reward':[176] no 'compliment', nor patronage, but only a transaction between free men on the labour market. The old labour leader T. J. Dunning drew the right conclusion when he wrote that rural trade unionism – though representing a great victory for the working men – was not likely to prime any rural revolution, but to have the opposite effect:

the landowners and farmers ought to rejoice that it has taken place, for it is of all others a circumstance which if successful, will give stability to their position and render impossible to them a similar fate to that of the French nobility and farmers who were swept from the face of the earth for the same kind of oppression. To avert such a catastrophe, success must attend the movement of the agricultural labourers . . .[177]

THE 'COMING REPUBLIC'?

Dunning was not the only labour leader who thought that social and political democracy were the antidotes to revolution: indeed, this was a common assumption, as illustrated by trade-union attitudes to revolutionary socialism and the First International. The latter was appreciated so long as it was seen as a sort of 'international trade union congress',[178] but when Marx gave it an unmistakably socialist and revolutionary character, British popular radicals became increasingly hostile.[179] It was not fear, but contempt that inspired this hostility: if Marx's socialism appeared credible to Continental workers, it was not to the credit of Marx,

---

[176] [Rep.], 'The Warwickshire Labourers' Union', *BH*, 13 Apr. 1872.

[177] T. J. Dunning, 'Strike of Agricultural Labourers', *BH*, 6 Apr. 1872, p. 2; and see 'The Agricultural Labourer', *BH*, 13 Jan. 1872, p. 1.

[178] [L.a.], *BH*, 18 Sept. 1869, p. 4.

[179] Marx himself was quite unpopular because of his disparaging comments on the British trade union leaders: [l.a.], 'Carl [*sic.*] Marx on Working Men's Leaders', *BH*, 14 Sept. 1872, p. 9.

but the consequence of the reactionary and anti-liberal politics of many European governments, which blinded labour leaders and prevented free discussion. When the General Council of the International was moved from Geneva to New York, in 1872, some prophesied that the organization would find a much less congenial atmosphere there and would soon disintegrate as 'The free people and the free Government of the great Republic render extravagance of thought harmless by permitting men to get weary of their own ludicrous follies'.[180] For precisely the same reasons the International had not been successful in Britain:

> Our working men need for the improvement of their social and political condition, serious, honest, open work; nothing else profits them. Preposterous shams, serving only the sinister purposes of despots, are things to be avoided. We have neither time nor inclination to play at hide and seek with reactionary Governments. Our labours as a people on behalf of political and social progress must be honest, open, and above-board. Our highest advantages will be found in the peaceable improvement of the laws and usages of society, and we can best succeed in this by taking the whole world into our confidence, and thus finding auxiliaries everywhere amongst the friends of even-handed justice and rational liberty.[181]

Not only the methods, but even the language used by the members of the International were disparaged as totally 'un-English':

> We know of no such thing as 'the Revolution' belonging to the present or to the future of England, nor do we want to have paraded before us any indefinite phrase which excites alarm without possessing meaning or purpose . . . The working men of England know what they want, and can express themselves in relation to their wants in their native language.[182]

The British working classes faced real practical problems, for which they already had the best solutions without any need for the interference of foreign middle-class intellectuals:

> It would be no difficult matter to name every question that at the present moment occupies the thoughts of English working men. Trade unionism is an absorbing thought, with good practical work allied to it, but no sensible man would think of calling it 'the revolution'. Co-operation engages the serious attention of tens of thousands of working men, and although it may be regarded as the commencement of a mighty change, the man who called

---

[180] [L.a.], 'The International', *BH*, 21 Sept. 1872, p. 9.
[181] *Ibid.*
[182] [L.a.], 'John Stuart Mill and the International', *BH*, 9 Nov. 1872, p. 9; Mill replied to Thomas Smith, Secretary of the Nottingham section of the International.

it 'the revolution' would be laughed at. We want still a thorough recasting of our representative system, but people would as soon think of calling such a change the 'ticket', the 'go', or the 'cheese', as they would of calling it 'the revolution'. We require from the root up an improvement in our land laws, and those who oppose this will call it 'spoliation', 'flat burglary' and all else that might be discrediting, but men friendly to the change, because they think it will be of advantage to the nation, will not play into their opponent's hands by calling it 'the revolution'.[183]

One of the most resolute attacks against the International was written by the former Owenite Lloyd Jones. He deprecated even the publicity that the Internationalists received in the British press, and claimed that it was due to Tory propaganda aiming at discrediting the labour movement:

Under ordinary circumstances, these Geneva ravings would not be worth notice; but at the present day, when the labour question is commanding the attention of the public in all directions, and when the enemies of labour are unusually active in misrepresenting it, and defaming those actively engaged in its promotion, foolish and pretended friends should not be allowed to give countenance by their folly to the evil representation of open enemies.[184]

As for Marx's socialism, Lloyd Jones described it as a grotesque edifice: 'If the despots of Europe, if the worst foes of popular liberty in Europe, had swept together their paid agents, and instructed them to gibber the wildest nonsense as popular faith, such persons could not have exceeded in folly what these half-insane patriots uttered.'[185] Similar doctrines would be met with scorn and derision by the British working classes, if only the latter had time to spare for such nonsense. Hostility towards revolutionary socialism could not have been more determined, and similar attitudes character-ized other radical leaders, such as G. J. Holyoake and even G. Odger, who resigned from the presidency of the International in protest against the socialists.[186]

Since this was the general mood, it is not surprising that the prevailing attitude to the Paris Commune of 1871 was one of

---

[183] *Ibid.*
[184] Lloyd Jones, *BH*, 20 Sept. 1872, p. 2.
[185] *Ibid.* Marx's lack of influence contrasted with the wide dissemination of J. S. Mill's ideas. 'Littlejohn's' articles in the *Weekly Times* were often elaborate masterpieces of populari-zation of Mill's proposals for social, political and economic reform: see e.g. Littlejohn, 'Social Equality', 12 Apr. 1868, p. 6 (dealing with the issues of education and equality between the sexes).
[186] Royle, *Radicals, Secularists and Republicans*, p. 200.

disapproval,[187] and even of hysterical anti-communism.[188] However, as Professor R. Harrison has demonstrated,[189] there was also a considerable minority of working-class radicals who supported the new French revolution. This sympathy may seem difficult to explain in the light of what we have seen so far, especially if we follow Royden Harrison's view that British support for the Commune was a sort of 'prelude to socialism' spearheaded by the Postivist intellectuals. The main body of evidence for his interpretation is derived from Frederic Harrison's private letters to John Morley, in which he uses a language with almost socialist overtones.[190] Royden Harrison concludes that the Positivists inclined towards revolutionary socialism, but did not reveal their convictions in their public writings in case they scared away the middle-class radicals, whose support they needed. This suggestion is fascinating, but has a number of flaws. First of all, the Positivists used a liberal-radical interpretation not only when writing for middle-class periodicals, but also in their contributions to the working-class press, which presumably addressed not middle-class radicals, but precisely the potential constituency of an allegedly embryonic socialist party. Second, in spite of his 'anti-bourgeois' rhetoric, even Frederic Harrison's private letters to Morley show that he admired the Commune not as a social revolution, but as a political one; indeed, far from supporting democratic socialism, he hoped that the new government would take a Positivist-elitist line and persuade France to rid itself of universal suffrage and pseudo-democratic Caesarism based on the votes of the 'abject' and 'ignorant' masses of the countryside; he maintained that men were not equal, and that a good government should consist of leadership by 'the most capable

---

[187] Even in the *Bee-Hive* there were articles by labour leaders who were bitterly opposed to the *Commune*: e.g. T. J. Dunning, 8 Apr. 1871, pp. 1–2; J. R. Hollond, 'The Commune', 20 May 1871, p. 2; J. Aytoun, 'Republicanism v. Communism', 10 Jun. 1871, p. 3.

[188] [L.a.], 'The Massacre in Paris', *WT*, 26 Mar. 1871, p. 4, describing the Communards as murderers and anarchists. For examples of hysterical anti-communism, see [l.a.], 'The New Reign of Terror', *LW*, 26 Mar. 1871, p. 6. For an openly Bonapartist and anti-republican comment (based on Napoleon's support for free trade) see [l.a.], 'The Coming Events in Paris', *LW*, 22 Oct. 1871, p. 6. The 'anti-communism' of *Lloyd's* remained unchanged over the years, and as late as 1879 this newspaper protested against an amnesty being given to the Communard prisoners: [l.a.]. 'The Return of the Communists', *LW*, 14 Sept. 1879, p. 6; [l.a.], 'The Plenary Amnesty', *LW*, 19 Oct. 1879, p. 6.

[189] See the relevant sections of Harrison, *Before the Socialists*, and his introduction to *The English Defence of the Commune*.

[190] Harrison (ed.), *The English Defence of the Commune*, pp. 17–8; *Before the Socialists*, pp. 235–6.

and energetic' members of society, the urban workers.[191] As for 'social reform', Frederic Harrison mentioned solely 'a system of social taxation';[192] he had little to say about communism, and what he did say was condemnatory. His friend E. S. Beesley in the *Bee-Hive* insisted on the distinction between 'Commune' and 'Communism': 'the former means municipal or local self-government as distinguished from the central or national Government'.[193] He admitted that there was a minority of 'communists' amongst the Paris insurgents, but stressed that they were opposed by the majority of the Communards as much as by the Versailles republicans.[194]

This was also basically the line taken by most working-class sympathisers with the Commune. From the proclamation of the republic the radicals had supported the French cause with a series of great meetings in London, Bradford and Newcastle upon Tyne.[195] Later on some transferred their support to the Commune;[196] however, they were inspired not by hopes for socialism, but rather by the conviction that the people of Paris were the only true friends of liberty and republican ideals, and were fighting to achieve what the British had *already* obtained generations before: namely civil and religious liberty, real representative and elective local government and the overthrow of 'priestly rule' and 'sacerdotal superstition'.[197] The war in Paris was seen as a political struggle between 'Privilege' and the 'People', in the tradition of 1689 and 1776, rather than 1793. Thus, the Parisian revolution was 'a tremendous protest against centralization',[198] that hideous system which 'smothers all independence, all local life; develops functional action in exorbitant proportions; paralyses the initiative freedom of citizens; entangles all France in the meshes of an

---

[191] F. Harrison to J. Morley, 28 Jan. 1871, in *F. Harrison Papers*, 1/53, pp. 21, 26; see also F. Harrison to J. Morley, 22 Mar. 1871, in *ibid.*

[192] F. Harrison to J. Morley, 30 Mar. 1871, in *F. Harrison Papers*, 1/53, pp. 29–30.

[193] E. S. Beesley, 'Professor Beesley on the Communists', *BH*, 29 Apr. 1871, p. 1.

[194] E. S. Beesley, 'Professor Beesley and the Defence of the Commune', *BH*, 20 May 1871, p. 1.

[195] Collins and Abramsky, *Karl Marx and the British Labour Movement*, p. 182.

[196] The exception being a 'Republican demonstration' which took place in London on 16 April, a Sunday. Organized by the International Democratic Association – a society composed mainly of English radicals and Polish refugees – this meeting was possibly the least British of all the demonstrations in support of the *Commune*, both because of the participants and the ideology they expressed. The leaders of the British labour movement were remarkable for their absence. See [rep.], 'English Sympathy with the French Communists', *BH*, 22 Apr. 1871, p. 13.

[197] [L.a.], *RN*, 2 Apr. 1871, p. 1.

[198] [L.a.], 'Paris and Versailles', *LW*, 2 Apr. 1871, p. 6.

immense net, whose strongest cord is at the Ministry of the Interior'.[199] The only republics then flourishing – Switzerland and the United States – had federal constitutions, and this was what the Parisians were trying to achieve for the threatened French Republic. Federalism was the only real alternative to the monarchist restoration then plotted by the General Assembly.[200]

The workmen of Paris were the first to detect the sham, and they sought to correct its action by setting up a municipal government, which unfortunately for the English intellect, was called the Commune. If the Parisians had called it the City Corporation, and had fought against centralization, the English people would have been better able to remember how glorious are the chapters in the history of the City of London in its passage of arms with the despot who ruled at Whitehall.[201]

Thus, the Communards' struggle was likened to that of the English Puritans in the seventeenth century, and both found their justification in the Lockian right to resistance, rather than in the proletarian revolution.[202] As a consequence, G. J. Holyoake wrote that the Commune could be seen as the 'most English' thing that the French had ever done.[203] This interpretation was shared by radicals of different inclinations, such as Thomas Smith, secretary of the Nottingham section of the International,[204] W. J. Linton,[205] W. E. Adams,[206] and even the more moderate *Nonconformist*.[207]

[199] [L.a., n.t.], *NW*, 29 Apr. 1871, p. 4, citing from E. Tenot, *Étude historique sur le coup d'État*, Paris, 1868; see [l.a.], 'The Evils of France', *Leeds Evening Express*, 19 Apr. 1871, p. 2; [l.a., n.t.], *DN*, 30 Mar. 1871, p. 5. It is noteworthy tht such an interpretation was also consistent with the public declarations of the Communard envoys to Great Britain: see [rep.], 'Nottingham West End Club' [lecture by Monsieur J. S. Prichard, Mechanical Engineer of Paris. Lieutenant de la Garde Nationale], *NR*, 7 May 1871, pp. 302–3.

[200] Ironside, 'The Triumph of the Red Republic', *NW*, 1 Apr. 1871, p. 4.

[201] [L.a.], 'The Retrospect of 1871', *RN*, 31 Dec. 1871, p. 1. A similar interpretation was made in the *Co-operative News* ([l.a.], 'The Paris Commune and the International Working Men's Association, and Mr. A. B. Cochrane, M.P.', 11 Nov. 1871, p. 109):

> the French word *Commune* does not mean a Communist or Socialist establishment, but simply a municipal district, such as the City of Manchester, or the Borough of Salford . . . And the demand of the *Commune* of Paris was not for the abolition of private property, and the establishment of socialism; but simply that the people of each district or township should appoint its own magistrates and other officials, instead of having them appointed by central government.

[202] J. A. Partridge, '1815 and 1871', *BH*, 18 Feb. 1871, p. 1.

[203] Holyoake, *History of Co-operation*, (1906), p. 511.

[204] Cit. in Harrison, *English Defence of the Commune*, p. 266.

[205] Smith, *Linton*, (1973), p. 175.

[206] Ironside, 'Paris and Versailles', *NW*, 22 Apr. 1871, p. 4; and 'The Fall of the Commune', *NW*, 27 May 1871, p. 4.

[207] [L.a.], *Nonconformist*, 24 May 1871, pp. 516–17. Though this paper was by no means sympathetic to the *Commune* on account of the violence and anarchy advocated by some of the Parisian revolutionaries.

All this may sound like another manifestation of the famous 'peculiarities of the English', but in fact many radicals in Continental Europe took a similar line,[208] which, as recent studies have suggested, was actually more accurate than both contemporary and modern Marxist interpretations of the Commune.[209] There is now little doubt that the Communards were concerned first and foremost with 'preserving the Republic and the "rights of Paris"', and that they, like their British working-class friends, feared that without a federal constitution another *coup d'état* would soon suppress the republic, as had happened in 1851.[210] Their programme, far from being socialist, resembled that of the French parliamentary Radical party, and indeed reproduced 'the main themes of Gambetta's Belleville Programme in 1869', with priorities like 'the democratization of the machinery of the state, . . . disestablishment of the Church and compulsory lay education'.[211] Even on the issue of State intervention for social reform there was strong resistance among the Communards,[212] whose emphasis was rather on the defence of peasant, artisan and shopkeeping property against exploitation by the big capitalists, in the conviction that only the Commune 'can make of each individual a citizen and a proprietor, sovereign master of his person, of his conscience, of his home, of his product, of his destiny'.[213] The management of the Commune's finance ought to be an example of 'order, economy, honesty and strict control'[214] – virtues which sounded quite Gladstonian, and in any case had little to do with 'communism'.[215] This

---

[208] Like the Italian federalist republicans of *La Plebe*: Giovannini, *La cultura della 'Plebe'*, pp. 31–3.

[209] As voiced by Haupt, *Aspects of International Socialism*, pp. 23–47.

[210] Tombs, 'Harbingers or Entrepreneurs?', pp. 976–7.

[211] *Ibid.*; for surveys of recent interpretations see Tombs 'History and the French Left, 1830–1981', pp. 733–44, and Magraw, *France 1815–1914*, pp. 199–205.

[212] Price, 'Ideology and Motivations in the Paris Commune of 1871', p. 81.

[213] *Ibid.*, p. 80.

[214] Edwards, *The Paris Commune 1871*, p. 217.

[215] One of the budgets of the Commune (for the period 20 March–30 April) has been published in Jellinek, *The Paris Commune of 1871*, pp. 393–4: it shows the limits of the Paris government's commitment to expenditure for social purposes: only 1,000 f. was spent on education and the department of Labour had no budget at all, while 240,000 f. was given to justice and police, 103,000 f. to the home office, 112,000 f. to the foreign office, and 50,000 f. to the department of trade. Revenue was still based on a typically nineteenth-century structure: apart from extraordinary sources (like confiscation of pre-existent municipal funds, and the money of the Bank of France), only 373,813 f. was obtained through direct taxation, while 4,298,446 f. was raised through indirect taxes (of this 2,629,123 f. from tobacco duty). For the popularity of 'minimalist' budgets among British working-class radicals see below, chapter 2 section 3, pp. 93–103.

zeal for retrenchment was duly praised by British defenders of the Commune, Cobdenite to a man, who stressed that

The Parisian Government is one elected by the poor for the poor . . . It is cheap, progressive, and would be endurable if left to himself. But such an example of good and economic government by the people and for the people is an eye-sore to kings, nobles, and all those who fatten and thrive in luxury and indolence on the tools of others . . . The longer it exists, the more striking will become the contrast between good and economical, as typified by the Commune; and bad and expensive government, as typified by empires and monarchies.[216]

Such were the real terms of the debate: the British working-class defenders of the Commune did not go beyond the traditional Whig-Liberal support for overseas constitutional movements. Their motivations were no different from those inspiring sympathy for other contemporary republican revolutions, including Juarez's government in Mexico[217] and the First Republic in Spain.[218]

THE 'GREAT REPUBLIC OF THE WEST'

But it was with the oldest republican models – the United States and Switzerland – that the Commune was frequently compared.[219] Switzerland was then quite a unique case in Europe, a 'political island among a whole ocean of monarchies',[220] a country which

---

[216] Gracchus, 'The Commune', *RN*, 9 Apr. 1871, p. 2.

[217] George Howell described the late Maximilian as 'an executed murderer' (G. Howell to J. W. Probyn, 9 Jul. 1867, in *G. Howell Collection*, IX, Letter Bk. 777).

[218] See the resolutions of the Executive Committee of the Labour Representation League of 14 Feb. 1873 and 21 Feb. 1873, the latter undersigned by A. M. Latham, J. Ryan, G. Potter, Lloyd Jones, and H. Broadhurst: *Labour Representation League, Minute Book 1873–1878*, R. (S.R.) 61, pp. 9–10 and pp. 11–12 respectively. See also [rep.], 'Annual Festival of Messrs. Reynolds' and Dicks' Establishments', *RN*, 12 Jul. 1874, p. 1, [speech by G. W. M. Reynolds].

[219] Cit. in Harrison, *The English Defence of the Commune*, pp. 246–7. See the letters by T. Smith to the *Nottingham Daily Express* (in *ibid.*): in particular, the letters dated 31 May 1871 (p. 250), 7 Jun. 1871 (p. 256), n.d. (p. 265). See also [l.a.], 'The Use and Cost of Republics', *RN*, 22 Nov. 1872, p. 1.

[220] Bill Blades, Bricklayer, 'Voices from the Workshop', *RN*, 2 May 1880, p. 2. The revolution of 1847 had excited the enthusiasm of British radicals: 'The ring of the first Austrian shot fired against Switzerland would reverberate through Germany, Poland, Bohemia, Hungary and Italy, and not Swiss rifles alone would answer the volleys of the armed slaves of a detested despotism' (*Fraternal Greeting from The Democratic Friends of All Nations in London*, 13 Dec. 1847, cit. in Halperin, 'The Transformation of Switzerland', in Fejto (ed.), *1848*, p. 50).

could offer 'a great lesson to continental Liberals'.[221] It was
admired for its representative institutions, its systems of primary
education, and the principle of a 'citizens' army'[222] – 'very powerful
in defence, cheaper than any other country in the world'.[223] The
Helvetic Confederation was seen as a contented country: it had
neither 'feudalism'[224] nor starving proletarians.

neither poorrates nor poorhouses, no king, no aristocracy, or any of those
institutions which materially tend to impoverish a people . . . Switzerland
is out of debt; her people are happy, prosperous, and contented. There is
very little political agitation, simply because there is no cause for the
existence of political parties, hankering and clamouring after the loaves
and fishes of office.[225]

In short it enjoyed most of the advantages attributed to the 1871
Commune, without the latter's disadvantages. The recipe for the
Swiss success was the traditional Chartist one: political democracy
was the source of prosperity and social justice.[226] At the time of the
constitutional referendum of 1874 *Lloyd's* commented:

The voters are at their looms by the streams, or by their cattle on the hill;
wise, sober men, who know exactly what Switzerland wants to keep her
free and keep her strong, and who are not bad workers because they are
fair scholars and have a hand in the government of the commune where
they were born and within the narrow bounds of which they will
contentedly die. If only France could get its peace and prosperity, by
deigning to copy the wisdom displayed by the Switzers last Sunday! If only
England could reach such a content and virtue as may be found in the rural
communes of Helvetia, in common with hard work from dawn to dusk![227]

---

[221] [L.a.], 'The Swiss Plebiscitum', *LW*, 26 Apr. 1874, p. 6.

[222] 'The fact of every man keeping his rifle at home, was a great safeguard of liberty' ([rep.],
'Tarlington Hall' (Mr H. Jung's lecture on 'The Institutions of Switzerland'), *NR*, 6
Mar. 1870, p. 156; italics in the text). This was also supposed to be the principle of the
British democratic tradition, as Lloyd Jones wrote:

> The English bowmen . . . were the best fighting men in the world. Their arms were playthings
> carried about with them from childhood up; they practised in sport at the village butts, and they
> performed in earnest on such fields as Cressy and Poitiers; but when doing this they knew they were
> paying for the homesteads where the women and children they loved lived in safety, defended by
> their arms from the attacks of foreign foes, and by their service from eviction and dispossession by
> hard-handed landlords with the power to throw them homeless on the world. (Lloyd Jones, 'Political
> Economy, Labour, and Trade', *NW*, 19 Mar. 1881, p. 4)

[223] Littlejohn, 'The Working Men of Switzerland', *WT*, 15 Oct. 1871, p. 6.

[224] *Ibid.*

[225] Gracchus, *RN*, 30 Jan. 1873, p. 3.

[226] 'It is impossible to arrive at social reforms except through political reform' (Littlejohn,
WT, 15 Oct. 1871, p. 6).

[227] [L.a.], *LW*, 26 Apr. 1874, p. 6.

However, it was the United States that was most admired by British democrats. North America and Switzerland shared many features, and both countries were seen as unrivalled models of democracy, on a level with Athens in Pericles' day.[228] But the United States was closer to the sensitivity of the British subaltern classes because of the links of culture and language between the two nations;[229] in addition, the British and the Americans shared political traditions, and the United States was founded on what some considered sound Chartist doctrine, that is, that 'the principle of sovereignity is lodged in the people . . . by the very fact of a free government'.[230] It also provided a shelter for the persecuted and destitute from all over the world,[231] and offered hope to the rest of humanity, 'a home and a refuge for free men, for all the members of the great army of industry, whose work in Europe is honeycombed with schemes for the sustenance of idlers, but which in the West . . . is all their own'.[232] This interpretation – based on the tradition of Jacksonian democracy – was reinforced in the 1860s by the victory of the Northern States in the Civil War. To democrats and radical Liberals the slaveholding and aristocratic South represented the American version of the *ancien régime*, while the North fought to preserve a nation 'conceived in liberty, and dedicated to the proposition that all men are created equal'.[233] Bright became the British interpreter of the American ideology of 'Free Soil, Free Labor, Free Men', and the apologist of Lincoln, the son of 'honest industry and toil'.[234] To Bright the war was not only about the emancipation of the negro slaves in America, but also about the defence of labour and democracy all over the

---

[228] Littlejohn, 'Defects of the American and Swiss Republic', *WT*, 26 May 1872, p. 6; the defect of the ancient Greek republics was slavery; that of the Swiss Confederation was the excessive powers of the cantons, which generated fragmentation; the problem with the United States was the opposite one, centralization of power into the hands of the President, who was not responsible to Congress.

[229] Berridge, *Thesis*, p. 290.

[230] Northumbrian, *RN*, 19 Nov. 1871, p. 3.

[231] See the poem by J. M. Peacock, 'The Centennial of the Great Republic, July 4th 1876', *NR*, 2 Apr. 1876, pp. 14–15.

[232] [L.a.], *RN*, 17 Jul. 1874, p. 1.

[233] From Lincoln's Gettysburg address, as quoted in Ironside, 'The Centenary of the American Republic', *NW*, 26 Dec. 1874, p. 4. For similar interpretations of the American war, see J. S. Mill, from Avignon to the Philadelphia Sanitary Fair, 25 May 1864, item 2, p. 3. in *Mill-Taylor Collection*, vol. 45; and G. Mazzini in Jordan and Pratt, (eds.), *Europe and the American Civil War*, p. 266.

[234] See Foner, *Free Soil, Free Labor, Free Men*, pp. 16, 17, 11–39.

world:[235] if the United States disintegrated, 'then European Democracy would be silenced and dumb-founded for ever'.[236] As Bright repeated to his working-class audiences,

Privilege thinks it has a great interest in this contest, and every morning, with blatant voice, it comes into your streets and curses the American Republic. Privilege has beheld an afflicting spectacle for many years past. It has beheld thirty millions of men happy and prosperous, without emperor, without king, without the surroundings of a court, without nobles, except such which are made by eminence in intellect and virtue, without State bishops and State priests.
'Sole venders of the lore which works salvation',
without great armies and great navies, without great debts and without great taxes. Privilege has shuddered at what might happen to Old Europe if this grand experiment should succeed. But you, the workers, – you, striving after a better time – you, struggling upwards towards the light . . . you have no cause to look with jealousy upon a country which, amongst all the great nations of the globe, is that one where labour has met with the highest honour, and where it has reaped its greatest reward.[237]

Most contemporaries – including Lincoln[238] – and many historians since, have thought that Bright's appeal was enormously successful. However, other scholars have suggested that it was only after the 1863 Emancipation Proclaim that a majority of the British working classes became sympathetic to the North; they maintain that during the first years of the war the workers had been quite inclined to support the South.[239] In particular, Royden Harrison has focussed on the older generations of trades union activists – Thomas Wright's 'old school' – those who 'had been born before 1820 and had been influenced by the Napoleonic Wars and a particularly harsh political and economic climate'.[240] Harrison has

---

[235] *Ibid.*, p. 62. The importance of the Civil War for the emancipation of labour and democracy all over the world has been assessed in a similar way by Barrington Moore, *Social Origins of Dictatorship and Democracy*, p. 153. For a different interpretation, see Ellison, *Support for Secession*, p. 7.

[236] Bright, *Speeches*, 1 (1868), pp. 224–5, 233–4; Gracchus, 'The Reconstruction of the Union', *RN*, 30 Apr. 1865, p. 3.

[237] Cit. in Trevelyan, *Bright*, p. 307. See also the speech of 3 Feb. 1863 (Bright, *Speeches*, 1 [1868], pp. 233–4), and that at the meeting of the London trade unions at St James' Hall (26 Mar. 1863, *ibid.*, pp. 252–3).

[238] 'Letter of President Lincoln to the working men of Manchester', *BH*, 14 Feb. 1863, p. 1.

[239] Harrison, *Before the Socialists*, pp. 42–55.

[240] Reid, 'Intelligent Artisans and Aristocrats of Labour', in Winter (ed.), *The Working Class in Modern British History*, p. 181; see Wright, *Our New Masters* (1873).

pointed out that several prestigious trade union leaders and plebeian journalists – including T. J. Dunning (1799–1873),[241] W. Newton (1822–76),[242] G. W. M. Reynolds (1814–79) and J. F. Bray (1809–97)[243] – supported the independence of the South and were hostile to the North as it represented the American equivalent of the 'Manchester school'.[244] According to Harrison one of the effects of the American Civil War on the British labour movement was to replace these survivors of the 'anti-capitalist' struggles of the 1830s and 40s with a younger generation, readier to co-operate with employers because they had accepted the bourgeois-industrial organization of society and work relations. He maintains that these new leaders reached their political maturity through this confrontation with the leaders of the Chartist generations over the issue of the American Civil War.[245] Harrison's interpretation is also strengthened by the fact that many of the later Lib-labs had their formative experiences in these crucial years, and were influenced by the question of the emancipation of the slaves much more than by the comparatively remote Chartist struggles: such was, for instance, the case of G. Howell (b. 1833), T. Burt (b. 1837),[246] J. Wilson (b. 1839) and R. Applegarth (b. 1834),[247] the co-operators T. Cheetham (b. 1828),[248] J. C. Edwards (b. 1833)[249] and G. O. Greening (b. 1836),[250] all of whom were always inflexible 'Northerners'. The cases of Burt and Howell are particularly interesting, since both were converted to abolitionism during the 1850s, after reading Beecher Stowe's *Uncle Tom's Cabin*; negro emancipation was probably the first political cause they ever supported.[251]

---

[241] DLB, II, *sub voce*.

[242] *Ibid.*, *sub voce*; Newton was later active in the movement for electoral reform and became a staunch supporter of Gladstone from the mid-1860s (*ibid.*).

[243] DLB, III, *sub voce*.

[244] T. J. Dunning went as far as comparing Lincoln to Xerxes: 'Emigration to America – Mr. G. Troup', *BH*, 5 Mar. 1864, p. 7.

[245] Harrison, *Before the Socialists*, p. 39; see also pp. 4, 55, 68.

[246] DLB, II, *sub voce*.

[247] Wilson, *Memories* (1910), pp. 172–80; for Applegarth see DLB, II, p. 17.

[248] During the Lancashire Famine he opened a small pub which he called 'The Lincoln' (DLB, I, *sub voce*).

[249] DLB, I, *sub voce*.

[250] DLB, I, *sub voce*. Greening and Edwards were also the organizers of the first meetings in support of the North in Lancashire, and founded the Union and Emancipation Society of Manchester.

[251] See G. Howell, 'Autobiography of a Toiler ...', p. 38(c), *G. Howell Collection*, I, 2/16; Burt, *Autobiography*, (1924), pp. 105ff. *Uncle Tom's Cabin* enjoyed a great success in Great Britain: published in 1852, it had sold over a million copies by the end of that year

Their contemporary W. E. Adams – Chartist and then Gladstonian Liberal – spoke on behalf of their generation when he maintained that the issue at stake in the Civil War 'was the greatest
question of the centuries. It was greater than the Great Rebellion,
greater than the French Revolution, greater than the war of
Independence . . . as great as any that has been fought out since
history began'.[252] These men believed firmly in the benefits that
the working men were receiving through the 'new model' unions,
co-operation, and free trade. To them the arguments of the British
supporters of the Confederation – that waged labour in Britain
and the Northern States was no better off than slave labour in the
South – was just empty rhetoric,[253] or worse, a betrayal of the true
cause of the people.[254] Thus there was little sympathy or even
communication between these young radicals and some of their
older colleagues.

However, it would be misleading to rely totally on this generational contrast, because one of the most important effects of the
American Civil War was to *unite*, rather than divide, the labour
leadership in Britain. Thus, though some of the men of the 'old
school' spoke out against the North and John Bright, many
(perhaps the majority) of their contemporaries joined the cause
of radical Liberalism precisely in these years, as a consequence of
their sympathy for the North and free labour: these men included the ex-Chartists G. J. Harney (1817–97), Ernest Jones
(1819–1869), John Donald (1804–1893),[255] Henry Vincent

(Adams, *Great Britain and the American Civil War*, i, p. 33). It was possibly appropriate
that a man of such a Puritan background as Burt should read *Uncle Tom's Cabin* in
between *Pilgrim's Progress* and Milton's *Paradise Lost*. As the radical journalist Aaron
Watson wrote: 'Before long a copy of it [*Uncle Tom's Cabin*] had made its way to Seaton
Delaval, and to the house of Peter Burt, where, being regarded as a sort of religious
book, it was read aloud in the family circle, arising in the mind of at least one of the
hearers [T. Burt] a craving to read other books of the same kind, as well as a passionate
longing for the liberation of the American slaves.' This happened in 1852. (Watson, *A
Great Labour Leader*, [1908], p. 58). On the popularity of Beecher Stowe's work, see also
the testimony of another artisan Liberal: Williams, *Some Reminiscences*, (1918), p. 42.

[252] Adams, *Memories* (1903), II, pp. 420, 422–3. Adams wrote several pamphlets on the
theme of slave emancipation and had one of them translated into one of the languages of
India.

[253] Harrison, *Before the Socialists*, pp. 57–8.

[254] Thus G. Howell, who, defending the cause of the North against G. Troup on the *Bee-
Hive*, wrote: 'Perhaps Mr. Troup will be taking his politics and ideas of Trades' Unions
from the *Morning Post* or the *Times*. But they will scarcely fit us as Trades' Unionists . . .':
G. Howell, 'Emigration to America – Mr. G. Troup', *BH*, 5 Mar. 1864, p. 7.

[255] Paterson, 'Newmilns Weavers and the American Civil War', p. 99.

(1813–78),[256] and Benjamin Lucraft (1809–97);[257] the Owenites William Cooper (1822–68);[258] Lloyd Jones (1811–86),[259] and Robert Cooper (1818–68);[260] the Christian Socialist J. M. F. Ludlow (1821–1911),[261] the republican shoemaker and future President of the First International George Odger (1820–77).[262] George Cooper, only slightly younger (b. 1824), was in America when the war broke out, joined the US Cavalry, and fought on various fronts until 1865 'because he detested slavery of every kind'.[263] John Ward (b. 1810), of Clitheroe in Lancashire, from the very beginning of the war had no doubt that 'the rebels' were wrong, and that the cause of Lincoln and the Union was absolutely right, independent of the issue of slave emancipation;[264] he did not change his mind even when he went through the hardships and unemployment of the cotton famine.[265] Likewise the ex-Chartist 'Scourge' (alias Robert Hartwell) described the Secession as 'a fratricidal attempt . . . by slave owners and slave breeders to overthrow the glorious American republic'.[266] Cases like these seem to point, not to the withdrawal from politics of the Chartist

---

[256] Who 'Throughout the American Civil War . . . consistently defended North against South, and greatly admired Abraham Lincoln and American political institutions' (DLB, I, *sub voce*).

[257] DLB, VII, *sub voce*.

[258] DLB, I, *sub voce*.

[259] 'I remember once that he was very angry upon being charged with being a Southerner in the great American Civil War, a question which for a long time was regarded as a test of radicalism in English politics. Jones declared the statement to be absolutely false, and gave proofs to show that from the first he was on the side of the North in the great struggle' (G. Howell, 'Autobiography of a Toiler . . .', MSS in *G. Howell Coll.*, I, I, 12. In fact, in 1863 Lloyd Jones resigned from the *Glasgow Sentinel* rather than write articles against the North, as the editor expected of him (DLB, I, *sub voce*).

[260] He sat on the executive committee of the Union and Emancipation Society and was active in discouraging any attempt to support the South (DLB, II, *sub voce*).

[261] He too was an active abolitionist and passionate admirer of Lincoln (DLB, II, *sub voce*).

[262] Soutter, *Fights for Freedom*, (1925), p. 115.

[263] DLB, II, pp. 102–3.

[264] 'The Diary of John Ward', entry for 4 May 1861, pp. 161ff. Ward did not change his mind nor did he lose his 'Northerner' faith after Bull Run (entries for 10 and 17 Aug. 1861, *ibid.*, pp. 166–7).

[265] These are documented in the diary with great simplicity: see entry for 10 Apr. 1864, 'The Diary of John Ward', p. 176:

It is nearly two years since I wrote anything in the way of a diary . . . It has been a very poor time for me all the time due to the American war, which seems as far off being settled as ever. The mill I work in was stopped all last winter, during which time I had three shillings per week allowed by the relief committee, which barely kept me alive. . . . I have not earned a shilling a day this last month, and there are many like me. My clothes and bedding is wearing out very fast and I have no means of getting any more, as what wages I get does hardly keep me, after paying rent, rates and firing.'

[266] Scourge, 'The Prince of Wales and the Tenant Farmer', *BH*, 17 Jan. 1863, p. 1.

generation, but to the fact that many of them became increasingly aware of the affinities between Chartism and Liberalism[267] as the supporters of the two movements joined in admiration for the American Republic.[268]

In conclusion, it is likely that the Civil War did not split plebeian radicalism by separating the two younger 'schools' from the old one. On the contrary, it is probable that it rekindled the commitment of all – 'young' and 'old' – who looked to the future of the labour movement. Only the impracticable line of a 'no politics' trade unionism was swept aside: labour leaders were increasingly aware that many of the then crucial questions for the organized workers – like democracy and legal equality between employers and employees – admitted solely of political solutions.[269] Support for the North was also encouraged by the fact that these labour questions were clearly at stake in a war to end slave labour. Co-operation with John Bright in the effort to prevent an intervention on the side of the South, and the impact of the final success of the North, contributed towards teaching an important lesson to British labour leaders, both 'old' and 'new': namely, that reformers could be successful only if supported by a movement which included both middle- and working-class radicals.[270]

Thus it is likely that a majority of working-class *leaders* were

---

[267] See the case of George Webber – a one-time stern supporter of 'physical force' Chartism – who at a 1885 meeting to celebrate the passing of the Third Reform Act praised Gladstone and his government for having enacted the principles of Chartism (Thompson, 'Homage to Tom Maguire', in Briggs and Saville (eds.), *Essays in Labour History*, pp. 281–82). On this topic see also below, chapter 5, p. 297.

[268] Indeed some famous Chartist documents sound almost like the Jeffersonian Declaration of Independence of 1776: see 'The First Principles of Government', *The Northern Star*, 2 Jan. 1841, republished in Mather (ed.), *Chartism*, pp. 48–50. Moreover several ex-Chartists, who were aware of the similarities between the Charter and Jacksonian democracy, had emigrated to the States, where they often prospered: H. Vincent, 'The Western States of America', *BH*, 14 Mar. 1868, p. 3.

[269] G. Howell, 'Autobiography of a Toiler . . .', 2nd draft, chapter 6, in *G. Howell Coll.*, 2nd page (not numbered).

[270] One of the first plebeian radicals to become aware of this necessity was the former Owenite Robert Cooper, a man of the 'old school' who was born in the year of Peterloo in a family of thorough-going Painites. In 1862 he wrote to Joseph Cowen:

> Experience has demonstrated that the middle class – whether justly or unjustly is not now the question – exercise, in the present political scale, a determining power in settling national concerns. If they and the aristocracy unite, they beat the people – if they and the people combine, they defeat the aristocracy, and the *latter* are the natural enemies of popular power. Is it not worthwhile, therefore, to make some sacrifice to secure the help of that class which would give the preponderance in the political scale in favour of popular interest? (R. Cooper to J. Cowen, 28 Jul. 1862, cit. in DLB, I, p. 105).

'Northerners' and liberals. But how far is this true for the *rank-and-file*? Several scholars have maintained that, though the workers wished to see slavery abolished, they tended to support the South rather than the North. In particular, this thesis has been maintained by Mary Ellison in a well-documented study based mainly on the evidence of leading articles in the local press and popular meetings in Lancashire.[271] The main flaw in her work is that, while she focusses on the pro-Confederation meetings, she forgets to assess the number of pro-Union demonstrations. This is quite serious, since her figures – insofar as it is possible to extract them from the text – seem to contradict her own thesis: in the first three chapters of her book (which deal with the crucial questions of the cotton famine, the secession, and the emancipation of the slaves) she lists forty-seven meetings in support of the South, but as many as fifty-one in support of the North;[272] then, in the chapter in which she tries to destroy the 'myth' of Lincoln's popularity in Lancashire, she only mentions one meeting which expressed any strong opposition, but as many as twelve which praised and supported his work.[273] She refers to cases in which pro-Union meetings failed, but there were also cases in which pro-Confederation demonstrations were turned into spontaneous demonstrations in support of the North: this happened, for example, at Stalybridge in September 1862. There a 'Southerner' meeting – whose organizers included such an influential friend of the labour movement as J. R. Stephens – was shipwrecked as the workers approved, by a majority of 100 to 1, the following amendment to a resolution asking for British military intervention against the Federal blockade of the South: 'That in the opinion of this meeting, the distress prevailing in the manufacturing districts is mainly owing to the rebellion of the Southern States against the American constitution'.[274] At another meeting at Blackburn, in July 1862, the formerly eminent Chartist leader Mortimer Grimshaw had his proposed resolution in support of the South defeated by 5,000 to

---

[271] Ellison, *Support for Secession*; but see also Lorimer, 'The Role of Anti-Slavery Sentiment in English Reactions to the American Civil War', pp. 405–20.

[272] See Ellison, *Support for Secession*, pp. 5–94: without taking into account the meetings whose outcome was either controversial or not clear from Ellison's account.

[273] *Ibid.*, 173–88. About the one hostile meeting she writes that it 'ended riotously with at least as many against as for him [Lincoln]' (*ibid.*, p. 177).

[274] Harrison, *Before the Socialists*, pp. 65–6; see [rep.], 'Meeting at Stalybridge on Intervention in America', *BH*, 4 Oct. 1862, p. 1.

12 by a resolution in support of the North, moved by the leader of the local branch of the weavers: the meeting then passed a motion of no confidence in Grimshaw (who was the chairman) and declared their complete support for Abraham Lincoln.[275]

Thus, Lancashire was by no means so 'Southerner' as Mary Ellison has suggested. Moreover Britain cannot be reduced to Lancashire, and the evidence from other regions seems further to corroborate the traditional interpretation that a majority of the workers supported the North from an early stage of the war: this seems to have been the case in Yorkshire,[276] Northumberland and Durham. It was in the north-east that the ex-Chartist George Julian Harney exercised his well-established influence to defend the cause of the North from 1861: like Bright, he thought that the victory of the Federals was necessary to ensure the survival of democracy in the rest of the world.[277] This was also the position of the English Mazzinians,[278] to whom Harney was linked. In London, the *Bee-Hive* was, as usual, an open forum: especially between January 1863 and spring 1864 the 'Southerners' – led by G. Troup and T. J. Dunning[279] – and the 'Northerners' – led by E. S. Beesley, T. Hughes, and the newspaper's editors, Potter and Hartwell[280] – waged a relentless verbal war in its pages. But by February 1863 the famous mass meetings at Exeter Hall and St James' Hall had defined once and for all the attitude of the London working-class radicals. These demonstrations – in which participation was so great that the Strand was jammed with people well

---

[275] Harrison, *Before the Socialists*, p. 66; Wright, 'Leeds Politics and the American Civil War', pp. 96–122.

[276] Adams, *Memoirs* (1903), II, p. 435.

[277] Schoyen, *Harney*, p. 258. Cf. Todd, *Cowen*, pp. 70–1.

[278] Smith, *Linton*, p. 136. Jordan and Pratt (eds.), *Europe and the American Civil War*, p. 266. Linton (b. 1812) should therefore be added to the group of radicals of the 'old school' who supported the North. Linton favoured a British military action against the Union during the Trent incident: but as soon as the crisis was over he went back to the cause of the North, which he had supported from 1861.

[279] See G. Troup, 'The Price of Labour in the Colonies and the States', *BH*, 20 Feb. 1864, p. 4; T. J. Dunning, 'Emigration to America – Mr. G. Troup', *BH*, 5 Mar. 1864, p. 7.

[280] There are many articles, but see e.g. [l.a.], 'An Editorial Explanation. Mr. Troup and the American Working Man', *BH*, 27 Feb. 1864, p. 1; E. S. Beesly, 'The Working Man in America', *BH*, p. 4; E. Beales, 'Mr. Troup and the Federal States', *BH*, p. 7; G. Howell, 'Emigration to America – Mr. G. Troup', *BH*, 5 Mar. 1864, p. 7; D. Stainiby *et al.* [shareholders of the *Bee Hive*], 'The Southern Sympathies of Messrs. Troup and Denning', *BH*, 12 Mar. 1864, p. 6.

before the beginning of the proceedings[281] – showed the virtually unanimous support of the artisans for the cause of emancipation and the Union. The proceedings were particularly interesting because of the large number of workers who stood up and spoke. The enthusiasm was such that some speakers found it difficult to complete their addresses as they were interrupted by 'ringing cheers for PRESIDENT LINCOLN'.[282] 'Unanimously amidst loud cheering' the meeting approved W. R. Cremer's proposal:

> That we altogether repudiate the statement, that the war now raging in America is the result of Republican or Democratic institutions, but rather do we believe that the liberty arising out of such institutions has made it impossible for slavery longer to exist there; and we further believe that; should the South be successful in setting up a government founded on human slavery, to recognise such a government would be to take a step backwards in civilization ... And we hereby tend our thanks to the President, Government, and the People of the Northern States for the firmness they have displayed and the sacrifices they have made to restore the Union, and to consolidate the liberty of the Republic; and as the cause of labour and liberty is one all over the world, we bid them God speed in their glorious work of Emancipation.[283]

Cremer had no doubts that the question of slavery directly concerned British workers as well: 'The South not only upheld the doctrine of the slavery of the blacks, but also of the labouring whites, and had, in fact, thrown down the gauntlet to the free labourers of the world.'[284] Immediately afterwards another artisan expressed his support for Lincoln, describing the secession as a 'diabolical attempt' and the British supporters of the Confederates 'an arrogant' and 'liberty-hating aristocracy': his resolution was also approved unanimously, 'the whole audience rising *en masse*, and cheering for several minutes'.[285]

Other great meetings in support of the North took place all over the country, with a maximum of fifty-six working-class demonstrations in 1863,[286] and a renewal of the popular upheaval in 1865

---

[281] [Rep.], 'Negro Emancipation – Great Meeting at Exeter Hall', *BH*, 31 Jan. 1863, p. 2.

[282] E. S. Beesly, 'The Exeter Hall Meeting', *BH*, 7 Feb. 1863, p. 1.

[283] See [rep.], 'Negro Emancipation – Great Meeting of Trades' Unionists', *BH*, 28 Mar. 1863, p. 5.

[284] *Ibid.*

[285] Speech by Mr Petherbridge (joiner), *ibid.*, p. 6; see E. S. Beesly, 'Working Men's Emancipation Meeting', *BH*, 14 Mar. 1863; and 'The Meeting in St. James' Hall', *BH*, 4 Apr. 1863.

[286] Harrison, *Before the Socialists*, p. 65.

after the murder of the President. At that time popular emotion was so great that in London the special editions of the newspapers were quickly sold out, the last copies were going for a price thirty or forty times higher than normal. In Manchester trade came to a standstill,[287] and all over the country there were held great working-men's meetings during which various spokesmen of the labour movement – from the journalist Robert Hartwell to the porter Whitlock – commemorated the late President and the republican virtues he had personified.[288] Emotion was heightened by the fact that Lincoln's murder coincided with the final victory of the North.[289] Resolutions and addresses of sympathy were sent to Mrs Lincoln and the US Government by British workers belonging to various associations from different parts of the country.[290] The London Working Men's Association declared

We feel that the loss of such a man is not only a loss for the nation over which he presided, but a loss to the world at large. Raised by the force of his own character and genius from a humble position in the ranks of industry to be the first citizen of a great and glorious republic, his memory will be endeared to, and enshrined in, the hearts of the toiling millions of the world. Abraham Lincoln has been sacrificed in the cause of negro emancipation, and the freedom of the slave has been consecrated by the blood of his deliverer.[291]

But Lincoln's personal popularity was merely increased, not created, by his death. It would be very useful to know the exact number and the provenance of the letters which were sent to the President by British workers during the four years of the Civil War

---

[287] Jordan and Pratt (eds.), *Europe and the American Civil War*, p. 261.

[288] [Rep.], 'Assassination of President Lincoln – Great Meeting of Working Men', *BH*, 6 May 1865, pp. 5–6. Meetings of radicals were held also at Newcastle upon Tyne, Gateshead, North Shields, Sunderland (see [rep.], 'The Assassination of President Lincoln – Meetings of Sympathy', *NW*, 6 May 1865, p. 7.

[289] [L.a.], 'The Assassination of President Lincoln – The Surrender of Lee', *RN*, 30 Apr. 1865, p. 1.

[290] And not only British, since admiration for Lincoln unified plebeian radicals all over Europe: see the example of the Società Italiana dei Meccanici Uniti of Turin 'to the Citizen George Perkins Mash, United States Envoy to Italy', of 30 Apr. 1865:

the officers of our society beg you to act as an interpreter to your countrymen, to express to them our high regard, particularly for one mechanic like us, who was born in Kentucky, and whose genius elevated him to the highest rank in the nation that trusted his destinies to his care; who served his country so well that the enemies of all good were forced to arm the hand of a hired assassin to take his precious life. (Cit. in Becker Sidemann and Friedmann, *Europe Looks at the Civil War*, p. 299)

[291] [Rep.], 'Assassination of President Lincoln – Great Meeting of Working Men', *BH*, 6 May 1865, p. 6: [address] 'To the President, Government, and People of the United States'.

to express esteem and political support. They included the famous address of December 1862 from the Manchester workers,[292] and the letter from the Newmilns weavers, who played on the Biblical meaning of the President's name, declaring that Lincoln was 'Abraham, the Father of the Faithful, whose name will be handed down to posterity by the echoes of one generation after another, until the oppressors of mankind shall vanish from the face of the earth, amidst the execration of a noble and patriotic people'.[293] As the struggle between 'Northerners' and 'Southerners' focussed attention on the President,[294] both friends and foes – wittingly or otherwise – prepared for Lincoln's eventual triumph as an abolitionist hero.[295] After the war, framed prints of his severe, bearded face became common ornaments in artisans' homes: like a 'modern saint' 'Lincoln came to typify some of the most noble ideals of the common man',[296] and was sometimes pointed to as the epitome of the sober, honest worker, independent, intelligent and with a clear mind about his own duties, rights and interests.[297] Typical of the new mythology was a lecture for the members of the Turners' Burial and Sick Society of Longton, in 1873: the speaker emphasized Lincoln's humble origins, his life as a pioneer and woodsman in the Far West, his education in a family of strong Baptist convictions, and God's clear 'election' of this man in His plan for the raising of the class he came from. He concluded:

But why be astonished at a man rising from cabin life in the backwoods of America and springing from low degree? Really great men had always sprung from the ranks. Biblical as well as secular history proved this. David, the shepherd boy, became the king of Israel, and why? Because

---

[292] See 'To His Excellency, Abraham Lincoln, President of the United States of America' (31 Dec. 1862), cit. in Becker Sideman and Friedman (eds.), *Europe Looks at the Civil War*, pp. 198–201.

[293] Paterson, 'Newmilns Weavers and the American Civil War', p. 102.

[294] [L.a.], 'An Editorial Remark', *BH*, 5 Mar. 1864, p. 4; G. Troup, 'The Editor, Professor Beesly, and Mr. Beales', *ibid.*, p. 1; T. Hughes, 'Mr. Dunning and President Lincoln', *BH*, 12 Mar. 1864, p. 6.

[295] See [rep.], 'President Lincoln on Emancipation', *BH*, 21 May 1864, p. 6.

[296] Jordan and Pratt (eds.), *Europe and the American Civil War*, p. 262.

[297] In 1872 *Lloyd's* declared that 'Mr. Arch . . . would steadily peg away in Abe Lincoln's rough fashion, at a good day's wage for a good day's work' ([l.a.], 'Hodge in Vanity Fair', 9 Jun. 1872, p. 1.). There was also a Smilesian component in British admiration for Lincoln, but the President was not primarily admired for his social success (in contrast, for instance, to other American statesmen, like the Vice-President Henry Wilson, who rose from farm labourer to the White House ([l.a.], 'An American Worthy', *BH*, 28 Nov. 1875, p. 6).

he had the ability to govern. As David was to Israel, and Moses to the
Israelites, so was Abraham Lincoln to the American slaves, for he came
with power to strike down the chains that fettered the black race, and bid
them go free.[298]

By the end of the century 'honest Abe, the rail-splitter, who piloted
[the United States] through the hours of their greatest trial'[299] was
a classic subject of democratic literature. His biographies and
speeches were read with emotion and great enthusiasm by radicals
of the younger generation, like George Ratcliffe – who took pride
in being born in 1863, the year of Gettysburg[300] – and George
Barnes, whose biography begins with a quotation from one of
Lincoln's speeches.[301] John Wilson of the Durham Miners' Association wrote in his memoirs:

Stern, indomitable 'Old Abe'. There was no compromising or evasion
with him to catch votes and secure another term of Presidential office.
Equality and the love of human right and a recognition of the fundamental truth that the colour of the skin ought not to differentiate the human
race weighed more with him. Freedom was with him an eternal principle;
to live in the White House was a temporary fleeting. Speaking to one of
the regiments at this particular and important juncture he said, 'I happen
temporarily to occupy this big White House. I am a living witness that
any one of your children may look to come here, as my father's child has.
It is in order that any one of you may have, through this free government
which we have enjoyed, an open field and a fair chance for your industry,
enterprise and intelligence; that you may all have equal privileges in the
race of life, with all its desirable human aspirations – it is for this that the
struggle should be maintained, that we may not lose our birthright.'[302]

With this tribute to the greatly admired President, Wilson also
enunciated his own ideals for society and politics, based on liberty,
equality and fraternity. From a similar point of view Andrew
Carnegie – a man of plebeian and radical background[303] – wrote
that 'it [wa]s impossible to imagine anyone a valet to Mr Lincoln:

---

[298] [Rep.], 'W. Mayer, "Lecture on President Lincoln"', *Potteries Examiner*, 17 May 1873,
     p. 7.
[299] [L.a.], 'The American Presidential Election', *LW*, 20 Jun. 1880, p. 6; the same
     description was used by C. Bradlaugh, 'The Radical Programme', *NR*, 26 Apr. 1885,
     p. 321.
[300] Ratcliffe, *Sixty Years of It* (1935), p. 79.
[301] Barnes, *From Workshop to the War Cabinet* (1924), p. 1.
[302] Wilson, *Memories* (1910), pp. 173–4.
[303] Carnegie's father was a damask weaver, and one of his uncles was a free trade Chartist,
     an admirer of the United States and also of Brutus, the Roman republican tyrannicide:
     Carnegie, *Autobiography* (1920), p. 10.

he would have been his companion. He was the most perfect of democrats, revealing in every word and act the equality of men.'[304] Lincoln had become a symbol.

Another effect of Lincoln's victory was to revive the old Painite image of the United States as the paradise of democracy,[305] with 'a government, not of a class, but of the people – a government of the people, for the people, and by the people'.[306] The Reconstruction administrations, by giving the vote to the negroes, seemed to vindicate the principle of manhood suffrage and anticipated the full emancipation of the British workers.[307] As Harney wrote in 1867,

Our interest in American politics has been mainly that of a desire to see the disenthrallment of an oppressed and cruelly-wronged race. The victory for humanity we at length witness. What a revolution in six years! Will the British working men occupy as proud a political position as that now held by the negroes of the States, within six years to come? There is stinging humiliation for us as Englishmen in the very question.[308]

In 1873 Thomas Wright wrote that 'the creed of the political section of the working classes is at present republicanism, or ultra-liberalism broadening down towards republicanism'.[309] There was considerable exaggeration in his words, though it was true that admiration for the United States was widespread, as was demonstrated not only by the celebrations in honour of William Lloyd

---

[304] *Ibid.*, pp. 101–2.
[305] Gracchus, 'Republican France', *RN*, 28 Dec. 1873, p. 3.
[306] Ironside, 'The Declaration of American Independence', *NW*, 1 Jul. 1876, p. 4.
[307] E. Jones, 'Democracy Vindicated', *EC*, 18 Dec. 1880, p. 3 [a reprint of lectures delivered in 1867]; G. J. Harney, 'State of Parties and Progress of Republicanism in America', *NW*, 30 Mar. 1867, p. 4; J. S. Mill, letters: from Avignon, 13 May 1865, [item 5, p. 21; from Blackburn Park, 1 Sept. 1865, it. 6, pp. 23–5, in *Mill-Taylor Collection*; [l.a.], 'The Fear of Democracy', *NW*, 17 Nov. 1866, p. 4; this article celebrated the return of two black representatives to the Massachussets Congress. See John Bright to the Reform League (*BH*, 26 May 1866, p. 1):

> The Tory party and those from the Liberal ranks who join it . . . regard the workmen here as the Southern planter regards the negroes who were so lately his slaves. They can no longer be bought or sold; so far they are free men. They may work and pay taxes, but they must not vote. They must obey the laws, but must have no share in selecting the men who are to make them. The future position of the millions of working men in the United Kingdom is now determined if the opposition of the Tory party is to prevail – it is precisely that fixed by the Southern planters for the negro.

[308] G. J. Harney, 'Mr G. Julian Harney on Negro Suffrage in America', *NW*, 13 Apr. 1867, p. 4. Cf. [rep.], 'The Miners and the Franchise – Demonstration at Morpeth', *NW*, 5 Oct. 1872, p. 8.
[309] Wright, *Our New Masters* (1873), p. 11. He went as far as proposing a 'Confederation of Great Britain, the United States, and the Colonies': letter to the *BH*, 18 Feb. 1871, p. 14.

Garrison during his 1867 visit to England,[310] but especially by the mass meetings to welcome Ulysses Grant in 1877. At that time the country witnessed scenes of popular enthusiasm unparalleled since Garibaldi's 1864 tour;[311] the labour movement – through its national leaders and organizations – again expressed its admiration and support for all that the United States and Grant personally stood for.[312] On that occasion even the moderate, and hardly republican, *Lloyd's Weekly* was ready to acknowledge that 'the mighty Republic of the West' held a special place in the history of liberalism:

> To those who have reviled liberal and democratic institutions as leading to confusion and misery, the United States have been a standing, irrefutable, answer. If the aristocracies of the old world still disdain the political forms, and deride the social customs which have grown under the Star and Stripes; the vigorous middle and working classes of Europe – the sap and sinew of our modern life – contemplate them with sympathy, and accept them as guides, in many directions.[313]

Thus, republicanism expressed deeply-rooted aspirations for a more egalitarian society, and in this sense was a wider phenomenon than the membership of Bradlaugh's organized following would suggest. However, it did not become a feasible programme for institutional change, nor did mass enthusiasm for the United States ever generate any large support for a republic in Britain. What most supporters of the 'Americanization' of British society wished for was the democratization of the political system and the institutionalization of social conflict. After the reforms of 1867–75 the opinion of most radicals was that these aims could be achieved without drastic changes in the unwritten constitution.

Revolutions seemed anachronistic: in 1872 the funeral of the

---

[310] See [rep.], 'Mr William Lloyd Garrison at Leeds', *LM*, 22 Oct. 1867, p. 8.

[311] Brewster, 'Ulysses Grant and Newcastle upon Tyne', pp. 119–28; on Garibaldi's visit to England see below, chapter 7.

[312] 'Presentation of an Address to General Grant by a Large Deputation of Representative Workmen', [3 Jul. 1877], in *Labour Representation League Minutes*, p. 265.

[313] [L.a.], 'The Lexington Letter', *LW*, 9 May 1875, p. 6. *Lloyd's* contains also interesting examples of liberal hostility to the United States, especially on account of the caucus system: when the latter was 'imported' – as many thought – to Great Britain by Chamberlain, those who wanted to attack the new Birmingham machine attacked the American 'prototype' as well (see [l.a.], 'The American Presidential Election', 25 Feb. 1877, p. 6). Another reason why *Lloyd's* was hostile to the States was protectionism, which was also its reason for attacking the French Republic (see [l.a.], 'The Republican Platform', *LW*, 25 Jun. 1876, p. 6).

Peterloo hero, Samuel Bamford, provided an occasion for the reassessment of the 'revolutionary' years between 1816 and 1848. As Bamford was greeted as an old patriot even by the Bishop of Manchester, 'Littlejohn' explained that the agitations of the 1810s were caused by 'war-taxation', protectionism, 'Misgovernment' and a non-representative electoral system: the reforms of 1846 and 1867 had changed all that, and the ideals of the Chartists were now the law of the country.[314] By then many thought that Great Britain had already been virtually 'Americanized', and that it had become 'a Republic with an hereditary President'.[315] Enthusiastic rank-and-file republicans like Edward Rymer could delude themselves that the day would come when Gladstone would play 'the glorious part of a Washington' as the first president of the British republic;[316] but Charles Bradlaugh himself was a firm 'constitutionalist' who stressed the peculiarities of the British case in contrast to those of the Continent, and declined even to consider the applicability to Britain of the republican solutions which he recommended for France or Spain.[317] Likewise, the 6–10,000 members of the republican and secularist clubs were important as a pressure group within popular liberalism: but what they meant by 'republic' became increasingly indistinguishable from the fuller implementation of Gladstone's programme of 'Peace, Retrenchment and Reform'.[318] An apt comment on this development could be provided by extending to Britain what *Lloyd's* had written about the first municipal elections at Paris after the fall of the Commune: 'The Red Spectre has been annihilated . . . by the very weapon which . . . is supposed, by not a few, to best serve its cause . . . the practical operation of the Ballot'.[319]

[314] Littlejohn, 'The Burials of Bamford – Old Radicals and New', *WT*, 28 Apr. 1872, p. 6; [l.a.], 'Radical Bamford', *LW*, 28 Apr. 1872, p. 6. Cf. [l.a.], 'The Death of Ernest Jones', *WT*, 31 Jan. 1869, p. 4.

[315] Littlejohn, 'The Republican Agitation – Utility and Froth', *WT*, 19 Nov. 1871, p. 6; see Plain Dealer, 'American and English Working Men', *BH*, 14 May 1870, pp. 201–2.

[316] Fisher and Spaven, 'Edward Rymer', in Harrison (ed.), 'Independent Collier, p. 256.

[317] Royle, *Radicals, Secularists, and Republicans*, p. 199.

[318] C. Watts, 'Republicanism and Monarchy', *NR*, 2 Apr. 1871, pp. 210–11; see also [rep.], 'Birmingham Republican Conference . . . Public Meeting in the Town Hall', [speech by C. Watts], *NR*, 18 May 1873, p. 318.

[319] [L.a.], 'The Reds and the Ballot', *LW*, 30 Jul. 1871, p. 6.

CHAPTER 2

The social contract

Ill fares the land to hastening ills a prey,
Where wealth accumulates and man decay;
Princes and kings may flourish or may fade,
A breath can make them and a breath hath made.
But a bold peasantry, the country's pride,
When once destroyed can never be supplied[1]

Free Trade, like religion, hath doctrines of love,
And the promise of plenty and health;
It proclaims, while the angels look down from above,
The marriage of Labour and Wealth.[2]

INDEPENDENCE AND *LAISSEZ-FAIRE*:
THE 'PASTORAL DREAM'

Whether the government was republican or monarchist, plebeian radicals did not expect to 'get millennium by act of Parliament'.[3] In particular, they suspected that government intervention would ultimately and almost inevitably lead to oppression, repression, and moral degradation[4] unless it was kept within its legitimate sphere, that of 'a power delegated from the people for the preservation of right and justice'.[5] Virtually any form of government

---

[1] O. Goldsmith, 'Deserted Village', a poem very popular among working-class radicals: cf. Gracchus, 'The People and their Persecutors', *RN*, 20 Jun. 1875, p. 3, and Wright, *Our New Masters* (1871), p. 46.

[2] Ebenezer Elliott, *Corn Law Rhymes and Other Verses*, London 1904, p. 3, in *J. Johnson Coll.*, 'Free Trade and Protection', box 7: this late edition, published as a collection of electoral songs for the anti-tariff campaign, provides an appropriate illustration of the continuity in popular perceptions.

[3] [L.a.], 'Millennium by Act of Parliament', *NW*, 3 Aug. 1872, p. 4.

[4] Tholfsen, *Working Class Radicalism*, p. 295; see McCord, *The Anti-Corn Law League*, p. 28: 'To the great majority of the people in the 1830's our Welfare State would be no more than national pauperism'. The issue is more extensively discussed below, pp. 173–83.

[5] Lovett, *Social and Political Morality* (1853), p. 147.

intervention beyond this modest aim was regarded with suspicion, to the extent that the 1864 Annuities Bill – enabling small savers to invest in government bonds – was criticized as an attempt to pre-empt friendly societies and destroy the workers' independence. The *Bee-Hive* declared that the Bill was unacceptable 'on account of its centralization principle':

our sincere conviction [is] that, if successful, it will not be industrial companies and friendly societies only, that will be taken under the paternal care of the Government; Trades Unions and Co-operative societies also will be taken under the Government patronage, as in France, and they will be, as they are in that country, emasculated for any political purpose. . . . Granted that all the benefits predicted from the Annuities Bill may come to pass . . . they are not worth the loss of that manly independence principle and self-government, which must be the inevitable consequence of the Bill.[6]

Thus, government intervention was resisted because of its feared political consequences, rather than because of the workers' commitment to economic *laissez-faire*. This coincided with the traditional claim to the fullest possible autonomy of society, already articulated by Godwin and Paine, and ultimately inspired by the polity and history of congregational Dissent.[7] But it is to be observed that similar attitudes also characterized artisan politics in other European countries as well as in America,[8] from the heyday of the French *sans-culottes*[9] at least until the end of the 1860s.[10] As John Breuilly has shown in his comparison with Germany, the fact that these attitudes survived for longer in Britain was not an indication of the weakness of labour, but a consequence of its strength, the timely winning of important reforms, and its success in democratizing the political system; in contrast, what turned continental plebeian radicals into socialists was the experi-

---

[6] [L.a.], 'The Government Annuities Bill', *BH*, 19 Mar. 1864, p. 4.
[7] Ruthven, *The Divine Supermarket*, pp. 305ff.
[8] Peterson, *The Jefferson Mind*, pp. 80, 84; Hugins, *Jacksonian Democracy and the Working Class*, p. 143.
[9] Soboul, *Les sans-culottes parisiens*, pp. 471–2; Breuilly, 'Artisan Economy, Artisan Politics, Artisan Ideology', in Emsley and Walvin (eds.), *Artisans, Peasants and Proletarians*, p. 214.
[10] For a significant Italian parallel see the co-operative programme of the federalist and republican group 'Liberta' e giustizia', in [l.a.], 'Le associazioni operaie', *Liberta' e giustizia*, n.1, 17 Aug. 1867 (cit. in Romano, *Storia del movimento socialista in Italia*, II, p. 251). It is remarkable that the same content, expressed in similar words, can also be found in Holyoake, *History of Co-operation* (1906), II, p. 587.

ence of defeat, repression, and frustration.[11] Paraphrasing Gwyn
Williams,[12] it could be said that the differences in tone, tempera-
ment and development among the various plebeian movements in
Europe were dependent on the cultural and constitutional environment in which each movement happened to operate, rather than
on inherent differences in popular aspirations and ideals.

What is really remarkable in the British case is not the liberalism
of the subaltern classes, but the populism of the ruling elites. The
latter made the Liberal coalition viable and lasting. In particular
there were marked 'elective affinities' between plebeian radicals
and left-wing intellectuals. The economists of the J. S. Mill 'school'
consistently subordinated economic considerations to political and
moral imperatives. Mill himself openly expressed his contempt for
the very idea of a highly competitive, profit-oriented society, to
which he preferred the 'stationary state' of peasant and artisan
contentedness.[13] Like the *Bee-Hive*, he supported *laissez-faire* out of
hatred for political centralization, Bonapartism and authoritarianism, and insisted on individual and community self-determination
as vital to the survival of liberty.[14] To him *laissez-faire* was mainly
'an ideology of local self-government'.[15]

Typical of this frame of mind was Mill's sympathy for peasant
proprietorship. Though he admitted that – from a purely economic
point of view – large farms would be more productive,[16] he was
committed to peasant proprietorship on moral and political
grounds.[17] Like Thomas Jefferson, Mill praised the homestead
farmer as the model citizen. While the factory proletarian was
trained to work as part of a machine, the farmer was employed
from childhood in an activity fostering independent thinking and
creativity, and was free from the anguish and crushing misery that
affected the factory worker:

[11] Breuilly, 'Liberalism and Social Democracy', pp. 26–31. See also Roth, *Social Democrats
in Imperial Germany*, pp. 127–35; it is noteworthy that even in Germany the culture of the
politically aware working man was liberal (*ibid.*, pp. 40–1).
[12] Williams, *Artisans and Sans-culottes*, p. 5.
[13] *Principles of Political Economy*, in *Collected Works*, III, 2, p. 754. See Halliday, *John Stuart Mill*,
chapter 4; and Dewey, 'The Rehabilitation of Peasant Proprietorship', pp. 17–47.
[14] Mill, *On Liberty*, in *Collected Works*, XIX, 1, pp. 306, 308–10; *Principles of Political Economy*,
in *Collected Works*, III, 2, pp. 943–4; Schwarz, *The New Political Economy*, p. 147.
[15] Halliday, *John Stuart Mill*, p. 104.
[16] Mill, *Principles of Political Economy* in *Collected Works*, III, 2, p. 768.
[17] *Ibid.*, 1, pp. 254–5. For the Jeffersonian rejection of productivity as a 'test of a good
society' and the preference for the 'happy classless state', see Marx, *The Machine in the
Garden*, pp. 126–7.

His anxieties are the ordinary vicissitudes of more and less; his cares are that he takes his fair share of the business of life; that he is a free human being, and not perpetually a child, which seems to be the approved condition of the labouring classes according to the prevailing philanthropy.[18]

Judging from the frequency with which this passage was cited in the popular press, Mill's eulogy of the 'independent peasant' was one of the elements which most endeared him to working-class spokesmen.[19] The latter thought that democracy was ultimately viable only if based on a society dominated by property-owning producers such as Switzerland or the United States[20]. This was the classical republican ideal of Xenophon, Cicero and Cato present in all the principal European and American popular radical movements.[21] It was also one of the components of popular admiration for the United States, a country that Priestley had celebrated as one whose

inhabitants consist . . . of an independent and hardy YEOMANRY, all nearly on a level – trained to arms . . . clothed in homespun – of simple manners – strangers to luxury – drawing plenty from the ground – and that plenty gathered easily by the hand of industry . . . the rich and the poor . . . protected by laws, which, being their own will, cannot oppress.[22]

Later the same ideals inspired Feargus O'Connor, with his projects of allotments for factory workers – who would thus be turned into

---

[18] Mill, *Principles of Political Economy*, in *Collected Works*, III, 2, pp. 280–81.

[19] Lecture by C. Bradlaugh, in [rep.], 'Plymouth', *NR*, 28 Aug. 1870, p. 142; see his article in *NR*, 3 Apr. 1870, pp. 214–15. On the popularization of the economists' views on peasant proprietorship, see also [l.a.], 'A Peasant Proprietary', *NC*, 15 Apr. 1885, p. 2, which discusses not only the ideas of Mill, but also those of other scholars like Thornton, Laveleye, H. Fawcett, Sir Henry Maine, and McCulloch. In addition, Joseph Arch mentioned the importance of open lectures, like those given by Thorold Rogers at Oxford in 1878 (*The Story of His Life* (1898), pp. 318–22).

[20] Foner, *Free Soil*, p. 21 and pp. 26–9; Epstein, *O'Connor*, p. 253; Peterson, *The Jefferson Image*, pp. 79ff. See also Palmer, 'Popular democracy in the French Revolution', pp. 453–4; Soboul, *Movimento popolare*, p. 75; Beard, *Economic Origins of Jeffersonian Democracy*, p. 435; Zahler, *Eastern Working Men and National Land Policy*, p. 10; Romano, *Storia del movimento socialista*, I, p. 39.

[21] See Foshee, 'Jeffersonian Political economy', p. 527; Marx, *The Machine in the Garden*, pp. 122, 127–30.

[22] Cit. in Marx, *The Machine in the Garden*, p. 105; the mention of military drilling as a component of the good patriot's education is significant: like the French *sans-culottes* of the 1790s, many Victorian radicals thought that 'the sovereign people' ought to be armed (Soboul, *Movimento popolare*, p. 96). Indeed, the decay of the British peasantry was often linked to the decline of the defensive capacities of the country: see Ironside, 'The Gracchi', *NW*, 19 Mar. 1881, p. 4, drawing a parallel between modern Britain and ancient Rome, and warning that the disappearance of the independent peasant may have the same effect on the former as it had on the latter.

a 'virtuous yeomanry'.[23] O'Connor himself boasted that he was 'an open-air, a work-when-I'm-able-and-work-for-myself-and-my-family-Radical', claiming that 'the sum and substance of my Chartism is independence and contentment'.[24] Both at the same time and for decades to come many other less resolute radicals – including Thornton, Fawcett and Cowen – cordially agreed that this was the safest basis for liberty as well as social reform.[25] Their envisaged 'state of rational simplicity'[26] was also the ideal of Gladstonian popular journalists such as 'Littlejohn'. It was not by chance that the latter chose a pseudonym evoking the bucolic liberty of Robin Hood and his merry men: Robin's foresters had been a band of yeomen, the people's champions in a struggle to recover their lost lands.[27] Allegedly there existed – in the second half of the nineteenth century – countries in which the equivalents and successors of Robin Hood's freedom fighters had not been defeated. Such countries were supposed to be 'structurally democratic' societies, exemplified by Switzerland, America, and France under the Third Republic. In these countries 'the cultivators own their land, have no landlords over them, are happy, industrious, educated, orderly, law abiding, and rich'.[28] The French farmer – a character surprisingly popular among British radicals[29] – was his own master. His small cottage was

invariably comfortable and clean; he has his little bits of furniture, his small stock of linen, and an old stocking pretty well filled with a mixture

[23] Zahler, *Eastern Working Men*, pp. 76–9.

[24] Epstein, *O'Connor*, p. 253; see Stedman Jones, *Languages of Class*, p. 137. For the 'equivalence' between independent farmers and craftsmen in popular radicalism, see Foner, *Paine and Revolutionary America*, p. 102.

[25] Thornton, *A Plea for Peasant Proprietors* (1848), pp. 41–114, 167–85; J. Cowen, jr., speech in Newcastle Democratic Reading Room (6 Jun. 1852), *Cowen Papers*, C59; Fawcett, *Pauperism* (1871), p. 208. See also Stedman Jones, *Languages of Class*, pp. 102–5.

[26] Littlejohn, 'Land and Law in Belgium', *WT*, 11 Jan. 1880, p. 6; this article was in fact a review of the greatly admired E. L. V. de Laveleye, *Essai sur l'Économie Rurale de la Belgique* (Paris, 1862).

[27] See Hilton, 'The Origins of Robin Hood', pp. 36–7. Also important friendly societies – like the Foresters and the Shepherds – testified to those bucolic aspirations of the working men.

[28] [Rep.], 'The British Democratic Convention', lecture by T. Mooney on the theme 'Fifteen Cardinal Principles of Democracy', *NR*, 24 Aug. 1873, p. 124; see P. J. Smyth, 'A Peasant Proprietary', *NW*, 26 May 1877, p. 4, which places Norway next to Switzerland; and G. Potter, 'The First Point of the New Charter. Improved Dwellings for the People', *Contemporary Review* (1871), pp. 556–8.

[29] [L.a.], 'Small Farms and Peasant Proprietors', *NW*, 17 Aug. 1867, p. 4. This admiration for French farmers was also shared by Littlejohn ('The Workmen of France', *WT*, 22 Oct. 1871, p. 6) despite his contempt for the French referred to above, chapter 1, pp. 45–6.

of gold, silver and copper coin. This depository of precious metal is only opened on occasions when more is put in, and when the opportunity presents itself of laying out the whole ... in a thoroughly safe and advantageous manner.[30]

In Britain these idyllic conditions had been destroyed by the 'land-robbers', who were Tory by definition,[31] With the enclosure of most of the commons, the ancient village community based on fraternity and co-operation among freemen had disappeared.[32] There was an immense nostalgia for the golden age preceding this corruption, a sentiment which animated the struggle to preserve the remaining commons.[33] The latter provided another rallying point for classical economists and plebeian radicals.[34] It represented a further eloquent illustration of the strength of the 'rural' component in urban popular politics: especially in London, the signatures under petitions for the preservation of green areas, like Wimbledon Common and Richmond Park, look almost like a 'Who's who' of working-men's clubs.[35]

The 'pastoral dream' also inspired the emigration movement. The 'Frontier' countries would become the promised land of the

---

[30] Gracchus, 'Our "bold peasants" – Our Nation's Pride', *RN*, 8 Sept. 1872, p. 3. See very similar comments in [rep.], 'Mr. Boon's Sunday Morning Lectures', *NR*, 16 May 1869, p. 317; Littlejohn, 'The Workmen of France', *WT*, 22 Oct. 1871, p. 6; Arch, *The Story of His Life* (1898), p. 4. See also the parallel celebration of the 'race of small proprietors' in the *Leeds Mercury* ([l.a., n.t.], 11 Oct. 1866, p. 2), which confirms how close middle- and working-class radicals were on this issue. Plebeian liberals resolutely dismissed the then current suspicion that peasants tended to be conservative or reactionary: if they had been so in France before 1871, it was because of the state of illiteracy and appalling ignorance in which the farmers had been kept by the Orleanist monarchy and Napoleon's regime: but the Third Republic would soon change all that, and bring the peasants 'to the light of political knowledge and unite them in action with the progressive classes of the towns' ([l.a.], 'The Land Question in England and France', *WT*, 12 Jan. 1873, p. 1).

[31] Northumbrian, 'The Robbery of the Peasantry', *RN*, 29 Aug. 1872, p. 3; see also *RN*, 27 Feb. 1876, p. 2; 'The poor peasant, who has been degraded into a labourer . . . is able to trace his degradation to Toryism . . . the wholesale confiscation of land by Toryism – for in land even Whigs are Tories.'

[32] [L.a.], 'Village Life', *NW*, 11 May 1872, p. 4, which quotes the famous book by H. Maine, *Village Communities in East and West* (London 1871) and Mill's review of it ('Maine on Village Communities', *Fortnightly Review*, (1871): a remarkable case of popularization of politico-literary works.

[33] For the most famous expression of this tradition, see Eversley, *Commons, Forests & Footpaths* (1910).

[34] [L.a.], 'The "Epping Forest" Question', *LW*, 9 Jul. 1871, p. 6. For the radical economists' commitment to the preservation of the commons, see Fawcett, *Pauperism* (1871), pp. 237–66.

[35] See 'Open Space for the People', a printed petition, n.d., in *James Bryce Papers*, 'Political Work', UB31, Bodleian Library, Oxford.

new yeomanry: thus, Australia was sometimes described as the labourers' 'Pastures New'[36] and as having an abundance of food and free lands;[37] Canada was recommended by the 1875 Trade Union Congress to the agricultural labourers,[38] and celebrated as the country where the workman 'may own land on which no castle frowns, and where certain prosperity will smile upon his labour.[39] In this sense, emigration was not only a desperate attempt at a self-help solution to poverty, but also the extreme protest of the subaltern classes against the British social system, a sort of 'definitive strike' against the farmers and a 'weapon to smite the landed monopolists'.[40] As 'Gracchus' wrote in 1875:

A large majority of the agricultural population now-a-days looks upon a landlord as nothing else than a land robber. Instead of bending the knee and bowing the back to titled descendants of Norman thieves, as in former times, they would rather souse them into the horseponds their ancestors purloined, and they have inherited.

This alteration of feeling, this sense of independence, this outspreading of manliness and intelligence is manifested in many ways. Here for instance, I find in the *Lincolnshire Times*, a letter from a village called Laceby, written by 'A Thrasher', wherein are expressed feelings and sentiments that would do honour to Hampden himself. He says:

'In your last week's paper I saw a motto "Everyone for himself". What does it mean? Formerly the motto was "Live and let live"; but it appears very plainly to me and others that if the peasantry want to live they must leave the country and go to New Zealand, Australia and America; and month after month are the "bold peasantry" of England leaving for foreign lands. The recruiting-sergeants cannot get men for soldiers; the farm labourers' motto is now "Let those who claim the land and property

---

[36] [L.a.], '"Pastures New" in Australia', *LW*, 11 Aug. 1867, p. 6. For the strong feelings excited by environment conservationism, see [l.a.], 'Save the Forest', *LW*, 20 Oct. 1867, p. 6; [l.a.], 'Social Irritants', *LW*, 16 Jul. 1871, p. 6.

[37] [l.a.], 'Finding Mouths for Food!', *LW*, 28 Jul. 1867, p. 1.

[38] *Minutes of the Eighth Trade Union Congress Glasgow*, 11–16 October 1875, *Report*, p. 25.

[39] [L.a.], 'The Valleys of the West', *LW*, 16 Nov. 1879, p. 6.

[40] [L.a.], 'The Nonconformist on wholesale emigration', *Labourers' Union Chronicle*, 13 Dec. 1873, p. 1; the article concluded with the motto: 'THREE CHEERS FOR THE UNIONS AND ENDLESS GROANS FOR A GREEDY LANDED ARISTOCRACY.' See also [l.a.], 'The "Home across the seas"', *LW*, 21 Dec. 1873, p. 6. Again parallels to this attitude can be traced in the history of continental labour movements; for the Italian case, see Brunello, 'Agenti di emigrazione, contadini e immagini dell 'America nella provincia di Venezia', pp. 95–122. Yet, while Italian emigrants had to face upper-class hostility and resistance – as employers were concerned about possible increases in wage rates – in Great Britain the ruling elite 'philanthropists and social reformers' were expected to become the organizers of emigration as an alternative to the Poor Law: see [l.a.], 'The Tide of Emigration', *LW*, 25 Aug. 1867, p. 6.

fight for the country, and we that have no home or political rights must go to where we shall be better treated.'[41]

In similar vein, one who described himself as an emigrated 'Northumberland Ploughman' invited a friend to join him in the United States and farm a plot of good land under the Homestead Act: what did he have to lose if he left Great Britain? Son and grandson of farm labourers, he had no prospect but that of dying a labourer himself; no social or economic improvement was to be expected at home, however hard he worked.[42] 'Ploughman' warned his friend that the pioneer's life was difficult, but exertion would reap its reward: 'with a house on the Cumberland Mountains or on Sand Mountain, you could literally 'sit under your own vine and your own fig tree' in all the pastoral dignity of an ancient patriarch.[43] These sentiments were widely echoed in the mass press and associated with all the themes of traditional anti-aristocratic and even republican radicalism.[44]

Such an emphasis on the 'return to the land' in a highly urbanized and industrialized country is somehow surprising: certainly few Victorian factory workers would have been able to farm a plot, let alone settle in the primitive conditions of the 'Frontier'. It is likely that for many of them – as for the New England Jacksonian democrats they so much admired – the language and rhetoric of the 'yeoman' represented an attempt to 'exorcise the monster' of urban industrial civilization.[45] However, the Victorian 'pioneer' perspective was not simply escapist: it was first and foremost normative, for the moral and civic virtues it celebrated, and the kind of relationship between State and society which it implied. With its stress on society being independent of, and existing before, the State, this perspective was also linked to the

---

[41] Gracchus, 'The People and their Persecutors', *RN*, 20 Jun. 1875, p. 3.
[42] 'A Northumberland Ploughman', 'The Prospects of the Peasant at Home and Abroad, by Joseph Watson, Horton Grove, Alabama, U.S.'. Supplement to *NW*, 23 Apr. 1870, p. 4. It was an essay submitted for a competition organized by the *Newcastle Weekly Chronicle*, and was awarded first prize.
[43] *Ibid.* The passage in inverted commas is from Zechariah 3:10. See also A. S. Macmillan, 'Advice to Emigrants', *NW*, 11 Sept. 1869, p. 4; and 'A Northumbrian', 'Queensland – Letter No. I', *RN*, 9 Dec. 1871, p. 4. For more examples, see Erickson, *English Women Immigrants*, pp. 12–3.
[44] [L.a.], 'The Exodus of the people', *RN*, 23 Aug. 1874, p. 1; [l.a.], 'Mr. Arch on his Travels', *LW*, 2 Nov. 1873, p. 1.
[45] Significantly, such was also the case with the Jacksonian artisans in the United States: Meyers, *The Jacksonian Persuasion*, pp. 140–1.

perpetuation of popular versions of the doctrine of the 'social contract'.[46]

John Locke's thought had inspired early-nineteenth-century artisan radicalism both directly[47] and through its reformulation by Thomas Paine.[48] In the 1870s 'Northumbrian' followed up this tradition when he popularized a vision of history which recalled the seventeenth-century discussions on the origins of civil society and the State: he maintained that from a 'state of nature', characterized by free and independent hunters and fishers, there developed a society based on equality and reciprocal obligation, with a simple elective government dependent on the voice of the people. In those days the right to property was limited to the fruits of one's labour, as in the Lockian 'original society':[49] a picture which looked remarkably like a Victorian version of Paine's ideal of a co-operative, self-helping society which made State agency superfluous by performing 'for itself everything which is ascribed to government'.[50] This was the positive side of popular *laissez-faire*; a libertarian, egalitarian, fraternal and 'State-less' cantonal democracy, in which highly patriotic, independent citizens served the common good like unpaid representatives in local offices: a dream which looked like a democratic version of the traditional English constitution, or an idealized image of what happened in the United States.[51]

But the golden age had come to an end when this 'well-regulated commonwealth' had been subverted by violent people – robbers and murderers – who had begun to accumulate wealth and power on the principle that might was right: thus the first landed aristocracy was established. This situation led to a *bellum omnium contra omnes*, an endless sanguinary struggle for greater wealth and supremacy, which only ended when the various lords – tired of cutting each other's throats – decided to entrust a superior power to one of them: hence the first monarchy. The latter was

---

[46] J. Aytoun, 'It's Kings and not Republics which cause Revolutions', *BH*, 25 Nov. 1871.

[47] Stedman Jones, *Languages of Class*, p. 138, n.16; Thompson, *The Making*, pp. 841–2; Prothero, *Artisans and Politics*, p. 78.

[48] Pelling, *Popular Politics*, pp. 3–5; Stedman Jones, *Languages of Class*, p. 111.

[49] Northumbrian, 'Why We are Over-Governed', *RN*, 24 Aug. 1873, p. 3.

[50] Paine, *Rights of Man* (1791–2), p. 163; see also pp. 68, 70, 163, 164–5; see Holyoake, *History of Co-operation* (1911), p. 610.

[51] [Rep.], 'Bristol Operatives' Liberal Association', *NR*, 20 Mar. 1869, p. 201; see Godwin, *The Friends of Liberty*, p. 199.

thus to be considered totally 'artificial', in the sense of being contrary to those social relationships which would be in accordance with reason and morality.[52] In the endless struggle for liberty that had followed, the primaeval democracy – identified with Saxon England – had been temporarily restored under the Puritan Commonwealth, then had fallen again: but nineteenth-century radicals campaigning for manhood suffrage were trying to re-establish it on a stronger foundation.[53]

THE 'MORAL ECONOMY' OF FREE TRADE

If society was at peace and in a generally healthy condition, the services of the State were hardly required, and its branches could virtually be disbanded; if, on the other hand, society was unhealthy, then political reform and democracy were needed, and not State patronage of an impoverished population. Such was the Victorian summary of the Jeffersonian and semi-anarchist part of Paine's thought. Keeping the State economical was a crucial means of constitutional control: government expenditure appeared to be aimed mainly at providing 'fuel' for a 'class' machinery whose purposes were war abroad, repression and economic exploitation at home, and the general preservation of a system based on privilege and injustice. This impression was based on the fact that at that time the largest portion of the revenue was absorbed by items offering little social benefit to the common people: the national debt, army, navy, police, diplomatic service, Civil List and other establishments which 'as the late Mr Cobden very pithily expressed it, have for their real object the granting of out-door relief for the younger sons, poor relations, and favourites of the aristocracy',[54] but offered to the people 'nothing except debts, taxes, obligations and bad trade'.[55] Particularly hated was the national debt; not only did it represent a major obstacle to fiscal reform,[56] it also compounded the material burden with an ideologi-

---

[52] Northumbrian, *RN*, 24 Aug. 1873, p. 3.
[53] Plain Dealer, 'The Working Men's Meeting at Guildhall', *BH*, 11 Aug. 1866, p. 4.
[54] Northumbrian, 'National Extravagance and Popular Wretchedness', *RN*, 4 Mar. 1866, p. 3. On the composition of national expenditure, see Matthew, *Gladstone 1809–74*, p. 111.
[55] Northumbrian, 'Cutting contrasts', *RN*, 7 Dec. 1879, p. 3.
[56] Plain Dealer, 'The State of the Revenue', *BH*, 6 Jan. 1866, p. 4 and [l.a.], *RN*, 22 Apr. 1866, p. 4. See also [anon.], 'Mr Gladstone's New Financial Policy', *Macmillan's Magazine*, XIV (May–Oct. 1866), pp. 130–4.

cal affront, as it had been raised mainly during the 1790s, 'in order that the aristocratic Government of France might be kept up – that the Bourbon might be sustained and the Republic kept down'.[57]

This being the situation, the art of good government consisted 'in the lowest possible interference with the people'.[58] Strongly held – despite the economists' refutation[59] – was the view that all taxes, both direct and indirect, tended to limit popular consumption, reduce capital, and consequently diminish the demand for labour.[60] This led to the conclusion that the redistribution of the burden between forms of taxation was not enough: 'The real point is expenditure, for seventy-two millions paid in one form, are equivalent to the same sum paid in another form. The remission we obtain from the abolition of the duty on corn is only temporary; the relief of a reduction of expenditure . . . is permanent'.[61] According to Howell, taxation was 'like a huge rental, or heavy mortgage upon industry. This amount has to be paid before profits can be made, or even wages paid. To say that this taxation has no prejudicial effect upon industry, is equivalent to saying that a heavy mortgage, or ground rent, makes no difference in the income to the owners of property'.[62] In contrast, 'Light taxation – other things being equal – implied unfettered industry, enterprising and

[57] [Rep.], 'Mr. Baines, M.P., and Mr. Alderman Carter at New Wortley', *LM*, 6 Oct. 1868, p. 8. Cf. [l.a.], 'How Public Money Goes', *WT*, 18 Jul. 1869, p 4; 'Chacun a son gout', 'Monarchy or Republicanism', letter to *RN*, 12 Feb. 1871, p. 3.

[58] [L.a.], 'National Expenditure on the Rack', *RN*, 23 Feb. 1873, p. 4; Northumbrian, 'The Money Value of the People', *RN*, 28 Oct. 1877, p. 3. See [l.a.], 'The Way to Economy', *LW*, 4 Mar. 1866, p. 1; Northumbrian, 'The Principles of Taxation', *RN*, 31 Jan. 1869, p. 3; Plain Dealer, 'The State of the Revenue', *BH*, 6 Jan. 1866; [l.a., n.t.], *LM*, 19 Feb. 1870, p. 5; Northumbrian, 'National Extravagance and Popular Wretchedness', *RN*, 4 Mar. 1866, p. 3.

[59] See Mill, *Principles*, in *Collected Works*, II, pp. 88–90, who stressed that part of the taxes on the wealthy was not paid out of their capital, but out of their income which would be spent on commodities; moreover, he pointed out that in any case part of the revenue was used 'in the direct purchase of labour' (soldiers, sailors, shipwrights in Royal Arsenals, public works, etc.).

[60] [L.a.], 'Tory Extravagance and Working-Class Indulgence', *RN*, 10 May 1868; [l.a.], 'John Stuart Mill on the Malt Tax and the National Debt', *RN*, 22 Apr. 1866, p. 4; [l.a.], *LW*, 29 Dec. 1867, p. 1.

[61] [L.a.], 'National Expenditure on the Rack', *RN*, 23 Feb. 1873, p. 4; Northumbrian, 'The Money Value of the People', *RN*, 28 Oct. 1877, p. 3. See [l.a.], 'The Way to Economy', *LW*, 4 Mar. 1866, p. 1; Northumbrian, 'The Principles of Taxation', *RN*, 31 Jan. 1869, p. 3; Plain Dealer, 'The State of the Revenue', *BH*, 6 Jan. 1866; [l.a., n.t.], *LM*, 19 Feb. 1870, p. 5; Northumbrian, 'National Extravagance and Popular Wretchedness', *RN*, 4 Mar. 1866, p. 3.

[62] G. Howell's contribution to Bernard and Reid (eds.), *Bold Retrenchment* (1888), p. 48.

profitable trade, a well-fed, well-clothed, and well educated people'.[63]

Expenditure was due to the fact that 'We are over-ruled by law, over-regulated by police', and money was lavished 'upon idlers, who, but for that expenditure, would be productive workers':[64] 'there [wa]s waste everywhere', indeed 'organized waste', '"knots, groups and classes" who prey upon the public purse',[65] causing the poor to become poorer, pauperism to increase, and the poor rates to grow. The first enemy of the public good was a profligate government, which was ultimately incompatible with liberty and democracy, as illustrated by the cases of Austria and Napoleonic France. In contrast, real democracies were economical,[66] the prime example being the United States, who 'commenced their retrenchment the moment their [Civil] war was over', and by 1869 were 'paying off their national debt at a rate of ten millions a month, while we can hardly reduce ours a stives in ten years'.[67] Real reform would cut down all the unproductive branches of the State,[68] 'spend as little as possible, and . . . collect that little from the people better able to pay'.[69] To achieve the latter aim it was necessary to start by repealing all taxation on necessities – that most unpleasant government interference with the life of the labouring poor. This was the basic reasoning behind popular commitment to free trade.

Free trade had a long tradition in plebeian radicalism, going back to the Levellers[70] and Thomas Paine, who developed it into a

---

[63] [L.a.], 'John Stuart Mill on the Malt-Tax and the National Debt', *RN*, 22 Apr. 1866, p. 4.

[64] [L.a.], 'National Expenditure on the Rack', *RN*, 23 Feb. 1873, p. 4; Northumbrian, 'The Money Value of the People', *RN*, 28 Oct. 1877, p. 3. See [l.a.], 'The Way to Economy', *LW*, 4 Mar. 1866, p. 1; Northumbrian, 'The Principles of Taxation', *RN*, 31 Jan. 1869, p. 3; Plain Dealer, 'The State of the Revenue', *BH*, 6 Jan. 1866; [l.a., n.t.], *LM*, 19 Feb, 1870, p. 5; Northumbrian, 'National extravagance and popular wretchedness', *RN*, 4 Mar. 1866, p. 3.

[65] *Lloyd's Weekly* quoting Gladstone: [l.a.], 'The Spendthrift of the Nation', 26 Feb. 1871, p. 1; [l.a.], 'Waste of Public Money', *WT*, 26 Apr. 1868, p. 4.

[66] [L.a.], 'Retrenchment', *NW*, 22 Jan. 1870, p. 4.

[67] Gracchus, *RN*, 19 Sept. 1869, p. 3.

[68] Northumbrian, 'The Principles of Taxation', *RN*, 31 Jan. 1869, p. 3.

[69] Northumbrian, 'The Money Value of the People', *RN*, 28 Oct. 1877, p. 3; see Gracchus, 'Ducal Drones and Despots, and What they Cost', *RN*, 16 Aug. 1868, p. 3, and C. Bradlaugh, 'To the Right Hon. W. E. Gladstone, MP', *NR*, 28 Nov. 1869, pp. 337–9.

[70] See *To the Supream Authority of England, the Commons Assembled in Parliament. The Earnest Petition of Many Free-Born People of This Nation* (London 1648), in Wolfe, *Levellers Manifestoes*, pp. 263–72.

sort of pre-Cobdenite philosophy based on peace, retrenchment, and disarmament.[71] But it was especially after the end of the Napoleonic wars that the question assumed a political relevance. The repeal of Pitt's Property Tax and the introduction of the new Corn Laws 'meant dearer bread and increased indirect taxation, both of which hit the poor disproportionately hard'.[72] The Corn Laws were further hated because they limited and controlled the import of food, representing a policy of 'starvation' of the workers for the benefit of the landlords. Not surprisingly, agricultural protectionism soon became the symbol of the iniquity of the political system:[73] John Buckmaster, the free-trade agitator, well expressed the anger of the labouring poor when he wrote that he 'was doing a religious work, as holy in the sight of God as any missionary. To see the families of a bold peasantry, their country's pride, reduced to living for days on bread and turn-tops, gathered by permission, was enough to drive men to acts of violence'.[74] The working men claimed cheap food as 'a moral right . . . in return for the sweat of their brows'.[75] This suggests that, despite their emphasis on the virtues of the 'independent producer', nineteenth-century plebeian radicals were increasingly concerned with the working man as consumer – a change of emphasis parallel to the one which had taken place among Jacksonian radicals a few years before.[76] But in fact, in Britain the struggle for free trade also had a producers' viewpoint, since from the days of John Gast working-class radicals had denounced the effects of protectionism not only on prices, but also on trade and employment:

Whenever the taxes press upon any species of manufacture, so as to diminish its consumption, they destroy the market for your labour, and you are deprived of work and of bread. Such is the case at the present time; the load of taxes upon goods of British manufacture has nearly destroyed our Foreign commerce; distress has reduced our Home consumption to almost nothing; by this means you are thrown out of employment, which means nothing less than you are deprived of your bread.[77]

[71] Paine, *Rights of Man* (1791–2), pp. 210–34, in *The Complete Works of Thomas Paine*, pp. 371, 358–9, 416, 424.
[72] Belchem, *'Orator' Hunt*, p. 50.
[73] Tholfsen, *Working-Class Radicalism*, p. 51. Cf. Barnes, *English Corn Laws*, pp. 231 ff.
[74] Buckmaster, *Village Politician* (1897), p. 178.
[75] Burnett, 'Introduction' to Buckmaster, *A Village Politician* (1897), p. xxi.
[76] Hugins, *Jacksonian Democracy*, p. 152.
[77] Belchem, *'Orator' Hunt*, pp. 110–11; see Prothero, *Artisans and Politics*, p. 77.

The demand for 'cheap bread' and 'cheap government' contributed powerfully towards stirring up popular unrest during the agitation of 1830–2, when 'Reform' was equated with financial probity.[78] Later, the Chartists reiterated these arguments: their petitions contained long and bitter protests against the burden of taxes under which both workers and manufacturers were 'bowed down'.[79] In January 1842 the *Scottish Chartist Circular* declared:

It is not of over-production that we have to complain; it is of our utter inability in consequence of the oppression we endure to obtain the means requisite for a sufficient consumption of the fruits of our national industry. An enlightened and popular Legislation would by securing to us the blessings of good and cheap government, and by encouraging trade at home, have placed within our reach, the abundant means of supplying all our reasonable wants, which would have rendered the power of production by automaton agency, a blessing instead of a curse; but the heathen 'Exclusives' who superintend the destinies of this injured nation instead of giving any possible facility to industry, have by enormous taxes which they have imposed on every necessary of life, rendered the working millions unable to purchase the products of their mutal labour.[80]

Thus, in spite of their differences,[81] many Chartists were quite close to the Cobdenite radicals; the main divergence between them did not concern the desirability of the repeal of agricultural protection, but whether this reform should and could come before political democracy.[82] As 3,000 Rochdale workers put it in 1839 in a resolution of no-confidence in John Bright, 'though the Corn Law is an injurious tax, yet the present House of Commons constituted on the present suffrage, will never repeal that law so as to be beneficial to the working classes'.[83] Eventually, however, Bright managed to defeat the intransigent wing of Rochdale Chartism, and gain considerable support among local artisans and workers. Just one month after the aforementioned resolution, he collected 9,700 signatures – virtually all the adult males in the town – on a

---

[78] Gash, *Pillars of Government*, pp. 43–6. See Place, 'National Political Union, on the Pledges to be Given by Candidates' (1832), in Rowe (ed.), *A Selection from the Papers of Francis Place*, p. 104; Lovett, *Social and Political Morality* (1853), p. 191; see also Thompson, *The People's Science*, pp. 129–30.

[79] From a petition of the period 1838–9, cit. in Trevelyan, *Bright*, p. 45; see also Weaver, *John Fielden*, pp. 229, 234.

[80] Cit. in Gash, *Sir Robert Peel*, p. 361.

[81] Brown 'Chartist and the Anti-Corn Law League', in Briggs, *Chartist Studies*, pp. 350–1.

[82] Buckmaster, *A Village Politician* (1897), p. 186.

[83] The event took place on 2 February 1839: cit. in Trevelyan, *Bright*, p. 31.

free-trade petition, and soon a local working men's Anti-Corn Law Association was established.[84] These achievements anticipated what would happen later at a national level.[85]

Though the history of plebeian anti-protectionism in the Chartist period is still largely to be written[86] – mainly because it has so far appeared unattractive to scholars of the labour movement – its existence and strength cannot be questioned. Indeed, when considered in the light of the Liberal and Labour fiscal policies of the following eighty years, workers' support for free trade would seem to be a phenomenon as significant as their commitment to democracy. As Ernest Jones admitted, after 1846 'there [would be] little use in holding before them the Cap of Liberty, unless you hold THE BIG LOAF by the side of it'.[87] The repeal of the Corn Laws thus became one of the major turning points in popular radicalism. This can be fully appreciated when we consider it against the background of the 1848 revolutions: while in famine-stricken continental countries unjust and heavy taxation was one of the factors which contributed towards the outburst of popular resistance,[88] in Britain a policy of cheap food helped to contain unrest within the limits of constitutional demonstrations. What the Chartists had thought impossible did in fact happen, and the psychological impact was considerable;[89] as *Lloyd's Weekly* put it rather crudely when recalling the events in the 1870s, 'the great, practical, easily-understood Anti-Corn Law League, which had the cheap loaf on its banner, drowned the clamour of Chartism . . . The Big Loaf had the better of the Big Talk.'[90]

Over the next twenty years the rhetoric and promises of the free traders seemed to be corroborated by improvements in working-class living standards, and at the end of the century Holyoake

---

[84] Trevelyan, *Bright*, p. 32.

[85] In fact, even in 1839 working-class support for Bright at Rochdale was not an isolated case, as Anti-Corn Law League 'operative' associations were established in many other towns as well: in April 1839 another was founded in Manchester, with 4,000 members, and others at Leicester (750 members) and Carlisle: McCord, *The Anti-Corn Law League*, p. 97.

[86] But see Brown, 'Chartists and the Anti-Corn Law League', in Briggs (ed.), *Chartist Studies*, pp. 342–71.

[87] Cit. in Tiller, 'Late Chartism in Halifax', in Thompson and Epstein (eds.), *The Chartist Experience*, p. 320.

[88] See Augulhon, *The Republican Experiment*, p. 29; Candeloro, *Storia dell'Italia moderna*, III, pp. 105–7.

[89] Stedman Jones, *Languages of Class*, p. 177.

[90] [L.a.], 'John Frost, Chartist', *LW*, 5 Jul. 1877, p. 1.

claimed that free trade had made 'the English nation heavier. Every man that you meet in the streets now is stouter, and weighs two stones more than he would have done but for Mr Cobden and Mr Bright.'[91] Contemporaries were so impressed that there were ex-Chartists who tried to re-interpret the history of the movement of which they had been members, exaggerating its commitment to free trade;[92] one of them, Francis Soutter, went as far as to write that Chartism had been a consequence of the 'Tax upon Bread'.[93] Many working-class biographies published in the second half of the century registered the repeal as a great liberation, and described the early 1840s as a 'dark age' when 'protection was at its zenith ... [and] the state of the people at its nadir'.[94] From a Primitive Methodist pulpit, the miners' leader John Wilson recalled those grim days when the government 'taxed the coal to save the landlords' pockets ... taxed the sugar to save the pockets that might bear the taxation ... put a corn tax on, and it was a burden to the widow and orphan to save the rich. They had filled the rich with good things, and the poor they had sent empty away.'[95] From this persecution and martyrdom the people had been rescued by

---

[91] Holyoake, *History of Co-operation* (1906), I, p. 297; 'National Income and Expenditure', *The Co-operative Wholesale Society Ltd., Annual for the Year 1884*, Manchester 1884, pp. 554–5, 586; see Gillispie, *Labor and Politics in England*, pp. 198–201. Recent research on army recruits has indicated a slow increase in height from the eighteenth century, halted between the 1830s and the 1850s and resumed in the 1860s, as a consequence of juvenile nutrition: Floud *et. al., Height, Health, and History*, pp. 317–19.

[92] See G. Howell, 'The Free Trade Movement and Chartism', in 'The Autobiography of a Toiler . . .', p. 116, in *G. Howell Collection*, I, 3, p. 116, where he mentions the case of E. Jones to maintain that Chartism and the free trade movement were close allies: their divergences were limited to marginal details. J. B. Leno recalled that in the 1840s, after a soul-searching time,

> In the end my allegiance went to the Chartists, and with them I opposed the Free Trade of Cobden and Bright. It is a mistake to suppose that the Chartists were in favour of Protective duties on corn, or that they had the least sympathy with landlord Protection. Their doctrine was Free Trade in corn, raw materials of all kinds, and in all articles of foreign growth and manufacture that did not run counter to English production. They were in favour of protection duties on silk manufactures, watches, and indeed all manufactured articles that needed protection. In fact they were believers in neither Free Trade or Protection, wholly and solely, but in an adjustment of both. Whether they were right or wrong, I will not stay to argue. All I can say is that I have, for many years, been a Free Trader. (Leno, *The Aftermath* (1892), pp. 18–19).

[93] Cf. Soutter, *Fights for Freedom*, pp. 29–30.

[94] Wilson, *Memories* (1910), p. 40; see also pp. 42–3; Hawker, *James Hawker's Journal* (1961), p. 95.

[95] J. Wilson about the 1840s, in a sermon: 'The New Primitive Church at Amble – Opening Ceremony', in *Wilson Papers*, D/X 188/ 12, issue 151. See similar remarks T. Rogers, 'A Century of English Labour', *The Co-operative Wholesale Society Ltd., Annual for the Year 1885*, Manchester 1885, pp. 339, 350.

the heaven-sent crusaders, Cobden and Bright,[96] who in the popular imagination soon became semi-mythical hero-figures, comparable with Wilberforce and Cobbett.[97]

If repeal of the Corn Laws was a victory for the 'Left' as a whole, the fact that it brought with it the general conviction that the cause of 'cheap food' needed thorough-going free trade, and that protectionism was synonymous with taxation of the necessities of life, was Cobden's personal triumph. The case of Joseph Gutteridge, a Coventry silk-weaver was significant. He – though ruined by the French Treaty of 1860 – remained dogmatically committed to free trade as the poor man's best hope.[98] For generations after 1846, free trade was to the labouring people a 'bread and cheese' question.[99] Hatred for the very word 'protectionism' was such that it remained in their political vocabulary only as a term of abuse.[100]

The success of free trade was one of the key factors in opening up the working classes to a formal alliance with the parliamentary Liberal party, and to the influence of current Liberal thought.[101] Among the various branches of the organized working classes, the co-operative movement was the one most completely committed to free trade: its members had been 'ardent advocates of the repeal of the Corn Laws' from an early stage;[102] after 1846, they supported the systematic dismantling of the protectionist duties; they then followed Cobden's and Gladstone's initiatives and particularly the French Treaty and the free trade budgets of the 1860s, later campaigning for the 'free breakfast table' and the abolition of all residual indirect taxation.[103] They consistently rejected economic nationalism in all its forms.[104] The Rochdale Pioneers, in particu-

---

[96] Arch, *The Story of His Life* (1898), pp. 6, 10, 151, 312; Wilson, *Memories* (1910), pp. 42–3; Hawker, *James Hawker's Journal* (1961), pp. 72–3, 95.

[97] Report of the Labour Representation League dinner at Anderton's Hotel, in *Labour Representation League Papers*, 7 Jan. 1875, p. 114.

[98] 'The Autobiography of Joseph Gutteridge', in Chancellor (ed.), *Master and Artisan in Victorian England*, p. 178; see also Chancellor, 'Introduction', pp. 5–6.

[99] [L.a.], 'The Story of Free Trade', *LW*, 28 Oct. 1866, p. 1.

[100] [L.a.], 'Free trade and the revivers', *WT*, 7 Nov. 1869, p. 4; [l.a.], 'Reciprocity', *Co-operative News*, 1 Feb. 1879, p. 74. See Semmel, *Imperialism and Social Reform*, p. 108.

[101] Semmel, *Imperialism and Social Reform*, pp. 106–7.

[102] [L.a.], 'Co-operators as Financial Reformers', *Co-operative News*, 9 Mar. 1872, pp. 114–15.

[103] Cole, *A Century of Co-operation*, pp. 188, 322; Barou, *The Co-operative Movement*, p. 101; Bonner, *British Co-operation*, pp. 126, 459.

[104] Cole, *A Century of Co-operation*, p. 353; Bailey, *British Co-operative Movement*, pp. 112–13. Besides seeing free trade as a form of international co-operation, each co-operative congress devoted a section of its proceedings to the time of the 'Progress of Co-operation in Foreign Countries'.

lar, became identified with Liberalism at least from the time they supported Cobden's candidature at the 1859 elections.[105] Assisted by Liberal support of their claims to legal protection and fiscal reforms,[106] the organized agencies of the consumers' interests maintained their allegiance to Liberalism till the end of the 1910s.[107]

Besides the material advantages it offered, free trade also implied a relationship between the State and society based on 'fair play', impartiality, and the withdrawal of the State from the market. In this way it provided an effective back-up to the liberal rhetoric of 'national' – in contrast to 'class' – policies.[108] Fairness and impartiality also seemed to characterize free trade as a regime of international exchange, and there was a great expectation it would be conductive to permanent peace as well as to the liberalization of the despotic governments of continental Europe.[109] Though the Franco-Prussian war of 1870–1 marked a crisis for this optimism, it did not shake the faith in free trade. Indeed, the war was seen as a further illustration of the urgency of extending the system to prevent further outbursts of national selfishness: as a *Bee-Hive* correspondent put it, 'If we had the [free trade] treaties . . . twenty years sooner, it is very likely the awful war which broke out between France and Germany in 1870 would have been averted'.[110]

In their enthusiasm for the repeal of indirect taxation, working-class radicals were close to extreme free-trade pressure groups. The Liverpool Financial Reform Association had many working men amongst its supporters,[111] though it had debarred itself from

---

[105] Cole, *A Century of Co-operation*, pp. 94–5. With the exception of some Lancashire societies: see the lively debate between the latter's delegates and the Liberal majority of the co-operators, led by Lloyd Jones, in *Proceedings of the Co-operative Congress held at Manchester, 1870*, Manchester 1870, pp. 33–5.

[106] Cole, *A Century of Co-operation*, pp. 310–11.   [107] *Ibid.*, pp. 191, 192, 276.

[108] [Rep.], 'West Riding – Eastern Division – Mr Thompson and Mr Holden, MP, at Selby', *LM*, 13 Oct. 1868, p. 5.

[109] [L.a.], 'The Revenue, Taxation, and National Despotism', *LW*, 7 Jan. 1866, p. 1; T. Briggs, 'Universal Free Trade, the First Condition of Universal Peace', *BH*, 3 Dec. 1870, p. 660; [l.a.], 'Mr Gladstone's Guildhall Speech', *BH*, 15 Nov. 1873, p. 7.

[110] 'A Cobden's disciple', *BH*, 24 Jul. 1875, p. 3; see [l.a.], 'Free Trade at Whitebait', *LW*, 25 Jul. 1875, p. 6. It is quite significant that during the last quarter of the century, when nationalism and protectionism came to dominate the greater part of the western world, working-class movements in Britain as elsewhere in Europe remained or became passionately free trader: see Fletcher, 'Cobden as Educator', pp. 561–78; Spriano, 'Introduzione' to Einaudi (ed.), *Le lotte del lavoro*, p. xi.

[111] See Calkins, 'A Victorian Free Trade Lobby', p. 91). The programme of the FRA was also closely similar to the financial proposals of working-class newspapers like *Reynolds's* (ibid., p. 99), as well as to those of popular reformers like John Noble (Noble, *National Finance* (1875), pp. 126–8; on Noble's career as a radical, see *DNB*, *sub voce*)..

co-operation with corporate labour because of its avowed hostility to trade unions.[112] In addition, the *Bee-Hive* widely reported the activities of a parallel organization, the London Financial Reform Union; its programme – inspired by Cobden's 'National Budget' of 1848–9 and built on halving the military estimates and on massive reductions in taxation[113] – was hardly distinguishable from the platform of the mass-circulation plebeian press.[114] Their affinities were also increased by the fact that both used the same language which consisted of a mixture of economic populism, moral emphasis and religious overtones,[115] and agreed that 'complete' free trade – the abolition of all forms of taxation on the necessaries of life[116] – was the first step towards 'real' social reform.[117]

[112] In 1871, a discussion took place between the secretary of the FRA and G. Howell, then secretary of the TUC, when the former charged the trade unions with being 'in restraint of trade' and protectionist, and invited the workers to leave them and join instead the FRA to struggle for the 'real' interests of labour – namely a 'real free trade' based on the repeal of indirect taxation; Howell rejected the charges and stressed that the TUC was already committed to obtaining the reform of the fiscal system (cf. [rep.], 'Trades Unions and the Financial Reform Association', *Potteries' Examiner*, 7 Apr. 1871, p. 2). This discussion was re-opened, in more bitter tones, in 1873, following an article against trade unions published by the editor of the *Financial Reformer*, to which Lloyd Jones replied in the *Bee-Hive* ('The "Financial Reformer" and Trades Unions', 22 Nov. 1873, p. 2). For the Association's interest in involving the workers on a mass scale, see C. Robertson, President of the FRA, 'The Financial Reform Association to the Unrepresented Working Classes. Why do you want Parliamentary Reform?', *BH*, 9 Jul. 1864, p. 6).

[113] *Financial Reform Union – Papers on taxation and Expenditure, No. 3. A Budget for 1869 Based on Mr. Cobden's 'National Budget' proposed in 1849*, n. d. [but 1869], in Bishopsgate Institute, London. Cf. Morley, *Life of Richard Cobden* (1879), pp. 498–9. The 'wasteful expenditure' of money unjustly obtained through 'the taxation of the humblest classes' by the Liberal government was one of the reasons why Cobden declined to enter Palmerston's last Cabinet in 1865 (*ibid.*, p. 929).

[114] *Report on Taxation: Direct and Indirect Adopted by the Financial Reform Association*, Liverpool, 1859, p. 8; (Unsigned article in the correspondence section], 'A Free Breakfast Table', *Co-operative News*, 13 Jan. 1872, p. 21.

[115] For two examples, see *ibid.*, p. 9, and the address of the Free Breakfast Table Association, *Co-operative News*, 20 Jan. 1872, p. 28.

[116] [L.a.], 'A Free Breakfast Table', *LW*, 28. 1872, p. 1; see the poem by 'W.B.', 'A Free Breakfast Table', *BH*, 3 Jan. 1874, p. 10.

[117] Noble, *Fiscal Legislation 1842–1865* (1867), pp. 162–72; Briggs, *Poverty, Taxation and the Remedy; Free Trade, Free Labour or Direct Taxation* (1883), *passim.*

GLADSTONE AND THE PLEBEIAN FINANCIAL REFORMERS

Though as early as 1866 the *Times* could claim that this work had been virtually completed,[118] working-class radicals begrudged the fact that a few items of widespread consumption – like sugar, tea and coffee – were still taxed. The opportunity for the removal of these taxes and for further fiscal reform seemed to come when Gladstone formed his first government.[119] Great expectation had been generated by Gladstone's unparalleled reputation as a financier,[120] as his chancellorships in the 1860s had come to symbolize the State's commitment to doing its share of reducing the cost of living and improving the lot of the labouring poor.

According to Schumpeter's classical analysis, Gladstonian finance was based on three principles: retrenchment and rationalization of State expenditure; a system of taxation which would interfere as little as possible with industrial and commercial operations; and the production of balanced budgets with surpluses to allow for fiscal reforms and the reduction of the national debt.[121] This scheme, however, does not account for Gladstone's sensitivity to the political importance of the distribution of taxation, and tends to confuse the attempts to minimize central government's expenditure with a 'minimalist' approach *tout-court*. In fact Gladstone's financial strictness was compatible both with non-expensive forms of state intervention (like factory legislation),[122] and with an expanding scope for local government, the responsibilities and budget of which continued to grow throughout his Parliamentary career. Thus, while *laissez-faire* and retrenchment were preached at Nos 10 and 11, Downing Street, the organization of social services was carried out by 'municipal socialists' in town councils and local school boards, under the supervision of central government inspectors and with the help of the loans and 'grants in aid' which Gladstonian surpluses made available.[123] At all levels the principles

---

[118] [L.a., n.t.], *TI*, 27 Feb. 1866, p. 9; see Buxton, *Gladstone as Chancellor of the Exchequer* (1901), p. 39.

[119] [L.a.], 'The People's Food and Taxation', *BH*, 3 Jan. 1874, p. 8.

[120] [L.a.], *Labour Standard*, 11 Feb. 1882, p. 4. See G. Howell, 'Taxation – How Levied and How Expended', *Industrial Review*, 12 Jan. 1878, p. 3.

[121] Schumpeter, *History of Economic Analysis*, pp. 403–5.

[122] Hilton, *Age of Atonement*, p. 268.

[123] As happened in 1892, when a former Liberal minister, Goschen, provided the money to make primary education free: P. Marsh, *Discipline of Popular Government*, p. 171. See also below, chapter 3, pp. 173–91.

of *laissez-faire* were applied in a pragmatic way and with due attention to what economists called the 'exceptions' to the principles themselves,[124] including the nationalization of 'natural monopolies', like the telegraphs[125] or even the railways.[126]

However, it was neither on occasional great measures of State intervention nor on the spending of public money that Gladstone's popularity was based: rather, as Colin Matthew has shown, it was his work on the public revenue side which brought him greatest credit, generating psychological expectations of balance, social equity, and political justice.[127] His budgets coupled a symbolic component with a degree of material relief. In choosing which taxes and duties to abolish Gladstone followed criteria more complex than that of merely encouraging consumption. He maintained that it would be 'a mistake to suppose that the best mode of giving benefit to the labouring classes is simply to operate on the Articles consumed by them. If you want to do the maximum of good, you should rather operate on the articles which give them the maximum of employment';[128] this constituted the only kind of employment policy devised by financiers and asked for by plebeian radicals[129] in times of economic expansion. Thus, while 'every encouragement [was] given to trade and personal expenditure', the fiscal load on 'the small people and the working classes' was rendered less grievous.[130] By the time of his first retirement, Gladstone's achievements included – in principle or in practice – most of what plebeian radicals considered good and useful:

Taxation has been removed from the necessaries of the poor and the luxuries of the rich . . . the great bulk of our trade has been liberated from fiscal exactions which hindered its development. The growth of commerce can be traced, step by step, as the direct consequence of the remission of indirect taxation, the Income-tax has been the instrument of effecting

[124] See below, chapter 3, pp. 166–8.
[125] See Cohen, 'Toward a Theory of State Intervention: The Nationalization of the British Telegraphs', pp. 176, 183; Hutchinson, 'Economists and Economic Policy in Britain after 1870', p. 237.
[126] Gladstone contemplated their purchase in 1844 and again in 1864: Matthew, *Gladstone 1809–74*, p. 119; Vincent, 'Gladstone and Ireland', p. 200; Parris, *Government and the Railways*, p. 8.
[127] Matthew, 'The Politics of mid-Victorian Budgets', pp. 615–18.
[128] Cit. in Buxton, *Gladstone as Chancellor of the Exchequer* (1901), p. 45; see Northcote, *Twenty Years of Financial Policy* (1862), p. 69; Matthew, *Gladstone 1809–74*, p. 213.
[129] [L.a.], 'Tory Extravagance and Working Class Indulgence', *RN*, 10 May 1868; Noble, *National Finance* (1875), p. 144.
[130] [L.a.], *TI*, 15 Feb. 1860, p. 8.

those remissions, and has thus conferred substantial benefit upon every section of the community.[131]

The popularity of these reforms was increased by the fact that some of them had assumed a more markedly 'democratic' flavour because of the way in which they had been carried. In particular, the repeal of the paper duty involved a famous fight with the Lords over the 1860 and 1861 budgets: it was then that Gladstone first became 'the idol' of working-class radicals.[132] 'The people' saw the abolition of the last vestiges of 'taxation upon knowledge' not only as a 'great boon to the working class, opening out to them the avenues of learning and mental culture',[133] but also as a powerful vindication of the 'Saxon constitution', because the will of the Commons had been enforced on the recalcitrant Lords.[134] *Reynolds's* explained that Gladstone had earned the artisans' confidence because he had demonstrated that he was 'a conscientious man ... an advocate of political progress and financial honesty': his moral worth was confirmed by the fact that he had become 'naturally hateful to the pack of howling, ravenous, coroneted wolves' in the Upper House and the Conservative party.[135] Gladstone's work as the 'liberator' of British trade survived his elaborate plan to relate taxation and the electoral franchise – which plebeian liberals never did accept as a substitute for democracy[136] – and remained the corner stone of British fiscal policy for generations, even under Conservative and Labour governments.[137]

From the viewpoint of popular success it was important that the central tenets of Gladstone's finance were easy to understand. Gladstone's stress on the need for balanced budgets was in tune with popular views of financial morality as consisting in 'making

[131] J. Noble, 'Taxation – Imperial and local. No. viii – The Income Tax', *BH*, 12 Aug. 1876, p. 3.

[132] Royle, *Victorian Infidels*, p. 265.

[133] Wilson, *Memories* (1910), p. 137; see pp. 133–7 for a working-class interpretation of the budgets of 1860–61. See *Gladstone the Friend of the People, by George Potter – Leaflets for the New Electors – Price One Penny*, n.d. [but 1885], p. 2, in *Collection of Electoral Propaganda Material*, Nuffield College Oxford.

[134] Wilson, *Memories* (1910), pp. 134–7.

[135] Northumbrian, 'Mr Gladstone for Premier', *RN*, 10 May 1868, p. 2.

[136] For Gladstone's plan, see Matthew, *Gladstone 1809–74*, pp. 110–14, 123–37; for the reaction of popular liberals, see below, chapter 5, pp. 258 ff.

[137] The former were long dominated by 'Gladstonian' Chancellors of the Exchequer like Northcote and Goschen (Cowling, *1867*, pp. 93, 179–80); the latter had in Snowden a most intransigent defender of the orthodoxy Skidelsky, *Politicians and the Slump*, pp. 327, 393; Snowden, *Autobiography*, vol. 2, pp. 622–59, 839–73.

expenses fall within the limits of a fixed income';[138] moreover, as an assimilation of national finance to that of a well-managed family, it seemed rational and verifiable. The classical principles of taxation which the 'People's Chancellor' applied were also deeply rooted in popular expectations through readings and popularizations of Adam Smith.[139] Moreover, Gladstone's businesslike mottoes of 'small profits and quick returns', and of leaving 'the money to fructify in the pockets of the people', seemed to contain the secret of 'a flourishing national exchequer, coeval with the diminution of taxes on the necessaries'.[140] The labouring poor were thankful for both prosperity and cheap food, as the poetess Janet Hamilton wrote in her 'Rhymes':[141] her words were an apt comment to the triumphal welcome that 'the Chancellor of the People'[142] was granted by the Tyne workers during his 1862 visit to radical Northumberland.

Given the tone of this popular reaction to his policies, it is not surprising that before 1867 the Liberal leader hoped to be better able to achieve retrenchment with a more democratic electorate,[143] and it is significant that working-class radicals were of the same opinion.[144] In fact, financial enthusiasm ran high during the months that led to the Liberal victory at the elections of 1868, the first to be held under the new dispensation of the household franchise. As a consequence, the 1869 'popular' parliament was expected to be the harbinger of an era of unprecedented economies and fuller free trade. And though plebeian radicals were eventually to discover that the financial millennium was not at hand[145] this realization and the political and electoral vicissitudes of 1868–74

---

[138] [L.a.], 'Proletarians and the Budget', *BH*, 20 Jul. 1872, p. 10.

[139] For Smith's abiding influence, see *Report on Taxation: Direct and Indirect Adopted by the Financial Reform Association*, Liverpool, 1859, p. 5; A Working Man, 'The ABC of Social Science, in Twenty Lessons – Taxation', *BH*, 12 Sept. 1868.

[140] [L.a.], *LW*, 29 Dec. 1867, p. 1; [l.a.], 'The Revenue, Taxation, and National Prosperity', *WT*, 7 Jan. 1866, p. 1; see also the address presented to Gladstone by the Whitby Liberal Working Men's Association, in [rep.], 'The Premier at Whitby', *LM*, 4 Sept. 1871, p. 3.

[141] Hamilton, 'Rhymes for the Times, 1865', in *Poems and Ballads* (1868), cit. in Matthew, *Gladstone 1809–74*, p. 132. For a very different poem on another Chancellor of the Exchequer, see 'A. Syntaxis', 'Ex LUCE Lucellum', *BH*, 10 Jun. 1871, p. 14 (a satirical poem on Robert Lowe).

[142] G. J. Holyoake, 'The Liberal Situation, or the Parliamentary Treatment of the People, II', *NW*, 18 Mar. 1865, p. 4.

[143] Vincent, *The Formation of the British Liberal Party*, p. 250; Matthew, *Gladstone 1809–74*, p. 128; Leathers, 'Gladstonian Finance', pp. 520–1.

[144] [L.a.], 'Next Year's Question', *LW*, 29 Dec. 1867, p. 1.

[145] I have discussed popular attitudes to Liberal Finance in 1868–74 in 'Popular Liberals and Gladstonian Finance' in Biagini and Reid (eds.), *Currents of Radicalism*, pp. 134–62.

did not modify their approach to the question: rather, it made them more militant in their pursuit of long-established goals.

Certainly in the 1870s there was abroad among the working classes an as yet unarticulated discontent. Ultimately, this was to become an aspiration to greater security and to release from the straight jacket of an uncontrolled market economy. Free trade had achieved many improvements; yet, more than twenty years after the repeal of the Corn Laws, poverty and pauperism were far from disappearing, and the economy was still going through periodical slumps. However, these problems had technical aspects linked to the as yet very limited knowledge of the working of an industrial economy in a world still undergoing industrialization: there was no credible recipe for getting out of the cyclical recurrence of slumps, apart from the remedies offered by collective self-help, trade union organization,[146] and free trade itself.

On the other hand, in some sectors unemployment was caused by unrestricted foreign competition, a factor which generated occasional waves of doubts about the actual desirability of a unilateral and unconditional free trade system:[147] this happened, for example, in 1866,[148] 1869,[149] and 1870[150] – when the number of those in receipt of relief was higher than in any year since 1849.[151] However, 'reciprocity' was regularly dismissed by plebeian radicals as the claim of sectional selfishness against the interests of the community as a whole,[152] and, in particular, of the great majority

---

[146] For these aspects, see below, chapter 3.

[147] Letter by T. W. Fenton, *BH*, 22 May 1869, p. 7; letter by J. Chapman, 'The French Treaty and the Macclesfield Silk Trade', *BH*, 9 Oct. 1869, p. 7; W. Johnson, [poem], *BH*, 10 Jul. 1869, p. 7.

[148] [L.a.], 'Untaxed Paper and Taxed Rags', *LW*, 18 Feb. 1866, p. 6: 'The foreigner takes advantage of our liberality . . .'

[149] Paper by Mr Bray of Coventry, *Proceedings of the London Co-operative Congress, 1869*, London, 1869, p. 53.

[150] 'A Trade Unionist', 'The Poor Englishman and the Prosperous Foreigner', *BH*, 15 Jan. 1870, p. 1.

[151] With the exception of the period of the Cotton Famine: Harrison, *Before the Socialists*, p. 221.

[152] [L.a.], 'The Revivers', *BH*, 6 Nov. 1869, p. 4; [l.a.], 'Commercial Treaties', *BH*, 5 Mar. 1870, p. 9; Northumbrian, 'Free Trade and Protection', *RN*, 10 Oct. 1869, p. 3, which defended the workers against the charge of being protectionists. This charge was also indignantly refuted by George Odger, in a letter to the *Times* and the *Bee Hive*, in which the new tendencies towards protectionism were described as 'weaknesses and follies' (G. Odger, *BH*, 25 Sept. 1869, p. 7). See also [l.a.], 'The Opening of the Session', *LW*, 13 Feb. 1870, p. 1; and 'Death of Mr John Snowden', *Halifax Courier*, 6 Sept. 1884, p. 7, for Snowden's defence of free trade during a debate in the Mechanics' Hall in 1870.

of the working classes. There is little doubt that the *Daily News* was right when it wrote that

The attempt to impose [new customs duties on the necessaries of life] . . . would at once bring back the time when budgets were political manifestoes and would produce an agitation from one end of the Kingdom to the other; unless, indeed, that agitation were averted, as it most likely would be, by the downfall of the administration which was so unadvised as to make the proposal.[153]

Most radicals remained totally unsympathetic towards economic nationalism, and indeed were horrified at the sight of Liberal governments in foreign countries moving away from free trade[154] – the American case being especially painful.[155] Even from the point of view of the economic contest with other advanced industrial countries, the safest course was free trade, as the 'free breakfast table' would decrease the cost of living and make British labour more competitive.[156] Indeed, slumps were due to excessive indirect taxation, which debilitated industry by keeping prices too high, prevented popular consumption from increasing, and eventually affected the market to the extent that many factories closed down and thousands of workers lost their jobs. At this stage, the half-ruined British producers were totally crushed by the growing burden of the poor rates necessary to provide relief for the unemployed.[157] In conclusion, unemployment was sup-

---

[153] [L.a., n.t., on some Conservative proposals of fiscal reform], *DN*, 27 Apr. 1871, p. 4.

[154] [L.a.], 'Free Trade in France', *WT*, 24 May 1868, p. 4.

[155] Gracchus, 'England on the Road to Ruin', *RN*, 13 Apr. 1879, p. 3; [l.a.], 'America and England', *NW*, 3 Apr. 1869. In any case – Gracchus stressed – 'Neither with "reciprocity" or protection can we possibly compete successfully with America and other nations, where the people can live on the land, and where they are not burthened with a thousand encumbrances in the shape of princes, peers, prelates, parsons, &c., dead weights upon the back of the people' (Gracchus, *RN*, 13 Apr. 1879, p. 3). Such was the importance ascribed to these factors that – even when commercial rivalry embittered the tone of other observers – it continued to praise the growing living standards of the American workers, and their 'fast decreasing' taxation (Gracchus, 'The Impoverishment of the Poor', *RN*, 23 Mar. 1879, p. 3).

[156] Letter by 'Patriot', *BH*, 27 Nov. 1869, p. 7; 'A Working Man' to J. Bright, n.d., in Dixon papers.

[157] Northumbrian, *RN*, 15 Aug. 1869, p. 3. In adition there was hostility to financiers, which was one of the recurrent themes in European and in particular American radicalism: Jacksonian democrats were especially hostile to banks: 'as "A Journeyman Printer" emphasized, the banks "assist great wealthy employers to compete and crush little ones – and prevent honest industrious journeymen from becoming employers"' (Hugins, *Jacksonian Democracy*, p. 194; see also pp. 28 and 131). The Jacksonian cause of 'free trade in banking' was not unpopular in Britain either (see letter by 'A Scotch Hawker', 'Professor Rogers and Adam Smith on Money', *NW*, 13 Feb. 1869, p. 4; Northumbrian, *RN*, 25 Nov. 1866, p. 3; [l.a.], 'The Nincompoops of Politics', *LW*, 3 Nov. 1867, p. 1).

posed to be caused by the 'monstrous load of taxation' under which the British worker languished[158] rather than by free trade.[159] Though the situation was bad, the fact that the 'Reciprocitarians' admitted that it would have improved if only the Americans and the French had opened their markets, refuted their own arguments in support of 'fair trade', as it implied that the slump would have been even worse had Britain joined the protectionist fold.

Discontent was voiced with increasing energy in 1872. In June the representatives of 'Trade Unionism in all its branches', of the Labour Representation League and of the ultra-radical Land and Labour League met in London to discuss several proposals for radical reform: under the heading of 'Finance questions' they required, not 'fair trade', but the 'reduction of expenditure in all departments of the State', the replacement of indirect with direct taxation, the reduction of the national debt, and 'readjustments in the Income-tax, so as to relieve incomes derived from industrial or professional pursuits from the same percentage as incomes derived from real property'.[160] Though it may seem surprising that the reform of the income tax was also supported by an allegedly 'proletarian' organization like the Land and Labour League, the items listed were traditional components of the arsenal of anti-State, anti-taxation, free-trade radicalism. In the same period, George Howell strove 'to disseminate the knowledge of Cobden's principles',[161] both to provide inspiration for this protest, and to counteract resurgent protectionism.

---

[158] [L.a.], 'Very Liberal Government', *LW*, 2 Apr. 1871, p. 1; *1871 TUC Minutes. 6th Day (11 Mar. 1871), Howell Coll., TUC PC*, p. 46.

[159] Actually, 'it is too little Free Trade that oppresses us!' [L.a.], 'Answers to the Reciprocitarians', *LW*, 9 Jan. 1870, p. 1; [L.a.], 'The French Treaty in Danger', *LW*, 16 Jan. 1870, p. 1. Cf. Also [l.a.], [Cobden Club dinner], *BH*, 17.17.;1869, p. 4; T. J. Dunning, 'Emigration as an Imperial Question', *BH*, 8 Jan. 1870, p. 7.

[160] [Report], 'A New Political Alliance', *TI*, 24 Jun. 1872, p. 13.

[161] G. Howell to J. Thompson, 22 Jun. 1872, letter accompanying a copy of Cobden's *Essays* in 2 vols., for the use of Thompson and his friends: in *G. Howell Coll., Letter Bks*, 103b. Howell sent several other copies of the same volumes to representatives of working-class institutions elsewhere in the country: cf. items 102a, 102b, 103a, 104a (to John Kane, Darlington), 106a, (to Daniel Guile), 106b (to William Allan), 108 (to Hogdson Pratt, for his Club and Institute); all these letters are dated 22 Jun. 1872, in *ibid*. See also G. Howell to T. B. Potter, MP, 17 Apr. 1872, in *ibid*., 606, concerning the distribution of 'some 50 copies of the Pamphlets on the teachings of Mr Cobden' received from the Cobden Club, as well as the *Essays*, which he used 'almost daily' 'as I have frequently to speak to large meetings of working men.'

When the Liberal government entered into a serious crisis in 1873, the *Bee-Hive* suggested that revival should be pursued through bold initiatives of fiscal reform: the latter should start with the full implementation of the 'free breakfast table' – 'the deserted flag of free trade'.[162] According to Thomas Briggs – a financial reformer of working-class origin who co-operated with the Labour Representation League[163] – indirect taxation 'robbed' the worker of one third of his wages by 'pretending' to obtain revenue under the principles of free trade:[164] but there was no real free trade yet, as on some items of heavy consumption there still survived taxes which provoked a general increase of prices and adulteration of food.[165] In particular, he denounced the Malt Tax which, like the old 'bread tax', was 'equivalent to step[ping] in between the tiller of the soil and the allwise Ruler of the Universe, and robbing them both'.[166] George Potter, addressing a labour conference on the 'free breakfast table', castigated the fiscal system as 'wicked' for taxing the necessities of life to the extent that every working man spending 7s 10½d of his wages on tea, coffee, sugar, beer and alcohol, paid 1s 9¼d in duties.[167] The final resolution passed on that occasion maintained

That this conference, having duly considered the present mode of taxation, is of the opinion that the method pursued in taxing the food of the people is pernicious in its incidence, unjust in operation, repugnant to the best interests of society, and injurious to agriculture, trade, and commerce. This conference is further of the opinion that in any readjustment of the system for raising Imperial revenue, the claims of the people for a 'free breakfast table' and the removal of all taxes from their food, should have the first consideration.[168]

Thus, by 1873 popular radicals were demanding a new Liberal crusade of fiscal reforms. This would also include changes in the

---

[162] [L.a.], *BH*, 15 Nov. 1873, p. 7.
[163] The meeting was held at Rainbow Tavern, Fleet Street in [rep.], 'Free Breakfast Table', *BH*, 28 Mar. 1873, p. 5; participants included Thomas Briggs, John Noble, the editor of the *Bee-Hive* and the leadership of the Labour Representation League; the purpose was the organization of a Free Breakfast Table League.
[164] T. Briggs, 'Free Breakfast Table', *BH*, 25 Oct. 1873, p. 9; and., 'Direct v. Indirect Taxation', *BH*, 28 Oct. 1871, p. 2.
[165] T. Briggs, 'The Budget', *BH*, 30 Mar. 1872, p. 3.
[166] T. Briggs, 'The Malt Tax Deputation to Mr Lowe', *BH*, 18 Jan. 1873, pp. 4–5.
[167] [Rep.], 'Free Breakfast Table', speech by G. Potter, *BH*, 25 Oct. 1873, p. 3.
[168] *Ibid.*, final resolution.

income tax,[169] which was increasingly disliked as it seemed grossly unequal in its incidence on lower incomes; moreover, because of inflation, it was beginning to impinge upon wider social groups.[170] However, in general, what was demanded was reconstruction, rather than repeal: at least in principle the income tax was preferable to most other taxes, as it was to some extent proportional to actual wealth, and had 'the exceptional merit of being direct. The taxpayer feels its pressure as soon as it is collected. He can therefore estimate at once how much an expedition or a war is likely to cost him every year'.[171] One of the proposals, advanced by the London Financial Reform Union, was to raise the whole revenue through a more rational and equal, but not graduated, income tax; this also would be imposed on incomes below £100, so that all working men would come within its reach.[172] Through the preliminary repeal of all indirect taxation, the worker would still be better off than under the existing system, as the new income tax would claim only 7.5 per cent of his wages, rather than the 15 per cent he was said to be paying under the then current system.[173] Even a progressive income tax was sometimes requested,[174] though this platform was not very common yet. Another plan – reminiscent of the radical bias against the agricultural interest – was to replace all indirect taxation with a 5 per cent tax on landlords and tenants.[175] None of these proposals was successful in attracting mass support in the early 1870s, and most of them posed difficult political and technical problems.[176]

More feasible, and also interesting because it prefigured Glad-

---

[169] [L.a.], *RN*, 2 Nov. 1873, p. 1. This topic has been discussed in detail in my 'Popular Liberals and Gladstonian Finance', in Biagini and Reid (eds.), *Currents of Radicalism*, pp. 148–62.

[170] See Biagini, 'Popular Liberals and Gladstonian Finance', in Biagini and Reid (eds.), *Currents of Radicalism*, p. 150.

[171] [L.a.], *NW*, 16 Apr. 1868; Northumbrian, 'The Weight of Taxation', *RN*, 14 May 1871, p. 3; [l.a., n.t.], *LM*, 28 Apr. 1871, p. 2.

[172] [Rep.], 'Free Breakfast Table – Exclusive Report of Deputation to Mr Lowe', *BH*, 2 Apr. 1870, p. 101. The deputation included delegates from the Financial Reform Union, the Leeds Liberal Registration Association, and the 'sugar interest'. The average income of a working man was assessed at £50–60.

[173] [L.a.], 'The Coming budget', *BH*, 9 Apr. 1870, p. 121. Obviously, this reform would be accompanied by some drastic reduction of public expenditure, in the tradition of working-class Cobdenism: 'J. B.', *BH*, 29 Apr. 1871, pp. 2–3; T. Briggs, *BH*, 23 Oct. 1871, p. 2.

[174] W. Cobbett, 'Taxation of the Poor', *BH*, 1 Mar. 1873, p. 12.

[175] See the pamphlet by Noble, *Fiscal reform* (1865).

[176] Anderson, 'Wage earners and Income Tax', pp. 189–92.

stone's abortive 1874 proposals, was Briggs' project of abolishing the income tax along with all indirect taxes: they would be replaced by a tax of 10 per cent on realized property, and by a graduated tax on houses, called 'Personal or Householders' Tax'; this system would raise a somewhat rigid revenue of about £73 million, within which the cost of government could be contained, thus imposing a sort of 'fiscal constitution' on State expenditure.[177] George Howell basically followed this approach when, at the end of 1873, he spoke against the repeal of the income tax 'before there was a freedom of the breakfast table from taxation':[178] the implication being that a satisfactory fiscal settlement should include both measures.

By the end of 1873 the 'free breakfast table' and the abolition or drastic reform of the income tax was becoming the dual platform of the radical working-class newspapers. It is noteworthy that, though the income tax as a whole was criticized, popular hostility was actually directed against the 'inquisitorial and vexatious', 'abominable schedule D . . . which stands as a monument of injustice to industry'.[179] Either because the best paid artisans and many shopkeepers were coming within the £100 exemption limit, or because 'schedule D' was perceived as a threat to employment because of the burden it imposed on small businessmen, there was a growing demand that the relative fiscal load be transferred onto realized property.[180]

When examined against this background, Gladstone's 1874 manifesto looks remarkably like an attempt to meet some of these popular demands. In fact the programme of the 'People's William' included both an important step towards the 'free breakfast table' – the repeal of tea and sugar duties – and the replacement of the income tax with new taxes on realized property.[181] Moreover, he

---

[177] T. Briggs, *BH*, 13 Sept. 1873, p. 3. Briggs maintained that his proposal relied on 'a much higher authority than Mr Gladstone . . . viz., the late Richard Cobden' ('Taxation', *BH*, 18 Oct. 1873, p. 3). For the concept of 'fiscal constitution', see Baysinger and Tollison, 'Chaining the Leviathan', and Leathers, 'Gladstonian Finance and the Virginian School of Public Finance', and ref.

[178] [Rep.], 'Free Breakfast Table', [speech by G. Howell, *BH*, 25 Oct. 1873, p. 5.

[179] [L.a.], 'The Veneered and Polished Cabinet', *RN*, 31 Aug. 1873, p. 1.

[180] [L.a.], 'John Bright', *BH*, 1 Nov. 1873, p. 8; [l.a.], 'Mr Gladstone at Whitby', *LW*, 14 Sept. 1873, p. 6; [l.a.], 'Reform of the Income Tax', *WT*, 28 Sept. 1873, p. 1.

[181] W. E. Gladstone, 'Dissolution of Parliament', *TI*, 24 Jan. 1874, p. 8. I have analysed these proposals in detail in 'Popular liberals and Gladstonian finance', in Biagini and Reid (eds.), *Currents of Radicalism*, pp. 152–6; Matthew, *Gladstone 1809–74*, p. 222; Buxton, *Finance and Politics*, II, (1888), p. 167.

envisaged important changes in local taxation, then weighing upon the poorer ratepayers with increasing severity. These proposals were accompanied by a commitment to avoiding 'the first entrance into equivocal and entangling engagements' in foreign affairs.[182] In his readiness to re-mould the consensus politics of his own making, Gladstone seems to have been quite sympathetic to the viewpoint of his plebeian supporters. In addition, the latter rejoiced at the prospect of the promised county franchise and reform of local government – measures deemed to be conducive to stricter financial probity, and welcomed as equivalent to 'deposing the landowning oligarchy from the government of the counties . . . a far vaster change than the abolition of the House of Lords'.[183]

However, the electors were left insufficient time to realize the full implications of the Liberal programme. Dissolution came suddenly and totally unexpectedly. As late as 21 January Gladstone received a delegation of miners from the North of England and the South of Scotland, representing – they said – 400,000 men: they interviewed the premier on the issue of county household franchise, and were satisfied with his answers; but no hint was given to them of the possibility of an early election.[184] On 23 January, commenting on this meeting, the *Manchester Guardian* wrote that the session of 1874 would be a preparatory one.[185] This also was the opinion prevailing in the mass-circulation press: elections were expected by autumn, no earlier than November. Then, on Saturday, 24 January, *The Times* announced that the House of Commons would be dissolved immediately. The *Manchester Guardian*, communicating the news to the mystified electors of the North, wrote:

---

[182] W. E. Gladstone, 'Dissolution of Parliament', *TI*, 24 Jan. 1874, p. 8. For an instance of the financial reformers' interest in the kind of foreign policy to which Gladstone wanted to commit his party in 1874, see the *Petition of the Financial Reform Union, presented by Mr S. Morley, on Friday, the 12th March, 1869*, in *Papers on Taxation and Expenditure issued by the FRU*, No. 6, p. 16 (Bishopsgate Institute, London).

[183] E. S. Beesley, *BH*, 31 Jan. 1874, pp. 1–2. About the possibility of electoral alliances between the trade unions and Conservative candidates who declared to be ready to endorse labour law reform Beesley wrote: 'The common-sense answer is that any one who honestly accepts that programme is no Conservative, and that no honest Conservative will accept that programme' (*Ibid*).

[184] [Rep.], 'Mr Gladstone and the County Franchise', *TI*, 22 Jan. 1874, p. 8; [rep.], *MG*, 22 Jan. 1874, p. 4.

[185] [L.a., n.t.], *MG*, 23 Jan. 1874, p. 5.

The announcement, we must confess, takes us by surprise, a day having actually been fixed for the opening of the House [of Commons], and all the usual preparations made for private legislation. The determination of the Government may be accounted for on the supposition of some great personal quarrel in the Cabinet. In a hasty review of what might be deemed possible causes of dissension, we fail to find one likely to have so starking an effect . . . An immediate dissolution is apparently so uncalled for that Mr GLADSTONE will need all his eloquence to justify it to his party and to the country.[186]

Working-class newspapers – most of which were weekly and published on Saturdays (like the *Bee-Hive*) or on Sundays (like *Reynolds's*) – were so surprised that they had hardly any time to express an opinion on Gladstone's programme before the election was over. Only on 30 January was the *Forest of Dean Examiner* able to write on the election, mainly to express surprise and astonishment: 'That [the dissolution] came upon the Foresters like a thunder-clap will only be saying what are the experiences of other districts throughout the length and breadth of the land'.[187] It was too late for mounting a campaign in the weekly press: on that very day, 30 January, the names of the first fourteen MPs returned for uncontested seats were published.[188] On 31 January, as the *Bee-Hive* and the Saturday weekly press began their propaganda, also a few constituencies where the election had been contested were able to declare the poll. A fortnight later, on Monday, 9 February, the Conservative victory was already clearly delineated, even though their majority was expected to be slight. On 14 February the working-class weeklies were able to begin the analysis of the Liberal defeat. Only three weeks had elapsed since the announcement of the dissolution of Parliament, and only two since the start of radical propaganda by the Saturday weeklies. In order to assess the handicap that such a short campaign must have represented for the Liberals it should be recalled that the elections of 1868 and 1880 were so long overdue that their campaigns virtually lasted for several months, and had been prepared for by one or two years of radical agitation.

That Gladstone dissolved Parliament so suddenly and without giving due forewarning to the press was bitterly resented by some of the mass-circulation newspapers. In particular, *Lloyd's Weekly*

---

[186] [L.a., n.t.], *MG*, 24 Jan. 1874, p. 5. See [l.a., n.t.], *DN*, 26 Jan. 1874, p. 4.

[187] [L.a.], 'Forest of Dean', *Forest of Dean Examiner*, 30 Jan. 1874, p. 4.

[188] [L.a., n.t.], *MG*, 2 Feb. 1874, p. 5; it was a Monday, and many newspapers did not have a Sunday edition.

described the premier's course as a 'Ministerial *Coup d'Etat*'[189] and commented disparagingly on Gladstone's programme.[190] However, it is likely that *Lloyd's* was not so much outraged by the alleged violation of the constitutional procedure, as by Gladstone's comparative neglect of the press,[191] and the fact that the swiftness of the election had not afforded 'thinking hours to the elector and candidate':[192] apart from anything else, this had deprived newspapers of the huge profits usually associated with long electoral campaigns.

The reaction of another great weekly, *Reynolds's*, was different, but also very interesting. At first, with typical admiration for the 'sovereignty of the people', it had welcomed the dissolution and forecast that the Liberals would obtain an easy victory, while the Whigs would meet with their final extinction.[193] Yet, a week later, as the first polls were being declared, *Reynolds's* concluded that the electoral campaign had been too short. Gladstone's programme was good – 'It is years since the income tax ought to have been abolished' – but his 'blunder consisted in making a dissolution so sudden, and issuing a manifesto so prolix, that no time was given to the country to appreciate the policy which he indicated, or to contrast it with the stagnation of the Conservatives'.[194]

---

[189] [L.a.], 'The Ministerial Coup d'Etat', *LW*, 25 Jan. 1874, p. 6. This was one of the earliest reactions of the popular press to the announcement of the dissolution, typical of the efficiency of *Lloyd's*; to ensure the greatest possible circulation even among those non-habitual readers of this newspaper who would buy it on the special occasion of the run-up to the election, this article was republished without alteration the following week: see [l.a.], *LW*, 1 Feb. 1874, p. 6. Even later *Lloyd's* continued to react against the government: [l.a.], 'Candidates' Addresses', *LW*, 1 Feb. 1874, p. 1. For Gladstone's lack of care for the national press during the last period of his government, see Matthew, *Gladstone 1809–74*, pp. 227–30.

[190] [L.a.], *LW*, 25 Jan. 1874, p. 6; [l.a.]. 'The Elections – So Far', *LW*, 8 Feb. 1874, p. 6.

[191] Matthew, *Gladstone 1809–1874*, pp. 228–30.

[192] [L.a.], 'A Rough-And-Tumble Election', *LW*, 8 Feb. 1874, p. 6.

[193] [L.a.], 'The Dissolution of Parliament', *RN*, 1 Feb. 1874, p. 1.

[194] [L.a.], 'The General Election', *RN*, 8 Feb. 1874, p. 1. It was only after the general election that *Reynolds's* became critical of Gladstone's government:

He offered a magnificent bribe to the middle class in the proposed abolition of the income-tax; but the middle class had some doubts whether this did not mean the substitution of other taxes which they would be called upon to pay, and the working classes not unnaturally suspected that the income-tax payers were to be relieved at the expense of consumers of taxable article ([l.a.].

('The licensed victuallers' Parliament', *RN*, 15 Feb. 1874, p. 1). Significant also was what 'Northumbrian' wrote the following year: 'When we are wealthy, we care little or nothing about politics, and we were in this position in February, last year, when Mr. Gladstone called upon us to go to a general election' (Northumbrian, *RN*, 6 Jun. 1875, p. 3).

In fact, the brevity of the electoral campaign had meant the impossibility of co-ordinating the actions of the Liberal electors. Moreover, one of the party's assets, the rhetorical power of leaders like Gladstone and Bright, had not been exercised. Virtually no national debate had taken place. Not surprisingly, the poll was quite poor by Victorian standards, and – as usual – the lower turnout helped the Conservatives.[195] In this situation party machinery and the electoral registers were bound to be the foremost factor: and it is well-known that the constituency organization of the Liberal party had much deteriorated since 1868, and that the decay of the registers was a universal complaint among Liberal agents.[196] On the contrary, thanks to the efforts of Gorst, the Conservative party had raised itself to maximum of efficiency and had taken particular care in renewing the registers.[197] As George Howell wrote to Gladstone, 'There is one lesson to be learned from this Election, that is Organization . . . We have lost not by a change of sentiment so much as by want of organized power'.[198] And to John Bright he wrote that 'There is no Tory reaction as understood by newspaper writers, as the future will prove': the problem was that organization and propaganda had been overlooked because 'We have been too secure with our great majority'.[199]

From our vantage point, the mistakes of the Liberals may look astonishing, but contemporaries saw things in a different light. Following the introduction of 'democracy' in 1867 and the ballot of 1872, another Liberal victory was expected to be the 'natural' and almost inevitable outcome of an election under virtually any circumstance. After all, the Liberals had been the usual ruling party between 1832 and 1865, and electoral reform had strengthened their traditional supporters – the Nonconformists, the artisans, the Irish, the Scots, and the Welsh. Gladstone himself was apparently confident of success: as he wrote in a memorandum on 20 January, 'I think our victory is as likely in an immediate as in a postponed Dissolution. While we run fewer chances of a crushing defeat'.[200] In this document the strength of the Conservative party was not

---

[195] See Cornford, 'The Transformation of Conservativism', pp. 37–66.
[196] See for example Williams, *Quarryman's Champion* (1978), p. 100.
[197] Feuchtwanger, *Democracy and the Tory Party*, pp. 121–4; Maehl, 'Gladstone, the Liberals and the Election of 1874', pp. 67–8.
[198] G. Howell to W. E. Gladstone, 12 Feb. 1874, *G. Howell Coll., Letter Bk.*, 304.
[199] G. Howell to John Bright, 14 Feb. 1874, in *G. Howell Coll., Letter Bk.*, 456.
[200] W. E. Gladstone, memorandum of 20 Jan. 1874, in *Diaries*, VIII, p. 444.

taken into serious consideration, almost as if it did not represent a real threat. Gladstone dissolved 'against the defence departments'[201] – with which he was at odds – and what he really feared were the internal divisions of the Liberal party and the possibility of a split. He was trying to square the circle by strengthening his own personal position with a fresh mandate from the electors, without going through the ordeal of a proper electoral campaign, which would have exposed his differences from both much of the front bench and many of the Radicals.[202] Had such a test taken place, even if it had not resulted in a split, it would have involved serious consequences, as a long electoral campaign on the issue of retrenchment could have increased the representation of the Radicals to the extent of compromising traditional balances within the Parliamentary party. A way out was to obtain a personal victory with a short campaign and without any huge majority, and then rule from No. 11 as well as from No. 10 through the 'fiscal constitution' envisaged in his manifesto. Thus Gladstone tried to offer a 'ready-made' solution to what he saw as the difficulties of the time, rather than 'elaborating' one through the national debate which would have accompanied a long electoral campaign with mass meetings and endless press reports. Gladstone relied on the people's blind trust in him: it is noteworthy that he was substantially correct, but only as far as the 'militants' were concerned;[203] the less committed stayed home, or split their votes. In conclusion, in January 1874 the Liberals were defeated not because of the Greenwich manifesto, but because of the way in which it was presented to the country; it was not a problem of content, but of political communication and propaganda.

Thus, Gladstone's manifesto did not play a major role because,

---

[201] Matthew, *Gladstone 1809–74*, p. 225.
[202] See *ibid.*:

> 6. The formidable divisions in the party would be aborted[?] or held in suspense if we have an immediate Dissolution upon a question of universal & commanding interest.
> 7. If the internal difficulty be only adjourned till after this dissolution, still we should be in a stronger & fresher condition to face it. But it might have disappeared.

[203] [Rep.], *NW*, 31 Jan. 1874, p. 3. even such a committed supporter of direct taxation as E. S. Beesley wrote that, though the 'total repeal of the income tax [was] not in itself a measure which can be satisfactory to workmen',

> Nevertheless I believe that in financial matters Mr Gladstone may be trusted to move in a right direction. Looking at his past career, and remembering that he has given very vague indication of what he intends to do, I do not expect that we shall find him proposing any financial scheme which, as a whole, will amount to relieving the rich at the expense of the poor. (E. S. Beesley, *BH*, 31 Jan. 1874, pp. 1–2).

in a sense, he deliberately avoided it. On the other hand, neither did Disraeli's manifesto have any influence, partly because he did not have a real programme, apart from saying that he too – like Gladstone – was ready to abolish the income tax. In particular, the Tory manifesto did not contain a word about social reform or any of the other major reforms that Disraeli's government was actually destined to implement; it only reached a high pitch in denouncing the allegedly weak and careless foreign policy of the Liberal government.[204] This being the case, even if Gladstone had explicitly committed himself to satisfying all the requests of the TUC, the supporters of county franchise, and any other popular cause, the result would hardly have been different: the basic problem was that working-class radicals were not given time to organize, and many of them were no longer on the register anyway.

The Liberals were potentially much stronger than the elections showed: this is also demonstrated by the fact that they obtained a majority of the popular vote in each of the kingdoms, and about 189,000 votes more than the Conservatives in the country as a whole.[205] But their majority in the polling booths was turned into a hopeless minority in the House of Commons because of the peculiar unfairness of the distribution of seats.[206] Moreover, it seems likely that the Liberal electoral majority would have been greater had there not been so much fragmentation in the party at constituency level, with internecine fights between moderates and radicals, all of whom were over-confident of the strength of Liberalism as a whole.[207] Meanwhile those regions such as the mining north-east – where the labour movement was strongly organized and not split by religious sectarianism – remained strongly Liberal.

The size and consequences of the defeat caused dismay among popular liberals, particularly because disaster had come after

---

[204] Blake, *Disraeli*, p. 534.

[205] That is, 1,281,159 votes (52.7%), against 1,091,708 for the Conservatives (43.9%). The Home Rulers obtained 90,234 votes, mainly from electors who had previously voted Liberal. In 1868 the Liberals had obtained 1,428,776 votes (61.5%), against 903,318 (38.4%) for the Conservatives. (Craig (ed.), *British Electoral Facts 1832–1980*, pp. 10–11, 67).

[206] As G. Howell considered in one of his lectures to working class clubs: MSS, n. d. (but 1874), in *G. Howell Coll., Letter Bk.*, 360.

[207] See Hurst 'Liberal versus Liberal', pp. 669–713; Temmel, 'Liberal versus Liberal', pp. 611–22.

several years of frustration.[208] It was the realization that the new 'democracy' was not invincible, the 'forward march of liberalism' could be stopped, and Toryism was far from dead. 'Ironside' wondered in amazement that 'Neither Mr Gladstone's magnificent record nor Mr Gladstone's magnificent programme' – 'perhaps the completest that could at this moment have been devised'[209] – had carried the election. It was then that, to explain this extraordinary reversal, there was first formulated the 'conspiracy theory', which was also to be long accepted by modern historians[210] – that the Liberal defeat was due to an unholy alliance between publicans and priests.[211]

TORY 'PROFLIGACY' AND LIBERAL CRUSADES

Disraeli's government was a success in many respects, but finance was certainly not one of them. Northcote's first budget offered short-term solutions to the problems of the unequal incidence of the income tax and the rates, and abolished the sugar duty.[212] On the whole this was welcomed as a measure of moderate Gladstonianism, an administrative implementation of the easier part of the programme of the 'People's William' – who had provided the necessary surplus in the first place. However, Northcote's popularity began to decline sharply during the following months: the earliest symptoms of the discontent which eventually led to the 1880 rout began to show less than a year after the election. Already by the end of 1874 the government was being criticized for the

---

[208] Lloyd Jones, 'The Oldham Election and its Moral', *BH*, 7 Jun. 1872, pp. 1–2; [l.a.], 'The Barren Session', *LW*, 10 Aug. 1873, p. 1.

[209] Ironside, 'The Liberal Defeat', *NW*, 14 Feb. 1874, p. 4. Out of all the observers only *Lloyd's Weekly*, full of resentment against Gladstone, ascribed the Liberal defeat to the Greenwich manifesto, and in particular to the proposal for repealing the income tax ([l.a.], 'The Old Ministry and the New', *LW*, 22 Feb. 1874, p. 6): however, the pages of *Lloyd's* itself offer evidence that this tax as it stood had long been perceived as iniquitous and 'brutal' for the way in which it was collected (see also the reactions to a meeting between Gladstone and a delegation from the Income and Assessed Tax Payers' Association in [l.a.], 'Where the Income Tax Shoe Pinches', *LW*, 30 Dec. 1866, p. 6.)

[210] Ensor, *England 1870–1914*, pp. 21–2; Lloyd, *Election of 1880*, pp. 3–4; but see Hanham's effective refutation in *Election and Party Management*, pp. 222–6.

[211] Ironside, 'The Liberal Defeat', *NW*, 14 Feb. 1874, p. 4; A. A. Walton, 'The Bung and Tap Parliament', *BH*, 21 Feb. 1874, p. 9; Littlejohn, 'The Forces that Won', *WT*, 22 Feb. 1874, p. 6; [rep.], 'London Patriotic Society's Club and Institute: Mr. Wynne', *NR*, 22 Feb. 1874, p. 124. Gladstone was described as a martyr: Ironside, 'The Government and the Landed Interest', *NW*, 4 Apr. 1874, p. 4. Cf. also below ch. 4, pp. 161–5.

[212] Buxton, *Finance and Politics*, II (1888), p. 187.

apparently uncheckable increase in public spending, and especially
in the cost of the defence departments.[213] In January 1875 Henry
Broadhurst warned the Trade Union Congress that 'It was their
duty to see to the purchasing power of their wages, as much as to
their increase. Working men had a deep interest in the immense
extravagance in connection with the expenditure of the country.
This, he considered to be a scandal and a shame . . .'.[214] Furthermore, the Labour Representation League also recommended the
strictest economy as 'a question of the utmost importance to small
traders, all classes of workpeople, and those of limited and fixed
incomes'.[215] In contrast, the growing expenditure – then amounting
to 'the monstrous sum of SEVENTY-FIVE-MILLIONS-STERLING' – represented 'nothing but wasteful extravagance, inefficiency, and gross
incompetence in every spending department of the State'.[216] Popular radicals began to denounce this 'profligacy' in moral tones
which anticipated the 'language of Midlothian'. Even *Lloyd's Weekly*
– the only mass-circulation newspaper to be quite sympathetic to
Disraeli – had no doubt that the financial policy of the new
government showed clear signs of moral perversion:

The evil, the sin of all this is the lavish and wanton outlay of the millions
which are drawn from the pockets of the people. There is never any
question now of decreasing that outlay. In the presence of a bad financial
year a Conservative Government has actually increased it! Last year they
were generous with a surplus: this year they are lavish with a deficit.[217]

As a consequence, John Bull 'must no longer think of remission of
taxes . . . he must be content rather to pay a little more for the
social blessing of having a Conservative Government in office'.[218]
As the so-called 'Great Depression' manifested itself with falling
wages, strikes and growing unemployment,[219] Gladstone's old
policy seemed to offer the only hope. But while he had 'got his
savings out of the spending departments' – 'Army, Navy, and Civil
Service'[220] – the government steadily increased military expendi-

---

[213] [L.a.], 'The Ministry of the Rich', *LW*, 6 Dec. 1874, p. 6.
[214] *Seventh TUC (Liverpool, 18–23 January 1875), Minutes*, p. 19.
[215] 'An Address to the People of Great Britain', n. d. [but Summer 1875]. *Labour Representation League Papers*, pp. 142–3.
[216] *Ibid.*
[217] [L.a.], 'The Financial Year', *LW*, 28 Mar. 1875, p. 1.
[218] [L.a.], 'The Opening of Parliament', *LW*, 6 Feb. 1876, p. 6.
[219] Lloyd, *Election of 1880*, pp. 12–3.
[220] [L.a.], 'The Trick of Budgets and Finance', *RN*, 9 Apr. 1876, p. 1.

ture, thus reinforcing the radicals' conviction that 'Tories have to pay friends . . .'.[221] Then came the Prince of Wales' costly visit to India, which further exasperated plebeian radicals. In the House, the two working-men's MPs emphatically declared that the people were not willing to meet the expense proposed by the special vote of credit: McDonald warned that 'Votes of this description tend more to bring the Crown of England into disrepute than anything else I know of. [No, no!] . . . Votes of this character tend more to create disloyalty than all Republicanism, internationalism or any "ism" put together'.[222]

Nostalgia for the previous government grew on financial grounds: as *Lloyd's* complained in 1876, 'that with which Mr. Gladstone would have made a handsome surplus shows us, in Sir Stafford Northcote's budget, a deficit'.[223] *Reynolds's* echoed: 'We need what Mr. Gladstone proposed in 1874 – a remission of taxation; but above all we need a revision of expenditure'; the latter was the crucial point, because while 'the Liberals . . . left behind them an overflowing Treasury', the Tories continued to increase expenditure to the extent that they 'rendered a future surplus next to impossible'.[224] Besides the deficit in the ordinary budget, 1876 also brought in a supplementary military budget to provide for British involvement in the Eastern crisis.[225] The radical press complained that the country was well on its way towards 'the abyss':

Let us ask ourselves how long can this country go on paying £77,000,000 taxes, £38,000,000 of local rates, and some £6,000,000 for a State Church.

---

[221] [L.a.], 'The Weak Point of the Tories – Increased Expenditure', *WT*, 20 Feb. 1876, p. 4.

[222] See the speech by Alexander McDonald (8 Jul. 1875) *Hansard PD*, ccxxv, 1875, col. 1153; and Thomas Burt, *ibid.*, col. 1157. In previous years there had been several other cases when working-class radicals had vociferously shown their hostility to increases in the Royal expenditure; in 1871 the dowry for Princess Louise had occasioned much discussion and even riotous meetings ([rep.], 'Another Stormy Political Meeting', *RN*, 23 Apr. 1871, p. 1); in 1874 the grant for Prince Leopold had attracted criticism even of the two working men's MPs, guilty of not opposing at any cost such a 'waste', of public money: Gracchus, 'A Wasted Session', *RN*, 9 Aug. 1874, p. 3; see the letters of protest by G. E. Merry and 'S.D.S.', 'Political Apostacy'; and 'A Warwickshire Labourer', 'When Will the Right Be Done?', both in *RN*, 9 Aug. 1874, p. 3.

[223] [L.a.], 'The Budget', *LW*, 9 Apr. 1876, p. 6.

[224] [L.a.], 'The Crime of Seventy-Eight Millions', *RN*, 21 May 1876, p. 1.

[225] Education expenditure had also increased by almost one million, but significantly this was not regretted: 'if this is well spent we ought not to grudge it', ([l.a.], 'The more-Income Tax budget', *WT*, 9 Apr. 1876, p. 1). Between 1870 and 1895 the total cost of the education system of England and Wales was £219,000,000, plus £11,000,000 invested in the building of voluntary schools (Smith, *History of English Elementary Education*, p. 314).

Why, this is a total of £120,000,000 a-year, or about a seventh or eighth part of the income of the British people. Insolvency must be produced, and the symptoms of national insolvency do not appear in the form of bankruptcy, and of the payment of a dividend, although we have large bankruptcies and small dividends in commerce, but in poverty, pauperism, and even crime.[226]

Over and over again the readers of the mass-circulation newspapers were invited to reflect on the 'astonishing' figures of the government's 'reckless profligacy'. After having been in power for three years, and in the midst of an economic crisis, the Conservatives asked 'the people' to pay five and a half million more than the Liberals had done during the last year of their government, when trade had been prosperous. According to some commentators, while the total of the surpluses of the Liberal administration had been £16,947,000, the surplus after three years of Tory government amounted to only £1,000,000: the difference between these figures allegedly indicated the extra amount of taxation that the people were due to pay under the Conservatives.[227]

Plebeian radicals thus came to think that the economic expansion of the period 1850–73 had been rendered possible by the 'sound' financial policy of the Gladstonian budgets, and linked the successive 'depression' years to Exchequer mismanagement. The extent to which Gladstone's financial style was then being idealized is suggested by the fact that the 'Model Budget under Perfect Free Trade' proposed by Thomas Briggs in 1876 looked remarkably similar to Lowe's actual budget for 1872–3 on the side of expenditure, including the provision of a huge surplus 'to pay off the national Debt . . . or to lighten the burden of taxation where it might be found to bear unfairly on any class'.[228] Indeed, the discussion of the income tax was also revived: in spite of Northcote's 1874 increase of the exemption limit and the deduction from the taxable income[229] – which had fully redressed the grievances of the poorer taxpayers – some plebeian liberals asked for further

[226] Northumbrian, 'Taxes Paid by the People', *RN*, 9 Aug. 1874, p. 3.

[227] [L.a.], 'The Tory Extravagance and Income-Tax', *WT*, 21 May 1876, p. 1; [l.a.], 'The Financial Results of a Spirited Foreign Policy', *Northern Echo*, 23 Oct. 1876, p. 2.

[228] T. Briggs, 'The Budget for 1877–8', *Industrial Review*, 5 May 1877, pp. 3–4; on this side of revenue Briggs reiterated his proposal to abolish all indirect taxation. See also Briggs, *Poverty, Taxation and the Remedy; Free Trade, Free Labour or Direct Taxation* (1883), pp. , 55–7. For Lowe's 1872–73 budget, see Buxton, *Finance and Politics*, II (1888), p. 348.

[229] Biagini, 'Popular Liberals and Gladstonian Finance', in Biagini and Reid (eds.), *Currents of Radicalism*, p. 162.

relief for those whose income was variable and insecure. Moreover
– following the example of what was then being done by Gambetta
in France[230] – they asked for an increase in the taxation of urban
and rural rents[231] 'to set industry free from every species of custom
and excise duty'.[232]

Meanwhile the Conservatives seemed to be going from bad to
worse: the deficit for 1877 was one million, and the expectation for
1878 was that there would be another, and even greater deficit.
Some suspected that Beaconsfield was also planning to accept
liability for the bankrupt Ottoman Empire, 'because the Jews wish
to "finance" Turkey'.[233] Eventually the 1878 budget looked like the
1874 one turned upside down: while in 1874 there had been a
surplus of five and a half million, allowing for a remission of
taxation of over four million which still left a large surplus, 1878
offered a deficit of five and a half million, and new taxes of over
four million which still left a large deficit for which provision was
postponed to the future.[234] Even the reform of the rates – which
satisfied Sir Massey Lopes' requests and transferred four million of
the cost of country prisons from the rates to the Consolidated Fund
– seemed aimed only at reducing the fiscal burdens of squires and
landed aristocrats.[235] The conclusion was that 'this is government
by the Land – this is government taxing the people for the benefit
of a class'.[236] At the Durham Gala of July 1878 – at the height of
Disraeli's success – W. Patterson declared that 'he believed that
until they got rid of Mr Disraeli and the Conservative Government,
the wheels of British commerce and prosperity for the benefit of
the working class of the country could not take place'; he went on
to say that they should reinstate 'the greatest statesman the world
ever knew – that was their tried and noble leader, Mr Gladstone'.[237] And in November, *Reynolds's* summarized popular discon-

---

[230] Gracchus, *RN*, 30 Apr. 1876, p. 3; also Disraeli in his 1852 budget had proposed a
   similar scheme, but 'Gracchus' did not mention this precedent.
[231] See J. Noble, 'Taxation – Imperial and local – No. 11, *BH*, 4 Mar. 1876, pp. 1–2; and
   Gracchus, 'Tricks of Toryism', *RN*, 30 Apr. 1876, p. 3.
[232] Northumbrian, 'Labour Paying for Landlords', *RN*, 6 Aug. 1876, p. 3; Northumbrian,
   'The People Taxed for Land', *RN*, 4 Jun. 1876, p. 3.
[233] [L.a.], *RN*, 1 Apr. 1877, p. 1.
[234] Buxton, *Finance and Politics*, 11 (1888), p. 249.
[235] Northumbrian, 'The Trick of Taxation', *RN*, 4 Mar. 1877, p. 3. See also note 181 above.
[236] Northumbrian, *RN*, 31 Mar. 1878, p. 2.
[237] In [rep.], 'Annual Demonstration of the Durham Miners', *DC*, 12 Jul. 1878, p. 6.

tent, prefiguring some of the arguments later used by Gladstone in Midlothian:

Six years back, when Mr. Gladstone left office, we were at peace with the whole world. Trade and commerce were fairly prosperous. Working men could obtain work, and wages were nearly twice as high as at present. Taxation was eight million less than now. Taxes were being remitted, instead of, as at present, being imposed. The Chancellor of the Exchequer met the House of Commons with a surplus, whereas poor Sir Stafford Northcote has never faced it except with an actual deficit, and a requirement of raising more money somehow or another. These are the results of Tory government. Are they, I ask, such as will warrant the working men of England, who live by labour and wages, voting for another six years' spell of Toryism?[238]

What residual popularity the Conservative government had preserved collapsed in 1879 and 1880, during the months leading up to the general election. Baconsfield's success at the Berlin Congress removed that sense of 'emergency' – the danger of a war with Russia – which had created a wave of nationalist support for the government between 1876 and 1878. On the other hand, especially from 1877 unemployment had been rising steadily among trade unionists[239] – many of whom were electors. Moreover, agriculture was depressed, and the government was at one and the same time unable to consider protection and to satisfy the free traders by repealing the Malt Tax.[240] Finally, it was difficult to justify the persistently high military expenditure: the Empire was no longer 'in danger', though the economy was, and the prevailing opinion was that the only remedy was a policy of peace abroad and retrenchment at home. As Buxton put it,

Great expenditure and high taxation necessarily curtail the powers of production and consumption. Trade and capital are beyond everything timid. At the first whisper of war, confidence, commerce and investment cease or are greatly curtailed. Indeed it is not so much war itself, as the fear of war, which disastrously affects trade.[241]

And in 1879–80 two new colonial wars were started, in Zululand and Afghanistan: ascribed to Beaconsfield's 'spirited foreign policy', these conflicts were unfortunate and of doubtful utility, but

---

[238] Gracchus, *RN*, 24 Nov. 1878, p. 3.
[239] Lloyd, *Election of 1880*, pp. 12–13.
[240] Blake, *Disraeli*, pp. 656, 697–8.
[241] Buxton, *Finance and Politics*, ii (1888), p. 251.

kept expenditure growing. Thus, even allowing for the cost of the organization of the system of primary education – admittedly, 'a legitimate expenditure, and a beneficial expenditure'[242] – the largest part of the increase was in the defence departments.[243] Moreover, as the military operations continued, it was difficult to say when this increase could be stopped,[244] and even the government seemed unable to budget in the traditional way. This engendered further political protest, as the working-class press opted for Gladstone's argument that repeated votes of credit and supplementary budgets constituted a breach of the constitution – they were equivalent to depriving the House of Commons of its most basic function, control of the 'ways and means' of running the nation.[245]

Fearing popular hostility, the government tried to avoid the imposition of fresh taxation by releasing what were described as 'Exchequer bonds and other devices of impecuniosity'.[246] According to the plebeian press Northcote's last budget embodied 'the miserable revelations of financial failures, blunder, and disaster',[247] and his proposal to deal with the deficit by adding to the National Debt was something of which he ought to feel 'ashamed'.[248] As the management of the national finance continued to be closely assimilated to that of private enterprise,[249] this procedure was disparaged as the 'art' of 'putting off the evil day'.[250]

Some of the shrewdest Conservative candidates unsuccessfully tried to present Northcote's policy as an alternative to Liberal

---

[242] Gladstone, *Midlothian Speeches* (1879), p. 135.

[243] *Ibid.*, pp. 135–8.

[244] [L.a.], 'The Budget Debate', *LW*, 4 May 1879, p. 6.

[245] [L.a.], 'Vote of Credit', *English Labourers' Chronicle*, 16 Feb. 1880, p. 1. As early as April 1879 the mass press had criticised this aspect of Northcote's policy as reminiscent 'too much of the Supplementary Budgets of France under Louis Napoleon'; see [l.a.], 'The Budget', *NW* 5 Apr. 1879, p. 4; and [l.a.], 'The Budget', *LW*, 6 Apr. 1879, p. 6.

[246] [L.a.], 'The Budget Debate', *RN*, 4 May 1879, p. 6. See Buxton, *Finance and Politics*, II (1888), p. 266.

[247] [L.a.], *RN*, 14 Mar. 1880, p. 4; [l.a.], 'The Budget', *LW*, 14 Mar. 1880, p. 6.

[248] [Rep.], 'The East Retford Election. – Messrs Foljambe and Mappin at Retford', *Sheffield and Rotherham Independent*, 17 Mar. 1880, p. 3.

[249] 'If we had a man at the head of any large and important concern, who told us that he had made a deficit of not £3,000,000 [Northcote's deficit for 1880], but I will say one-tenth of that sum, £300,000, what should we do with him? (Loud cries of "sack him", and laughter)' [Rep.], 'The Borough Election. – Arrival of Mr. Mundella and Mr. Waddy. – Great meeting in the Albert Hall' [Waddy's speech], *Sheffield and Rotherham Independent*, 15 Mar. 1880, p. 3. col. 3.

[250] [L. a.], 'The Quarterly Returns', *LW*, 5 Oct. 1879, p. 6.

'financial rectitude', stressing that the government had avoided imposing fresh taxation in times of crisis.[251] Similarly, modern historians like Trevor Lloyd and P. Ghosh have tried to re-evaluate this approach by showing its 'modernity' as 'deficit finance', which almost anticipated 'counter-cyclical' public expenditure through loans to municipal enterprises.[252] However, as Lloyd has put it, 'at the time so much attention was paid to a balanced Budget, and the Government's direct effect on the National Income was so slight', that these positive aspects were outweighed by the crisis in business confidence which was the consequence of lack of 'financial rectitude'.[253] At the same time, given the moderate level of public expenditure and Britain's wealth, any deflationary implications of the tax increase necessary to balance the budget would have been marginal. Moreover, far from appearing socially oriented, Conservative expenditure allegedly dried up what little money had been set aside for extraordinary poor relief in India, 'having . . . taken for war purposes a million and a half that was raised a year or two ago on the pledge and honour of this country that it should be used for famine purposes only – (cries of "Shame")'.[254] If Northcote's approach appeared to offer an 'alternative' to Gladstonian 'rectitude', it was only in the sense of seeming 'immoral', of reaching 'the lowest depths of debt and dishonour':[255] 'That's Jingoism',[256] one from the crowd cried at a Liberal meeting. Even had the concept of 'counter-cyclical expenditure' been known, the Conservative way of using public money could hardly have suited the case.

As newspapers kept writing of growing deficits and taxation, of 'nearly seventy millions of money paid or to be paid as the wages of imperialism'[257] – figures 'more eloquent than the most glowing rhetoric'[258] – the prevailing impression was that Gladstone's orthodox finance would be not only socially and economically beneficial,

[251] See [rep.], 'Conservative Meeting at the New Drill Hall', *Sheffield and Rotherham Independent*, 15 Mar. 1880, p. 3.
[252] Lloyd, *Election of 1880*, p. 55; Ghosh, 'Disraelian Conservatism', pp. 284–7.
[253] Lloyd, *Election of 1880*, p. 56.
[254] [Rep.], 'Great Meeting in the Albert Hall', [Waddy's speech], *Sheffield and Rotherham Independent*, 15 Mar. 1880, p. 3.
[255] 'The Dissolution . . . Special telegram from a London Correspondent', *Sheffield and Rotherham Independent*, 15 Mar. 1880, p. 6.
[256] [Rep.], 'East Retford Election . . . Enthusiastic Liberal Meeting at Workshop', *Sheffield and Rotherham Independent*, 18 Mar. 1880, p. 2.
[257] [L.a.], 'Imperial Insolvency', *RN*, 22 Mar. 1880, p. 1.
[258] [L.a.], 'Six Years of Toryism', *NW*, 19 Mar. 1880, p. 4.

but also politically wiser, as it would effectively curb Jingoism by the simple device of making the country pay at once for the cost of a 'spirited foreign politics'. Thus, if Shannon has suggested that enthusiasm for Gladstone in Midlothian derived more from concern for finance than from the appeal of a moral foreign policy,[259] reports of working-class meetings south of the border suggest that his conclusion can be extended to the general situation in Britain. People were concerned with depression and unemployment, and voted for a return to mid-Victorian prosperity and for the Liberals as 'the party of cheap food and high wages'.[260] However, it should be remembered that international morality and economic prosperity were closely correlated: 'peace and plenty' went together, and were contrasted with the policy – crudely summarized as 'bloodshed and crime' – of the Conservatives, who had met their retribution in the form of trade crisis and financial disorder.[261] Discontent was so widespread within the labour movement that when the Durham miners set up their Political Reform Association, they were spurred on by the increase in the 'fearful National Debt, which, incubus like, weights the wheels of industry'.[262] Candidates addressing working-class meetings at by-elections exploited the alleged connection between trade instability, low wages and growing unemployment, on the one hand, and the Tory 'enormous expenditure' and 'exciting policy' abroad, on the other.[263] This argument was convincingly recapitulated by the influential Yorkshire miners' leader, Benjamin Pickard, in March 1880, when he declared that

The present Government have fully demonstrated their incapacity to manage the great and growing affairs of this great country, and unless the Liberals are returned at this present time, the Tories in the next Parliament will nearly, if not absolutely, ruin its trade and commerce if they continue disturbing every country on the face of the earth. The

[259] Shannon, *Gladstone and the Bulgarian Agitation*, p. 157.
[260] Resolution passed by 2,500 Salford electors: [rep.], 'Open Air Demonstration of Liberals', *MG*, 20 Mar. 1880, p. 12.
[261] [Rep.], 'The Liverpool Election' ['very large' gathering of working men' in the Liverpool docks], *LM*, 2 Feb. 1880, p. 8. See R. Bailey Walkers, FSS, 'Three Laws of a Healthy State: That Trade be Free, Clean and Beneficient', *Co-operative News*, 20 Mar. 1880, p. 177.
[262] Wilson, *Memories*, (1910), p. 243. See G. Howell, 'TAXATION LIBERAL AND CONSERVATIVE', Ms notes for a lecture to working men's clubs, in *G. Howell Coll., Letter Bk.*, 364 bis.
[263] [Rep.], 'The Liverpool Election' [meeting at the Bramley Moor Dock], *LM*, 3 Feb. 1880, p. 5. For a precedent, see [rep.], 'The Representation of Leeds – The Liberal Candidate', *LM*, 10 Aug. 1876, p. 5; and [rep.], 'The Leeds Election', *LM*, 15 Aug, 1876, p. 5.

foreign policy has made a much greater effect upon the trade of this country than many so-called Tories imagine. Working men, examine for yourself the cost of the present Government . . . And where does all this money come from? I answer for you, out of the blood, bone, and sinew of the working classes.[264]

This message was echoed over and over again at popular meetings throughout the country. At a demonstration at Withington a man stood up from the crowd and declared that, though he had always voted 'blue' in previous elections, he was now going to vote 'red' because of the 'reckless extravagance' characterizing the Conservative management of the public purse.[265] At Hackney a meeting chaired by Sir Stafford Northcote himself was repeatedly interrupted by cheers for Gladstone.[266] At Nottingham, at a Conservative meeting held in the yard of a factory whose owner was also a Tory, a few hundred lace makers unanimously passed a resolution of no confidence in the local candidates, amidst laughter and cheers for Gladstone and Bright:[267] an episode which illustrates the limits of the 'politics of deference'. Many Conservative meetings ended in riot, as their speakers were frustrated by strong groups of radicals in the audience.[268] The presence of a restless, impatient and undaunted plebeian crowd was ubiquitous, hypercritical of the 'mismanagement' of the Exchequer, and asking all sorts of embarrassing questions to disoriented Tory candidates.[269] Even a social group which in the past had been one of the safest mainstays of the Conservative party – the farmers – was very responsive in 1880 to the fiscal and financial appeal of the Liberals.[270]

---

[264] B. Pickard, 'The Appeal to Sheffield', *Sheffield and Rotherham Independent*, 18 Mar. 1880. p. 8.

[265] [Rep.], 'South-East Lancashire. The Liberal candidates at Withington', *MG*, 29 Mar. 1880, p. 7.

[266] [Rep.], 'Sir Stafford Northcote on Conservative Achievements. Stormy Meeting in Hackney', *MG*, 24 Mar. 1880, p. 5.

[267] [Rep.], 'Nottingham. The Conservative Candidates "trapped" by the working men', *Sheffield and Rotherham Independent*, 17 Mar. 1880, p. 3.

[268] See for another example [rep.], 'The General Election' [Pontefract], *LM*, 22 Mar. 1880, p. 6.

[269] [Rep.], 'The Conservative Candidates at Pendlebury – Disorderly Meeting', *MG*, 25 Mar. 1880, p. 6; [rep.], 'Mr Wortley's Candidature. Ticket Meeting at Attercliffe', *Sheffield and Rotherham Independent*, 18 Mar. 1880, p. 2.

[270] [Rep.], 'East West Riding. The Liberal Candidates at Knaresborough', *LM*, 18 Mar. 1880, p. 7; there was a fair going on, and the audience included a great number of farmers who were so sensitive to these issues that some of them corrected, from the floor, the Liberal candidates' statements about the increase in the income tax, high-way rates, and other taxes, maintaining that the situation was even worse than the Liberal candidates had suggested.

The fact that public interest concentrated on financial recovery powerfully promoted Gladstone's – rather than Hartington's or Granville's – candidature for the premiership, as the logical alternative to Beaconsfield – Northcote.[271] The Conservatives themselves contributed to this phenomenon, as they implicitly recognized Gladstone's hegemony by making his budgets and strategy the standards for their own achievements.[272] Thus, the role of Gladstone's famous Midlothian campaigns was one of articulating and giving expression to widespread popular concern and exasperation. His speeches – published and re-published several times to meet mass demand[273] – provided a focus which turned such inchoate sentiments into votes. In this sense, the 1879–80 campaigns were similar to the 1876 Bulgarian agitation, which, as Shannon has demonstrated, had started as a spontaneous popular protest, and was supported by Gladstone only at a later stage – but with decisive effects.

In contrast, the Conservative propaganda was totally out of tune with the mood of the nation. Beaconsfield's manifesto contained no hint that he was sensitive either to the general demand for a speedy return to a policy of 'Peace, Retrenchment, and Reform', or to the growing protest against what was perceived as the government's 'indifference to the principles of sound finance, and to the claims of domestic legislation'.[274] Moreover, though the Conservatives did not intend to make free trade an election issue,[275] plebeian radicals took the contemporary revival of 'reciprocity' sufficiently

---

[271] See letter by W. Warburton, 'Facts for voters', *MG*, 22 Mar. 1880, p. 8; letter by 'A Working Man', 'The Tories and Bad Trade', *Sheffield and Rotherham Independent*, 31 Mar. 1880, p. 5; letter by 'Veracity', 'Mr Gladstone's surplus', *MG*, 25 Apr. 1880, p. 7; letter by J. Watts, 'Tory Finance', *MG*, 1 Apr. 1880, p. 7.

[272] See the Conservative electoral pamphlet *Financial Catechism for Electors; giving 'Chapter and Verse' for the statements made, by 'A Voter for South-East Lancashire'*, Southport 1880, 3rd edition, price 1d., in *Gladstone Papers*, 44462, f. 98.

[273] See the second 'Introduction' to Gladstone's speech at the Edinburgh Stock Exchange (29 Nov. 1879), republished as a pamphlet. The *Sheffield and Rotherham Independent* also republished it ('Mr. Gladstone and the Government's Finance. – A reply to the Chancellor of the Exchequer', 15 Jan. 1880, p. 6. The fact that it was reprinted in the Saturday issue [17 Jan. 1880, p. 11] suggests that the second edition was aimed at working-class readers, many of whom bought the *Independent* only on Saturdays, as if it were a weekly. A similar behaviour in its working-class readership is suggested by the editorial policy of the *Newcastle Chronicle*).

[274] [Rep.], 'Liberal Demonstration at Wakefield', *LM*, 21 Jan. 1880, p. 7; see also the canvassers' report in Ecclesfield', *Sheffield and Rotherham Independent*, 19 Mar. 1880, p. 3, col. 5. See Lloyd, *Election of 1880*, pp. 20, 59; Blake, *Disraeli*, p. 709.

[275] Blake, *Disraeli*, p. 698; Lloyd, *Election of 1880*, p. 49.

seriously[276] to make the defence of free trade one of their election slogans.[277] Protectionist criticism could not even dent working-class support for free trade: to them the latter remained 'the Big Loaf Question', an issue which excited strong emotional reactions among women as well as men.[278]

The outcome of the elections was a plebiscite in favour of 'Peace, Retrenchment and Reform'. The Conservatives were defeated all along the line, including in some of the one-time faithful shires, and suffered major setbacks 'in the great centres of population and industry, where the working-class vote was largest'.[279] They lost not only the seats gained in 1874, but even some of the positions held in 1868.

Gladstone resumed the party leadership and premiership[280] – as well as the Chancellorship of the Exchequer – with the specific mandate of restoring the 'good old times' and cutting down the 'upas tree' of Beaconsfieldism. His first budget seemed to justify popular expectations. By increasing the income tax to sixpence, Gladstone immediately achieved important successes: not only were part of the debts paid off and the budget balanced, but he also raised enough revenue to repeal the Malt Tax. The latter was

---

[276] On the popular discussion of the revival of protectionism, see [l.a.], 'Protection in Germany', *LW*, 29 Dec. 1878, p. 6; and the debate between C. H. Thompson ('Reciprocity', *Industrial Review*, 23 Feb. 1878, pp. 2–3) and the uncompromising free-trader Lloyd Jones ('Whom are We to Believe?', *Industrial Review*, 13 Jul. 1878, pp. 1–2). See also the discussion of Fawcett's dogmatic defence of free trade: Littlejohn, 'Professor Fawcett on obstacles to free trade', *WT*, 28 Oct. 1877, p. 6; 'D', 'Professor Fawcett on Free Trade', *NR*, 28 Oct. 1878, p. 723. Though he went as far as justifying anti-labour practices, like the importation of foreign workers to break strikes and lower the wages, his lectures also contained many features that pleased working-class liberals, to the extent that H. Broadhurst congratulated the author on their publication: H. Fawcett to H. Broadhurst, 29 Sept. 1878, in *Broadhurst Papers*, item 46, pp. 66–7.

[277] [Rep.], 'National Secular Society', *NR*, 19 Sept. 1880, p. 237:

I have acknowledged another parcel of books from the Cobden Club, through Mr. T. B. Potter, M.P. This parcel consists of 100 copies, by 'Economist', of 'The New Protection Cry'; 100 copies of 'Free Trade, Reciprocity, and Foreign Competition' by T. P. Whittaker; 50 copies of 'Free Trade and English Commerce', by Augustus Mongredien; 48 copies of 'The Western Farmers of America', by the same author; and 21 copies of 'Goldwin Smith's Lecture on England and America'. This last parcel will enable us to furnish other copies of these books to branches that have already sent applications for more copies to be accompanied with two penny stamps for booking.

Cf. [rep.], 'Hall of Science Club and Institute' [lecture by J. H. Levy on 'Free Trade, Reciprocity and Protection'], *NR*, 29 Feb. 1880, p. 141; 'he explained the principles of free trade and exposed the fallacies of the opponents'.

[278] *To the Mothers, Wives and Daughters of Ipswich*, by 'An Elector's Wife', Gladstone Papers, Add Mss 44462, f. 228.

[279] Smith, *Disraelian Conservatism*, p. 314.

[280] For a discussion of this aspect, see below, chapter 7, pp. 412–6.

a considerable achievement rendered spectacular by the fact that the Tory government had been singularly ineffective in dealing with the issue. Repeal enthused the farmers, appealed to free traders, and was sanctioned by the labourers as the abolition of 'a vexatious restriction, not merely upon brewing, but upon the production of articles which are more widely consumed even than beer'.[281]

This resolute policy was continued in 1881. However, it was evident that the situation was very different from that of 1874, and did not allow for any easy restoration of mid-Victorian finance. Accumulated debts and war scares contributed towards rending traditional retrenchment hardly feasible, and also social legislation was becoming increasingly expensive. What is striking is that awareness of the changing times was a ruling-elite phenomenon, while the prevailing opinion among the working classes was still that it was necessary to bring 'the expenditure within income' by whatever sacrifice was required 'in order to afford the Chancellor opportunities for financial reform'.[282]

This did not imply popular indifference to further experiments in social legislation, but the search for alternatives to the protectionist cure took priority. The persisting 'Depression', rather than shaking popular support for Cobdenite economics, stimulated the beginning of the typical Liberal trend towards radical taxation on property in order to shore up the free trade system – a trend which would culminate in the 'People's Budget' of 1909. At the end of the 1870s and in the early 1880s this mainly produced requests for better and free education for the workers,[283] taxation of rent and the reform and proper cultivation of land:[284] but Henry George would soon extend the scope of 'free trade socialism'. Gladstone's ruthlessness in dealing with financial disorder aroused hopes that eventually he would be able to implement more ambitious reforms, including the organization of a system of life insurance through the

---

[281] [L.a.], 'The Budget', *English Laborers' Chronicle*, 26 Jun. 1880, p. 1.

[282] [L.a.], 'The Government's Financial Opportunities', *LW*, 9 May 1880, p. 1.

[283] Littlejohn, 'The Technical Education Cry', *WT*, 20 May 1877, p. 6; [l.a.], 'The Scientific Instruction of the Artisan', *LW*, 23 Mar. 1879, p. 6.

[284] J. Arch, 'Would Protection Remove the Present Distress and Benefit the Working Man?', *Cobden Club Leaflet No.* xviii, n. d., cit. in Arch, *The Story of His Life* (1898), pp. 231–2; Joseph Arch, 'Would Protection Remove the President Distress, and Benefit the Working Man?', n. d., but 1885, *John Johnson Coll.* 'Free Trade and Protection', box 3, Cobden Club leaflets.

Post Office, completely free primary education, a State-funded system of emigration, and even direct State intervention in agricultural and industrial enterprises. It is interesting that these daring reforms were to be funded not through increased taxation, but through retrenchment in the army, navy and civil service; they would also be accompanied by the repeal of the income tax and of all the remaining taxes on the necessities of life.[285] These proposals may seem eccentric and self-contradictory, and to some extent they were. However, they were not devoid of logic, and indeed reflected a shrewd assessment of working-class interests during the 'Great Depression', when free trade represented the best guarantee that the diminishing costs of production and transport would benefit real wages rather than just capitalists' profits. On the other hand, working-class liberals were not motivated by any hatred for the employers, and were aware of the importance of preserving the latters' profits as a requisite of economic prosperity – a consideration that helps one to understand their support for the repeal of the income tax. That social reforms would hardly be feasible with the reduced revenue resulting from such a policy was evident, but working-class radicals did not want to increase the burden on industrial wealth, and moved instead towards the obvious alternative – the old proposal of Thomas Paine and J. S. Mill – heavy taxation of ground rents.

What is peculiar to the British case is that the subaltern classes rejected any compromise with protectionism and abhorred economic nationalism. As the trade crisis continued, popular radicals faithfully echoed the ageing John Bright in their advocacy of undiluted Cobdenism. The first commandments in the economic decalogue were clear to them:

Capitalists should invest their capital in the classes of manufactures most suitable to the climate, the soil, and the genius of the people; they should not be encouraged to start naturally unremunerative industries by bounties, or by import duties on the foreigners; such protection puts money into the pockets of the capitalist for a time, but it taxes the community for their benefit, and ultimately injures even themselves by

---

[285] S. Price, 'What Could They do for the People?', *English Laborers' Chronicle*, 12 Jun. 1880, p. 2; Bill Blades, Bricklayer, 'Words from the Workshop', *RN*, 20 Jun. 1880, p. 2. The request for a post-office life insurance was really remarkable step towards the acceptance of State interventionism, as similar proposals had been rejected by the managers of the friendly societies only a few years before: see below, chapter 3, pp. 114–5.

drawing them away from occupations wherein the same amount of labour would produce more wealth.[286]

The fact that protectionism was identified with the landed aristocracy and the Conservative party – despite the latter's disclaimers – was in itself sufficient to discredit it:[287] as Annie Besant wrote, 'fair' trade was 'the Landlords' Attempt to Mislead the Landless',[288] and was virtually equivalent – according to the *Labour Standard* – to Tsarist despotism and 'Cossack government'.[289] Besides being politically and socially unjust, protectionism was seen as economically counterproductive: as 'Littlejohn' put it, by imposing retaliatory duties against the most damaging of Britain's protectionist partners, the United States,

we should punish ourselves tremendously. We import from America . . . 25 millions worth of cotton, and if we made their cotton dearer by taxing its importation, not only our great Lancashire industry would be damaged, but the clothing of our whole population would be more costly. Still worse would it be if we taxed their wheat, of which we take 12 millions worth, or their bacon, pork, &c. Nine tenths of what we take from them consists of food, and it would be disastrous to keep any quantity of it out, and starve our poor.[290]

These sufferings would outweigh the expected material benefits of some categories, so that the policy of reciprocity 'becomes simply a selfish one, both in a national and personal point of view'.[291] This understanding, which was very widely held in plebeian radical circles,[292] was ultimately based on a realistic evaluation of Britain's position in the world economy.[293] But the mainstays of working-class free trade remained the consumers' 'moral economy', and the claim to a more equal division of the fiscal load: the fate ultimately

[286] A. Besant, *Free Trade versus 'Fair Trade', being the substance of Five Lectures delivered at the Hall of Science, London, in October, 1881, with Appendix*, London 1881, p. 4; in *John Johnson Coll.*, 'Free Trade and Protection', box 1.
[287] See the debate between the free-trade co-operators and a protectionist employer in [rep.], 'The Seventeenth Annual Co-operation Congress', *Co-operative News*, 6 Jun. 1885, p. 520.
[288] Undertitle of Besant, *Free Trade versus 'Fair Trade'* (1881), see no. 286 above.
[289] [L.a.], 'Free Trade and Self Government', *Labour Standard*, 1 Oct. 1881, p. 7.
[290] Littlejohn, 'Fawcett on Free Trade and Protection', *WT*, 7 Jul. 1878, p. 6.
[291] *Ibid.*
[292] See [l.a.], 'Low Rents and Cheap Beef', *LW*, 6 Jul. 1879, p. 6, and Id., 'The Little Loaf and the Big Rent Roll', *LW*, 13 Jul. 1879, p. 1. [l.a.], 'Reciprocity', *Co-operative News*, 1 Feb. 1879, p. 74; [l.a.], 'The Anglo French-Treaty', *NW*, 27 Jun. 1881, p. 4; [l.a.], 'The Fair Trade Fallacy', *Co-operative News*, 15 Oct. 1881, p. 698.
[293] Hobsbawm, *Age of Empire*, pp. 39-41.

attending on any departure from a policy of cheap bacon and eggs seemed to be a return to the 'hungry' 1840s.[294] As the *Co-operative News* concluded,

Call it Fair Trade, call it retaliatory tariffs, or call it suicidal policy – for that is the right name – nothing good can come out of Protection. In France – protected France, the land of sugar bounties – there are riots for bread. Riots of this kind were frequent enough in this country about fifty years ago ... 'The greatest good of the greatest number' is possible through co-operation, but Protection means only the good of the few at the expense of the many. The only Fair Trade is Free Trade ...[295]

As for the persistent trade crisis and unemployment, the accepted diagnosis was that they had little to do with British fiscal policy: they were general phenomena affecting protectionist as much as free trade countries.[296] Moreover, it was pointed out that during the period 1846–60 Britain had achieved prosperity by resolutely resorting to free trade, 'irrespective of reciprocity or any other consideration', in a world dominated by protectionism:[297] allegedly, there was a parallel with the 1880s, and it was hoped that sooner or later trade would revive, as it had done in the 1850s, provided the British stuck to the right policy. As in the 1870s, the popular remedy for trade slumps remained free trade and more free trade: free trade in land, the free breakfast table, and the repeal of any 'Excise restrictions upon industry'.[298]

But the following years were even more difficult. Though Gladstone still maintained that he was committed to the classical principles of public finance,[299] by 1882 plebeian journalists read scepticism in his declarations,[300] as his twelfth budget – like his

---

[294] [L.a.], 'The Fallacies of Protection', *NW*, 28 May 1881, p. 4. Readers were also advised to read appropriate books on the subject, like Mongredien's *History of the Free Trade Movement* ([l.a.], 'Is Toryism Protectionism?', *WT*, 11 Sept. 1881, p. 4). See also Littlejohn, 'Free Traders in France', *WT*, 19 Oct. 1884, p. 6, exposing the doctrines supported in an article then published in the *Revue Scientifique*). See also [l.a.], 'Protectionist Devices', *WT*, 7 Aug, 1881, p. 4; [l.a.], 'The Fair Trade Delusion', *NW*, 17 Sept. 1881, p. 4; [l.a.], '"The Tariff that Robs"', *LW*, 1 Jan. 1882, p. 1.

[295] [L.a.], 'The Protection Cry', *Co-operative News*, 5 Dec. 1885, p. 1907.

[296] [L.a.], 'Fair Trade', *NC*, 1 Dec. 1884, p. 2.

[297] Gracchus, 'England on the Road to Ruin', *RN*, 13 Apr. 1879, p. 3.

[298] J. Hampden Jackson, 'LESS Free Trade or MORE. Which shall it Be?', n. d., (but 1885), in *J. Johnson Coll.*, 'Free Trade and Protection', box 3, Cobden Club leaflets.

[299] There were three main ones: 'First, whatever the charge, there should be a surplus. Secondly, in time of peace and comparative prosperity we should reduce our debt. Thirdly, we ought to try to reduce expenditure' ([rep.], 'The Budget. Speech by Mr Gladstone', *NC*, 25 Apr. 1882, p. 2).

[300] [L.a.], 'Budgets, Monarchical and Republican', *RN*, 30 Apr. 1882, p. 1.

eleventh – offered only a small surplus. The years of prosperity were definitely over, as was the elasticity of the revenue. Now, far from being able to offer great surpluses, Gladstone had to struggle even merely to balance the budget. Yet working-class radicals still prescribed the old Cobdenite recipe, the universal panacea:

We wonder why trade does not improve; but can it possibly do so when every year we absorb eighty-five millions, and abstract it for the time from the wage fund? It is clear as any proposition of Euclid that labour and the source of industry are the sources of all wealth; but if eighty-five millions of the earnings of the workers are to be devoted to the sustenance of idle soldiers, useless ships, and an army of civil servants, all of them non-producers, we have only to ask ourselves a simple question, how long will it take in point of time for the non-producers to eat up the producers?[301]

Such had been the hostility towards alleged Tory responsibility for the trade crisis, and expectations of Gladstone's return to the 'helm of the ship', that plebeian radicals were now disappointed by the Liberal government's inability to re-create the atmosphere of the early 1870s. These sentiments were even reflected in popular political poetry: if in the 1860s Janet Hamilton had celebrated Gladstone's 'boons' to the 'people', in the 1880s an anonymous working-class poet listed only unfulfilled hopes.

> We dreamed of large exemptions,
> Of duties lighter made,
> We trusted that exceptions
> Would now be made for trade.
> 'The income tax' we whispered,
> 'Must clean be wiped away.'
> But we found the bill
> At the old rate still,
> And the old sums all to pay.
>
> Still on the poor man's bacoy
> Lies heavy fiscal weight
> Nor can his one pet doggie
> The tax-man's calls abate;
> Our breakfast table groaning
> But fills us with dismay

---

[301] [L.a.], *RN*, 30 Apr. 1882, p. 1. Note the persistence of the 'wage fund' theory, which had been refuted a few years before by Mill (see Biagini, 'British Trade Unions and Popular Political Economy', pp. 822–32).

As we find the bill
At the old rate still,
And the old rates all to pay.

We fancied trade revival
Would free our trade beer;
That something might be done by G.
Beefsteaks to make less dear.
'At last' we sighed, 'we've done with
The tithe tax on our hay;'
But we found the bill
With the parson still,
And the dearned lot yet to pay.

To pay for all the nonsense
Our fathers left behind,
And for a million useless shows
The exes aye to find
Once more we said, 'It's nonsense
To think a single pin'
Of stopping the bill
Of figures so ill,
Till a people's chief gets in.[302]

The conclusion was not that free trade and Cobdenism were outdated, but that the Liberals had betrayed their mandate:

'Peace, retrenchment and reform' was the party cry which carried the Liberals into power in the spring of 1880. Nearly three years have elapsed since then and the country has not had peace, but war, not retrenchment, but increased expenditure, not reforms, but a Babel of talks . . . The Government are to blame for the increased expenditure. It is no use to say that the increase is due to the fact of the present Government having to pay off the debts incurred by their predecessors. This amounts only for a small portion of the increase. Mr Gladstone's Government expended in 1882 5¼ millions over the estimates of the last year of Lord Beaconsfield's Administration. We believe it was Bright who once said that if a Liberal Government could not carry on the government of the country for seventy millions annually, such a government, whatever it called itself, was not deserving the support of the English people. But Mr Bright has lived to be a member of a Liberal Government that spent eighty-five millions in one year. So it comes to this, that no matter what the Government may

---

[302] [Anon.], 'A Budget Lay', *RN*, 30 Apr. 1882, p. 2.

style itself that chances to be in power, taxation goes on increasing despite all the promises of leading statesmen and protests of political reformers.[303]

Fiscal revolt was beginning to spread because – as in 1868 and 1874 – rank-and-file liberals were more Gladstonian than Gladstone. Significantly, the way out of the economic crisis was looked for, not in social, but in political reform, just as plebeian radicals had done in the days of Chartism: eventually popular exasperation found an outlet in the enthusiastic twelve-month franchise reform campaign of 1884. But it is also remarkable that – as in 1871[304] – so also in 1882 there were some who suggested that the only solution to 'profligate expenditure' would come from the foundation of a parliamentary Labour party: this would not be a socialist party, but one of strict retrenchment, and would stand 'for sweeping fiscal reforms ... the total abolition of all taxes on industry and commerce',[305] and the real implementation of the programme of 'Peace, Retrenchment, and Reform'.[306] It is also characteristic that in dreaming of this new political force plebeian liberals did not draw their inspiration from the German Social Democrats, but from the American and French Republicans:

We must be a party and a power in parliament. We must go for cabinet rank, and, if possible, for a radical working man Premier. We have our Garfields, our Gambettas, and our Lincolns at the bench and in the factory. Let us pick them out and return them as our representatives, with definite instructions to stop all jobbing, to reduce expenditure, to lighten our bonds, and to closely watch, not the interests of the aristocracy, but those of the overworked multitudes who are to be met with all through the realm.[307]

However, no new party was set up. One of the reasons was that the election of 1874 had taught a lesson that the radicals had not yet forgotten, namely the persistent strength of Conservatism and the need to keep the 'forces of progress' united. But there was also the fact that the proposed 'labour' party was not to embody trade union or class representation: rather it was to be – as the quotation

---

[303] [L.a.], 'Increase of the National Expenditure', *RN*, 4 Mar. 1883, p. 4.

[304] Biagini, 'Popular Liberals and Gladstonian Finance', in Biagini and Reid (eds.), *Currents of Radicalism*, p. 147.

[305] E. Copland, independent labour candidate, 'To the electors & non-electors of Newcastle-upon-Tyne', *NC*, 19 Feb. 1883, p. 2.

[306] [Rep.], 'Newcastle election – Mr Copland's candidature – Open-air meeting in Haymarket', [concluding words in the chairman's speech], *NC*, 19 Feb. 1883, p. 3.

[307] Northumbrian, 'Drones and Bees', *RN*, 4 Feb. 1883, p. 3.

shows – a more democratic version of the Gladstonian Liberal party. This further reduced the scope of the enterprise, especially because in the early 1880s – and indeed for a long time afterwards – the road to greater democracy passed through electoral and parliamentary reform: and this was just what Gladstone had promised and was implementing from 1883. Thus, the obvious strategy for popular radicalism was to keep Gladstone in power until reform had been achieved, and then give him a more democratic – and economic – House of Commons. It was but a revised version of the platform of 1867–8.

CHAPTER 3

The social question

Brethren in this life's existence,
Though but humble being your parts,
Let no fear upbuild resistance
To the dictates of your hearts.
Fear of ridicule and scorning,
Of oppression's thralling band,
For a better time is dawning,
Brighter moments are at hand,
Come they fast, or come they slowly,
It depends alone on you;
If we are but somewhat lowly,
There is something ye may do.[1]

The central principle of Land Reform is also the central principle of the English Land Law: namely the supreme right of the State, as represented by parliament, to control the conditions on which land may be held. The object of modern Reformers is not to introduce a new principle, but to apply and enforce the old.[2]

THE SEARCH FOR 'INDEPENDENCE': THE WAYS OF SOLIDARITY

In the last analysis, the 'minimalist' State was popular because it fitted in with the artisan ideal that the relationship between government and citizen ought to be based on the former's respect for the latter's 'independence'. 'Independence' was not only a dream of the recovery of the yeoman's 'paradise lost'; it was also the aim of the working man's daily struggle. Though ultimately utopian, some kind of 'independence' was actually achieved by

[1] F. Enoch, 'There is Something Ye May Do!', *BH*, 28 July 1866, p. 6.
[2] A. Besant, 'The English Land System', *NR*, 18 Jan. 1880, p. 33.

139

several million workers who became members of co-operatives and friendly societies – organizations proud to offer a shelter from the strains of the market, the vicissitudes of life and the expenses of a dignified death.[3]

In recent years, some historians, emphasizing the 'anti-capital-ist' aspects of the co-operators' programme, have suggested that the socialist tradition somehow survived mid-Victorian compla-cency and eventually sprang up again in the 1890s.[4] In many respects such an approach seems convincing, especially if one considers the affinities between the Victorian co-operators and their continental, socialist equivalents. In particular, both groups maintained that the misery and degradation of the working classes under capitalism could be eliminated by changing the mode of production and ending the system of waged labour 'by taking the workman and the customer into partnership',[5] and rendering labour 'a human service rather than a compulsory obligation'.[6] Both suggested that co-operation should be extended to embrace the whole national market, in order to bring to an end the problem of the so-called crises of over-production.[7] There would then take place the 'transition of trade from a fierce and savage competition between capital and labour, to a general harmony in which the greatest good of all w[ould] be the interest and care of all'.[8] The British shared these 'socialist' hopes, but they were nevertheless fiercely hostile to virtually anything else that their continental socialist counterparts stood for.[9] State intervention was anathema

---

[3] [Rep.], 'Leeds and District Trades Council', *LM*, 16 Oct. 1873, p. 7. See Tholfsen, *Working Class Radicalism*, pp. 262, 288–96; Crossick, *An Artisan Elite*, pp. 174–98.

[4] Kirk, *Working Class Reformism*, p. 166; Lancaster, *Radicalism, Co-operation and Socialism*, pp. 134–5.

[5] Holyoake, *History of Co-operation* (1875), p. 306; see also p. 342.

[6] [L.a.], 'The Contests of Labour and Profit', *RN*, 10 Sept. 1871, p. 1.

[7] Lloyd Jones, 'Co-operation in England', *BH*, 29 Apr. 1871, p. 1.

[8] [L.a.], 'The Bolton Co-operative Congress', *LW*, 7 Apr. 1867, p. 5; *Proceedings of the London Co-operative Congress 1869*, London, 1869, p. 49. Working-class co-operators believed that such a development was indeed possible, and were unimpressed by the gloomy forecasts of their Positivist allies: Lloyd Jones, 'Mr. Lloyd Jones' reply to Mr. Frederic Harrison', *BH*, 2 Nov. 1872, p. 1.

[9] See above, chapter 1, pp. 60–2. However, not all continental co-operators were socialists, as is illustrated by the case of Giuseppe Mazzini, the instigator of the Italian co-operative movement. With the support of some of his English friends, including G. J. Holyoake and W. J. Linton, he conducted a long polemic against the French socialists (Della Peruta, *I democratici e la rivoluzione italiana*, pp. 167–72). Mazzini's articles in support of co-operation, but against socialism, were posthumously published in the *Bee Hive* under the general title of 'Joseph Mazzini on the social question' (*BH*, 20 July 1872, p. 11, and 10 Aug. 1872, p. 3).

to them, and they thought that rejection of 'unlimited competition and unrestricted rivalry' was quite compatible with liberalism and free trade. Indeed, they maintained that co-operation required a substantial amount of *laissez-faire*.[10]

To some extent this attitude was built into the Owenite model, but from 1844 it had been strengthened by the tradition of the Rochdale Equitable Pioneers. Extraordinarily successful from the beginning,[11] the Pioneers had created a 'new model' of co-operation, seen as a system of property management within a market society, rather than as an alternative model of global economic organization.[12] The response of the political economists was enthusiastic, and amounted to a complete reversal of their previous position; while in the 1820s they had attacked Owenism as a 'heresy',[13] from 1848 they celebrated the Pioneers' experiment as one of the hopes of the working classes.[14] This in turn encouraged a favourable response to political economy by co-operators: they were still ready to acknowledge their debt towards Owen and Louis Blanc, but came to trust J. S. Mill as a better guide.[15] The latter, as we shall see, exercised a pervasive influence on popular-liberal attitudes to social policies.

Thus revived and revised, co-operation promised to transplant liberal democracy into the world of industry and trade, pulling down the 'despotic master–servant relationship': 'The immense mill is a harmonious and thriving republic. The master is the

---

[10] [Rep.], 'Co-operative Congress', opening speech by the chairman, J. Cowen jr., *NC*, 14 Apr. 1873, p. 8; see Backstrom, *Christian Socialism and Co-operation*, p. 140.

[11] Kirk, *Working-Class Reformism*, pp. 149–50. See Clapham, *Free Trade and Steel*, pp. 308–11.

[12] Holyoake, *History of Co-operation* (1875), p. 674. On the development of the attitude of the economists, see Schwartz, *New Political Economy*, pp. 30–2 and 221–6.

[13] Bonner, *British Co-operation*, pp. 14–18.

[14] See Mill, *Principles of Political Economy*, in *Coll. Works*, III, 1, pp. 791–4. The notion that 'labour . . . is the source of all wealth' ([l.a.], 'The Contest of Labour and Profit', *RN*, 10 Sept. 1871, p. 1) nevertheless remained.

[15] If nobody practised thrift and self-denial in order to create capital society must remain in a state of perpetual barbarism; and if capital is refused interest as compensation for its risk, it would never be available for the use of others; it would simply be hoarded in uselessness, instead of being the great instrument of civilization and national power. The class of reformers who made this mistake were first reclaimed to intelligent appreciation of industrial science by Mr. Stuart Mill's 'Principles of Political Economy, with some of their applications to Social Philsophy'. Most of these 'applications' were new to them, and though made with the just austerity of science, they manifest so deep a consideration for the progress of the people, and a human element so fresh and sincere, that prejudice was first dispersed by sympathy, and error afterwards by argument. (Holyoake, *History of the Rochdale Pioneers* (1893), p. 25).

For Holyoake's rejection of socialism see *ibid.*, p. 94.

elected of the men whom he governs.'[16] Furthermore, in some respects the co-operative factory or store could be seen as the industrial version of the 'pastoral dream' described in the previous chapter: the co-operators, like the 'independent yeomen',

> not only provide themselves with work; they grind their own flour, have their own malting establishment, kill their own meat, and live on the best food provided by their own buyers . . . the Co-operator is his own master; and is elevated by the sense of his independence, and steadied by the responsibilities which independence brings with it.[17]

The idea of co-operative property no longer seemed socialist,[18] to the extent that in 1884 Thomas Burt described the Owenite New Lanark as the radicals' 'earthly paradise':

> For 29 years they did without the necessity of legislators, or lawyers, without the burden of poor rates, without religious animosities; they reduced the hours of labour, educated all their children, gradually improved the conditions of the adults, and acquired upwards of £300,000 profits.[19]

The marriage between co-operation and Liberalism was sealed by free trade – especially important for wholesale organizations[20] – and fully consummated during the 1850s, with legal protection for co-operatives.[21] By that time the movement's new friends – Gladstone, Cobden, John Bright and J. S. Mill – had replaced the socialist leaders in the co-operators' pantheon.[22] Towards Mill, in particular, there was a two-fold debt of gratitude: on the one hand, he had authoritatively supported and helped the movement in his public statements, which culminated in the evidence he gave to the

[16] [L.a.], 'The Great Experiment', *LW*, 3 Sept. 1871, p. 1 (about one of the workshops of the Rochdale Pioneers). See Mayor, *Churches and the Labour Movement*, pp. 167–8.

[17] [L.a.], 'The Great Experiment', *LW*, 3 Sept. 1871, p. 1.

[18] See F. Harrison, 'Industrial Co-operation', *Fortnightly Review*, III (1865–66), pp. 489–90; T. Brassey, 'Co-operative Production', *Fortnightly Review*, XXIV (1874), pp. 213–34.

[19] Speech by T. Burt in [rep.], 'Durham Co-operative Society. – Mr. Burt, M.P., and Mr. Acland on Co-operation', *DC*, 18 Apr. 1884, p. 6.

[20] [L.a.], 'Co-operation', *NW*, 19 Oct. 1867, p. 4. On these issues, see above, chapter 2, pp. 100–1. See also Bailey, *The British Co-operative Movement*, pp. 112–13.

[21] See [rep.], 'Co-operative Congress. – Public Meeting in the Lecture Room', *NC*, 14 Apr. 1873, p. 3; *The Co-operative Wholesale Society Ltd., Annual for the Year 1884*, Manchester, 1884, p. 2.

[22] See *The Co-operator*, 15 Nov. 1866, pp. 184–5 (on Cobden); G. J. Holyoake, 'John Stuart Mill. The Threefold Memorial of Him', *Co-operative News*, 28 Aug. 1873, pp. 417–18; G. J. Holyoake, 'Completion of the History of Co-operation', *Co-operative News*, 25 Jan. 1879, p. 1 (on Bright's support for the movement). See Cole, *A Century of Co-operation*, pp. 94–5.

1850 Select Committee;[23] on the other, his *Principles* – with the distinction between the laws of production and those of distribution – provided a new basis and a 'scientific' respectability to co-operation.[24] As in the case of his attitudes to trade unions – which I have discussed elsewhere[25] – Mill had modified his position to suit social and economic changes, especially when the latter were brought to his attention by working men themselves. In this way he helped to establish a typically two-way relationship between 'official' and popular economic culture, and considerably extended his own influence, as well as the respect he enjoyed in the labour movement. Indeed, eventually Mill became an honorary member of the 'London Association for the Promotion of Co-Operation',[26] and went as far as declaring that he thought that the co-operative model would eventually absorb and replace the private ownership of the means of production.[27]

Thus, during the second half of the century no ideological barrier had been left between Liberalism and co-operativism: as Cole wrote, the latter 'was just as much on the side of Liberalism as was the weight of Nonconformity'.[28] The two movements also shared the same attitudes and a frame of mind: the strong sense of social solidarity typical of the Owenites could easily be translated into a liberal idiom, as 'self-defensive Individualism, made attractive by amity, strengthened by interest, and rendered effective by association'.[29] Both liberals and co-operators celebrated the 'love of labour' as 'the foundation of civilization',[30] and to a large extent it was something like 'the Protestant work ethic' which stood in the background of both movements.[31] Moreover, co-operation was

---

[23] Bonner, *British Co-operation*, p. 66. See 'Minutes of Evidence taken before the Select Committee on Savings of Middle and Working Classes', *PP*, 1850, xix, 253–66, now also in J. S. Mill, *Coll. Works*, v, pp. 408–29.

[24] Holyoake, *History of Co-operation* (1875), p. 291.

[25] 'British Trade Unions and Popular Political Economy', pp. 811–40.

[26] Holyoake, *History of Co-operation* (1875), p. 386.

[27] *Ibid.*, p. 447.

[28] Cole, *A Century of Co-operation*, p. 102; see also pp. 188, 191–2, 310–1; see Bailey, 'The Consumers in Politics' in Barou (ed.), *The Co-operative Movement in Labour Britain*, pp. 101–2; Bonner, *British Co-operation*, pp. 83, 131; Backstrom, *Christian Socialism and co-operation*, p. 66. See Holyoake, *History of Co-operation* (1875), pp. 608, 655: and 'George Jacob Holyoake', in A. Reid (ed.). *Why I Am a Liberal* (1885), pp. 57–8.

[29] Holyoake, *History of Co-operation*, pp. 666, 669.

[30] Holyoake, *Self-Help a Hundred Years Ago* (1888), p. 164.

[31] The co-operators had many Nonconformists among their most enthusiastic supporters; Mayor, *Churches and the Labour Movement*, pp. 152–3.

likely to prosper among the same sort of people who joined the various 'currents of radicalism':[32] 'thrifty, sober men, who can look beyond the morrow and curb their selfish appetites for the good of those who belong to, and depend upon, them'.[33] These attitudes may have attracted the admiration of the ruling elites as embodying the spirit of private enterprise: however, Pat Thane has rightly observed that they were 'as essential to a successful workers' movement as to successful capitalism';[34] in fact, they were shared even by those who belonged to the most 'proletarian' mass organizations, the burial and friendly societies, with their huge membership of over four million people.[35]

An expression of this frame of mind can be seen in the fact that both co-operatives and friendly and burial societies always remained opposed to State intervention except for the punishment of dishonest practices.[36] In this sense too they were in tune with contemporary Liberalism.[37] To the 1871 Royal Commission on Friendly Societies H. Liversage, of the Royal Livery, declared:

> As a rule the working classes have a natural dislike of officialism; and moreover I think, speaking generally, that the less Government interference there is with these societies and the people, the better. If sufficient or rather comprehensive laws are framed, and sufficient penalties are enforced against the [dishonest] office bearers in the various societies, I think that that is all that can be required . . .[38]

The prevalent opinion was that the State ought to limit itself to playing the role of 'nightwatchman'. The Register of Friendly Societies was accepted as an established practice, but any further

---

[32] Thompson, *The Chartists*, p. 301; Lancaster, *Radicalism, Co-operation and Socialism*, pp. 55–62, 135; Gurney, 'Holyoake', in Yeo (ed.), *New Views of Co-operation*, pp. 52–72.

[33] [L.a.], 'Co-operative Marketing', *LW*, 7 Jan. 1866, p. 1.

[34] Thane, 'The working class and State welfare', p. 884.

[35] 'Appendix (I) to Fourth Report', *P.P.*, 1874, xxiii, part 1, 243. Crossick, however, has suggested that this assessment grossly exaggerated the actual membership of such societies (*An Artisan Elite*, p. 181).

[36] Gracchus, 'Mismanagement of the friendly societies', *RN*, 28 June 1868, p. 3. From a very early stage the government took a keen interest in regulating the activities of friendly societies; after some discussion in the 1780s, the first Act of Parliament dealing with these organizations was passed in 1793. However, from the very beginning State intervention generated negative reactions and widespread fears among society members, who, in 1819, obtained a reduction of the public controls enacted the year before on their finances (see, Blake and Moore, *Friendly Societies*, pp. 4–5).

[37] G. Howell to W. MacCall, 4 June 1868, in *G. Howell Coll.*, Letter Bks. See Gosden, *Friendly Societies*, p. 92; Crossick, *An Artisan Elite*, p. 195.

[38] *Royal Commission on Friendly and Benefit Building Societies (RCFS)*, PP, 1872, xxvi, H. Liversage (9 Feb. 1871), q. 1452, see also q. 1345.

extension of State control was controversial. At most, some would tolerate a more active role of 'prevention and information', what Mill called 'unauthoritative interference':[39] the government could inform the public about the solvency of the societies which applied to be registered,[40] but would not be entitled to refuse registration to those whose rules were not in agreement with the guidelines laid down by the Board of Trade. In this matter many managers of the most widespread working-class societies exceeeded even Robert Lowe in their zeal for *laissez-faire*.[41]

In contrast, those who cherished greater public control were upper-class philanthropists or social reformers like the Hon. Edward Stanhope, who was a vigorous supporter of a national system of 'Post Office Friendly Societies'.[42] But even Stanhope acknowledged the strength of the objection that the workers who subscribed to a friendly society 'do so from a feeling that it is something of their own, which is under their control, and in which they have a sort of social intercourse', and that such an incentive would be destroyed by the kind of public intervention that he recommended.[43] This was in fact the issue at stake: friendly societies were proudly defined by the workers as 'great self-governing institutions'[44] and – one of the witnesses declared – were 'so much better managed by the people themselves that I cannot see my way to the Government undertaking any part in the management of them'.[45] To proposed interference from above the response was that 'the people should take their affairs in their own

---

[39] Mill, *Principles of Political Economy*, in *Coll. Works*, III, 2. p. 937.

[40] *RCFS, PP*, 1873, xxv, E. Rendle, Friendly Union Benefit (10 Apr. 1872), qq. 24, 728–24, 731; C. Burls, Mutual Provident Alliance Society, (6 June 1872), qq. 25, 821, 25,822. See the discussion of the various possible alternative forms of State intervention in the evidence given by the Radical MP J. Stansfeld (*ibid.*, 2 Apr. 1873, qq. 28,516–518).

[41] For the extent of 'minimalism' recommended by Lowe, see the evidence he gave in *RCFS, PP*, 1873, xxii, 6 July 1873, q. 28,312; *ibid.*, 6 March 1873, q. 28,349. As in the case of trade union legislation, Lowe became the champion of working-class rights and 'independence' (Gosden, *Friendly Societies*, pp. 162–3; see below pp. 157–8).

[42] *RCFS, PP*, 20 June 1873, q. 24,374, Hon. E. Stanhope, Assistant Commissioner to the Commission on the Employment of Women in Agriculture, 20 June 1872, q. 24,374.

[43] *Ibid.*, q. 26,447. For a similar project, which proposed not only the integration of the private system, but also its compulsory nationalization, see *ibid.*, 'Appendix to the Evidence of Mr. J. W. Williams', President [of the] Association of Warehousemen, Travellers and Clerks, 8 July 1872, Appendix No. 2.

[44] *Ibid.*, J. Shepherd and H. Murphy, 24 Feb. 1871, q. 2396. For the importance of 'independence', see Gosden, *Friendly Societies*, p. 18.

[45] *RCFS, PP*, 1873, xxii, A. Doyle 6 March 1873, q. 28,379.

hands, and not allow themselves to be deceived'[46] by 'the wealthy'. Traditional plebeian anti-statism came to the fore, as *Reynolds's Newspaper* protested that

The honest and solvent societies which working men have successfully conducted for half-a-century do not need any legislation whatever. They only seek to be released from the shackles which law has provided, and to be allowed to carry out that doctrine of freedom of contract which finds so much favour with the upper classes.[47]

In contrast to 'doctrinairism of the Downing Street kind'[48] many workers asked for a legislative intervention similar to that embodied in the 1867 Companies Acts. This law, in dealing with middle-class societies,

does not bristle all over with pains and penalties, is not restrictive at every turn, does not cramp and disable those who seek to conform to its requirements. Any seven or more men can form a company for almost any purpose and having done so they are left free so long as they conform to a few provisions of the most necessary kind, provided the intentions of the parties entering on such a work are fair and honest. Our legislators take for granted that the capitalists of the country are grown men with mature understanding, and, as a rule, quite capable of taking care of themselves. Whilst, on the other hand, on the business of life insurance, working men seem to be regarded as children too careless to look after their own interests, and too simple minded to understand them, even though they were so disposed.[49]

In particular there was widespread hostility towards the kind of social reform that Pat Thane has defined as 'inquisitorial, "anti-working class"',[50] and based on the assumption that the labourers were unable to act in a rational or honest way. A typical example would be the 1875 proposal of a legal limit of 30/- (later increased to £3) on the life insurance for children. As the thinking behind it was that the higher sums previously allowed had encouraged poor parents to commit infanticide for the sake of gain, such a suggestion was inevitably unpopular, and the rising tide of working-class

---

[46] [L.a.], 'Self-help and Labour', *RN*, 31 May 1874, 1. See Crossick, *An Artisan Elite*, p. 185; Thane, 'The Working Class and State Welfare', p. 878.
[47] Gracchus, 'The Government and the Friendly Societies', *RN*, 15 July 1874, p. 3.
[48] [L.a.], 'Friendly Societies Bill', *BH*, 30 Jan. 1875, p. 9.
[49] [L.a.], 'Friendly Societies Bill', *BH*, 9 Feb. 1875, p. 9.
[50] Thane, 'The Working Class and State Welfare', p. 895; MacDonagh, *Early Victorian Government*, pp. 47–8. It was a common saying that 'social reform means "police"' (Hay, *Origins of the Liberal Welfare Reforms*, pp. 28–9; Reynolds and Woolley, *Seems So!* (1911), p. 118).

indignation soon forced the Chancellor of the Exchequer to give in.[51]

The reactions to these government initiatives showed that it was the poverty-stricken societies which were the most hostile to State intervention. In contrast, the most prosperous and stable organizations, whose membership was made up of the better-paid workers, were in favour of forms of stricter government control on solvency and the criteria of financial administration. The reason was that these societies were aware that their criteria of management were decidedly above any standard the government might like to fix,[52] and looked down on the other associations,[53] believing that the bankruptcies and irregularities that characterized their management discredited the whole movement and limited its extension.[54] On the other hand, the societies which catered for the poorest workers and those whose jobs were irregular or dangerous, could attract customers only by offering a wide range of different agreements, drawn up in an empirical way and taking little note of the current criteria of statistical calculation. Hence, the high percentage of bankruptcies, which in general were not due to the managers' irresponsibility or dishonesty, but to the rigid limits of the contributive capacities of the members of their associations. Had the criteria of the wealthier organizations been forced upon them, many small friendly and burial societies would soon have collapsed under the strain, and their wretched members would have lost their only opportunity of subscribing to an insurance fund, albeit a fortuitous and unreliable one. Unfortunately there was little alternative to this situation so long as the poor were so hopelessly poor.

[51] See [rep.], 'Friendly Societies Bill. – Deputation to the Chancellor of the Exchequer on Infant Insurance', *BH*, 13 March 1875, pp. 11–12; [l.a.], 'The Friendly Societies Bill', *BH*, 20 March 1875, pp. 9–10; [l.a.], 'The Friendly Societies Bill and Infant Insurance', *BH*, 12 June 1875, pp. 9–10.

[52] See *RCFS, PP*, 1873, xxii, W. Mortimer, Western Provident Association, 10 Apr. 1872, qq. 24,538–24,550; A. Blyth, Northumberland and Durham Permanent Relief Fund, 6 Nov. 1872, qq. 27,216–27,226.

[53] *Ibid.*, A. Blyth, qq. 27,155–27,173.

[54] See the interesting remarks on the 'universalization' of labour insurance in [n. s.], 'Side Views of Social Life. Mutual Help', *NW*, 17 Apr. 1869, 4. The *Newcastle Chronicle* was notoriously close to the miners' unions.

TRADE UNIONS AND CIVIL LIBERTY

Therefore, in the last analysis, the heart of the problem was that some sections of the working classes were not paid enough to look after their own welfare effectively. It is not surprising that the prevailing opinion among the workers was that the solution was to be found not in State-controlled compulsory insurance, but in the collective action of the labour movement to obtain higher wages and more regular jobs, 'to elevate workmen up to a certain minimum'.[55] The main instruments in this struggle were the trade unions.

During the 1860s the latters' role and legitimacy was accepted by the most important economists, who indeed declared that they were necessary to the proper working of the market. These developments, opportunely incorporated into trade union ideology, contributed towards stimulating the emphasis on conciliation, arbitration and peaceful collective bargaining, which was to dominate the following two decades.[56] However, the trade unions still had to overcome one major obstacle, namely that of ambiguous or restrictive legislation, like the unequal Master and Servant Act or the application to trade unions of the common law of conspiracy.[57] These laws still preserved the flavour and some of the content of old measures limiting the rights of meeting, speech, and demonstration, and – as T. J. Dunning complained – tended to categorize industrial labour almost under 'the old feudal notion of serfdom'.[58]

The issue came to a head in 1867, with the Royal Commission's

---

[55] 'Report of the Conference of Trades Delegates, held in the Town Hall, Leeds, on December 2nd, 1871 . . .', in *G. Howell Coll.*, 'TUC Parliamentary Committee Papers', 9, 11; a similar point of view prevailed until the end of the century: Thane, 'The Working Class and State Welfare', p. 880.

[56] I have discussed these aspects, including the ideology of conciliation and arbitration, in 'British Trade Unions and Popular Political Economy', pp. 811–40. See also Dunbabin, 'The "Revolt of the Field"', pp. 76–8. For a different interpretation, see Clements, 'British Trade Unions and Popular Political Economy', pp. 93–104. For the relationship between economic thought and the labour movement in previous decades, see Webb, *British Working-Class Reader*; and Thompson, *The People's Science*.

[57] For the check on trade union activities exercised by this law, see Daphne Simon, 'Master and Servant', in Saville (ed.), *Democracy and the Labour Movement*, pp. 160–200; and Curthoys, *Thesis*, pp. 21–3, 116–20.

[58] T. J. Dunning, 'Restraint of Trade', *BH*, 17 Apr. 1869, p. 1; see also E. S. Beesly, 'Professor Beesly on the new Law of Conspiracy, No. II', *BH*, 21 Sept. 1867, p. 4 and No. III, *BH*, 21 Sept. 1867, p. 5.

enquiry into the famous Sheffield 'outrages'.[59] and with the Hornby
v. Close judgement. Both seemed to pose serious threats to trade
unions: the former again raised the question of the legality of their
methods; the latter suggested that they were 'in restraint of trade',
and deprived their funds of the legal protection accorded to those
of friendly societies. At this stage legislative intervention to restore
and secure the legal standing of the unions became an absolute
priority for the organized labour movement. The recently formed
Liberal government was quite willing to comply, though it had to
choose between two approaches, corresponding – respectively – to
the recommendations of the Majority and Minority Reports of the
Royal Commission.

The majority of the commissioners had proposed that trade
unions should not be exposed to prosecution as organizations 'in
restraint of trade', but that the privileges of registration under the
1855 Friendly Societies Act should be reserved only to those
societies whose aims did not include limitations on apprentices or
on the use of machines in their respective branches of industry. A
minority of three commissioners – Thomas Hughes, Frederic
Harrison and Lord Litchfield – recommended instead that the
provisos of the Friendly Societies Act be extended to all trade
unions unconditionally, and that the latter be given immunity from
being sued in a corporate capacity. Their recommendations were
adopted by the trade unions as the basis of their requests, and this
provided a precise reform programme for the alliance between
parliamentary radicalism and the labour movement.[60]

Eventually the Minority Report also inspired the proposal
presented in 1871 by H. A. Bruce, the Home Secretary. The
government Bill was completely satisfactory as far as statutory
protection of trade unions was concerned. However, it also contained recommendations for the prevention and punishment of
intimidatory practices by trades union members, and it was this
section that generated much opposition from organized labour.[61]
Because of this opposition, historians have tended to undervalue

---

[59] See Pollard, *The Sheffield Outrages*, pp. v–xvii and references; cf. also Webbs, *History of
Trade Unionism*, pp. 251–3; McCready, 'The British Labour Lobby, 1867–1875',
pp. 141–60.

[60] See Harrison, *Before the Socialists*, pp. 287–8; Spain, 'Trade Unions and Gladstonian
Liberals', in Biagini and Reid (eds.), *Currents of Radicalism*, pp. 109–33.

[61] The text of Bruce's Bill was commented on in detail in the *Bee Hive*: 'The Government
Trade Union Bill', 18 Feb. 1871, pp. 6–7.

both the actual importance of the Bill for the workers, and the difficulties that Bruce had to overcome.[62] Public opinion had been so shocked by the Royal Commission's revelation about violence and blackmail at Sheffield and elsewhere, that even trade union spokesmen and 'advocates' had recognized the necessity of modifying the Common Law in order to punish these criminal practices:[63] indeed, clauses to this effect had been included in the private Bills they had sponsored in 1867–8[64] and 1869.[65] The problem with the 1871 government Bill was rather that it seemed biased against the workers, on whom it picked as a sort of 'specially criminal class'. Moreover, it did not define with sufficient precision those cases in which a judge could intervene, and indeed was worded in such a way as to allow contrasting interpretations. Thus, to 'persistently follow' a working man or employer from place to place, or to 'watch and beset' a house or a place where such a worker or employer resided or worked or happened to be – objectively, two of the most common intimidatory practices then used in strikes – became criminal offences if carried out by two or more workers 'with a view to coerce': the Bill, however, was not clear about the meaning of 'coercion'. It introduced the notion of intentionality – always difficult to evaluate – in a casuistry in which offences were vaguely described.[66] As George Howell lamented, there was the risk that over-zealous magistrates would

[62] See Tholfsen, *Working-Class Radicalism*, pp. 275–76, who mentions only the controversial Criminal Law Amendment Act, without making any reference to the Trade Union Act. Also Harrison, *Before the Socialists*, pp. 288–91, who not only contrasts Bruce's Bill with the Mundella-Hughes' 1869 one, but also identifies the rights of the trade unions with those of workers in general, forgetting both the limited dimensions of Victorian trade unionism, and the criminal enterprises which had characterized trade unions activities in some parts of the United Kingdom, in order to increase their effectiveness.

[63] Cf. [l.a.], 'The Trades Union Bill', *BH*, 25 Feb. 1871, p. 8; T. J. Dunning, 'Trades Union Bill', *BH*, 4 March 1871, p. 1.

[64] The text of the Bill had been prepared by Beesly and H. Crompton: see 'The Proposed Act of Parliament Relating to Combinations and Trade Societies', *BH*, 27 Nov. 1867, 1; the final draft of this Bill and the discussion of its merits among the trade union leaders was published in [rep.], 'Important Delegate Meeting of the London Trades', *BH*, 17 Oct. 1868, 5. For the successive developments, see [l.a.], 'The London Trades and the Trades Societies Bill', *BH*, 24 Oct. 1868, p. 5, and [rep.], *ibid.*, p. 1; and [rep.], 'The Trades Societies Bill – Adjourned Meeting of the Trades Delegates', *BH*, 31 Oct. 1868, p. 5.

[65] For labour comments on this Bill, see [l.a.], 'The Trades Union Bill', *BH*, 24 Apr. 1869, 4; T. J. Dunning, 'Trades Union Bill', *BH*, 10 July 1869, p. 5.

[66] On the details of the Bill see Spain, 'Trade unions and Gladstonian Liberals', in Biagini and Reid (eds.), *Currents of Radicalism*, pp. 110–2.

construe the Bill in such a way as to make a criminal offence anything which could be done in the course of a strike.[67]

When the TUC met, it noticed with satisfaction that the Bill offered full protection to the workers' organizations[68] in line with the Liberal policy of government 'neutrality' and non-interference in the labour market.[69] However, it devoted little time to the positive aspects of the government proposal not because it underestimated their importance, but because – as Mark Curthoys has demonstrated[70] – the Bill looked more like a return to normality and the restoration of a well-established practice only recently endangered by the judiciary, than a new major concession. Moreover, as early as 1869 Parliament had passed a temporary measure for the protection of trade union funds, giving the impression that this question was no longer controversial. Expectation had focussed on the issue of the unions' right to strike and the relative modification of the criminal law:[71] now, however, the relevant part of the Bill – the famous 'section 3' – seemed to be making things worse.[72] The campaign against this section absorbed much of the energy of organized labour for the next four years.

As Jonathan Spain has illustrated,[73] trade union spokesmen made effective use of traditional liberal concepts in this endeavour: they presented their struggle as a crusade to clear the labour market of State interventionism,[74] and to obtain 'perfect equality before the law'.[75] Whereas in a previous stage some labour leaders had accepted the necessity of 'special measures' for the trade

---

[67] G. Howell to Goldwin Smith, 25 Feb. 1871, in *G. Howell Coll.*, Letter Books. 450.

[68] *Third Annual Trade Union Congress*, London, March 6th to 11th Inclusive 1871, 2nd day 7 March 1871, discussion and resolution moved by Lloyd Jones, in *Minutes, G. Howell Coll.*, TUC Parliamentary Committee Papers (hence forward cited *TUC PC*).

[69] Curthoys, *Thesis*, pp. 265, 271.

[70] *Ibid.*, pp. 223, 231.

[71] See G. Howell to Goldwin Smith, 19 July 1869; 'The Government has dealt very well with the question of Trades' Union funds, and next session they will deal with the Combination Laws' (*G. Howell Coll.*, Letter Bks).

[72] Though actually the CLAA limited, rather than extended, the criminal law directed at trade unions: see Curthoys, *Thesis*, pp. 269–71.

[73] Spain, 'Trade Unions and Gladstonian Liberals', in Biagini and Reid (eds.), *Currents of Radicalism*, pp. 114–15.

[74] Harrison, 'The Trades Union Bill', *Fortnightly Review* (1869), p. 30; *TUC PC*, 'The Trades Union Bill – A Protest', 23 March 1871, MS in *TUC PC*; see also G. Howell to W. Owen, 19 Feb. 1871, in *G. Howell Coll.*, p. 443. The argument was obviously taken up by libertarian friends of the unions: T. Hare, letter to the Editor, *DN*, 11 March 1871 [newspaper cutting] in *TUC PC*, p. 67.

[75] [L.a.], 'The Trades' Union Bill', *Leeds Evening Express*, 5 Apr. 1871, p. 2.

unions, they now adopted a more aggressive stance, almost echoing the contemporary Nonconformist campaigns for religious equality.[76] 'We ask no privileges – no exemptions; but we protest against any exceptional legislation for Trades Unions as such; give us the protection of law, and make us amenable to law, as citizens of a free State; we ask nothing more, and shall be content with nothing less'.[77]

However it was not possible to obtain from the government anything more than the grouping of the penal clauses in a separate Criminal Law Amendment Bill: in this way, the Trades Union Bill could be accepted as a final settlement,[78] while the more controversial part of the new labour legislation could be more easily amended or even repealed, if further discussion and examination showed that such a course was appropriate. This could have been a reasonable compromise for the government as well as for the trade unions, had it not been for one of the Lords' amendments, which made peaceful picketing punishable even when attempted by *one* person. At this point the workers' suspicions and fears about the real aims of State interference seemed confirmed. As the TUC commented, the new law

enacts that if any one workman watches or besets a house or other place where any person resides or works, or carries on business, or happens to be, or the approach to such house or place, with a view to coerce, he shall be liable to be tried summarily before the magistrates, to be sentenced to three months hard labour. Any workman loitering anywhere while a strike is going on or impending will be liable to be a convicted criminal. Waiting at the door of a shop or public-house would be just the same. If arrested upon such a charge how could he possibly prove that he did not intend to coerce? No workman, unionist or non-unionist, is safe for a moment while this law is in existence.[79]

---

[76] See below, chapter 4, pp. 220–4, 228–51. See also Brown, 'The Nonconformists and the Sheffield Outrages', in Biagini and Reid, *Currents of Radicalism*, pp. 86–105.

[77] G. Howell, 'The Trades Union Bill', *BH*, 25 Feb. 1871, pp. 2–3; under the same title there also appeared an article by Lloyd Jones (*ibid.*, p. 3), For the popularity of this approach, see [l.a.], 'The Trades Union Bill', *BH*, 4 March 1871, p. 9; A. Crompton, 'The Trades Union Bill', *BH*, 1 Apr. 1871, 1; F. Harrison, 'The Trades Union Bill', *BH*, 1 July 1871, 1; T. J. Dunning, 'The Trades Union Act', *BH*, 16 Sept. 1871, p. 2.

[78] A. Crompton, 'The Trade Union Act', *BH*, 22 July 1871, 2.

[79] 'The Criminal Law Amendment Act', *BH*, 5 Aug. 1871, p. 12, signed by H. Crompton, F. Harrison, A. Crompton, and, 'on behalf of the Trade Union Congress', by A. McDonald, Lloyd Jones, Joseph Leicester, G. Potter, Chairman, G. Howell, Secretary.

Not only was the Act likely to result in arbitrary prosecutions, but also to perpetrate injustices even when applied in its proper context: that the criminal character of any action depended on one person's 'intention' to exert an undefined 'coercion' on other people, meant that this law could be interpreted 'in such a way as to include moral coercion, that justifiable and proper influence which each citizen is entitled to exercise over others'.[80] Almost paraphrasing J. S. Mill's *On Liberty*, the TUC protested that 'An act ought not to be a crime, merely because it is morally wrong, or because it is an annoyance', and that the issue at stake was no longer the right to strike, but 'the personal freedom of the working classes'.[81] Howell invited trade union leaders to provide the newly-established TUC Parliamentary Committee with figures and details of prosecutions and convictions which could be used as evidence for the oppressive character of the Criminal Law Amendment Act (CLAA).[82] A few, well advertised cases of clearly unjust court rulings – like the Bolton one, described as 'absurd' by the Home Secretary himself[83] – forwarded their efforts.

Yet Parliament had reached a wide consensus on the necessity of new penal laws: and – as far as the principle, rather than the precise form, was concerned – such necessity was never questioned,

---

[80] *Ibid.*

[81] Resolution moved by A. A. Walton, passed by the 1872 TUC: *Minutes of Trades' Union Congress 1872*, Nottingham, 2nd day (9 Jan. 1872), p. 21, in *TUC PC*.

[82] G. Howell to W. Hicking (Nottingham), 23 Feb. 1872, in *G. Howell Coll.*, Letter Bks, 557; see 'Memorial to the Home Secretary Incorporating a Synopsis of all the Prosecution under the Criminal Law Amendment Act', 26 Feb. 1872, in *TUC PC*.

[83] Bruce expressed this opinion during a meeting with a delegation of the TUC at Nottingham: [rep.], 'The Criminal Law Amendment Act', *TI*, 22 Mar. 1872, p. 11. Thomas Wearden, of the Operative Stonemasons, had been sentenced to one month imprisonment by the Bolton Petty Sessions because he had tried to collect a fine from another member of the same trade union, who had declined to comply, and because the episode had been followed by a strike:

They have decided that the occurrence of a subsequent strike is evidence that the accosting and demanding payment was 'with a view to coerce'. That is to say, the magistrates have not merely decided that subsequent acts done by other persons may be given in evidence to show what was the intention of the accused . . . Their decision goes far beyond this; it lays down that any act, however innocent, may become criminal by a subsequent strike taking place. It necessarily follows that the notice of a strike . . . would . . . be held to be done 'with a view to coerce'. So that though the demand is legal, and the strike legal – yet the demand plus the strike constitutes a crime punishable with three months hard labour. ('The Operation of the Criminal Law Amendment Act', [newspaper cutting in] *TUC PC*, p. 80)

From August 1871, a few days after the passing of the Act, the *Bee-Hive* had begun to record similar cases: see a Leeds episode commented in [l.a.], 'The Law and Trade Unionists', *BH*, 19 Aug. 1871. See also Spain, 'Trade Unions and Gladstonian Liberals', in Biagini and Reid (eds.), *Currents of Radicalism*, p. 121.

not even in 1875. What happened instead was that repeated abuses and injustices helped the Parliamentary Committee to demonstrate that the new law had to be modified in order to avoid misinterpretations or excessive liberty of interpretation on the side of the magistrates. In 1872 and 1873 the TUC organized a series of petitions and sent delegations to meet the Home Secretary,[84] while leaders and spokesmen for the labour movement argued their case in very moderate language in the most 'respectable' newspapers.[85] *Causes célèbres* like the convictions of the Oxfordshire female farm-workers – one of whom was suckling a baby[86] – and the mass trial of the London gas workers – some of whom were condemned to even more severe penalties than the law actually warranted[87] – excited public indignation, even though such injustices were due more to the excessive severity of the magistrates, than to the iniquity of the law itself.[88] However the TUC's campaign for full juridical equality gained momentum and credibility as a result of these excesses, which highlighted the fact that many judges were biased against the working classes, and were likely to exploit any ambiguity in the statutes.[89]

This campaign was successful. Soon those who disregarded the CLAA 'were considered, and justly so, as "heroes and martyrs"'.[90] At the end of 1872 an observer wrote that 'Labour . . . is now a

[84] See the reports in *The Times*: 'What is Liberty' [Mundella presenting a petition with 5,000 signatures], 25 Apr. 1872, 9; 'Molesting Workmen' [delegation meets Stansfeld], 28 Sept. 1872, 6; 'Mr. Lowe and the Working Classes', 4 Sept. 1873, p. 9; 'Mr. Lowe and the Criminal Law Amendment Act', 6 Nov. 1873, p. 8.

[85] G. Potter, 'Mr. George Potter on Trades Unions', *TI*, 22 Jan. 1873, p. 7; F. Harrison, 'Workmen and the Law of Conspiracy', *TI*, 24 March 1873, p. 7.

[86] W. MacKenzie, 'Imprisonment of Women', *BH*, 5 July 1873, p. 8.

[87] Spain, 'Trade Unions and Gladstonian Liberals', in Biagini and Reid (eds.), *Currents of Radicalism*, p. 112.

[88] Howell defined this decision as 'a cruelly vindictive piece of Broadheadism' (G. Howell to J. D. Prior, 21 Dec. 1872, in *G.Howell Coll.*, Letter Bks; for other similar comments, see the reports of meetings in London, Stafford and Manchester: 'The Imprisoned Gas Stokers', *BH*, 1 Feb. 1873, pp. 2–3. See also the resolution passed by a workers' meeting at the Patriotic Club of Clerkenwell-Green, on the gas-stokers judgement in [rep.], 'The Imprisoned Gasmen and the London Trades', *RN*, 22 Dec. 1872, p. 1; and 'Draft Resolutions for Meeting at Lambeth Bath, Feb. 12th, 1873', MS in *G. Howell Coll.*, Letter Bks).

[89] 'Look at what the landlords are doing in Warwickshire! Evicting labourers for joining a union, whereas if a unionist threatens a non-unionist, he gets three months imprisonment' (A. J. Mundella to G. Howell, 7 Apr. 1872, cit. in Armytage, *Mundella*, p. 119; see W. R. Cremer, 'The Conspiracy of Gas Stokers and the Conspiracy of Coal Owners', *RN*, 5 Feb. 1873, p. 1; Northumbrian, 'Capital Up and Labour Down', *RN*, 21 Dec. 1873, p. 3).

[90] Thomas Burt, in *Hansard PD*, 3rd. series, ccxxv, 682 (28 June 1875).

great power, because it is associated with opinion'.[91] Pressure was kept high with a series of peaceful and well-ordered demonstrations,[92] culminating in the 1873 trade union processions in London, Edinburgh and Glasgow, in which there took part, respectively 10,000, 15,000 and 18,000 people.[93] The employers felt threatened and organized counter-petitions and delegations to the Home Secretary.[94] But given the comparative strength of the TUC members in the electorate of the time, and the fact that some of the requests of the trade unionists were undeniably legitimate, the government could not ignore the labour unrest without incurring serious electoral risks.[95]

Thus, things soon began to move again in the House of Commons. By June 1872 the Parliamentary Committee, in co-operation with a few Liberal MPs, prepared an amendment to the CLAA which would have made peaceful picketing legal, provided it was limited to mere 'watching or observing' without verbal communication of information.[96] This was a very moderate measure: indeed trade union leaders supported it only as a temporary settlement and a step towards the full repeal of the CLAA;[97] but it was nevertheless unsuccessful. A few months later, Harcourt and Mundella – with Gladstone's support – presented a new and more

[91] [L.a.], 'The Retrospect of the Year', *RN*, 22 Dec. 1872, p. 1; [l.a., n.t.], *LM*, 22 Jan. 1873, p. 2.

[92] [Rep.], 'The Criminal Law Amendment Act' [2,000 trade unionists at Nottingham], *TI*, 13 Aug, 1872, p. 9; [rep.], 'Trades Union Demonstration' [1,000 trade unionists at Blackburn], *TI*, 18 Aug. 1873, p. 10; [rep.], 'The Criminal Law Amendment Act' [a 'great' demonstration at Dundee], *TI*, 5 Jan. 1874, p. 12.

[93] According to *The Times*; see [rep.], 'Trades Union Demonstration', 3 June 1873, p. 6; [rep.], 'Trades' Demonstration in Edinburgh', 25 Aug. 1873, p. 4; [rep.], 'The Criminal Law Amendment Act' [Glasgow], 3 Nov. 1873, p. 10. The figure of 100,000 demonstrators at Hyde Park supported by R. Harrison *(Before the Socialists*, p. 298) is probably exaggerated. For the accurate propaganda preparation behind the Hyde Park demonstration, see the series of reports with which the London Trades Council tried to inform the middle- and upper-class public about the trade unionists' intentions and methods: [rep.], 'The Demonstration of the London Trades', *TI*, 10 Apr, 1873, p. 7; [rep.], 'The Forthcoming Trades' Demonstration', *TI*, 22 May 1873, p. 11; [rep.], 'The Trades Demonstration', *TI*, 2 June 1873, p. 8.

[94] [Rep.], 'The Criminal Law Amendment Act' [delegation of the Master Engineers], *TI*, 15 June 1872, p. 11; [rep.], 'The Criminal Law Amendment Act' [the Council of the Sheffield Chamber of Commerce expresses its disapproval for the possible repeal of the CLAA], *TI*, 2 June 1873, p. 8.

[95] Winter, *Lowe*, pp. 304–5; Spain, 'Trade Unions and Gladstonian Liberals', in Biagini and Reid (eds.), *Currents of Radicalism*, p. 123.

[96] V. Harcourt, 'The Criminal Law Amendment Act', *BH*, 28 June 1872, p. 1.

[97] See 'The Criminal Law Amendment Act 1871 Amendment Bill', MS in *TUC PC*, p. 2.

advanced Bill: this would have been substantially satisfactory as far as the interests of labour were concerned,[98] had it not been heavily amended by the House of Lords. Finally, in October 1873 Lowe produced a memorandum containing the guidelines for a broad settlement of the whole issue[99] but the sudden dissolution of the Commons in January 1874 prevented the Liberal government from carrying this last attempt further.

As Jonathan Spain has stressed,[100] at the ensuing elections, many candidates – both Liberal and Conservative – promised to satisfy the requests of the TUC, and some were explicitly committed to the full repeal of the CLAA.[101] However, after the Conservative victory, Disraeli – running the gauntlet of labour indignation[102] – declined even to consider any reform before a new Royal Commission had investigated the actual working of the labour laws.

This inquiry has traditionally been considered as a Disraelian device to gain time, and almost a formality.[103] Still, its findings could have been very damaging to the trade unions, and could have prevented the repeal or satisfactory amendment of the CLAA. The Commission did in fact reveal a situation which was quite different from the image of respectability and law-abidingness so successfully popularized by the TUC Parliamentary Committee; not surprisingly, George Howell was pessimistic on the eve of the publication of the reports.[104] What the Royal Commission showed was that between 1871 and 1875 the application of the CLAA had

---

[98] 'Mr. Harcourt's Bill will give the workmen complete and final protection' (F. Harrison, 'Mr. Harcourt's Conspiracy Bill', *BH*, 5 July 1873, p. 8).

[99] Matthew, *Diaries*, VIII, pp. 417–18; Spain, 'Trade Unions and Gladstonian Liberals', in Biagini and Reid, *Currents of Radicalism*, pp. 123–5.

[100] Spain, 'Trade Unions and Gladstonian Liberals', in Biagini and Reid (eds.), *Currents of Radicalism*, pp. 125–7.

[101] See [rep.], 'Manchester Reception of Sir Thomas Bazley, Bart.', *MG*, 31 Jan. 1874, p. 8; and [rep.], 'The Liberal Candidates and Tory Trade Unionists', *MG*, 4 Feb. 1874, p. 6.

[102] See 'Resolution Passed by the Trades Union Congress Parliamentary Committee', in 'Appendix Part IV', 4b., p. 105, *Second and Final Report of the Commissioners Appointed to inquire into the Working of the Master and Servant Act, 1867, the Criminal Law Amendment Act, 34 & 35 Vict. Capt. 32, PP*, 1875, XXX.

[103] Harrison, *Before the Socialists*, pp. 302–3.

[104] G. Howell to W. V. Harcourt, 30 Jan. 1875, and G. Howell to H. James, 30 Jan. 1875, both in *G. Howell Coll.*, Letter Bks, p. 663 and 665. Probably something of these terroristic connotations of trade-unionism was preserved even in working-class usage, as can be deduced from the use of the expression 'trade union' to mean 'a clique to confer unfair privileges to a specific group of people': for example, both the Church of England and the landed aristocracy were defined as 'trade unions' in this sense (Littlejohn, 'The Union of Church and State', *WT*, 17 May 1868, p. 6; [l.a.], 'Federate! Federate! Federate!', *RN*, 29 Aug. 1875, p. 1).

punished mainly physical violence and a series of threats of violence. Abuses of the law had indeed taken place, but had been the exception, rather than the rule. On the whole, it seemed that the 1871 criminal law was necessary if the basic civil liberties of non-organized workers (still a majority of the workforce) were to be guaranteed, and if violent, semi-criminal union practices were to be discouraged.[105]

However, the Commission also demonstrated that other civil liberties – those of the trade unionists – were threatened by the arbitrary powers which the Lords' amendment had given to the magistrates.[106] Moreover the wording of the law was unnecessarily discriminatory: the offences punished under the CLAA between 1871 and 1875 were crimes in themselves, independent of the occupation of the offenders. What was therefore required was a modification of the ordinary criminal law, rather than a measure explicitly aimed at trade unionists. Finally, it was difficult to deny that the prohibition of peaceful picketing endangered the freedom of meeting.

Successive developments showed that three years of trade union progaganda had not in the end been nullified by the revelations of the new Royal Commission. The general trend both in public opinion and in Parliament was in favour of a generous settlement. In preparing his Bill, Cross virtually accepted most of the arguments of the one dissenting Commissioner, the miners' leader Alexander McDonald, who had ably expounded the trade unions' case in the language of the most traditional political economy.[107] Cross' approach came as a pleasant surprise to the trade unionists, but what most astonished them was the easy acceptance by both Houses of Parliament of the new Bills in an amended, improved form.[108] It was Robert Lowe – the former Liberal Home Secretary

---

[105] *Royal Commission on the Working of the Criminal Law Amendment Act, PP* 1874, xxiv, E. Johnson, Honorary Secretary to the Master Builders' Association, Manchester, qq. 672–676. See also H. Crompton to G. Howell, 6 Sept. 1875, in G. Howell Coll. Intimidatory practices, much violence and even looting continued to take place in connection with strikes during the following decades, in spite of all the efforts of trade union officials (*Royal Commission on Labour, PP* 1894, xxxv, p. 353).

[106] *Royal Commission on the Working of the Criminal Law Amendment Act, PP* 1874, xxiv, W. Paterson, Secretary to the Associated Carpenters and Joiners of Scotland, q. 173. See H. Crompton, 'The Trial of the London Cabinet Makers', *BH*, 15 May 1875, p. 1.

[107] See *Royal Commission on the Working of the Criminal Law Amendment Act, PP* 1874, xxiv, A. Macdonald, 'Dissent', pp. 28–9.

[108] Smith, *Disraelian Conservatism*, pp. 215–16.

– who seized the initiative when he proposed removing all the legal anomalies of which the trade unionists were victims:[109] acting in close consultation with the TUC Parliamentary Committee,[110] and driven by his zeal for rationalizing the law and implementing *laissez-faire*, he became the most authoritative spokesman for labour.[111] The final *coup de théâtre* came when Lowe proposed, and Cross accepted, the complete repeal of the CLAA:[112] what Cross had hitherto consistently and categorically excluded,[113] and George Howell had described as the maximum that the labour movement could hope to obtain,[114] was suddenly incorporated into a bipartisan proposal. It was not the abolition of all the measures enacted by the CLAA: rather, faced with the difficulties involved in amending the 1871 Act, Cross had preferred to replace it with a completely new proposal, the Conspiracy and Protection of Property Bill. This was to apply to all citizens, rather than to just a 'discriminated class'; moreover, though it included most of the text of the CLAA, the wording was no longer ambiguous, especially in the definition of the kinds of association which were to be deemed 'conspiracies'. In its final version, it also legalized peaceful picketing.[115] This Bill was accompanied by a parallel measure, the Employers and Workmen Bill, which repealed the Master and Servant Act and placed the two roles on a legally equal footing.[116]

In these new laws there was nothing that the Liberals could not have accepted in 1871, and in particular there was no trace of any 'social paternalism', from which front-bench Conservatives were no less alien than the Liberals.[117] These laws simply provided for full legal equality between employers and employees, still 'having due regard' – as the TUC itself had recommended – 'to the

---

[109] Winter, *Lowe*, p. 217; Spain, 'Trade Unions and Gladstonian Liberals', in Biagini and Reid (eds.), *Currents of Radicalism*, pp. 129–30.

[110] See G. Howell to R. Lowe, 27 Feb. 1875, in *G. Howell Coll.*, Letter Bks p. 683.

[111] H. Crompton, 'Henry Crompton on the Government Labour Laws', *BH*, 3 July 1875, pp. 3–4.

[112] Smith, *Disraelian Conservatism*, p. 216.

[113] See Cross's reply to a delegation of the ASE in [rep.], 'The Labour Laws', *NW*, 10 July 1875, p. 5. For the sudden change in Cross' position see Spain, 'Trade Unions and Gladstonian Liberals', in Biagini and Reid (eds.), *Currents of Radicalism*, pp. 130–2.

[114] G. Howell, 'George Howell on the Labour Laws', *BH*, 3 July 1875, p. 4.

[115] H. Crompton, 'Digest of the New Labour Law', *BH*, 18 Sept. 1875, pp. 2–3.

[116] Smith, *Disraelian Conservatism*, p. 216; Spain, 'Trade Unions and Gladstonian Liberals', in Biagini and Reid (eds.), *Currents of Radicalism*, pp. 131–2.

[117] Smith, *Disraelian Conservatism*, pp. 203–4; Roberts, 'Tory Paternalism and Social Reform', p. 326.

freedom of the individual, to the protection of persons and property, and other civil rights'.[118] The new legislation – just like the CLAA – included penal sanctions against 'those who attempt[ed] to violate the personal liberty of another, whether by threat, coercion, intimidation, or personal violence': but the leaders of the TUC had never objected to this part of the law.[119] On the whole, the 1875 acts were judged a consistent expression of juridical liberalism,[120] and were acclaimed by the TUC as representing 'emancipation from the remains of the old barbarous feudal laws of the past'.[121]

Though the reform of trade union legislation had enormous importance for the labour movement from the point of view of the arguments used and the principles at stake, the series of events leading to it fit rather better into the history of struggles for civil liberties, than the contemporary debate on social legislation. The closest parallel to it can be found in the long campaign for the repeal of the Contagious Diseases Acts (CDA). Like the CLAA, the CDA were 'special legislation': they applied only to a few garrison towns and aimed at controlling venereal diseases – always common among the military – by checking the prostitutes' state of health. To this end the police were given power to detain prostitutes and suspected prostitutes, and to subject them to compulsory medical visits. Since prostitution was then widespread among the poor, all working-class women were potentially exposed to a treatment considered outrageous and dishonouring.[122] The CDA represented a serious violation of civil rights against a specific section of the female population of the country: hence the charge that they were another instance of 'class legislation'.[123] As 'Gracchus' wrote,

---

[118] TUC Parliamentary Committee, 'The Labour Laws. A memorial to the Right Honourable Richard Assheton Cross, MP', MS, n. d., in *G. Howell Coll.*, Letter Bks, 709ff. See Webbs, *History of Trade Unionism*, pp. 294–7.

[119] Howell, 'Intimidation and Picketing', *Fortnightly Review* (1877), p. 608.

[120] See the important observation in Smith, *Disraelian Conservatism*, pp. 216, 217 and note 1.

[121] G. Howell, 'The Trades Union Congress Parliamentary Committee and the Labour Laws', in *G. Howell Coll.*, Letter Bk. 754.

[122] [Rep.], 'The Contagious Diseases Acts', *BH*, 19 Aug. 1871, p. 4. For the widespread character of prostitution in Victorian Britain, see McHugh, *Prostitution and Victorian Social Reform*, p. 18.

[123] [L.a.], 'Repeal of the Contagious Diseases Act', *BH*, 7 Feb. 1872, 9; [l.a.], 'Judicial Murder', *RN*, 3 Apr. 1870, p. 4; letter by 'An Indignant Englishman', *RN*, 28 Aug. 1870, p. 3.

All exceptional laws are objectionable, and none more so than those which give the police additional powers over the liberties and persons of the defenceless portion of the community . . . Assuredly, this violation of an Englishwoman's person, never mind in how low scale of life she may move, no matter what her mode of life may be, is a monstrous and abominable outrage upon the first principles of liberty, of decency, and of propriety. The person of a prostitute should be as sacred from harm or touch as that of a duchess, or of the Queen herself.[124]

Another parallel between the CDA and the CLAA was the uncertainty of the law:

It is left absolutely to the discretion of the police, to determine what constitutes a 'common prostitute', and . . . it is clear that their definitions vary, and that one policeman would hold himself justified in charging, as 'a common prostitute', a woman whom another policeman would not allow to come within that category. Further than this, the duty of the Justice is very loosely explained in the act . . . The accused woman has no notion as to the fact which the police intend to prove; a special hardship in this case, since proof of prostitution usually depends not on direct, but on circumstantial evidence. Often it consists of facts susceptible of an innocent explanation, yet for want of notice of the facts to be produced, and for want of legal assistance the women may fail to rebut the presumptions based on these facts. Now the women most likely to be charged by the police are, as a rule, far too poor to engage legal assistance, even if they are not altogether too ignorant to know how to set about it.[125]

Like the CLAA between 1871 and 1875, the CDA between the 1860s and 1886, when success was finally achieved,[126] also gave rise to a coalition of 'repealers', including trade unionists,[127] parliamentary and intellectual radicals, and outraged Nonconformists.[128] Besides the moral aspects, their arguments were the

---

[124] Gracchus, 'An Appeal to British Womanhood on the Contagious Diseases Act', *RN*, 29 May 1870, p. 2.

[125] Elizabeth C. Wolstonholme, Contagious Diseases Acts', *BH*, 4 May 1872, pp. 2–3.

[126] McHugh, *Prostitution and Victorian Social Reform*, pp. 227–8.

[127] Humphrey, *Applegarth*, pp. 240–4. See also Howell's notes in *G. Howell Coll.*, Letter Bks, 9/75, n. d. [but October 1874].

[128] The CDA were condemned as 'Unrighteous, Unconstitutional, Oppressive, One-sided, Cowardly; Pernicious in their operation, and calculated to undermine all that is good and holy in the relationship between Man and Woman. Let no one be deceived. These Acts have introduced into the British Islands nothing more nor less than LICENSED PROSTITUTION!!' ('What Are the Contagious Diseases Acts?', leaflet of the National Association for Repeal, n. d., in *Solly Coll.*, III, 3, 2. See also, H. Solly, 'The Contagious Diseases Acts', *BH*, 14 June 1872, p. 3). The Methodist Conference took a clear position on this issue from 1870: Plain Dealer, *BH*, 6 Aug. 1870, pp. 394–5. The composition and vicissitudes of the repeal movement are studied in detail in McHugh's excellent study, *Prostitution and Victorian Social Reform*; see also Walkowitz, *Prostitution and Victorian Society*, pp. 90–136.

classical ones of liberal radicalism.[129] More particularly, they were
similar to those used by the labour opponents of the CLAA, being
based on the old Whig cry of 'equality before the law'. They
requested equality for all, not only for rich and poor, but also for
men and women, since 'all women are human beings, even
prostitutes . . . [who] are not one bit worse than the men who seek
them'.[130]

Thus, between 1871 and 1873 the Liberal government missed
the opportunity of settling two questions involving important issues
of civil liberty. However, in neither case can the reason be found
in some alleged adherence to the 'dogmas' of *laissez-faire*: what
needs to be explained is rather why the Liberal government did *not*
abide by such 'dogmas'. This apparent inconsistency was criticized
from the very beginning by some Parliamentary Radicals,[131] as
J. S. Mill became one of the chief inspirations for the campaign for
the repeal of the CDA.[132] However, the majority of MPs thought
that both the CLAA and the CDA were necessary either to curb
criminal offences or to prevent greater social evils, two spheres in
which by general admission even the 'State nightwatchman' had a
role.[133] Thus, it was not over general principles, but over the
assessment of specific cases, that the advocates and repealers of
these laws disagreed. This further enhanced the importance of
propaganda and pressure groups, who effected the conversion of
Parliament as the mood of public opinion swung. In the case of the
labour laws, the change took place in a comparatively short time,
because of the exceptional influence exercised on MPs and govern-

---

[129] Cf. McHugh, *Prostitution and Victorian Social Reform*, esp. pp. 244–63; and Walkowitz, *Prostitution and Victorian Society*, pp. 108–12.

[130] Lucy Wilson, 'The Contagious Diseases Acts', *BH*, 25 May 1872, p. 5; Josephine Butler, 'The Contagious Diseases Acts', *BH*, 6 Apr. 1872, p. 3; Id., *BH*, 18 May 1872, pp. 2–3. For the links between this campaign and the wider issues of women's emancipation, see Kent, *Sex and Suffrage*.

[131] Of particular interest on the reform of the Labour Laws is a leading article in the *Daily News* of 1868, published on the eve of the elections, already containing all the arguments which would eventually be used by the various TUC spokesmen between 1871 and 1875:

> We want no special legislation for Trade Unions, except so far as these unions are subject to special disabilities. It is not class legislation, but the abolition of class distinctions as grounds of legal difference between persons and organizations, which will characterize the legislation of the future. Working men do not want to be legislated for as working men, but as British subjects and citizens. Any contracts between them which the law may enforce it must equally enforce between other persons, and any combinations it may forbid must be equally forbidden to all ranks in the social order. [l.a., n.t.], *DN*, 27 Oct. 1868, p. 4.

[132] Cf. St John Packe, *Mill*, pp. 437, 501–3.

[133] See section 4 of the present chapter, and especially pp. 173–8.

ments by the strong and well-organized trade union lobby. This transformation was also facilitated by the fact that industrial relations between 1871 and 1874 had been relatively peaceful.[134] In the case of the CDA the abolitionist lobby was much weaker, and, since these laws did not have any national application, it was more difficult to whip up popular support. Finally, the question of venereal diseases and the best way to cure them was not only an issue of civil liberty, but also a 'technical' question, on which the medical profession had an important say. But the latter was hopelessly divided, and this further contributed towards confusing public opinion.

As the campaigns against these forms of State intervention could be quite comfortably fought under the colours of Liberalism, they had the effect of strengthening the links between popular radicalism and the Liberal party. The repealers of the CDA were predominantly Liberal, and it was Gladstone's third government which accepted their claims in 1886. But even the 1875 labour laws were interpreted as an instance of the Conservatives' acknowledgement that the 'forward march' of Liberalism had not been checked by their 1874 'Beer and Bible' victory: while the working-class press gave credit to the Liberals and the Radicals,[135] Disraeli was treated with undeserved contempt.[136] The *Bee-Hive* even went as far as publishing a satire on the cynical opportunism alleged to be the real motivation behind his and Cross' acceptance of the reforms.[137]

The realignment of the labour movement with the Liberal party did not follow the 1875 Acts, but preceded them. More precisely, at no stage did organized labour waver in its allegiance to liberalism as a set of values. And though in the early 1870s

---

[134] *Royal Commission on the Working of the Criminal Law Amendment Act, PP* 1874, XXIV, q. 469.

[135] F. Harrison, 'Frederic Harrison on the Labour Bills', *BH*, 3 July 1875, pp. 2–3. See also [l.a.], 'The Labour Law Bills', *BH*, 24 July 1875, p. 10; F. Harrison, 'The New Labour Bills', *BH*, 7 Aug. 1875, p. 1; [l.a.], 'The New Labour and the Parliamentary Committee', *BH*, 4 Sept. 1875, pp. 2–3; and the message of thanks sent by Broadhurst, on behalf of the Parliamentary Committee, to Mundella, quoted in Armytage, *Mundella*, p. 152. This interpretation was obviously strengthened by the fact that it was the Liberals who extended the benefits of the new legislation to the seamen, in 1880: a measure then judged as especially generous since 'the seamen were practically voteless' (T. Burt, 'The Merchant Seamen Act', *NW*, 21 Aug. 1880, p. 4).

[136] G. Howell to J. Fitzpatrick, 19 March 1875, in *G. Howell Coll.*, Letter Bks. 686.

[137] 'The Labour Laws. An Unreported Scene in the House', *BH*, 24 July 1875, pp. 6–7. The article was not signed but the author was G. Howell: see the original MS in *G. Howell Coll.*, Letter Bks. 738–744. About this attitude see Smith, *Disraelian Conservatism*, p. 261.

criticism of the Gladstone government was often expressed in bitter tones, this happened only because the trade unions – like Chamberlain, the Nonconformists and other components of the Liberal alliance – were over-confident about the strength of the Radicals within both the Parliamentary party and the electorate. When the 1874 elections brought sudden disillusionment, even the most influential labour spokesmen answered with a renewed commitment to Gladstonianism. In the aftermath of 1874, Howell – who had played a crucial role in the campaign against the CLAA – declared that, in spite of the 'wreck' of the 'Liberal ship', 'the rank-and-file will not leave her even should the Captain desert his post'.[138] And in June 1874 Lloyd Jones – one of the most independent labour journalists – in answering Gladstone's reprimand of a group of miners who tried to enforce a 'closed shop', used tones of great respect and showed admiration and even veneration for the former Liberal leader.[139] Certainly in that period the Liberals did not go out of their way to please the trade unions, as confirmed by John Bright's unfortunate remark about the workers' organization being a form of 'protectionism'; yet, if these allegations were much resented, they only provoked renewed protests of the workers' loyalty to liberalism and free trade.[140] When, at the end of the 1875 parliamentary session, the Queen's Speech offered the opportunity to assess Disraeli's achievements – including the recently passed Labour Laws – the *Bee-Hive* was surprisingly critical.[141] By 1880 any trace of gratitude to the Conservatives had completely disappeared: Thomas Burt, addressing his Morpeth electors, seemed to have no doubt that the 'two or three good laws' passed by the government in seven years were actually the product of the efforts of the Radicals, and had been passed by parliament in spite of, rather than because of, the Beaconsfield government.[142] It was not

---

[138] [MS of a post electoral speech, n. d. but early Feb. 1874], in *G. Howell Coll.*, 5, 360.

[139] In the case of the attempt of the miners of Aston Hall Colliery to impose the closed shop: Lloyd Jones – though trying to defend the miners – made it clear that 'We entirely agree with Mr. Gladstone as to the right of individual action on the part of the working men out of the union', and that this, rather than the closed shop, was the foundation of the action of trade unions ('Mr. Gladstone on Trade Unionism', *BH*, 20 June 1874, p. 1). On the incident, see Matthew (ed.), *Diaries*, VIII, p. 499 and footnotes 7 and 10.

[140] Lloyd Jones, 'John Bright on Trades Unions', *BH*, 8 May 1875, pp. 3–4 and 15 May 1875, pp. 2–3.

[141] [L.a.], 'Great Statesmanship', *BH*, 21 Aug. 1875, pp. 10–1.

[142] [Rep.], 'General Election. Morpeth', *NW*, 27 March 1880, p. 5; the point of view of the Durham miners was analogous: W. Crawford, 'The Conservative Working Man', in *Durham Miners' Association Circular*, 1880, pp. 444–456 D/DMA 7.

a fair assessment, but it was indicative of the mood of the working-class electorate, as would be revealed in the forthcoming elections.

'EXCEPTIONS TO THE RULE' OF *LAISSEZ-FAIRE*: FACTORY LEGISLATION

The labour laws provide a good illustration of how liberal doctrines could be used to forward trade union interests. But a defence of civil liberties was not all that Liberalism had to offer to organized workers. On the contrary, without disclaiming any of their avowed 'sound economic' principles, labour leaders could argue in favour of considerable central and local government intervention, and claim 'special legislation' in certain fields, while pressing for more *laissez-faire* in others.

Sometimes what organized labour demanded was public action to enforce the market's 'normal' operation, or even to 'liberate' it from institutional or customary fetters. The main example of this is provided by the campaign for the abolition of the so-called 'truck' system. In some regions and trades a substantial part of the weekly wage was paid not in cash, but in goods, purchase 'orders' or 'tickets' in company shops, or even loans, 'advance notes', and other devices which disrupted the regularity of weekly income, and tended to cause improvidence, accumulated debt, and increasing dependence on the employer. The system had been declared illegal by a special law in 1831, but in many regions it had survived.[143] In 1871 a Royal Commission revealed that it was still rooted in some industries in the west of Scotland, Wales, the west of England, and the Midlands.[144] Considerable injustice was involved, and in some cases the workers – heavily indebted to their companies – turned out to have been reduced to a condition of semi-slavery.[145] Though the Commission managed to examine many witnesses, including 194 workers and 31 workers' wives, many others were afraid to give evidence, knowing that they would probably be sacked in retaliation, and become 'marked men' in the eyes of all the other employers in the neighbourhood as well:[146] appropriately enough,

---

[143] See the evidence given by Alexander McDonald, *Royal Commission on the Trade Unions*, PP 1867-8, xxxix, qq. 15,526–15, 544 (29 Apr. 1868).
[144] See *Report of the Commissioners appointed to Inquire into the Truck System*, PP 1871, xxxvi, pp. v, xxv, xxx.
[145] *Ibid.*, pp. xi–xii.
[146] *Ibid.*, p. xxxii.

Alexander McDonald described the 'truck system' as the employers' 'absolute despotism'.[147] Men like the miner Thomas Price – who had resolutely faced the agents and managers of his company and forced them to pay his wages regularly and in cash[148] – personified the ideal of economic liberalism; the fact that there were so few of them confirmed that only in exceptional cases was a working man able to have the law enforced. What the Commissioners found was that the intimidatory practices of many 'truck' employers prevented the majority of the working men both from resisting such injustices, and from suing their 'masters' on the basis of the 1831 Act.[149]

Not surprisingly, the TUC expressed its 'abhorrence' at the revelations of the Royal Commission. The only way to eradicate the truck system was to make it legally compulsory for employers to pay wages in cash and at regular intervals. This proposal, embodied in the TUC request,[150] coincided in essence with the *Recommendations* of the Royal Commission. Accordingly, the Home Secretary Bruce presented a Bill enacting 'that wages shall be paid weekly, without deductions'; inspectors of mines, factories and workshops would be responsible for the enforcement of the law.[151] Though this proposal was supported by the unions,[152] it was not allowed to reach the Statute Book without important amendments, particularly a series of exceptions to compulsory cash payment.[153]

[147] *PP* 1871, xxxvi, A. McDonald (5 Sept. 1870), and in particular q. 8684. See also [l.a.], 'The Truck System', *NW*, 17 Aug. 1878, p. 4.
[148] Cf. the evidence he gave on 3 Oct. 1870, and in particular qq. 25,506–518 and 25,602–604, in *PP*, 1871, xxxvi.
[149] *Report on . . . the Truck System*, p. xx. See the evidence given by J. Gilliver, miner, 3 Jan. 1871, q. 36,200; and T. Connor, labourer, (3 Jan. 1871), qq. 36,255–237.
[150] See the two resolutions from Kane-McDonald, both unanimously approved, in the 'Minutes of the Trades Union Congress of 1871, 5th day, March 3rd, 1871', p. 35, MS in *TUC PC*.
[151] *Hansard PD*, 3rd Series, 1872, ccx, col. 220 (18 March 1872).
[152] See the text of the Bill in *PP* 1873, iii, Public Bills 3, pp. 13–22. For comments by some of the spokesmen of the trade unions, see *A Memorial to the Right Honourable Henry Austin Bruce*, circular signed by 11 of the members of the Parliamentary Committee of the TUC, n. d., in *TUC PC*.
[153] Namely: 1) school fees; 2) rents; 3) loans and advance payments; 4) medicines; 5) 'fuel, materials, tools, implements, hay, corn, provender or victuals', provided that the sums deducted 'do not exceed the real and true value of the articles so supplied to or consumed by the workman'. Moreover it was agreed that the law should not deprive 'a master who sells goods manufactured or adapted for sale by such a master to a workman, for the use of the workman or his family, at a price not exceeding the real and true value of such goods, of any right to sue for any sum due to him in respect of such goods, or prevent the payment of wages to such workmen on the premises of the master on which such goods are sold. (*PP* 1872, iii, Public Bills 3, pp. 25–6).

The workers immediately complained that these exceptions rendered the Bill ineffective and easy to evade.[154] Yet the problem posed by the 'truck system' was more complicated than had at first appeared. On the one hand, the government was reluctant to interfere further with the freedom of contract of workers all over the country in order to find a fully satisfactory remedy to a question which concerned only a minority in certain regions. On the other hand, the working classes were increasingly well organized and able to look after themselves, and, as they often claimed, did not need government patronage;[155] in fact, the Royal Commission had shown that wherever the workers were strongly unionized, the 1831 Truck Act could be applied and was effective.[156] Another aspect which the government had to take into consideration was the fact that, in some cases, particular local conditions or generous paternalistic employers actually rendered the 'truck system' advantageous to the workers, who in one instance asked that it should be continued.[157]

As far as the present study is concerned, the importance of this discussion is that it shows that the differences between the government and the TUC were not over the principles of State intervention, but over the evaluation of specific cases. This was not only because in the case of 'truck' the workers stood for the 'free market' and tried to have it imposed on reluctant employers. It was also because some public regulation of the market was recommended by the economists. J. S. Mill – whose name 'stood for political economy'[158] – had listed a series of important 'exceptions to the rule' of *laissez-faire*: these included education,[159] poor relief, hospi-

[154] A. A. Walton, 'The Truck Act and Wages Bill', *BH* 31 May 1872, pp. 2–3.
[155] See the report in *TUC PC* of a meeting between a TUC delegation and Bruce, which took place on 13 June 1872.
[156] See *Royal Commission on the Truck System, PP*, 1871, xxxvi, the evidence given by John Price, Secretary to the Nailmakers Association, South Staffordshire (4 Jan. 1871), qq. 37,546–553; D. Sandford, former Secretary of the Anti-truck Association 4 Jan. 1871, qq. 37,649–656.
[157] See in *ibid.*, the evidence given by J. Brogden, employer, qq. 43,466–467; qq. 43,529–530; and J. Smith publican (3 Jan. 1871), q. 37,393, p. 1014.
[158] Clapham, *Free Trade and Steel*, p. 390. Admiration for Mill was widespread among the working classes, many of whom regarded him as 'the masterly thinker – the chief political economist of the day' ([l.a.], 'Artisan Electors and Representatives', *NW*, 21 Apr. 1866, p. 4). For Mill's popularity, see De Marchi, 'The Success of Mill's *Principles of Political Economy*', pp. 119–57; and Biagini, 'British Trades' Unions', pp. 811–40. On the general problem, see Brebner, 'Laissez-faire and State Intervention', pp. 59–73; Robbins, *Theory of Economic Policy*, pp. 89–92, 101–3.
[159] Mill, *Principles of Political Economy*, in *Coll. Works*, iii, 2, pp. 947–50.

tals and other public services, the limitation of the hours of labour, and the regulation of conditions of work.[160] Not only did these 'exceptions' cover factory legislation, but also, freely interpreted, provided Radicals like Chamberlain with arguments justifying their 'municipal socialist' experiments.[161] In 1868 Mill went beyond his classical analysis when he recommended land nationalization in Ireland. Not surprisingly, this generated much polemic and discussion, as the proposal was questionable not only from a political but also from an economic and methodological point of view. But when Robert Lowe – the sternest defender of *laissez-faire* – criticized Mill's audacity as economically heretical, Mill replied that legislation should not be bound by dogma since economic analysis did not provide any 'set of maxims and rules, to be applied without regard to times, places and circumstances'.[162] This reply contributed towards establishing the important methodological criterion of the non-normative character of economics, which was to become very influential with economists of younger generations.[163] In fact, for years to come Mill's hegemony was such that whoever wanted to attack public intervention started from the 'exceptions' laid down in his *Principles*.[164] But apart from a few critics, contemporary thinkers and economists followed in Mill's footsteps, and even surpassed him in interventionist zeal.[165] Thus, as had happened previously in the debates on trade unions and the co-operative movement,[166] the alteration of perspective caused by Mill's influence was deep, far-reaching, and – as Clapham observed – 'far more effective in keeping men's minds open to possibilities of social change than any socialist dogmatics'.[167]

---

[160] *Ibid.*, pp. 950–71; for a discussion of this issue, see Petrella, 'Individual, Group, or Government?', pp. 157–65.

[161] Gulley, *Chamberlain and English Social Politics*, p. 44.

[162] *Hansard PD*, 3rd Series, cxc, 1525–26 (12 Mar. 1868).

[163] See A. Marshall's famous 1874 articles in the *Bee Hive*, now republished by R. Harrison in Wood (ed.), *Alfred Marshall, Critical Assessments*, iv, pp. 119–31; see also Jevons, *The State in Relation to Labour* (1882), p. 9.

[164] See [Anon.], 'Popular Fallacies Concerning the Function of Government', *Westminster Review* (1877), pp. 332–33.

[165] See Sidgwick, *Principles of Political Economy* (1883), pp. 420, 426; Keynes, *End of Laissez-Faire*, p. 26; Hay, *Origins*, p. 34. For a working-class appreciation of some of these developments, see [l.a.], 'The People's Political Economy', *Co-operative News*, 3 Oct. 1885, pp. 908–9.

[166] On Mill's contribution to Victorian trade unionism, cf. Biagini, 'British Trade Unions and Popular Political Economy', esp. pp. 814–7, 820–2; for his intervention in the debate on the co-operative movement see above, section 1 of this chapter.

[167] Clapham, *Free Trade and Steel*, p. 482.

Besides there was the fact that economists as well as politicians operated under the influence of strong moral and religious convictions: *laissez-faire* was qualified in practice by the Christian concern to preserve the life, health and morality of the workers.[168] Whatever the logic of the economic 'laws', politicians were always aware that behind *homo œconomicus* were real people with flesh, blood and soul: in many cases the *economic* justification for certain kinds of State intervention was questionable, but intervention was nevertheless accepted on *moral* grounds.[169] Even economically orthodox politicians like Gladstone, considered moral constraints so important that, whenever necessary, they were ready to 'banish to Saturn' the logic of the economic laws.[170] Once it was admitted that the magistrate's duty was not only to punish crime, but also to prevent evil and 'discourage sin', the door was opened to a greater degree of public intervention.

This frame of mind was shared by working-class radicals.[171] They claimed that, without some legal restraint, the 'tyranny of capital' would threaten even the most elementary human rights and moral principles which should be enforced for 'the promotion of justice and of peaceable order in life'.[172] As the miner Edward Rymer put it,

If the Government is not really responsible for bad trade the Government must have some controlling power over the trading and commercial system, by which all our trade is carried on. And in so far as the Government neglects to enforce just conditions between labour and capital, and watching over the equitable distribution of wealth, then the Government must be responsible, for no other power can enforce right where wrong exists. The Corn Laws, Merchant Shipping Acts, and all other legislative enactments relating to companies, banks, railways, &c., &c., prove this to be so.[173]

---

[168] Lubenow, *Politics of Government Growth*, pp. 178–9; Armytage, *Mundella*, p. 115; contrary to what some historians seem to think, to acknowledge the influence of this factor does not necessarily imply the acceptance of 'a Tory interpretation of history' (Hart, 'Nineteenth-Century Social Reform', pp. 39–61; see also the schematic definition of Oastler and his followers as 'reactionaries' in Lubenow, *Politics of Government Growth*, pp. 52–3).

[169] Taylor, *Laissez-faire and State Intervention*, p. 44.

[170] From Gladstone's famous reply to the economist Bonamy Price who criticized the Irish Land Bill, 1881: cit. in Clapham, *Free Trade and Steel*, p. 396.

[171] Watson, *A Great Labour Leader*, p. 233; 'Burt, Thomas', in DLB, I, p. 62.

[172] Lloyd Jones, 'Working Men's Claims and Duties', *NW*, 9 Jan. 1886, p. 4; Littlejohn, 'The Tyranny of Capital', *WT*, 10 June 1883, p. 6.

[173] E. A. Rymer, *NW*, 24 Feb. 1877, p. 2.

Hence the need for comprehensive factory legislation was not presented as a form of special pleading, but rather as the extension to the working classes of rights which other categories of citizens normally enjoyed;[174] like, for instance, the right to education,[175] which could not be guaranteed without interfering with the child labour market. It was similar with other measures:

> Is a man free to commit suicide? If not he is hardly free to contract to go down into a coal pit. Talk of freedom, indeed! – why, if a man brought up as a collier refuses to go down a pit which he knows to be fiery, he starves on the ground that he will not work, and if he works he is suffocated or burnt. A puddler is perfectly free to contract to produce iron, but his freedom is to work at an occupation that tends to shorten his life; and has a man the right to enter into a contract to shorten his days? Let us go to the case of the sailors . . . They are free to contract with a shipowner, and they discover after they have contracted that the ship in which they have contracted to sail is rotten, unsound, overloaded, badly provisioned, or under the command of a tyrannical master, and their free contract is held to compel them to serve under conditions by which their lives may be sacrificed, or at least rendered miserable.[176]

On the authority of the Bible and Mill's *Principles of Political Economy*, the answer to each of these questions was an emphatic 'no'. Though there was disagreement over the specific measures which should be adopted in the various cases, the principle was clear: 'We should begin from one point – the sanctity of life'. If 'A life lost by the ignorant administration of a coal-mine [wa]s no less than a murder',[177] then the 'State-nightwatchman' should be ready to act. Thus, factory reformers and trade union leaders could claim that they demanded nothing new, nothing more than what morality, reason and the 'English constitution' commanded: in other words, they argued that factory reform – like many other Victorian

---

[174] As in the case of the extension to railwaymen of the passengers' insurance against accidents ([l.a.], 'Employers' Liability for Injuries to Workmen', *LW*, 23 Apr. 1876, p. 1); or the extension to seamen of the insurance against shipwreck which already covered the goods transported ([l.a.], 'Watching the Ministry', *LW*, 7 Feb. 1875, p. 1). An Employers' Liability Bill was passed by Gladstone's second government during its first session: see the very favourable comments by T. Burt, 'Employers' Liability', *NW*, 28 Aug. 1880, p. 4.

[175] An argument often used by the workers: see [rep.], 'Miners' Conference on Education', *LM*, 20 Oct. 1869, p. 3; [rep.], 'Important Meeting of Miners at Bolton', *LM*, 7 March 1871, p. 8.

[176] Northumbrian, 'Freedom and Tyranny of Contract', *RN*, 20 June 1875, p. 3.

[177] Gracchus, *RN*, 9 Jan. 1870, p. 3; and 'The "Right of Property" and the Right of Life', *RN*, 2 May 1870, p. 3.

reforms – was not innovative, but 'restorative'.[178] Indeed, what was at stake was one of the basic rights defended by the laws of the Kingdom, namely property: the working man's life, health, industry, and skill were 'his property', and employers should not be allowed to abuse their freedom to the extent of interfering 'with the property of others'.[179] This approach may seem old-fashioned and naïve, but was in fact directly paralleled by the line then taken by radical economists, who likewise concluded that 'When looked at from the right point of view, factory legislation confers or maintains, rather than destroys, rights and liberties'.[180] Once established, this principle could be applied to a wide range of cases. For example, defending an Act obtained by the Glasgow Corporation to prevent overcrowding, the *Newcastle Chronicle* observed that

Some people may consider the act as an invasion of the rights of property; but the rights of the individual must be sacrificed to the community – if an individual has any 'right' to let a house that is not fit for human habitation. Railway companies are required to take every care and make every provision for the safety of their passengers, and it is no greater hardship to require the owners of property to make the provisions that are absolutely necessary to the health and comfort of their tenants and the safety of the people generally. It is as wrong to let houses under unsanitary conditions as to send an unseaworthy ship on a voyage; and there can be no greater hardship in limiting the number of occupants of tenemented houses than in prescribing the number of passengers an omnibus or a passenger ship shall carry. In all these cases the public safety requires that a limit should be placed upon the cupidity or necessities of owners or occupiers.[181]

In this way, the conviction that the law should protect certain God-given rights, was gradually extended – via housing, public health, and adulteration Acts – over a much wider area; the Biblical principle that the State should restrain evil and promote good (Rom. 13:1–7) could be stretched to the point of becoming a battlecry for new generations of working-class radicals in their struggles on behalf of welfare legislation.

---

[178] See on this subject A. McDonald's speech on the Employers' Liability Bill of 1876, in *Hansard PD*, 3rd Series, ccxxxi, 1155 (24 May 1876). As always, working-class rhetoric on the 'ancient rights' could be extended indefinitely, to the extent of inviting almost socialist measures in the same breath in which theoretical socialism was rejected. See also Littlejohn, 'Home Labour and Foreign Labour', *WT*, 2 Sept. 1866, p. 6.

[179] Northumbrian, 'Wages and Markets', *RN*, 14 March 1875, p. 3.

[180] Jevons, *Methods of Social Reform* (1883), p. 178.

[181] [L.a.], 'Social Legislation', *NW*, 30 May 1868, p. 4.

Yet, especially in the case of regulation of conditions of work, the foundations and main structures of Victorian social legislation had been erected before the period studied in the present book. Many important measures were indeed passed between the 1860s and the 1880s: the 1867 Factory Acts Extension and Workshops Regulation Acts, the 1874 Factory Act (which shortened the working day of women and children), the comprehensive 1878 Factory Act, to mention just a few. However, they were not new in principle, but aimed rather at extending, completing and consolidating the already existing framework.[182] They were no longer considered 'romantically philanthropic' as the laws of the first half of the century had been, but rather 'were taken as a mere matter of common sense and economic prudence'.[183] Often the legislators operated along guidelines proposed by the Parliamentary Committee of the TUC.[184] And though government Bills usually did not fully satisfy the workers, in some cases they went beyond the trade unionists' basic expectations. One example of this is provided by the 1872 Mines Regulation Bill.

The original government Bill aimed – among other things – at increasing the pitmen's safety at work, and further limiting the employment of boys, by incorporating the recommendations of the TUC.[185] It was, to use Howell's words, 'first rate'; the trade union delegates were 'thoroughly satisfied with the Bill',[186] and anonymous miners wrote enthusiastic letters to their local newspapers to encourage their fellow-pitmen to support the government with the greatest energy.[187] However, the miners' spokesmen, McDonald

---

[182] Clapham, *Free Trade and Steel*, pp. 413–20.

[183] Hutchins and Harrison, *History of Factory Legislation*, p. 167.

[184] Compare the list of the laws asked for by the TUC in 1871, with the assessment of the work of the Liberal Government in 1872, respectively, in: 'The Third Annual Trades Union Congress, Portland Rooms, March 6th to 11th Inclusive 1871', pp. 1–2, MS in *TUC PC*; and Meeting of the General Committee on June 13 and 16, 1872, *ibid.*

[185] See 'Minutes of the 1871 Trades Union Congress', 3rd day 8 Mar. 1871, p. 22, resolution moved by Lloyd Jones and W. Allan and passed unanimously (MS in *TUC PC*). See Smith, *History of Elementary Education*, p. 190.

[186] G. Howell to Mr R. Byron of Sheffield, 23 Feb. 1872, in *G. Howell Coll.*, Letter Bks, 7/557. On the same day A. McDonald declared that 'the Mines Regulation Bill was an exceedingly good Bill, and that the Committee should ask for the support of the Trades Secretaries to enable the Government to pass it' (*TUC PC* Committee meeting of 23 Feb. 1872).

[187] Letter by 'End and Bord', 'Yorkshire Miners and the Mines Regulation Bill', *Leeds Evening Express*, 5 Apr. 1872, p. 2; letter by 'A Silverdale Miner', 'The Mines Regulation Bill', *BH*, 16 March 1872, p. 13.

and Halliday, in order to reduce friction with the coal-owners over the clauses substituting payment by weight for payment by measure, gave in on the clauses imposing penalties on the owners.[188] Thus the Home Secretary Bruce – caught between the pressure of the coal-owners and the unsolicited surrender of the miners' leaders – was unable to prevent his Bill from being made less effective, though he did manage to stop one of the amendments.[189] Admittedly, this incident was quite unusual, but was nevertheless indicative of the extent to which working-class liberals were able to see eye to eye with the parliamentary party, and in some cases even be more moderate. In spite of the amendments, the 1872 Mines Act was welcomed as an important improvement by the miners,[190] who, for the first time had the impression that they were considered '*human* men, whose lives and limbs are actually of importance to the State'.[191] Obviously, however, the measure did not represent a final settlement, and during the ensuing years labour spokesmen and parliamentary radicals resumed their campaign, focussing especially on the right to appoint check-weighmen and on the civil and penal liability of employers for accidents.[192]

The parliamentary and national debate on this Act, as well as on most other social measures passed during the 1870s, confirmed the existence of a broad, bi-partisan, consensus based on a blend of the precepts and 'exceptions' of classical economy with Christian moral concern.[193] Consequently many forms of social legislation

---

[188] Fisher and Smethhurst, 'War on the Law of Supply and Demand', in Harrison (ed.), *Independent Collier*, p. 132.

[189] '. . . here we find him [Bruce] fighting the battle of the miners without the support which he had a right to expect. [. . .] the miners are deeply indebted to Mr. Bruce for saving them from the results of the mistake committed by their representatives' (E. S. Beesly, 'The Mines Regulation Bill', *BH*, 6 July 1872, p. 1. See Harrison, *Before the Socialists*, pp. 296–7; and the detailed discussion in Fisher and Smethurst, '"War on the Law of Supply and Demand"', in Harrison (ed.), *Independent Collier*, pp. 130–3).

[190] T. Burt, 'The Mines Regulation Bill', *NW*, 14 Sept. 1872, p. 4. See Fisher and Smethurst, 'War on the Law of Supply and Demand', in Harrison (ed.), *Independent Collier*, p. 133; Evans, *Miners of South Wales*, p. 117.

[191] J. Holmes, 'Mines Inspection Act', *BH*, 2 March 1872, p. 3. (italics in the text).

[192] See the Lloyd Jones' resolution passed by the DMA at the 1878 gala; it was A. McDonald – one of the men responsible for the mistakes of 1872 – who stressed the necessity of prosecuting irresponsible masters as 'murderers', and compelling them 'to compensate the injured and the friends of those destroyed; O'Connor Powell and J. Cowen proposed compulsory insurance at the employers' expense. See their respective interventions in [rep.], 'Annual Demonstration of Durham Miners', *DC*, 12 July 1878, p. 6.

[193] [L.a.], 'Legislation for the Working Class', *WT*, 28 June 1874, p. 1.

began to be seen as almost purely 'technical' and virtually 'non-political', as George Howell observed as early as 1871.[194]

There were still lively controversies on important questions of detail and on the evaluation of specific issues. Such was the case with the regulation of female labour: the question was whether women should be 'let alone', being persons 'able to look after themselves', as the supporters of female emancipation maintained, standing on the high grounds of moral principle and equality before the law;[195] or whether they needed government protection more or less like children, as the trade union leaders tried to argue, combining pragmatic social reformism and 'male chauvinism'.[196] Yet, this remained a debate within liberalism: it confirmed that middle-class radicals and trade union leaders agreed on the final aims of reform, and differed only on the means of achieving them. In their controversies it is not always easy to tell who stood for the real, long-term interests of labour or democracy. However, there is little doubt that the workers' attachment to Liberalism was greatly encouraged by the economists' sincere concern for the claims of labour.[197]

EXCEPTIONS TO THE RULE OF *LAISSEZ-FAIRE*:
POOR RELIEF, THE DRINK QUESTION, AND
'MUNICIPAL SOCIALISM'

In addition to factory legislation, there were several other areas in which government intervention was normally expected to take place. For example, while the discipline of charity and the organization of poor relief were defensible on the basis of political economy,[198] they were even more so on moral grounds: for they aimed at alleviating what contemporaries considered the consequences 'of moral evils . . . which must be resolutely grappled with by moral forces'.[199]

---

[194] G. Howell to the Editor of the *Daily News*, 'The New Social Movement', *DN*, 2 Nov. 1871, p. 6.
[195] Radical emancipation through full equality before the law was the line particularly recommended by Mill (*Principles of Political Economy*, in *Coll. Works*, III, 2, p. 953).
[196] See A. McDonald's speech in reply to H. Fawcett, in *Hansard PD*, 3rd Series, CCXIX, 1874, 1448–50; see also Smith, *Disraelian Conservatism*, pp. 213–14.
[197] See Jevons, *Methods of Social Reform* (1883), pp. 172–5.
[198] See Crouch, 'Laissez-faire in Nineteenth-Century Britain', pp. 210–11, 213.
[199] [L.a.], 'Voices from the Hive', *BH*, 26 March 1870, p. 1.

As far as poor relief was concerned, plebeian liberals were not much ahead of current legislation, and they shared the Victorian conviction that it was necessary to distinguish 'between that kind of poverty which is disgraceful, and that which deserves benevolent aid'.[200] Thus people as different as Robert Lowe and Alexander McDonald could share a genuine horror of what they saw as the 'communistic' character of the Poor Law.[201] Indeed, working-class radicals were emphatic in rejecting any system of relief which might increase the paupers' dependence on public charity: they looked forward to their ideal society of 'independent producers', and insisted that social reforms were good only if they increased the citizens' self-reliance and ability to help themselves; the State should 'educate rather than relieve the masses'.[202] Thus, though they hated the workhouse system, they seemed to have had no strategy for, and little interest in, reform.[203] What plebeian liberals demanded in practice was that workhouse inmates be treated more humanely, so that their indigence should not be further punished by persecutory public relief.[204] They supported improvements like the supply of better sanitary services,[205] the separation in different buildings of inmates by sex, age, moral character, and state of health,[206] and permission for elderly couples to live together.[207] However, these were moderate measures which did not go far beyond a more compassionate interpretation of the existing poor law.[208]

Moreover, though they asked for greater liberality towards the helpless, they tended to be particularly severe towards the 'voluntary pauper'. The latter was seen as no better than 'a thief in

---

[200] Littlejohn, 'How to Make Paupers. – A Hint for Mr. Goschen', *WT*, 13 March 1870, p. 6.

[201] See *Royal Commission on the Friendly Societies, Minutes of Evidence, PP* 1873, XXII, qq. 28,318–329 (R. Lowe, 6 March 1873); Hansard PD, CCXX, 271–2 (A. McDonald, 22 June 1874). McDonald declared that 'He, for one, looked with detestation upon the Poor Law as the edge of Communism . . .' See also the evidence given by A. McDonald to the Royal Commission on trade unions, in 1867 (*PP* 1867–8, XXXIX, 59, q. 15,744 [29 Apr. 1868]).

[202] Gracchus, 'The Cause of Commercial Depression', *RN*, 18 Jan. 1879, p. 3.

[203] Crowther, *Workhouse System*, p. 79.

[204] *Report of the 15th Trades Union Congress* (Manchester, 18–23 Sept. 1882), p. 37.

[205] Northumbrian, 'Atrocious Treatment of the Poor', *RN*, 3 Nov. 1867, p. 3; 'Side Views of Social Life – The Dispensary and Fever Hospital', *NW*, 9 Jan. 1869, p. 4.

[206] Littlejohn, 'The Workhouse System and Its Reformation', *WT*, 21 Jan. 1866, p. 6; 'WP', 'A Radical Programme', *NR*, 13 Feb. 1881, pp. 102–3.

[207] 'King of Norfolk Poachers', *I walked by Night* (1961), p. 105.

[208] See Crowther, *Workhouse System*, pp. 41–2.

disguise . . . [who] lives by wrongfully appropriating the earnings of the industrious'.[209] His problems were essentially moral, and lay in sloth, improvidence, and vice: short of 'repentance' from his 'ways of sinfulness' 'There [wa]s no hope whatever for the drunken or the idle workman. No plan for raising the condition and the wages of the labourer c[ould] apply to him'.[210] That the 'undeserving poor' were regarded more or less as criminals, helps to explain why it was readily accepted that the 'State nightwatchman' had a wide scope for direct action in the regulation of their behaviour. Indeed, as Alfred Marshall declared later in the century, there was 'a large majority among the working classes in support of a stern administration of the Poor Law in cases of all people who do not deserve well'.[211]

That 'police' control and repression of vice and immorality spearheaded the raising tide of 'collectivism' is also illustrated by the case of drink legislation. In an age when alcoholism seriously affected the common people's standards of living and health,[212] militant temperance or teetotalism were virtually a necessary article in the radicals' creed. Many of the plans then discussed involved some legal restriction and control over working-class habits and lifestyles.[213] As teetotalism was probably the most popular platform,[214] its legal enforcement through forms of 'local

---

[209] Littlejohn, 'Labour Tests and Pauperism', WT, 23 Jan. 1870, p. 6.

[210] [L.a.], *LW*, 7 Jan. 1866, p. 1; See Gilbert, *Evolution of National Insurance*, p. 21. A similar attitude had characterized some sections of the Chartist movement: Tholfsen, *Working-Class Radicalism*, p. 109.

[211] *Royal Commission on the Aged Poor*, PP, 1895, xv, q. 10,232. This conviction derived from his correspondence with Thomas Burt (A. Marshall to T. Burt, 11 May 1892; and T. Burt to A. Marshall, 14 May 1892, in *A Marshall Papers*, 1[7], as well as from his experience as a member of the 1894 Royal Commission on Labour (Pigou, 'In Memoriam', in Pigou (ed.), *Memorials of Alfred Marshall*, p. 85). Almost in the same period 'undeserving' pauperism became the object of even more repressive 'collectivist' proposals pioneered by socialists and artisans radicals alike: cf. Stedman Jones, *Outcast London*, pp. 302–14, and Haw, *Crooks* (1907), p. 246.

[212] Dingle, 'Drink and Working-Class Living Standards', pp. 621–2; Hurt, 'Drill, Discipline, and the Elementary School Ethos', in McCann (ed.), *Popular Education*, p. 198.

[213] Harrison, *Drink and the Victorians*, pp. 19, 204–5.

[214] Shiman, *Crusade against Drink*, pp. 29–30; many of the labour leaders were rigid teetotallers, including Burt, John Wilson, Burns, Mann, and Tillet: See Kent, *Burns*, p. 12; Mayor, *Churches and the Labour Movement*, p. 158. The reasons for the popularity of teetotalism were various: it was recommended by many Nonconformist bodies, it implied the assertion of one's personality through a radical commitment which reflected the strength of the temptation to drink (Shiman, *Crusade against Drink*, p. 245), and it had the effect of stimulating the formation of communities alternative to those which centred on the pub (Harrison, *Drink and the Victorians*, p. 32).

option' prohibitionism – like the Permissive Bill of the United Kingdom Alliance – were also passionately supported. 'Local option' was approved because it was democratically-managed, and had anti-aristocratic and anti-clerical implications;[215] in fact, according to this scheme, control of licensing would be taken away from the magistrates (all of whom belonged to the ruling elites and established church) and conferred on the ratepayers (among whom people belonging to the working classes were a majority).[216]

However, support for the Permissive Bill was not uniform, and indeed attitudes to it varied considerably from region to region: it was widely accepted in the north-east of England, and in Wales and Scotland,[217] wherever the workers were heavily organized and uniformly Nonconformist or Presbyterian; on the other hand, it was fiercely resisted in other parts of the country, particularly the London area, where both religion and workers' organizations were comparatively weak, and a sense of community lacking.[218] While in the north the ratepayers' majority which could impose a teetotal 'dictatorship' was likely to be controlled by the labour organizations, in the south the weaker and fragmented working classes would not be able to wrest control of local government from middle-class politicians. Perhaps in London something more democratic than Lawson's household suffrage prohibitionism was needed to attract popular interest: significantly, at one stage the *Bee-Hive* declared that it would support a Permissive Bill only if the electorate included all adult males.[219]

But in general, southern plebeian radicals were too aggressively libertarian to tolerate coercive social reform.[220] Following Mill,[221] they stressed 'science and education' in contrast to the Puritan

---

[215] Lambert, *Drink and Sobriety in Victorian Wales*, p. 169; see Harrison, *Drink and the Victorians*, pp. 29, 117–18, 198–201.

[216] See Lawson's speech in [rep.], 'Great Temperance Demonstration', *RN*, 28 Aug. 1875, p. 1.

[217] Kirk, *Working Class Reformism*, p. 202; Harrison, *Drink and the Victorians*, p. 254; Hutchinson, *A Political History of Scotland*, pp. 137–9; Smout, *A Century of the Scottish People*, pp. 141–4, 241.

[218] Davis, *Reforming London*, pp. 5.

[219] [Editor's comment to the letter by] J. R. Taylor, 'The Public Conscience and the Drink Traffic', *BH*, 21 March 1868, p. 7; about this objection to the Permissive Bill, see Harrison, *Drink and the Victorians*, p. 200.

[220] See, for a typical example, [l.a.], 'The Morality of Coercion', *RN*, 16 Apr. 1871, p. 4; see also Reid, *Social Classes and Social Relations in Britain* (forthcoming).

[221] See Mill, *On Liberty* in *Coll. Works*, XVIII, pp. 276–91.

self-policing community,[222] and they regarded prohibitionism and the other great 'cause' of the northern workers, Sabbatarianism,[223] as forms of 'tyranny' and expressions of 'religious fanaticism'. They were readier to support – as both more effective and more rational – the line of the 'counter-attractionists', who proposed the organization of alternative centres for working-class social life: an interesting experiment in this field were the 'Working Men's Clubs' of George Howell and Henry Solly.[224]

These contrasting approaches were illustrated by popular reactions to the introduction of Bruce's 1872 Licensing Bill. Apart from the fact that the principle of local option was only partly embodied in the Bill, many objected to another aspect of it, the sale of licenses by auction, because it was to the advantage of big companies and would eventually create a situation of virtual monopoly.[225] However, in contrast to what Brian Harrison has suggested,[226] the Bill was not uniformly resisted by the workers' organizations. In reality, while criticism was voiced by the radical press addressing a London or southern readership,[227] reactions in the north were very different: there Bruce's policy was comparatively popular, especially among the big trade unions in heavy industry.[228] Some leaders – like Thomas Burt of the coalminers

---

[222] Littlejohn, *WT*, 4 Oct. 1868, p. 6.

[223] [L.a.], 'Brewers and Magistrats – Publicans and the Public', *RN*, 3 Feb. 1867, p. 4; [l.a.], 'Fashionable Sabbatarians. – A Nuisance Which Ought to Be Abated', *RN*, 22 March 1868, p. 4.

[224] Littlejohn, 'The Suppression of Drunkenness and Sabbath Breaking', *WT*, 10 March 1867, p. 6;[[l.a.], 'Sunday's Beer', *LW*, 22 March 1868, 6. G. Howell to David Hack, 8 June 1868, in *G. Howell Coll.*, 9, 491. *Minutes of Evidence Relating to Friendly Societies*, PP, 1872, xxvi, H. Solly (29 June 1871), qq. 8354–8356; see also Solly, *These Eighty Years* (1893), pp. 244–57.

[225] [L.a.], 'New Government Measures', *NW*, 8 Apr. 1871, p. 4; [l.a.], 'The First Stage to Easter', *RN*, 5 Apr. 1871, p. 1. Along these lines, *Reynolds's* supported instead the old platform of 'free trade in drink': see [l.a.], 'The Monopoly of Publicans and Sinners', *RN*, 21 Apr. 1872, p. 1; [l.a.], 'Our Adulteration Government', *RN*, 3 May 1874, p. 1. On the background of 'free trade in drink', see Harrison, *Drink and the Victorians*, pp. 64–70.

[226] Harrison, *Drink and the Victorians*, pp. 268, 275–6.

[227] [L.a.], 'The Law of Liquor', *LW*, 3 Dec. 1871, p. 6; [l.a.], 'Compensation for the Officer and Confiscation for the Publican', *LW*, 7 May 1871, p. 1; see also the very positive comments on the succeeding amendments introduced Disraeli's government to relax licensing legislation: [l.a.], 'The Conservatives and the Public House', *LW*, 3 May 1874, p. 1.

[228] [L.a., n.t.], *LM*, 13 Apr. 1871, p. 5; [l.a.], 'The Licensing Bill', *BH*, 6 May 1871, p. 9; letter by 'Omicron', 'Mr. Bruce's Licensing Bill', *BH*, 6 May 1871, p. 14; [l.a., n.t.], *NW* 20 May 1871, p. 4; [l.a., n.t.], *BH*, 24 Aug, 1872, p. 4; the whole text of the Bill was published on p. 6, in six columns.

and John Kane of the ironworkers – included the Licensing and Permissive Bills in their electoral programmes, and emphasized their importance as measures of social and moral reform.[229] Reports of electoral meetings in 1874 also show evidence of militant mass commitment to temperance.[230] This posture continued to be one of the features of northern popular politics even after the Liberal defeat: then the labour stance on drink regulation became even stronger,[231] and in Parliament Cowen himself promoted a scheme of local option.[232]

The issue was so strongly felt in working-class circles, that the two Lib-lab MPs – Burt and McDonald – were ready to quarrel over it. Their respective stances reflected the division in the labour movement, and, possibly, also the difference between Burt's Methodist constituency of Morpeth, and McDonald's Stafford, where less collectivist shoemakers constituted a powerful section of the electorate.[233] For Burt local option was a question of 'confidence in and . . . respect for the working men', because of the extensive powers they would be given; in contrast, for McDonald it was a threat to the working man's freedom of choice, equivalent to 'asking Parliament to do that for the people which the people could, if they pleased, do for themselves'.[234] Both stressed the importance of workers being able to keep the situation under their own control, but disagreed on the means. In fact, this aim could be pursued either through a complete rejection of any encroachment on the life of the working-class family; or through a commitment to bringing whatever public action there was under the management of the elected representatives of the working men.

[229] Cf [rep.], 'Representation of Morpeth. – Mr. Thomas Burt at Blyth', *NC*, 14 Nov. 1873, p. 3; and one of the electoral speeches of J. Kane in [rep.], 'Middlesborough', *NW*, 31 Jan. 1874, p. 3.

[230] First and second resolutions passed by the meeting: [rep.], 'The Publicans and the Late Elections', *NW*, 31 Jan. 1874, p. 8.

[231] Cf. [l.a.], 'The Tory Licensing Bill', *NW*, 16 May 1874, p. 4; Ironside, 'Our Pot-House Parliament', *NW*, 9 May 1874, p. 4.

[232] *Hansard PD*, 3rd Series, ccxxix, cols. 848–867, (17 May 1876).

[233] Wilson, *McDonald*, pp. 148–9.

[234] For the debate McDonald-Burt, see *Hansard PD*, 3rd Series, ccxxvi, cols. 70–74 (16 June 1875). Burt also maintained that there was a close connection between, on the one hand, 'Intemperance', alcoholism, and ignorance, and, on the other, the difficulties that the labour movement was facing in its struggle to enlarge the parliamentary franchise: see Burt's speech in [rep.], 'Liberal Demonstration at Newcastle', *LM*, 20 Sept. 1875, p. 4. See for a similar debate the letters by J. Leicester of the glass-blowers, *BH*, 20 May 1871, p. 13; and by R. Hartwell, 'Teetotal Intemperance', *BH*, 3 June 1871, p. 11.

The latter approach was really acceptable only in regions where intense community life and high unionization had already accustomed the workers to forms of collective control on individual and family behaviour. But in contrast to both of these positions, working men had no trust at all either in professional bureaucrats or in ruling-elite philanthropists, an attitude also confirmed by widespread popular resistance to compulsory vaccination.[235]

The fact that property qualifications made town councils and poor law boards middle-class preserves[236] ensured that workers looked with suspicion at their activities as well. More generally, the chaotic state of the system of local government – saddled with a multitude of elective authorities with conflicting and overlapping competence and jurisdiction[237] – and the related intricacies of local taxation, were also major hindrances to social reform. Public revenue was inefficiently managed, and self-help solutions seemed at one and the same time more economic and more effective.[238]

It is true that there were cases – notably water and gas[239] – in which municipal intervention was endorsed or accepted by organized labour, because it was the only alternative to either private monopoly or total anarchy. Furthermore, in the case of services relevant to the safeguard of public health – for example, the disposal of sewage and the supply of pure water – intervention was upheld even if it took the form of State coercion of reluctant local authorities.[240] But in many other instances plebeian radicals were

---

[235] For a few examples see [rep.], 'Vaccination', *Co-operator*, 13 Feb. 1869, p. 105; and [rep.], 'Martyrs', *Co-operator and Anti-Vaccinator*, 26 June 1871, p. 387. See Pelling, *Popular Politics and Society*, p. 1; Lambert, 'State Vaccination', pp. 1–18.

[236] On this topic, see below, chapter 4, pp. 215–6, and Chapter 6, pp. 319–28.

[237] See Chalmers, *Local Government* (1883).

[238] In 1872 a contributor to the *Bee Hive* wrote that if the millions of pounds paid in poor rates were deposited in a private insurance company people would realize that the money collected 'would keep all our poor, not from starvation only, but in comparative comfort' ('Improvidence of the Working Classes', *BH*, 10 Feb. 1872, p. 3).

[239] Cf. [l.a.], 'The Water Supply', *NW*, 6 Sept. 1866, p. 4; and Neville, 'Introduction' to Rymer, 'The Martyrdom of the Mine', p. 222. But see below for an instance of popular reservations about a water municipalization project.

[240] See A. McDonald's speech on the question of water supply and the Hucknell Torkard Board, on 9 July 1875; *Hansard PD*, 3rd Series, ccxxv, 1875. This was not a particularly radical position, as it was quite similar to what *laissez-faire* reformers like Fawcett were ready to support: see Fawcett, *Labour and Wages* (1881), p. 56. For similar examples, see [l.a.], 'Gateshead and Its Corporation', *NW*, 27 Oct. 1866, p. 4; [l.a.], 'The Water Companies and the Public', *LW*, 14 Dec. 1884, p. 6. One of the most 'socialist' plebeian radical documents in our period concerned the problem of health, and was written by Littlejohn, 'Parliamentary Aid Towards Improved Labourers Dwellings', *WT*, 16 Feb. 1866, p. 6. However, this article was written in the extraordinary circumstances of a

totally unsympathetic towards excessively enterprising councils. In particular, they had no time for the aesthetic ambitions of middle-class municipalities: as one indignant ratepayer expressed himself,

They launch into extravagant schemes of so-called improvement, building themselves palatial town-halls, purchase sites for public parks at absurdly high prices, and indulge in other feats of reckless expenditure – borrow money at high rates to cover that expenditure, utterly regardless of the wants or wishes of the ratepayers, and, instead of diminishing the rates, increase them to such an extent as to rouse the hatred and hostility of the overburdened and struggling class of persons who have to pay the piper.[241]

Nor did slum clearances receive much popular sympathy, because they were seldom followed by the timely provision of a sufficient amount of cheap accommodation for the evicted proletarians.[242] Thus 'improvement schemes' might well make towns more attractive, but did not necessarily mean an 'improvement' in living standards of the poor: even the famous 1875 Artizans' Dwellings Act – which the Conservative government prepared with some Radical assistance[243] – turned out to be 'a heavy tax instead of a blessing on the working men of London'.[244] Once the old slums had disappeared, it was left to building societies and charitable trusts to provide new housing over the years: so that public intervention, rather than heralding the coming of the welfare state, constituted one of the stimuli to the extension of self-help solutions.[245]

cholera epidemic. In general, 'Littlejohn' disparaged 'State socialism' as a product of poverty and political despotism: see Littlejohn, 'The Causes and Kinds of Socialism', *WT*, 30 June 1873, p. 6; Littlejohn, 'German Socialism', *WT*, 15 May 1881, p. 6.

[241] [Letter by] G. Humphries, newspaper cutting, n. d., in *G. Howell Coll.* 'Community Env.' I have discussed in more detail the issue of local taxation reform in 'Popular Liberals and Gladstonian Finance', in Biagini and Reid (eds.), *Currents of Radicalism*, pp. 148–9, 151–5.

[242] See Wohl, *The Eternal Slum*, pp. 29, 34, 37; Stedman Jones, *Outcast London*, pp. 166–71, 188–89; Pelling, *Popular Politics*, pp. 3–4. Some of these improvement programmes provoked energetic popular reactions; in November 1872, the inhabitants of Clerkenwell met in the 'large room' of the Workmen's Club to protest against the proposed 'clearance' of a few working-class quarters to make room for the Holborn Viaduct [rep.], 'Improving Away', *TI*, 13 Nov. 1872, p. 4.

[243] Gulley, *Chamberlain and English Social Politics*, p. 54.

[244] [Rep.], 'General Election. Morpeth', *NW*, 27 Mar. 1880, p. 5. Stedman Jones, *Outcast London*, pp. 200–2.

[245] R. G. Gammage, Surgeon, 'Working Men's Dwellings' [prize essay], *NW*, 8 June 1867, p. 4. See [l.a.], *RN*, 2 Aug. 1874, p. 1: 'The Artizans' and Labourers' Dwelling Company has succeeded in doing more, without aid of legislation, than all the governments we have ever had, put together'.

But the most fundamental cause of popular hostility towards enterprising local administrations was concern about high rates: moreover, without direct representation on town councils, working-class radicals were unable to prevent municipal corporations from giving over-generous compensation to private companies.[246] Though there was a comparatively positive attitude to local, in contrast to national, taxation,[247] the fact remained that the rates were paid by the poor as well as by the rich. This meant that an increase in the rates could easily jeopardize the living standards of those families managing to keep themselves just above the level of pauperism.[248] Thus the first condition for municipal reforms to be really popular was that they were not funded out of the rates. Such was the case in Birmingham, where Chamberlain's reforms had been made possible by the profits of the municipalized gas company; in contrast, attempts to increase the rates had generated ratepayers' revolts in 1855 and 1874.[249]

However, most municipalities were less fortunate than in Birmingham: this left the radicals facing the alternative of whether to give priority to reforms or to safeguard the ratepayers' family budgets. There were two viable solutions to this deadlock. First, it was possible to ask the Exchequer for ever-increasing 'grants in aid' for local finance. Second, it was possible to pursue a complete reform of the system of local taxation. The two solutions were compatible, the former also being inevitable because of the growing complexity of the public services and the technical skills required to provide them, which meant growing co-operation and interdependence between local and central government.[250] In fact, 'grants in aid' were resorted to increasingly after the 1870 Education

---

[246] The municipalization of the Middlesborough and Stockton water company cost 'a sum of money amounting to five times the total rateable value of the property of the two towns', as the worried local radical paper pointed out: [l.a.], Middlesborough and Stockton Joint Board', *Northern Echo*, 21 Aug. 1876, 2. See also the fierce opposition of the plebeian *Leeds Evening Express* to the acquisition by the Town Council of the Quebec Building, a proposal supported by the middle-class *Leeds Mercury*: [l.a.], 'Leeds Street Decision', *Leeds Evening Express*, 29 June 1871, pp. 2–3. For the expression of similar concerns in the case of popular housing in London, see Littlejohn, 'Housing the Poor: Who is to Pay?', *WT*, 9 March 1884, p. 6.

[247] [Rep.], 'Working Men and Local Taxation' [meeting of the Labour Representation League], *BH*, 3 June 1871, p. 4, speech by Sir Henry Hoare, chairman.

[248] McCord, 'Ratepayers and Social Policy', in Thane (ed.), *Origins of British Social Policy*, pp. 24–5; Pelling, *Popular Politics*, p. 12 note 3; Crowther, *The Workhouse System*, p. 51.

[249] Hennock, 'Finance and Politics in Urban Local Government', pp. 218–21.

[250] Lambert, 'Central and Local Relations in mid-Victorian England', pp. 133–4, 148–50.

Act.[251] However, this form of State 'interference' was not always reconcilable with the widespread passion for local autonomy[252] – especially cherished by some working-class leaders[253] – and generated the fear that the increase of Exchequer grants and loans would eventually cause an increase in Imperial taxation.[254] Moreover, subsidization without reform would mean perpetuating the uncontrolled waste and inequalities by rendering them more tolerable to the local ratepayers.

A reform of the system of local taxation was much more agreeable in theory, but very difficult to pursue in practice. For one thing, as an observer wrote, 'the general public . . . regard[ed] rates as a subject of considerable mystery':[255] the technicalities of the matter were so intricate that very few plebeian radicals – and in fact few people of any class – were able to make sense of them, let alone suggest any reforms. Moreover, the problem was posed in different ways in different places. While incorporated towns had councils, the counties did not yet have elective boards, so that rate reform required a similtaneous reform of local government. In addition, London had peculiar problems: because of the lack of a central municipality and a system of equalization of the rates, there was a wide divergence of resources between authorities expected to fulfil the same statutory duties. A substantially higher rate in the pound was required to raise a given sum in a poor parish – where expenditure for poor relief etc., was also higher – than in a rich one: hence the amounts and incidence of London rates were highly regressive.[256] Another and more general problem was the distribution of the fiscal burden: the rates weighed on the occupiers rather than the owners as such, despite the fact that any improvement increased both the commercial and rateable value of the property, and benefited the owners at the expense of the tenants. Those who suffered most were 'the small struggling tradesmen . . . and others

---

[251] Page, *Local Authority Borrowing*, pp. 146–51.
[252] *Vigilance Association for the Defence of Personal Rights, Report* (1872), pp. 4–7, in Cambridge University Library, 'Secondary Material'; see Row-Fogo, *An Essay on the Reform of Local Taxation* (1902), pp. 284–5; Fraser, *Power and Authority in the Victorian City*, p. 169.
[253] Brown, *John Burns*, p. 200.
[254] [L.a.], 'Local Taxpayers' Grievances', *WT*, 30.5.1875, p. 1; [l.a.], 'The Clever Foot of Tory Taxation', *RN*, 22 April 1883, p. 1.
[255] Row-Fogo, *Essay on the Reform of Local Taxation* (1902), p. 155.
[256] 'First Report from the Select Committee on Metropolitan Government . . .', *PP*, 1866, xiii, p. xi.

who might be described as the working classes'.[257] The latter groups paid an amount of local taxation out of all proportion to their means, as the 1866 Select Committee and labour spokesmen pointed out emphatically at different stages.[258] This situation resulted in continual resistance to even necessary expenditure by the occupiers.[259] Yet proposals to increase the load of taxation on property-owners met with only marginal support,[260] because of the fear that landlords would then transfer the additional load on to their tenants by increasing their rents. Eventually, both redistribution and reform of local taxation survived well into the 1900s among the unresolved questions of radical politics.

Not only were these questions arduous to solve, but they were also difficult to argue at a popular level, and did not provide any viable focus for starting a mass agitation, because – in contrast to free trade and the 'free breakfast table' – local taxation did not involve clear-cut issues along the simple lines of 'public morality'. The question was so complicated that retrenchment – 'the greatest possible economy compatible with efficiency'[261] – remained the first concern of working-class radicals:[262] reducing public expenditure was the only readily understandable criterion of tax reform, the only 'battle-cry' to which the poorer ratepayers could rally with some enthusiasm. But even retrenchment had obvious limitations because local taxation and expenditure were necessary for

---

[257] *PP*, 1866, XIII, evidence given by Sir J. Thwaites, Chairman of the Metropolitan Board of Works (15 Mar. 1866), qq. 614–17.

[258] *Ibid.* For the complaints of organized labour, see the speech by Mr. Savage, in [rep.], 'Working Men and Local Taxation' [meeting of the Labour Representation League], *BH*, 3 June 1871, p. 4.

[259] Cf. *Royal Commission on Local taxation*, *PP*, 1899, XXXVI, qq. 20,364–80 (30 June 1898); see also *PP* 1898 LXI, qq. 1841–2 [26 Mar. 1897], and 9995–10,013 [7 Jul. 1897]; Murray, *The People's Budget*, pp. 40–3.

[260] [L.a.], 'Taking Care of the Spoons', *LW*, 30 Apr. 1876, p. 1.

[261] G. Howell, 'Ratepayers' Association Dinner, July 13th [18]69 – Toast of the Evening – "Success to the Ratepayers' Association of St Mary's Newington"'. MS, n. d., in *G. Howell Coll.*, Letter Bks, 151.

[262] See Howell's programme for a 'Ratepayers' National Protection League' (in fact, a London organization), in the late 1870s:

    1. 'Reduction of Local Taxation and consequent Relief of the Ratepayers.
    2. Revision of the incidence of Local Rating, with a view to the more equal distribution, and appointment, of its burdens, on real and personal estate.
    3. Reform in the Mode of Assessing and Levying the Local Rates.
    4. To enforce economy in administration, and expenditure, in all departments.'

Of these points, Howell expanded only on retrenchment and reduction of the rates, leaving the others as general statements. (MS in *ibid.*, 294). See also *Report of the 15th Trades Union Congress* (1882), p. 37.

funding essential social services deemed to be the specific responsibility of the municipality, rather than the State.[263] In this sense, the rates were the only tax whose practical utility was immediately and universally recognized by the poor.

The best card plebeian radicals could play was the 'Chartist' one: that was the democratization and rationalization of the whole system of local government, to give 'to any resident Householder a more direct and practical control as to the mode of levying and expending our vast local income and expenditure'.[264] Many were convinced that the problems of social reform would become less difficult once the relevant authorities were unified and democratically elected.[265] But it took a long time before popular opinion was stirred up even about this issue, because the problems of the reform of local government were different in different parts of the country. Moreover in some regions where the need for reform was greater, popular apathy was prevalent: this was the case for a long time in London, where – in spite of the report of the Select Committee of 1866 and the commitment of many Parliamentary Radicals[266] – the cause of municipal reform seemed of interest almost only to the middle classes.[267]

'EXCEPTIONS TO THE RULE' OF *LAISSEZ-FAIRE*: THE LAND QUESTION

At the end of the day, self-help remained the easiest option for social reform. However, voluntaryist remedies appeared totally inadequate to deal with the great Victorian problem of the semi-permanent unemployment of a considerable number of people. It was generally assumed that part of them – hampered by moral or

---

[263] Brown, *John Burns* (1977), p. 200.

[264] 'Report of the Sub-Committee appointed by the Financial Committee [of the Labour Representation League], at its meeting on Aug. 12th [18]75, to inquire into the Report upon the Conditions and Future Prospects of a Number of Parliamentary Boroughs to be selected by the Committee'. Labour Representation League Papers, 'Appendix', p. 26. See also the *Report of the 15th Trades Union Congress* (1882), p. 13.

[265] This was the platform of mass newspapers in London and the north: cf. [l.a.], 'Mr. Goschen's "Astounding Totals", *LW*, 9 Apr. 1871, p. 1; [l.a.], 'Local Taxation', *NW*, 4 Mar. 1871, p. 4; [l.a.], 'Local and Less Taxation', *LW*, 27 Apr. 1873, p. 1.

[266] *PP*, 1866, xii, cit., pp. xi–xii; Stedman Jones, *Outcast London*, p. 250; for a contemporary plebeian comment, see Northumbrian, 'The Equalization of the Poor Rates', *RN*, 18 Oct. 1868, p. 3.

[267] Davis, *Reforming London*, pp. 28–9, 73, 168; the equalization became a point in Will Crooks' programme in 1892: Haw, *Crooks* p. 91.

mental defects – constituted the 'residuum' of the virtually unemployable, to be dealt with through the poor law.[268] But the question was too big to be so simplistically dismissed. In particular, when cyclical trade crises generated waves of mass unemployment, great hardship was endured by hundreds of thousands who clearly were not responsible for their predicament.

In these cases local authorities and the government could resort to extraordinary public works to create temporary jobs, as happened in 1886 at the time of the 'Chamberlain circular'. Though much publicized,[269] this episode did not mark a new beginning in social welfare policies, nor was it an antecedent to the 1905 unemployment insurance Act: it was just a modest, occasional attempt to provide a palliative to an abnormal situation.[270] Similar initiatives had also been taken during previous crises from the time of the 1863 'Cotton Famine', when – with the blessing of the apostles of the 'Manchester School'[271] – Parliament had passed a Public Works Act to enable Poor Law unions to raise cheap loans.[272] From then on, this special form of public intervention was solicited to shore up emergency situations;[273] indeed, the practice was so established and 'respectable' that Henry Fawcett included it in his very conventional *Manual of Political Economy*.[274] Other devices were untried and virtually unknown, though during the 1880s the idea that the rates could be used to raise an insurance fund was circulated in extreme-left circles.[275]

Yet many believed that a permanent and virtually definitive solution to the problem of mass unemployment did exist: however, it was expected to come not from within industrialized urban

---

[268] Lynd, *England in the Eighteen-Eighties*, pp. 86–90; see also Brown, *Labour and Unemployment*, p. 13; and 'Conflict in Early British Welfare Policy', pp. 628–9; Emy, *Liberals, Radicals and Social Politics*, p. 34.

[269] Gilbert, *National Insurance in Great Britain*, p. 39.

[270] [L.a.], 'Work for the Unemployed', *LW*, 7 Feb. 1886, p. 6.

[271] Hinde, *Cobden*, pp. 312–3.

[272] Henderson, *The Lancashire Cotton Famine*, p. 67; Crowther, *The Workhouse System*, p. 63.

[273] See E. S. Beesly, 'The Social future of the Working Classes', *Fortnightly Review*, v (1869), p. 362: 'Voices from the Hive', [to Goschen, President of the Poor Law Board], *BH*, 12 March 1870, p. 1.

[274] Fawcett, *Manual of Political Economy* (1863), p. 212.

[275] See 'W. T.', 'A Radical Programme', *NR*, 20 Mar. 1881, p. 203; Annie Besant, 'A Reply', *NR*, 25 Jan. 1885, p. 55. The popularity of these proposals remained minimal until well into the new Century: Pelling, *Popular Politics and Society*, pp. 1–18; Thane, 'The Working Classes and State "Welfare"', pp. 885ff.

society, but from the countryside, through land reform.[276] In many ways this was not surprising, especially as far as working-class radicals were concerned: besides their emphasis on rural themes already discussed,[277] they had always complained that urban overcrowding and unemployment had been caused by 'landlord-ism', which had 'driven the people into the cities'. Nothing seemed more logical than to try to reverse this evil by attracting people back to the countryside.[278] Hence, the apparent paradox that land reform was seen as one of the crucial issues for the welfare of industrial workers in the most urbanized country of Europe.[279] This conviction was so widespread that at the general election of 1885 'The references of the Liberal orators to the rural land question [we]re enthusiastically received by audiences who ha[d] no direct interest therein'.[280] The enthusiasm was even greater among farm labourers, as well as among miners, potters, and other industrial workers who resided outside the main urban centres, and also had an easy access to the countryside and a certain familiarity with small-scale agriculture.[281]

Land was seen as a special case, different from other forms of property, first of all because of its limited and non-renewable character. Radicals warned of the danger of 'monopoly',[282] and their fears were increased by the results of the 1874 inquiry, which showed that a quarter of the surface of the Kingdom was owned by 1,200 people, and one half by 7,400.[283] Like other 'natural monopolies', this situation evoked demands for public control or reform of the laws which regulated property. Once more popular radicals found their most influential allies in the political econom-

---

[276] *Report of the Seventeenth Trades Union Congress* (Aberdeen, Sept. 1884), Simmons' resolution, pp. 37–8.

[277] See above chapter 1, pp. 50–60 and chapter 2, pp. 84–93.

[278] *Report of the 19th Trades Union Congress*, (Hull, November 1886), speeches by Snow (Middlesborough), and Drummond (Glasgow), p. 39.

[279] [L.a.], 'The Land Question', *NW*, 20 May 1871, p. 4; [L.a.], 'The Work of the Future', *NW*, 1 May 1880, p. 4. See Jones and Keating, *Labour and the British State*, p. 24ff.

[280] [L.a.], 'The Crofters and the Land', *LW*, 18 Oct. 1885, p. 6.

[281] Evidence given to the Royal Commission by A. McDonald in 1868 (*PP*, xxxix, 1867–68, 56–8, qq. 15,686–15,688); [rep.], 'Mr. Burt, MP, on Sliding Scales', third resolution (George Taylor), *NW*, 8 May 1880, p. 8; *Report of the 19th Trades Union Congress* (Hull, November 1886), speech by Snow, p. 39.

[282] See 'Land Monopoly', *Co-Operator*, 29 May 1869, pp. 350–1; A. A. Walton, 'Land Monopoly', *ibid.*, 7 Aug. 1869, p. 565. See also – for a later period – 'The Land Question', *The Co-operative Wholesale Society Ltd., Annual for the Year 1884*, pp. 257ff.

[283] *Returns of the Owners of Land, PP*, 1874, lxxx, parts 1, 2, 3.

ists, as their ideology was related to the Ricardian criticism of rent.[284] Paid to the landlords for the use of the soil, rent was equivalent to the profit above the market average, given by the most fertile lands as the least productive ones were brought into cultivation. Since the latter process followed the rising demands of a growing society, rent increased spontaneously, and the landlords prospered at the expense of those classes engaged in production: as Mill put it, the landlords 'grow rich in their sleep, without working, risking, or economizing'.[285] An important, very radical implication was that – since work was the source of the right to property – such a right could hardly be extended to rent, or even to land itself. Arguably, if private ownership of land was legitimate at all, any right to it depended on whether its productivity was increased by the landlord through investment of work and capital. In fact, in cases in which such investment did not take place, Mill asserted that the State could even expropriate the land, with due compensation, and dispose of it in such a way as to increase agricultural productivity: as already mentioned, in 1868 he recommended that the British government should do this in the case of Ireland[286] – a proposal which was then seen as less revolutionary than we might expect.[287]

Against this background the popularity of proposals of 'home colonization' and the fact that they were not considered especially alarming or revolutionary, becomes more easily understandable. 'Home colonization' implied that 'waste lands' – that is, lands which were 'permitted to lie either waste or reserved for the exclusive use of the landed aristocracy' as hunting grounds – should be 'brought into profitable cultivation'.[288] In order to carry out this 'reclamation', the supporters of 'home colonization' were

---

[284] For the importance for both earlier and later land reform movements of Ricardo's criticism of rent, see Thornton, *A Plea for Peasant Proprietors*, (1848); and Collier, 'Henry George's System', p. 70.

[285] Mill, *Principles*, in *Coll. Works*, II, 2, pp. 819–20.

[286] Cf. Mill, *England and Ireland* (1868), pp. 37–41.

[287] For the impact of this essay on the contemporary debate, see Steele, 'John Stuart Mill and the Irish Question', pp. 419–50; and Vogel, 'The Land Question', pp. 106–36. Land nationalization had been recommended by Herbert Spencer in *Social Statics* in 1851 (Burrow, 'The Village Community', in McKendrick (ed.), *Historical Perspectives*, p. 256).

[288] Northumbrian. 'Have We a Surplus Population?', *RN*, 16 Jan. 1870, p. 3; this request was consistently advanced throughout the period: see [rep.], 'New Herrington' [Durham Miners' Lodge: lecture on the 'Land Question' by Mr Tweedle of Gateshead], *NR*, 25 Jan. 1880, p. 63; 'A Trade Union Official', in 'The Ideas of the New Electors', *Fortnightly Review* (1885), p. 156.

ready to warrant State direct intervention on an unprecedented scale: for example, the anti-socialist Cobdenite George Howell suggested to Gladstone that the whole enterprise be funded by the government;[289] Bradlaugh, Labouchere, Arch and Burt – all of them also very hostile to socialism – proposed that persons holding more than 100 acres of land in waste condition were to be judged 'guilty of misdemeanor and thereby ejected' with compensation.[290] In fact, more or less radical plans of 'home colonization' were supported and cherished by all sorts of people, from *laissez-faire* political economists like Fawcett,[291] to trade union leaders,[292] and even some of the very poor, like the members of the London 'Unemployed Labour League'.[293]

However, 'home colonization' was to be just a step in the right direction, since all radicals agreed that what was really needed was a comprehensive reform of the laws regulating the ownership of land. J. S. Mill was one of the most active supporters of this approach. Since he thought that it was possible to distinguish – within the return of land – between rent properly speaking, and the profit from capital improvements, he proposed to tax the former as an 'unearned increment'.[294] This platform inspired many radicals. In particular, it was further developed by a man of working-class origins, Alfred Walton,[295] whose proposals are interesting as an anticipation of Henry George's 'Single Tax' programme. Walton proposed the complete 'nationalization' of rent through taxation:

---

[289] W. E. Gladstone to G. Howell, *N. D. 1. 1871* [n.d., January 1871?], *Gladstone Papers*, 44432, f. 210–1. Gladstone thought that the proposal 'would end in failure as to its immediate objects' and would cause a too heavy 'addition to the public burden'.

[290] *Bradlaugh Papers*, item 1243; the proposal is dated 22 Jan. 1886, the period in which Gladstone prepared his Irish Land Purchase Bill.

[291] Fawcett, *Economic Position of the British Labourer* (1865), p. 55; Fawcett's opinions were discussed and endorsed by T. J. Dunning in *BH*, 16 Jan. 1869, p. 1.

[292] See the resolution moved by Walton and Allan, *TUC, PC*, Business Committee 1871, p. 45.

[293] [Rep.], 'The Unemployed Poor League', *BH*, 17 Oct. 1868, p. 1: the meeting – which drew 'a large audience' – asked that Parliament set up 'a self supporting system of home colonisation . . . in the cultivation of well selected waste lands, for all the unemployed and able-bodied poor'. The speaker was a man who – as he said – had been unemployed for five months.

[294] Mill, *Principles, in Coll. Works*, II, 2, pp. 819–22.

[295] On Walton – a builder, then architect, active in free trade and labour campaigns – see Anderton, *Thesis*, p. 106. For his political activities as a Lib-Lab candidate to parliament, see below, chapter 6, pp. 343–4.

Let any man picture to himself the immense benefits that would be conferred upon all nations by the enormous revenues derived from land ... being diffused among the different populations. For instance, the whole of the taxation of the country would then be taken from the land, which would be the only rent payable by the tenants to the State, inasmuch as there would be no landlords either to claim or receive rents when the land became public property. Every nation adopting this principle would then be able to abolish all customs and excise duties, and a genuine free trade might then be everywhere proclaimed as the true commercial code of all the civilised nations of the earth.[296]

Thus, the landed elites would be made to pay for a great economic and social reform: taxation of rent would complete the work begun in 1846 with the repeal of the Corn Laws, and deliver the country from the persistent effects of the 'Norman Yoke'. Walton's plan differed from Mill's project for Ireland, because, as he wrote, 'while Mr. Mill proposes to make the compulsory sale of land in favour of the present tenantry, I propose that the purchase shall be made on behalf of the nation'.[297] It is noteworthy that by 'nation' he meant the workers, capitalist employers, and urban consumers in general.

It was a bold scheme, but did not find great support at the time. Most labour leaders were much more moderate. Old T. J. Dunning – 'the authoritative voice of the Trades Union oligarchy'[298] – regarded land nationalization as a nightmare, leading to an economically inefficient and politically dangerous government monopoly.[299] Instead, he proposed the abolition of primogeniture and the laws of settlement and entail – the basic requests of Mill's Land Tenure Reform Association[300] – in order to liberalize the market and allow the gradual transfer of land from the idle to the industrious, from large landowners to independent yeomen. Most other 'labour intellectuals' – including Howell, Potter, and Odger

---

[296] A. A. Walton, 'The Land Question', *BH*, 5 Sept. 1868, p. 4. He had presented part of his proposals in a letter to the *Bee Hive* the year before (28 Sept. 1867, p. 7). See also A. A. Walton, 'The Land Question', *BH*, 3 Oct. 1869, p. 7.

[297] A. A. Walton, *BH*, 20 June 1868, p. 7.

[298] Harrison, *Before the Socialists*, p. 233.

[299] T. J. Dunning, 'Land Tenure and the Principle of Exchange', *BH*, 13 Nov. 1869, p. 7. That nationalized enterprises could be politically dangerous was a recurrent theme in Victorian labour anti-socialism: see Reid, 'Robert Knight', in Biagini and Reid (eds.), *Currents of Radicalism*, pp. 214–43.

[300] J. S. Mill, *'Land Tenure Reform Association'. Copy of the Resolutions submitted and agreed to Aug. 7th 1869* in *G. Howell Coll.* (Howell's materials for a history of the Land Tenure Ref. Ass.).

– also remained close to this model.[301] Its popularity was increased by the fact that it had long been recommended by charismatic leaders such as John Bright and Ernest Jones,[302] and was supposed to have been successfully operated in Prussia from the 1800s by Stein and Hardenberg, the liberal ministers who had become almost legendary among British plebeian radicals.[303] The only alternative to individual peasant property was in fact, not nationalization, but – as Mill had suggested[304] – co-operative ownership. The interest in the latter was further revived by the contemporary eulogies of the mythical 'village communities' of the ancient Germans,[305] reviewed by the *Bee-Hive* as a model of liberal and democratic social organization, a form of primitive, 'freedom-loving', co-operative farming.[306]

But whether they desired individual or co-operative peasant proprietorship, most leading plebeian radicals – including Walton[307] – as well as the mass-circulation radical newspapers,[308] gravitated towards Mill as their mentor, and tended to support the Land Tenure Reform Association.[309] In contrast, before the 1880s the popularity and credibility of the more collectivist proposals was limited: even in the case of Ireland working-class newspapers tended to support Bright's old plan for the gradual formation of independent peasants.[310] More 'advanced' proposals were debated

---

[301] See Odger, 'The Land Question', *Contemporary Review*, XVIII (1871), pp. 23–42.

[302] *The Co-operator*, April 1864, pp. 164–5.

[303] See [l.a., n.t.], *LM*, 1 Nov. 1867, 2; [l.a.], 'Landed Tenure – Tenant Farmers versus landed proprietors', *RN*, 29 Sept. 1867; A. A. Walton, 'Strike among the Agricultural Labourers of Warwickshire', *BH*, 6 Apr. 1871, pp. 3–4; [l.a.], 'Stein and the Prussian Land Reform', *NW*, 11 Oct. 1879, p. 4.

[304] Mill, 'Professor Leslie on the Land Question', *Fortnightly Review*, VII, (1870), pp. 641–54.

[305] See Burrow, 'Village Communities', in McKendrick (ed.), *Historical Perspectives*, pp. 255–84.

[306] [L.a.], 'Land Tenure Reform', *BH*, 27 May 1871, p. 1; see also [l.a.], 'Voices from the Hive – To John Stuart Mill, Esquire', *BH*, 11 June 1870, p. 1. Co-operative farms were supported also by H. Fawcett (*Pauperism* (1871), p. 200).

[307] Walton supported the programme of the Land Tenure Reform Association as a step in the right direction: see A. A. Walton, *BH*, 3 Jun. 1871, p. 12; in the same spirit he also supported Bright's schemes for 'free trade in land' 'Mr. Bright on the Land Question', *BH*, 1 Nov. 1873, p. 3).

[308] See Littlejohn, 'Just Dealing with Land', *WT*, 16 Apr. 1871, p. 6; and [l.a.], 'The Opening of the Land Campaign', *LW*, 21 May 1871, p. 1, which represents a very interesting example of popularization of Mill's economic doctrines.

[309] G. Howell to J. S. Mill, 16 Sept. 1869, in *G. Howell Coll.*, Letter Bks, 194. Howell, Potter, and Odger had been among the Association's founding members: see Land Tenure Reform Association, Provisional Committee, leaflet in *G. Howell Coll.*

[310] See [l.a.], 'The Frightful Condition of Ireland – The Impending Insurrection', *RN*, 2 Dec.

in the most 'intellectual' of the working-class newspapers – like the *Bee-Hive* and the *National Reformer*, which aspired to offer an open forum for discussion – but did not provide inspiration for the masses. Thus, it is not surprising that such an extremist group as the Land and Labour League – which maintained that no measure short of nationalization would solve the problem[311] – always remained small, received little or no support from organized labour, and soon disappeared. In spite of Royden Harrison's spirited attempt to rescue it as the organization of 'proletarian Republicanism',[312] the League turns out to have been either indistinguishable from working-class liberalism, or much more elitist and sectarian than any of the contemporary currents of radicalism.[313] Not surprisingly it was 'ousted' by the Land Tenure Reform Association.[314]

It was not until the early 1880s that the land question really came to the forefront of mass politics – significantly, at a time when a substantial democratization of the representative system was being achieved. But in the decade which followed the labourers' 'Revolt of the Field' – that of their struggle for the franchise[315] – the stress on 'social' reform typical of the 1870s was replaced by a more traditional emphasis on 'political reform first'. Even the most radical tended to support this 'Chartist' approach, arguing that adequate social measures would become feasible only after the representative system had been completely democratized[316] and working-class MPs returned in sufficient number.[317] This also implied that, whatever change might be necessary, it should be managed 'from below', rather than administered 'from above'. And, as we have seen, such was indeed the central principle of the whole plebeian radical approach to the 'social question'.

1866; [l.a.], 'Aristocracy and the Irish Land', *RN*, 3 Oct. 1869, p. 1. In contrast the publication of Mill's clamorous essay, *England and Ireland*, did not receive much attention, apart from an unsigned review ('Mr. Mill on England and Ireland', *RN*, 23 Feb. 1868).

[311] F. Riddle, 'The Land and Labour League and Mr. John Stuart Mill', *NR*, 22 March 1873, pp. 182–3.

[312] Harrison, *Before the Socialists*, p. 215.

[313] By Harrison's own admission: *Before the Socialists*, pp. 238–9.

[314] *Ibid*, p. 243.

[315] On the labourers' role in this campaign see below, chapter 5, pp. 295–302.

[316] See letter by 'A Warwickshire Labourer', 'The Land – The Coming Republic', *RN*, 17 Nov. 1872, p. 3; speech by J. Arch in [rep.], 'Land Law Reform', *NR*, 22 Feb. 1880, p. 113; [rep.], 'Mr. Burt, MP. On Sliding scales', 3rd resolution, *NW*, 8 May 1880, p. 8; letter by 'Bill Blades, Bricklayer', *RN*, 16 Jan. 1881, p. 3.

[317] See the speeches by A. A. Walton and G. Odger in [rep.], 'National Congress of Trades Unions', *LM*, 30 Aug. 1869, p. 3.

CHAPTER 4

Anti-clericalism

Religion ought to be too sacred for State patronage, and where divers religions co-exist in the same community, none should be petted and none coerced.[1]

The main feature of the agitation is the abrogation of the ecclesiastical system, which exalts or depresses men according to their religious beliefs, and compels pecuniary support for a particular sect from those who hold its tenets and ritual in utter abhorrence.[2]

EDUCATION AND HUMAN EMANCIPATION

In his reply to an employer who had charged the trade unions with training youth for crime, a shoemaker wrote: 'Let "J.W." give us good wages, and we can afford to send our children to school, and keep them from picking and stealing.'[3] Most plebeian radicals agreed with him in establishing a close connection between ignorance, crime and the 'social question';[4] uneducated people were supposed to be more vulnerable to the temptations of a criminal life, and more likely to sink into pauperism – a conviction then generally accepted, and apparently cooroborated by freshly-researched statistical evidence.[5] Educational zeal was also reinforced by the political economists' insistence on the link between mass schooling and national performance,[6] which was

[1] [L.a.], 'Priestcraft in Ireland', *WT*, 20 Oct. 1867. p.1.
[2] [L.a.], 'The General Election', *NW*, 31 Jan. 1874. p. 4.
[3] Edwin Hiley, letter to *LM*, 26 Jan. 1869, p. 7.
[4] G. Howell, 'Technical Education', MS in *G. Howell Coll.*, Letter Bks, 880; [l.a.], 'Lord Shaftesbury's Scholars', *LW*, 19 Nov. 1871, p. 6. Adams, *Free Schools of the United States* (1875), p. 250; Chamberlain, 'Free Schools', *Fortnightly review* (1875),
[5] McCann, 'Artisans and the Education Act', p. 147.
[6] Jevons, 'Inaugural Address', p. 187; Fawcett, *Pauperism*, pp. 122–63; and *Manual*, pp. 232–37; See West, 'The Role of Education', pp. 161–5. For similar opinions expressed

already being debated during the 1850s and 60s.[7] Artisan reformers shared this conviction as well, but insisted on more immediate applications: to them education seemed necessary first and foremost to the success and expansion of trade unionism, the co-operative movement and other enterprises of collective self-help.[8] Moreover, contemporary events – like the 1866 Royal Commission on trade unions – had demonstrated the importance of having highly educated leaders to speak out on behalf of the workers. Indeed, self-taught, 'organic intellectual' trade union secretaries like Thomas Burt, Alexander MacDonald and Robert Applegarth were living testimonies to the importance of education; they stood up – in the words of Alfred Marshall[9] – as a new sort of 'gentleman' whose ability, intelligence and worth commanded the admired respect of public opinion. Thus, though basic literacy was all that many working men desired or thought necessary for themselves and their children,[10] the more ambitious artisans demanded a longer and more formal education, which could be expected to provide them with the means of upward social mobility.[11] As an anonymous poet wrote.

> All are born with a right to be all that they can.
> Free to rise to the height they are fitted for, mated
> To all they can win by the full powers of man.[12]

This attitude was also encouraged by religious convictions: for those influenced by the Nonconformist tradition education was a moral duty, that of self-improvement. They believed that 'God has sent man into the world to be developed, and the more you can

in the popular press, see [l.a.], 'Ragged Schools', *NW*, 12 Oct. 1867, p. 4; [l.a.], '"Inopportune Popular education"', *LW*, 8 Dec. 1867, p. 1; [l.a.], *RN*, 12 Jun. 1870, p. 4.

[7] Cobden, *Speeches*, II (1870), p. 606; [l.a.], 'National and Technical Education', *NW*, 30 Nov. 1867, p. 4; see [l.a., n.t.], *LM* 29 Nov. 1867, p. 2. See also Jones, 'Socialization and Social Science', in McCann (ed.), *Popular Education*, p. 113; Armytage, 'The 1870 Education Act', p. 122. The military victories of the 'well educated' armies of the Union over the Confederates and of the Prussians over the Austrians were often discussed in this context: see e.g. [l.a.], *RN*, 18 Nov. 1866, p. 1.

[8] J. K. Gough, printer, to H.Solly, 17 May 1873, in *Solly Coll.*, sec. 11c, item k 97: [rep.], 'The Leeds Trades Council and the Education Bill – Speech by Mr. George Odger', *LM* 10 May 1980, p. 3.

[9] Marshall 'The Future of the Working Classes' (1873), p. 105.

[10] Hurt, *Elementary Schooling and the Working Classes*, p. 30: Silver, *English Education*, pp. 68–9.

[11] See [l.a.], 'The Right and Wrong of National Education', *RN*, 26 Dec. 1869, p. 1; 'Mid-Durham Election 1892', electoral leaflet in *J. Wilson Papers*, Durham Co. Rec. Off., 13/4.

[12] [Poem by] 'One of the People', 'To Certain Opponents of the Education of the People', *BH*, 5 Feb. 1870, p. 6.

develop him, the better he is for himself, and the better it will be for the world at large'.[13] Such an attitude was widespread especially in the northern coalfields, where Primitive Methodism had moulded the community identity of the pit villages.[14] As John Wilson – quoting Mazzini – observed,

Your liberty, your rights, your emancipation from every injustice in your social position, the task each of you is bound to fulfil on earth; all these depend upon the degree of education that you are able to attain.

Without education you are incapable of rightly choosing between good and evil; you cannot acquire a true knowledge of your rights; you cannot attain that participation in political life, without which your complete social emancipation is impossible[15]

Some artisan radicals were carried further by their enthusiasm and maintained that what was at stake was actually 'the advancement of humanity itself'.[16] To them, education was the universal panacea, leading to the formation of that active, intelligent and 'independent' citizenry[17] which – as we have seen in chapter 2 and 3 – was regarded as the essential prerequisite for both 'good government' and a successfully self-helping society. This was the heritage of Paine and Richard Carlile, which had been passed on to the Victorian generations through Lovett's brand of Chartism[18]

---

[13] [Rep.], 'The Leeds Election – . . . Liberal Meeting at the West End' [speech by Ald. Barran], *LM*, 12 Aug. 1876, p. 10.

[14] Hurt, *Elementary Schooling and the Working Classes*, p. 46.

[15] Wilson, *Memories* (1910), pp. 319–20 (a quotation from G. Mazzini, *Duties of Man* (1894), p. 83). Wilson was always very active on the issue of primary education: see his speeches in 24A and 151, 'The New Primitive Methodist Church at Amble, Opening Ceremony', in *J. Wilson Papers*, D/x, 188/12. See T. Burt's speech in [rep.], 'Mass Miners' Meeting – The Cramlington Strike', *BH*, 6 Jan, 1866.

[16] 'Report of the Conference of the Trade Delegates held in the Town Hall, Leeds, on December 2nd, 1871, called to consider the statements made by Wm. Newman, Esq., in his address to the Social Science Congress lately held in Leeds. Published by the Leeds and District Trades Council', p. 7, in *G. Howell Coll.* IV, Trades Union Congress Parliamentary Committee.

[17] Halliday, *Mill*, p. 98.

[18] See Royle, *Victorian Infidels*, pp. 32 ff., pp. 44, 128, 134; Wiener, *Lovett*, pp. 76–138, and pp. 110–11 for the influence of Mazzini. McCann has argued for a decline of popular interest in education in contrast to Chartist chiliastic expectations ('Artisans and the Education Act'. p. 149). However, he generalizes Lovett's particular strand of Chartism, forgetting that other leaders were not so enthusiastic: in fact, O'Connor and O'Brien were extremely antagonistic, thinking that that 'educationalism', like Owenism and free trade, was just a 'distraction' from the main struggle for the political Charter: (Silver, *Education and the Radicals*, p. 80). It was the latter attitude – rather than Lovett's – which appears to have no parallels among plebeian liberals: see Silver, *Popular Education*, pp. 56, 87; and *Education and the Radicals*, p. 10.

and the English 'Mazzinians'.[19] Consequently, support for education was motivated by political as well as by social considerations: 'the school house' was seen as 'the stronghold of liberty and independence, and . . . the source of all progress'.[20] Others put it even more emphatically:

In education, in light, in knowledge, in wisdom lies the watchword of the free . . . You must free men from within, ere you can free them from without: or you can only release them from an outward yoke to plunge them into the sea of their own unbridled passions, to make them slaves of their own ignorance and folly . . . To be free we must be enlightened.[21]

This mass appetite for more and better education was rendered possible by the fact that basic literacy was comparatively widespread even before the 1870 Education Act: indeed, by the late 1860s about three-quarters of all working-class adults were able to read after a fashion.[22] In spite of Lowe's rhetoric about the urgency of 'educating' the allegedly unschooled new electors, as early as 1851 there was substantial evidence that 'very few children [were] *completely* uninstructed', while 'nearly all, at some time or another of their childhood, see the inside of a schoolroom',[23] even if only to scrub its floor. This was one of the achievements of the voluntary day[24] and Sunday schools, further expressions of working-class commitment to self-help.[25] E. G. West and – especially – P. Gardner have convincingly demonstrated the importance of private working-class day schools both as a means of mass education, and as an expression of popular culture.[26] Gardner has pointed out that, from the viewpoint of working-class parents, the distinction between private and public schools was far from technical: rather, it involved important questions of control, discipline, and relation-

[19] On this group, see above chapter 1, pp. 46–50.
[20] [L.a.], 'Earl Russell and the Borough-Road School', *WT*, 16 May 1869, p. 4.
[21] Fanny H. Jennings, *BH*, 30 Sept. 1871, p. 8; See A. Holyoake, 'What Freethinkers Gain by the New Education Bill', *NR*, 28 Aug. 1870, p. 129; [l.a.], 'A Century of American Independence', *LW*, 26 Dec. 1875, p. 1; Littlejohn, 'The Tricks with Education', *WT*, 30 Jul. 1876, p. 6. See Royle, *Victorian Infidels*, p. 128; Salt, 'Isaac Ironside 1808–1870', p. 192; and Howkins, *Poor Labouring Men*, pp. 53–4.
[22] McCann, *Thesis*, p. 4; West, *Education and the State*, p. 134; Read, *England 1868–1914*, p. 94; See also McCann, 'Spitalfield 1812–1824', in McCann (ed.), *Popular Education*, p. 3.
[23] Horace Mann, cit. in Gardner, *Lost Elementary Schools*, p. 75; see also p. 85
[24] Smith, *Conflict and Compromise*, pp. 104–5.
[25] Berridge, *Thesis*, pp. 209, 364.
[26] West, *Education and the State*; and *Education and the Industrial Revolution*; Gardner, *Lost Elementary Schools*, pp. 50, 96. See also Wardle, *Education and Society*, pp. 37–81; Stephens, *Education, Literacy and Society*; Murray, *Thesis*, pp.54–60.

ship to the community;[27] popular preference for family-managed
dame schools reflected the same basic attitudes to 'independence'
and State interference, and the same 'free-trade' mentality towards
social reform as those which have been described in the preceding
two chapters. Yet, just as in the case of drink regulation and local
prohibitionism, the crucial issue was not so much government
intervention, as *who* would control and administer those institutions which affected working-class life-styles – regardless of
whether such institutions were private or public, secular or
religious.

Political control was the crucial issue. This also is illustrated by
the case of Sunday schools, which – though closely linked to church
organisations – were extremely popular, to the extent that they
reached virtually all the children of the poor[28] and exercised a
strong influence on working-class culture and politics.[29] One of the
reasons for their success was that they tended to be lay-dominated,
'local, even neighbourhood organization[s] in which a distant
authority could only play a minimal role';[30] thus, these schools
enjoyed a substantial independence whether they were within the
Establishment or outside it.[31] That local independence was a factor
in the popularity of Sunday schools is possibly also reflected in the
fact that Nonconformists were more successful than the Church,
especially in 'recruiting those untouched by organized religion' in
the new industrial towns.[32] As a result, by 1851 Dissent was the
dominating influence in the movement: though Anglicans controlled 54 per cent of all church and chapel sittings, they catered
for only 42 per cent of the children in Sunday schools.[33] Staffed by
weavers, blacksmiths, shoemakers and pitmen[34] and spreading 'the
art of community self-government',[35] Dissenting Sunday schools

[27] Gardner, *Lost Elementary Schools*, pp. 14 n, 95, 100, 157–8, 235.
[28] Laqueur, *Religion and Respectability*, pp. xi, 89. There were as many as 7,500,000 pupils in
Sunday schools in 1897: Smith, *History of English Elementary Education*, p. 220.
[29] See the evidence given by the trade unionist W. Pickard before the 1867 Royal
Commission: *PP*, 1867–1868, xxxix, 6, qq. 15,919–15921; and *G. Howell Coll.*, Letter Bk.
171.
[30] Laqueur, *Religion and Respectability*, p. 33.
[31] *Ibid.*, pp. 77–8.
[32] *Ibid.*, p. 3.
[33] *Ibid.*, pp. 43–4, 46. Of the rest, only about 2 per cent attended Roman Catholic Sunday
Schools: *ibid.* p. 48. Of the six national Sunday school organizations four were Nonconformist and one interdenominational (*ibid.*, p. 33).
[34] Bamford, *Passages*, p. 14; Laqueur, *Religion and Respectability*, pp. 3, 189, 194.
[35] Silver, *Concept of Popular Education*, p. 36.

became one of the channels through which the ethos of Nonconformity was being extended to the masses outside formal chapel
membership.[36] They had a reputation for political radicalism
which, though sometimes exaggerated by paranoic Churchmen,
was nevertheless deserved.[37] By rejecting the Church's ecclesiology
and social doctrines, and bypassing its educational institutions,
Nonconformist Sunday schools defied the Establishment in two
ways. In a militant, self-conscious form plebeian Dissenters voiced
the widespread suspicion that the aim of Anglican involvement in
popular education was not so much to instruct but to make sure
that 'the children of working people should be so educated as to
perform obediently such humble duties as may fall to their lot in
life; or, in other words, that they may order themselves reverently
before their pastor and masters'.[38] Allegedly, Anglican 'pastors'
and Tory 'masters' dreaded *real* education as conducive to

anarchy, and revolution, and confusion. Yes, for well they know that an
educated people cannot be led by the nose ... They well conceive the
influence of education in levelling social distinctions, and overthrowing
castes. They have no objection to a little learning, such as is obtained in
parish and charity schools, and which rather warps than expands the
mind. But they have every objection to an educational code which tends
to bring the common mind on an equality with their own.[39]

These opinions were strengthened by the fact that social control
was admittedly one of the main functions of the Church.[40] As
Kitson Clark has written, though the Anglican contribution to the
education of the people was very considerable, and the commitment of many clergymen complete, the problem was that the
Established Church as a whole was 'based on the principle of
inequality'.[41] This principle and its legal embodiments represented
the first targets of radical criticism. For centuries Dissent had

---

[36] McCann, *Popular Education*, p. 9; Cowherd, *Politics of English Dissent*, pp. 36ff; Mathews,
Methodism and the Education of the People, p. 52. Silver, *Concept of Popular Education*, p. 23.

[37] Silver, *Concept of Popular Education*, p. 41; and *Education and the Radicals*, p. 18; Smith,
Conflict and Compromise, p. 125; McCann, 'Spitalfield 1812–1824', in McCann (ed.),
Popular Education, p. 11; Frith, 'Elementary Education in Leeds before 1870', in *ibid.*,
p. 80; Laqueur, *Religion and Respectability*, p. 105.

[38] [L.a.], *BH*, 11 Jul. 1874, pp. 7–8; Northumbrian, 'The Tory Fear of Education', *RN* 30
Jul. 1876, p. 3; [l.a.], *BH*, 9 May 1874, p. 8. Silver, *The Education of the Poor*, p. 30; Griggs,
Trades Union Congress and the Struggle for Education, p. 85.

[39] [L.a.], *RN*, 23 Jan. 1870, p. 4.

[40] Best, *Temporal Pillars*, p. 152.

[41] Kitson Clark, *Churchmen and the Condition of England*, p. 265.

consistently voiced its opposition: now it inspired and gave lead to
a general radical upheaval which was making it clear that 'the old
hierarchy would no longer be tolerated'.[42] To the radically-minded
artisan – who was a Nonconformist either by formation or by
conviction – the reform of the school system was as much a political
as an educational issue.[43] He insisted that education should be 'the
handmaid of freedom', and that every means should be employed
to prevent it from remaining 'the servant, whether of tyranny or
superstition'[44] – both of which were allegedly embodied in the
system of Anglican schools. Thus reform was about dismantling
the ecclesiastical Establishment and its system of spiritual 'monopoly' and clerical privilege, as much as about schooling the
children of the poor.[45] Indeed, as Hurt has put it, the 1867 Reform
Act gave new urgency to the 'education question' not because the
new working-class electors had to be educated, but because 'they
wanted the same semblance of control over the nation's schools
that they now had over parliament'.[46] In this sense the establishment of a national system of education was seen as a step in the
'forward march' of democracy, and one of the top priorities on the
plebeian radical agenda in the aftermath of the general election of
1868.[47]

THE 1870 EDUCATION ACT AND ITS AFTERMATH

Thus the newly-enfranchised artisan reformers demanded not just
'education', but a specific kind of education, one which would be
emancipated from ecclesiastical control, and be managed and
administered locally in a democratic way. The radicals' models
were provided – in education as well as in politics – by the
democracies of the time: Switzerland[48] and the United States. In

---

[42] *Ibid.*
[43] Hurt, *Elementary Schooling and the Working Classes*, p. 61.
[44] [L.a.], 'The Education Conflict in America', *NW*, 9 Oct. 1875, p. 4.
[45] See Howell, *History of the Working Men's Association*, pp. 36–7, 39, 52–3; Northumbrian, *RN*, 22 Sept. 1878, p. 3; Joseph Chamberlain's programme for the Sheffield election in 1874: Briggs, 'Introduction' to Adams, *Elementary School Contest*, p. xxxvi.
[46] Hurt, *Elementary Schooling and the Working Classes*, p. 67.
[47] [Rep.], 'Barnsley Working Men's Liberal Association', *LM*, 29 Sept. 1869, p. 4; McCann, 'Artisans and the Education Act', p. 134.
[48] R. Applegarth's ideal: see his 'Education in Switzerland', *BH*, 19 Feb. 1870, pp. 12–13. Typically, Applegarth stressed that in Switzerland 'The cost of government is very moderate amongst these simple and reasonable people, one of their largest items being

particular, they admired America's 'free and common schools', where 'the son of the senator and the son of the artizan s[a]t side by side'[49] and were both taught 'a more correct knowledge of the duties belonging to them as men: a higher estimate of the dignity and rights of labour'.[50]

Though they had this general model, views were still quite confused on the practicalities of transplanting it into Britain. For example, while everybody agreed on the necessity of some public intervention,[51] opinions varied a great deal on the crucial issues of religious education, compulsion and even payment of fees.[52] Compulsion was enthusiastically supported by Applegarth and many other labour leaders[53] and 'organic intellectuals' like Lloyd Jones and George Odger;[54] but, as Hurt has written, it is very likely that such people and those who shared their views were already sending their children to school 'without intervention of any coercive agency interfering in their daily lives', and tended 'to share the middle-class attitude that compulsory education was for somebody else's children'.[55] Not surprisingly, the parents of children directly involved held different views: in fact, compulsion was stubbornly

for education, which they know is money invested well.' See also [l.a.], 'The New Swiss Constitution', *WT*, 20 Apr. 1874, p. 1. Switzerland had long been a source of inspiration to British Liberals: see Brent, *Liberal Anglican Politics*, p. 246.

[49] [L.a.], *BH*, 13 Jan. 1866; Adams, *Free Schools of the United States*, *passim*.

[50] [L.a.], 'The New Labour Movement', *BH*, 13 Jan. 1866, p. 4; [letter by] 'A Worker', *BH*, 13 Mar. 1869, p. 7. T. J. Dunning was one of the few who disagreed: in 1863 he wrote that in the United States boys grew up

Well indoctrinated as to [their] own rights, but . . . kept in ignorance of the duty of respecting the rights of others . . . As the masses, when children, condemned the authority of their parents, so, when grown up, they condemn the counsel and authority of their superiors in intellect and morals, and will have none of them. (Cit. in Harrison, *Before the Socialists*, pp. 43–4)

[51] [Rep.], 'Working Men's Opinions on Education', *BH*, 30 May 1868, p. 5. Typically, there was much concern over the fact that 'the taxes levied on the people of this country were very oppressive, and any increase of the burden would lead to great evils': the chairman of the meeting, one Gilliver, asked that education be financed through massive retrenchment in central government expenditure, in order to contain the increase in taxation. J. Collings mentioned the disendowment of the Church as a future source of income for educational purposes: 'Endowments should be dealt with, after very careful deliberation, for the good of a nation. (Hear, hear.)'

[52] See the debate at the Birmingham Trades Council in [rep.], 'Working Men's Opinions on Education', *BH*, 30 May 1868, p. 5.

[53] [Rep.], 'Working Men's Conference on Education in Leeds', *LM*, 11 Nov. 1869, 3; [l.a.], 'National Education', *NW*. 24 Jul. 1869, p. 4; McCann, 'Artisans and the Education Act', pp. 136–7, 146.

[54] See their respective speeches in [rep.], 'national Education League', *BH*, 18 Jan. 1870, p. 1.

[55] Hurt, *Elementary Schooling and the Working Classes*, p. 62.

resisted by many working-class families who objected to any interference in the artisan's private life, as well as by the multitude of those radicals – including even such an ardent educationist as William Lovett[56] – who first and foremost were concerned for the preservation of 'English ideas of Liberty'.[57]

Such hostility was reinforced by the fact that education was not free.[58] Yet, the proposed abolition of school fees was still controversial, and this represented a second area of debate. For example, a group of artisan educational reformers meeting in Leeds in 1869 were unable to agree on this question.[59] In 1868 even the *Bee Hive* – usually one of the most 'advanced' working-class newspapers and later fully committed to free education[60] – wrote that 'Nine-tenths or nineteen-twentieths of parents prefer to pay a moderate fee for the instruction of their children . . . The school-fees should be devised to press lightly, if possible, but it would be an imprudence that cannot be afforded to abandon entirely this source of revenue.'[61] On the one hand popular opposition to free education is surprising in view of the fact that as early as 1851 even stern supporters of self-help like Cobden had emphatically recommended the establishment of 'a system of schools free to all, paid by all'[62] to give 'everyone the opportunity to attend gratis'; [63]certainly any stigma of social degradation should have worn off by the late 1860s. Moreover, fees – however low – did represent a significant burden, especially for very poor parents with many children: and

[56] Old Reformer, 'Memorandum for Reformers', *BH*, 4 Jul. 1868, p. 4.

[57] See [rep.], 'Mr. Trevelyan, MP., on Elementary Education', *NW*, 2 Feb. 1867, p. 4; [l.a.], 'The Education Debate', *NW.* 9 Mar. 1872, p. 4. See Silver, *Education and the Radicals*, p. 48; Armytage, 'The 1870 Education Act', p. 128; McCann, *Thesis*, p. 40. For the persistence of this attitude to the end of the century, see Rubinstein, 'Socialization and the London School Board', in McCann (ed.), *Popular Education*, pp. 244–45.

[58] [L.a.], 'The School Board Visitor', *LW*, 27 Sept. 1874, p. 1; [l.a.], 'The Education Embroglio', *RN*, 26 Jun. 1870, p. 1.

[59] See [rep.], 'Working Men's Conference on Education in Leeds', *LM*, 11 Nov. 1869, p. 3.

[60] See [l.a.], 'The Religious Difficulty in National Education', *BH*, 10 Mar. 1870, p. 10.

[61] [L.a.] *BH*, 22 Feb. 1868, p. 4.

[62] Cobden, *Speeches* II (1870), p. 605 (speech delivered on 1 Dec. 1851).

[63] *Ibid.*, p. 580 (speech delivered on 22 Jan. 1851). On the other hand, as late as 1869 other leading radicals – like Mill and Fawcett – held 'a rather strong opinion in favour of making parents pay something for their children's education' (Mill to Fawcett, 24 Oct. 1869, in *Later Letters, Coll. Works*, XVIII, 4, p. 1658). Though it would seem that Mill had not yet fully made up his mind on the subject – as he would have liked to have kept the issue of payment of fees 'an open question' – in this letter he pointed out that opposition to gratuity had been the main reason why he had not joined the National Education League.

since the number of people belonging to this category was large, the radicals' campaign for free education in rate-supported schools was likely to be popular in the long run.[64] On the other hand, the above-mentioned reservations became more understandable when we consider the strength of working-class 'voluntaryism'. Resistance to a totally free, compulsory public education could be inspired by a wish to preserve private schools: such concern was voiced, for example, by the ironfounder D. Guile, who – speaking at a meeting in London in June 1870 – 'bore testimony to the many obligations working men were under to the voluntary system, and hoped the [1870 Education] Bill would not dry up that source of educational means'.[65] Many working-class families still preferred to send their children to these 'private' schools because they were less disciplinary than 'public' schools, very flexible in timetable and syllabus, and community-centred: parents appreciated these aspects and were willing to pay fees whenever they could afford it, even if this meant their children's schooling was intermittent.[66] They also felt a strong attachment to such institutions because they considered them 'their own' property, to be guarded jealously against any State 'interference'.[67]

In contrast to these grass-roots attitudes, by the late 1860s the most important trades unions had taken a definite stand in favour of wide-ranging public intervention: in 1869 the TUC – expressing its support for the programme of the National Education League – asked for the establishment of a 'national . . . and compulsory' school system, 'unsectarian' but not purely secular.[68] Besides the

---

[64] [L.a.], 'The weak points of the Education Bill', *NW*, 26 Feb. 1870, p. 4; Humphrey, *Applegarth* (1914), p. 225.

[65] [Rep.], 'Government Education Bill – Working Men's Meeting at Exeter Hall', *BH*, 18 Jun. 1870, p. 277.

[66] Gardner, *Lost Elementary Schools*, pp. 95, 100, 174, 235; See also pp. 157–8 for working-class dislike of drill and discipline in the much more formal board schools.

[67] Silver has observed:

So proud [. . .] were working men of their self-acquired accomplishments that there was sometimes in working class organizations an uncritical acceptance of the low level of attainment in the schools, and in fact an interpretation of it as a virtue [. . .] it was enough for schools to teach working class children the letters, the rest was best acquired independently. Working class radical resistance to middle class philanthopy, and even to middle class radicalism, led not only to an independent movement for education, but also to independent casts of mind, which saw Sunday and monitorial schools as useful preliminaries to what [Thomas] Cooper called 'larger acquirements' (Silver, *English Education*, pp. 68–9)

[68] Interventions by G. Howell, W. R. Cremer, and Mr. Connolly (London), and final resolution passed by the TUC, in *Second Annual Congress of Trades Unions*, Birmingham 23–28th August 1869, *Minutes*, p. 26.

great 'amalgamated' societies and the Dissenting miners, the
League's platform attracted the self-educated workers who provided the local (formal and informal) leadership of the labour
movement: these workers did not constitute an 'aristocracy of
labour', but a multitude of individuals who were to be found in
most factories and workshops, were looked up to by their fellow-
workers as 'scholards', and 'constantly in demand to read or write
letters, settle disputes, draw up petitions or addresses and act as
spokesman in putting forward demands or grievances to the
employer'.[69] Also, national leaders such as Howell, Lloyd Jones,
Odger and Applegarth were all committed to the League, and
some of them sat on its Executive Committee.[70] Their enthusiasm
carried many of the rank-and-file,[71] to the extent that as early as
1869 nineteen local branches of various trade unions, and sixteen
'Working Men's Auxiliaries' were affiliated to the League.[72]

Thus, though those likely to form the bulk of the activists of the
Liberal party in the constituencies were solidly behind public
intervention, working-class opinion on the whole was still divided
when W. E. Forster presented his Bill. Forster's first objective was
to cater for all unschooled (or 'improperly' schooled) children as
quickly as possible and at the lowest cost to both the taxpayer and
the various educational agencies involved in existing schools:
accordingly, the Bill aimed at integrating, rather than replacing,
the voluntary system. His second objective was to strike a balance
between the various approaches to the religious question, by
'keeping the Bible open' in the new public schools and by trying to
guarantee liberty of conscience as well.[73] The third was the
decentralization of choices and responsibilities. Forster proposed to
devolve the setting up of the new system on to local school boards by
granting them the power to raise taxes for educational purposes, and
to decide whether or not attendance should be compulsory.

This Bill produced a variety of reactions in the country and

---

[69] McCann 'Artisans and the Education Act', p. 135.
[70] G. Howell to J. Collings, Hon. Secretary of the National Education League, 23 Dec.
1869, in *G. Howell Coll.*, Letter Bk, 269; Adams, *The Elementary Education Act, 1870*, p. V;
Levanthal, *Howell*, pp. 137, 191; McCann, *Thesis*, p. 22; and 'Artisans and the Education
Act', pp. 137, 141. In addition Joseph Cowen jr. was a member of the Executive
Committee.
[71] [Rep], *BH*, 16 Oct. 1869, p. 1; [rep.], *BH*, 20 Nov. 1869, p. 1; Jones, *The Making*, p. 59;
Levanthal, *Howell*, p. 125.
[72] McCann 'Trades Unions, Artisans, and the 1870 Education Act', pp. 138–43.
[73] *Hansard PD.*, 3rd Series, cxcix, cols. 438–66. See Parry, *Democracy and Religion*, p. 296.

popular press, ranging from moderate support,[74] to outright hostility.[75] Besides, as the debate went on in Parliament and the Bill was considerably amended, opinions and positions kept changing. Yet, throughout the debate there were several issues which seemed paramount in the minds of plebeian radicals: their criticism concentrated on the clauses which, in the original Bill, provided for the appointment of school boards by town councils and vestry meetings – bodies which were still far from being fully democratic – [76] as well as on those which allowed for the funding of voluntary schools and sectarian religious instruction from the education rate,[77] seen as an attempt at establishing concurrent endowment. Not surprisingly, in the wake of the anti-clerical crusade which accompanied Irish disestablishment,[78] concern for the complete separation of State and Church was quite widespread. The strength of popular feeling was shown by the campaign of meetings – widely supported by working men[79] – organized by the National Education League throughout England and Scotland during the first six months of 1870.

When in June the Bill was amended to the effect that the denominational education should be completely separated from the board school system, and that school boards could decide whether rate-supported education would be undenominational or purely secular,[80] some of the radicals' objections were met. Yet, the government continued to fund denominational schools with an Exchequer grant (independent of the rates) which covered 50 per cent of the maintenance costs, and was a measure hardly reconcilable with anti-clerical demands. What was worse, 'clause 25' of the Bill laid down that boards could fund denominational schools by paying the school fees of needy children attending them. Inevitably, Nonconformists complained that the Bill required ratepayers to fund the 'teaching [of] the religion of some with the money raised by the taxation of all'.[81] and many compared the new school rates

---

[74] [L.a.] 'The Education Bill', *LW*, 27 Feb. 1870, p. 6; [l.a.], *RN* 13 Mar. 1870, p. 1; See Adams, *Elementary School Contest*, p. 212.

[75] [L.a.], 'The Education Bill', *BH*, 12 Mar. 1870, pp. 8–9.

[76] On the limits to popular representation on town councils, see below, chapter 6.

[77] Cruickshank, *Church and State in English Education*, p. 24.

[78] See below, section 4 of this chapter.

[79] McCann, 'Artisans and the Education Act', pp. 139–40.

[80] *Ibid.*, pp. 29–30.

[81] Morley, *The Struggle for National Education*, p. 74; poem by W. Owen, 'National Education', *BH*, 19 Mar. 1870, p. 71. Gladstone too was very worried about these aspects: see his memorandum, 'Rate Provided Schools', 29 May 1870, in *Diaries*, VII, pp. 297–98.

to the then recently-abolished compulsory Church rates.[82] Indeed the first cases of passive resistance through non-payment were celebrated as a new page in the Dissenters' martyrology.[83]

But perhaps the question on which plebeian radicals placed the greatest emphasis was whether school boards should not be appointed by the existing local authorities – as the government Bill proposed. Their view was that they should be directly elected by the ratepayers. One of the speakers at the great working men's meeting at Exeter Hall in June 1870 asked for the compulsory establishment of 'school boards . . . in every parish and district immediately after the passing of the bill', as 'our municipal and parochial institutions do not command sufficent confidence to be entrusted with the education of the people'.[84] This request – 'a vindication of the principle of self-government'[85] – implied that 'all ratepayers and heads of families [should] have the power of voting in the election of such boards, the votes being recorded by ballot'.[86] It is significant that these workers believed that – thus constituted – school boards would be democratic enough not only 'to be entrusted with the education of the people', but also to exercise the 'imperative' mandate 'to enforce the attendance of the national schools of every child who is not elsewhere receiving a satisfactory education'.[87]

Eventually – in July – the government incorporated in its proposal the principle of direct election, and indeed extended eligibility to both male and female ratepayers without any property qualification – thus making the boards the most democratic local representative assemblies in the country at the time. This development considerably increased the legitimacy of the new school authorities among working men. Moreover, the cumulative vote – by offering a sort of proportional representation to minority groups – was welcomed by Secularists, women and others who saw it as an effective guarantee that the 'intensity' of their desire to be directly represented would be taken into proper consideration.[88]

[82] Northumbrian, *RN*, 22 May 1870, p. 3.
[83] [L.a.], 'School Boards and Denominational Fees', *NW*, 30 Sept. 1871, p. 4; [rep.], 'Refusing to Pay the School Board Rate', *Potteries Examiner*, 24 Feb. 1872, p. 3. See Royle, *Victorian Infidels*, p. 267.
[84] Lucraft, chairmaker, second resolution, in [rep.], 'Working Men's Meeting at Exeter Hall', *BH*, 18 Jun. 1870, p. 277.
[85] Hales, elastic web weaver, in *ibid.*
[86] Lucraft, chairmaker, second resolution, in *ibid.*
[87] *Ibid.*
[88] *Hansard PD.*, 3rd Series, ccii cols. 1398–1425 (4 Jul. 1870). See [l.a., n.t.], *LM*, 6 Jul.

At this stage the points of the Act on which plebeian criticism focussed were the permissive character of the clause for the establishment of school boards, the weak approach to the issue of compulsory attendance, and the fact that school boards could indirectly finance denominational schools.[89] The latter was the most controversial issue. Though Applegarth maintained that the 'religious difficulty' had 'been created for and not by the working class',[90] what he really meant was that there would have been no difficulty had everybody accepted his own 'secularist' approach. However, this was not the case. The cynical indifference later paraded in *Seems So!*[91] was far from typical among working people, and there is no doubt that the question of religious education was felt as strongly by the subaltern classes as by other social groups, especially in the sectarian north-west, the Black Country, Wales, and many other areas where Dissent was particularly strong and popular.[92]

The issue was complicated by its connection with Church endowment, then passionately discussed as the radicals tried to achieve complete separation between Church and State.[93] The Church of England controlled – through various agencies – most of the existing schools, which received the bulk of the Government grants.[94] Many reformers – and especially the most radical Nonconformists – had hoped that the organization of a national system implied that public funding for denominational schools would become superfluous and so be discontinued. This would have diminished not only the Church's wealth, but also its scope

---

1870. p. 2; A. Holyoake, 'What Freethinkers gain by the new Education Bill', *NR*, 28 Aug. 1870, p. 129. For working-class support for the system of the cumulative vote, see the declarations of the miner Samuel Neil in 'Select Committee on School Board Elections', *PP*, 1884–5, xi, q. 5, 136ff., pp. 635–8.

[89] Cf. McCann, 'Artisans and the Education Act', p. 142.

[90] R. Applegarth, 'Education in Switzerland', *BH*, 19 Mar. 1870, p. 76; See [l.a.], 'The Question of Education', *NW*, 5 Nov. 1868, p. 2.

[91] Reynolds and Woolley, *Seems So!* (1911), p. 40:

> ... about the religious education difficulty we don't care two pins ... Secular education does not shock us. Differences of creed do not trouble us. What concerns us here, in a working-man's family, is how the education, to which the children are bound to submit, is going to help them to live; to earn their bread-and-cheese, and to live useful, happy, *fitty* lives.

[92] McCann, *Thesis* pp. 27, 41, 52, 57–9.

[93] See below, section 4 of the present chapter. For the strict correlation between the issues in the sources, see Derrington, *Thesis*, p. 389.

[94] Jones, *The Making*, pp. 9, 13.

and influence; and in fact, as a corollary to this, the Nonconformists assumed that they themselves would become more influential through the operation of democratically elected school boards, on which the Dissenters' numerical strength would become fully evident.[95] However, Forster's compromise and especially 'clause 25' disappointed such hopes.[96] The problem was further complicated by the fact that the 'conscience clause' – designed to protect religious minorities in denominational schools – seemed insufficient and was likely to be totally unworkable in country districts, which would still be devoid of any representative assembly, unless the establishment of school boards were rendered compulsory.[97]

Popular opposition to the religious aspect of the Education Bill was not only one more episode in the long struggle for 'civil and religious liberty'.[98] but also voiced the claim of the new electors to exercise effective political control over the way public money was spent and their children educated. They came to identify the struggle against 'sectarian' education with the parallel campaign for Church disestablishment, and indeed with the wider struggle against the 'cruel and selfish principles of feudalism, of aristocracy, of the plutocracy, of capital, and of masterdom'.[99]

This also meant that the object of their hostility was not religious teaching as such, but its manipulation as an instrument of political and social control.[100] Indeed, while all popular liberals insisted on religious liberty and equality, few went so far as to recommend that their children's education should 'exclude the Bible';[101] for instance, both at Manchester and Birmingham – strongholds of the Education Union and the Education League respectively – the Trades Councils refused to take sides and remained neutral,[102]

---

[95] Roland, *Thesis*, I, p. 36.
[96] Machin, *Politics and the Churches 1869–1921*, p. 34.
[97] [L.a.], *BH*, 12 Mar. 1870, pp. 8–9; A. A. Walton, 'The Second Session of the Reformed Parliament', *BH*, 21 Aug. 1870, p. 3. For an example of the inefficacy of the conscience clause in the rural districts, see Roland, *Thesis*, II, p. 721.
[98] [Rep.], 'The Education Question – Conference of Nonconformists' [speech by Rev. H. T. Robjohns (Congregationalist)], *NW*, 23 Apr. 1870, p. 7; [rep.], 'Mr. R. W. Dale on National Education' [final resolutions], *ibid*. See also J. S. Mill, 'The Education Bill', *Spectator*, p Apr. 1870, p. 465, now in *Coll Works*, xxv, 4, p. 1,222.
[99] Northumbrian, *RN*, 17 Jul. 1870, p. 3.
[100] H. W. Holland, 'The Education Crisis of the Country, No.1', *NW*, 9 Apr. 1870, p. 4.
[101] Reid, *Forster* (1888), pp. 489–90. See Smith, *History of English Elementary Education*, pp. 288–9; Roper, 'Forster's Memorandum', p. 70; Parry, *Democracy and Religion*, p. 304.
[102] McCann 'Artisans and the Education Act', p. 140.

while the working-men's Auxiliaries of both cities declared themselves against the exclusion of the Bible.[103] In some places, such as Salford, a strong working-class Orange faction emerged.[104] When the most radical trade unionists decided in favour of a fully secular education, they lost part of their rank-and-file support. As far as working-class liberals were concerned, a consistent criticism of the Government measure was probably developed only by the trade union leaders who belonged to the Education League.[105] By contrast, the most common attitude among less committed labour spokesmen seemed characterized by a certain confusion and readiness to change. For example, a barometer of the popular mood as *Lloyd's Weekly* initially condemned Forster's Bill and supported secular education,[106] but later switched to 'unsectarian education, "but not to the excusion of the Bible"'.[107] Then, in November 1870 the first school board elections demonstrated that the 'sectarian party' could count both on the determined support of many working-class ratepayers, and on the benevolent indifference of many others.[108] On the whole, it is likely that the *Leeds Mercury* spoke for a very large number of people of all social classes when it declared that 'We would rather that the truth of CHRIST was preached by a Baptist, a Methodist, or Churchman, than not preached at all'.[109] A similar position was eventually taken by other popular newspapers of a marked Nonconformist tradition, like the *Newcastle Chronicle*,[110] as well as by the *Bee-Hive*.[111] In the latter's

[103] *Ibid.*, p. 145.
[104] *Ibid.*, p. 141.
[105] G. Howell to Mr. Bartlett, in *G. Howell Papers*, IX Letter Bk, 350.
[106] [L.a.], 'Progress of the Education Bill', *LW*, 26 Jun. 1870, p. 6; [l.a.], 'The Secular Schoolmaster', *LW*, 19 Jul. 1870, p. 6.
[107] [L.a.], 'The London School Board Election', *LW*, 30 Oct. 1870, p. 6.
[108] H. W. Randal, 'Education', *BH*, 6 Jun. 1868, p. 7; this article was part of an exchange with 'The Raven', who in a letter had maintained the opposite thesis (see *BH*, 30 May 1868, p. 4).
[109] [L.a., n.t.], *LM*, 3 Dec. 1869, p. 2; see [l.a.], 'School Board Elections', *LW*, 20 Nov. 1870, p. 6.
[110] [L.a.], 'The Position of the Nonconformists', *NW*, 23 Apr. 1870, p. 4; H. W. Holland, 'The Educational Crisis of the Country, No.II. – The Union Speeches in Newcastle', *NW*, 16 Apr. 1870, p. 4; and 'The Education Crisis of the Country – No.4. – The Bible and the New National Schools', *NW*, 7 May 1870, p. 4. Between 1867 and 1869 the newspaper had taken different positions (cf. [l.a.], 'An Educated Democracy' *NW*, 24 Nov. 1867, p. 6; [l.a.], 'The Education Conference', *NW*, 27 Nov. 1869, p. 4). Afterwards only occasional contributors wrote in favour of a purely secular education.
[111] [L.a.], 'To Samuel Morley – The Education Bill and Social Reform', *BH*, 30 Jul. 1870,

case, by the time the Bill was passed Potter had been joined on the editorial board by Henry Solly, who – though a Unitarian minister – was sympathetic to the Forster compromise. In fact the divergence between supporters and opponents of the government measure went beyond the well-known disagreement between 'old' Dissent and Methodists: various influential Congregationalist and Baptist leaders – like Baines, Samuel Morley, and to some extent C. H. Spurgeon – were openly in favour of the Act and ready to defend it against thorough-going supporters of purely secular education.[112] Such being the case, not only did Gladstone have good reason to say in January 1870 that the Dissenters as a body had not yet made up their minds,[113] but possibly they never did, 'as a body'. It was 'unsectarian education with the open Bible' – a platform supported by moderate nonconformists like Samuel Morley and adopted by the London School Board in 1871[114] – which eventually became the most widely-accepted solution throughout the country, and one of the options preferred by working-class ratepayers. The law also gave local educational authorities the choice of offering a purely secular education in board schools, as it 'rest[ed] exclusively with the school boards to determine whether or not there [should] be any religious observance or instruction in the schools provided by them'.[115] However, as it turned out, most Nonconformist parents were in favour of 'unsectarian' religious teaching: 'practically the whole of the children attended religious instruction'.[116] The latter was provided in the great majority of board schools outside Nonconformist

p. 369; see also [l.a.], 'Letters to Statesmen. The Right Hon. W. E. Forster, M.P.', *BH*, 18 Jun. 1870, p. 273. However, the newspaper's correspondents voiced all sorts of contrasting positions: *e.g.* see the letters by L. Davies (*BH.* 16 Dec. 1874) and by 'Omicron' (*BH*, 23 Dec. 1874).

[112] See Binfield, *So Down to Prayers*, p. 90; Cruickshank, *Church and State in English Education*, p. 34 and pp. 26, 45.

[113] W. E. Gladstone to J. Bright, 27 Jan. 1870, in *Gladstone Papers*, Add. Mss. 43385, p. 241

[114] Richards, 'Religious Controversy', p. 190. For Samuel Morley's view, see Hodder, *Morley*, pp. 337–9.

[115] Owen, *The Elementary Education Act, 1870* (1871), pp. 56–7, n.3.

[116] Adams, *Elementary School Contest* (1882), p. 282; 'Select Committee on School Board Elections', *PP*, 1884–5, xi, q. 369 (evidence given by Sir Francis Sandford), p. 414; 'the parents who professed never to come to church, and did not care for religion themselves, insisted on their children having a religious education'.

Wales,[117] and even in Chamberlain's Birmingham the school board went back to Bible reading 'without note or comment' in 1879, after a six-year experiment of complete separation.[118]

In spite of its limits, the other leading features of the 1870 system – legislative decentralization, direct representation, and the fact that it was rate-funded – were much appreciated by plebeian liberals and encouraged full acceptance.[119] Moreover, the Act's effectiveness as a measure to 'carry forward popular education with rapid strides' was soon realized[120]: well before 1874 the mass press began to praise the spectacular increase in the number of pupils both in London and in major cities like Sheffield.[121] Birmingham,[122] Leeds and Manchester.[123] After a few years, the defects which at first had been bitterly criticized seemed almost forgotten even by the sternest supporters of the League.[124] Inflexible 'secular' educationalists like Frederic Harrison – whose mottoes were 'No Bible' and 'No State Religion'[125] – and labour leaders like William Owen and George Potter were equally convinced by the democracy of the new system: they insisted on the extension of the school boards to all districts, but generally accepted Bible reading and 'unsectarian' education with the 'time clause'. The latter ensured that religious instruction was given at the beginning or end of the day, so that children of Dissenter or atheist parents might avoid it by arriving later or leaving earlier.[126] No drastic modification of the Forster settlement was necessary to satisfy this group of radicals.

In fact, interest in further educational reform began to decline:

---

[117] Machin, *Politics and the Churches 1868–1921*, p. 39.

[118] Cruickshank, *Church and State in English Education*, pp. 44–5.

[119] Richards, 'Religious Controversy', p. 187, 196; Smith, *Conflict and Compromise*, p. 210.

[120] [L.a.], 'The Progress of the Education Bill', *LW*, 3 Jul. 1870, p. 6; See A. Holyoake, *NR*, 28 Aug. 1870, pp. 129–30.

[121] [L.a.], 'Mr Forster at Sheffield', *LW*, 30 Aug. 1874, p. 6.

[122] [L.a., n.t.] *MG*, 4 Nov. 1876, p. 7.

[123] [L.a., n.t.] *LM*, 28 Jun. 1873, p. 5; [rep.], 'Leeds School Board – Review of Three Years' Work', *LM*, 20 Oct. 1885, p. 3. For the official figures, see 'Select Committee on School Board Elections', *PP*, 1884–5, XI, Appendix No.2, p. 671.

[124] 'London School Board Election, 1888', by George Howell, MP., in *G.Howell Coll.*, Misc. 1888.

[125] Harrison's: F. Harrison to E. S. Beesly, n.d (but November 1870), in *Harrison Papers*, 1/16, pp. 98–101.

[126] 'London School Board. George Potter, Candidate for Westminster', poster in *John Johnson Coll.* Educational, II W. Owen, 'Burslem School Board Election. To the Ratepayers of the Parish', *Potteries Examiner*, 7 Mar. 1874, p. 4.

at the 1871 TUC, it was realised only at the eleventh hour that no paper had been prepared on the education issue,[127] and the delegates unanimously supported a hastily-framed resolution in favour of 'universal' primary education and technical schools: no mention was made of the 'religious difficulty'.[128] At the 1872 TUC a paper was duly prepared by one A.W. Bailey, but its presentation was relegated to the last day of the congress, and eventually not read for lack of time: the issue was not otherwise mentioned.[129] This evidence suggests that a majority among the subaltern classes desired only universal, cheap education, 'no matter whether it is "denominational", "unsectarian", "secular", compulsory, or voluntary, *with only one condition the election of the school boards by the people, voting equally, by ballot*'.[130] Again, more than anything else, it was the question of political control through local representative bodies which was paramount, to the extent that all the other considerations – in this case even consistency – were almost disregarded.

Thus it was not indifference, but local democracy which helped to push aside the 'religious difficulty': true to the Chartist tradition, plebeian radicals believed that democracy would sort out any problems, especially when administered by 'local option', rather than by some distrusted 'central authority'.[131] Their optimism was also encouraged by the knowledge that for the first time they had become eligible for membership of local representative bodies.[132] Soon their attention focused solely on the problem of extending the still modest school board framework throughout the country.[133] Moreover, despite the allegations of the most extreme supporters of the National Education League, the Act was also a popular

---

[127] *Ibid.*, p. 10. It must be remembered that the Trades Union Bill was then absorbing the attention of the organized workers.

[128] *The Third Annual Trades Union Congress*, London, March 6th to 11th Inclusive 1871, *minutes*, p. 43, in *G. Howell Coll.*

[129] 'Secretary's MS Notes of Proceedings of the Fourth Annual Trades Union Congress held at Nottingham, Jan. 8th, 9th, 10th, 11th, 12th, and 13th 1872', p. 9, in *ibid*; See Griggs, *The Trade Union Congress*, p. 245.

[130] [L.a.], 'The Education Embroglio', *RN*, 22 Jun. 1870, p. 1. My italics.

[131] For the popularity of the 'local option' as a general principle, see [rep.]. 'Mr Copland's Candidature'. *NW*. 17 Feb. 1883, p. 3; and (l.a.), 'The School Board Debate', *LW*. 10 Mar. 1872, p. 1.

[132] Littlejohn, 'The Working Class and the Education Board', *WT*, 2 Oct. 1870, p. 6.

[133] Ibid.; See [l.a.], 'Another Education Muddle', *LW*, 22 Jun. 1873, p. 1. At the end of 1871 more than half of the boroughs and 98 per cent of the parishes did not have a school board: Adams, *Elementary School Contest*, p. 269.

success because it preserved the denominational schools: in relation to their children's education many parents valued the possibility of choice offered by the 'dual' system of board and private schools.[134]

For all these reasons, it is likely that Forster's solution was well-suited to meeting the needs and desires of *urban* workers and their families, as well as of public opinion at large. Of course the situation with *rural* workers was different: they did not yet have the vote, and their political impotence frequently expressed itself in extreme anti-clericalism.[135] At the same time, the petty persecutions which still took place in the countryside were no longer national, but local grievances, and could thus in principle be solved by the extension of local democracy. Consequently the focus of the debate even in rural areas began to shift from the proposed reforms of the 1870 Act, to the establishment of new school boards. This still involved some difficulty, because the new Tory government was trying to prevent it, being convinced – as Lord Sandon declared – that the school boards

will produce very serious political results. They will become the favourite platform of the Dissenting preacher and local agitator, and will provide for our rural population, by means of their triennial elections and Board meetings, exactly the training in political agitation and the opportunity for political organization which the politicians of the Birmingham League desire, and which will be mischievous to the State.[136]

---

[134] 'Royal Commission on the Elementary Education Acts', *PP* 1887 xxx, qq. 898–900, p. 401 (evidence given by T. E. Powell). The number of pupils in denominational schools – including Wesleyan and British schools – kept increasing even after 1870 (Silver, *Education of the Poor*, p. 119; Sutherland, *Elementary Education*, p. 351), rising from about 1,200,000 to 2,000,000 by 1880 (Cruickshank, *Church and State in English Education*, p. 47). The competition of the public system – which in only ten years had increased so as to cater for 750,000 children – became more difficult to resist during the 1880s (Cruickshank, *Church and State in English Education*, p. 48). Yet, in the light of the above considerations, Kenneth Wald's hypothesis that the 'end' of denominational education was one of the main factors in the decline of the Liberal party (*Crosses on the Ballot*, pp. 162–254) does not look very convincing. Indeed, the Nonconformists – besides running many of their own day schools and extending their Sunday schools – were heavily involved in the school boards (Cox, *Churches in a Secular Society*, pp. 184–9). The education of children between the 1870s and the 1910s did not take place in a 'secularized' environment.

[135] See below, section 4 of the present chapter.

[136] Cit. in Smith, *Disraelian Conservatism*, p. 246. See the Tory electoral poster denouncing the school boards as instruments of state repression, cit. in [Anon.]. 'The Government and the Education Act', *Westminster Review*, (1872), pp. 167–8. For other instances of anti-board activitists, see Adams, *Elementary School Contest*, p. 309. For the bishops' opposition to the school boards in the Lords, and the branding of Nonconformity as 'heresy' in Anglican catechism, see *ibid.*, pp. 242–48.

A crucial stage in these vicissitudes was the discussion of Sandon's Education Bill of 1876. This measure represented an important step towards compulsory attendance because it provided for the needs of primary education in the rural districts. Sandon, however, did not propose to extend the school board system, but rather to confer the power of passing by-laws on borough councils and poor law boards. This aroused radical opposition on two grounds: first, the violation of the principle that the school system should be managed by directly-elected educational authorities, and second the exclusion of working people from the poor law boards and town councils by a property qualification.[137] Popular opposition became more vocal when Sandon's Bill was amended to enable local authorities to enforce compulsory attendance even when the only schools in the district were denominational, or, in other words, Anglican.[138] In this new context Forster's Act seemed much more democratic than it had done in 1870–4, and in fact came to be exalted as the bulwark of religious liberty.[139]

Thus, by 1876 popular liberals had completely re-aligned themselves on the education question. It was an important change, but had already been on its way before 1874. Traditionally, historians have maintained that radical opposition to the Forster Act was one of the causes of the Liberal defeat in February 1874.[140] Undoubtedly there was such opposition, and it involved working-men too; this was especially evident at Bradford, a Nonconformist stronghold and Forster's own constituency,[141] and even elsewhere the mass press accused him of having 'treacherously' re-enacted the 'vicious ecclesiasticism' of 'the old heathenish principle of compulsory contribution to religion'.[142] More generally, the success of the

---

[137] On the attitudes of working-class liberals to the reform of local government, see below chapter 6, pp. 319–28.
[138] 'Meeting of General Council, 21 Apr. 1874', *Labour Representation League Papers*, p. 87; Northumbrian, '"Society" and the Workers', *RN*, 3 Dec. 1876, p. 3.
[139] 'The Government Education Bill, Resolutions to be submitted to the conference at Canon Street, 19 Jun. 1876', in *Labour Representation League Papers*, p. 179. Cf. 'Meeting of General Council', 4 Aug. 1876, *ibid.*, p. 199; [l.a.], 'Mr Pell's Amendment', *LW*, 30 Jul. 1876. p. 1; [l.a.], 'The Tory Hatred of School Boards', *WT*, 28 May 1876, p. 6; Ironside, 'The Reactionary Policy of the Government', *NW*, 5 Aug. 1876, p. 4; [l.a., n.t.] *DN*, 21 Jul. 1876, p. 5. See also Adams, *Elementary School Contest*, p. 312.
[140] Machin, *Politics and the Churches 1868–1921*, pp. 40, 61–8.
[141] [Rep.], 'Mr Forster at Bradford'. *LM* 27 Jan. 1874, p. 8; [rep.], 'Mr Burt on Mr. Gladstone's Retirement', *NW*, 30 Jan. 1875, p. 5; [rep.], 'Mr. Forster at Bradford', *LM* 27 Jan. 1874, p. 8.
[142] [L.a.], 'The General Election', *NW*, 31 Jan. 1874, p. 4; See McCann, *Thesis*, pp. 74–5.

Conference of Nonconformist Committees and the National Education League in obtaining from 300 of the 425 Liberal candidates a promise to vote for the repeal of 'clause 25',[143] suggests that the League was still a powerful political influence. However, popular support for it had already considerably declined from the peak of 1870–1: by the end of the summer of 1872 the situation was so unpromising that the League discontinued its contacts with the trade unions.[144] Not only did working men no longer respond to the agitators' appeals in the way they once had done, but occasionally were even positively opposed to secular education, as Thomas Burt discovered when addressing his constituents at Morpeth in November 1873. On that occasion he was hissed when maintaining that 'the State should have nothing to do with the teaching of religion in any shape';[145] a minor incident, but nevertheless a significant one, because usually Burt was immensely popular in his constituency.[146]

In the light of this substantial acceptance of Forster's system, even the most extreme anti-clerical radicals eventually had to revise their positions. In 1877 the *Weekly Times* admitted:

The general rule is found to be, that parents neither desire the exclusion of religious teaching, nor object to the form in which it is usually given in Board Schools, or, where there are no Board Schools, in those of the various denominations, if they have any choice. Where theological quarrels are rife, the School Boards have, in some cases, enforced a very strict neutrality in religious teaching . . . but the most common plan is to leave the teachers a good deal of liberty in explaining Bible passages.[147]

Plebeian anti-clericalism was far from vanishing, as illustrated by the bitter controversies at election times and the continuous clashes between 'unsectarians' and Churchmen.[148] Yet school boards had deflated these conflicts politically by institutionalizing the procedure by which one policy or the other would prevail: Forster had devised a system whereby religious disputes over

---

[143] [Rep.], 'The Nonconformists and the General Election', *LM*, 26 Jan. 1874, p. 8; See [rep.], 'National Education League – Great Meeting in Newcastle', *NC*, 31 Jan. 1873, p. 7.

[144] McCann, *Thesis*, pp. 77–81; Balfour, *Chamberlain*, pp. 86–7; Judd, *Radical Joe*, pp. 72–3.

[145] [Rep.], 'Representation of Morpeth – Mr. Burt at Blyth', *NW*, 14 Nov. 1873, p. 3.

[146] For Burt's popularity, see below, chapter 6, pp. 347–51.

[147] Littlejohn, 'The Work of the School Boards', *WT*, 30 Dec. 1877, p. 6.

[148] Cruickshank, *Church and State in English Education*, pp. 46–7.

primary education could be accommodated at the local level,[149] rather than being turned into major contentions in national politics. Once again the ballot box effectively controlled political conflict. During the rest of the century 'sectarian' strife continued to characterize school elections,[150] but these formalized confrontations contributed towards satisfying the radicals' hatred for 'clericalism-Toryism' without upsetting the stability of the system.[151]

In fact, it was only as a result of the lesson of the polling-booth that the anti-clericals became aware that their political position was weaker than they had expected. Between 1870 and 1873 Nonconformist irritation had been exacerbated by the unexpected success of the Church party at the first school board elections,[152] when tactical mistakes under the new system of the 'cumulative vote' had led to the defeat of the 'unsectarians' in heavily Nonconformist areas like Birmingham, Newport and Merthyr Tydfil. At the succeeding elections, in 1873, these results were partly reversed,[153] and Chamberlain in particular triumphed at Birmingham, where he emerged both as mayor and president of the new school board. But while on the one hand these successes encouraged a more positive appraisal of the system,[154] on the other, many elections confirmed the popularity of religious education, as the 'unsectarian' party met with bitter disappointment in relation to important boards like London and Manchester.[155] Thus, on the whole there was no alternative but to accept that the elections had provided a fair test 'of what each party has of power'.[156] Once the radicals realized the modesty of the level of electoral support which

---

[149] See 'Select Committee on School Board Elections', *PP.*, 1884–5, XI, qq. 6, 7, 8 (evidence given by Sir Francis Sandford), p. 399.

[150] [Rep.], 'East Leeds – Mr. Lawrence Gane's Candidature – Open-Air Liberal Meeting' (speech by Mr Crawford), *LM*, 23 Nov. 1885, p. 7.

[151] See [Rep.], 'Tower Hamlets Radical Club and Institute Union' (lecture by G. Hales on 'The Aims and Objects of the Working Classes'). *NR*, 12 Nov. 1876, p. 317; letter by W. Tomaling, *RN*, 8 Nov. 1874, p. 3; Ironside, 'School Board Contests'. *NW*, 13 Jan. 1877, p. 4; [l.a.]. 'The National School Board Victory and What it Means'. *NW*, 27 Jan. 1877, p. 4.

[152] [L.a.], 'The Education Question', *NW*, 30 Jan. 1872, p. 4.

[153] Parry, *Democracy and Religion*, p. 398; Machin, *Politics and the Churches 1868–1921*, p. 38.

[154] See [l.a.], 'The National School Board Victory and What it Means', *NW*, 27 Jan. 1877, p. 4.

[155] See *Nonconformist*: 19 Nov. 1873, p. 1,155; 26 Nov. 1873, pp. 1,172–3; 3 Dec. 1873, pp. 1,189–90, 1,196; and Derrington, *Thesis*, p. 396.

[156] In the words of W. E. Forster: 'Select Committee on School Board Elections', *PP.*, 1884–5, XI q. 435.

they enjoyed, their militancy – previously stimulated by the impression that they were being defrauded of some of their due – declined. The 1873 school elections were thus a powerful call to political realism. In the summer of that year the League suspended its agitation against the government[157]: by then it was also evident that it would be easier to obtain further reforms by supporting a Liberal government, than by letting in a Conservative one,[158] and indeed when the general elections took place the regions where Nonconformity was strongest remained loyally Liberal.[159]

Another factor which encouraged acceptance was that, though by 1880 only about one third of the children went to board-controlled schools,[160] the latter were at first concentrated in urban centres: thus the effects of the Act were immediately felt in those districts where opposition to the Church was most powerful and better organized, and thus were marginally greater – from a political viewpoint – than the actual provision of school places would suggest.

As years went by it became increasingly clear that the Forster system was really popular. Working-class radicals valued the possibility of exercising political and financial control over education, as Thomas Smyth – plasterer and member of the London Trades Council – told the 1887 Royal Commissions: 'We pay for them', he said, 'and we feel that we have a right to them: and that they are partly our own'.[161] Thomas Powell – trade unionist, school board visitor, and father of 11 children, who gave evidence after Smyth – made a similar point and stressed that 'as the school board system continues it will be possible to create a still larger and more vivid interest on the part of the mass of the working population in the schools'.[162] Moreover, the fact that working-class

---

[157] McCann, *Thesis, p. 81;* Balfour, *Chamberlain,* pp. 86–7.

[158] [L]et us ask whether they [the Dissenters] are more likely to get either the repeal of this clause or the separation of Church and State from Mr. DISRAELI than from Mr. GLADSTONE. To suppose they can hesitate in the answer to such a question would be to insult alike their common sense and their virtue. From the Tories they can have nothing to hope for: from an enlightened Liberal Ministry with a powerful majority in the Lower House they can have no good grounds for despondency. The same argument may be urged on the supporters of the Permissive Bill, and also on those who urge the repeal of the Contageous Disease Acts. ([L.a.], 'The General Election', *NW,* 31 Jan. 1874, p. 4)

[159] Parry, *Democracy and Religion,* p. 398.

[160] Cruickshank, *Church and State in English Education,* p. 47.

[161] 'Second Report of the Royal Commision Appointed to Enquire into the Working of the Elementary Education Acts, England and Wales', *PP.,* 1887, xxx, q. 52,251, p. 379; cf. q. 52,613, p. 392.

[162] *Ibid.,* qq. 52,990–2, p. 403.

people felt that no charity or poor relief was involved in rate-supported schools encouraged further experiments in public intervention: as Annie Besant wrote in 1885, defending the abolition of fees and the provision of free meals at school, 'Nothing paid for out of rates is "given" to the ratepayers. It is paid for by them . . . Individual charity pauperises; the administering of the national fund for the national benefit does not'.[163]

Eventually, most plebeian liberals came to agree with the *Leeds Mercury*, which from 1870 had commented that the Education Act had 'excited much stronger opposition than it deserved'.[164] From the late 1870s, as growing numbers of working men's candidates began to be returned to school boards in spite of various difficulties,[165] opposition was limited to those families who resented compulsion and the policing of their lives it involved.[166] Forster's work was then given a honourable place among the Liberal triumphs of the century: it had been 'one of the earliest fruits of the Reform Bill of 1867', 'Ironside' declared in 1879; and he went on to say that 'If the Tories had been as powerful then as they are now, not one of the magnificent schools which have since been raised in all parts of the country would have been erected'. He admitted that it had been wise of Gladstone and Forster to reject the radicals' request to postpone the settlement of the question until public opinion 'matured':

As one of those who advocated this course, I am constrained to confess now that the postponement would have been a great mistake. Such a Bill as Mr. Forster's, if the work had to be done again, would not have the smallest chance of success in the present Parliament. It is only fair to admit, too, that the cause of education has received an immense impetus from the elaborate and comprehensive scheme which was adopted in 1870. School Boards have been formed in hundreds of towns and parishes where formerly the instruction of the children of the poor was left to mere accident . . . In fact, an almost perfect network of educational machinery has been spread over England . . . Ignorance was once the reproach of our country. That approach will soon no longer have been even a shadow of justice.[167]

---

[163] A. Besant, 'A Reply', *NR*, 25 Jan. 1885, p. 55.

[164] [L.a., n.t.], *LM*, 11 Aug. 1870, p. 5.

[165] *Ibid.*, pp. 86–9. Though Hurt places a great emphasis on the obstacles to working-class direct representation, especially in the 1870s, the fact remains that school boards were the most open elective assembly in the country: see below, chapter 6, p. 321.

[166] Hurt, *Elementary Schooling and the Working Classes*, pp. 82–3.

[167] Ironside, 'Tories and Education', *NW*, 14 Jun. 1879, p. 4; See [letter by] J. Lucas, 'Education', *NW*, 17 Jul. 1875, p. 4.

This remained the prevailing popular attitude to the Forster's system till its dismantling in 1902, which Labour and Liberal working men did their best to prevent[168] and which greatly revived the struggle between clericals and anti-clericals. By then even the agricultural labourers had reason to call the 1870 Act 'a priceless blessing';[169] the case of James Hawker, the Leicestershire poacher who at the end of the century was twice returned to his village school board, where he sat next to the 'Leading Gentlemen' on whose lands he poached,[170] seems well suited to illustrate the revolution which the extension of school boards had eventually brought about throughout the country.

THE DYNAMIC OF POPULAR-LIBERAL ANTI-CLERICALISM

Behind the 'religious difficulty' in education there stood the wider problem of the Established Church's legal claim to the monopoly of moral and spiritual authority, also involving the control of various forms of legitimate power. It was, again, a struggle about political control, involving two distinct general issues: that of the link between Church and State, and that of the relationship between ministers and laity, both within the Church itself and within the national community at large. Leaving the former question to the next section of the present chapter, let us now examine the latter one.

In sacerdotal religions – such as Roman Catholicism and High-Church Anglicanism – the ministers were members of a clerical order set apart from the congregations and appointed to be mediators between God and man. Theirs was a role to which some authoritarianism was intrinsic, and inevitably generated the hostility of the political left, both in Britain and on the continent.[171]

---

[168] Munson, 'London School Board Election of 1894', P.18; Griggs, 'Labour and Education', in Brown (ed.), *First Labour Party*, pp. 158–9; McCann, *Thesis*, pp. 342–4, 406–20; For contemporary views see Northumbrian, 'Popular Education', *RN*, 14 Sept. 1902, p. 1; Evans, *Price of Priestcraft* (1904), 155ff.

[169] Arch, *The Story of His Life* (1898), p. 246.

[170] Hawker, *Journal* (1961), pp. 94–5.

[171] McLeod, *Religion and the People*, pp. 130. For polemics against 'le joug du despotisme sacerdotale' in France, see Guerin, *La lutte de classe*, i, pp. 294ff., and Gadille, 'French Anticlericalism', pp. 128–9. In Britain this factor might have influenced the widespread popular liberal hostility towards Anglican ritualism: [l.a., n.t.], *LM*, 10 Nov. 1866, p. 2; See [l.a.], 'The Liberal Programme – Mr. Fawcett at Brighton', *WT*, 29 Jan. 1871, p. 1; [rep.], 'Ritualism in Lambeth', *BH*, 28 Mar. 1868, p. 1. For the importance of anti-ritualism as a political issue, see Machin, *Politics and the Churches 1868–1921*, p. 62.

However, while in continental countries – where there was no easily-accessible Christian alternative to the established churches – anti-clericalism tended to be free-thinking or atheistic, in Britain the churches closer to the tradition of the Reformation were able to take the lead in the anti-clerical protest,[172] and indeed – as Royle has demonstrated[173] – to influence even militant freethinkers. This could happen because Reformed denominations did not have either a sacerdotal theology or a powerful, hierachically organized clergy.

This contrast is underlined by the fact that anti-clericalism was much less pronounced in Scotland, where the Presbyterian Establishment allowed for a wider diffusion of power, and limited the ministers' role and authority. It is significant that the legitimacy and hegemony of the Auld Kirk was never really questioned in principle, not even during the Disruption crisis: it was rather the links between the Kirk and the *social and political* establishment – the issue of patronage of ecclesiastical appointments – which came under heavy criticism. Thus, while in the rest of the United Kingdom the question of disestablishment presented itself as a struggle against the supremacy of the Anglican Church, in Scotland it took the form of the issue of the Kirk's supremacy and independence from the civil authorities.[174]

South of the border, the Nonconformist churches were also virtually invulnerable to anti-clerical hostility. It could hardly have been otherwise since they did not have a real 'clergy': indeed the notion of universal priesthood was so solidly established that it would be more correct to say that the contrast between clergy and laity was absent not because there were no clergy, but because there were no laity. Some denominations – like the Primitive Methodists and the Plymouth Brethren – had very few or no full-time ministers at all. Others had pastors who did most of the preaching but were not in control of the congregations: on the contrary, it was the congregations – through their elders and general assemblies – who controlled their ministers' appointment,

---

[172] Evans, 'The Church in Danger?' p. 202. It is important to remember that Calvinist or 'fundamentalist' denominations played a similar role in continental countries as well: see, for the Italian case, Camaiani, 'Valori religiosi', pp. 232–41; and Hollenweger, *The Pentecostals*, pp. 252–66.

[173] Royle, *Radicals, Secularists and Republicans*, pp. 138–9.

[174] Machin, *Politics and the Churches in Britain 1832–1868*, pp. 112–47.

salary, tenure and dismissal.[175] Moreover, ministers and congregations were on a level of substantial equality even from the point of view of intellectual and cultural background, since pastors often had little or no formal education, and were just gifted churchmembers trained in the pulpit by other, more experienced churchmembers.[176] This was possible because the theology of the Dissenting denominations was simple, based on the Bible as the only source of authority, and on private analysis and judgement as the only method of study. In this way, a democratic form of church government was supplemented – as Barrow has written about another group of radical common people – by 'a democratic definition of knowledge', 'one . . . in which knowledge should be accessible' to all.[177]

But possibly the crucial factor was that the criteria of membership in Nonconformist churches were radically different from those of the Church of England: while the latter was a territorial church, and in theory included all English, Welsh and Irish citizens, independent of their religious opinions, the Dissenters formed churches of 'believers only', that is of 'volunteers'. Thus, *as churches* they did not claim any authority over secular society – though their members, *as citizens*, might aspire to impose some form of moral control on non-believers through the ordinary workings of democracy, as in the case of 'local option' prohibitionism in the drink trade. On the whole, the authority of the Nonconformist bodies depended on their moral prestige and force of persuasion, and as such was not as politically objectionable as the authority of the Established Church, which depended on the law of the country giving a privileged position to its bishops, clergy, and schoolteachers. This difference was but a further application of their respective and opposite epistemological stances: the Nonconformist one, that the truth was enshrined in the Scriptures and open to public enquiry through trial and error, and the Established Church's one, that emphasized – alongside the Scriptures – the role of the

---

[175] Possibly it is significant that the Chartist programme for the reform of the Church of England included – besides disestablishment and disendowment – that 'All ecclesiastics to be appointed in any way their respective congregations think fit, and to be paid voluntarily by the congregations that employ their services' (Faulkner, *Chartism and the Churches*, p. 35).

[176] Brown, *Nonconformist Ministry*, pp. 56–123.

[177] Barrow, *Independent Spirits*, p. 147.

traditions of the Church itself, the liturgy, and the leadership of the clergy.[178]

In this respect the contrast between Dissent and the Church was so complete that it was actually similar to the conflict between secular anti-clericalism and the established churches on the continent. Indeed, the greatest issue in English and Welsh anti-clericalism was the struggle for 'civil and religious liberty' for all non-Anglicans, including atheists. To some extent this liberty had long been achieved, but it had never been completely secured.[179] The Dissenters feared that there could be little room for real toleration so long as Anglicanism was part of the constitution itself[180] – as the existence of such a relationship implied that, in spite of toleration, Dissent and atheism were somehow treacherous and 'anti-constitutional'. In fact, the potential threat for religious liberty involved by the doctrine of the confessional State still materialized in specific instances, the most famous of which was the Bradlaugh case in the 1880s.

This question had a 'prehistory' which went back to 1868, when the atheist Charles Bradlaugh had unsuccessfully stood as a Parliamentary candidate for the borough of Northampton, provoking an upsurge of religious indignation. On that occasion intolerance had been so general that even J. S. Mill – who had endorsed Bradlaugh's candidature – was electorally damaged by the support he had given to 'the infidel': a factor which might have had some influence in his defeat at Westminster.[181] After several other attempts Bradlaugh was finally returned in 1880, only to discover that his atheism was still an obstacle to his admission to the House, as he was not allowed to take the oath. He appealed, protested, and was ejected from Parliament. This was not the end, however, but the beginning, as his cause resulted in a large-scale agitation throughout the country. Working-class radicals were outraged at

---

[178] This consideration did not apply to Evangelical Anglicans, whose theology was much closer to that of the more radical Reformed denominations. But it was the Anglican Church as a national institution – rather than specific clergymen and congregations – which attracted criticism.

[179] Addison, *Religious Equality in Modern England*; Royle, *Radicals, Secularists, and Republicans*, pp. 304–5; Machin, *Politics and the Churches 1868–1921*, p. 130.

[180] Best, 'Religious Difficulty in National Education', p. 162; and *Temporal Pillars*, p. 72; Kitson Clark, *Churchmen and the Condition of England*, pp. 24–5, 27.

[181] Mill, *Autobiography*, in *Coll. Works*, I, p. 289; St John Packe, *Mill*, pp. 474–6; Even a radical working-class newspaper like the *Bee-Hive* criticized Mill for his support of Bradlaugh: [l.a.], 21 Nov. 1868, p. 1.

this attack on 'civil and religious liberty', and – as they had done a few years before in the case of the 'Tichborne claimant'[182] – demanded 'fair play'. Soon a major campaign had begun. The workers supported Bradlaugh both because he was a very popular radical politician – a speaker in great demand at labour meetings[183] – and because many had the impression that the House was trying to impose strict religious standards that might also be applied to exclude working men's MPs in the future[184]: as 'Ironside' commented, the Establishment at that time seemed to imply that 'Those who believe certain doctrines, or profess to believe them . . . set up their doctrines as a test of admission to the Legislature – nay, as tests of other men's honour and integrity'.[185] Soon many trade unions – especially those of the miners[186] – and other working-class organizations joined in the fight, and all over the country radical clubs and associations held special meetings to condemn the behaviour of the House and claim the right of the constituencies to return whatever candidate they preferred[187] – as in the days of John Wilkes – against blatant attempts by 'London' to control 'local democracy'. In 1882 and 1883 demonstrations with thousands of participants – including corporate delegations from many labour associations[188] – were held in Leeds, Stockton, and Halifax, as well as in London, in Hyde Park and Trafalgar Square.[189] The agitation even involved some communities in the British colonies, where democratic societies were set up to defend

[182] See McWilliam, 'The Tichborne Case and the Politics of Fair Play', in Biagini and Reid (eds.), *Currents of Radicalism*, pp. 44–63.

[183] See below, pp. 358–9.

[184] [Rep.], 'Northampton's Constitutional Struggle' [declaration of the Boro' of Hackney Workmen's Club], *NR*, 11 Feb. 1883, p. 88.

[185] Ironside, 'Mr Bradlaugh and the Oath Question'. *NW*, 26 Jun. 1880, p. 4.

[186] E.g. *NR*, 15 May 1881, pp. 397–8, reports of meetings at Birmingham, and demonstrations by the Rossendale Union of Liberal Clubs, the North Yorkshire and Cleveland Miners' Association, the Southwark Club and Association. See also [rep.], 'Auckland Park Colliery', *NR*, 14 Aug. 1881, p. 174; [rep.], 'Constitutional Rights' Defence. St. James' Hall Demonstration' [speech by T. Burt], *NR*, 5 Aug. 1883, p. 84; [rep., n.t.], [mass meeting of the Forest of Dean miners], *NR*, 18 Feb. 1883, p. 104.

[187] [Rep.], '[Meeting at] Jarrow', *NR*, 4 Jul. 1880, p. 46. See Ironside, 'Bradlaugh and Liberty', *NW*, 3 Jul. 1880, p. 4; [l.a.], 'Mr Bradlaugh and the House of Commons', *NW*, ' Aug. 1881, p. 4. See [rep.], 'Lambeth Democratic Association' [lecture by W. Hasker, 'John Wilkes, Bradlaugh and Liberty'], *NR*, 14 Aug. 1881, p. 174.

[188] [Rep.], 'Trafalgar Square', *NR* 25 Feb. 1883, pp. 116–17 ['National Demonstration to protest against the continuous violation of Northampton's Constitutional Rights'].

[189] [L.a.], 'The Bradlaugh Demonstration', *Labour Standard*, 24 Feb. 1883, pp. 5; See Royle, *Radicals Securalists, and Republicans*, pp. 30–1.

'the inherent right of all individuals to hold, practice and proclaim any opinions on all subjects whatsoever which their conscientious convictions may demand'.[190]

The Bradlaugh case reproduced the alignment most typical of British anti-clerical conflicts, as Dissenters and Secularists were brought together in a campaign for civil rights,[191] while many Anglicans and Roman Catholics[192] maintained their traditional stance that the law of the country should embody and enforce Christianity. Indeed, Annie Besant wrote that it was the Catholics who were the most dangerous enemies of civil and religious liberty:

Such has been the spirit of Rome in all ages; legality and freedom are rubbish to her, and she is as tyrannical at heart to-day as she has ever been . . . It is perhaps well that we see the hideousness of Papal tyranny thus unveiled, for England is Protestant to the core, and will recognise the dangerous spirit whose outbreak in Parliament we have just seen.[193]

But blame on the 'Papists' reflected – more than the specific responsibilities attributed to the Catholic hierarchy in the Bradlaugh case – the broader context of contemporary European politics. Plebeian liberals thought that one of the most serious threats to democracy was posed by the 'Black International', the 'clerical conspiracy' involving, directly or indirectly, the despotic regimes of the continent.[194] In the latter category, 'Rome' and 'Popery' had always occupied first place, and appeared in an even more sinister light after 1849: then 'Liberal Catholicism' and the dream of a 'reformist pope' collapsed, as Pius IX was restored to his throne by French, Austrian and Neapolitan armies, and subsequently kept in power by foreign garrisons and mercenaries. In 1864 the publication of the Syllabus of Errors – which restated the Roman Church's absolute claims to the truth and condemned free enquiry, liberalism and democracy as 'heresies' – completed the break between radicalism and orthodox Catholicism. The scenario was ready for the age of *Kulturkampf*, which in different

[190] [Rep.], 'New South Wales', *NR*, 17 Jul. 1881, p. 78.
[191] Arnstein, 'The Bradlaugh Case, pp. 136, 157–61. For a few examples of. [rep.], 'Electioneering at Northampton' [speech by Rev. J. H. Williams], *NR*, 4 Apr. 1880, pp. 210–11; [rep.], 'Torquay Working Men's Liberal Association' [speech by Rev. W. Sawyers], *NR*, 1 Jul. 1883, pp. 8.
[192] Arnstein, *the Bradlaugh Case*, pp. 174–85, 261–2 for the Roman Catholic position, and pp. 165–73 for the Anglican one.
[193] A. Besant, 'Defence of Liberty', *NR*, 4 Jul. 1880, p. 51.
[194] Parry, *Democracy and Religion*, pp. 33, 125–6.

forms took place not only in Germany, but throughout Europe.[195]

This perspective was so central to British Liberal anti-Vaticanism that the latter – in contrast to Tory Orangeism – was constantly dominated by the problems of continental politics. During the 1860s it was the question of Italian aspirations regarding Rome, and Garibaldi's unsuccessful attempts to liberate it, which provided the focus.[196] Following the Aspromonte incidents in 1862 – when Garibaldi was wounded and arrested by Italian troops – popular demonstrations of protest took place all over Britain. In London a 'Working Men's Garibaldian Committee' organized meetings which culminated in the Hyde Park riots, involving British 'Garibaldians', Irish Catholics, and a large number of Londoners.[197] Sheridan Gilley has described the incidents almost as if they were an Orange tumult with a touch of *mafia* violence;[198] however, this episode was quite distinct from the traditional anti-Catholicism to which he alludes, at least as far as working-class radicals were concerned. The Risorgimento in general and Garibaldi in particular were extremely popular,[199] and not surprisingly the dramatic events of 1862 excited a large and heart-felt response. In London, artisan radicals were concerned not so much about the pope's religion, as about what they considered an 'object of vast importance to all those who love Civil and Religious Liberty . . . namely, the right of France to occupy Rome with her army'.[200] Thus, while they sympathised with Garibaldi as a democratic hero, they did not feel any hostility to the Irish or Roman Catholics as such;[201] rather, as supporters of religious equality, they distrusted both 'the rampant

---

[195] See Pirenne, *Histoire du Belgique*, VII, pp. 226–41; Mallinson, *Power and Politics in Belgian Education*; Magraw, *France*, pp. 193, 219ff; McLeod, *Religion and the People*, pp. 8, 15, 44; Della Peruta, *Democrazia e socialismo nel Risorgimento*, p. 128; Lyttelton, 'Italian Anticlericalism', p. 225; Ullman, 'Spain, 1808–1939', pp. 154–65; Freeze, 'Imperial Russia', p. 178.

[196] See McIntire, *England against the Papacy*, pp. 182–227.

[197] See Gilley, 'Garibaldi Riots', pp. 697–732.

[198] *Ibid.*, p. 710; though 'Murphy, Garibaldi and the Queen' became an Orange motto at the end of the century: Kirk, *Working-Class Reformism*, p. 334.

[199] See Beales, 'Garibaldi in England', pp. 184–216.

[200] [Letter by] W. Petherbridge, 'Garibaldi and Louis Napoleon', *BH*, 4 Nov. 1862, p. 5.

[201] Scourge [R. Hartwell], 'Hyde Park and the Garibaldian Committee', *BH*, 11 Oct. 1862, p. 1; [l.a.], 'Garibaldi and the Trades', *BH*, 1 Nov. 1862, p. 4. Indeed, the radicals often sought the electoral support of the Irish Catholic immigrants: such was the case of one of the most ardent British 'Garibaldians'. Joseph Cowen jr. (see [rep.], 'Mr. Cowen on Tory Treatment of Catholics & Dissenters. – Meeting at the Jubilee Schools', *NW*, 10 Jan. 1874, p. 2; Digamma, 'A Canvasser's Experience', *NW*, 14 Feb. 1874, p. 4). See also Macintosh, *Thesis*, p. 138.

Orangeman and the bigoted Papist' who worked 'upon folly to create delusion'; typically they concluded that a 'more thoroughly educated people would put them all down by contemptuous indifference to their jabber and their tricks'.[202]

It was not sectarian strife, but education, free enquiry, and the establishment of liberty and democracy which would inflict the death blow to Roman clericalism.[203] In this respect, British popular radicals shared the vision of some continental 'liberal Catholics': they hoped that the dismantling of the pope's temporal power pursued by the Italian patriots would pave the way for a complete transformation of the Church of Rome by restoring the ecclesiastical democracy of early Catholicism. This process would culminate in Roman Catholic congregations recovering their ancient right to elect priests and bishops[204] following the example then already being set by some Italian dioceses, such as Mantua.[205]

Thus, there was no contradiction between sympathy for Ireland, support for Catholic reformers, and hostility to the politics of the Roman hierarchy. The pope was attacked not as a religious leader, but as a temporal and spiritual despot, as the source of all arbitrary power in Europe and 'the paymaster of [the] mercenary troops'[206] necessary to keep down his Italian subjects; similarly, his priests were accused of being 'the most inveterate enemies to the just rights of men'.[207] Liberal anti-clericals also decried the poverty and ignorance then typical of many Catholic countries, whose clergy did not educate the people, but let 'the men grow indifferent and sceptical, the women keep superstitious',[208] and thus tended 'to create a nation of children and of sceptics'.[209]

---

[202] Littlejohn, 'Folly, Fraud, and Superstition', *WT*, 31 May 1868, p. 6; See [l.a., n.t.], *LM* 25 Apr. 1871, p. 5.

[203] [L.a. n.t.], *DN*, 10 Oct. 1868, p. 4; [l.a.], 'Religious Tendencies of the Continent', *BH*, 4 May 1872, p. 8.

[204] C. Larkin, 'The Plebiscite at Venice. – The Bishop of Newcastle and Victor Emmanuel', *NW*, 17 Nov. 1866, p. 4; [l.a.], 'The Popedom in Danger', *WT*, 7 Oct. 1866, p. 1.

[205] [L.a.], 'The Pope and the Jesuits', *WT*, 7 Jul. 1878, p. 4. Gladstone's aims for the reform of the Roman church were therefore less eccentric than Shannon thinks (Shannon, 'Gladstone, la Chiesa cattolico-romana e l'Italia', in Gherardi and Matteucci (eds.), *Marco Minghetti*, pp. 161–87), and indeed were shared by the Italian Liberal government: Chabod, *Politica estera*, pp. 246–7, 258–9.

[206] [L.a.], 'The End of the Roman Insurrection. – Who Has Gained by It?', *NW*, 9 Nov. 1867, p. 4; [l.a.], 'The Arrest of Garibaldi', *NW*, 28 Sept. 1867, p. 4.

[207] [L.a.], 'The Papal Policy in Italy', *BH*, 13 Jul. 1872, p. 10.

[208] Littlejohn, 'The Great Conspiracy of Priestcraft', *WT*, 27 Jun. 1875, p. 4.

[209] Littlejohn, 'The New Pope as Politician and Conspirator', *WT*, 5 May 1878, p. 6.

This ominous picture also had a conspiratorial aspect: the pope was charged with being the instigator of secret sects, brigands and various criminal organizations especially active in Spain and southern Italy.[210] Through the Jesuits, Ultramontane control on conscience was supposed to be at work in other parts of Europe as well, including France and Belgium,[211] Ireland and the whole of Britain.[212] A typical symbol and instrument of these 'Popish plots' was the practice of auricular confession, a 'device' for influencing women and especially effective in Catholic countries, where 'The wife is the priest's spy'.[213] So bad was the situation that

It is no fault of the priesthood of Rome – it is no fault of the violent adherents of the Papacy – that we are not at the moment engaged in new religious wars. While . . . poor deluded peasants in France are being enticed upon pilgrimages to the shrines of inspired lunatics, dethroned sovereigns are informing the Pope that if they had still the power they had lost he would soon be restored to his temporal dominions. Well, these things go to show that it is only to the impotence of the Infallibilists that society owes its immunity from the evils of militant fanaticism.[214]

Similar views were so prevalent on the left that they were heartily shared even by the International Working Men's Association, which described the pope and his protector, Napoleon III, as 'the Beast':

Rome and Paris are the capitals of the apocalyptic beast with two foreheads, the double tyranny crowned and mitred of this Catholic-Monarchical Janus – the Pope and Emperor. Fraud and force are the hyphen between the Siamese twins of divine right . . . Catholicism, in denying liberty of conscience, denies every other liberty, drives the subject to discipline and obedience, makes him pass . . . from the confessor to the *commissaire*, from one authority to another, automaton accustomed to

---

[210] [L.a.], *BH*, 4 Nov. 1873, p. 3; Ironside, 'Priestly Tyranny in Ireland', *NW*, 1 Jun. 1872, p. 4; Littlejohn, 'Gambetta's War with the Church', *WT* 29 Sept. 1878, p. 6; [rep.], 'A Modern Model Brigand', *WT*, 7 Apr. 1867, p. 1 (on the alleged conspiracy between brigands and clericals in Calabria); [l.a.], 'The Popedom in Danger', *WT*, 7 Oct. 1866, p. 1.

[211] [L.a.], 'The Riots in Belgium', *LW*, 25 Jun. 1876, p. 6; [l.a.], 'The Crisis in France', *NW*, 19 May 1877, p. 4; Littlejohn, 'France and the Jesuits', *WT*, 11 apr. 1880, p. 6.

[212] [L.a.], 'Mr. Gladstone on the Papacy', *NW*, 14 Aug. 1875, p. 4; Parry, *Democracy and Religion*, p. 349.

[213] Littlejohn, 'Priestcraft and Morals', *WT*, 24 Jun. 1877, p. 6. Auricolar confession was also a classic target for continental anticlericalism: see Michelet, *La Revolution Française*, I, Book 7, Chapter 2, pp. 1,144–70; and Lyttelton, 'Italian Anticlericalsim', p. 243.

[214] [L.a.], 'The League of Beggars', *NW*, 28 Sept. 1873, p. 4; [l.a.], 'Mr. Gladstone on the Papacy'. *NW* 14 Aug. 1875, p. 4.

serve, afraid of being free, delegating his sovereignity, and quickly electing Emperors instead of Presidents, Napoleons instead of Washingtons.[215]

The Vatican Council and the proclamation of papal infallibility contributed towards exacerbating these sentiments,[216] as they seemed to involve 'the elevation of a priest to the place of God'.[217] Infallibility was considered an insult not only to common sense and reason, but also to the Scriptures and the Catholic tradition, and indeed was 'a dream and delirium' of Pius IX's diseased imagination. Together with Ultramontanism, it was condemned as part of a wicked plan to establish a system of slavery comparable only with the ancient despotism 'of Xerxes'.[218] The fact that at the very moment infallibility was proclaimed the pope's temporal power finally collapsed, as the Italian army swept away the last shred of the Vatican States and Rome was forcibly annexed to the Kingdom of Italy, was interpreted as divine Providence's ironic comment on clerical arrogance and folly.[219]

If in the case of Italy the army had been required to subdue the Vatican, in other countries too public force might be necessary to control the 'clerical conspiracy'. In 1874 Gladstone's attack on 'Vaticanism' had great success among popular liberals, who acclaimed his denunciation of 'the civil dangers inherent in submission to an absolute Church . . . [and in] dictation by a foreign power'.[220] Similarly, Gambetta's 'war' against the Roman Catholic Church in France was greatly commended, and in 1877 the Italian

---

[215] 'International Working Men's Association' (deputation to the American minister and petition to President Grant). *NR*, 29 Mar. 1869, p. 199.

[216] Pirenne, *Histoire de Belgique*, VII, p. 219; Aquarone, *Italia liberale*, pp. 149–51.

[217] Ironside, 'The Infallibility of the Pope', *NW*, 11 Dec. 1869, p. 4.

[218] C. Larkin, 'The Infallibility of the Pope Laughed to Scorn', *NW*, 10 Aug. 1867, p. 4.

[219] [L.a.], 'The Position of Italy,', *NW*, 17 Sept. 1870, p. 4; [l.a.], 'Free Rome', *LW*, 25 Sept. 1870, p. 6; [l.a.], 'A "Heavenly Rome"', *LW*, 2 Oct. 1870, p. 6.

[220] [L.a.], 'Mr. Gladstone's Expostulation with the Pope and Ultramontane Catholics. A Home-Thrust in Favour of Civil and Religious Liberty'. *Forest of Dean Examiner*, 20 Nov. 1874, p. 4; Ironside, 'Mr. Gladstone's New Departure'.*NW*, 21 Nov. 1874, p. 4; [Rep.], 'Progressive Club' [speech by Mr. Galbraith], *NR*, 22 Nov. 1874, p. 333. An exception was represented by *Lloyd's Weekly* which criticized Gladstone's pamphlet as reactionary and intolerant ([l.a.], 'The Vatican Decrees', 15 Nov. 1874, p. 1): it did not deny that the pope and the Vatican were obscurantist and anti-liberal, however the fact that the Italians themselves enjoyed liberty and a constitutional government meant that Britons would be at least as free. This position would seem convincing, but the fact that in other articles *Lloyd's* approved of the German *Kulturkampf* leads one to think that its reaction to the 1874 pamphlet was due more to hostility towards Gladstone personally, than to his ideas. The Positivists also criticized Gladstone, only to be rebuked by the popular press ([l.a.], 'The Positivists and Mr. Gladstone', *NW*. 2 Jan. 1875, p. 4).

'Law against clerical abuses' was reviewed at length by the *National Reformer*.[221] In the case of the German Empire, the struggle of the 'Old Catholics' against Vatican autocracy was celebrated as the 'war of Catholic emancipation from the Papacy', leading to a new Reformation which 'will consummate the ends for which Luther fought'.[222] Even Bismarck's *Kulturkampf* was just a defensive operation:

It is the old game that Rome is playing; to set the spiritual above the temporal power being its life-long dream. The tactics which BISMARCK is combating are tactics with which Germany was familiar centuries ago. Fortunately, the civil power is in a better position to-day for resisting the pretensions of the Vatican than in days gone past. With the advance of civilization the State has been strengthened. It was in a semi-barbarous age that spiritual authority achieved its highest triumphs.[223]

Popular-liberal hostility to 'Rome' was such that the closing of a church in Germany might be celebrated with an especially composed poem.[224] Thus no sympathy was wasted on the Catholics who remained loyal to Rome:

Bismarck is no persecutor, but a prudent man, operating against traitors. He does nothing against freedom of conscience until conscience, or what is called so, takes the form of open hostility to the State. An Ultramontanist has a perfect right to his religious opinions, and so had the Thugs in India; but when he wants to destroy the safety of his neighbours, he must submit to restraining.[225]

It is difficult to assess how far popular liberals would go in their anti-Vaticanism when this tendency became clearly anti-liberal, especially in cases when disagreement emerged.[226] Anyway, the

---

[221] R. H. Dvas, 'The New Law Passed by the Italian Parliament against Abuses in Relgion', *NR*, 18 Feb. 1877, pp. 97–8.

[222] [L.a.], 'The New Reformation', *LW*, 26 Oct. 1873, p. 6.

[223] [L.a.], 'Ultramontanism', *NC* 1 Apr. 1873, p. 2.

[224] Elizabeth Cockron, 'The Wind of Bonn', *BH*, 28 Jun. 1873, p. 5; See H. Rylett, 'Church and State in Germany, and the Jesuits in England', *BH*, 6 Jun. 1874, p. 1; [rep.], 'The Jesuits in England', *RN*, 20 Jun. 1875, p. 1.

[225] Littlejohn, 'Irish Priests and Home Rule', *WT*, 5 Oct. 1878, p. 6; Bismarck was even compared to Garibaldi by Gracchus ('Things at Home and Abroad', *RN*, 5 Jan. 1873, p. 3).

[226] See the contrasting comments of Littlejohn, 'France and the Jesuits', *WT*, 11 Apr. 1880, p. 6 and [l.a.], 'The Expulsion of the Jesuits from France', *LW*, 4 Apr. 1880, p. 6. Interestingly enough, in contrast to the prevailing lack of sympathy for the Catholics, the persecuted Jews of Russia were pitied and even compared with the Waldensians during the seventeenth-century massacres celebrated in Milton's sonnet: [l.a.], 'Anti-Jewish Riots', *NC*, 15 Jun. 1884, p. 3.

libertarian critics of the *Kulturkampf* – like Beesley and the Positivists[227] – remained substantially isolated until Bismarck began to attack the Socialists as well, in 1878. It was then realized that the 'measures demanded against Socialism would strike, in general, at the freedom of speech, the freedom of the press, liberty of public meeting' and that 'what is actually wanted, is the suppression of liberty and Liberalism'.[228] The *Weekly Times*, which had consistently supported anti-Catholic legislation, declared that 'The timid liberal who is ready to consent to be unjust to the Socialists because he dislikes them, is in reality a cowardly tyrant.'[229]

This change of attitude was full of implications, but it must also be remembered that, from the viewpoint of British radicals, there were important differences between the Ultramontane Catholics and the Socialists – the former being regarded as an 'anti-national', 'subversive sect', the latter as a law-abiding parliamentary party. But in general, it would seem that British popular liberals tended to believe that in Catholic countries the best policy towards the Church was to enforce 'the complete subordination of the ecclesiastical to the civil authority',[230] as even such an ancient and stable democracy as Switzerland had done in 1874.

'FREE CHURCHES IN A FREE STATE':
THE DISESTABLISHMENT QUESTION

Interestingly enough, government control and the supremacy of the civil authorities was recommended not only in the case of the Catholic Church abroad, but also in that of the Church of England at home[231]. This might suggest that popular radicals shared some form of Erastianism. However, their view was different: it was the possibility that the Anglican Church might be disestablished *without* being disendowed which was feared, as leading to the creation of an irresponsible power within the State.[232] The ideal settlement of Church–State relationships should rather follow the

---

[227] E.S. Beesley, *BH*, 24 Jan. 1874, p. 1.
[228] [L.a.], 'The Policy of the German Government', *NW*, 14 Sept. 1878, p. 4.
[229] [L.a.], 'The Anti-Socialist Bill in Germany', 29 Sept. 1878, p. 4.
[230] Littlejohn, 'Defects of the American and Swiss Republics', *WT*, 26 May 1873, p. 6; [l.a.], 'The New Swiss Constitution', *WT*, 20 Apr. 1874, p. 1.
[231] Plain Dealer, 'The Church in Wales', *BH*, 28 Aug. 1869, p. 5.
[232] [L.a.] 'The Religious Equality Agitation', *WT*, 16 Feb. 1873, p. 1; Littlejohn 'Church Property and National Property', *WT*, 12 Mar. 1876, p. 6.

teaching of Congregational and Baptist polity: that all churches should be 'wholly liberated from State patronage and state control'.[233]

Disendowment and disestablishment – almost free trade in religion[234] – had been included in radical programmes since at least as early as the 1830s.[235] However, the issue became a political reality after the Second Reform Act had enhanced the influence and self-confidence of the Nonconformists. What was generally requested was a sort of British version of the policy of complete separation between Church and State that the radical press ascribed to Cavour and Ricasoli. For instance, in 1866 the Italian case became one of the arguments of the *Leeds Mercury* against any project of concurrent endowment.[236] This unofficial organ of northern moderate Nonconformity was readily echoed by the mass press, which often quoted 'Count Cavour's immortal sentence . . . – a Free Church in a Free State',[237] a motto which was so much a household word that it was sometimes quoted in the original Italian.

The reason for such an interest in 'Cavour's model' was that between the Church of Rome and that of England there were similarities, which went well beyond sacerdotalism and ritualistic practices.[238] The two crucial facts in which Canterbury was seen as similar to Rome were firstly clerical hierarchy and centralization to the exclusion of the laymen, and secondly the fact that – like Roman Catholicism on the continent – the Anglican Church occupied within British and Irish society a position of power and prestige which made it a 'natural' ally of the ruling elites. The latter point was much more important than the doctrinal differences between Anglicans and Dissenters,[239] and reveals the true nature of the conflict, which again was about political control.

---

[233] [L.a.] 'The Welsh Establishment', *NW*, 28 May 1870, p. 4.
[234] Matthew, *Gladstone 1809–1874*, pp. 172; Parry, *Democracy and Religion*, p. 23.
[235] Weaver, *Fielden*, p. 59.
[236] [L.a. n.t.], *LM*, 28 Dec. 1866, p. 2.
[237] H. W. Holland, 'The Education Crisis of the Country – No. vi – The Bearing of the Education Question upon Ireland', *NW*, 28 May 1870, p. 4.
[238] Which anyway provoked much radical opposition: see cf. [l.a.], 'The Liberal Programme – Mr. Fawcett at Brighton', *WT*, 29 Jan. 1871, p. 1; [rep.], 'Ritualism in Lambeth', *BH*, 28 Mar. 1868, p. 1; [l.a.], 'The Church in Danger', *BH*, 6 Jul. 1872, p. 8. Disestablishment was supposed to be 'the best cure for ritualism': [rep.]. 'Disestablishment of the Church of England' [lecture by Mr. Mason Jones]. *BH* 29 Nov. 1873, p. 9.
[239] Dunbabin, 'Farm Servants', in Dunbabin, [ed.] *Rural Discontent*, p. 248.

The political power of the 'State Church' was felt in many different areas. Of these one of the most sensitive was that of ecclesiastical taxation, especially compulsory church rates – levied in both urban and rural parishes for the upkeep of the church (including repairs, the purchase of materials such as prayer books and copes, etc., for services). The levying of a rate could be prevented by vestry meetings, if their Nonconformist members achieved a majority of the votes: this strategy was often followed by Dissenters seeking to redress this obvious injustice locally. Their opposition resulted in long and repeated disputes,[240] which were particularly bitter in those parishes where the majority of residents consisted of Nonconformists, but an Anglican minority dominated the assembly through the ecclesiastical chairman and the control of plural voting.[241] If vestry opposition failed and a rate was levied, the latter could become a source of considerable tension within the parish, and of oppression for local Dissenters: in particular, non-payment on conscientious grounds was not admitted, and people who resisted became liable to legal action, often resulting in seizure of property and even imprisonment.[242] In fact, attempts to levy the rate had actually been abandoned in many town parishes since the 1830s, though Anglican appeasement had been uneven, and had consequently excited still fiercer conflicts in the numerous parishes in which the rate continued to be enforced.[243] From the 1830s Radical, Whig, and even Tory statesmen had repeatedly attempted to exempt Nonconformists or to reform the rates, but all the Bills had been wrecked during the parliamentary debate. As a consequence this grievance remained unredressed till the end of the 1860s. The fact that the Lords was the main stronghold of the old system, while Disraeli was one of its most strenuous advocates in the Commons[244], confirmed working-class radicals in their conviction that there was a close alliance between the ecclesiastical and the political and social establishments, and that the Church was

---

[240] Machin, *Politics and the Churches 1869–1921.* p. 249.

[241] See Cf. [rep.], 'Church Rate Contest at Dorking', *BH,* 11 Oct. 1862, p. 1; Holyoake, *Bygones Worth Remebering,* I, Chapter p. 38, 'Penal Christianity'. For the situation during the 1830s. see Brent, *Liberal Anglican Politics,* pp. 9, 12. The abolition of the church rates had been included in the programme of some Chartists: Addison, *Religious Equality,* p. 65.

[242] Machin, *Politics and the Churches 1869–1921.* p. 259. In the 1840s this could also involve imprisonment: Binfield, *So Down to Prayers,* p. 110.

[243] Machin, *Politics and the Churches 1869–1921,* p. 105

[244] *Ibid.,* pp. 55–63, 317–9.

little more than the greedy clerical appendix to the landed aristocracy.

Another major grievance was tithing – a tax on owners and occupiers of land for the support of the rural clergy. Tithing had been one of the causes of the 'Swing Riots' during the 1830s, when the agricultural labourers were persuaded that it contributed towards keeping wages down and food prices high.[245] The fact that in some regions even poor fishermen were asked 'every tenth fish',[246] and that – though only sporadically – agricultural labourers were prosecuted for failing to give one tenth of their wages or of the product of their allotments for the Church[247] did not increase the latter's popularity among the subaltern classes. In 1836 the system had been reformed, and the hated payment in kind was commuted. During the second half of the century the tithe did not affect the labourers directly: still, it weighed on the farmers, thus reducing – so it was believed – the 'wage fund' out of which the labourers could be paid:[248] significantly, during the 'tithe war' of the 1880s riots in Wales involved miners and labourers, who took the opportunity to show their hostility towards the Established Church and ecclesiastical taxation.[249] Moreover, tithes could also weigh heavily on village artisans and shopkeepers, who provided the staff and leadership for various working-class organizations;[250] in fact, in 1855 even eminent plebeian radicals like E. Truelove and G. J. Holyoake were among those who had property seized for refusing to pay tithes.[251]

Tension was aggravated by the presence of many clergymen on the 'Great unpaid', the county bench which played an important role not only in quarrels over the payment of church rates and tithes, but also in cases of labour disputes or political unrest. Thus resentment towards clerical control of civil life was exacerbated by the fact that the clergy did exercise an influence which went well beyond the sphere of ecclesiastical matters. On several

---

[245] Ward, 'The Tithe Question in England'. pp. 78–9.

[246] In Cornwall, for example: Evans, *The Contentious Tithe*, p. 81.

[247] Evans, 'Growth of English Rural Anti-clericalism', pp. 90–1; See cf. Brent, 'Whigs and Protestant Dissent', p. 891.

[248] Machin, *Politics and the Churches 1868–1921, p. 47.*

[249] Dunbabin, 'The Welsh Tithe War', in Charlesworth [ed.], *An Atlas of Rural Protest in Britain*, p. 179.

[250] See for an example Buckmaster, *A Village Politician* (1897), pp. 42–3.

[251] Royle, *Victorian Infidels*, p. 267.

occasions clerical magistrates had shown an excessive and almost ruthless zeal in applying the law: the radicals had never forgotten that it had been a clergyman who had read the Riot Act at Peterloo.[252] Even in the milder climate of mid- and late-Victorian politics the clerical bench preserved a controversial reputation for judicial severity: this was displayed, in particular, in 1873, when, after a rural strike at Ascott (Oxfordshire), sixteen women were sentenced to hard labour for picketing by two Chipping Norton magistrates, both of whom were clergymen.[253] This case provoked much scandal among farm labourers, urban workers and radicals in general, resulting in a renewed anti-clerical crusade[254] and even a Bill 'to prevent the appointment as magistrates of any cleric with a cure of souls'.[255] The Chipping Norton verdict was not a totally isolated case,[256] and similar incidents – widely reported by the press – had a cumulative effect, giving the impression that the Church *as a whole* was hostile to labour. The *Labourers' Union Chronicle* effectively summarized the mood of plebeian radicals when it declared that since priests provided such 'un-Christian' magistrates,

Well may the labourers of England ask themselves . . . what is the value to them of the religion which such men as these parson magistrates teach: or what to them is the worth of a Gospel that is harsher than their country's law; that favours the wealthy in their selfishness and luxury: that consecrates not a few of the social and political iniquities of the age and that strains the law to crush the poor in their struggles to gain emancipation from a degrading and oppressive serfdom and to win from society and the country a recognition of their just and equitable rights? . . . The Church not only has itself large interest in the land, but is in close alliance with the great landowners of the country. It is the rich man's friend, but in the great struggle in which labour finds itself pitted

---

[252] Evans, 'Growth of English rural Anti-clericalism', pp. 84, 101–9; Brent, *Liberal Anglican Politics*, p. 13.

[253] [Rep.], 'The Chipping Norton Conviction [Special Report]', *Labourers' Union Chronicle*, 7 Jun. 1873, p. 7; 'Business Committee Meeting', 29 May 1873, in *Labour Representation League Papers*, RSR 61, 32. Cf. also Horn, 'Introduction' to id. [ed.]. *Agricultural Trade Unionism*, 14; Kitson Clark, *Churchmen and the Condition of England*, pp. 249–51; Evans, 'The Church in Danger?', p. 215.

[254] Horn, 'Introduction', in Hon [ed.], *Agricultural Trade Unionism*, p. 14. See Cf. [rep.], 'The Chipping Norton Conviction [Special Report]', *Labourers' Union Chronicle*, 7 Jun. 1873, p. 7; and 'Business Committee Meeting', 29 May 1873, in *Labour Representation League Papers*, RSR 61, p. 32.

[255] Kitson Clark, *Churchmen and the Condition of England*, p. 251.

[256] For another episode of this kind, see Evans, 'The Church in Danger?', p. 215.

against wealth, this Church, which will kindly patronise the contented serf, is fast proving itself to be the poor man's foe.[257]

For all these reasons throughout the nineteenth century, radicals of the subaltern classes – from William Lovett to Keir Hardie[258] – regarded the Church of England as one of the main bulwarks of social and political conservatism, almost on a level with the Church of Rome,[259] as 'an engine of the State'[260] and an illustration of the dangers of State intervention: given the strength of the free-trade and anti-State feelings among plebeian radicals, this form of intervention and religious 'protectionism' seemed both an iniquity to be abolished and an inconsistency to be rectified. This iniquity was especially evident in those regions, such as Wales and Ireland, where the majority of working people were not Anglicans. In particular, it was the Anglican Establishment in Ireland which became a favourite target for radical criticism in the second half of the 1860s.

Hostility to Vaticanism and Ultramontanism did not deter British plebeian radicals from asking for religious equality for the people of Ireland. As most of them – in England and Wales at least – shared the congregational polity of Dissent, they rejected the notion that Irish Protestantism relied on the Establishment.[261] Instead, many – including the most enthusiastic supporters of Bismarck's *Kulturkampf* – agreed with Bright that the Reformation in Ireland had been hindered, rather than helped, by the existence of a privileged church.[262] Indeed, religious inequality and the form of oppression which it generated seemed so important that disestablishment was expected to effect a decisive step towards national reconciliation.[263]

---

[257] [L.a.], 'The Church of England at the Bar of Public Opinion – The Clerical Outrage at Chipping Norton'. *Labourers' Union Chronicle*, 7 Jun. 1873, p. 1.

[258] Tawney, *William Lovett*, p. 155; Morgan, *Hardie*, p. 92. Cf. also Griggs, *Trades Union Congress and the Struggle for Education*, pp. 85–91.

[259] [L.a.], *BH*, 15 Nov. 1873, p. 8; lett. by 'The Raven', 'Education', *ibid.*, 30 May 1868, p. 4.

[260] [L.a.], 'The Pope, the Cabinet, and the People', *RN*, 19 Dec. 1869, p. 1.

[261] [L.a.], 'Specific Wrongs and Remedies', *LW*. 5 Apr. 1868, p. 6; [l.a.], *BH* 22 Aug. 1868, p. 4.

[262] [L.a.], *WT*, 20 Oct. 1867, p. 1; [l.a.], 'The Debate on the "Missionary Church"', *NW*, 4 Apr. 1868, p. 4.

[263] [L.a., n.t.], *LM*, 10 Oct. 1867, p. 2; C. Larkin, 'Mr. Gladstone and the Irish Church', *NW*, 28 Mar. 1868, p. 4; 'Robin Goodfellow', 'The Gossip's Bowl', *ibid.*; [l.a.], 'The Church Debates. – Opposition and Progress', *WT*, 9 May 1869, p. 1.

Next to religious equality there was the question of ecclesiastical property: in contrast to the property of the Nonconformist denominations, which was private, the endowment of the 'State Church' was 'State property'; consequently, the State had 'a moral right to secularize any portion of it, or the whole of it, as public interest may demand',[264] especially to fund education, poor relief, or even land reform.[265] But this argument did not lead to extreme Erastianism; it led rather to pure voluntaryism: once the Church of Ireland was disendowed, there would be no reason left to justify any further State interference in religion.[266]

Though the issue of Irish disestablishment had been repeatedly raised in Parliament in 1844, 1850–6,[267] and more successfully from 1865,[268] a mass agitation was started only when franchise reform was secured in 1867. The resolutions that Gladstone presented on 23 March 1868 were immediately taken up by popular radicalism.[269] From 31 March the issue was debated with enthusiasm by thousands of men at mass meetings successfully organized all over the country.[270] Gladstone's personal popularity again reached the highest peaks achieved during the previous campaign for the Reform Bill,[271] and he became the personification of this new 'great cause' as the Liberation Society distributed more than one million pamphlets, tracts and leaflets on the subject.[272] The Reform League and the London Working Men's Association (LWMA) readily declared their support for the Liberal leader's resolutions in favour of the abolition of the 'alien church'. The most enthusiastic and

---

[264] [L.a.], 'Priestcraft in Ireland', *WT*. 20 Oct. 1867, p. 1.
[265] [L.a.], 'The Irish Church Question', *LW*, 14 Apr. 1867, p. 6; [rep.], *BH*, 14 Dec. 1867, p. 1. speech by Mason Jones.
[266] [L.a.], 'Church Reform in Italy', *WT*, 3 Feb. 1867, p. 4; C. Larkin, 'A Free Church in a Free State', *NW*, 9 Feb. 1867, p. 4; See [l.a.], 'Mr. Disraeli's Manifesto', *NC*, 5 Oct. 1868, p. 2: 'the full-blown Erastianism in which he glories is at this moment esteemed by the majority of the inhabitants of the three kingdoms not the stronghold, but the tomb of spiritual liberty'.
[267] MacIntosh, *Thesis*, pp. 143–6.
[268] Machin, *Politics and the Churches 1832–1868*. pp. 311, 327, 352, 357.
[269] [Rep.], 'London Working Men's Association – The Irish Church Meeting', *BH*, 28 Mar. 1868, p. 1; [rep.], 'Working Men's Association [Pimlico branch]' [speech by the chairman and resolution], *BH*, 4 Apr. 1868, p. 1.
[270] Machin, *Politics and the Churches 1832–1868*, pp. 360–61, 368–69; MacIntosh, *Thesis*, p. 254.
[271] Contemporary enthusiasm is illustrated, for instance, in [rep.], 'The Irish Church Question', *NW*, 4 Apr. 1868, p. 8; and [l.a.], 'Mr. Gladstone's Resolutions', *LW*, 29 Mar. 1868, p. 1.
[272] MacIntosh, *Thesis*, p. 225.

radical of the two associations was the LWMA. It was also the first to organize demonstrations, starting from that of 31 March in the 'grand hall' of the Freemasons' Tavern. *The Times* described this meeting as 'enthusiastic' and 'very crowded': more than 2,000 people took part – all 'presenting the unmistakable working men's appearance' – as hundreds of other workers thronged through the neighbouring streets, unable to gain admittance.[273] This meeting was characterized by a high degree of participation in the deliberations from the floor, and the proceedings provide a vivid impression of what radical artisans thought of the various aspects of the issue. In his opening speech G. Potter mentioned four fundamental reasons why London working-class radicals were interested in the question of the church of Ireland: the first was that, after the Reform Act, they wanted to claim their right 'to have a voice in the making of law affecting the people of this country, whether the law refers to religious, social or financial matters (Cheers.)'.[274] The second was the enormous cost of the Establishment – and the audience punctuated Potter's list of figures with cries of amazement and indignation – totally out of proportion to the number of people who benefited from it. The third was that the Irish Establishment was the church of the privileged few:

The religion of these persons is sustained by the compulsory taxation of the poorest classes in Ireland. (Shame!) Has not the time come when it should be not merely denounced, but abolished? (Yes.) Can peace and happiness exist in Ireland so long as a small minority of the people are placed in a position of legal and political ascendancy? Would the people of England or of Scotland quietly endure such a wrong? (No. No.) Why then should it be inflicted upon Ireland. (Hear, hear.)[275]

There was also a fourth reason, the conviction that the Church of Ireland was 'the most fruitful source of the discontent which characterizes that unhappy country. (Hear, hear.)' These themes were repeated over and over again in Potter's speech, in order to stir up the enthusiasm of the audience, which welcomed with a 'loud and prolonged applause' the speaker's final appeal. The actual political content of the demonstration was summarized by the Secretary of the Tailors' Association, Druitt, who moved the

---

[273] See [rep.], 'The Irish Church', *TI*, 1 Apr. 1868. p. 10; [rep.], 'Great Meeting on the Irish Church Question – Mr. Gladstone's Resolutions', *BH*, 4 Apr. 1868, p. 1.

[274] [Rep.], 'Great Meeting on the Irish Church Question . . .', *BH*, 4 Apr. 1868, p. 1.

[275] *Ibid.*

first resolution. After stressing that he was a Protestant and indeed a Churchman, Druitt proposed that all the Irish churches be disestablished and disendowed, and that the Church endowment be used for 'promoting the secular interests of the Irish people'.[276] The resolution was supported by Upshall, a joiner, who began by stressing that he was 'an Englishman and a Protestant'. A proposed amendment in favour of leaving some of its endowment to the Church for the pastoral care of Irish Anglicans – moved, significantly, by a barrister, not an artisan – was rejected amidst 'continued uproar, groans, hooting, and yelling, which rendered the hearing of a complete sentence impossible':[277] a reception which further demonstrated the audience's strength of feelings.

This radicalism contrasted with the initial reactions of Edmond Beales and a few other leaders of the Reform League, who were reluctant to adopt such an aggressive line. But when the League's General Council met the following day, 1 April, to decide what course to follow, many of the delegates spoke strongly in support of the radical line of the LWMA: one of them declared that Gladstone had been 'a little too tender. . . by professing his respect for what was termed "vested rights or interest"', as 'in this instance "vested interests" meant the privilege of sharing in the plunder of the State', namely the endowment.[278] Though the issue was intensely debated for a few days,[279] eventually Beales and the 'moderates' were forced to go along with the national agitation as rank-and-file pressure indicated that no other course would be supported or indeed tolerated. 'Crowded', 'large and most successful' meetings took place in Manchester, Newcastle on Tyne, Sheffield, Leeds, Preston, Glasgow, and Edinburgh[280]: in Wales disestablishment 'was virtually the only aspect of politics which

---

[276] Druitt also alluded to the Jewish background of the greatest advocate of the preservation of the Church of Ireland: 'Mr. Disraeli would, in fact, be much better engaged in rebuilding the temple at Jerusalem than in propping up the Irish Church. (Hear, hear, and laughter.)' (*Ibid.*)

[277] *Ibid.*

[278] [Rep.], 'The Reform League. – Meeting of the General Council' [speech by Weston], *ibid.*

[279] See the reports of the meetings of the branches of Pimlico, Bloomsbury, and Marylebone in 'Meeting of Branches', *ibid.*; and [rep.], 'The Reform League – Meeting of the General Council', *BH*, 11 Apr. 1868, p. 1; see the speech of the delegate for Whitford and that of E. Beales.

[280] [Rep.], 'The Irish Church Question', *TI*, 2 Apr. 1868, p. 5; [rep.], 'The Irish Church Question', *TI*, 3 Apr. 1868, p. 12.

the body of electors and the populace in general could understand as an issue of principle, and to which they could engage themselves'.[281] These demonstrations took place throughout April 1868 amidst growing enthusiasm,[282] expressing unqualified support for 'the great principle of religious equality', for disendowment, and for Gladstone, who was seen as embodying these causes.[283] Yet the Reform League did not join the fight until after John Bright's Reform Union had organized its 'great public meeting', held on 16 April at St James' Hall – 'which was crowded in every part'. G. Potter, R. Hartwell and E. Beales shared the platform with Lord Russell, Lord Amberley, V. Harcourt and other Liberal leaders and MPs, effectively symbolizing the unity of all the currents within the Liberal party coalition on the disestablishment platform as the general election drew near.[284]

The position of the anti-clericals was morally and politically strong and difficult to challenge. This is also confirmed by the fact that the demonstrations in support of the Church of Ireland were comparatively few and far between, and attracted only limited participation (in some cases it was difficult to fill a meeting hall).[285] In contrast, disestablishment demonstrations attracted great concourses of working men. For instance, on 12 May 1868 – when the Reform League organized its first mass meeting – St James' Hall was so 'densely crowded' that the contingents of Clerkenwell and Holborn were unable to find a place, and moved to Waterloo-place to hold a parallel meeting.[286] On this occasion the LWMA and the Irish Reform League had sent delegations, and the meeting could claim a wide representativeness – though *The Times* reported that 'the people composing the assemblage were generally of a more respectable class than ordinarily attend large demonstrations'.[287]

---

[281] I.G. Jones, Cit. in Harvie, 'Gladstonianism', in Bellamy (ed.), *Victorian Liberalism*, p. 168.

[282] Cf. the reports of the meetings; 'The Irish Church', *TI*, 16 Apr. 1868, 10; 'The Irish Church', *TI*, 17 Apr. 1868, p. 5; 'The Irish Question', *TI*, 25 Apr. 1868, p. 12; 'The Irish Church', *TI*, 28 Apr. 1868, p. 12: 'The Irish Church', *TI*, 29 Apr. 1868, p. 9.

[283] Namely, 'that the State should resume the endowments of this Church and apply them – regard being had to existing interests – to national and unsectarian purposes': [rep.], 'The Irish Church Question'. *NW*, 4 Apr. 1868, p. 8.

[284] [Rep.], 'The Irish Church – Meeting at St. James's Hall', *BH*, 18 Apr. 1868, p. 1.

[285] [Rep.], 'The Irish Church', *TI*, 18 Apr. 1868, p. 12.

[286] [Rep.], 'The Irish Church. – The Ministerial Crisis'. *BH*, 16 May 1868, p. 5. The Proceedings began at 8:30 pm so that 'working men might have an opportunity of attending from the most distant parts of the metropolis'.

[287] [Rep.], 'The Ministry and the Church', *TI*, 13 May 1868, p. 5; Yet at a meeting of the General Council of the Reform League Beales declared that it had been 'a meeting exclusively of working men' ([Rep.], *BH*, 9 May 1868, p. 5).

The presence of Irish radicals was significant: in fact, one of the features of the agitation was that it by-passed religious and ethnic differences and brought together British and Irish working-class reformers, to the extent that meetings of Irish Catholic workers were sometimes addressed by Protestant spokesmen of the LWMA and the Reform League[288]. Indeed the vice-president of the Irish Reform League, Mowatt, a Wesleyan Methodist, belonged to one of the most anti-Catholic denominations: yet, his commitment to the separation of State and Church was complete, and he declared that the cause of religious equality in Ireland was not only that of the Roman Catholics, but also of the Nonconformists.[289] Moreover, because of the recent reconciliation between the Reform League and the LWMA,[290] demonstrators could claim to represent London popular radicalism as a whole.

On 13 May the LWMA organized another meeting in Trafalgar Square, with the participation of between 4,000 and 7,000 people,[291] and led by Potter, Hartwell, and various delegates, most of whom were leaders of small artisan unions.[292] Though numbers were comparatively small, the presence of these leaders lent some authority to this meeting. The alliance between the LWMA and Reform League was confirmed by the fact that the leader of the latter was one of the main speakers. Indeed, it was Beales who gave the most heated speech, thus demonstrating that he had relinquished his original moderation. Amidst 'loud cheers' he maintained that

The Irish Church was an insult to the great majority of the people of Ireland ... It was a monstrous enormity, a disgrace to Christianity – (Cheers.) – a foul blot upon Protestantism, and an obstacle to the proper advancement of the truth ... It was a barrier to the real, permanent, practical union between Great Britain and Ireland.[293]

Rejecting the Anglican rhetoric that Irish disestablishment would lead to the supremacy of Rome, Beales added that

---

[288] See [rep.], 'The Irish Church – Proposed Sunday Demonstration in Hyde Park', *BH*, 18 Jul. 1868, p. 1; [rep.], 'The Irish Church', *TI*, 20 Jul. 1868; p. 12: [rep.], 'The Irish Church Question ... Meeting in Hyde Park', *BH* 25 Jul. 1868, p. 1.

[289] [Rep.], 'The Ministry and the Church', *TI*, 13 May 1868, p. 5.

[290] [Rep.], 'The Reform League. Meeting of the General Council', *BH*, 9 May 1868, p. 5.

[291] [Rep.], 'The Ministry and the Irish Church', *TI*, 14 May 1868, p. 7.

[292] [Rep.], 'Great Meeting in Trafalgar Square', *BH*, 16 May 1868, p. 5.

[293] *Ibid.*

He said clearly to his Roman Catholic brethren, 'We are not going to put down one ascendancy in order to put up another.' (Cheers). The old Puritan spirit might, indeed, be dead, – (No) – in their own State Church, but it was not dead in the hearts of the English people. (Hear, hear.) They objected to Protestant ascendancy in Ireland because it was an injustice and a reproach to their Protestant faith, and they were prepared to free their consciences from participating in that great injustice. But they would battle at the same time to the very death against the supremacy of every other Church, Roman Catholic or not . . . What they claimed, asked, insisted upon, what they would have, was perfect, complete, religious freedom and equality for all. (Loud cheers).[294]

The reactions of the audience are a clear indication of the extent to which these words expressed the views of the meeting. These arguments were also powerfully echoed in newspaper leading articles. The *Bee-Hive* wrote that

The Irish Church is doomed in spite of the 'No Popery' cry attempted to be raised by Mr D'Israeli [*sic*] . . . Yes, the Irish Church is doomed to fall by the weight of its own corruption and rottenness . . . The united power of the Crown, the House of Lords, the Lord Mayor of London, the Conservative 'Working Men's' Associations, and of all those who have so long fattened upon its corruption, will not avail to save it from disestablishment and disendowment . . . When it falls, as fall it will, we shall cordially say – Amen![295]

One aspect of the process of radicalization was that at this stage anti-clericalism became identified with the 'constitutional question' of Disraeli's minority government resisting the will of the nation and the decision of the majority in the House of Commons.[296] The agitation continued unabated during the following months up to the general elections,[297] and indeed so dominated popular attitudes that it seemed as if Irish disestablishment and disendowment had subsumed all the other traditional liberal causes, like 'retrench-

---

[294] *Ibid*
[295] [L.a.], 'The Irish Church Meetings', *ibid.*, p. 4.
[296] For example, these sentiments were expressed by the inscription on a banner hanging over the entrance to a new branch of the LWMA: [rep.], 'London Working Men's Association', *BH*, 27 Jun. 1868, p. 1.
[297] See 'Large and enthusiastic meeting' at Blackburn, *TI*, 12 May 1868, p. 12; [rep.], 'Meeting at Blackheath', *BH*, 30 May 1868, p. 7; [rep.], 'The Reform League – Meetings of Branches . . . Pimlico Branch' [lecture by C. Bradlaugh, 'The Past and the Future of Ireland'], *BH*, 6 Jun. 1868, p. 5; [rep.], 'The Irish Church Question', *BH*, 25 July 1868, p. 10.

ment' and 'peace'.[298] In some regions – especially around Liverpool – the confrontation assumed almost 'continental' overtones, with the exacerbated contrast between Secularist Liberals and Christian Conservatives.[299] However, in general the contest was not between 'Free Thought' and 'Christianity', but between 'two religions, that of the Church and that of Christ',[300] between the 'church of the State' and the 'church of God'. Thus at Huddersfield – where E. A. Leatham spoke to about 10,000 people in a hall decorated with mottoes like 'Gladstone and Free Churches' – neither 'Popery' nor 'Protestantism' were at stake: answering the objection that disestablishment 'would extinguish the light of the Reformation in Ireland', Leatham 'denied that this would be the result and instanced the case of the Free Church of Scotland. Was the Free Church of Scotland a failure? Was Nonconformity itself a failure?' And the audience cried: 'No, no':

And yet when two centuries ago their forefathers – and he was proud to say his forefathers – (Cheers) – separated themselves from the communion of the Church of England were they richer or stronger than the Church of Ireland would be if she were disendowed or disestablished tomorrow? (Hear, hear.) Strip the Church of Ireland of every scrap of endowment – rob her of every character [sic] which had been bequeathed to her, turn every congregation out of their church and every clergyman out of his parsonage, shut the doors of the national Universities against her, deprive her of every social advantage, of every privilege of the citizen, and of every franchise of the freeman – add to all this fines, imprisonment, stripes, and they would but reduce the Church of Ireland to the condition by which the Church of England . . . reduced their ancestors and his. (Hear. hear.) And where was Nonconformity now? Not fretting out their soul about the light of a candle, or the cut or tint of a vestment – (hear, hear) – but then their forefathers had this advantage – they placed their reliance not upon the loaves and fishes which came down from Parliament, but upon 'the bread which cometh down from heaven'. (Cheers).[301]

Popular enthusiasm did not decline after the Liberals' electoral victory. In fact, the agitation was renewed in 1869, when working-

---

[298] See [rep.], 'Great Liberal Demonstration in the Tyne Theatre', *NC*, 6 Nov. 1868, p. 3; see also [l.a.], 'The Irish Church and the Election', *BH*, 26 Jun. 1868, p. 4.

[299] E.A. Rhymer, Miner's Agent, 'A Word to the Liberal Freethinkers of Manchester and Liverpool', *NR*, 2 Aug. 1868, p. 92.

[300] G. Howell to E. Corner, 4 May 1870, in *G. Howell Coll.*, p. 331.

[301] [Rep.], 'Mr. E. A. Leatham, M.P., on Expenditure and the Irish Church', *LM*, 5 Nov. 1868, p. 3; see [rep.], 'Great Liberal Demonstration in Tyne Theatre, Newcastle', *NC*, 6 Nov. 1868, p. 3.

class radicals earnestly supported the government's Irish Church Bill against the Lords' opposition: the threat of a constitutional confrontation generated further mass response culminating in an enthusiastic open air meeting at Leeds, which about 15,000 attended.[302]

By then, disestablishment had virtually replaced – though only temporarily – 'manhood' suffrage as the panacea of popular radicalism. On the eve of the great reforms of the first Gladstone government, plebeian liberals had come to see the issue of Irish disestablishment not only as the first step towards a complete separation between Church and State in the whole of the United Kingdom,[303] but also as the key to the final amendment of all that was wrong in society and politics.[304]

On the wave of this enthusiasm, during the early 1870s, the cause of English, Welsh and Scottish disestablishment seemed on the verge of generating a popular movement of the same strength as the 1868–9 one, parallel to the struggle for the Education Bill, which also encouraged the popular request that Church property be used to fund secular enterprises.[305] That this agitation took off so well in spite of further important ecclesiastical reforms, including the 1869 Endowed Schools Act – which for the first time 'breached the Anglican hold on education'[306] – the repeal of the University Tests Act in 1871, and the bipartisan abolition of the compulsory payment of Church rates in 1868,[307] indicates the extent to which anti-clericalism was rooted in radical politics. On the other hand, these reforms could in no way satisfy popular requests for ecclesiastical reform: the first two were of limited or symbolical significance to plebeian radicals, as neither secondary

---

[302] See [l.a.], 'The Message from Englishmen to Irishmen', *RN*, 14 Mar. 1869, p. 1; [l.a.], *BH*, 13 Mar. 1869, p. 4; [rep.], 'The Irish Church Bill. – Town's Meeting in Leeds', *LM*, 14 Jul. 1869, p. 3; Balfour, *Chamberlain*, p. 77.

[303] [L.a.], 'Mr. Gladstone's Motion', *NW*, 28 Mar. 1868, p. 4; 'Robin Goodfellow', 'The Gossip's Bowl', *NW*, 4 Apr. 1868, p. 4; [l.a.], 'The Welsh Church Grievance', *NW*, 11 Apr. 1868, p. 4.

[304] Plain Dealer, 'The State Church', *BH*, 19 Sept. 1868, p. 4; [l.a.], 'The Irish Church Funds', *BH*, 26 Jun. 1869, p. 4.

[305] [L.a.], 'The Established Church in Wales', *WT*, 29 May 1870, p. 1.

[306] Fletcher, *Feminists and Bureaucrats*, p. 7.

[307] See Anderson, 'Gladstone's abolition of Compulsory Church Rates', pp. 192–95; Machin, *Politics and the Churches 1832–1868*, pp. 337–43, 349–51; see the contemporary comment of [l.a., n.t.], *LM*, 11 Jul. 1868, p. 5; 'The Church Rate Act', *TI*, 21 Aug. 1868, p. 7.

education[308] nor admission to 'Oxbridge' were questions which involved the masses.[309] The third failed to eliminate completely one of the longest-standing causes of anti-clerical strife: in spite of the 1868 Act, some churchwardens continued trying to collect the rate from Nonconformist parishioners, especially in the country-side, exploiting their ignorance; others kept imposing church rates legally, relying on local Acts which had escaped the 1868 measure. The amendment of such anomalies required the attention of Nonconformist politicians for a good many years.[310]

These incidents renewed memories of past persecutions and revived rancour, which was further stimulated by surviving griev-ances like the question of burial rights. Nonconformists could be denied the right to hold funeral services in chuchyards according to their own rites. The setting aside of 'unconsecrated' public cemeteries for the use of non-Anglicans from 1853[311] did not remove discrimination, but made it even more evident; moreover it com-pounded the grievance of Dissenters in rural districts, where generally no alternative 'unconsecrated' burial ground was avail-able. Burial rights also involved the question of Church endow-ment, as the radicals claimed that 'churches and churchyards were not the property of a sect, but of the nation, and all the Dissenters asked was the preservation of their rights as citizens in the national churchyards'.[312] Thus, the 'secularization' of Church property –

---

[308] Balls, 'The Endowed Schools Act of 1869, II', pp. 223, 225. In spite of its radical implications for Church endowment and the uproar which it then excited, this measure generated only marginal interest among plebeian liberals; in fact it was not even mentioned by William Lovett in the article he published in the *Bee-Hive* on 'Education of Women' (See 'An Old Reformer', *BH*, 30 Oct. 1869, p. 1; on the details of the Act See – besides Balls' articles – Parry, *Democracy and Religion*, pp. 309–11, and Fletcher, *Feminists and Bureaucrats*).

[309] Though at least in the case of one future leader of popular radicalism exclusion from 'Oxbridge' was relevant. Howard Evans wrote:

> I wanted to go on and compete for an Oxford scholarship, but my father told me that if I wanted to go forward then I must conform to the Established Church. As he had brought me up to regard Cromwell and Milton and Bunyan as the great heroes of the Primitive Apostolic and Puritan faith, he was not surprised that I answered 'Never! Never!' Ever since then I have done my best to avenge that wrong, and have taken a keen delight in standing by other victims of priestly arrogance, which does the devil's work in the outraged name of the God of all goodness. (Evans, *Radical Fights*, p. 17)

In general, the abolition of the Tests Acts generated popular sympathy, but not enthusiasm: [l.a.], 'The University Test Bill', *LM*. 19 Jun. 1870, p. 6.

[310] Machin, *Politics and the Churches 1832–1868*, p. 355.

[311] See MacIntosh, *Thesis*, pp. 199–200.

[312] [L.a.], 'The Burials Bill', *BH* 17 Feb. 1872, p. 10; [l.a.], 'The Burials Bill', *NW*, 17 Feb. 1872, p. 4. See MacIntosh, *Thesis*, p. 515.

the reassertion of the nation's political control over it, the reversal of decisions taken by aristocratic rulers in past ages – was definitely the main aim of plebeian liberals in the agitation.

The peak was reached in 1871–3. The membership of the Liberation Society had long included a lively plebeian component,[313] but from 1871 artisans and trade unionists like Potter, Howell and other working-class activists – and eventually, in the 1880s, even representatives of the Democratic Federation – were also appointed to its executive committee.[314] Popular support for the Society was also voiced in the correspondence columns of the working-class press,[315] as Liberationist conferences were carefully reported and reviewed,[316] and Miall's resolutions earnestly supported.[317] Moreover, 'Working Men's Committees for Promoting Separation between State and Church' were set up in London and many other towns,[318] led by Howell, Potter, Applegarth and Henry Broadhurst.[319] This mobilization resulted in an impressive series of meetings,[320] of which 250 were held in 1871, 222 in 1872 and 269 in 1873.[321]

However, it is also clear that the Church – just like the Conservative party – had not only opponents, but also faithful supporters among the working people, who set up the 'Working

---

[313] Thompson, 'The Liberation Society', in Hollis (ed.), *Pressure from Without*, p. 229.

[314] Machin, *Politics and the Churches 1868–1921*, p. 46; Ingham, 'The Disestablishment Movement', pp. 47–50.

[315] [Letter by] T. G. Headley, 'The State Church – A Failure', *BH*, 3 Feb. 1872, pp. 6–7; H. S. Skeats, 'Did Jesus Christ or His Apostles Covet Seats in the Senate of Rome?', *BH*, 9 Dec. 1871, p. 1; G. Howell, T. Guile, G. Potter, 'Working Men's Committee for the Separation of Church and State', *BH*, 3 Fe. 1872, p. 8.

[316] See [rep.], 'Church and State', *BH*, 18 Apr. 1868, p. 1; [rep.], 'The Irish Church – Great Meeting at the Metropolitian Tabernacle', *BH* 25 Apr. 1868, p. 5; [rep.], 'The Disestablishment of the English Church', *BH*, 22 Apr. 1871, p. 13; [l.a.], 'Disestablishment of the English Church', *BH*, 6 May 1871, p. 9; [rep.] 'The Disestablishment Movement' [7 columns]. *BH*, 11 Nov. 1871, pp. 13–4. See also Newton, 'Edward Miall and the Diocese of Durham', pp. 164–65.

[317] [L.a.], *BH*, 2 Nov. 1872, p. 10; 'Church and State', *BH*, 13 May 1871, pp. 8–9; [l.a.], 'Thorough Disestablishment', *LW*, 16 Apr. 1871, p. 6; [l.a.], 'Mr. Miall's Defeat', *LW* 7 Jul. 1871, p. 6; [l.a.], 'Lord Salisbury on the Church', *BH*, 19 Oct. 1872, p. 8.

[318] 'Working Men's Committee for Promoting the Separation of Church and State', *BH*, 27 Jan. 1872, p. 4; [rep.], 'Bradford', *Nonconformist*, 27 Mar. 1872, pp. 315–16.

[319] Machin, *Politics and the Churches 1868–1921*. p. 46; Ingham, 'The Disestablishment Movement', p. 47.

[320] For a few of them see [rep.], 'Disestablishment – Working Men's Meeting in Sheffield', *Nonconformist*, 24 Jan. 1872, pp. 82–3; [rep.], 'Meeting At Darlington', *ibid.*, 13 Mar. 1872, p. 268; See also Ingham, 'The Disestablishment Movement', p. 48.

[321] Ingham, 'The Disestablishment Movement', p. 52.

Men's Church Defence Association'. Their activities included –
among other things – disrupting disestablishment meetings.[322] In
one case a 'Church mob' went as far as trying to set fire to the
building in which 2,000 Liberationists were deliberating.[323] However, in some instances at least popular supporters of the Church
seemed interested in defending, not so much the Anglican Establishment, as the working man's right to his beer;[324] this was what
Potter called the 'infamous' connection 'between Church and the
beer-barrel',[325] and suggests that popular animosity against the
Liberation Society was motivated, at least in part, by hostility to
Nonconformist prohibitionism. Still, in general, the Liberationists
managed to keep the situation under control: their strength and
self-confidence was such that in some cases, instead of preventing
the admission of opponents to their meetings, they even allowed
them to present amendments.[326] Artisan Liberationists strived to
emphasize the national – rather than 'sectarian' – relevance of the
issue. They focused on the 'wickedness' of a system in which 'The
State pays the Church . . . and punishes those who are not of the
Church',[327] thus reminding their audience that the Church represented a form of state intervention and political control,[328] which
had opposed every popular movement of the century.[329] They also

---

[322] See [rep.], 'The Disestablishment Movment – Uproarious Meeting at Chester'. *Nonconformist*, 20 Jan. 1873, p. 106; [rep.], 'Riotous Proceedings at Exeter', *ibid.*, 26 Feb. 1873,
p. 204.

[323] [Rep.], 'Disturbances at Wakefield', *Nonconformist*, 26 Feb. 1873, p. 204; [rep.], 'The
Disestablishment Movement. – Great Meeting at Northampton', *ibid.*, 12 Mar. 1873,
p. 252; 'Disorderly Meeting at Openshaw – Another Meeting Broken Up'. *ibid.*, 19 Mar.
1873, p. 274.

[324] [Rep.], 'Northampton – Church Defence Opposition', *Nonconformist*, 5 Feb. 1873, p. 132;
'The Disestablishment Movement. – Wigan. – More Riotous Proceedings', *ibid.*, p. 133.

[325] [Rep.], '[Working men's meeting at] Norwich' [speech by G. Potter], *Nonconformist*, 24
Jan. 1872, p. 83.

[326] See 'Disestablishment – Working Men's Meeting at Sheffield', *Nonconformist*, 24 Jan.
1872, p. 83; '[Working men's meeting at] Derby', *ibid.*, 28 Feb. 1872, p. 211. Perhaps
significantly, in both cases these amendments, which were moved by professional
middle-class people or clergymen, were rejected by the meetings.

[327] Citizen, 'Letters on Church and State, I', *NW*, 22 Apr. 1871, p. 4; the following 'letters'
were published on 29 Apr. 1871, 4 and 6 May 1871, p. 4; [l.a.], 'Ecclesiastical
Cormorants and National Education', *RN*, 12 Nov. 1871. See Parry, *Democracy and
Religion*, p. 235.

[328] G. Potter, in a speech cit. in Ingham, 'The Disestablishment Movement', p. 47.

[329] [Rep.], 'Great Meeting at Leicester', *Nonconformist*, 28 Feb. 1872, p. 211; see also H.
Broadhurst's speech, see [rep.], 'Meeting at Newcastle' [speech by G. Howell],
Nonconformist, 13 Mar. 1872, pp. 267–68; G. Howell, (notes for a speech on Church
disestablishment, n.d., but 1875), MSS in *G. Howell Coll.*, IX, Letter Bk, 861, p. 17; and
Littlejohn, 'The Land and the People', *WT*, 19 Mar. 1876, p. 6;

emphasized the traditional social antagonism between clergymen and plebeian radicals, who denounced the 'class prejudices' of 'the white chokered, immoral, wine-swilling, degraded clergy, backed by debauched aristocrats and degraded wives and daughters'.[330] The Church

> has long been considered a feeding ground for lean members of our great houses, and these people have carried with them into the fold of the Church, not the humility taught by the Apostles, not the sense of human equality and justice which the founder of the Christian religion died to establish, but rather the pride of the old pharisees and the worldly greed which in the old days hated the new light and sought to trample it out with all the hard relentless of bigotry and pride.[331]

Not surprisingly, the poor '[went] to the Methodist chapel, where they th[ought] they hear[d] something that does them good'.[332] In contrast, the wealthy forced the State to pay for their religion: the latter argument was also often stressed to bring home – to a people deeply concerned with the cost of central government – the financial implications of the endowment.[333] In fact, the cost of the Established Church was the factor which excited the most furious reactions among working-class radicals.[334]

Yet, after 1874 the participation of urban workers in the disestablishment campaign began to decline: indeed, Machin has argued that as early as 1873 the alliance between the Liberation Society and plebeian radicalism 'petered out, and the Working-men's Committee ceased to function',[335] just as the parallel co-operation between the National Education League and the trades unions had come to an end. He has explained this crisis as the inevitable epilogue of a movement which did not really have deep roots, since 'urban workers in general showed little positive zeal either for or against the establishment', tended to be indifferent to

---

[330] [Letter by] 'A Reynoldist', 'The Education Bill', *RN*, 12 Jun. 1870, p. 3; see also [letter by] 'Cromwell', 'The Parsons and their Compeers', in *ibid.*, the latter being a list of insults more than a proper letter.

[331] [L.a.], 'The Church and its Ministers', *BH*, 7 Jun. 1873, p. 7; Gracchus, *RN*, 18 Oct. 1874, p. 3.

[332] [L.a.], *BH*, 9 Dec. 1872, pp. 8–9; H. Crompton, *BH*, 30 Dec. 1872, pp. 1–2.

[333] 'Disestablishment and Disendowment of the Church', *BH*, 20 May 1871, pp. 1; see G. Potter, 'The Church of England and the People', *Fortnightly Review* (1872), pp. 176–7 and 189–90.

[334] Lloyd Jones, 'Disestablishment and Disendowment of the Church', *BH*, 20 May 1871, pp. 1–2.

[335] Machin, *Politics and the Churches 1868–1921*. p. 47.

religion, and 'were scarcely affected by any "social oppression" which might be attributed to the established Church. It was not clear what material or religious benefit disestablishment could give them'.[336] However, if these really were the reasons it would be difficult to explain why urban workers had been interested in disestablishment at all, even in 1868–72. Moreover, Machin agrees that 'the link between the Society and some working-class organizations persisted for a long time',[337] especially in the industrial regions of the north.

Keeping these considerations in mind, an alternative explanation is to be found in the specific political context of 1873–4: for by then it had become clear not only that the Conservatives were much stronger than previously anticipated, but also that the Liberal front bench would not consent to go any further in the policy of disestablishment. Moreover, because the legislation of 1868–74 had made the Church less vulnerable – by abolishing its Irish branch, removing some Nonconformist grievances, and shifting the 'religious difficulty' in education from the level of national to that of local politics – the issue of disestablishment in England was less urgent. It was certainly not important enough to cause any major revolt against the Anglican Liberal leadership: indeed, both at parliamentary and constituency level, the radicals were generally ready to conciliate and compromise, especially when the general elections drew near.[338] As far as urban radicals were concerned, it would seem that by the end of the 1870s the focus of the agitation was moving from 'big' national grievances, which appealed to the masses, to less spectacular questions of principle, which appealed especially to the activists.[339] Possibly this was also reflected in a change of emphasis in Liberationist arguments, which during the second half of the 1870s showed a growing concern for issues of civil liberty. Similar components in the Liberationist rhetorical arsenal were not new; indeed, civil liberty causes had always been linked to anti-clericalism, through – for example – questions like the repeal of the law forbidding marriage

[336] *Ibid.*
[337] *Ibid.*
[338] 'The Representation of Newcastle. Address by Mr. Cowen in the Lecture Room. Tuesday, December 30, 1873'. TS copy in *Cowen Coll.*, B 159; 'A Member of the Church of England', 'Twelve Reasons for Disestablishing the Church of England', *NW*, 31 Jan. 1874, p. 5.
[339] Ironside, 'Mr. Miall's Motion', *NW*, 6 Jul. 1872, p. 4.

to a deceased wife's sister,[340] and of the Contagious Diseases Acts. However, from the late 1870s they seemed to acquire a greater emphasis. In particular, the notion of the non-confessional State, which 'exists only for secular purposes' and whose duty 'is done when it secures entire freedom of worship',[341] was quoted with increasing frequency well before the beginning of the Bradlaugh agitation in 1880. When Howell recapitulated the principles of the Liberationists in a speech in 1878, he listed four points:

1. That religion is a matter of conscience between man and his Maker; it cannot be defined by statute, nor enforced by law.
2. In all matters of conscience the State should recognize perfect equality before the law for all Sects, Parties, and Persons.
3. In a Church which is State created, endowed, and maintained, there may be, to a certain extent there now is, liberty of conscience, but equality there is not, and never can be.
4. There is in the nature of things a violation of equality in the constitution and government of a church which, by its position, 'lords' it over all other sects in the country . . . there has been a constant and persistent effort on the part of the Established Church to crush even liberty of conscience, as her past history, and even her present action clearly shows.[342]

Another factor was that the Anglican revival in the industrial towns had changed the relationship between the Church and the working-class community.[343] This change was accentuated by the fact that both Evangelical and liberal Anglicans were increasingly concerned about the social problems of the inner cities, and readier to co-operate with other Christians in evangelization and charity. Anti-labour prejudice was still entrenched in certain Anglican quarters, as illustrated in 1872 by the bishop of Gloucester's harsh words against rural trade unionists[344] and in 1879 by a National Society schools' textbook which described the trade unions as semi-

---

[340] John Bright described it as 'the work of priests' reflecting their thirst for 'domination and tyranny', rather than any Biblical teaching (cit. in [l.a.], 'A Great Social Wrong', *NW*, 24 Apr. 1869, 4). See [l.a.], 'Breaking Up the Family', *LW*, 8 May 1870, p. 1; [rep.], 'Marriage with a Deceased Wife's Sister', *BH*, 11 Mar. 1871, p. 11: 'A large and Enthusiastic Meeting . . .' On the issue, see Pearsall, *The Worm in the Bud*, pp. 138–40.
[341] [L.a.], 'Disestablishment', *NW*, 19 Feb. 1876, p. 4.
[342] [G. Howell on Church disestablishment, n.d., but spring 1878], MSS in *G. Howell Coll.*, IX Letter Bk, 198.
[343] Yates, 'The Religious Life of Victorian Leeds', in Fraser (ed.), *History of Modern Leeds*, p. 254.
[344] Kitson Clark, *Churchmen and the Condition of England*, pp. 247–8.

criminal organizations: however it is significant that in the former case the bishop felt ashamed of his own words and tried to make reparation,[345] and in the latter the offensive textbook was withdrawn following remonstrations by the TUC.[346]

Thus, the decline in popular urban participation during the late 1870s was not due to the indifference of popular liberals, but to the successes that they had already achieved and were then achieving – especially through school board politics – and to the changes in the general political climate. In itself, the separation between Church and State still excited strong feelings,[347] also because it was linked to the struggle against ritualism – then fiercer than ever – as a means of leading the Church back to orthodox Protestantism.[348] Far from disappearing, between the Liberal defeat in 1874 and the Bulgarian agitation in 1876 this branch of anti-clericalism remained one of the few political causes which still excited the enthusiasm of plebeian radicals. Indeed, the Liberation Society became the focus of their hopes for 'the resurrection of the Liberal Party'.[349]

The really new factor in the 1870s was not the decline of urban anti-clericalism, but – as Machin admits[350] – the political awakening of the farm workers. Most of them – and especially the activists in the trade union movement – were ardently Nonconformist, fiercely anti-clerical, and committed to the principle of total separation between Church and State.[351] Strife between the politicized countryfolk and the Church had many causes, since evils that had declined in the towns had survived in the countryside, and were aggravated by the fact that in rural districts social and political conflicts were mediated neither by strong and recognized trade unions, nor by representative local government, not even

---

[345] *Ibid.*, p. 248.
[346] See *Minutes and Report of the 12th TUC* (Edinburgh 15–20 Sept. 1879), pp. 34–5; Griggs, 'The Trades Union Congress and the Controversy over the National Society', 240–44; and *Trades Unions Congress and the Struggle for Education*, p. 77.
[347] MacIntosh, *Thesis*, p. 384.
[348] G. Howell Coll., Letter Bk, n.d. [but 1875], 852–62. The stress on the success of voluntary efforts as a system of evangelization was typical of the Nonconformist anti-Church propaganda of the day: Machin, *Politics and the Churches 1832–1868*, p. 345.
[349] [L.a.], *BH*, 9 May 1874, p. 8; [l.a.], 'Disestablishment and Disendowment', *LW*, 8 Nov. 1874, p. 6.
[350] Machin, *Politics and the Churches 1868–1921*. p. 47.
[351] See for a few examples [l.a.], 'The House of Lords and Church Reform', *Labourers' Union Chronicle*, 20 Mar. 1875, p. 1; [rep.], 'The National Agricultural Labourers' Union – Meeting of the Executive Council. – Mr. Holloway's visit to New Zealand . . . – Civil and Religious Privileges', *Labourers' Union Chronicle*, 3 Apr.1875, p. 6.

school boards. Especially when looked at from a rural perspective, the Church appeared the main obstacle to progress both in Parliament, through the alliance between spiritual and temporal Lords, and in the country. Its influence was particularly resented in villages and small towns that were under the influence of what the *Daily News* stigmatised as 'the Political Parson . . . little else than a [Tory] squire in black coat',[352] exclusively concerned with the preservation of his privileges and ready to act as the religious arm of the Conservative party.[353] To the 'political parson' was generally ascribed a distinct anti-labour bias, and he often seemed to side with the farmers and landlords in every way: indeed Frederic Harrison wrote that the rural incumbent, like the Roman Catholic priest in rural France, was just a kind of 'black spiritual police'.[354] Thus it is not surprising that the organized agricultural labourers were strongly hostile to the 'State Church':[355] as 'One from the Plough' wrote to Gladstone, 'We know, sir, and these poor men know, who are their enemies . . . many of the clergy of the Established Church are tyrants of the worst class'.[356] On the other hand, Anglican ministers complained that the setting up of local sections of the National Agricultural Labourers' Union, or even simply the circulation of copies of their newspaper, was accompanied by a decline in the labourers' attendance at Church services.[357] The *Labourers' Union Chronicle* – which was very sympathetic towards the radical ecclesiastical policy advocated by the *Nonconformist* newspaper[358] – was committed to 'the British Toilers'

---

[352] [L.a. n.t.], *DN*, 27 Oct. 1868, p. 4.

[353] [L.a.], 'Parliamentary Manners', *LW*, 24 May 1868, p. 1. See the case of the vicar who – on the eve of the 1885 elections – sought Salisbury's advice as to how to be more effective when preaching to the labourers on why they should vote for the Conservative party: Pugh, *Making*, p. 70.

[354] F. Harrison to J. Morley, 22 Mar. 1871, *F. Harrison Papers*, 1/53, pp. 19–28.

[355] See the series of articles published in 1873 in the *Labourers' Union Chronicle* under the general title of 'The Church of England in Its Relation to the Working Classes': see esp. 5 Jul. 1873, pp. 1–2; 19 Jul. 1873, 4; 26 Jul. 1873, p. 4; 9 Aug. 1873, 4; 1 Nov. 1873, 2 subtitled 'Episcopal Plunder'; 22 Nov. 1873, 1 subtitled '"Episcopal Scoundrelism" – Simony.'

[356] G. Mitchell, 'One from the Plough', 'To the Right Hon. W. E. Gladstone, M.P.', *Nonconformist*, 22 Mar. 1876, p. 277.

[357] See 'Extracts from Incumbents' Answers to the Bishop of Oxford's Visitaton Questions for the Archdeaconry of Oxford', and particularly M.Talmage Fifield with Idbury and V. Pearse Hanwell, in Horn (ed.), *Agricultural Trade Unionism*, pp. 132–3 and 136.

[358] See 'The Nonconformist Newspaper and the National Agricultural Labourers' Union', *Labourers' Union Chronicle*. 14 Jun. 1873, p. 8; and 'The *Nonconformist* on Wholesale-Emigration', *ibid.*, 13 Dec. 1873, p. 1. The *Nonconformist* had supported the Chartists as

Right to Free Land, Freedom from Priestcraft, and from the Tyranny of Capital': and it is interesting that the labourers saw a clear connection between these questions, to the extent that in some areas they were reported to say that they intended to have 'their share' of tithe and glebe.[359] The occasions for clashes between trade union activists and rural parsons multiplied especially from the mid-1870s, when Arch's trade union began its ten-year agitation for the county franchise.[360]

From the point of view of the Liberation Society and the Radicals, this political awakening meant the infusion of much new blood into the anti-clerical movement: however, it also meant that the epicentre of the latter was moving away from the cities, at a time when the rural working men did not – as yet – have the vote. However, this contributed towards re-unifying the Liberal party during the second half of the 1870s, because Radicals and Nonconformists began to set aside their differences and rally round the cause of county franchise as the necessary preliminary step towards further reforms. As always when a major political problem was hard to solve, popular radicals went back to the Chartist recipe of more democracy. A turning point was the general election of 1874, which demonstrated that the Church was well rooted and supported in urban constituencies, and that its opponents were not strong enough to carry disestablishment in England in the way they had done in Ireland.[361]

Thus, the succeeding general election – in 1880 – was fought on issues that had little bearing on the question, though eighteen members of the Executive Committee of the Liberation Society were returned to parliament in the wake of the huge Liberal majority.[362] Gladstone's triumph was promptly followed by the Burials Act: this relieved another old grievance,[363] though – as in

well, and, because of its democratic principles, had been praised by *The Republican* during 1840s (Faulkner, *Chartism and the Churches*, pp. 100–1).
[359] Cit. in Dunbabin, 'The "Revolt of the Field"', p. 73.
[360] See e.g. [rep.], 'Labourers' Demonstration – Mr. Arch at Hugendorf, Berks.', *Labourers' Union Chronicle*, 24 Apr. 1875, p. 5. See Griggs, *Trades Union Congress and the Struggle for Education*, pp. 78–81. Cf. below pp. 291–302.
[361] [L.a.], *BH*, 5 Oct. 1872, pp. 8–9.
[362] MacIntosh, *Thesis*, p. 423.
[363] For examples of local conflicts on this issue during the late 1870s, see [l.a.], 'The Government Defeat on the Burials Bill', *NW*, 23 Jun. 1877, p. 4; [l.a.], 'Lord Harrowby's Clause', *LW*, 24 Jun. 1877, p. 1; Resolution of the Council of the LRL, 20 Apr. 1877, in *Labour Representation League Papers*, p. 250; [l.a.], 'The Battle of God's Acre', *LW*, 6 Jun. 1880, p. 6.

the case of previous reforms – many country parsons managed to disregard the law and 'continued to deny the Nonconformist ministers and chapel families the right to a decent burial in the churchyard' well into the 1890s.[364] The Burials Act, like the abolition of the compulsory rates in 1868, illustrated the ambiguous operation of moderate reforms, which reduced the momentum of popular anti-clericalism without sorting out the problem of religious equality in a definitive way.

Yet by the early 1880s, as the county franchise approached, it seemed that the prospective new electors would do for the Church of England what the urban householders had done for the Church of Ireland in 1869. Liberationist expectations were reinforced as outstanding leaders of county radicalism confirmed their hostility to the Anglican Establishment, to its endowment, and to the hauteur characterizing the lifestyle of many rural clergymen.[365] More than ever the contrast between plebeian Dissenters and the Church was social and political, rather than theological. Besides, recurrent petty persecutions still reminded the countryfolk of the injustice of an 'ecclesiastical system, which exalts or depresses men according to their religious beliefs'.[366] As one Anglican minister admittd, commenting on the political feeling of the rural workers in 1885. 'Religious liberty exists in the great centres, while it is stifled in the villages, and though I'm a strong Tory, if I were a labourer in the country this alone would have made me plump Liberal'.[367]

Max Weber has written that 'what gave the [seventeenth-century] Puritans, and above all the Baptist sects, their insuperable power of resistance, was not the intellectualism of the elite but rather the intellectualism of the plebeian and occasionally even the pariah classes'.[368] Though he argues that this 'mass intellectualism'[369] was a somewhat unique historical phenomenon, Victorian popular

---

[364] Hollis, *Ladies Elect*, p. 363. One of these cases, in Caernarvonshire in 1888, helped 'to launch the young Baptist lawyer David Lloyd George in his Parliamentary career' (Machin, *Politics and the Churches 1868–1921*, p. 132).

[365] 'The Church and the Working Classes', *Durham Miners's Association, Monthly Report*, January 1884, No. 44, pp. 4–5, in D/DMA 7. (Italics in the text).

[366] [L.a.], 'The General Election', *NW*, 31 Jan. 1874. p. 4.

[367] Cit. in Simons, 'Church Disestablishment', p. 819.

[368] Weber, *Sociology of Religion*, p. 134.

[369] *Ibid*, p. 135.

liberals seem to present a closely parallel case:[370] not only were they imbued with Puritan religious and ethical values, as we have seen in chapter 1, but also many of them showed an impressive grasp of contemporary economic, social and political theories, a sophisticated understanding of political strategies, a taste for controversy, discussion, and participation in political decisions, and indeed a sense of being 'called' to a mission. Their 'mission' was the replacement of privilege with democracy, or, as some said, the 'Americanization' of Britain.

To them democracy was a religious heritage, a culture, a language, a habit of mind, a set of attitudes to everyday problems, an end in itself. However, chapters 2 and 3 have shown that it was also a means to an end, since it was related to the fiscal 'social contract', and ultimately instrumental in the hoped-for realization of the Jeffersonian utopia – a society of independent producers, unimpeded by either aristocratic or State oppression[371].

Such a society would need no government intervention: that was the ideal. The reality was admittedly quite different. For one thing, as we have seen in chapter 3, the market was rendered 'unfair' by customary practices and legal restrictions which could be amended only through Parliamentary action. Moreover, many people were *not* 'independent producers' – nor indeed even independent at all. Hence, popular liberals, like their contemporaries in North American populist movements,[372] in order 'to attain the goal of the yeoman republic . . . called on the aid of government intervention . . . [though] this intervention was envisaged as temporary'.[373] It was in this spirit that land reform, 'national' education, and the disestablishment and disendowment of the Church of England were conceived, all intended to replace the old system of 'aristocratic monopoly' with a more open society based on liberty, equality and fraternity.

Among the various forms of public intervention requested by plebeian liberals, primary education was the one which they hoped

---

[370] Weber himself goes some way towards acknowledging this when he writes that Gladstone's 'charisma of rhetoric' was 'irresistible in its appeal to puritan rationalism' (Weber, *Selections*, p. 248); for a detailed discussion of this topic, see Chapter 7 below.

[371] For Parallel attitudes among north American populists, see Worsley, 'The Concept of Populism', in Ionescu and Gellner (eds.), *Populism*, p. 220.

[372] It is significant that the latter were also reared in the traditions of Independent Nonconformity: *ibid.*, p. 221.

[373] MacRae, 'Populism as an ideology', in Ionescu and Gellner (eds.), *Populism*, p. 160.

would be most effective: it was close to the spirit and aspirations of Puritan 'mass intellectualism' and was aimed at changing not only institutions and situations, but also the people themselves. In this sense, to the radical plebeian reformer of Puritan background education was the secular parallel to, and complement of, evangelism. Yet, even education could be foiled by the fact that the aristocratic forces that the radicals attacked extended their 'monopoly' to the existing school system through the 'State Church – itself a 'monopolistic' institution. Hence, the inevitable politicization of the education question, and the various anti-clerical crusades to dismantle the Church and loosen its stranglehold on the schools. For, as the ex-Chartist Robert Sykes put it in 1874, radical working men were convinced that 'this education question (education free from priestly and sectarian bias) lies at the basis of true liberty'.[374]

Thus anti-clericalism occupied a crucial and emblematic position in the ideology of popular liberals. On the one hand, it summed up both their commitment to democracy, and their attitudes towards the reform of society and the economic system; it also reflected the separatist polity of congregational Dissent, with its concomitant rejection of central government intervention and parallel support for the locally-managed action of community or representative bodies. On the other hand, the attitudes associated with popular-liberal anti-clericalism explain why further advances in public intervention in social and economic matters were ultimately dependent on political democracy: if public intervention was – in the end – an unpleasant necessity, it was imperative that 'the people' were given political control of the government machine, to ensure that only the 'right' kind of intervention took place, and that both aristocratic patronage and political control from Whitehall were excluded. In this way the traditional Chartist emphasis on democracy as the first cause of all things good and desirable was reinforced by the development of more advanced approaches to social reform: more than ever before, democracy turned out to be both the means to an end and an end in itself.

[374] R. Sykes to J. Chamberlain, 11 Feb. 1874, in Chamberlain Papers, 6/5/2/58.

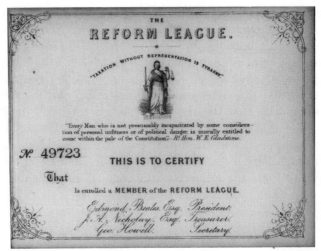

1a Membership card of the Reform League, 1864–8. Note the Whig motto and the quotation from Gladstone's famous speech (see p. ooo). The card was signed by E. Beales, J. A. Nicholas and G. Howell.

1b Membership card of the National Liberal League. A London-based radical-labour association, set up in 1877, as an alternative to the Birmingham National Liberal Federation. Note that the motto is, again, based on the tradition of Whig radicalism. The portraits are also very significant: from bottom left, anti-clockwise, J. S. Mill, R. Cobden, Oliver Cromwell and an unidentified Puritan leader. This card and 1a are in the G. Howell Collection, Bishopsgate Institute, London. The card was signed by the labour leaders Howell and Broadhurst, and by W. Morris.

MANHOOD SUFFRAGE.

GREAT

DEMONSTRATION

ON NEWCASTLE TOWN MOOR.

SPECIAL NOTICE !

All the Men that intend to join in the Procession, especially the Marshals, Captains, and other active Promoters of the Demonstration, are requested to give particular attention to the instructions laid down in the following Programme. The order assigned to each Body by Ballot must be strictly adhered to. The Regulations as to the Streets in which the different Bodies are to meet, and the manner in which they are to be reached, must also be observed. It is the earnest wish of the Committee that as little interruption to the Ordinary Traffic of the Town should be occasioned by the Prossession as possible, and they appeal to the men who join in the proposed gathering to assist in PRESERVING ORDER, and attending to the Regulations laid down.

ON SATURDAY, APRIL 12, 1873,

A Great Radical Reform Demonstration will be held at Newcastle-on-Tyne.

The PROCESSION will start from Neville Street, opposite the Central Railway Station, punctually at One o'Clock.

The Procession will proceed along Collingwood Street and Mosley Street, up Grey Street, past Earl Grey's Monument, along Blackett Street West, then up Percy Street, through the Haymarket, and along Barras Bridge to the Town Moor.

There will be Six Platforms, from which Addresses will delivered by Fifty different Speakers, Four Resolutions will be moved affirming the justice and necessity of basing the Electoral Franchise in both Counties and Boroughs on Manhood. A Petition to Parliament in favour of Manhood Suffrage, and a Memorial to Mr. GLADSTONE will also be submitted to the Meeting.

The Members of all organised Political Bodies, of all Trade and Benefit Societies, and Workmen in different Factories and Collieries, with their Trade and other Emblems, Banners, and Bands, are invited to join in the Procession, and attend the Meeting on the Town Moor.

GENERAL ORDERS.

1.—The Procession must walk Four Deep.

2.—Each Body of Men must have at least Two Captains—one to walk at the head, and the other to walk at the end of each Section.

3.—In addition to the Captains, for every Forty Men there must a Marshal, to walk by the side of the Procession and keep the men in line.

4.—The Captains and the Divisional Marshals must be appointed by each body of men themselves. The Mounted Marshals will be appointed by the Executive Committee.

5.—Each distinct body of men must carry at their head a board, with the name of the Society they belong to, and the Number of the Place they are to take in the Procession printed or written in large letters.

6.—The entire Procession will be under the direction of Twelve Mounted Marshals, whose duty it will be to bring the different divisions into their proper places in the Line of March.

7.—Each Marshal and Captain should Wear or Carry some Badge or Wand to indicate his Office and his Duties.

ORDER OF PROCESSION.—FIRST SECTION.

The Chairmen of the different Platforms and the Speakers will walk at the head of the Procession. They must meet and form in line in Neville Street, opposite the Portico of the Central Station. When the Procession reaches the Town Moor the Chairmen and Speakers must take up their positions on the platforms assigned them, and commence the business of the meeting with as little delay as possible.

SECOND SECTION.

The Northumberland Miners will walk after the Chairmen and Speakers. They will form in Rye Hill Street, Maple Street, Wharncliffe Street, and the cross streets adjacent to the Grammar School. The head of the Procession—the Bebside men—will stand at the bottom of Rye Hill, next to Scotswood Road, and the other collieries, according to the order of the ballot, will fall in behind. It is absolutely necessary to keep the main thoroughfares of the town clear till the Procession starts. If any of the Northumbrian Collieries, therefore, walk in procession from the Blyth and Tyne Station, they must proceed by way of Blackett Street, Gallowgate, Corporation Street, past Dr. Rutherford's Church, and Elswick Lane; if they walk from the Central Station, they must go up Westgate Road, and along Elswick Lane, to the place of rendezvous in Rye Hill and adjoining streets.

The following is the order in which the men from the Northumberland Collieries have been balloted to walk :—

The Men from these Collieries will form in Rye Hill Street.	The Men from these Collieries will form in Maple Street and Around the Grammar School.	The Men from these Collieries will form in Wharncliffe Street.
1.—Bebside Colliery.	16.—New Delaval.	32.—Mickley, Prudhoe, and West Wylam.
2.—Pegswood and Longhirst.	17.—Seaton Burn.	33.—Plashetts.
3.—Coxlodge and North Fenham.	18.—Dinnington.	34.—Acombe and Fourstones.
4.—Cambois.	19.—Barrington and Choppington.	35.—Walbottle, Throckley, and Old Throckley.
5.—Dudley.	20.—Nedderton.	36.—South Benwell, Delaval, Benwell, Elswick, and
6.—Broomhill.	21.—West Cramlington.	Montague.
7.—West Moor.	22.—Shilbottle.	37.—Ridsdale.
8.—Ashington.	23.—North Seaton.	38.—Wylam Wylam Hills, and Heddon.
9.—Old Delaval.	24.—Gosforth.	39.—Lumbley, Midgeholme, and Byron.
10.—Sleekburn.	25.—Seghill.	40.—Coanwood.
11.—Widdrington.	26.—Hartford and Cramlington.	
12.—Newsham.	27.—New Backworth, Old Backworth, and East Holywell.	
13.—Cowpen.	28.—Ratcliffe.	
14.—Walker.	29.—Burradon.	
15.—West Sleckburn.	30.—Preston.	
	31.—Scremerston, Berwick Hill, Fordmoss, Barmoor, and Shoreswood.	

THIRD SECTION.

The Durham Miners will walk third in the procession (after the Northumberland Miners), and will form in the following streets as the different bodies arrive:—Blenheim Street, Blandford Street, George Street, Westmoreland Street, and the cross streets adjacent thereto. If the Durham Miners walk in bodies from the Central Station, or from either the Tyne Bridge or the High Level, they must walk up Westgate Street past the Tyne Theatre to Blenheim Street, Blandford Street, Westmoreland Street, and George Street, The men from Milkwell Burn Colliery will stand at the foot of Blenheim Street, and the other collieries will fall behind them in the order of the ballot.

The following is the order in which the men from the Durham collieries have been ballotted to walk :—

1.—Milkwell Burn and Hamsterley.	20.—Harraton.	38.—Cornsay Colliery.
2.—Hunwick.	21.—West Pelton.	39.—Ryhope.
3.—Tudhoe and Spennymoor.	22.—Monkwearmouth.	40.—Harton.
4.—Haswell.	23.—Ravensworth.	41.—Shipcote.
5.—Chophill, Beamish Air Pit, and West Stanley.	24.—Houghton-le-Spring.	42.—Pensher.
6.—Heworth.	25.—Old Durham.	43.—New Lambton.
7.—North Hetton.	26.—South Derwent.	44.—Adventure, Middle Rainton.
8.—North Brancepeth.	27.—Burnopfield.	45.—Wheatley Hill.
9.—Marley Hill.	28.—Quarrington Hill.	46.—Edmonsley and the Byron.
10.—Sunnyside and Hedley Hope.	29.—Modomsley.	47.—Springwell.
11.—Hetton.	30.—Westwood.	48.—Chester, South Moor, and Waldridge.
12.—Marton.	31.—Wardley.	49.—Eden, &c. (two or three collieries in the neighbour-
13.—Kibblesworth.	32.—Usworth.	hood of Consett, all ballotted for in one body).
14.—Lizzie, Pontop, and East Pontop.	33.—Lilly and South Medomsley.	50.—Felling and Tyne Main.
15.—Water Houses.	34.—Tanfield, Tanfield Moor, and Tanfield Lea.	51.—East Castle (near Consett).
16.—Townley, Addison, &c.	35.—Lintz Colliery.	52.—Broom Drift.
17.—Boldon.	36.—Felton Fell and Cragg Head.	53.—Tin Mill.
18.—Washington.	37.—Framwellgate Moor.	54.—Bewick Main. [that neighbourhood.
19.—Philadelphia.		55.—Sunnybrow, and three or four other collieries in

As the number of men that will walk in the Procession from some of the Durham Collieries is not yet known, it has been found impossible to name the exact list of collieries that will form in each street. All that can be said at present is that the head of the Procession will stand in Blenheim Street opposite Harry Kelly's, and that the other Collieries must fall in behind, filling Blenheim Street first, Blandford Street second, George Street third, and then Westmoreland Street.

FOURTH SECTION.

¶The members of the different Organised Trades and the men from the various Factories on Tyneside will form in Gloucester Street, Park Road, and adjacent streets. After the Northumberland and Durham Miners have moved away, the Men of the different Trades must move forward to Harry Kelley's, and follow the last of the Durham Miners in the order of ballot, the Chainmakers heading the trade procession. The following is the order in which the men belonging to the different Tyneside Trade Societies and Factories have been ballotted to walk :—

The Men belonging to these Societies and Factories will form in Gloucester Street, Park Road, and neighbouring streets.	10.—Cabinetmakers.	22.—Patternmakers.
1.—Chainmakers.	11.—T. Clark and Co.'s Works.	23.—Amalgamated Engineers.
2.—Bricklayers.	12.—Newcastle and Gateshead Tailors.	24.—Joiners of Newcastle and District.
3.—Hawthorn's Works.	13.—Brass and Copper Trade.	25.—Bakers.
4.—Printers' Machinists.	14.—Moulders.	26.—Painters.
5.—Joicey's Works.	15.—Shoemakers.	27.—Quarrymen.
6.—Newcastle Trades Council.	16.—Tanners.	28.—Boilermakers.
7.—Tyne Shipwrights' Provident Society.	17.—Masons of Newcastle and District.	29.—The Jarrow Workmen (Messrs. Palmer & Co.'s Works.
8.—Workmen of Newcastle and District Saw Mills.	18.—Gateshead Pipemakers.	30.—The Blaydon Workmen.
9.—Elswick Works.	19.—River Tyne Commissioners' Men.	31.—Workmen unconnected with any Trade Society, and
	20.—Ouseburn Engine Works and Co-operative Smiths.	the Men from such Factories as have not had any
	21.—Tyne Shipwrights.	special organisation for joining the Procession.

All other bodies of Workmen that join the Procession will have to fall in behind the last body named above.

TRAIN ARRANGEMENTS.

The North-Eastern Railway Company will run SPECIAL TRAINS on their various Lines to accommodate the Men joining in the Procession. The Hours of Running these trains will be announced in a few days.

On the Blyth and Tyne Railway RETURN TICKETS will be issued by all Ordinary Trains during the day, and also by SPECIAL TRAINS, as under :—

Leaving at or about	a.m.	a.m.	a.m.	a.m.	Leaving at or about	a.m.	a.m.	a.m.	a.m.	a.m.	Leaving at or about	a.m.	a.m.	a.m.	a.m.	a.m.
Bedlington	8·0	9·15	—	10·30	10·46	Hartley	8·15	9·30	—	10·45	11·0	Backworth	8·31	9·46	10· 7	11·1	11·16
Bebside	8· 4	9·19	—	10·34	10·49	Benton Delaval	8·20	9·35	—	10·50	11·5	Benton	8·38	9·53	10·14	11· 8	11·23
Newsham	8·10	9·25	—	10·40	10·55	Seghill	8·24	9·39	10·0	10·54	11·9	Gosforth	8·43	9·58	10·19	11·13	11·28

Available for Return by Ordinary Trains, and by Special Trains from New Bridge Street at 4.30, 5.0, 6.30, and 7.0 p.m, the same day. The Return Special Trains will Run as far as Choppington.

Passengers from the Blyth and Newbiggin Branches will avail themselves of the Ordinary Trains.

An Adjourned Delegate Meeting, to complete the arrangements for the Demonstration, will be held in the Mechanics' Institution, New Bridge Street, on Saturday first, April, 5, at Three o'clock.

J. McKENDRICK, A. SCORER, Hon. Secs.

THOS. BURT, Treasurer.   JOS. COWEN, Jun., Chairman.

Newcastle-upon-Tyne, March 31, 1873.

NORTH OF ENGLAND CO-OPERATIVE PRINTING WORKS, 40, HIGH BRIDGE, NEWCASTLE-ON-TYNE.

2 Poster of the 1873 Newcastle suffrage demonstration (see pp. 283–7). There is an impressive list of the trade unions involved (the miners are listed in the second and third sections, the artisans in the fourth.

3 Popular liberalism: some leaders. Standing are the shepherd T. Eley, and J. Arch, with two urban trade unionists.

4 Popular liberalism: the rank and file, celebrating a Lib-lab victory at Swanton Morley.

5 Farmworkers' demonstration at Ham Hill, Yeovil, Whit Monday 1877, one of the many discussed on pp. 291–3. Platform men numbered include Joseph Arch (1), and T. Halliday (2) of the miners.

6 The great London Franchise demonstration of 21 July 1884. None of these
photographs has previously been published. They are preserved in the Bishopsgate Institute, London. These photographs were taken from Cockspur Street, as
the procession was leaving Trafalgar Square. Visible in the background are
Nelson's Column and the Grand Hotel. Note the typical banners (a) and (b), the
model which probably represented the House of Lords as a target of radical
hostility. (c) The Kent & Sussex Agricultural Labourers' Union. Note the

American spelling of the word 'laborers' on the banner. The American spelling was widely used in republican circles (e.g. *The National Reformer*) and by the organized farmworkers who were strong admirers of the United States. The picture on the banner in (d) shows Gladstone as an agricultural labourer. It is interesting that by the 1880s the bowler hat had become the working man's standard 'Sunday' headgear. (e) shows again the Kent & Sussex Agricultural

Labourers' Union with their brass band. The relaxed atmosphere is evident, and large numbers of women can be seen in the crowd.

PART II

Reform

CHAPTER 5

The franchise question

We want Reform because we see
Some men with too much money.
While some fall in our streets and die
For want of food and shelter.[1]

Whereas it hath been the Ancient Liberty of this Nation,
that all the Free-born people have freely elected their
Representers in Parliament, and their Sheriffs and Iustices of the Peace, &c. and that they were abridged of
that their native Liberty, by a Statute of the 8.H.6.7.
That therefore, that Birth-right of all English men, be
forthwith restored to all which are not, or shal not be
legally disenfranchised for some criminal cause, or are
not under 21 years of age, or servants, or beggers . . .[2]

THE APPEAL OF THE REFORMERS

No single issue illustrates the continuity between Chartism and
working-class liberalism better than popular commitment to the
enlargement of the franchise.[3] After Kennington Common pressure
for reform was kept alive by regional organizations throughout the
1850s,[4] but it was only in the 1860s that the movement took off
again at a national level, spurred on by the direct involvement of
the trade unions[5] and the influence of continental and American

---

[1] J. P. Williams, 'Why Working Men want Reform', *BH*,9 Feb. 1867, p. 6.
[2] *To the Supream Authority of England, the Commons Assembled in Parliament. The Earnest Petition of many Free-born People of this Nation*, London, 1648, in Wolfe (ed.), *Leveller Manifestoes*, p. 269.
[3] Tiller, 'Late Chartism in Halifax', in Epstein and Thompson (eds.), *The Chartist Experience*, pp. 311–44.
[4] See Gillespie, *Labor and Politics*, pp. 13, 178–85; Muris, *Thesis*, pp. 32–3.
[5] As early as November, 1861 the Glasgow Trades Council favoured trades unions' involvement in politics, on the grounds that, since they were under the law, they had an interest in its amendment: Gillespie, *Labor and Politics*, pp. 206–7. London trade unionism followed suite only in 1864.

democratic thought.[6] As in previous reform agitations, the 'sheet anchor' of the cause of reform was not some Mazzinian idea of democracy, but the old Whig rhetoric of 'no taxation without representation'.[7] However, behind it there stood more radical notions, like pride in contributing to the support of the *res publica* and the concept of an active citizenship which identified freedom with being 'governed by laws to which we have *ourselves* assented, either in person or *by representatives* for whose election *we have actually voted*'.[8] The latter idea, remarkably close to what Benjamin Constant had called 'the liberty of the ancients' – the classical concept of a participatory democracy – implied that all those without 'a right of suffrage [we]re *slaves*'.[9] Thus, the franchise was at one and the same time the means of liberty and its substance and symbol: a citizen could not be really free so long as he remained unenfranchised. This concept was especially appealing in the immediate aftermath of the American Civil War,[10] when, in the wake of the emancipation and enfranchisement of the 'negroes', the suffrage was easily identified with equality, justice and respect,[11] and expressed in highly moral and emotional language.

Indeed the language of reform was a moral language, the language of Gladstone's 'flesh and blood' speech,[12] of the 'moral right' of every citizen 'not presumably incapacitated by some consideration of personal unfitness or political danger'.[13] The

---

[6] For these leaders' involvement in European radical movements, see Gillispie, *Labor and Politics*, pp. 257–58; McKay, 'Joseph Cowen e il Risorgimento'.

[7] [Rep.], 'The Reform Movement – The Reform Conference', *BH*, 3 Mar. 1866, p. 1, speech by E. Beales; see Muris, *Thesis*, pp. 42, 44. The fiscal argument was also the strongest link with middle-class radical organizations: see Taylor, *Thesis*, pp. 140–79.

[8] G. J. Holyoake, 'The Liberal Situation, or the Parliamentary Treatment of the People, II, *NW*, 18 Mar. 1865, p. 4. See J.B. Leno's motion approved at a meeting of London working-class radicals: [rep.], 'MANHOOD SUFFRAGE – Great Demonstration of the Middle and Working Classes at Freemasons' Hall', *BH*, 25 Jun. 1864, p. 1.

[9] G. J. Holyoake, *NW*, 11 Mar. 1865, p. 4. For the continuity with Chartism, see Wiener, *Lovett* (1989), p. 66.

[10] [Lett. by] J. Bright to the Reform League, *BH*, 26 May 1866, p. 1.

[11] Tholfsen, *Working-class Radicalism*, p. 315.

[12] See his speech in the Commons on 23 Mar. 1866 (Morley, *Gladstone*, II, p. 203).

[13] Morley, *Gladstone*, II, p. 126. For the immense success of these speeches, see some of the paraphrases in working-class songs, e.g.:

> 'Gladstone has said – 'O brother band,
> Our flesh and blood througout the land,
> Workmen, of England's State and strength,
> Your right is, to the front at length,'
> (Cit. in Smith, *Second Reform Bill*, pp. 140–1).

emotionalism and moralism of popular politics was well known to contemporary Liberal leaders,[14] yet the specific development of the arguments for Reform in 1866–7 owed much to the Adullamite and the Conservative opponents to it. Robert Lowe in particular, with his arrogant comments on the alleged immorality and debauchery of the 'inferior' classes became the focus for popular hatred,[15] and so inadvertently helped Bright to work up mass support for 'Reform'.

On the other hand, Bright's isolation as the only national leader who led a campaign of meetings throughout the country[16] contributed to the generation of a democratic mythology,and his ambiguous commitment to 'democracy'[17] roused the hopes of the most radical without driving away the moderates. According to Trevelyan,[18] the most complete exposition of his arguments in support of 'democracy' is to be found in his speech of 16 October 1866,[19] delivered in Glasgow in front of a huge audience. Bright concentrated on the poverty and deprivation which characterized the life of the working classes, and stressed the hope of improvement through democracy in his famous appeal 'to the nation':

I believe that ignorance and suffering may be lessened to an incalculable extent, and that many an Eden ... might be raised up in the waste wilderness which spreads before us. But no class can do that. The class which has hitherto ruled in this country has failed miserably ... If a class

For other paraphrases of Gladstone's speeches see [l.a.], 'Mr. Gladstone on the Franchise', *BH*, 14 May 1874, p. 4; [l.a., n.t.], *BH*, 21 May 1864, p. 4; 'The New Reform Movement' (*BH*, 11 Jun. 1864, P.1), a proclamation 'To the People' signed by George Odgers [sic.], W. R. Cremer and others, to encourage the organization of a national agitation; the reformers' motto was 'The suffrage for every man not morally or intellectually disqualified'. This motto was even printed on the membership cards of the Reform League (Crossick, *An Artisan Elite*, p. 219). The York working men wrote to Gladstone: 'You have spoken words that have sunk deep into the heart of every working man in every corner of the land' (from the address to W. E. Gladstone, June 1864, cit. in Vincent, *Formation of the Liberal Party*, p. 266).

[14] In 1863–5, Lincoln's readiness to acknowledge the virtues of the Lancashire workers was one of the factors responsible for his popularity in Britain: see [rep.], 'Assassination of President Lincoln – Great Meeting of Working Men', *BH*, 6 May 1865, p. 6. speech by Mason Jones.

[15] E.g. the comment by *Lloyd's Weekly* on the Tory *Standard*, which defined a Leeds' 'monster meeting' as a 'meeting of monsters', representing only the 'poverty and ignorance' of the country ([L.a.], 'Reform at Leeds', *LW*, 14 Oct. 1866, p. 6). See also Joyce, *Visions of the People*, pp. 53–4.

[16] Trevelyan, *John Bright*, p. 363.

[17] See e.g.: [l.a., n.t.], *LM*, 29 Aug. 1866, p. 2; Bright, *Speeches*, II, pp. 222–23, 234.

[18] Trevelyan, *John Bright*, p. 365.

[19] Bright, *Speeches*, II, pp. 199–211.

has failed, let us try the nation. That is our faith, that is our purpose, that is our cry – let us try the nation. This is what has called together these countless numbers of people to demand a change; and, as I think of it, and of these gatherings, sublime in their vastness and in their resolution, I think I see . . . above the hill-top of time, the glimmerings of a dawn of a better and nobler day for the country and for the people that I love so well.[20]

This rhetoric was similar to that of Gladstone, and had millenni-alist overtones especially effective with the crowds. It was powerful because it used the evangelical–apocalyptic language which was familiar to the majority of the audience: in fact it appealed to convictions which were deeply rooted even among old anti-Whig radicals such as Linton.[21] At the same time Bright was also effective in addressing the 'countless numbers' of those who were politically apathetic and 'indifferent', because he stressed that it was their self-respect as 'independent' men which had been challenged, and invited them to 'arouse and resent as one man the insults to which you have been, and are about to be, subjected'.[22]

   The reports of the demonstrations of 1866–7 and the leading articles in plebeian newspapers suggest that these arguments reached their target: the will to vindicate the moral character of the 'people' against Lowe's allegations soon became even more important than the reform programme itself, to the extent that the latter was sometimes left undeveloped in a set of general declar-ations of principle.[23] Both at the meetings organized by the Reform Union and at those called by the Reform League, there were two typical resolutions: the first invariably expressed the workers' protest against the Adullamite charges; the second their thanks to Gladstone, Russell, Bright and Mill, who had vindicated the moral

---

[20] *Ibid.*, p. 211.

[21] Especially on the issue of the contrast between 'class government' and government by the 'nation': Smith, *Radical Artisan*, p. 30.

[22] [L.a.], 'The Reform Bill in Danger', *BH*, 24 Mar. 1866.

[23] E.g. [rep.], 'The Reform Bill – The London Working Men's Association – Great Aggregate Meeting of Working Men at St. Martin's Hall', *BH*, 7 Apr. 1866, p. 1; the hall was 'densely crowded' and many were unable to enter. The meeting was chaired by George Potter, and it was on that occasion that T. J. Dunning pronounced 'his first political speech', declaring that it was high time that the trade unions abandoned the principle of 'no politics'. Possibly it was also to please difficult converts like Dunning that the resolutions were kept very general in tone; but what was emphasized was the trade unionists' indignation against Lowe and the other enemies of reform, whose names, whenever mentioned, were received by a chorus of whistles and groans.

character of 'the People'.[24] The chronology of popular mobilization also strengthens the impression that sensitivity to the 'provocations' played an important role: it was only after the moderate Reform Bill proposed by Russell and Gladstone was endangered[25] and eventually rejected, that the first great mass demonstrations took place.[26] The Russell-Gladstone government fell on 18 June, and on the 27th, 10,000 demonstrators accompanied by a brass band and red flags congregated in the centre of London to the cry of 'Gladstone and Liberty!', 'Gladstone for ever'.[27]

Meanwhile the irritation and irritability of the populace had also been increased by the cholera epidemic which claimed thousands of victims in London and other cities.[28] Such was the background to the great demonstrations of 2 July[29] and 23-4 July (which mobilized hundreds of thousands and culminated in the famous Hyde Park riots).[30] Police repression – unsuccessful in preventing the demonstration – had instead the effect of increasing the sense of moral outrage felt by the working classes: it seemed that the upper classes threatened even the freedoms of meeting and discussion. This stimulated more mass meetings which took place on 30 July,[31] the 31st (10–12,000 demonstrators in Victoria Park and as many at Lincoln's-Inn-Fields),[32] and 8 August (6,000 people at the

---

[24] See [rep.], 'Meetings in the Provinces', *BH*, 5 Jan. 1867, p. 1; Resolutions voted on at Blackburn by 15,000 demonstrators, and at Rochdale by '3–4,000' people 'chiefly working class', organized by the Reform Union: and at Torquay by about 1,000 people organized by the Reform League. For the use made of Lowe's insults in the popular press, see also [l.a.], 'Mr. Disraeli and the House of Commons – Mr. Lowe and the Working Classes', *RN*, 26 May 1867, p. 1, which shows that this episode was remembered and brought to people's attention till the achievement of final victory.

[25] See [rep.], 'Government Reform Bill', *BH*, 31 Mar. 1866, p. 1, for the early mass reactions which burst out almost simultaneously at Birmingham, Manchester, Brighton, Derby and the West Riding.

[26] See Harrison, *Before the Socialists*, pp. 83–5.

[27] [Rep.], 'Reform Demonstration in Trafalgar Square', *BH*, 30 Jun. 1866, p. 1.

[28] Smith, *The Second Reform Bill*, pp. 125–6.

[29] [Rep.], 'Reform Demonstration', *TI*, 3 Jul. 1866, p. 12.

[30] [Rep.], 'The Reform Demonstration in Hyde Park', *TI*, 24 Jul. 1866, p. 9; [rep.], 'The Rioting in Hyde Park', *TI*, 25 Jul. 1866, p. 9.

[31] [Rep.], 'The Reform Meeting Demonstration in the Agricultural Hall', *TI*, 31 Jul. 1866, p. 3.

[32] [Rep.], 'Meeting in Victoria Park', *BH*, 4 Aug. 1866, p. 1; [rep.], 'Meeting of the London Working Men's Association in Lincoln's-Inn-Fields', *ibid.*; see [rep.], 'Reform Meeting in Lincoln's Inn Field', *TI*, 1 Aug. 1866, p. 10, which does not contain any assessment of the number of the demonstrators, but disdainfully emphasizes their rough and proletarian appearance.

Guildhall).[33] Contemporaneously dozens of other impressive demonstrations took place in Birmingham, Bristol, Leicester, Norwich,
Tiverton, Ashton-under-Lyne and Rochdale.[34] Some of these
equalled or even exceded the London demonstrations in magnitude:
on 27 August, 250,000 participated in the Birmingham demonstration organized by the Reform League and the Birmingham Liberal
Association;[35] on 22 September, 25–30,000 Reform League workers
marched through the streets of Liverpool[36]; while two days later, in
Manchester, a Reform Union procession comprised 80–100,000
people,[37] with perhaps another 100,000 lining the streets.[38]

These were not 'spontaneous' demonstrations, since each of
them was carefully organized by the League, the Union and other
radical and liberal associations. But if such organization was
successful, it was because the urban working classes had been
deeply upset by the events of the previous months. To many
workers without any precise political consciousness, the series of
insults collectively received were a more effective and eloquent
illustration of the need for Reform than the speeches of the
radicals.[39] In all demonstrations anger and indignation featured
prominently: the workers wanted vindication of their moral character against the charges of chronic drunkenness and depravity.
Resolutions approved at meetings,[40] leaders' speeches, occasional

---

[33] [Rep.], 'Reform Meeting in the Guildhall – Great Meeting of the London Working Men's
Association and the Reform League', *BH*, 11 Aug. 1866, p. 6.

[34] [Rep.], 'Meetings in the Provinces', *BH*, 4 Aug.1866, p. 1.

[35] [Rep.], 'The Great Reform Demonstration in Birmingham', *BH*, 1 Sept. 1866, p. 6; see
[rep.], 'The Reform Demonstration at Birmingham', *TI*, 28 Aug. 1866, p. 4.

[36] [Rep.], 'The Reform Movement – Reform Demonstration in Liverpool', *BH*, 29 Sept.
1866, p. 6.

[37] [Rep.], 'Reform Demonstration in Manchestr', *ibid*.

[38] According to *The Times*: [rep.], 'The Reform Demonstration at Manchester', 25 Sept.
1866, p. 7.

[39] E.g. Benjamin Lucraft's speeches to the Clerkenwell Green weekly meeting in April,
which possibly sparked off the mobilization of London workers: [rep.], 'Open Air
Meeting at Clerkenwell Green', *BH* 21 Apr. 1866. p. 1; [rep.], 'Working Men's Meeting
on Clerkenwell Green', *BH*, 28 Apr. 1866, p. 1; [rep.], 'Open-Air Meeting on Clerkenwell
Green', *BH*, 5 May 1866, p. 1 (1,500 workers took part in the latter).

[40] The resolutions approved during the great London demonstrations of 3 Dec. 1866 were
especially significant: ([rep.], 'The Great Reform Demonstration by the London Working
Men's Association and the Trades' Societies, Monday, December 3rd.', *BH*, 8 Dec. 1866
p. 5): '1. That this meeting enters its solemn protest against, and its denial of the charges
of venality, ignorance, drunkenness and indifference to Reform brought against the
working classes during the last session of Parliament; and hereby declares that no Reform
Bill falling short of the principle of registered residential manhood suffrage and the ballot
will be satisfactory to the people, or accepted as a final settlement of the Reform question.'
The second resolution was, as usual, of thanks to Russell, Bright, and J. S. Mill.

comments by anonymous workers from the floor, as well as leading articles in the popular press, regularly placed great emphasis on the respectability of the working classes.[41]

That the importance of protesting their 'respectability' was felt intensely by the great mass of those who took part in these demonstrations – the anonymous rank-and-file who marched through the streets and in the parks without making any speeches – is also shown by the discipline and decorum that the demonstrators strove to show,[42] and by the fact that most of them had put on their best clothes.[43] Tholfsen has written of this as one of the symptoms of the permeation of the values of 'middle-class progressivism', of the embourgeoisement which distinguished the reformers of 1866–7 from those of previous radical movements.[44] However, he seems to forget that throughout the nineteenth century radicals of the subaltern classes taking part in public demonstrations always tried to present themselves as 'respectable' people, especially when the issue at stake was that of the enlargement of the franchise. In fact even those who organized and took part in the meeting in St. Peter's Field in 1819 shared similar concerns: in the words of Samuel Bamford,

It was deemed expedient that this meeting should be as morally effective as possible ... We had frequently been taunted by the press, with our ragged, dirty appearance, at these assemblages; with the confusion of our proceedings, and the mob-like crowds in which our numbers were mustered; and we determined that, for once at least, these reflections should not be deserved, – that we would disarm the bitterness of our political opponents by a display of cleanliness, sobriety, and decorum, such as we never before had exhibited. In short, we would deserve their respect by shewing that we respected ourselves, and knew how to exercise our rights of meeting, as it were well Englishmen always should do, – in a spirit of sober thoughtfulness; respectful, at the same time, to the opinions of others.[45]

---

[41] [Rep.], *BH*, 8 Dec. 1866, p. 5: the reporter stressed that the procession took place in the greatest order and that none had shown signs of intoxication, though the cold and frequent showers would have encouraged some use of alcoholic drinks.

[42] See [l.a.], 'Last Monday', *LW*, 9 Dec. 1866, p. 1. The editorial stressed the 35,000 people who took part in it did not represent 'mere numbers', but also millions of pounds 'of landed property, and millions invested in government securities, as well as the earnings of the entire working-clas of the community'.

[43] [Rep.], *BH*, 10 Aug. 1867, p. 1; See [rep.], BH 8 Dec. 1866, p. 5.

[44] Tholfsen, *Working-Class Radicalism*, pp. 322–4.

[45] Bamford, *Passages* (1844), p. 131; Thompson, *Making of the English Working Class*, pp. 745–6, 758.

In 1819 as in 1866–7 ex-drill sergeants were employed to ensure that the workers were properly disciplined and organized in their processions.[46] In 1819 as in 1866–7 the watchwords were: '"CLEANLINESS", "SOBRIETY", "ORDER", . . . "PEACE"'.[47] Contemporary prints of 'Peterloo' confirm Bamford's testimony, showing a crowd of men and women dressed up, including a number of men in top-hats.[48] Likewise, the prints and the only photograph[49] of Chartist meetings show contingents of well-dressed people, many of them wearing top-hats, collars and ties. Both when marching through the towns in well-drilled battalions, with bands playing and colours flying,[50] and when grouped around the platforms from which they were addressed by their leaders, the Chartists manifested no appreciable difference in cermonial or political liturgy from their sons and grandsons who organized themselves for 'Reform' during the 1860s.

THE PLATFORM OF PLEBEIAN 'REFORM'

Though the moral-emotional character of the agitation contributed towards ensuring mass support, it did not help to clarify either the programme or the issues at stake. The first popular reactions to the 1866 Liberal proposal showed hatred for the enemies of reform rather than support for the actual Bill.[51] Gradually, however, indignation against the Adullamites generated a growing commitment to even such a moderate proposal as the Gladstone-Russell Bill.[52] Plebeian radicals were fighting, in the first place, over a

---

[46] For 1819, see Bamford, *Passages* (1844), pp. 132–3; for 1866 see [rep.], *BH*, 8 Dec. 1866, p. 5.

[47] Bamford, *Passages* (1844), p. 131.

[48] See 'Manchester Heroes, 1819', a contemporary print of Peterloo, Manchester City Libraries, published as cover illustration of Bamford, *Passages* (1844).

[49] See the reproduction in Morgan (ed.), *Illustrated History of Britain*, p. 443.

[50] Wilson, *Struggles of a Chartist*, in Vincent (ed.), *Testaments of Radicalism*, p. 197; according to Tholfsen even brass bands are a mark of the 'embourgeoisement' of the post-Chartist radicals (see *Working Class Radicalism*, pp. 322–3).

[51] See [l.a.], 'Class against Class', *LW*, 25 Feb. 1866, p. 6; [l.a.], 'The Reform Bill in Danger', *BH* 24 Mar. 1866, p. 4; [l.a.], 'Reform' *NW*, 10 Mar. 1866, p. 4, [l.a.], 'The Bill', *NW*, 17 Mar. 1866, p. 4.

[52] 'Against this arrogant, selfish and unscrupulous cabal, it is the duty of all sections of the people to make war with the utmost energy' [L.a.], 'Mr. Bright's Letter', *LW*, 1 Apr. 1866, p. 6; See Plain Dealer, 'The Working Man and the Reform Bill', *BH*, 31 Mar. 1866, p. 1; [l.a.], 'The Great Debate', *LW*, 6 May 1866, p. 1; [l.a.], 'Politics', *WT*, 6 May 1866, p. 1.

question of honour:[53] the typical rank-and-file participant in the reform demonstrations seemed anxious to proclaim 'that he stood there to tell the country that he was not, as Mr. Lowe had said he was, a drunken man, a venal man, or a man who intimidated his fellows. (Loud cheers.)'.[54] The modern observer may have the impression that by then the assertion of the 'faith' had become – as in some religious movements – an end in itself:[55] however, the Bill was still considered as just a first step in the 'right direction'.[56] The problem was that it was not clear how far to go in that 'direction' (i.e., in terms of extension of the franchise).

A good example of this problem is provided by the demonstration held in Newcastle upon Tyne in February 1867. On that occasion the resolutions passed expressed the workers' protest against Lowe's charges, and their gratitude towards Russell, Gladstone, Bright, J. S. Mill and others 'who have supported the people's claims'.[57] As far as positive proposals were concerned, the resolutions were ambiguous. A 'registered, residential manhood suffrage' was proclaimed to be 'the only just and proper basis for representation': this meant something less than the vote for all adult males, and was a *qualified* 'manhood' suffrage,[58] while other demands were only for a 'fair' share in the franchise. Closer examination of the speeches does not solve these ambiguities: the majority of the speakers laid great emphasis on rejecting Lowe's claims, but either referred only in general terms to the reforms that

---

[53] [L.a., n.t.], *LM*, 17 Mar. 1866, p. 3. The *Mercury* stressed that the traditional 'constitutional balance' of classes would be preserved under the Reformed system [l.a.,n.t.], 6 Mar. 1866, p. 2): its ideal was a £6 rental franchise' [l.a., n.t.], 13 Jan. 1866, p. 4), one pound lower than the one proposed in the Russell-Gladstone Bill. Typical of this paper is the predilection for the use of the language of the 'people' in these discussions (cf. [l.a., n.t.], 22 Feb. 1866, p. 2).

[54] [Rep.], 'Great West Riding Demonstration', *LM*, 9 Oct. 1866, pp. 7–8, speech by a certain 'Mr. Mark Porrit, a working man'.

[55] Tholfsen, *Working Class Radicalism*, p. 325.

[56] [L.a.], 'The Whole Bill', *LW*, 13 May 1866, p. 1.

[57] See [Supplement, rep.] 'GREAT REFORM DEMONSTRATION IN NEWCASTLE – Monster Meeting in the Town Hall', *NW*, 2 Feb. 1867. This supplement was distributed 'gratis' together with that week's issue. For the resolutions, see p. 1.

[58] That 'manhood' suffrage should be residential and registered was one of the points strictly adhered to not only by the Newcastle demonstrators and the Reform Union in general, but also by the Reform League: see G. *Howell Coll.* IX, *Letter Box*, p. 538, Resolution No. 2. The length of the residential qualification was not specified in the case of the Newcastle demonstration: in other cases we find different periods defined as appropriate: according to Ernest Jones it should be four months in order to implement one of the points of the old Charter (Harrison, *Before the Socialists*, p. 117).

they wanted to implement, or even remained silent on the issue,[59] possibly for fear of rocking the boat.[60] Among the orators, one (R. Robson, painter) was a survivor of the 1819 agitation, another a veteran of 1829–32 (T. Gregson, watchmaker), and a third (P. Doyle, labourer) had taken part in the struggle for the repeal of the Act of Union:[61] each interpreted the Reform agitation as the natural continuation of the battles of their youth, though such movements might appear to have had little in common. Even those who went into more detail made use of a moral-sentimental rhetoric aimed at stirring up the emotions of the audience, rather than clarifying their programme.[62] A brassfinisher, Robert Warden, defined the aims of the agitation in negative terms, saying that

Their opponents were afraid that if the working classes were admitted to the franchise, they would Frenchify or Americanise the institutions of the country. But he could assure those opponents that the working men were too much endeared to liberty and institutions for which their forefathers fought and laboured, to change them for those of France; and however much they may sympathise with their American brethren, they still loved the glorious constitution of their own country. (Cheers.) No, the working classes valued too highly the liberties for which their forefathers fought and bled to change them for those of any foreign land.[63]

This refusal to 'Americanise' the constitution did not imply the acceptance of a less democratic platform, but rather the celebration of the Saxon and 'early English' roots of 'manhood' suffrage and annual parliaments.[64] However, in this specific case Warden

[59] See the interventions by Ralph Currie, millwright ([Supplemnt, Rep.], *NW*, 2 Feb. 1867, p. 1), John Keir, shipwright (*ibid.*, p. 2); A. M'Laughlin, boilersmith, (*ibid.*); A. Schorer, engineman (*ibid.*); J. Nixon, cooper (*ibid.*); J. Charlton, tailor (*ibid.*); J. Daglish, waterman (*ibid.*); and T. Walton, house carpenter (*ibid.*).

[60] E.g. J. Aitken, joiner (*ibid.*)

[61] *Ibid.*

[62] Like Thomas Burt, who gave one of his first political addresses on this very occasion (*ibid.*).

[63] *Ibid*

[64] See Thomas Doubleday's letter to the organizers of the evening meeting in the Newcastle Town Hall to apologize for his absence. He wrote that the proposals in the radical platform 'cannot justly be called "innovations". I am well convinced that manhood suffrage was the practice under the original English Constitution for more than two centuries; and that Parliaments were sessional and ended with the business which they were convened especially to transact. . . . The ballot was not employed anciently because it was unnecessary. Where all adult males voted, and when every head of a family had more or less of property, intimidation, if it were wished, was impracticable' (*Ibid.*). It is interesting to note the connection between property and the alleged invulnerability to intimidation.

concluded on a more modest note, saying that they only wanted the country to have 'a cheaper and better Government – (cheers) – and that would not be attained until the working classes had a *fair share* in the representation in Parliament. (Cheers.)'.[65] The exact meaning of 'a fair share in the representation' was not clear, though it implied some willingness to accept something less than 'manhood' suffrage. Thus, the ambiguity of the motions was mirrored by some at least of the speakers. A taylor, John Davy, probably summed up the prevailing attitude among the Newcastle demonstrators by remarking that

When Mr. Gladstone introduced his Reform Bill, the people expressed their willingness to accept it, though it was but a small instalment of their just rights; but the contemptuous manner in which the bill was thrown out aroused the popular indignation, and they were now determined to have nothing short of manhood suffrage. (Loud cheers.) . . . Give the man a vote for his manhood, and it would be a stimulous to him to become a worthy citizen. (Cheers.) Instead of excluding as many as possible, he thought it was political wisdom to rest the constitution of the country upon as broad a basis as possible, for the essence of good legislation was to seek the happiness of the greatest number rather than the aggrandisment of any particular number.[66]

Thus, Davy maintained that it had been the arrogance of the Tories and their allies which had made it impossible for the workers to accept a compromise solution.[67] Once again it would seem that the radicalization of the position of the reformers was due to emotional factors, which had transformed what had initially been the radicalism only of the militants into the platform of the

---

[65] *Ibid.* (my italics).

[66] *Ibid.* Bentham's motto was often used as the standard of good government in the popular demonstrations of the period.

[67] See also the following speech at another meeting: 'Mr. W. H. Arnold (a working man) supported the resolution. He observed that the political character of either the supporters or the opponents of the Bill was an additional assurance to him of the honesty of the measure. He advised his fellow working men to unite to give an earnest support to the Bill. It was not so good as they expected, let them, nevertheless, do all in their power to ensure its success. (Cheers.)' ([Rep.], 'Reform-Meeting at Bradford', *LM*, 22 Mar. 1866, p. 4); it is remarkable that in this case support for the Bill was argued on the basis of the moral character of those who asked for it, and the immoral one of those who opposed it. A similar argument was contained in the anonymous poem 'A reform Bulletin!' (*NW*, 21 Apr. 1866, p. 2):

> We can see that 'the Bill' is quite safe in the fight,
> By the relative health of its friend and its foe;
> For the spirit that burns in the former, is Bright,
> While the pulse of the last is decidedly, Lowe!

masses. We may conclude that, if it is true that Bright was deliberately vague about the aims of the agitation, it is also true that it was not clear what kind of 'democracy' the mass of plebeian reformers were seeking, or were ready to accept. 'Manhood' suffrage was certainly the most popular slogan: but that was due not to a Jacobin commitment to principle, but to a pragmatic appreciation of the simplicity of the concept, which made 'Reform' readily understandable.

Moreover, it is certain that by 'manhood' suffrage the majority meant something less than 'universal adult male suffrage'. The two qualifications regularly associated with the expression ('registered and residential') had a restrictive character which was not general and shaded – as suggested by R. Harrison[68] – but socially focused and precise, often quite explicitly: thus, a contributor to the *Bee-Hive* wrote that 'The franchise is the manhood right of every moral, educated, and sane minded Englishman . . .';[69] and 'Littlejohn' of the *Weekly Times* protested that 'the men upon whom we bestow the franchise must be possessed of sound common sense and honest intention': this meant that he intended to exclude from 'manhood' suffrage

the agricultural labourer of Dorsetshire or Suffolk in his present degraded state, who, with his family, drags out a miserable existence upon eight or nine shillings per week, and is, to all intents and purposes, as much the bondslave of his employer as if he had been bought in a public market . . . It would simply seem to be giving the ignorant lout, who looks upon the fox-hunting squire as a demi-god, the power to do mischief.. . . [70]

'Littlejohn' consoled himself at the thought that 'Happily, however, all our working men are not poor Dorsetshire and Suffolk labourers; and no true reformer would desire to clothe with political power the man who is unfitted to wield it aright'.[71] From a similar point of view, the editor of *Lloyd's Weekly*, rejecting Lowe's

[68] Harrison, *Before the Socialists*, p. 117.
[69] [Lett. by] J. Rowe, *BH*, 26 May 1866, p. 7.
[70] Littlejohn, 'Reform and the Working Classes', *WT*, 11 Mar. 1866, p. 6.
[71] *Ibid.* This contempt for the agricultural labourers was very common in the 1860s. Frederic Harrison was one of those who shared it: in his speech at St James's Hall on negro emancipation, on 28 March 1863, he declared, speaking to London trade unionists, 'There are two classes of workmen, both infinitely below you in intelligence, in organization, and in social position, but still workmen, and therefore irrevocably bound up with you. I mean the agricultural workers of England and the negro slaves of America' (cit. in Harrison, *Before the Socialists*, p. 73).

allegations, explained that 'Mr. GLADSTONE spoke of the right of every *morally sound man* to the franchise',[72] rather than of any person, and that the purpose of Reform was to restore the spirit of the *Petition of Rights*, the *Declaration of Rights*, and the *Bill of Rights*.

The frequency with which the argument of the 'constitutional tradition' was appealed to suggests that a clarification of the actual content of the reformers' platform may be found in the plebeian interpretation of this 'tradition'. 'Littlejohn' was a committed supporter of the 'manhood' suffrage in the sense of the 'constitutional tradition'. Writing just two months after the article quoted above, 'Littlejohn' commented;

The plain and simple old plan – which the good sense of Simon de Montfort imported into this country, and which the manly vigour of the Gothic nations settled in Spain first invented of the entire manhood selecting their best men to assemble and make laws for all, is just as good now as it was six hundred years since . . . what we want is an Act which will enable *the common sense and the common honesty of the nation to express itself*.[73]

To 'Littlejohn', 'manhood' suffrage had limits, being co-extensive with the 'common sense' and 'common honesty' of the nation – which clearly, in the context of 1866, excluded the agricultural labourers[74] on the ground that 'the popular vote may be made the instrument of despotism',[75] as in France after 1851. A few months afterwards, a *Newcastle Chronicle* leading article declared that the fact that the British did not enjoy the same electoral rights as the Americans and the French (i.e., 'manhood' suffrage) was a scandal and a national shame, but concluded: 'As long as there is a man on British soil from whom is kept back that which is acknowledged on every hand to be the due of thousands at least – the suffrage – we are a party to that wrong, and his disgrace is ours'.[76] The interpretation of this ambiguous passage is helped by what he declared later, namely: 'The peasantry of Northumberland and

---

[72] [L.a.], 'Mr. Lowe's Explanation', *LW*, 3 Mar. 1867, p. 6; my italics.
[73] Littlejohn, 'The Second Part of the Reform Bill', *WT*, 13 May 1866, p. 6; my italics.
[74] Yet it is certain that 'Littlejohn' considered himself a thorough-going radical, which in many respects he actually was. In an 1866 article he went as far as to invoke the advent of a 'new Cromwell' to dissolve the House of Commons as 'a self-seeking and corrupt set'. 'Littlejohn' asked for a 'Convention Parliament' to vote for a new Bill of Rights: Littlejohn, 'Is There a Genuine Political Agitation?', *WT*, 12 Aug. 1866, p. 6.
[75] [L.a., n.t.], *NW*, 16 Apr. 1870, p. 4.
[76] [L.a.] 'The Demonstration: Our Glory and Our Shame', *NW*, 2 Feb. 1867, p. 4.

Durham [who] have never been reduced to that state of abject
slavery and poverty in which the agricultural labourers of the
southern counties are found to this day'.[77] This meant that the
rural workers of the north east 'deserved' the vote because they –
in contrast with the labourers of the south – had always demonstrated a 'sturdy independence'[78] 'which has gained them rights
and privileges which men of other districts of the country have not
possessed'.[79]

All these themes were further developed in another issue of the
Newcastle Weekly Chronicle by 'Britannicus',[80] who wrote a detailed
eulogy of the constitution of Edward I, describing the 'ideal' body
politic. A surprising feature of this perfect State and citizenry is
the parallels with one of the Levellers' manifestoes. To 'Britannicus' 'the pith and kernel of all free governments' and 'the consum-
mation of the English Constitution'[81] was the statute *De Tiellagio
non concedendo*, which laid down that no tax might be imposed by
the king without previous consent of the nation expressed by a
parliament elected by 'manhood' suffrage. On this basis there
would stand a justice open to all, rapid, and free (also a Leveller
claim),[82] a foreign trade free of duties,[83] and a fiscal system
localized in collection and administration.[84] But the crucial point
for 'Britannicus' was the distribution of property: in the 'golden
age' which he described

The people were almost universally owners of their own houses, shops,
warehouses and manufactories; so that all men had solid means . . . All
this real property . . . arose . . . out of the observance, by our ancestors,
of the primary conditions of all good government, which are safety to life,
to person, and to property: which last included safety from fiscal extortion
of all kinds – which they held as only legalised brigandage . . .[85]

---

[77] *Ibid.*
[78] *Ibid.* The Northumberland labourer had a real reputation of being 'most independent in
word and action' (A.W. Fox, 'Summary Report', *Royal Commission on Labour, PP.* 1893–4,
xxxv, p. 322).
[79] [L.a.], 'The Demonstration: Our Glory and Our Shame', *NW*, 2 Feb. 1867, p. 4.
[80] Britannicus, 'The English Constitution. What It was and What It is', *NW*, 19 Oct. 1867,
p. 4.
[81] *Ibid.*
[82] *Ibid.* (See *To the Supream Authority*, point 6, p. 267).
[83] Ibid. (See *To the Supream Authority*, point 9, p. 268).
[84] *Ibid.* (See *To the Supream Authority*, points 10 and 14, p. 268–70.
[85] *Ibid.*

This 'ideal' society was made up of 'independent' artisans or small producers secured in the enjoyment of their own property by the rule of law. According to 'Britannicus' the right to property was of crucial political importance. It seems that to him as to the Levellers it was clear that

To every individual in nature is given an individual property by nature, not to be invaded or usurped by any. For every one as he is himself, so he hath a self propriety, else could he not be himself . . . No man hath power over my rights and liberties, and I over no man's . . . For by natural birth all men are equally and alike born to like propriety, liberty, and freedom, as we are delivered by God into the hands of Nature into this world, every one with a natural innate freedom and propriety . . . even so are we to live, everyone equally and alike to enjoy his birthright and privilege, even all whereof God by nature hath made him free.[86]

Prothero and Stedman Jones have shown that this concept of property had survived within popular culture from the seventeenth century and had been passed on to nineteenth-century radicals;[87] indeed, as we saw in chapter 3, it was central to the 1860s discussions on labour legislation and factory acts. As a consequence, nobody was supposed to be really property-less. Another consequence was that those who did not work abdicated one of their natural rights, and deserved to be considered with hostility (as in the case of the 'royal paupers'), or with suspicion and contempt (as in the case of the real 'paupers'), or at least with the commiseration reserved for underdeveloped human beings.[88] If the alleged lack of independence of the agricultural labourers of the south was to some radicals a sufficient reason for excluding them from 'manhood' suffrage, the prevailing opinion was that the franchise ought to be reserved for everybody 'who is not a pauper or a criminal'.[89] This was not a further consequence of the

[86] *An Arrow against All Tyrants and Tyranny, shot from the prison of Newgate into the prerogative Bowels of the arbitrary House of Lords . . . by Richard Overton, 10 October 1647*, cit. in Brailsford, *The Levellers*, p. 140. n.30.

[87] Prothero, *Artisans and Politics*, p. 27; Stedman Jones, *Languages of Class*, pp. 107, 156; See Thompson, *The Chartists*, p. 237.

[88] Stedman Jones, *Languages of Class*, p. 170; Prothero, *Artisans and Politics*, p. 311.

[89] [L.a.], 'Let Us Try the Nation', *NW*, 20 Oct. 1866, p. 4. This was the context in which the expression was used, in the comment to the Glasgow demonstration of 16 October: 'The standard under which the masses of the west of Scotland assembled was that of the Reform League – "Manhood suffrage and the ballot". These are terrible words to some people; but what do they imply? Simply that every man who is not a pauper or a criminal, and has reached the years of discretion, shall have a voice in the government of the country, and the freedom of his vote shall be maintained by the only effectual guarantee – the ballot.'

embourgeoisement of the British working classes: criminals and paupers were considered as beyond the pale of social outcasts even in the 'uncorrupted' times of John Gast, Samuel Bamford, and 'Orator' Hunt.[90]

In this respect the advanced platform of the nineteenth-century radicals had remained substantially similar to that of the Levellers,[91] with their concept of a 'manhood' which was not co-extensive with the whole population of 'adult males'. Though apparently ambiguous, this distinction did not represent a breaking away from original ideals, but rather their consistent application: to Victorian radicals, as to the Levellers, *real* 'manhood' ought to be accompanied by 'independence'. The latter implied primarily the full control of the most basic form of property – the property of one's self, one's will and one's work;[92] without this control a man was not recognized as being fully adult, as possessing that 'manhood' which gave the right to full citizenship.

From the seventeenth century there thus survived a tendency to exclude from the vote those who showed themselves unable or lacking the intention to preserve their 'independence'. This tendency was universal, apart from the Chartists, who were ready to admit workhouse inmates to the franchise – [93] this 'exception' probably being a consequence of the application of the New Poor Law during the difficult 1830s and 40s,[94] when the chance of ending up in a workhouse became a real possibility for groups who both before and after were relatively safe from that danger. The spread of this fear in the Chartist period caused a temporary 'civic

---

[90] Prothero, *Artisans and Politics*, pp. 83–6; Bamford, *Passages* (1844), p. 4; Belchem, '*Orator* Hunt, p. 224.

[91] See *To the Supream Authority of England*, p. 269 (the passage from the 1648 Agreement quoted at the beginning of the present chapter). As early as 1647 the Rainsborough group had declared: 'That all soldiers and others, if they be not servants or beggars, ought to have voices in electing those which shall represent them in Parliament, although they have not forty shillings per annum in freehold land.' (Cit. in Brailsford, *The Levellers*, p. 288, my italics). See MacPherson, *Political Theory of Possessive Individualism*, p. 158.

[92] MacPherson, *Political Theory of Possessive Individualism*, pp. 140–1; see also pp. 148–9.

[93] See Gammage, *The Chartist Movment* (1854), pp. 416, ad 90; Lovett, *Life and Struggles* (1876), p. 139ff. However, some leaders, like Edward Miall, excluded from the franchise all 'whose actions are under the legal control of others, who, in the eye of the law, are not their own masters ... [namely] all minors and paupers. [as well as] ... Vagrants, foreigners, and criminals whose term of imprisonment had expired ...' (Miall, *Edward Miall* (1884). p. 77).

[94] Of course it was the agitation against the New Poor Law which was one of the main impulse behind Chartism: see Thompson, *The Chartists*, pp. 30–1.

rehabilitation' of the paupers, but the old discriminatory attitude again became prevalent once the difficult years were over.

Indeed a close examination of the meetings on franchise reform in the 1860s suggests that the paupers' exclusion occurred only gradually, with the clarification of the issues at stake. In 1864 J. R. Taylor reproposed the platform of the 1840s, asking that only convicted criminals be excluded from 'manhood suffrage'.[95] But even then the terms of the debate were being modified towards a more restrictive approach: at the Manchester conference, in April, alternative interpretations of the aims of reform were proposed by Robert Cooper – who asked that the vote be given to 'every person rated, or liable to be rated, for the poor' – and by Ernest Jones – who askd for a '*registered* manhood suffrage'.[96] In June, at another demonstration, J. B. Leno requested the vote for all those who 'contribute[d] to the real strength and wealth of the nation, and who, as liable to the duties and obligations of citizens, have a well founded right to the franchise . . .';[97] Howell – who spoke immediately afterwards – maintained that the vote was a right for 'all resident and registered male persons of sound mind and unconvicted of crime'.[98] In December, at the time of the great meetings at Manchester and Bradford, the *Bee-Hive* admitted that a man could be morally and intellectually unworthy of the vote.[99] The constitution of the Reform League – published in April 1865 – claimed the vote for 'every *resident* and *registered* adult male person *of sound mind*, and unconvicted of crime',[100] and at the great St Martin's Hall meeting, in May, Beales took care to give a precise interpretation of these words. He said that Gladstone had presented the franchise question in its proper terms when he defined it as a 'moral' right, since such was the spirit of the 'ancient electoral laws':

[95] [Rep.], 'Mr. Gladstone's Annuities Bill – Monster Meeting at Exeter Hall' [speech by J. R. Taylor], *BH*, 12 Mar. 1864, p. 6.

[96] [Rep.], 'National Reform Conference' [speeches by R. Cooper and E. Jones], *BH* 23 Apr. 1864, p. 1. It is significant that Jones insisted that it was a case of asking the maximum in order to obtain 'Mr. Baines' Bill, or Mr. Lock King's Bill, or any other moderate franchise . . .'. See also E. Jones to K. Marx, 25 Feb. 1865, cit. in Harrison, *Before the Socialists*, pp. 117–18.

[97] [Rep.], 'MANHOOD SUFFRAGE – Great Demonstration of the Middle and Working Classes at Freemason's Hall' [resolution moved by J. B. Leno], *BH*, 25 Jan. 1864, p. 1.

[98] *Ibid.*, speech and resolution by G. Howell; he quoted Blackstone and Bentham.

[99] [L.a.], 'The Franchise Movment', *BH*, 10 Dec. 1864, p. 4.

[100] [rep.], 'The Reform League', *BH* 1 Apr. 1865, p. 1, my italics.

there existed, up to the time of the Reform Bill of 1832, various rights of voting for towns and boroughs, which were . . . very unconstitutionally . . . swept away by that bill, and which were also so many proofs of the franchise as having been formerly very extensive, and probably from time to time infringed or narrowed, through usurpation or carelessness, in violation of the constitutional principles; such rights being those of inhabitants householders, without regard to the amount of rent, rates, or taxes paid by them: inhabitants housekeepers paying scot and lot – that is, assessed to the poor rates – being tenant at a very low rent, sometimes a rent of no more than a few pence; inhabitants generally, whether householders or not; and potwallers, or persons furnishing their own diet, whether householders or lodgers: the two latter rights of voting being, in fact, identical with manhood suffrage.[101]

It is noteworthy that Beales restricted his aims to the boroughs, without mentioning the counties, thus avoiding the difficult question of the agricultural labourers. But even within the urban context, only one of his 'traditional' franchise – that of the 'inhabitants generally, whether householders or not' – could be interpreted as inclusive of all adult males, while the others implied the exclusion of paupers. However, to avoid misunderstanding, Beales went on to say that representation should follow taxation: he declared that the 'manhood suffrage' of which he was speaking was also

in accordance with what Sir William Blackstone . . . describes as the true theory and genuine principle of liberty, upon which every member of the community, however poor, *who is not under undue influence*, should have a vote in electing those delegates, to whose charge is committed the disposal of his property, his liberty, and his life. (Cheers.)[102]

This meant that the Reform League activists 'did not want the vote to be given to paupers, to beggars, or to convicts; but only to men who registered themselves as residing in place'.[103] The right to the vote under 'manhood suffrage' was not consequent on one's humanity: rather it was a right which the working man claimed because he: 1) paid taxes and rates; 2) obeyed the laws; 3) contributed to the defence of the country; 4) demonstrated his moral and intellectual independence by means of his capacity for

---

[101] [Rep.], 'Great Reform Meeting in St. Martin's Hall' [speech by E. Beales], *BH*, 20 May 1865, pp. 5–6.
[102] *Ibid.*, my italics.
[103] [Rep.], 'The Reform League – Deputation to Mr. Gladstone', *BH*, 6 Apr. 1867, p. 6.

organization, self-help, and other individual and collective virtues.[104]

Since this was the background to the agitation, it is not surprising that the reformers were ready to accept Disraeli's Bill. If in March 1867 the *Bee-Hive* considered household suffrage simply as a first instalment of the suffrage of the 'manhood',[105] in the same period Howell described it as all that could then be obtained, and not even for every kind of constituency but only for the boroughs.[106] Generally, the Reform League leaders shared this view: the only chance of obtaining more depended on the reaction of the Tory government to popular pressure and Radical amendments in Parliament. Writing to Howell Beales declared: 'If Mr. Bright can carry household suffrage with a large lodger franchise I shall not be very dissatisfied. But I think he will find himself compelled as the struggle goes on to rank himself with us'.[107] Beales' hopes did not come true because in one sense the struggle did *not* go on, since the flexibility of the Conservatives and the effectiveness of the parliamentary Radicals took the initiative away from the League. Not only did the final draft of the Reform Bill placate popular anger by satisfying the self-esteem of the urban workers; it also enfranchised an electorate which was substantially representative of the forces which had animated the 1864–67 movement.

Disraeli's Bill – in its original draft – was condemned as 'partial and oppressive' by the executive of the Reform League.[108] However, from the beginning the most important objections were directed not against household suffrage as such, but against both the incomplete way in which the household qualification was

---

[104] This was one of the points that Howell, secretary of the Reform League, also stressed on other occasions: see G. Howell, 'The Reform League – To the Trades' Unionists of the United Kingdom', *BH*, 17 Jun. 1865, p. 1. See also F. Harrison, 'The Suffrage – No.II', *BH*, 2 Jul. 1864, p. 4. Paying the poor rates was generally considered to be an act of great civic importance not only at the time, but even as later, in the 1900s: see Matthew *et al.*, 'The Franchise Factor', p. 724.

[105] [L.a.], 'Are We to Have an Honest Reform Bill?' *BH*, 2 Mar. 1867, p. 2; see [l.a.], 'Extra Parliamentary Utterances', *NW*, 27 Apr. 1867, p. 4.

[106] G. Howell to E. Jones, 6 Mr. 1867, *G. Howell Coll. Letters Book*, 300.

[107] E. Beales to G. Howell, 14 Jan. 1867, *ibid.*, 11.

[108] Smith, *Second Reform Bill*, p. 188.

applied, and the lack of a 'lodger franchise'.[109] As soon as the Bill became more widely known, Beales expressed the League's point of view by listing a series of amendments which were to be introduced in order to make the Bill not only acceptable, but 'in substance' *equivalent* to 'residential manhood suffrage'.[110] The amendments required were: 1) inclusion of the compound house-holders; 2) a lodger franchise; 3) abolition of plural voting; 4) the abolition of the qualification of two-year residence; 5) a secret ballot.[111] In effect, the principle of mahood suffrage as the basis of reform was being abandoned, and the new strategy of the League was to obtain something like an empirical surrogate for it by carving out as much as possible from the government Bill.

The essential point was the enfranchisement of the compound householders[112]. As for the lodger franchise – dear to some of the agitators[113] – plebeian reformers could not agree on the appropriate level of the rent qualification. The delegation of the London Working Men's Association which met Gladstone at the end of March declared that the workers might consider temporarily abandoning manhood suffrage if the Bill incorporated a franchise for lodgers paying a rent of at least 4 or 5 shillings per month (about £10 per year), the then average rent paid in London by working-class lodgers.[114] But when a delegation of the Reform League was received by Gladstone at the beginning of April, Beales declared that only a lodger franchise without any rent qualification would be acceptable: he asked for the enfranchisement of all rate-paying lodgers and householders.[115] The LWMA, however, appar-

---

[109] See [rep.], 'The Reform League', *BH*, 2 Mar. 1867, p. 1, [speech by Mr. Richardson, gas-fitter]; the official position of the *Bee-Hive* was similar: [l.a.], 'The Government Reform Bill', 16 Mar. 1867, p. 4. Obviously the activists of the National Reform Union were more easily satisfied and readier to accept the government proposal: cf. [rep.] 'The Country and Reform', *BH*, 9 Mar. 1867, p. 1.

[110] [Rep.], 'The Reform League – Meeting of General Council and Delegates', *BH*, 23 Mar. 1867, p. 1.

[111] *Ibid.*

[112] Blake, *Disraeli*, pp. 471 ff. The Reform League asked that no discrimination be applied against those who paid the rates with the compound system, thus extending the practice already in use for municipal elections (cf. *Howell Collection*, 'Reform League', iii, 1 Jul. 1867). This system was eventually adopted in 1869.

[113] For instance George Potter, who was himself a lodger: see [rep.], 'Deputation to Mr. Gladstone from the Working Men's Association', *BH*, 30 Mar. 1867, p. 1.

[114] *Ibid.*, speech by G. Troup; See also [rep.], 'Working Men's Association – Important Conference on the Lodger Franchise', *BH*, 6 Apr. 1867, p. 1.

[115] [Rep.], *BH*, 6 Apr. 1867, p. 6; the League's greater radicalism on the lodger franchise was probably due to the fact that it represented not only workers from London, but also from the North, where rents were lower.

ently stuck to its proposal of a £10 qualification,[116] which was eventually accepted by all the reformers when the fear arose that the Lords were going to increase it to £15.[117] At that stage even the secretary of the Reform League – Howell – thought along these lines: in a series of letters to several Liberal and Radical M.P.s he asked their advice 'as to what should be done to obtain a clause giving the vote to all lodgers paying a bona fide annual *rent* of £10 for apartments occupied by them during twelve months'.[118] Thus, the Reform League was unable to pursue effectively its 'empirical' way to 'manhood' suffrage. In fact the Bill's final draft limited the lodger qualification to rents of an annual value of £10 net from the rates, which was virtually equivalent to a qualification of £15.[119]

Yet when the Reform Bill was passed reactions were generally – if not unanimously – euphoric, as illustrated by the great Manchester demonstration of June 1867 when Samuel Bamford and other survivors of Peterloo symbolically joined Robert Cooper, Ernest Jones and Jacob Bright.[120] At meetings of the Reform League the focus then switched from the franchise to the secret ballot, redistribution, and the right of meeting in parks: further extension of the suffrage was no longer of immediate interest.[121] The *Newcastle Weekly Chronicle* commented that with the Reform Act,

As householders or as lodgers, the great bulk of the inhabitants of the boroughs will certainly be admitted to a right of which they have only too long been deprived ... a principle which really opens Parliament to the people ... Great as were the effects the Reform Bill of 1832 produced, we are perfectly satisfied that the Reform Bill of 1867 will produce still greater effects. Progress in all directions will presently be registered. Ignorance will give place to education, prejudice to justice, peace and good will to hostility and contempt ... a glorious future is before us.[122]

---

[116] [Rep.], 'The Lodger Franchise', *BH*, 13 Apr. 1867: the lodger franchise should be 'certainly not higher than £10 a year'.

[117] See [rep.], 'The Reform Movement – Meeting on Blackheath', *BH*, 15 Jun. 1867, 1, motion No. 1; and [rep.], 'The Reform League – Demonstration in Hyde Park – The Lodger Franchise', *BH*, 3 Aug. 1867, p. 1.

[118] G. Howell to John Bright, 8 Jun. 1867, *G. Howell Coll. Letter Book*, 754. See also similar letter to W. E. Gladtone (15 Jun. 1867, *ibid.*, 736), and to McCullagh Torrents, Sir John Roll, Sir Randall Palmer.

[119] Blake, *Disraeli*, p. 470.

[120] [Rep.], 'The Manchester Reform Demonstration', *BH*, 8 Jun. 1867, p. 1.

[121] [rep.], 'The Reform League. Meeting of the General Council', *ibid.*

[122] [L.a.], 'The Triumph of Reform', *NW*, 13 Jul. 1867, p. 4.

On the topic of qualifications it concluded:

Ministers were perfectly consistent when they insisted that the franchise should be rendered dependent on the performance of a public duty. No other public duty is so generally performed as the payment of the rates for the relief of the poor. Whatever defect may attach to the rating principle, therefore, it is clear that it is neither narrow nor inflexible. Henceforth no class, as a class, will be excluded from the franchise; except it may be for the impoverished peasants of our rural districts. The time will come when even the peasants will be entrusted with the suffrage. But sufficient for the present the victory achieved.[123]

One year later, when the new electoral registers had been completed and the country was on the eve of the first general elections with a larger franchise, the tone of the most radical newspaper of the north was no less enthusiastic:

We are 'recurring to the ancient principle of the Constitution' – returning to the 'wisdom of our ancestors'. The inhabitant-householders have recovered their long-lost rights; and wherever there is a contested election, they will exercise them today at the poll. About six centuries ago our forefathers in Newcastle – the heads of households in our good old town – were sending their representatives to a Parliament of EDWARD THE FIRST; and now, after all the storms and shocks of time – after civil war, and revolution, and change of dynasty – the Constitution is still with us and we are electing representatives to a Parliament of QUEEN VICTORIA . . . the People's Parliament is coming into life. The principles of the old Reformers are triumphant. The franchise for which they contended amid obloquy and proscription, is now in the hands of the people . . .[124]

That this attitude was shared by a majority of the reformers is suggested by the fact that a few months later the Reform League was disbanded.[125]

THE REVIVAL OF 'MANHOOD SUFFRAGE'

In spite of all the enthusiasm of 1867–8, a new popular reform movement began to take shape in the early 1870s, asking, once again, for manhood suffrage. The heart of this new agitation was

---

[123] *Ibid.*

[124] [L.a.], 'Constitutional Reformation', *NW*, 17 Nov. 1868, p. 4.

[125] Harrison, *Before the Socialists*, pp. 211–2. The Refrom League was especially keen on the 1868 Scotch Reform Act, which enacted 'pure and simple household suffrage – unfettered by the odious ratepaying clause which still defaces our English Reform Act . . .' ([rep.], 'The Reform League', *BH*, 23 May 1868, p. 5).

in Northumberland and Durham, traditional hotbeds of working-class radicalism.[126] The miners became the spokesmen for the unenfranchised multitudes of both counties and boroughs, and organized a series of mass meetings, the most important of which took place in Newcastle and Durham city in 1873. Superficially this movement could be mistaken for an illustration of the plebeian radicals' attachment to manhood suffrage, as well as of their dissatisfaction with household franchise. However, a more careful analysis suggests that the situation was quite different.

The agitation of the north-eastern miners was sparked off by a series of judicial incidents at Morpeth. Following the 1867 reform, the boundaries of the borough had been extended to include a few mining villages and the mining port of Blyth. As a consequence, the borough included a comparatively high proportion of miners who, as householders, were eligible to register as electors. However, the revising barristers interpreted the law in a restrictive way. The question was whether it was possible to assimilate the miners' case to that of servants lodging with their employers without formally paying a rent: according to the law, such servants were not 'independent' and thus were excluded from the franchise. There were affinities between the two cases since in Northumberland miners usually lived in cottages owned by the mining companies without being charged for their use: the rent was counted as part of the pitmen's wages.[127] On the basis of this analogy the Morpeth revising barristers declared that the miners were not householders in the sense of the law and should not be registered.

This decision occasioned a series of appeals by the miners, who also started a political agitation. To this purpose in 1872 they set up a Working Men's Franchise Association and announced that they would present one of their leaders – Thomas Burt – as the working man candidate for Morpeth as soon as they had obtained their registration as electors.[128] In the meantime the movement became more radical.

---

[126] For the strength and vitality of Chartism in this region, see Maehl, 'The Northeastern Miners', pp. 212–13. Within the Northern Reform Union – which continued the Chartist tradition – the most active were the metal workers, though their arguments were no different from the mainstream moral and fiscal ones (see rep. of NRU meetings, speech by J. Rayan [meeting of 4 Dec. 1866] and 'A Working Man' [meeting of 11 Feb. 1866], in *Cowen Coll.*, C 1174). Thomas Burt one of the speakers (rep. of NRL meeting of 9 Jan. 1867, in *ibid.*, C 1174).

[127] Fynes, *The Miners* (1873), pp. 269–70; Maehl, 'The Northeastern Miners', pp. 198–202.

[128] Maehl, 'The Northeastern Miners', p. 203.

When a similar case in the nearby borough of South Shields was resolved in favour of the miners it became evident that the law had virtually assigned arbitrary powers to revising barristers and Poor Law Guardians. The miners could complain ironically that 'there were scarcely two revising barristers now travelling the country who would agree in their definition of what a house was'.[129] Moreover, the contrast between the 'democratic' qualification for the boroughs and the restrictive one for the counties generated puzzling distinctions between householders who lived in villages within the bounds of a borough, and their neighbours who lived in similar villages which happened to be outside the borough bounds: 'Why not disfranchise people because they have black hair or blue eyes?', Howell had complained as early as 1867, 'We must go on for justice to all.'[130]

But the question was just *what* was meant by 'justice for all'. After the beginning of the 'revolt of the field' in the early 1870s the most common tendency – supported with great fervour by G.O. Trevelyan – was towards extending the household franchise to the counties, since by then the labourers' political awareness and 'independence' seemed guaranteed by the success of Arch's union.[131] Even the Durham miners spoke in favour of this option[132] and eventually set up the Durham County Franchise Association to further it.[133] However, the Morpeth incident had the consequence of pushing them towards the more radical solution supported by their fellow-miners in Northumberland.

It was in the course of a series of meetings of the representatives of the two pitmen's communities that the problem of defining a common platform was examined in detail. Interestingly enough, one of the arguments in favour of manhood suffrage was that the Morpeth revising barrister had insulted the dignity of the miners by ruling that 'they were not occupiers of the houses in which they lived, but that the colliery owners were the occupiers. It seemed, then, that the men were no more the occupiers of their houses than

---

[129] [Rep.], 'Manhood Suffrage Demonstration – Shadon's Hill', *NC*, 31 Mar. 1873, p. 3, speech by Joseph Cowen.

[130] G. Howell to J. Nicholson, 20 May 1867, *G. Howell Coll. Lett. Book*, 664.

[131] [L.a.], 'The Extension of Household Suffrage to the Counties', *Potteries Examiner*, 26 Jul. 1873, p. 4: [l.a.], 'The Federation of Labour', *LW*, 18 Jan. 1874, p. 1.

[132] [Rep.], 'Great Demonstration of Miners at Durham', *NW*, 10 Jul. 1875, p. 5.

[133] Maehl, 'The Northeastern Miners', p. 207.

the pit galloways, and in fact the men were included in along with the colliery machinery'.[134]

When such objections were brought against their claims under the Household Suffrage Act it was time they advocated some more satisfactory franchise. The revising barrister had determined that if two or three went into a house by the same door, even though they occupied different rooms, they were all disqualified, and in that manner 500 men were struck off the list in Bedlington alone. It was ridiculous for the working men to go in for any such franchise as that . . . Mr. Gladstone admitted that there was a great difficulty in defining what a house was, and even the judges and the legal authorities had not yet settled the point. . . . There would not be the same difficulty in defining what was meant by a man; and therefore manhood suffrage would be the easiest suffrage imaginable.[135]

This opinion was largely shared by the miners, and was echoed at the numerous meetings held in those months. It implied a rejection of the household suffrage on pragmatic grounds rather than on principle: the 1867 Act was ineffective and seemed just 'a piece of barefaced bunkum to gammon the people into quietness',[136] which 'profusely gave household suffrage to boroughs, but practically excludes a very large number of householders upon the most frivolous and vexatious pretexts'.[137] Northumberland radicals had become so hostile to household franchise that they could not avoid violent discussions with the Durham supporters of the extension of the provision of the 1867 Act to the counties.[138] However, even they were not fully committed to manhood suffrage: for instance, one of the delegates of the Northumberland miners maintained that 'he should have a vote because he was a man, and it was right that he should have a voice in the government of the country because he contributed to the taxation of the country'.[139] Similarly, Elliott, who was one of the most intransigent supporters of manhood suffrage, declared that

[134] [Rep.], 'Manhood Suffrage – Proposed Demonstration on the Town Moor', *NC*, 10 Feb. 1873, p. 3; speech by R. Elliott.
[135] *Ibid.*
[136] [Rep.], 'The Miners and the Franchise – Demonstration at Morpeth', *NW*, 5 Oct. 1872, speech by R. Trotter.
[137] [Rep.], 'Manhood Suffrage Demonstration – Shadon's Hill', *NC*, 31 Mar. 1873, p. 3, motion voted by the miners.
[138] See in [rep.], *NC*, 10 Feb. 1873, p. 3, the speeches by Grieves (who supported county household franchise) and T. Brown, R. Elliott, and J. Cowen (who maintained the principle of 'manhood' as the only acceptable basis for a permanent settlement).
[139] [Rep.], *NC*, 10 Feb. 1873, p. 3, speech by M. Batey.

They ought not to give a man a vote because he had a house, for that was enfranchising the house, and they might just as well give a man a vote because he possessed a horse, or a gig, or something of that sort. (Laughter). But men ought to have votes because they were men. (Loud applause.)[140]

But concluded with an anticlimax, proclaiming that

a man who had to obey the laws of his country, and to contribute towards the taxation of his country, ought to have a voice in the making of the laws and in the levying of the taxes. It was an old Whig maxim, and it was perhaps a radical maxim too, that representation and taxation should go together.[141]

Neither Elliott nor his colleagues who expressed a similar opinion seemed to realize that there was a difference between the first and second parts of their argument – between asking for the franchise for every man as such, and asking for it for every man as a tax-payer, the latter being very similar to household franchise. Possibly such inconsistency was inevitable, since the miners wer not really interested in the rights of man, but only in their birthright as 'free Englishmen', as John Pritchard proclaimed[142] and Robert Elliott declaimed in a poem.[143] It should also be noted that, while asking

---

[140] Elliott's democratic radicalism was perfectly compatible with his passionate devotion to 'Mr. Gladstone', whom he energetically defended as

the best Minister England had ever had. They had great reasons to be grateful to him for the Mines Regulation Bill, which was one of the best measures ever carried through Parliament. Though there might not be a great amount of pressure required to bring Mr. Gladstone round to their views on manhood suffrage, they must remember that many of his colleagues were not nearly so far advanced as himself, and he was compelled to adapt himself to the circumstances of the case.' (*Ibid.*)

[141] *Ibid.*

[142] [Rep.], 'Manhood Suffrage Demonstrations – . . . Brandon', *NC*, 31 Mar. 1873, p. 3. Pritchard was one of the leaders of the Durham miners and president of the Durham County Franchise Association.

[143] This poem – read from a waggon at a meeting at Morpeth – was quoted in one of the reports of the Northumberland miners' demonstrations: [rep.], 'A London Correspondent's Account of the Morpeth Meeting', *NW*, 5 Dec. 1872, p. 8: 'Ye hardy sons of toil arise, ye Miners of the North, / To claim the rights of labour in your majesty come forth; / Come forth, come forth in thousands, and let your watchword be, / That you will not pose a moment in your struggle to be free. / In your struggle to possess what belongs to you by birth, / As a portion of the nation and as dwellers of the earth; / Be faithful, never faulter, in this truly noble cause, / And we'll win our rights as freeman, for to make our country's laws; / To make these laws that others too long have made for you, / For too long we have borne submission by the many to the few. / [. . .] We'll labour long and patiently, we'll labour one and all, / To send a toiler like ourselves within St. Stephen's Hall. / We'll try no more the wealthy, no more the 'Upper Ten', For what know they of the struggles or the wants of the lowly men? / [. . .] But can't we find a toiler, a man of lowly birth, / A one with scant possession of the good things of the earth? / Who has toiled as we have toiled in a region far away / From the fields and woods and

for manhood franchise, the miners insisted that 'real manhood' was qualified by certain intellectual and moral characteristics.[144]

All these themes found their fullest exposition in the two most spectacular demonstrations of 1872–4, which took place on the Newcastle Town Moor on 12 April and on the Durham Racecourse on 14 June 1873. Both were popular festivals in the style of the annual miners' galas. The Newcastle one was the most imposing, with a procession of 80,000 people including delegations from the unions of almost all the trades present in the north east, as the streets were thronged with something like 200,000 spectators. The main organizers of the demonstration were Joseph Cowen and a group of radicals of the Northern Reform Union. A Manhood Suffrage Committee was set up with the participation of delegates from all the workshops, shipyards and mines of Northumberland and Durham, and was entrusted with the task of co-ordinating the activities of the lodges of the different participating trades.[145]

In view of the difficulties involved in organizing such a huge number of demonstrators, each lodge was asked to specify how many representatives it would send. The lodges' replies provide evidence of the extent to which the cause of suffrage was felt by the anonymous rank-and-file plebeian radicals in the north-east: before replying each union held a general assembly of its members, who discussed the question, voted on the proposal to participate in the demonstration and defined the method and the form of their involvement. Writing in an English solemn in tone but with uncertain spelling and grammar, often betraying the strong influence of the local dialect, the secretaries of the great majority of the societies announced to the organizing Committee that their members had expressed the unanimous desire that their entire membership should participate, with banners and brass bands;[146] such was the case, for instance, of the lodge of Ryhope Colliery, which

flowers, and the blessed light of day / Who can rise and give expression in language clear and strong, / To our hatred of oppression and every form of wrong. / Yes, we have found a Miner, a man of sense and worth, / A one to nobly represent the Miners of the North. / Possessed of high intelligence, with culture much refined. / Whose labours in the past have been to elevate mankind; / To banish strikes for ever from every form of trade, / Where they of peace and happiness have often havoc made. / Then let us pledge ourselves to right, to do what'er we can, / To send to famed St. Stephen's this true-hearted working man.'

[144] [Rep.], *NC*, 31 Mar. 1873, p. 3, speech by John Lucas.
[145] Fynes, *The Miners* (1873), pp. 272–3.
[146] See *J. Cowen Coll.*, C 1760–C 1799.

brought to Newcastle all its 1200 members and their families.[147] In all, about 130 working-class societies decided to participate.[148]

There was great concern for the practical aspects of the demonstration; one problem was how to organize the rapid transport of tens of thousands of men, women and children from remote mining villages to Newcastle, in such a way as to allow them to congregate from the early morning. Several societies had to decline the invitation because they were unable to face the difficulties and cost of the transport,[149] while many lodge secretaries anxiously inquired about the possibility of organizing special trains to provide a sufficient number of seats.[150] In the end the number of partipants was so great that the railway companies had to set up many such special convoys: not only were all the carriages normally in service reserved, but also all the old ones were taken out of the depots for the occason, in addition to hundreds of other carriages having to be hired from rail companies in other regions of the country.[151]

All the details of the demonstration were carefully organized, with a meticulous marshalling service and a plan of the exact position which each of the delegations ought to occupy during the procession and on the moor. Six platforms were set up, on each of which three resolutions were to be proposed and voted on by the whole assembly. The text of each of the resolutions – manhood suffrage and redistribution of seats in proportion to the population – and the men who were to move and second them (all eminent trade union leaders) were proposed by the Manhood Suffrage Committee and communicated to each society by means of a circular.[152]

When the day arrived the organization bore the expected fruits. In spite of all the difficulties, the movement of this army of workers with their wives and children took place according to plan. There was no apprehension among the townsfolk: that Easter Saturday looked like a civic festival rather than a political demonstration. The balconies along the streets were crowded with ladies and

---

[147] *Ibid.*, C 1759, Ralph Anderson to McKendrick, 12 Mar. 1873.
[148] *Ibid.*, C 1808, poster of the demonstration with a list of the participants (see illustration 2 below).
[149] E.g. *ibid.*, C 1796.
[150] See the case of the lodge of Hetton Colliery, *ibid.*, C 1789.
[151] [Rep.], 'The Great Demonstration in Favour of Manhood Suffrage on the Town Moor', *NC*, 14 Apr. 1873, p. 4; the North Eastern hired 550 extra coaches.
[152] *J. Cowen Coll.*, *C 1821*.

gentlemen, and the women had dressed up for the occasion.[153] The windows of pubs and many private houses had been rented out to spectators, and the crowd lined up along the streets. For over three hours the demonstrators, in their Sunday attire, with banners and bands, marched through the city before the gathering on the Town Moor was complete. At the end, according to one witness, 'the eye had become weary with colours, the ear of sweet and stirring music, and the heart of such unremitting appeals to its choicest sympathies and most powerful emotions'.[154]

The banners themselves would provide enough material for a chapter on the political culture of the subaltern classes. One of them, from Newsham Colliery, woven in blue silk with yellow edges, bore words which effectively summed up the meaning of the demonstration and its cultural background: the motto on the front was 'We claim Manhood suffrage', and on the back it had verses which expressed the anti-aristocratic sentiments of the 'independent collier':

> Parsons and peers may preach,
> And endless falsehoods teach.
> Think for yourselves,
> And let your watchword be,
> Justice and liberty,
> And tell unweariedly to save ourselves.[155]

All the platform orators spoke energetically in favour of manhood suffrage, but nobody defended it as an 'inalienable right'. The reasons invoked were rather of an empirical[156] or historical-

---

[153] Fynes, *The Miners* (1873), pp. 274-5.

[154] *Ibid.*, p. 275. The Durham demonstration in June replicated the success and features of the Newcastle one, though its organization was less efficient. The most serious problem was that rail transport had been organized for only 35,000 people, whereas the number of participants was much greater, and as a consequence trains were overcrowded with miners and their families: according to one assessment 85,000 people congregated on the Racecourse (the Durham Miners' Association had 48,000 members): [rep.], 'Great Demonstration of Miners at Durham', *NC*, 16 Jun. 1873, p. 3.

[155] [Rep.], *NC*, 14 Apr. 1873, p. 6.

[156] E.g. the speech by W. Grieves, miner and president of the Northumberland Miners' Association (*ibid*). Another empirical argument was that a parliament elected on manhood franchise would pass more liberal legislation: particular mention was made of the full enactment of the programme of the National Education League: see the speeches by Andrew Steel (miner, Helburn), and R. Ellioss (miner, Choppington), *ibid*. The demand for 'manhood' suffrage had generally been argued on empirical grounds also by Cowen, in spite of the influence of continental democratic thought: see his text of the petition 'To the honourable commons of great britain and ireland, in parliament assembled', *J. Cowen Coll.*, C 1749. n.d., but *c*.1870).

constitutional kind.[157] Thomas Burt mentioned examples of countries where manhood suffrage had already been achieved (among which he mistakenly included Italy), stressing the case of the United States where – he said – even ex-slaves were admitted to the vote.[158] Another orator vigorously attacked household suffrage on Evangelical grounds, maintaining that it was a 'materialist' qualification, unworthy of a Christian country, since it valued property more than humanity.[159] And of course there were interventions by people who appealed to the 'Constitution of Edward I' as a model to be emulated.[160]

Once again, as in 1864–7, the appeal to the 'ancient constitution' singled out the core of the workers' conception of democracy: they wanted the franchise for all 'free-born' Englishmen, rather than for all Englishmen. In 1873, 'manhood' suffrage was not equivalent to universal male suffrage. The problem is well illustrated by Thomas Beckwith (joiner, Newcastle), who declared:

Some people ask the nonsensical question 'In what does manhood consist?' Well, certainly not in walking the streets with a cigar and a silver-headed cane. (Hear, hear, and laughter.) As the poet said –
> 'Honour and fame from no condition rise,
> Act well thy part, 'tis where true honour lies.'
(Cheers.) The men who swept the streets or shaped the wood, or hammered the iron, or hewed the coal, were men honourably doing their duty, and men who ought to possess the rights of citizenship. If any one ought to be excluded from the exercise of these, it ought to be those men who did nothing for the benefit of society.[161]

---

[157] E.g. the speech by W. Steel (miner, West Moor):

Forty per cent. of all taxes were contributed by the working classes, and yet they were debarred having a say as to the manner of its distribution. As a principle of justice, representation ought to be co-extensive with taxation. They affirmed the right of manhood suffrage because every man paid taxes to his country.

See also the speeches by T. Burt and T. J. Bayfield (moulder, Gateshead in ([Rep.], *NC*, 14 Apr. 1873, p. 6).

[158] [Rep.], *NC*, 14 Apr. 1873, p. 6.

[159] Speech by J. Birkett (moulder, Newcastle), *ibid.*

[160] Thus T. Thompson (weaver, North Shields), and W. Huntor (smith, Newcastle), *ibid.* All those elements were collected and published by J. Pritchard in a circular to the non-electors ('The Durham Franchise Association and Manhood Suffrage', *NC*, 5 May 1873, 4). Pritchard reminded them that it was the King's refusal to respect the fundamental principle of 'no taxation without representation' that had brought to the forefront 'the immortal Cromwell' as well as, later, forced the thirteen American colonies to proclaim their independence in 1776.

[161] [Rep.], *NC*, 5 May 1873, p. 4.

As Burt recalled on another occasion, the principle of manhood implied that

every man who had fulfilled the common duties of citizenship ought to possess and exercise the common rights of citizenship. If they had to apply a test at all, he thought they had to exclude everybody who did not work either in one way or in another for his livelihood. (Laughter, and applause.) If a man was not of some use to the community he ought not – if anybody ought not – to have any recognised right.[162]

It is clear that both Burt and Beckwith meant to attack the privileged 'drones' first and foremost, but their words had wider implications. In fact, just like the reformers of 1866–7, they defined the 'manhood' which entitled one to the vote not as the natural state of an adult male, but as that of the adult male who was *socially useful*. Their 'manhood' concerned only 'every man who was not a pauper, a criminal, or a lunatic'.[163]

On this point the reformers of 1872–4 were always clear and totally unanimous. Even on those few occasions when the suffrage was defined as an inalienable right, it was readily specified as 'the inalienable right of every man who has attained the age of 21 years, who is not tainted by crime, or is a pauper or a lunatic'.[164] This was exactly the formula adopted by the Durham miners as the text of the second resolution voted on during the great demonstration on the Racecourse on 14 June 1873[165]: only those who paid taxes and rates ought to have a say in the way in which the revenue was used.[166] Focusing on the question of the exclusion of paupers from 'manhood' suffrage, one of the orators said:

Although they objected to paupers, they sympathised with them on account of their poverty, and readily admitted that they might have as

---

[162] [Rep.], 'Northern Reform League', *NC*, 12 Nov. 1873, p. 3, speech by T. Burt.

[163] [Rep.], *NC*, 14 Apr. 1873, p. 6 (speech by T. Brown miner, Dinnington).

[164] [Rep.], 'Manhood Suffrage Demonstrations – . . . Blaydon', *NC*, 31 Mar. 1873, p. 3.

[165] See [rep.], 'The Great Demonstration of Miners at Durham', *NC*, 16 Jun. 1873, p. 3, resolution No.2:

> We regard the reduction of the Franchise to Manhood and Suffrage as both just and politic. Just – because it is the inalienable right of every man of mature years, and who is neither a pauper, a lunatic, nor a criminal; and 2) it will tend to increase the interest of every man in the moral and material welfare of his country.

> This had become the standard platform of the miners by then, and was even presented and approved by other meetings without modification: See for instance [rep.], 'Cleveland Miners Demonstration', *NW*, 19 Jun. 1875, p. 5).

[166] See speeches by C. Simpson (Lanchester), and J. Thompson (Tow Low) in [rep.], *NC*, 16 Jun. 1873, p. 3.

good principles at heart as any on that ground: but still, being under the control and influence of the poor law authorities, it was felt that they could never exercise their will like free men, and might thus be used to check the good which free men in other ranks of life might be striving for. (Hear, hear.) [167]

It would have been difficult to express more thoroughly the alignment of the plebeian supporters of manhood suffrage with the old Leveller and radical tradition, a tradition which even the agricultural labourers accepted, as Joseph Arch made clear [168]. The interventions of the miners at the 1872–4 demonstrations added no new elements to the popular debate on the franchise question, but only clarified the extent to which ideas which were two-centuries old were rooted in working-class culture.

THE MISSING REVIVAL OF 'MANHOOD SUFFRAGE'

The reform movement of those years remained limited to the north-east and ran out of steam when the original requests of the miners were satisfied, a decision which made Burt's election at Morpeth possible. [169] Resolutions in favour of a further enlargement of the franchise were presented at successive annual meetings of their organizations, but agitation was not resumed.

Meanwhile popular radicals in the rest of the country remained quiet, with the important exception of the agricultural labourers. Part of the explanation is that in this period most trade unionists were concentrating their energies on the reform of trade union laws. [170] Yet it is surprising that even in zones with a socio-economic structure similar to that of Northumberland and Durham, labour radicals did not show much interest in franchise issues. For instance, the Forest of Dean miners – a lively community with established radical traditions – devoted all their meetings and demonstrations exclusively to social and industrial issues. Towards the end of 1873 in West Gloucestershire an attempt was made to

---

[167] Speech by C. Kidd (Hanwick Lane Ends.), *ibid.*

[168] Arch though that 'manhood suffrage' was 'the inalienable right of every man of mature years, and who is neither a pauper, a lunatic or a criminal'. [Rep.], 'Cleveland's Miners Demonstration', *NW*, 10 Jun. 1875, p. 5).

[169] Mahel, 'The Northeastern Miners', p. 217.

[170] See [rep.], 'Demonstration of the London Trades', 7 Jun. 1873, pp. 9–10. Though the republican Odger was again the main speaker, no mention was made of the franchise question.

organize an agitation to return a working-man candidate,[171] but no practical result was achieved and no mention was ever made of any further enlargement of the franchise.

In Staffordshire, too, the workers were well-organized and resolute, with a long radical tradition,[172] but during the early 1870s they seemed almost exclusively concerned with industrial questions.[173] When political issues were raised, attention focused on the need for the secret ballot (until 1872) and direct representation of labour; political questions seemed partially or totally subordinate to labour ones.[174] The issue of the extension of the franchise was never taken into serious consideration, and was discussed only occasionally.

According to Broadhurst – then campaigning in the Potteries – the aim of direct labour representation was to extend household franchise to the counties;[175] possibly, he did not realize that he was reversing the terms of the question as it was being presented during the agitation of the north east, when working-class radicals realized that a wider franchise was the preliminary condition, not the consequence, of the election of working-class MPs. Yet Broadhurst's opinion was somehow representative of the convictions prevailing among the Potteries' workers, who seemed to think that the borough household franchise on its own would be enough to allow the return of working-class MPs.[176] Their view derived from

---

[171] See [l.a.], 'Labour Representation in West Gloucestershire', *Forest of Dean Examiner*, 14 Nov. 1873, p. 2; e [l.a.], 'Mr.George Howell a Candidate for West Gloucestershire', *ibid.*, 19 Dec. 1873, p. 4. Possibly it was the publication of T. Burt's address to the electors of Morpeth which sparked off the interest of the *Forest of Dean Examiner* in 'direct' labour representation: [l.a.], 'Labour Representation', *ibid.*, 25 Oct. 1873, p. 2.

[172] See Anderton, *Thesis*.

[173] Such were the points in the platforms of the main meetings: cf. [rep.], 'Mass Meeting of Miners at Henley', *Potteries Examiner*, 15 Mar. 1873, p. 7 (when the strike of the South Wales' miners was discussed and supported, but franchise reform was not mentioned): and [rep.], 'Miners' Meeting at Burslem – The Recent Advance of Ten Per Cent . . . The Government Inquiring into the High Price of Coal', *ibid.*, p. 8; 'The Third Annual Demonstration and Tea Meeting of Engineers', *ibid.*, 17 May 1873, pp. 6–7; [rep.], 'The Annual Demonstration and Tea Meeting of Engineers', *ibid.*, p. 8; [rep.], 'Miners Demonstration and Gala at Longton'; *ibid.*, 21 Jun. 1873, p. 3, [rep.], 'Miners' Mass Meeting', *ibid.*, 7 Jun. 1873, p. 7; [rep.], 'Overmen's Grand Annual Demonstration', *ibid.*, 9 Aug. 1873, p. 5. In each of these demonstrations, the only questions discussed were economic and industrial.

[174] [Rep.], 'Trades' Union Meeting at Hanley'. *Potteries Examiner*, 25 Apr. 1873, p. 3.

[175] *Ibid.*

[176] This was the general tone of several speeches at the meetings: see Stoke-on-Trent Labour Representation League. Nomination of Candidates for the Parliamentary Borough', *ibid.*, 15 Mar. 1873, p. 8; [rep.], 'Stoke-on-Trent Labour Representation League', *ibid.*, 29 Mar. 1873, p. 6.

the fact that many of them were already 'heads of families and householders' in the sense of the 1867 law:[177] though many labourers were still excluded from the franchise,[178] the number of electors seemed so great that the success of a working-class candidate was considered certain. Indeed, the leader of the Potteries miners, William Brown, declared that the working classes would soon return as many as 100 labour MPs.[179] He was not the only optimist: at the 1873 TUC Alfred A. Walton – prospective 'working man' candidate for the Potteries – maintained that the trade unions would easily be able to set up an 'independent industrial party of labour Members of Parliament' forty or fifty strong.[180]

Walton voiced the typical Positivist delusion that the working classes were 'naturally' unified in politics on the basis of shared material interests, and therefore could organize a 'labour and industrial' political party.[181] The vicissitudes of the succeeding fifteen years showed that the reverse was true.[182] The working classes were *not* politically unified or unifiable on a purely economic platform, and direct representation of labour was possible only in those regions where workers were ideologically and culturally unified.

Furthermore, the 1874 election showed that working men could vote Conservative as readily as any other class of electors. The self-confidence of the Staffordshire men was based on the Liberal victories of 1867–68, which seemed to promise the imminent triumph of the 'forces of democracy' and the inexorable decline of

---

[177] [Rep.], 'Labour Representation in Stoke-upon-Trent', *ibid.*, 4 Oct. 1873, p. 6, speech by W. Owen. Among the speakers at this meeting were Howell and Broadhurst, who stressed the urgency of a series of labour law reforms, but did not mention the enlargement of the franchise. Significantly both Howell and Broadhurst came from, and were politically active in, regions where the 1867 reform had enfranchised a conspicuous section of the working classes.

[178] In fact, 82,000 labourers signed a petition in support of Trevelyan's Bill in 1873: [l.a.], 'The Extension of Household Suffrage to the Counties'. *Potteries Examiner*, 26 Jul. 1873, p. 4.

[179] See his speech in 'Miners' Meetings – Silverdale', *Potteries Examiner*, 15 May 1873, p. 3.

[180] A. A. Walton, 'Representation of Labour in Parliament. The Best Means to Secure It. A Paper Taken and Read at the Trades' Congress', *ibid.*, 22 Feb. 1873, p. 3.

[181] See [l.a.], 'The Direct Representation of Labour', *RN*, 15 Dec. 1872, p. 1: 'The working classes have only to be united in one general election, daring to disregard party cries, and the battle is won.'

[182] As early as June 1873 the *Bee-Hive* observed that the Durham and Northumberland miners' unions could afford the luxury of direct political involvement because 'They have no fear of political divisions in their unions, as they are all liberal' [l.a.], 'Durham Miners' Demonstration', *BH*, 21 Jun. 1873, pp. 7–8.

the Tories. In this way they were blind even to the reality of the restrictive and undemocratic character of the 1867 franchise. The fact that so many important legislative achievements had been obtained with a limited electorate contributed towards restricting the interest in further franchise reform. In general, interest in extending the vote was not much greater than support for the women's franchise,[183] and even *Reynolds's Newspaper* remained substantially apathetic.[184]

However, it was not simply that the cause of further franchise reform did not find much support: the problem was that it even faced some working-class opposition. Though officially the farm workers were considered politically redeemed by the 'revolt of the field', [185] there were observers who remained sceptical about them: 'Littlejohn' of the *Weekly Times* observed that 'There are . . . many labourers who are greatly wanting in intelligence', and these could not be given the vote before education 'resurrected' them from abject slavery;[186] and as late as 1875 E. A. Rymer, the radical secularist miner, wondered how Joseph Arch 'or any other patriot' could possibly support the labourers' claim to the franchise 'when so many are mere drunken idiots and hardly capable of understanding wrong from right in political matters'.[187]

Despite these disparaging comments about the ability and awareness of the farm workers, the only section of the labour movement really committed to enlargement of the franchise after 1874 was the agricultural workers themselves. It is significant that they represented the group which had benefited least of all from the 1867 Reform; it is also significant that their platform was not manhood suffrage, but the extension of household franchise,[188]

---

[183] See [rep.], 'The Women Suffrage Movement', *BH*, 28 Jun. 1873, p. 4. Both causes were scarcely reported.

[184] Apart from some editorial support for the Newcastle demonstration ([l.a.], 'Political Incidents of Easter', *RN*, 20 Apr. 1873, p. 1),

[185] See Lloyd Jones, *BH*, 16 Nov. 1872, p. 1; [l.a.], *ibid.*, p. 9; [l.a.], 'Electoral Reform', *LW*, 17 Nov. 1872; [l.a.], 'The New Reform Movement', *NW*, 16 Nov. 1872, p. 4.

[186] Littlejohn, 'The Labourers and the Land', *WT*, 7 Apr. 1872, p. 6. 'Littlejohn' compared this resurrection to that of the 'dry bones' of Ezekiel 37 – a fact which in itself shows the low esteem in which the labourers were held by London plebeian radicals.

[187] E.A. Rymer, *Barnsley Chronicle*, 4 Dec. 1875, cit. in Fisher and Spaven, 'Edward Rymer', in Harrison (ed.), *Independent Collier*, p. 256. Traces of similar prejudices against the labourers were still to be found as late as 1881, when *Lloyd's Weekly* suggested balancing the county household franchise by the introduction of 'manhood' suffrage in the boroughs (see [l.a.], 'Town Manhood Suffrage', *LW*, 4 Dec. 1881, p. 1).

[188] See the resolution approved – two months after the Newcastle demonstration – by a

though occasionally they also voted for resolutions in favour of manhood suffrage.[189] The political content of their agitation was remarkably similar to that of 1866–7: they shared the conviction that 'Taxation without representation is tyranny',[190] and that the franchise was both the symbol of full citizenship,[191] and a necessary step towards the realization of one of their political ambitions, namely that of returning 'Joe' Arch to Parliament.[192]

These were the elements recurring in most addresses given in village market places week after week and in the petitions that thousands of agricultural labourers signed.[193] Thus the real peculiarity of the labourers' agitation was their perseverance. Between the beginning of the 1870s and 1884, year after year – in spite of the weakness of their trade union – the labourers never ceased to organize demonstrations in support of the county household fran-

---

meeting of labourers at Stratford: [rep.], 'National Agricultural Labourers' Union – Public Meeting at Stratford-upon-Avon, Warwickshire', *Labourers' Union Chronicle*, 14 Jun. 1873, pp. 5–6. Household, rather than 'manhood', franchise was also asked the following month at a great demonstration at Cottenham (see [rep.], 'Great Demonstration in Cambridgeshire', *ibid.*, 12 Jul. 1873, p. 7). Both instances took place in the period when the labourers' union was strongest and most self-confident. See also [l.a., n.t.], *PE*, 19 Apr. 1873, 9; [l.a.], 'Manhood Suffrage', *BH* 26 Apr. 1873, pp. 7–8.

[189] See [rep.], 'Labour Demonstration at Peterborough', *BH* 2 Aug. 1873, p. 3: the resolution in favour of 'manhood' suffrage was moved by G. Odger, the demonstration being organized by the Peterborough Labourers' Union.

[190] Cf. [rep.], 'Speech of a Union Delegate at Blockley, Worcestershire – The Franchise for the Labourer', *Labourers' Union Chronicle*, 2 Aug. 1873, pp. 7–8. W. Howard declared that 'One reason why the working man should have a vote is because he is taxed on nearly all that he requires. When he buys his tea, beer or tobacco, or almost anything, he pays the tax as well as the price of the article. This is taxation without representation.'

[191] [L.a.], 'Our First Anniversary', *ibid.*, 7 Jun. 1873, p. 1.

[192] See the following poem by Howard Evans, and compare it with Robert Elliott's work quoted above. (This poem was published in *BH*, 21 Jun. 1873, p. 10, and also in Arch, *Life* (1898), p. 273): 'The Franchise'.

There's a man who represents our shire / In the Parliament House, they say. / Returned by votes of farmer and squire / . . . / And farmer and squire when laws are made. / Are pretty well cared for theirs; / But the County Member, I'm much afraid, Has but little care for us.

[. . .] Whenever the rights of labour need / A vote on a certain day / The County Member is sure to plead / And vote the contrary way.

We asked for the vote, and we have good cause / To make it our firm demand; / For ages the rich have made all the laws / And have robbed the poor of their land. / The Parliament men false weight have made, / So that Justice often fails: / And, to make it worse, 'the Great Unpaid'. / Most always fiddle the scale.

So we ought to vote, deny it who can / 'Tis the right of an honest Englishman.

[193] A typical labourers' petition began by solemnly declaring that it was 'a monstrous grievance that they, who are the producers of so large a portion of the national wealth, and who are heavily taxed in proportion to their means, should have no voices in the imposition of those taxes, and that they should be called upon to obey laws in the making of which they have no share.' (cit. in Arch. *Life* (1898). p. 330).

chise in general and Trevelyan's Bills in particular. Dozens and dozens of franchise meetings took place throughout the rural counties of the Midlands, East Anglia and the south. The widespread geography of the demonstrations, the high level of participation of the labourers – in spite of the hostility of farmers and clergymen, and the difficulties involved in walking miles to reach the places where the meetings were held – are evidence of the popularity of the cause of franchise reform among this section of the working classes.

Their situation was very different from that of the miners because their bargaining power was smaller, they were much poorer, and were also scattered throughout the countryside rather than concentrated in compact villages. With the coming of the agricultural depression only politics offered any way out for the labourers: through the support of the Liberals, the hope of obtaining legal guarantees against the landlord persecutions, and eventually through the appointment of some labour leaders as Justices of the Peace.[194] All this helps to explain the labourers' prolonged and tenacious commitment to reform and – indirectly – also the lack of a similar commitment on the part of other sections of the labour movement and plebeian radicalism. During the 1870s the geography of the agitation for further reform faithfully followed the social geography of the non-elector householders.

One may wonder why the urban radical workers did not support the programme proposed by the Northumberland men in 1872–74. The reality is that nobody really wanted *universal* male suffrage, and indeed even the most extreme radicals who asked for 'manhood' franchise, meant something limited: as *Reynolds Newspaper* declared, 'The man ought to vote because he is a man, a free man, unstained by crime and pauperism, or unhappily subject to lunacy'; 'nor have we any objection to add, so far as working women paying their lot and earning their independent livelihood, womanhood suffrage, too'.[195] This was the most advanced conception of the electoral basis of a 'complete' democracy: male and female citizens 'paying their lot and earning their independent livelihood'. The 'free-born Englishman' (and 'Englishwoman')

[194] Dunbabin, 'The "Revolt of the Field"', p. 90.
[195] [L.a.], 'Political Incidents of Easter', *RN*, 20 Apr. 1873, p. 1.

who ought to be enfranchised were people able to 'stand on [their] own feet'.[196]

Out of the six categories of citizens excluded from household franchise according to Matthew, McKibbin and Kay,[197] only three would have been included in the greatest possible extension of the franchise then advocated. Since this was the case, the difference between the maximalist and minimalist platform was – both in practice and in theory[198] – less wide than might at first appear. After 1867 'manhood' suffrage gained mass support only in the north-east, where the Reform Act had been applied in an exasperatingly restrictive way, and, as we have seen, even there it was a temporary phenomenon. When in January 1874 the miners and labourers met Gladstone to urge electoral reform, the issue was simple county household franchise; nobody mentioned manhood suffrage.[199]

The 1870s showed that the Second Reform Act had placed the suffrage on a basis which was substantially acceptable to the majority of plebeian radicals. Aspirations to further democratic reform were limited both in distribution and intensity. As a leading article in the *Newcastle Chronicle* commented, it was vain to expect 'any extraordinary enthusiasm among those who already possess full citizenship in behalf of their excluded fellow-countrymen'.[200] Significantly urban plebeian radicals believed that they had received 'full citizenship' with the household franchise, and were by then interested in other reforms, like longer hours for voting, the repression of electoral corruption, redistribution of seats, and especially the secret ballot.[201] Until its introduction in 1872, the

---

[196] 'Here he stands' – 'Northumbrian' wrote a few years afterwards, in a passage which recalls verses from Milton's *Paradise Lost* – 'a man among his fellows, in a world in which the Creator has ordained that he should get a living by his labour . . . He has no right to demand anyone else's earnings. He has no right to compel anyone else to work for his own benefit: nor have others a right to demand that he shall work for their benefit.' (Northumbrian, 'British Slaves', *RN*, 17 Aug. 1884. p. 2).

[197] Namely, paupers, servants living with their employers, sons living with their parents and not being able to claim the exclusive use of their room, poorer lodgers, the mentally ill, and women (Matthew et al., 'The Franchise Factor', pp. 725–6).

[198] See [l.a.], 'The Extension of the Household Franchise to the Counties', *Potteries Examiner*, 26 Jun. 1873, p. 4: 'By the measure that became law in 1857 [sic, sc. 1867] . . . the legislature has sanctioned the principle that every man who by his labour can pay his way and keep a house over his head is entitled to a vote.'

[199] [L.a.], 'Mr. Gladstone and the County Franchise', *NW*, 24 Jan. 1874.

[200] *Ibid.*

[201] See R. Marsden Latham, President of the Labour Representation League, 'Root

ballot represented the top priority:[202] this had been a classical radical request for generations, and though it had been set aside in 1867 in order to concentrate attention on franchise reform,[203] from the early 1870s[204] it again became the battlecry of all sections of plebeian liberalism.[205]

After the Ballot Act popular radicals were left without a unifying political cause. County household franchise, and even manhood suffrage, were supported in principle, but were considered, for the time being, only marginally relevant to the immediate needs of plebeian radicals: the repeal of the Criminal Law Amendment Act, educational reform, and the remission of indirect taxation represented objectives which were more popular, or at least, more popular with a greater number of borough radicals.

THE AGITATION FOR THE THIRD REFORM BILL

The defeat of the Liberals at the election of 1874 had important repercussions for British popular liberalism, the first of which was to dispel the delusion that a 'democratic' electorate was inherently progressive. Yet, while to some radical intellectuals the defeat came as the confirmation of the danger of enfranchising the 'residuum' of illiterate drunkards open to easy bribery,[206] a majority of observers were of a different opinion. Plebeian radicals stressed that Gladstone had not been abandoned by the popular electorate, but betrayed by the unequal distribution of seats.[207] The very limited success of the labour candidates, and the unpalatable perspective of a septennial parliament with a Tory majority, also stimulated interest in other reforms, including that of the restoration

Questions, No. VIII: Electoral Reform', *BH*, 8 Mar. 1873, p. 3. In this article the extension of household franchise to the counties was also mentioned, as one of five reforms requested.

[202] See [l.a., n.t.], *LM*, 20 Apr. 1872, p. 5; [l.a.], 'The Ballot Debate', *WT*, 21 Mar. 1869, p. 1; J. Aytoun, *BH*, 21 Jun. 1872, p. 2; [l.a.], 'The Ballot Bill', *PE*, 1 Jul. 1871, p. 4.

[203] 'Mr. Bright at Rochdale', *BH*, 6 Jan. 1866, p. 1; [l.a.], 'The Ballot Debate', *LW*, 22 Jul. 1866, p. 6; [l.a.], 'The Defeat of the Ballot', *NW*, 21 Sept. 1866, p. 4.

[204] Particularly after the victimization of some radical voters: see [l.a.], 'A Cry from Wales for the Ballot', *BH*, 12 Feb. 1870, pp. 4–5.

[205] See for example, [l.a.], 'Forward, for the Ballot', *LW*, 18 Jun. 1871, p. 6; and [l.a.], 'The Ballot Bill', *PE*, 1 Jul. 1871, p. 4.

[206] [Anon.], 'The Revolt of the Residuum', *The Westminster and Foreign Quarterly Review*, October 1, 1874, p. 303.

[207] 'A Real Representation, No.2'. *Labourers' Union Chronicle*, 2 Jan. 1875.

of the system of payment of members[208] and shorter parliaments.[209]

However, the section of the labour movement which continued to be more committed to reform – the agricultural labourers – still placed county household suffrage at the top of the agenda.[210] In 1877 a conference of trade unionists was held in London, with the purpose of asking for the enlargement of the franchise in the counties: it is remarkable that, out of a total of 2,594 delegates, as many as 1,218 belonged to the National Agricultural Labourers' Union,[211] which thereby contributed out of all proportion to its strength and resources. These men, as their newspaper stressed, did not hesitate to come to London 'at the loss of two days' work and at the sole expense of themselves and their fellow-toilers'.[212] Such a high level of interest was also confirmed by the number of signatures on the petitions in favour of the Trevelyan Bills: almost one third of the 153,216 signatures on the 166 petitions sent to parliament between 27 June and 3 July 1877 were those of agricultural labourers.[213] Between the April of that year and the April of the next, resolutions in favour of county franchise were passed in at least forty-two agricultural meetings, of which thirteen had been convened specifically for this purpose.[214]

In addition, the other great category of rural or semi-rural workers traditionally committed to franchise reform – the miners – was still in a state of political unrest, especially in the north-east. The men of Durham and Northumberland had never stopped asking for an extension of the franchise, though no real 'agitation' had taken place after 1874. The Durham miners were definitely

[208] 'A Real Representation, No.3', *ibid*, 9 Jan. 1875, pp. 1–2: again reform was restoration, this time of the seventeenth-century tradition.
[209] 'A Real Representation – No.4', *ibid*., 16 Jan. 1875, p. 1: it was a case of restoring the 'old' constitution of Edward III.
[210] See [rep.], 'Labourers' Demonstrations ... Mr. Arch at Diss, Norfolk', *ibid*., 24 Apr. 1875, pp. 4–5, see the resolution; 'From a Correspondent', 'The Labourers and Their Right to Vote', *ibid*., 1 May 1875, p. 5; [rep.], 'The National Agricultural Labourers' Union – Market Harborough District', *ibid*., 8 May 1875, p. 5: the resolution asked for the extension of the household franchise since 'the successful management of the National Agricultural Labourers' Union by its members is an entire justification of the labourers in their demand for the electoral franchise ...' See also 'The Demand for the Franchise' by the Wife of a Labouring Man in the Brailes Branch, Banbury District', *ibid*., 19 May 1877, p. 3.
[211] [L.a.], 'At the Halls', *ibid*., 26 May 1877, p. 1.
[212] [L.a.], 'The London Conference', *ibid*.
[213] [Rep.], 'Franchise Petitions', *ibid*., 14 Jul. 1877, p. 3.
[214] See the reports, *ibid*., 12 Apr. 1877–6 Apr. 1878. These meetings were continued, at the same pace, throughout the rest of 1879 and 1880.

committed to county household franchise,[215] while their colleagues from Northumberland – and Burt in particular – continued to adhere to the platform of manhood suffrage.[216]

One of the effects of this growth of rural radicalism was to whip up Liberal support for the county franchise.[217] Though opinions on the final settlement of the franchise questions still diverged, the extension of the franchise to the 'illiterates' ceased to be a divisive issue, especially among popular liberals.[218] Democracy was becoming very fashionable. Chartism, fully rehabilitated, was then being celebrated as a step in the 'forward march' of liberalism:[219] indeed at Liberal meetings 'venerable' ex-Chartists read resolutions which were concluded with the old motto of 'the Charter, the whole Charter, and nothing but the Charter'.[220] In the popular mind, Chartism, Liberalism and democracy seemed to have become completely identified.[221]

---

[215] [Rep.], 'The Durham Miners – Great Demonstration on Durham Race Course', resolution No. 3, *NW*, 8 Jul. 1876, p. 5; [l.a.], 'The Political Claims of the Miners', *ibid.*, p. 4; See 'Annual Demonstrations of Durham Miners', *DC*, 12 Jul. 1878, p. 6. The majority of the Durham miners lived in villages outside the bounds of boroughs, and felt that their situation was more similar to that of the labourers.

[216] Burt quoted Gladstone in support of his views that the vote was not a privilege, but a right for all those who were not 'incapacitated by some consideration of personal unfitness or political danger' [rep.], 'Miners' pic-nic at Morpeth', *NW*, 19 Jul. 1875, p. 5. However, at the 1877 London conference Burt was the spokesman for the proposal of a ' a uniform Parliamentary franchise for county and borough constituencies', which was equivalent to the extension of household franchise: [rep.], 'Great Public Meeting at St James' Hall', *English Labourers' Chronicle*, 26 May 1877, p. 4. Another advocate of manhood suffrage was Bradlaugh: see his speech in [rep.], 'Annual Demonstration of Durham miners', *DC*, 12 Jul. 1878.

[217] [L.a.], 'The County Franchise', *LW*, 20 May 1876, p. 6; [l.a.], 'County Household Franchise', *NW*, 24 May 1874, p. 6; [l.a.], 'The Borough and County Franchise', *NW*, 10 Jul. 1875, p. 4; [rep.], 'The Leeds Election – Alderman Barran's Candidature – Great Liberal Mass Meeting', *LM*, 15 Aug. 1876, p. 8.

[218] A similar evolution had also taken place in the *National Reformer*, which was very sensitive to individual liberties: while in 1866 it had contained an article suggesting that 'there is always a risk of an extension of the suffrage, coupled with ignorance, bigotry and improvidence, resulting in the people becoming slaves to despotism as in France' (Manu. 'The Reform Question', *NR*, 23 Sept. 1866, p. 204), in 1877 it published a programme of eight points, the first of which was universal suffrage for both men and women (C. Bradlaugh, 'A Radical Programme', *NR*, 21 Jan. 1877, pp. 33–4).

[219] See Frost, *Forty years Recollections* (1880), pp. 97–9, as an example of the 'Whig interpretation' of Chartism by a former Chartist.

[220] [Rep.], 'Revival of Chartism', *English Labourers' Chronicle*, 15 Mar. 1879, p. 2. A Manhood Suffrage League was established in London: its programme included 'the Charter and something else' [rep.], 'Manhood Suffrage League', *English Labourers' Chronicle*, 26 Jul. 1879, p. 6.

[221] [Rep.], 'Chartist Lecture', [by W. H. Chadwick], *English Labourers' Chronicle*, 18 Jan. 1879, p. 7.

Possibly it was because the cause of county franchise was so strongly identified with the Liberals and with Gladstone personally that popular liberals did not think that it deserved special discussion during the the 1880 election: rather the most recurrent themes were those of the Midlothian campaigns. Even Joseph Arch expanded on foreign politics and national finance, without entering into the question of county franchise;[222] a Lib-Lab candidate, he stood as 'the supporter of Mr. Gladstone' and did not promise county household franchise, but 'Peace, Prosperity, and Plenty of Labour and Food'.[223]

After the Liberal victory, county franchise,[224] redistribution of seats and a legal limit to electoral expenses became the radical watchwords,[225] but it was not until 1884 that the Liberal government introduced the Third Reform Bill. Gladstone wanted to sort out a number of other issues first, and to reserve a measure requiring new elections for the end of the legislature.[226] Incidentally, a franchise agitation in the last years of the 1880 parliament could also be expected to help in unifying and reinvigorating rank-and-file Liberalism in preparation for the electoral campaign. If these were Gladstone's intentions, he was completely successful. The Bill, introduced on 28 February 1884, was greeted all over the country with immense excitement by plebeian radicals, who saw it as the reform which would give the vote to 'every head of a household'[227] and which 'grasped the whole problem of taxation

---

[222] [Rep.], 'Mr. Arch at Wilton', *English labourers' Chronicle*, 3 Apr. 1880, p. 8.

[223] *Ibid.*, J. Arch's manifesto. Even Burt's electoral addresses supported Gladstone's Midlothian programme without mentioning the suffrage: [rep.], 'Morpeth', *NW*, 27 Mar. 1880, p. 5. However, the labourers kept organizing meetings to ask for county franchise: see [rep.], 'Labourers' Meeting at Lincoln', *English Labourers' Chronicle*, 6 Mar. 1880, p. 7.

[224] That it was necessary to concentrate on this immediate objective was stressed by the Durham miners ([rep.], 'The Durham Miners – Annual Demonstration', *NW*, 7 Aug. 1880, p. 8, resolution, and was not denied even by the supporters of universal (male and female) suffrage: 'D.', 'A Radical Policy. v. – Electoral Mechanism', *NR*, 26 Aug. 1883, p. 131).

[225] See the programme of the National Liberal League – a London working-class association founded by George Howell and Broadhurst: 'Report of the special committee Appointed to Consider and Report on the Future Work of the League', 22 Apr. 1880. *G. Howell Coll., Political Parties*; see also [l.a.], 'The Home Policy of the Government', *LW*, 21 Nov. 1880, p. 1; and Ironside, 'A Radical Programme', *NW*, 30 Apr. 1881, p. 4.

[226] Matthew 'Introduction', *Diaries*, x, pp. cii-ciii.

[227] [L.a.], 'Reform at Last', *NC*, 29 Feb. 1884, p. 2; [l.a.], 'The New Reform Bill', *RN*, 3 Mar. 1884, p. 4; See [rep.], 'Liberal Demonstration at Hanley', speech by H. Broadhurst, *Staffordshire Knot*, 17 May 1884, p. 3.

and representation'.[228] Particular enthusiasm was shown by the farm workers who started a frantic ten-month agitation throughout East Anglia and central and northern England.[229] If it is possible to judge the level of interest and participation from the number and geography of popular meetings, then no other issue ever raised such enthusiasm. Just like the urban working classes in 1866–7, the labourers in 1884 were very emotionally involved because they also felt that they were excluded from the 'pale of the constitution' as a 'class', an impression accentuated by the arrogance and contempt towards them shown by Lord Randolph Churchill, who played the role of a latter-day Robert Lowe. In May there took place, on average, two large meetings per week, all characterized by great enthusiasm and the virtual identification of the franchise with the cause of rural trade unionism.[230] The thirteenth *annual* franchise demonstration in June[231] marked a record for the farm workers: no other group could claim such a long and uninterrupted commitment.

Over the whole country the agitation reached its climax in July, when the Bill was introduced into the House of Lords. The Lords asked that redistribution be included in the Bill.[232] But redistribution was a delicate and difficult question, which for various reasons, including his concern to avoid mixing up complex issues with the simple franchise question, and to 'keep the government's supporters . . . in line for another session', Gladstone intended to solve at

---

[228] [L.a.], 'The Policy of the Tory Party', *RN*, 9 Mar. 1884. p. 1. For the persistent popularity of the fiscal argument, see 'The County Franchise A Reform Leaflet'. *English Labourers' Chronicle*, 14 Feb. 1884. p. 3: [the county householders only] 'ask only for their legitimate rights as free-born English subjects. They pay their taxes, they conduct their own business, they contribute their share to maintain our army, our navy, our civil service and the government of the country, and no small share too.'

[229] From March: [rep.], 'The Franchise Question – Important Meeting at Diss', *English Labourers' Chronicle*, 15 Mar. 1884, p. 2. The text of the Bill had been published on a previous issue: [rep.], 'The New Reform Bill – Speech of Mr. Gladstone'. *English Labourers' Chronicle*, 8 Mar. 1884. p. 3.

[230] [Rep.], 'The Franchise Demonstration at Leamington – Speeches of Mr. Joseph Arch, Dr. Dale, and Mr. Jesse Collings, M.P.', *English Labourers' Chronicle*, 19 Apr. 1884, pp. 4–5. At this stage the trade union and the political activities of the National Labourers' Union were so closely intermixed as to be indistinguisheable: see [rep.], 'Anniversary Meeting of the Union at Wellesbourne', *English Labourers' Chronicle*, 24 May 1884, pp. 2–3.

[231] [Rep.], 'Great Demonstration of Agricultural Labourers', *English Labourers' Chronicle*, 7 Jun. 1884, p. 7.

[232] Jones, *Politics of Reform*, p. 126.

a later stage.[233] He could have called a general election to force reform on the Lords as Bright and Collings suggested;[234] but though this course would possibly have commanded popular support,[235] it appeared unworkable because it would have precipitated the already impending crisis with the Whigs.[236] As an alternative, Gladstone tried to bend the Lords by 'appealing to the country' without dissolving the Commons.

And the 'country' responded: during the twelve weeks preceding the Autumn session between 1,200 and 1,300 meetings took place in support of the government and against the Lords.[237] Many of these were really mass demonstrations: if we consider those which took place in July and August, we find that at least three had more than 60,000 participants, eight had between 20 and 30,000, and eleven had 10 to 19,000.[238] By 1884 no one doubted the urgency and inevitability of reform,[239] and this made the Lords' veto even more exasperating,[240] especially since it tended to confirm the arrogant remarks of Churchill and Salisbury. Indeed, as William Crawford wrote, the Tory leaders and the Lords did more for the reform agitation than all the radical militants put together.[241] Popular hostility to the upper chamber was further exacerbated by the fact that their obstructionism was not unexpected, having been anticipated since at least 1880.[242] In February 1884, when the Bill was being introduced into the Commons, William Crawford warned the lodges to make ready for action against the Lords:

---

[233] Matthew, 'Introduction', *Diaries*, x, p. civ.

[234] Hayes, *Third Reform Act*, pp. 167–8.

[235] *Ibid.*, pp. 138–41.

[236] Chadwick, 'Role of Redistribution', p. 674; Matthew, 'Introduction', *Diaries*,x, p. cvii.

[237] 1,227 meetings according to Jones (*ibid.*, p. 162), 1,300 according to Marsh (*Discipline of Popular Government*. p. 41). The Conservatives tried to organize counter-demonstrations, but theirs were less spontaneous and less numerous than the Liberal ones; only 184 took place: the ratio was 1:7 in favour of the Liberals (Jones, *Politics of Reform*, p. 167).

[238] 'Meetings for and against the House of Lords', *English Labourers' Chronicle*, 6 Sept. 1884, p. 2.

[239] Jones, *Politics of Reform*, p. 142.

[240] See [l.a.], 'Warnings for the Lords', *LW*, 7 Sept. 1884, p. 6; [l.a.], 'The Lords' Decision', *NC*, 9 Jul. 1884, p. 3. Chamberlain told the Cabinet that 'Birmingham was "thirsting for the blood of the Lords"' (Gwynn and Tuckwell, *Dilke*, ii, p. 65).

[241] *Durham Miners' Association, Monthly Report*, September and October 1884, No. 49 and 50, p. 4, 'Reform Agitation', in D/DMA 8.

[242] [Rep.], 'The Durham Franchise Association', *NW*, 6 May 1880, p. 5. In these circumstances it is quite surprising that Gladstone did not anticipate such a course: Matthew, 'Introduction', *Diaries*, x, p. cvi.

The time is past for the Lords to exercise feudal powers by setting at defiance the will of the nation. To make this matter clear beyond doubt, you ought to hold meetings and pass resolutions, and forward copies both to Mr. Gladstone and your local member of Parliament . . . any appeal to the county working population will show men like Lord Salisbury, and the puppet, Randolph Churchill, that if quiet, it is the quiet of earnest determination which will shew itself in a way least desired by Tories, should this measure of reform, so long delayed, be rejected by the House of Lords.[243]

Throughout the year the lodges of the DMA worked hard doing the job of Radical clubs.[244] The structure of the agitation was based on local[245] and preparatory meetings[246] which kept the pot boiling during the intervals between one great demonstration and the next. This method had been tested in 1866–7, and also had the advantages of propagating popular excitement, and allowing a full expression to the feelings of working-class liberals. In the north-eastern upheaval the trade unions played the role that in 1866–67 had been taken by the Reform League, Northern Reform Union, and other associations.[247] The greatest and most spectacular demonstration occurred at Hyde Park on 21 July with the participation of more than 100,000 people.[248] It is interesting to note that the proceedings were publicly perceived as a popular festival rather than as a revolutionary threat,[249] though they gave expression to popular hostility towards the landed aristocracy and the House of Lords.[250] The demonstrators claimed that sovereignty resided in

[243] *Durham Miners' Association Monthly Report*, February 1884, No.45, p. 4, in Minutes and Balance Sheets from January to June, D/DMA, 7, Durham Co. Rec Off., p. 200.

[244] See in D/DMA 8, Durham Co. Rec. Off., 'Reform Demonstration – To the Members', signed by W. Crawford, 26 Aug. 1884: 'Gentlemen, As you will be aware, a series of local demonstrations will be held on Saturday, October 8th, and you are requested to attend these meetings. With this you will get a circular, pointing out to which meeting you have been appointed. Go in great numbers.'

[245] Like that of the Silverdale 1,000 miners: [rep.], 'Meeting at Silverdale', *DC*, 2 Aug. 1884, p. 4.

[246] See [rep.], 'The Franchise Demonstration', *DC*, 4 Oct. 1884, p. 3: these meetings were held in Primitive Methodist school, in a New Connexion chapel, and in Temperance Halls.

[247] See [rep.], 'Durham Miners' Annual Gala', *DC*, 11 Jul. 1884, p. 6.

[248] 150,000 according to one estimate: [rep.], 'Magnificent Demonstration of the people against the Peers – Monster Meeting in Hyde Park', *RN*, 27 Jul. 1884, p. 2. See Gwynn and Tuckwell, *Dilke*, II p. 65: 'I saw the Franchise Demonstration . . . from the Speaker's window, the procession passing from three till six.'

[249] [Rep.], 'The Great Reform Demonstration'. *DN*, 22 Jul. 1884. pp. 5–6.

[250] See [rep.], 'The Franchise Demonstration – Enthusiasm of the People', *English Labourers' Chronicle*, 26 Jul. 1884, p. 4; [rep.], 'The Great Liberal Demonstration in Hyde Park',

the people in the parks, rather than in the squires in the upper House: this was also the message of most of the other mass meetings,[251] like those of Glasgow (*c.*70,000 participants) and Victoria Park, in London (40,000 people)[252] – through which, as they said themselves, 'the people' made their voice heard.

THE END OF THE 'AGITATIONS'

During this long agitation, popular liberals struggled to affirm not only their right to the vote, but also a whole set of values, which the 20,000 men and women who marched through Stoke-on-Trent on 6 October expressed with the chorus:

> Give the countryman a vote,
> Though House of Lords should perish,
> And keep dear Gladstone at the helm,
> To make the nation flourish.[253]

The franchise for the countryman, the destruction of the Lords, and the GOM at 10 Downing Street, were causes closely linked to each other in popular perception. Following their own convictions and radical rhetoric, plebeian liberals do not appear to have seriously contemplated the possibility that suffrage and redistribution might be passed together as a result of an agreement between Gladstone and Salisbury. When events took precisely this course, the compromise was received as a welcome surprise by many, but not all. *Reynolds's* complained that

It was not for a paltry Franchise Bill which only enfranchises two millions of ratepayers instead of five millions of men; it was not for a Redistribution Bill which even at the best would give us by no means a complete representation of the people, that demonstrations of the most imposing

English Labourers' Chronicle, 2 Aug. 1884, pp. 2–5; [rep.], 'The Franchise Demonstration', *Staffordshire Knot*, 26 Jul. 1884, p. 2; [l.a.], 'The Political Crisis – The Hyde Park Demonstration and Tory Misrepresentation', *ibid.*, p. 1, where the workers' demonstration is described as their reply to Lord Salisbury's provocation. On the question of the cult of the GOM see below, chapter 7, pp. 395–425.

[251] [Rep.], 'The Franchise Bill', *Staffordshire Knot*, 2 Aug. 1884, p. 2; [rep.], 'The Peers and the Franchise', *English labourers' Chronicle*, 9 Aug. 1884, pp. 4–7; cf. [rep.], 'The Monster Anti-Aristocratic Demonstration at Birmingham', *RN*, 10 Aug. 1884, p. 1.

[252] [L.a.], '1819 to 1884', *RN*, 14 Sept. 1884, p. 4; [rep.], 'Great Franchise Demonstration', *ibid.*, p. 8.

[253] [Rep.], 'Great Franchise Demonstration – Reception of Mr. Chamberlain – Mass Meetings of Liberals – Speech by Mr. Chamberlain at Hanley', *Staffordshire Knot*, 11 Oct. 1884, pp. 2–3.

and impressive character were held between August and November ...
A great issue was presented to the people – should they put down their
heads for the Lords to put their heels upon their necks? The peers had
thrown down the gage; the people took it up and declared that the
Franchise Bill should be passed without any condition as redistribution;
either that or the abolition of the Lords of Parliament.[254]

This challenge was now being lost because of Gladstone's
'betrayal'.[255] According to *Reynolds's*, the real question was not the
Bill, but the power of the Lords, the House that Cromwell had
justly dissolved as a 'useless and dangerous' body.[256] By compromising with Salisbury the government had established a constitutional precedent and renewed the credibility of the upper chamber;
this was too high a price to pay for reform,[257] and the problem of
the Lords, *Reynolds's* prophesized, would soon re-emerge in a more
threatening form.[258]

However, the prevailing mood was one of relief and euphoria,
and it is likely that this reform more than any other single measure
helped to consolidate the Lib-lab alliance.[259] To celebrate, in
several parts of the country the labourers even planted Franchise
Trees,[260] just as the Jacobins had planted Liberty Trees in the
1790s. This triumphalism was also encouraged by the fact that, in
growing stronger, the agitation had assumed an increasingly
emotional character, a fact which did not encourage any critical
assessment of the result once achieved.

For a while the question of manhood suffrage thus seemed to
have disappeared from the programme of popular radicalism,
which devoted itself to questions like free and compulsory elementary education, reform of local government, and distribution of

---

[254] [L.a.], 'The Political Metz', *RN*, 23 Nov. 1884, p. 1.
[255] *Ibid.*
[256] [L.a.], 'The Gladstone-Salisbury Treaty', *RN*, 30 Nov. 1884, p.1 .
[257] Gracchus, 'Defeat, Disgrace, and dishonour', *ibid.*, p. 3; and 'The Conservative Cock-a
   Doodle-Doo', *RN*, 14 Dec. 1884, p. 3.
[258] [L.a.], 'The Abolition of the House of Lords', *RN*, 30 Nov. 1884, p. 4; [l.a.], 'The Leader
   of the People', *RN*, 27 Sept. 1885, p. 4.
[259] [Rep.], 'Miners' Demonstration at Chesterfield – Addresses by Miss H. Taylor and Mr.
   Bradlaugh', *Sheffield and Rotherham Independent*, 21 Jul. 1885, p. 2, resolution moved by
   Mr. Bailey; [rep.], 'Miners' Demonstration at Barnsley', *ibid.*, 11 Aug. 1885, p. 8,
   resolution moved by Rev. G. Hadfield.
[260] Ashby, *Joseph Ashby* (1961), pp. 112–13. Ashby claims that there are many photographs
   documenting this kind of event.

allotments.[261] Reforms of this kind were important especially for the farm workers who had made an important contribution to the movement for the Third Reform Act, but who now seemed fully satisfied with the result of the 1884–5 legislation. In 1885 for the first time franchise extension was not included on the agenda of the annual general meeting of the National Union of Agricultural Labourers,[262] and the Annual Council of the NALU did not contemplate any further extension of the vote.[263] In October 1885 the *Labourers' Chronicle* declared that the 1884 Act had 'crowned the edifice' of 'national freedom' whose foundation had been laid in 1832.[264] Apparently nothing more was required: Arch himself, in his electoral manifesto, seemed to consider the franchise question as resolved.[265]

It was only when the new electoral registers were complete that it became possible to evaluate the limits of the new law: then a few critical voices were sporadically raised. For instance, in Sheffield a certain Henry May lamented that there were many cases in which 'a *bona fide* working man in the receipt of weekly paid wages' was not among the £10 lodger electors: in order to enfranchise this 'very intelligent and meritorious portion of the community' May asked for a lower lodger qualification (£4), a halved residential qualification, and that electors should retain the franchise when changing residence, provided that there was continuity of employment.[266] A few months later, when the Home Rule crisis was already precipitating a new general election, the adequacy of household suffrage was seriously questioned for the first time: indeed, the Durham Miners' Political Reform Association passed a resolution which requested the vote for all 'adult males'.[267]

---

[261] [Rep.], 'Mr. Chamberlain at Hackney – The Liberal Programme – Tories and Imitative Legislation', *ibid.*, 25 Jul. 1885, p. 5.

[262] [Rep.], 'The National Agricultural Labourers' Union – Annual Council at Swaffham', *English Labourers' Chronicle*, 22 May 1885, p. 3.

[263] [Rep.], 'The National Agricultural Labourers' Union – Annual Council at Swaffham – Political Programme', *English Labourers' Chronicle*, 23 May 1885, p. 3.

[264] [L.a.], 'The Franchise Jubilee', *English Labourers' Chronicle*, 17 Oct. 1885, p. 1.

[265] J. Arch, 'An Address to the New Voters', *English Labourers' Chronicle*, 14 Nov. 1885, p. 1; and 'To the Electors of North-West Norfolk', *English Labourers' Chronicle*, 21 Nov. 1885, p. 5.

[266] H. May, 'The Lodger Franchise', *Sheffield and Rotherham Independent*, 1 Oct. 1885, p. 8. Significantly May's proposed franchise qualifications were somehow linked with the idea of 'independence' (as in the case of continuity of employment).

[267] [Rep.], 'Durham Miners' Political Reform Association', *DC*, 21 May 1886, p. 6. Here something more than the old 'manhood' suffrage was requested.

The unexpected disaster of the 'party of Progress' in 1886 stimulated popular reflection on the limits of the 'democratic' settlement of 1884–5. By then the revision of the registration procedures had become a common request.[268] At the Durham Miners Gala, in August 1886, a resolution was passed asking for the abolition of plural votes,[269] a request that soon became the established watchword of working-class radicalism,[270] and, by 1888, also a point in the official Liberal programme.[271] Another increasingly popular reform was that of the reduction of the residential qualification.[272] It was not until July 1891 that these points and manhood suffrage were voted on at a Gala of the Durham Miners' Association.[273] But even then these electoral reforms were listed in a long series of improvements dominated by the reform of the land laws, free secular primary education, and Home Rule.[274] In fact, in those years and till the defeat of the second Bill, Home Rule was the most popular political issue both among the Durham miners[275] and the agricultural labourers,[276] with the reform of local government coming in second place.[277]

In contrast, manhood suffrage never got much support after 1884. Although from 1886 to 1895 Howell introduced annual Bills to replace manhood for household in the existing legislation,[278] as

---

[268] [Rep.] *DC*, 21 May 1886, p. 6. This development went on hand in hand with a similar change in the official position of the Liberal party: see Clarke, *Lancashire and the 'New Liberalism'*, pp. 117–18.

[269] [Rep.], 'Durham Miners' Annual Gala', *DC*, 6 Aug. 1886, p. 6, resolution no.2.

[270] [Rep.], 'Liberalism in North Norfolk', *English Labourers' Chronicle*, 2 Jun. 1888, p. 2; [rep.], 'Mr. Sydney Stern's Candidature', *English Labourers' chronicle*, 15 Jun. 1889, p. 5: this candidature was supported by Arch, who stressed the question of the abolition of plural voting.

[271] See Barker, *Gladstone and Radicalism*, p. 259; Hamer, *Liberal Politics*, p. 182.

[272] From twelve to three months [rep.], 'London Liberal and Radical Union', *English Labourers' Chronicle*, 10 Mar. 1888, p. 7), or even to one month ([rep.], 'Mr. Arch, M.P., at New Bukenham', *English Labourers' Chronicle*, 24 Jun. 1893, p. 5). On this point too there was agreement with the official Liberal programme: see Clarke, *Lancashire and the 'New Liberalism'*, pp. 117–18.

[273] [Rep.], 'The Durham Miners' Association – Annual Gala – A Huge Throng', *DC*, 10 Jul. 1891, p. 6.

[274] *Ibid.*

[275] [Rep.], 'Great Demonstration of Miners at Durham', *English Labourers' Chronicle*, 30 Jul. 1887, p. 2: it was the Gala, and Home Rule was the subject of one of the resolutions approved.

[276] See [rep.], 'Mr. Joseph Arch at Terrington', *English Labourers' Chronicle*, 26 May 1888, p. 2; Howkins, *Thesis*, pp. 145–7.

[277] [L.a., n.t.], *English Labourers' Chronicle*, 25 Nov. 1893, p. 1.

[278] *DLB*, II p. 192. Howell's proposal also included the reduction of the residential qualification to 3 months. Manhood suffrage was also included in the 1885 Radical programme: Chamberlain, *The Radical Programme* (1885), pp. 106–7.

late as 1893 Arch considered the franchise as something which had already been achieved, implicitly admitting that no section of the working classes was excluded from it.[279] In these years even the Durham County Franchise Association – which in 1886 had passed a resolution in support of universal male suffrage spurring on the Miners' Association to pass a similar resolution in 1891 – insisted almost exclusively on the reduction of the residence qualification and the abolition of plural votes. Though the latter was the most important issue – as suggested by the resolutions regularly passed in 1891,[280] 1892,[281] 1893,[282] 1895,[283] and 1896[284] – plural voting also attracted considerable hostility: it represented an 'insult' against the dignity of the independent worker since it implied that one wealthy elector was worth several working-class ones.[285]

It can be concluded that, after the radical triennium of 1872–4, manhood suffrage was relegated to the margins of plebeian politics, having more or less the same position as women's suffrage and a wider lodger franchise, measures which few radicals objected to *in principle*, but which many did their best to obstruct *in practice*.[286] Just like manhood suffrage, these were therefore questions in which little effective progress was made after 1867–9.

An examination of the question of woman suffrage confirms the general picture of plebeian attitudes to the vote. Within Victorian liberalism there was a strong current in favour of women's eman-

[279] [Rep.], 'Mr. J. Arch, M.P., at Haywards Heath', *English Labourers' Chronicle*, 26 Aug. 1893, p. 5; See [l.a., n.t.], *English Labourers' Chronicle*, 16 Sept. 1893, p. 1, an article which condemned the miners' riot: since they now had the vote, they were expected to behave in a law-abiding way.

[280] *Durham County Franchise Association*, 'Programme of Council Meeting, To be held in the Miners' Hall, Durham, on Saturday, August 1st, 1891', Resolution No. 9 (Philadelphia), p. 3, in D/X 188/13/1.

[281] *Durham Political Reform Association*, 'Programme of Council Meeting, To be held in the Miners' Hall, Durham on Saturday, Aug. 2nd', Resolution No.3 (South Durham), p. 3, in *ibid.*

[282] *Durham County Franchise and Political Reform Association*, 'Programme of Council Meeting, to be held on Saturday, February 25th, 1893', Resolution No. 3., p. 2, in *ibid.*; the Liberal government was thanked for trying to introduce an appropriate Bill.

[283] *Durham County Franchise and Political Reform Association*, 'Programme of Council Meeting, to be held in the Miners' Hall, on Saturday, April 13th, 1895', Resolution No.6 (Ryhope), p. 3, *ibid.*, which asked the Unionist government to modify the electoral law.

[284] *Durham County Franchise and Political Reform Association*. 'Programme of Council Meeting, to be held on Saturday, April 4th, 1896', Resolution No.7, p. 4, in *ibid.*

[285] [Rep.], 'Mr. Sydney Stern's Candidature', *English Labourers' Chronicle*, 15 Jun. 1889, p. 5.

[286] It is significant that both at the 1882 and the 1883 TUC's amendments in support of 'manhood suffrage' were rejected with large majorities. (Webb, *History of Trade Unionism*, p. 368).

cipation and suffrage, also encouraged by the rise of new forms of party organization and the moral tone of politics in the age of Gladstone.[287] On several occasions between 1867 and 1884 the House of Commons witnessed the grouping of strong minorities in favour of amendments to the electoral laws to bring some women 'within the pale of the constitution'. Mill, Fawcett and Jacob Bright were the main spokesmen for this platform, and their efforts were partially successful in 1869–70, with the enfranchisement of female ratepayers for local elections.[288] The subsequent attempts to obtain the parliamentary franchise for at least some women were based on proposals to extend the norms accepted for town councils and school boards,[289] and employed the same arguments and rhetoric already used to foster the extension of male suffrage.[290] Even the most aggressive pioneers of female suffrage did not go beyond the radicalism of 'no taxation without representation',[291] and other similar appeals to the 'constitutional tradition'.[292]

In general, plebeian radicals looked at these proposals with sympathy,[293] and even supported Helen Taylor's attempt to stand as a candidate for one of the London constituencies in 1885.[294] The Primitive Methodists, in particular, had a traditional feeling for

[287] Hollis, *Ladies Elect*, p. 53.

[288] See [l.a., n.t.], *NW*, 6 Nov. 1869, p. 4, for a favourable comment on the first municipal elections in which women took part. On the eve on the 1918 Act 78 per cent of women above thirty years of age were local electors (Tanner, 'Parliamentary Electoral System', p. 214).

[289] E.g. [rep.] 'Meeting in Leeds in Support of Women's Suffrage', *LM*, 21 Feb. 1874, p. 3, and in particular Miss Lucy Wilson's speech.

[290] See Lydia E. Becker, 'Female suffrage', *Contemporary Review* (1967), pp. 307–16, Mill in 1867 used the Gladstonian theory of the 'moral right' and of the fact that any 'unfitness to the franchise' was yet to be proven against the women as much as against the working men who were then being enfranchised: Smith, *Second Reform Bill*, p. 204.

[291] See the then famous case of Miss H. Muller (who was also a radical member of London School Board) in [rep.], 'Taxation and Representation', *RN*, 6 Jul. 1884, p. 5; *Lloyd's Weekly* expressed the typical popular liberal reaction: approval for the principle, but disapproval for the methods [l.a.], 'Women and the Franchise', 13 Jul. 1884, p. 6).

[292] Maintaining that there was a time when widows had exercised the vote on behalf of their deceased husbands: (lett. by) H.D. Griffiths, '"Ye Ancient Method" of Holding Parliament in England', *BH*, 31 Oct. 1868, p. 7.

[293] See [l.a.], 'The Future of the Franchise', *NW*, 17 Oct. 1868; J. Cowen, 'Women's Franchise', 12 Jun. 1884, in *Cowen Coll.* B 319; G. Howell to Mrs. J. Butler, 22 Oct. 1870, in *G. Howell Coll., Lett. Book*, IX.; [l.a.], 'A Laugh at Women's Suffrage', *LW*, 12 May 1872, p. 6 (a protest against the rejection of Jacob Bright's Bill); 'A Real Representation – No.2', *Labourers' Union Chronicle*, 2 Jan. 1875, p. 2; 'Women Suffrage', *LW*, 9 Jan. 1875, pp. 1–2.

[294] See [rep.], 'The Metropolitan Election – No.II, Dr. Pankhurst and Helen Taylor', *MG*, 26 Oct. 1885.

the cause of women's emancipation, due to the prestigious positions held by women in their congregations,[295] as well as in many working-class families.[296] The *Bee-Hive* distinguished itself in this as in all radical campaigns by reacting enthusiastically to the publication of Mill's *Subjection of Women*,[297] and welcoming to its columns articles by leading exponents of women's emancipation.[298] As in the case of the agricultural labourers, the *Bee-Hive* maintained that women were first to be educated, and then given both the franchise and full legal equality.[299] The vote, however, was to be limited to 'independent', unmarried women and widows, since married women were supposed to be already 'represented by their husbands'.[300] This had been an established attitude for a long time in radical circles,[301] and was then predominant among working-class radicals.[302]

On the other hand, many liberals and radicals were opposed to female suffrage and used arguments similar to those which had been used to resist the enfranchisement of the agricultural labourers: lack of education and political awareness[303] were expected to make the women docile instruments in the hands of the Conservatives. Even George Howell thought that 'Most women have a kind of undefined Conservatism. Conservatism is uneducated thought,

---

[295] McCleod, *Religion and the Working Classes*, p. 28; Moore, *Pit-men, Preachers and Politics*, p. 171.

[296] In spite of common assumptions, mothers and wives were often in charge of the working-class family's education, both religious and secular, not simply because they spent more time at home, but also because they often had higher intellectual abilities than their husbands: see for two examples, Arch, *Life* (1898), pp. 16–22, 24; Edwards, *From Crow Scaring to Westminster* (1922), pp. 13, 32ff.

[297] [L.a.], *BH*, 13 Nov. 1868, pp. 4–5.

[298] See Rosamond Harvey, 'Women's Rights,' *BH*, 28 Oct. 1871, p. 3; Martha Hardcastle, 'Women's Suffrage', *BH*, 1 Mar. 1873, p. 3; [rep.], 'The Woman Suffrage Movement', *BH*, 28 Jun. 1873, p. 4 [a meeting in support of Jacob Bright's Bill]; Josephine Butler also often contributed to the *Bee-Hive*: See 4 Jun. 1872, p. 2.

[299] Plain Daler, *BH*, 16 Oct. 1868, pp. 4–5.

[300] [Lett. by] 'D', *BH* 25 Apr. 1868, p. 6; [l.a.], *BH* 26 Sept. 1868, pp. 4–5.

[301] James Mill had maintained 'that women's interests would be adequately represented by their husbands, and that men over forty would look after the interests of the youth' (Thompson, *Mill and Representative Government*, p. 19).

[302] [L.a.], 'Woman Suffrage', *NW*, 6 May 1871, p. 4; [l.a.], 'Women's Suffrage', *NW*, 4 May 1872, p. 4; [Unsigned review article], 'Woman Suffrage', *Labourers' Union Chronicle*, 9 Jan. 1875, pp. 2–3.

[303] See Littlejohn, 'The Woman of the Working Class', *WT*, 19 Apr. 1868; [l.a., n.t.], *LM*, 11 Jun. 1866, p. 2 (in answer to Mill's proposal); the same conviction was shared by Joseph Ashby as late as 1906 (Ashby, *Joseph Ashby* (1961), p. 247). For the point of view of the Liberal leaders see Pugh, *Making of Modern British Politics*, p. 93.

trusting to others rather than self-reliant. This is the secret of Priestly power over them.'[304] Women were expected to provide some 'proof' of their civic maturity before being enfranchised: the debate remained circumscribed within the perspective of a franchise linked 'with the performance of public duties, or the fulfilment of citizen's responsiblities'.[305]

In any case, during the campaign for the Third Reform the radicals were not ready to join the request for female franchise to their platform.[306] Indeed, male household franchise remained the only aim seriously pursued,[307] since even the high lodger qualification was tacitly tolerated until 1918, despite its total ineffectiveness being well-known. For example, in 1869 only 12,000 electors (out of a total of about two and a half million) were registered on the basis of the lodger franchise, and of these 8,000 resided in the West End of London, where rents were very high; in contrast, Manchester had only twenty-eight lodger voters, and Birmingham only one.[308] As late as 1884, as we have seen, the lodger electorate was extremely small even in cities like Sheffield. The most important category excluded was – as Thomas Wright wrote in 1868 – that of "single young fellows", the young unmarried men, who d[id] not rent apartments, but [we]re "taken in and done for" at from half-a-crown to three-and-six pence a-week'.[309] Thus, Wright complained, only married men, however miserable their conditions, had been enfranchised in 1867,[310] while bachelors had been

---

[304] G. Howell to Capt. F. Maxse, 31 Mar. 1872, in *G. Howell Coll., Lett. Book*, IX, p. 584.; however, Howell concluded: 'but if the right of voting is extended to all males it must be also to all females . . . I fear not the results'.

[305] G. Howell, 'Women's Suffrage Movement', MS, nid., in *G. Howell Coll.*

[306] [L.a.], 'At the Halls', *English Labourers' Chronicle*, 26 May 1877, p. 1; 'We have no objection whatever to female ratepayers having the franchise . . .' but labourers were not ready to tolerate interruptions of their meetings to obtain county franchise in order to accommodate suffragettes like 'a hysterical young person who shrilled out a lot of nonsense from the body of the hall . . .' In any case, these forerunners of the suffragettes did not seem to belong to the working classes. On this question, see Harrison, *Separate Sphere* and Ken, *Sex and Suffrage in Britain*, pp. 184–219.

[307] *Ibid.*; See [l.a.], 'Mr. Woodall and Women's Suffrage', *Staffordshire Knot*, 14 Apr. 1884, p. 1.

[308] Smith, 'Second Reform Bill', p. 195.

[309] Wright, *The Great Unwashed* (1868), p. 74. The same conviction was entertained by the radical miner T. Glassey, who said that even with household franchise in the counties 'there would still be hundreds of thousands of unmarried men and others who would not have votes' [rep.], 'Manhood Suffrage – Proposed Demonstration on the Town Moor', *NC*, 10 Feb. 1873, p. 3).

[310] Wright, *The Great Unwashed* (1868), pp. 73–4.

debarred, though they represented a class 'numerous . . . and, if intelligence, education, and independence are to be taken as qualifications for the possession of the franchise, one which is . . . better fitted than any other division of the working classes'.[311] This consequence of the Second Reform Act had not escaped the notice of the legislators either: while the Bill was still being framed, Henry Fawcett had proposed – unsuccessfully – to introduce a supplementary 'educational qualification' in order to enfranchise 'many young men of intelligence who could not easily gain a vote in any other way'.[312] Later W. Forster declared that the Second Reform Act had enfranchised 'the heads of our families',[313] and stressed that *that* was the 'right' electoral basis. This may suggest that the exclusion of bachelors was deliberate.[314] The legislators were suspicious of the economic and political independence of young workers who were emancipated from family authority, politically and socially aggressive,[315] and sometimes even identified with the *classe dangereuse*.[316] In contrast, married workers, weighed down with family responsibilities, might be expected to provide a more moderate, deferential, and thoughtful electoral body.

More generally, we must remember that the principle followed by the legislators was substantially that of enfranchising the smallest possible number of people, while making due allowance for the necessity of satisfying popular pressure and stabilizing the political situation. In many respects household franchise presented an ideal solution, a convincing compromise between a property qualification and universal male suffrage. Moreover, even from the point of view of the subaltern classes this franchise was highly acceptable because it did not appear to be class-biased, and, by

---

[311] *Ibid.*, p. 74.

[312] Cowling, *1867*, p. 226.

[313] [L.a.], 'The Extension of the Household Franchise to the Counties', *PE*, 26 Jul. 1873, p. 4.

[314] This was largely the case with Gladstone: Matthew, 'Introduction', *Diaries*, x, p. cv, n.3.

[315] Wright, *The Great Unwashed* (1868), pp. 75–6.

[316] See Smith, *Conflict and Compromise*, chapter 3. This radicalism of the young folk is confirmed by the fact that they had an important role in the rise of the Labour party after 1918, which was accompanied by a conflict of generations (Moore, *Pit-men, Preachers and Politics*, pp. 178–9). Were it possible to provide statistical evidence for Wright's observations, the impact of the new generations after 1918 might be seen as one of the main factors in the decline of the Liberals and the rise of Labour. In addition, the psychological effects of the First World War on these young people – widely known among historians of culture and mentality (see Hughes, *Consciousness and Society*, pp. 392–431) – have yet to be assessed by political historians.

enfranchising those who paid the rates, could be taken as giving the vote to full-manhood and independence.[317] Moreover, the household qualification was constitutionally prestigious because of its links with the 'democratic' tradition of the borough of Westminster before 1832,[318] and with local 'democracy', from the 1835 Act onwards.[319]

There may also have been elements of an anthropological nature. Patrick Joyce has maintained that one of the effects of industrialization was the reconstruction of the patriarchal structure of the family.[320] If married men found themselves newly invested with the role of leaders of the most elementary social structure, household suffrage would have recognized their hegemony by enfranchising them as a group. However, it must also be observed that this *res publica* of the heads of families was not a peculiarity of Victorian Britain, but was rooted deep in the culture of the radical common people throughout Europe even in the day of the first French Revolution.[321]

Finally, the voluntary character of registration and the possibility of losing one's vote even after having been registered, meant that only those who were really interested in using the vote were able to obtain it and to keep it.[322] Those who had no developed political consciousness were systematically excluded: but *they* were not the people likely to protest. In this way the 1884–85 system operated on a kind of 'survival of the fittest' principle; moreover it selected an electoral body which was both highly politicized and 'virtually' representative, as Duncan Tanner has shown,[323] both of women,

---

[317] In 1867 Disraeli had placed great emphasis on this point, maintaining that paying the rates was 'the best evidence of the trustworthiness of the individual', and that as an electoral qualification was 'a popular and a rational principle', indeed 'the constitutional principle of the borough franchise in use for centuries, extending back to the Normans, and even to the Saxons' (Cowling, *1867*, pp. 172–3). See Hobsbawm, *Worlds of Labour*, p. 238.

[318] Belchem, '*Orator*' *Hunt*, p. 80.

[319] On the links between parliamentary and local representation in the culture of popular radicalism see below, chapter 6, pp. 313–28.

[320] Joyce, *Work, Society and Politics*, pp. 110–15.

[321] See Cobb, *Les Armées*, p. 186; Viola, *Il trono vuoto*, pp. 76–87.

[322] In the eight elections which took place between 1885 and December 1910, the turn out varied from of 74 per cent (1886 and 1900), to 86 per cent (January 1910): see Cornford, 'The Transformation of Conservativism', p. 57; and Clarke, *Lancashire and the 'New' Liberalism*, p. 125.

[323] Tanners, 'Parliamentary Electoral System', p. 216; See Blewett, 'The Franchise in the United Kingdom', p. 52; Pugh, *Making of Modern British Politics*, p. 141.

young bachelors and even paupers.[324] It is not inappropriate to observe – by way of conclusion – that as early as 1868 authoritative spokesmen for popular radicalism had declared that 'The nation is now in power . . . .'.[325]

[324] Through those who paid for their maintenance: Smith, *The Second Reform Bill*, p. 26.
[325] [L.a.], 'The Progress of Society', *NC*, 7 Nov. 1868, p. 2.

CHAPTER 6

Parliament and community

That every County may have its equal proportion of
Representers; and that every County may have its
several divisions, in which one Representer may be
chosen, and that some chosen Representatives of every
Parish proportionably may be Electors of the Sheriffs,
Iustices of the Peace, Committee-men, Grand-jury men,
and all ministers of Iustice whatsoever, in the respective
Counties, and that no such minister of justice may
continue in his Office above one whole year, without a
new Election.[1]

> I love the village Hampden,
> He's a saviour to his race,
> (For he who saves a hamlet
> Saves the whole world from disgrace)
> Who ever calls a spade a spade,
> No matter who may frown,
> And tells the tyrant to his face
> I mean to pluck you down.[2]

PARLIAMENT AND ELECTORS

If households, rather than individuals, constituted the accepted
basis for the franchise, it should not surprise us that a community-
centred approach also dominated the discussion of representative
bodies, both central and local.[3] The general attitude was expressed
by Mill's contention that a 'well founded' public opinion – crucial
for a feasible liberal society – could develop fully only in face-to-

---

[1] *To the Supream Authority of England, the Commons Assembled in Parliament* (1648), in Wolfe,
Leveller Manifestoes, pp. 269–70.
[2] Leno, 'I Love the Village Hampden', in *Muscular Poetry* (1864), p. 69.
[3] Pugh, *Modern British Politics*, p. 4; Cowling, *1867*, p. 68.

face communities: community life was the safeguard against the degeneration of society into an anonymous mass of 'monads' in which individuals would be isolated and impotent,[4] and rational debate would be replaced by mere propaganda.[5] This attitude was encouraged both by the reality of contemporary British politics,[6] and by fact that Victorian radicals – like their admired Jeffersonians[7] – did not see any divergence of principle between direct and representative democracy. Following Mill and Grote,[8] they found their model in Pericles' Athens, the 'small State'[9] with its popular magistracies and participatory emphasis:

All the Greek free citizens were voters, legislators, jurists. . . . theirs was a pure democracy; the People was sovereign, all power was vested in the general assembly of the citizens; they administered the government not by deputy, but actually by themselves . . . DEMOS was himself King, Minister, and Parliament, his own Treasurer, Chancellor, Primate, and Commander-in-Chief. . . . It is responsibility like this that educates a people . . . By their continued attendance at the courts the Athenians learnt the art of hearing both sides . . . Athens was the first state to teach the world that the voice of persuasion could be stronger than a despot's will, that disputes could be settled in free debate and the rule of the majority be adopted without ruin to the minority . . . [10]

Plebeian liberals thought that the differences between direct and representative democracy resided only in their dimensions, modern states being – in general[11] – too large for direct popular government. Ancient and modern democracies alike were vulnerable to citizens' apathy and lack of interest in public business, but these dangers tended to be more serious under representative govern-

---

[4] Mill, *Autobiography*, in *Collected Works*, I, p. 151; Tocqueville, *La democratie en Amerique*, II, pp. 432–3; Hanham, 'Tra l'individuo e lo Stato', in Pombeni (ed.), *La trasformazione politica*, pp. 96, 98.

[5] Mill, 'On Civilization', in *Collected Works*, XVIII, p. 132; see Weber, 'Die protestantischen Sekten', p. 215.

[6] Clarke, 'Electoral Sociology of Modern Britain', p. 45.

[7] See Pitkin, *Concept of Representation*, pp. 60–1, 63, 191.

[8] See for J. S. Mill: Finlay, *Democracy Ancient and Modern*, pp. 31–3; Biagini, 'Mill e la democrazia ateniese', pp. 469–501, and esp. p. 495. More in general, see Turner, *The Greek Heritage in Victorian Britain*, pp. 187–233.

[9] [Rep.], 'Political Address by Mr. Cowen, MP', *NC*, 16 Feb. 1885, p. 2.

[10] [L.a.], 'Democracy in Olden Times', *NC*, 30 Oct. 1885, p. 4; see (L.a.], 'The People's Parliament', *LW*, 21 Dec. 1884, p. 6. See also [rep.], *BH*, 18 Jan. 1868, p. 1. For the persistence of the symbolism of the Roman republic, see the 1892 NALU card published in Hawkins, *Poor Labouring Men*, p. 58.

[11] With the exception of Switzerland: [l.a.], 'Representative Government in England', *NC*, 26 Oct. 1881, p. 4; [l.a.], 'The Jubilee Year of the "Reform Bill"', *NC*, 30 Jan. 1882, p. 2.

ments, where power was largely delegated to elected deputies. To counteract this danger, modern democrats had to devise schemes to increase popular opportunity and motivation for direct participation, by linking the national representative system to smaller units. This was the case even with Mill's proposed constitution of 'voluntary' parliamentary constituencies – almost ideal communities of citizen-philosophers – along the lines of Hare's project of proportional representation. Fawcett and Morrison tried to persuade their working class friends that this solution would provide a fairer chance for labour representation,[12] but, apart from some notable exceptions,[13] their efforts were unsuccessful: to their dismay, Victorians continued to favour representation not of persons, but of localities. In fact the prevailing trend among reformers was towards extending and rationalizing popular government by enfranchising – both in local and national government – 'legitimate communities', the communities into which national life was actually articulated.[14] This involved the complete reshuffling of ancient institutions, as well as the establishment of new ones.

At the level of national government the major problem was the archaic distribution of Parliamentary seats, which was so unequal that the ratio between the number of electors in the largest and smallest constituencies was 250: 1.[15] Though redistribution had been hotly debated from the 1830s, and 'equal electoral districts' had become a radical motto from the days of the Chartists,[16] in 1867 plebeian radicals did not press for a systematic reform, and eventually Disraeli's Act corrected the old system only marginally.[17] This settlement was clearly unsatisfactory, especially from a democratic viewpoint, but an analysis of the popular debate suggests that the question was pushed into the background –

---

[12] W. Morrison to G. Howell, 30 Nov. 1868, in *G. Howell Coll.*, *Ind.*, 43; see Fawcett's speech in [rep.], 'Reform League', *BH*, 28 Mar. 1868, p. 1.

[13] Howell was one of them (see notes dated 16 Nov. 1872 in *G Howell Coll.*, *Lett. Book*, 131); another was the loyally Millite Littlejohn (see 'True Principles of Representation', *WT*, 8 Mar. 1868, p. 6; but the most committed was probably Samuel Neil: see Neil, 'Miners' View of Proportional Representation', pp. 255–65.

[14] Moore, *Politics of Deference*, pp. 394–5.

[15] Chadwick, 'The Role of Redistribution', p. 683.

[16] Lovett, *Life and Struggles* (1876), p. 316; see Taylor, *Thesis*, p. 177.

[17] The Reform Act increased the county seats by twenty-six, and added sixteen seats to large boroughs and cities: Hanham, *Nineteenth-Century Constitution*, p. 274; for the 1866–7 debate, see Cowling, *1867*, pp. 8–9, 68.

despite the protests of a few[18] – first by the overriding concern for the enlargement of the franchise, then by the burning issues of 1868–73. Redistribution attracted mass support only at times of radical revival: for example, in April 1873 at a great Newcastle reform meeting several miners stressed the urgency of the question, and declared that they hoped 'to see the country divided into districts, and the members thoroughly distributed according to population'.[19] More generally, the slogan of 'equal electoral districts' remained as popular as ever.[20] Yet, in spite of Sir Charles Dilke's efforts, there is no evidence of working-class commitment to redistribution. Indeed, during the 1874 elections this question was not even included in the manifestoes of shrewd artisan candidates like Howell and Potter.[21] It would seem that the Liberal defeat had the effect of stimulating further reflection: this might help to explain why redistribution was the first point in the programme of the 'Democratic Union' of Howell, J. C. Cox and Dr Pankhurst in August 1874;[22] and in 1875 Thomas Burt, MP, presented a petition to Parliament on behalf of the Labour Representation League (LRL) – a detailed document denouncing 'a grievous inequality in representation' and supporting Sir Charles Dilke's motion for a Royal Commission.[23] But again, on the whole, working-class interest remained limited and occasional.[24] Trevor Lloyd has explained this apathy by referring to the technicalities and intricacies of the question, which allegedly kept the general public at bay[25] and his interpretation seems strengthened by the fact that those who took an active interest in

[18] See G. Troup, 'The Reform Bill', *BH*, 11 May 1867, p. 7; 'To the Working Men of England – The *Beehive*', *BH*, 10 Oct. 1868, p. 8. The Reform League seemed hardly interested in the issue, as suggested by their lukewarm response to Alison's proposal (Executive Committee, 7 Jun. 1867, in *Reform League Papers, G. Howell Coll.*), though in 1868 they examined Hare's redistribution scheme ([rep.], 'Reform League', *BH*, 7 Mar. 1868, p. 1). Mill and Fawcett were present at this meeting.

[19] [Rep.], *NW*, 14 Apr. 1873, p. 7, see esp. the speech by N. Wilkinson, Treasurer of the DMA, and J. Laverick.

[20] See Northumbrian, 'Proportional Household Suffrage', *RN*, 6 Oct. 1872, p. 3; Northumbrian, 'Equal Electoral Districts', *RN*, 17 Nov. 1872, p. 3; J. Aytoun, 'The Redistribution of Electoral Power', *BH*, 19 May 1873, p. 3.

[21] See G. Howell, 'To the Electors of the Borough and Hundreds of Aylesbury', *BH*, 31 Jan. 1874, p. 11; G. Potter, 'To the Working Men Electors of the Borough of Peterborough', *ibid.*

[22] 'Democracy', *Labour Press and Miners' and Workmen's Examiner*, 29 Aug. 1874, p. 4.

[23] See the text of the petition in 'The Labour Representation League', *BH*, 17 Jul. 1875.

[24] Crossick, *An Artisan Elite*, p. 222.

[25] Lloyd, *Election of 1880*, p. 54.

redistribution were 'intellectual' working-class leaders like Howell.[26]

However, there were also other reasons, which emerge from a consideration of the way in which the issue was discussed with in 1884–5. At that time, popular Liberals not only seemed to follow the initiative of parliamentary leadership – as Lloyd would have us expect – but also demonstrated that they shared traditional assumptions and convictions about representation, including Gladstone's 'tenderness' for the communitarian theory of representative government.[27] The *Newcastle Chronicle* declared itself to be

... especially pleased with the Prime Minister's observations concerning the constitutional basis of our system. He denies that numbers should be the only test of political power, and believes that parliamentary representation should bear the impress of local life and peculiarities. This is not only the essence of British constitutionalism, but it is the essence of all political liberalism that is worthy of the name. It will be an evil day for the country . . . when local idiosyncracies and the peculiar life of outlying constituency are swamped by numbers concentrated elsewhere . . .[28]

In spite of the rhetoric of 'equal electoral districts', redistribution could not be solved by a simple arithmetic equalization of constituencies: the 'collective personality' of the traditional constituencies had to be preserved.[29] The most radical spokesmen of plebeian liberalism were emphatic in maintaining the importance of the identification of each constituency with a historic community, to which an MP was expected to be closely related,[30] since he represented not individual electors but the borough or county as a whole. As a consequence, to be 'a stranger' could compromise a

---

[26] As a lecturer for Walter Morrison's Representative Reform Association: see his notes for a speech at Greenwich, dated 16 Nov. 1872, in *G. Howell Coll., Lett. Book*, IX, 131 (see also 161 ff.); and his letter to D. Guile, 9 Nov. 1872, in *ibid.*, 129: Howell included also 'a condensed abstract' of Morrison's proposal. However his efforts met with little practical success. (Leventhal, *Howell* (1971), p. 136). Yet, for an occasional positive reaction by the mass press, see Northumbrian, 'Proportional Representation', *RN*, 21 Jul. 1872, p. 3.

[27] For Gladstone's attitude, see Matthew, 'Introduction' to *Diaries*, x, p. cviii.

[28] [L.a.], 'Franchise at Last', *NC*, 29 Feb. 1884, p. 5; see also [l.a.], 'The Liberal Test', *LW*, 30 Mar. 1884, p. 1.

[29] See [l.a.], 'The Inequalities of the Electoral System', *Potteries Examiner*, 10 May 1873. Moves towards multi-member constituencies with proportional representation – obtained some working-class support, especially thanks to the efforts of the miner Samuel Neil: Parsons, *Thesis*, pp. 235–8.

[30] [L.a.], 'The Candidates', *NC*, 12 Feb. 1883, p. 2; J. Cowen, 'The Representation of Newcastle. Address by Mr. Cowen in the Lecture Room. Tuesday, December 30, 1873', TS, p. [ix], in *Cowen Coll.*, B 159.

candidate's success,[31] while an indisputable link with the local community was a very important advantage – as Joseph Cowen, jr., stressed when contesting Newcastle in 1874:

I was born in the vale of the Tyne, I have lived in it all my life. Since I left school I have not been a consecutive month absent from the sight of its waters. All the material and commercial interests I possess in the world are centred in this vale; and I believe I may say that I share the principles, and, perhaps the prejudices of Tynesiders. I share their feelings, and possibly, some of their failings.[32]

The fact that this approach was widely accepted helps to explain why criticism of the distribution of seats remained substantially marginal between 1866–7 and 1884–5. Though redistribution of seats as a motto was popular, one gains the impression that plebeian liberals – just like the front-bench Radicals[33] – were unable to make up their minds between the platform of 'equal electoral districts'[34] and the preservation of the communitarian features of the traditional system.

This uncertainty is evidenced by popular reactions to the Government Bill, a largely bipartisan solution which led to the redistribution of 120 seats[35] and the replacement of most large two- and three-member constituencies with smaller one-member ones.[36] Though the Bill was acclaimed as a resolute attempt to eliminate the old scandal of inequality,[37] some feared that the Liberals had paid too heavy a price for this settlement, not only because the urban electorate was still under-represented, but also because the old civic constituencies had been subdivided into smaller divisions, thus losing their community identity.[38] *Reynolds's* was so upset that

---

[31] Cf. for an example [rep.], 'The Nomination', *NC*, 17 Nov. 1868, p. 5; see also Fisher, *Custom, Work, and Market Capitalism*, p. 91; and Williamson, *Class, Culture and Community*, p. 68.

[32] J. Cowen, 'The Representation of Newcastle. Address by Mr. Cowen in the Lecture Room. Tuesday, December 30, 1873', TS pp. [ix–x], in *Cowen Coll.*, B 159.

[33] Hayes, *Third Reform Act*, p. 251.

[34] Included in the programme of the 'Manhood Suffrage League': cf. [rep.], *English Labourers' Chronicle*, 26 Jul. 1879, p. 6, point 4.

[35] See Hanham, *Nineteenth-Century Constitution*, pp. 281–2.

[36] Though some two-member constituencies survived: Ensor, *England 1870–1914*, p. 88.

[37] [L.a.], 'Redistribution', *RN*, 23 Nov. 1884, p. 4; [l.a.], 'The Redistribution of Seats Bill', *RN*, 7 Dec. 1884, p. 1; [l.a.], 'Counties versus Boroughs', *RN*, 14 Dec. 1884, p. 1. Though 'equal electoral districts' were still far from being achieved: Chadwick, 'The Role of Redistribution', p. 683.

[38] [L.a.], 'Redistribution and its Defects', *RN*, 21 Dec. 1884, p. 1. As early as 1874 Howell had pointed out the danger of breaking up large boroughs into small divisions, which 'would give us only more local noodles' (*G. Howell Coll.*, v, 361).

it suggested amending the Bill by assigning an extra MP to 'manufacturing and industrial townships' and 'old boroughs', as a representative for the corporate citizenship.[39]

Paradoxically, the strength of this approach is also confirmed by those who dismissed these concerns as 'sentimental prejudice'.[40] They stressed that radicals were likely to gain from the increase of the number of industrial seats and the constitution of many purely working class divisions, where labour candidates would find safe seats; and they argued that even in the counties, Liberalism would improve its position because small boroughs like Aylesbury – 'all of whom were essentially working men's constituencies' – were to be absorbed into the surrounding counties,[41] and would radicalize the rural vote. In both ways the effect of the Redistribution Act would be, not to disintegrate community representation into constituencies 'artificially chopped up' by demographic geometry,[42] but rather to enfranchise the real communities of modern Britain, the homogeneous social groups who lived in wards and county divisions. The system would improve the prospects of the Liberal party because the majority of the new electors were 'men who toil[ed] for their living with their hands',[43] and therefore 'natural' Liberals. In short, the Redistribution Act was praised because it had realistically chosen class rather than tradition as the basis for community representation.

THE LOCAL COMMUNITY AND ITS SELF-GOVERNMENT

Though the rise of class politics was not to take place in the immediate future, it was true that the liberal search for a surrogate for Periclean democracy was already being directed towards social units different from than the old constituencies. The revival of interest in traditional village life[44] was reflected in the debate on representation; in particular, the popular press celebrated hamlet fraternity and social integration, in contrast to urban alienation

---

[39] [L.a.], *RN*, 21 Dec. 1884, p. 1.
[40] [L.a.], 'A Fallacy Refuted', *LW*, 21 Dec. 1884, p. 1.
[41] [L.a.], 'What the Seat Bill does', *LW*, 7 Dec. 1884, p. 1. However, this urban presence in county elections was also a feature of the pre-1885 system, and was possibly one further reason for popular 'apathetic' attitudes to redistribution.
[42] Ensor, *England 1870–1914*, p. 88.
[43] [L.a.], *LW*, 7 Dec. 1884, p. 1.
[44] See above, chapter 2, p. 86–93, and 3 p. 184–91.

and anonymity.[45] Those most firmly committed to these ideals were the agricultural labourers, who asked for the preservation and restoration of village community life via self-government,[46] and who, like many other democrats, looked to the Swiss Confederation as a model.[47] To some extent their ideal was in accordance with the British tradition[48] as embodied in the municipal reforms of 1834–5.[49] This had an important influence on popular perceptions and expectations, for, though many were excluded from its benefits, local democracy was regarded thereafter not as an innovation to be introduced, but rather as a practice to be extended. As a consequence, reformers were not so interested in establishing general principles – which were already widely accepted – as in actually implementing them.

One of their problems was efficiency. Victorian Britain was characterized by an embarrassing proliferation of local authorities: for instance, the Sunderland Union, with an area of 11,497 acres and a population of 112,643 (in 1876), was ruled by 20 different elective assemblies with a total of 362 representatives.[50] Each of these assemblies held its elections on different dates, and in consequence the Millite ideal of an always deliberating *demos* was almost literally realized.[51] However, the quality of government was none the better for that, because most of the existing bodies had specialized aims, separate budgets and different claims upon the rates. Moreover, although their jurisdictions overlapped, some of the needs of the local community were cared for by none of them.

Another problem was that the 'traditional' system was far from being democratic: while the counties were still autocratically ruled by JPs at the quarter sessions, urban politics remained the preserve of the middle classes, not only in the small towns studied by Joyce

---

[45] [L.a.], 'Village Life', *LW*, 11 May 1872, p. 4.
[46] [L.a.], 'Local Self-Government in the Rural Districts', *National Agricultural Labourers' Chronicle*, 11 Dec. 1 1875, p. 1.
[47] *Ibid.*; see for a similar statement in the speech of the Sheffield Chartist Isaac Ironside in 1850, quoted in Smith, *Conflict and Compromise*, p. 75. For the popularity of the Swiss model see also above, chapter 1.
[48] Webb, *Our Partnership* (1948), p. 151.
[49] Hanham (ed.), *Nineteenth-Century Constitution*, p. 294. As in other fields, Britain was a model for European Liberals: for the Italian case, see Romanelli, 'Autogoverno, funzioni pubbliche, classi dirigenti locali', pp. 35–83.
[50] T. F. Hedley, Local Government and Taxation – from the 'Daily Express', April 5, 1876, handbill in *J. Cowen Coll.*, B 173.
[51] Chalmers, *Local Government* (1883), pp. 29–30.

but also in the large municipalities studied by Fraser. It is true that in the 1840s Leeds had Chartist councillors, guardians and churchwardens, but 'they were not necessarily poor men. To have participated in these township offices they had to be rated at £30 or £40, well above the 1832 parliamentary qualification, and some of those who became Chartist councillors were able to swear that they possessed £1,000 in real property'.[52] The poor were effectively excluded.[53] The difficulties faced by working men aspiring to enter local government are illustrated by the case of John Normansell, who, in 1872, was elected onto the Barnsley town council only because his trade union had deposited £1,000 in a local bank on his account.[54] Given the difficulties involved in collecting such a sum of money, it is not surprising that Barnsley remained one among very few exceptions,[55] and that even Normansell did not represent his candidature in 1875. Similar obstacles made it impossible for working-class radicals to be elected to most other local bodies, including the important Poor Law Boards. In the latter case the qualification was a £25 rating: 'Wheer is the workin' man so raated?' – an indignant pitman protested in 1872[56] – 'The chyce is sarcumscribed, and the man elected knaws little or nowt about the poor.'

Though eligibility for the school boards was open from 1870, it was only in 1878 that property qualifications for the other bodies were abolished. This reform was the result of years of patient 'pressure from without' organized by the Labour Representation League,[57] which conducted a detailed inquiry throughout the country to collect evidence on the injustice of the property qualification, and eventually prepared a draft Bill in collaboration with Mundella.[58] The LRL was able to argue its case on convincingly

[52] Fraser, *Urban Politics in Victorian England*, p. 258.
[53] T. Burt, 'The Property Qualification for Local Boards, Etc.', *NW*, 10 Mar. 1877, p. 4; see Fraser, *Urban Politics*, p. 14; Smith, *Conflict and Compromise*, p. 61.
[54] DLB, I, p. 256.
[55] Significantly, radical Birmingham was another, with an 'independent working man' on the town council from 1867 to 1876: Briggs, *History of Birmingham*, II, p. 193 n.
[56] [Rep.], 'A London Correspondent's Account of the Morpeth Meeting', *NW*, 5 Dec. 1872, p. 8. Cf. T. Burt, 'The Property Qualification for Local Boards', *NW*, 10 Mar. 1877, p. 4.
[57] 'Meeting of the General Council', 10 Dec. 1875, *Labour Representation League Minutes*, p. 145. Daniel Merrick, one of the League's leaders, was a councillor on the Leicester School Board and Town Council.
[58] 'Abolition of the Property Qualification for Town Councillors and Members of Local Boards', 20 Feb. 1876, p. 239, *Labour Representation League Minutes*; Broadhurst, *Life* (1901), p. 71.

empirical grounds, emphasizing that it was 'working men [who] suffered most from the burden of local rates, and no one would feel greater interest in keeping down excessive expenditure than they would'.[59] This stance – stressed by the Liberal press[60] – contributed to soothing the anxiety felt by the ruling classes about the protection of local property against 'rapacious' proletarian councillors.[61] It was clear that, far from dreaming of increased taxation, the poor thought of reform and meant retrenchment.[62] From this standpoint it is also interesting that the League claimed eligibility not for all citizens, but only for ratepayers: this confirmed that, as in the case of the electoral franchise, paying the rates was the basic criterion for full citizenship.

This qualification also had the ideological justification of reflecting the spirit of 'old' local democracy,[63] which in this case at least had not been lost completely. Indeed some of its relics were to be found in the vestry,[64] election to which was either open to all residents (when the procedure was by a show of hands), or to all ratepayers (when a formal poll was required). The vestry was the only rural representative body before 1889, and had quite an important role in the life of the common people, because it elected churchwardens, who were also overseers of the Poor Law and often took part in the management of local charities: as a consequence radicals were active propagandists of mass participation at the annual assemblies.[65] The newspaper of the labourers' union regularly published reports of the proceedings of meetings, and offered legal and practical advice to any readers facing intimidation and

---

[59] 'Abolition . . .', 20 Feb. 1876, speech by Mr Nyass, President of the London Plasterers' Association, p. 239, *LRL Minutes*.

[60] [L.a.], *DN*, 1 Mar. 1877, p. 5.

[61] [Rep.], 'Qualification for Members of Town Councils', *DN*, 26 Jun. 1876, speech of the Chancellor of the Exchequer.

[62] The opinion of *Lloyd's* was typical, maintaining that one of the aims of reform of London government was 'to make existence cheaper and more comfortable at any rate to ensure that not a single penny spent on rates shall be wasted' ([L.a.], 'The New Year's Programme', *LW*, 4 Jan. 1885, p. 1).

[63] [L.a., n.t.], *DN*, 1 Mar. 1877, p. 5. As always, radicals insisted that they were not 'so much innovators and aggressors as advocates of rights and privileges which have been wrested from the people by the force or fraud of their adversaries' (T. Burt in *NW*, 10 Mar. 1877, p. 4).

[64] Webbs, *English Local Government*, 1, p. 94.

[65] E.g. [l.a.], 'Easter Work', *English Labourers' Chronicle*, 2 Apr. 1877, p. 1.

threats.[66] Vestry meetings were often very lively. For instance, in the village of Crick, in 1877, the labourers asked for a formal poll to ensure the appointment of a union man as overseer. In response the vicar decided to hold the poll on that very day at 3 pm, hoping that, since the labourers were working in the fields, they would not be able to vote. But his plans did not take into account the labourers' militancy, which left 'no stone unturned':

Our informant says the blind were made to see, the lame to walk; poor women running in all directions to fetch their husbands to the poll, old men and maidens, young men and children were all in commotion, until, as our informant says, 'Old men and women said neither they nor their fathers ever witnessed such a day'. We are happy to say that the poor people carried the day.[67]

However, in many other similar cases the labourers – heavily penalized by victimization and plural voting – were easily defeated, and sometimes even their right to vote was questioned.[68] Therefore, radicals argued that counties needed not only democratization of the existing institutions, but also a comprehensive reform providing representative assemblies at various levels.

Though reform had been attempted as early as 1836,[69] the old county system was left untouched during most of the century. In the 1870s various schemes were presented, under the administrations of both Gladstone and Disraeli, but all were equally abortive.[70] During Gladstone's second government the issue – described by some as 'scarcely second in importance to the extension of the county franchise itself'[71] – continued to be debated. In 1885 Dilke proposed 'restoring' the 'Saxon constitution'[72] by replacing the old chaos with 'three sets of districts which never overlap' – namely, counties, districts and parishes, the latter incorporating the vestries. Radicals acclaimed this scheme as

---

[66] See H. Evans, 'The Franchise – Local and Imperial', *English Labourers' Chronicle*, 20 Apr. 1878, p. 1.
[67] [Rep.]. 'The Battle of the Vestries', *English Labourers' Chronicle*, 21 Apr. 1877, p. 2.
[68] E.g. 'From a Correspondent', 'The Labourers and their Right to Vote', *English Labourers' Chronicle*, 1 May 1875, p. 5.
[69] Maccoby, *English Radicalism 1832–1852*, pp. 386–9.
[70] See the programme of a working-class Liberal association, the National Political Union, in 1878, in G. Howell Coll., ix. *Lett. Book*, 284; and [l.a.], 'The County Boards Bill', *NW*, 22 Mar. 1879, p. 4.
[71] [L.a.], 'County Government', *NW*, 19 Nov. 1881, p. 4.
[72] [Rep.], 'Sir Charles Dilke on Local Government', *DN*, 14 Oct. 1885, p. 6.

embodying the principles of federalism and the delegation to local assemblies of greater responsibilities;[73] yet once more 'national' issues pushed local government into the background. It was only in 1888 that the Unionist government provided representative assemblies for the counties as well as for London, but without any proviso for parishes.

The County Council Act did not appeal to working-class radicals: as Davis has demonstrated, London government reform, though often campaigned for,[74] did not attract much popular support until later, when concern for growing fiscal burdens sensitized public opinion.[75] Even in the counties proper, the Act – in spite of its important consequences in the area of social reform and education[76] – was coldly received by the labourers: there were a few declarations of general approval,[77] but little real interest, and even Arch's paper limited itself to merely introducing the Bill to its readers.[78] Scant interest was reflected in the polling booth: in 1889 – though the labourers' vote was decisive in all constituencies – the newly elected councils retained in power the old elites of farmers and squires, with only a sprinkling of trade union leaders.[79].

This failure was partly due to the crisis of the labourers' trade unions, and the consequent disbanding of the farm workers as a political force.[80] It must also be remembered that participation in

---

[73] See J. Cowen, 'Speech on the Change in the Work and Ways of Parliament at the Sanitary Congress Banquet, Newcastle, September 29, 1882', TS, Cowen Coll., B 267; [l.a.], 'Liberal Views of Local Government', LW, 28 Jun. 1885, commenting with some approval on Harcourt's idea of a 'Home Rule all round'. See Williams, *W. J. Parry*, p. 148ff.

[74] Mill's 1866 proposals for the reform of London government were very favourably commented on by the popular London press (see [l.a.], 'The Government of London', WT, 4 Feb. 1866, p. 4; [l.a.], 'A New Government for the Metropolis', WT, 21 Feb. 1866, p. 4). Later proposals were also supported (cf. [l.a.], 'The Municipal Reformers', LW, 1 Nov. 1874, p. 1; [l.a.], 'The Municipality of London', LW, 21 Feb. 1875, p. 6; [l.a.], 'Mr. Gladstone as a Municipal Reformer', LW, 12 Mar. 1876, p. 1; [l.a.], 'London in the Future', LW, 13 Apr. 1884, p. 1). While none of the proposals was successful, the impression is that the press and the working-class associations followed the lead of party politicians, but never tried to take the initiative themselves.

[75] [L.a.], 'London Municipal Reform', LW, 7 Feb. 1886, p. 6; see Davis, *Reforming London*, pp. 110–14.

[76] Dunbabin, 'Expectations of the New County Councils', p. 376.

[77] [Rep.], 'Liberal Demonstration in Warwickshire', *English Labourers' Chronicle*, 30 Jun. 1888, pp. 4–5.

[78] 'A *Times* Correspondent', 'The Local Government Act', *English Labourers' Chronicle*, 13 Oct. 1888, p. 5.

[79] Arch, *Story* (1898), p. 379.

[80] Howkins, *Thesis*, p. 148.

county council meetings could involve expenses and material difficulties which would discourage labourer involvement. But there were also other factors, which from 1881 had convinced parliamentary radicals that a County Act without parish councils would end up as 'a small matter'.[81] The point was that the rural poor considered county councils as somehow alien to their 'real' interest: the heart of their community life was the village, which could be seen as a largely self-sufficient unit,[82] and what the labourers considered to be 'real' local government was the vestry. The requests of the country folk were made clear by Atherley Jones – son of the Chartist leader – at the 1891 Durham Miners Gala:

until they had established district or parish councils, where the working man, in his own village, might, without leaving his work, without going to the expense, say, of travelling from Consett to Durham, be able to go and look after his own district affairs, until then no system of local government would be a solution to the present difficulties.[83]

Jones offered a revealing view of the labourers' model of self-government: he did not ask for a salary for county councillors, to enable the poor to be elected and attend meetings. Rather, he asked for the reduction of the size of the units of self government: access to local representation would become open to the poor not by professionalizing politics, but by transforming representative into direct democracy. This aspiration to parish democracy was deep-rooted in popular radicalism: as early as the 1830s Francis Place had been agitating for reform, and in 1831 Hobhouse managed to obtain a 'permissive' Act which aimed at democratizing vestry government, with the enfranchisement of all ratepayers of both sexes, secret ballots and annual elections: the Act, however, was applied in very few cases, and on the whole remained without practical consequences.[84] When the issue was effectively resuscitated, sixty-two years later, rural radicals reacted with great enthusiasm:

Excepting the Franchise Bill – Arch's paper declared – there is no domestic measure to which the farm labourers attach a greater importance, and none which has so raised their hopes. It is that for which they

[81] Dunbabin, 'Expectations of the New County Councils', p. 356; and 'Establishment of County Councils', p. 231.
[82] Thompson, *Lark Rise*, p. 11.
[83] [Rep.], 'The Durham Miners' Association'. – Annual Gala. – A Huge Throng', *DC*, 10 Jul. 1891, p. 6, speech by Atherley Jones, MP.
[84] Maccoby, *English Radicalism 1832–1852*, pp. 380–2.

have toiled for twenty years past; for which they have waited with exemplary patience.[85]

The parish councils seemed to be the only institutions in which the labourers could realistically hope to make a stand against parson and squire, and fight to obtain control over the management of their daily life.[86] The Chartist faith in political power as the source of economic emancipation, and deep-seated Nonconformist 'localism',[87] contributed towards focussing hopes and expectations on the establishment of the new bodies. Indeed, some spoke as if all the farm workers' questions would be solved through village democracy:

The people will be their own landlords through their own directly elected representatives, chosen from their own neighbourhood, and deliberating and administering at their own doors ... No statute has ever been submitted to Parliament which more intimately concerns the welfare of farm-labourers. In its acceptance we recognize a harvest of blessings which will make the home and life of the agricultural labourer happier than it has been for centuries.[88]

Arch wrote:

By conferring upon these councils the control of the charities, and the administration of the Poor Law, many of the abuses at present existing will be disposed of. These councils, too, must take on the matter of rating and education in the villages. Then, above all, they must have the power to compulsorily acquire as much land for the labourer as he wants at the same rent as land is letting in the district.[89]

The labourers were not unaware of the Act's shortcomings,[90] but accepted it as the best settlement possible given the weakness of the Liberals,[91] they thought that extension of self-government to

---

[85] [L.a.], 'The Parish Councils Bill', *English Labourers' Chronicle*, 10 Jun. 1893, p. 1.
[86] See the interviews with workers, artisans, and shopkeepers published under the general title of 'The Parish Councils and the Villages.': *English Labourers' Chronicle*, 21 Oct. 1893, p. 7, and *English Labourers' Chronicle*, 28 Oct. 1893, p. 7.
[87] For the link with Nonconformist attitudes to central and local authorities, see Cox, *English Churches in a Secular Society*, p. 166.
[88] [L.a.], 'The Parish Councils Bill', *English Labourers' Chronicle*, 9 Dec. 1893, pp. 1–2.
[89] Arch, *Story* (1898), p. 390.
[90] 'The Parish Councils' Bill Explained', *English Labourers' Chronicle*, 11 Nov. 1893, p. 1; [l.a.], 'Mr. Arch and the Parish Councils Bill', *English Labourers' Chronicle*, 2 Dec. 1893, p. 1.
[91] [L.a.], 'The Parish Councils' Bill', *English Labourers' Chronicle*, 18 Nov. 1893, p. 1. Though, in fact, the limits on the councils' budgets was introduced in the Commons, not in the Lords, and the Liberals did not use their majority to stop the amendment. (Dunbabin, 'British Local Government Reform', p. 787 n.).

villages would achieve the essence of what was required,[92] the always sought-for integration between representative and direct democracy, almost a British version of the Swiss *Landesgemeinde*. The 1894 elections were fought with great vigour, and indeed in some parishes 'the contest turned savage' and became 'a battleground for lock-out farmers and labourers on strike'.[93] But many expectations were soon disappointed: as some feared, the new village democracy was seriously handicapped by the limits imposed upon council expenditure.[94]

The 1894 Act was not the beginning of the millennium for the labourers: however, it had an important influence on the democratization of the representative system because it involved the common people, on an unprecedented scale, in the management and organization of their community life. In the meantime hundreds of working-class leaders were also admitted into another vital sector of local government, the county bench, which had an important role in the settlement of industrial disputes.[95] These changes compounded the effects of the reforms of 1878 and 1888, and transformed popular attitudes to local government, which was increasingly considered as a genuine expression of the popular will. In the 1880s the biography of the 'typical' labour leader was enriched by participation in local government as an almost regular feature,[96] which reached a climax after 1894. The figures speak for themselves: working class representatives on local bodies grew from 12 to 200 between 1882 and 1892, while 'in 1895 there were six hundred Labour representatives on Borough Councils alone'.[97]

These reforms had an importance that cannot be assessed in terms of material advantages alone: in fact, as the labourer George Edwards wrote about the 1894 Act, a 'moral revolution' took place then. He himself was one of those who directly experienced its effects: in those years he became a councillor on the Norfolk County Council, a justice of the peace, a member of the Board of

---

[92] [L.a.], 'The New Parish Councils', *English Labourers' Chronicle*, 9 Dec. 1893, p. 2; '"Wait till we get the Parish Council" – What They Think of the Bill in East Anglia', *English Labourers' Chronicle*, 16 Dec. 1893, p. 1.

[93] Hollis, *Ladies Elect*, p. 364.

[94] Ensor, *England 1870–1914*, pp. 295–6.

[95] Powell, 'The Liberal Ministers and Labour', p. 417; Shepherd, 'James Bryce and Working-Class Magistrates', pp. 155–69.

[96] Shepherd, 'The Lib-labs and English Working Class Politics, 1874–1906', p. 166.

[97] Clegg et al., *History of British Trade Unions*, I, p. 286.

Guardians, and chairman of the Parish Council;[98] at the same time his wife was elected onto the latter, after defeating the vicar's wife.[99] In their village all the councillors but one (the schoolmaster) were labourers. Poor relief was put into the hands of other poor men and women, who used it to improve the quality of the assistance and of local sanitation, while the councils tried to obtain allotments.[100] In this exercise of authority and responsibility there took shape 'a village leadership which was not that of the land-owner or of the incumbent whom he could influence'.[101] Not surprisingly, to the end of his life George Edwards remembered the District and Parish Councils' Act as a great victory for the farm labourers, a success that – coming at a time when their trade unions were still in ruins – helped to alleviate the psychological and material difficulties of their situation.

THE PARTY AND ITS FORMS

Continuous local elections were one of the factors which stimulated the growth of another form of collective political identity: to some extent party associations had a role comparable to that of local government in providing 'intermediate bodies' – voluntary com-munities based on a shared ideology – between the individual and Parliament.[102] These institutions had of course a long tradition,[103] but their expansion during the second half of the nineteenth century was both stimulated by, and stimulated the democratiza-tion of the system.[104]

Party organization took two main forms: in the most famous and studied case, the urban caucus, the party became one of the instruments through which middle-class political elites confirmed their ability to provide a leadership for popular radicalism.[105] In the other case – which could be called the rural caucus – an analogous evolution took place, but with inverse social effects: it

---

[98] Edwards, *From Crow Scaring* (1922), pp. 6, 19.
[99] *Ibid.*, p. 67.
[100] *Ibid.*, pp. 68, 70, 84; Hollis, *Ladies Elect*, p. 28.
[101] Ashby, *Joseph Ashby* (1961), p. 183.
[102] Hanham, 'Tra l'individuo e lo Stato', in Pombeni (ed.), *La trasformazione politica*, pp. 97–8.
[103] See Money, 'Taverns, Coffee Houses and Clubs', pp. 15–47.
[104] See above, chapter 5, for the role of the Reform League in 1864–67; for municipal politics, see the Sheffield 'wardmotes' in the 1850s (Smith, *Conflict and Compromise*, p. 76).
[105] Tholfsen, 'Origins of the Birmingham Caucus', pp. 161–84.

was working-class radicalism which took control of the party and moulded Liberalism into its own image. Spokesmen for popular radicalism reacted to the growth of caucus politics in different ways, according to which of the two models they were dealing with, and more generally according their the local Liberal association's attitudes to working class representation. In this sense the caucus was 'morally neutral' from the point of view of organized labour, and only attracted systematic hostility from old-fashioned plebeian radicalism.

With the politicization of the rural masses party organization spread into the countryside, but generated new and more informal structures, focused on the village and practically independent from the official Liberal associations in the county capitals. The rural model was 'George Rix's inspired linking of the union to the Liberal Party at village level, so that a permanent triad – Liberal–union–chapel – was established among the Norfolk poor',[106] and indeed among those of many other regions.

In the first chapter we examined the ideological content of working-class Nonconformity: but chapel life also had an institutional impact. Its importance was greater in those regions where Nonconformity was a truly working class religion,[107] but Wald has demonstrated that at a national level there is a strong statistical correlation between Liberalism and Dissent,[108] the latter being 'the most potent variable in structuring the mass vote'.[109] The electoral effectiveness of Nonconformity derived from its intensely social character. In fact, religious conversion itself implied a complete involvement in a local congregation within which the values of co-operation and solidarity were much stressed: 'We manifest our love to God' – a 'Prim' wrote in 1873 – 'by the way in which we love each other . . . we are all united to alleviate suffering, to help the weak against the strong; we stand by our brother who is about to fall and support him'.[110] While these congregations provided a Weberian compensation for the marginalization and exclusion

---

[106] Howkins, *Poor Labouring Men*, p. 127; Dunbabin, 'The "Revolt of the Field"', p. 90.
[107] Pelling, *Popular Politics*, p. 20.
[108] Wald, *Crosses on the Ballot*, p. 67.
[109] *Ibid.*, p. 150.
[110] Cit in Scotland, *Methodism*, p. 33. A passage in the 'Union Hymn' reads: 'We thank Thee for the men who lead / Who fight our cause with tongue and pen; / Whose love to Thee – best shown in deed, / Breaks forth in love to me' (cit. *ibid.*). See Moore, *Pit-men*, pp. 226–7.

commonly felt by the poor,[111] the social intercourse they generated constituted what in more than one respect was a 'spiritual awakening', with the accompanying benefits of a habit of organization and exchange of ideas, some intellectual life, and 'a democratic structure for society'.[112] Strong community feeling seems to have accompanied popular Nonconformity from one end of the country to another,[113] to the extent that the chapel became a symbol around which both believers and non-believers tended to congregate,[114] and which provided an 'alternative culture, for it was genuinely that, [which] suffused their whole being and dominated the local world' of the worker;[115] such was its influence that the secularists felt it necessary to fill the psychological gap generated by the breaking up of chapel ties, by establishing institutions which were different in name and 'theology', but surprisingly similar in functions and style.[116]

If the chapel was the ideological and communitarian 'hinterland' of rural popular liberalism, the trade union was its 'strong arm'.[117] In this regard the case of the north-eastern miners is the most significant. In the atmosphere of chapel Puritanism, generations of miners grew up – as one of their leaders said – 'educated from boyhood in "sturdy Radicalism"';[118] at a later stage in their life, the union's executive stepped in, and told them who to vote for and how much money to invest in the party organization. From 1872 village political clubs had been established in Northumberland and Durham 'to keep the question of parliamentary reform prominently before the country, and to make arrangements for supporting Liberal candidates at the forthcoming general elec-

---

[111] Hammonds, *Town Labourer*, p. 186; Cox, *The English Churches*, p. 138.

[112] Cox, *The English Churches*, p. 195. On these aspects, see also Scotland, *Methodism*, pp. 43–56, 81; Moore, *Pit-men*, pp. 96, 226–7; Ashby, *Joseph Ashby*, pp. 113–15; Williamson, *Class, Culture, and Community*, p. 56.

[113] See Cox, *English Churches*, p. 141; Tiller, 'Late Chartism in Halifax', in Thompson and Epstein (eds.), *Chartist Experience*, p. 113; Epstein, 'Chartist Movement in Nottingham', *ibid.*, pp. 250–1, 257; Clarke, *Lancashire and the New Liberalism*, pp. 16–18; Morgan, *Wales 1880–1980*, p. 14; Hutchison, *Political History of Scotland*, pp. 139–40.

[114] Armstrong, *Pilgrimage from Nethead* (1938), pp. 72–3.

[115] Howkins, *Poor Labouring Men*, p. 56.

[116] Even Secularists had their Sunday services with hymns and 'sermons': see Royle, *Radicals, Secularists, and Republicans*, pp. 316ff.; Gould, *The Life Story* (1923), p. 91.

[117] Howkins, *Thesis*, pp. 143–45; Brown, 'The Lodges of the Durham Miners' Association, 1869–1926', pp. 138–52.

[118] Rubinstein 'The Independent Labour Party and the Yorkshire Miners', p. 113.

tions'.[119] The Durham County Franchise and Political Reform Association, which expressed the federated strength of these clubs, was in fact the political organization of the DMA,[120] the embodiment of the pitmen's 'home made' Liberalism. The leaders of the Franchise Association were also those of the union, its delegates were representatives of the various pits, and its meetings took place in the Durham Miners' Hall.[121] To some extent the Franchise Association reproduced the pyramidal structure of the Birmingham caucus. However, parallel to it, and in fact above it, there towered the DMA and the Miners' National Union, which often intervened directly, authoritatively taking the initiative at crucial times: not only in 1884, as we saw in the previous chapter, but also during elections. For instance, in March 1880 the union lodges received a circular and a letter instructing them to spare neither effort nor money to ensure the return of the two miners' MPs:

Fellow Workmen,
[. . .] we again send you, per this post, copy of a circular issued by the Miners' National Union. The case is so fully set forth in that circular, that any lengthened remarks by us would be superfluous. Let us say, however, that we regard the continuance of Messrs. Burt and Macdonald in the House of Commons, as an absolute necessity to the mining population. We, therefore, want you to help keep them there. To do this money must be sent, and sent at once. Let all lodges do whatever they can, by sending immediately their mite to Mr. NIXON, 35, Lovaine Crescent, Newcastle-on-Tyne. You can either send these from your local funds, or you can make a contribution among yourselves.[122]

This letter was signed by twelve of the main leaders, including Crawford, Patterson, Foreman, and Wilson. Naturally Burt and Macdonald were both returned: the trade union was their caucus. The 'caucusization' of the union characterized other regions too: particularly Yorkshire and the Midlands, stronghold of the Labour Electoral Association (LEA), which was led by staunch Lib-labs like William Bailey of Nottingham,[123] Joseph Toyn of Cleveland,[124]

---

[119] Fynes, *The Miners* (1873), pp. 276–7.

[120] See Nossiter, *Political Idioms*, pp. 96–7.

[121] See the Programmes of Council Meetings, 1882–1896, in Durham Miners' Association *Minutes*, in D/X (Durham Co. Rec. Off.).

[122] 'Messrs. MacDonald and Burt', in *Minutes and Balance Sheets from January to June 1880*, 16 Mar. 1880, *D/DMA 5*, for another example see *Minutes and Balance Sheets from July to December 1883*, 4 Sept. 1883, *D/DMA 6*, (Durham Co. Rec. Off.).

[123] DLB, II, p. 31.

[124] DLB, II, p. 396.

and William Millington of Hull.[125] But, as in Durham, even more important than the LEA was the direct political role of the Yorkshire Miners' Association and the Miners' Federation of Great Britain, led by Benjamin Pickard, who used union lodges as part of a Lib-lab electoral machine.[126] This phenomenon was directly related to the strength of the union: 'Where unions were well established . . . close Liberal links had usually developed'.[127] As correspondent for *The Times* wrote, 'It is difficult to convey to outsiders an adequate notion of the powers wielded by the Miners' Federation. It is to all intents and purposes a Radical organization in Parliamentary elections in South Yorkshire'.[128] And the complete identification of the miners with their union made it particularly effective since it was wholly integrated into the local community and provided with powers of coercion much greater than those traditionally ascribed to the caucus. Moreover, the workers had also permeated the official local Liberal Clubs: for instance, in 1897 out of 324 members of the 'Barnsley Three Hundred', 280 were described as working class, while at Shipley (West Yorkshire) 'the Lib-Labs had captured the Liberal Association'.[129] It is not surprising that a Liberal candidate for one of these Yorkshire constituencies 'was little more than the prisoner of the YMA leaders'.[130] Thus Liberal strength among the north eastern working classes was based almost on a sort of 'bloc vote'.

This situation could occur only in regions where the workers were strongly concentrated and politically unified by a hegemonic radical-Nonconformist cultural identity: in addition to the northeast, the Rhondda – the territory of William Abraham and his men[131] – or the Highlands, where the crofters obtained a spectacular success in 1885 with the election of five independent MPs.[132] In these regions, community feeling and the prevailing notion that the MP should be a man identified with it, was transformed into

---

[125] DLB, III, p. 137. On the LEA cf. below p. 342.
[126] Purdue, 'North East Politics 1900–1914', p. 23.
[127] Rubinstein, 'The Barnsley By-Election of 1897', p. 105.
[128] Cit. in *ibid.*, p. 112.
[129] Laybourn-Reynolds, *Liberalism and the Rise of Labour*, p. 83.
[130] Rubinstein, 'The Barnsley By-Election of 1897', pp. 120–1.
[131] Morgan, *Wales 1880–1980*, p. 49.
[132] Two for the 'Highland Land League' and three 'Independent Crofters': Crowley, 'The "Crofters" Party, 1885–1892', pp. 119–20.

labour power by the influence of the trade union caucus and the prestige of its leaders.

However, men like Benjamin Pickard and William Crawford did not isolate themselves in their regional strongholds, but also participated in the councils of the National Liberal Federation (NLF),[133] while other labour leaders cultivated links with the official caucus: for instance, Joseph Arch was President of the Birmingham Radical Union,[134] and Robert Knight was a member of the Newcastle 'Hundreds';[135] more generally, activity within a local Liberal Association became an almost regular feature of a labour leader's cv.[136] In fact, even very poor workers like George Lansbury[137] and chronically unemployed men like George Meek[138] used to look for temporary employment in one of the Liberal Clubs.

All this goes some way towards correcting the conventional picture of an incurable antagonism between Liberal party organizations and the labour movement.[139] However there is also something to be said in favour of the traditional interpretation. Its supporters have focussed on the clashes between local Liberal associations and working-class candidates,[140] and have implicitly or explicitly generalized these cases as if workers were uniformly hostile to the caucus: illustrations and examples abound, since even some confirmed Lib-labs like Howell were actively antagonistic to the caucus system. But this established interpretation and the revision proposed above are not really at variance, but rather are complementary, once placed in context.

---

[133] [Rep.], 'National Liberal Federation – Meeting at Bradford', *LM*, 2 Oct. 1885, p. 6. Broadhurst was also present, and moved a resolution in support of the decisions taken at this meeting.

[134] Arch, *The Story* (1898), 354.

[135] Waitt, *Thesis*, Appendix B.

[136] See the cases of: J. Wilson (Morpeth, DLB, II, p. 409); H. Hutchings (Cramlington, DLB, II, p. 201); S. Shaftoe (Bradford, DLB, III, 159); E. Trow (Darlington, DLB, III, p. 191); J. Shillito (Halifax; DLB, I *sub voce*); T. Sitch (Rowley, Staffords.; DLB, I, *sub voce*); E. Rymer (Wombwell, Yorks.: Neville, 'Introduction' to Rymer, 'Martyrdom of the Mine', p. 222); even Keir Hardie began his career as speaker of the Cumnock Junior Liberal Association in 1884 (Morgan, *Keir Hardie*, p. 14). See also Anderton, *Thesis*, p. 76.

[137] DLB, II, p. 215.

[138] Meek, *George Meek* (1910), pp. 112–14.

[139] Pelling, *Origins of the Labour Party*, p. 18 and *passim*; Barker, *Gladstone and Radicalism*, p. 131.

[140] Morgan, *Keir Hardie*, pp. 25–31.

Nobody – not even Howell[141] – questioned the importance and necessity of organizing Liberal electors, an activity which became increasingly important once the electorate grew to such an extent that it was beyond the reach of personal electioneering.[142] As early as 1868 Wright, the 'Journeyman Engineer', wrote that

An electoral or other purely political association open equally to all working men, whether unionists or non-unionists, mechanics or labourers, is what is wanted to give effect to the political power of the working classes.[143]

Working Men's Liberal Clubs and Associations tended to provide an answer to this need.[144] Their relationship with the official Liberal associations could be quite good, and in fact the Birmingham caucus itself sprung out of the merging of two such associations – the Working Men's Reform League and the St George's Reform League – with the local Liberal association;[145] even in the new organization the majority of the members were composed of manual workers.[146] Though criticized by some, the 'Birmingham Liberal Association of the 400' was praised by many traditional radicals: John Bright described it as made up of 'the popularly elected representatives of the 60,000 electors of Birmingham' and indeed 'perfect as a representation of the whole community – that is of the Liberal party in the town'.[147] A similar judgment was made by the radical press all over the country in the aftermath of the 1874 defeat. In those days even the paper of the caucus' most famous and implacable enemy, Joseph Cowen, eulogized the Birmingham Liberal Association, and wished its prompt extension to Newcastle.[148] Positive assessments continued to be heaped on it by many sections of the Liberal press throughout the 1870s and indeed even later, while Millite radicals such as 'Littlejohn' of the

[141] G. Howell to the Executive Committee of the R.L., 15 Jul. 1867, in *G. Howell Coll., Lett. Bk*, 779; see J. S. Mill to G. Howell, 22 Jul. 1867, in *ibid.*, Ind., 1562.

[142] Ostrogorsky, *Democracy*, I, p. 588; O'Leary, *Elimination of Corrupt Practices*, p. 208.

[143] Wright, *Great Unwashed* (1868), p. 68.

[144] See [rep.], 'Burley Working Men's Liberal Association', *LM*, 13 Jan. 1874, p. 8.

[145] Briggs, *History of Birmingham*, II, p. 192; this was not an isolated case: Hanham, *Election and Party Management*, pp. 327–28.

[146] Pugh, *Modern British Politics*, p. 30; also a great number of Conservative Associations were dominated by working men: Lloyd, *Election of 1880*, p. 67.

[147] [Rep.], 'Mr. Bright on Political Affairs', *NW*, 30 Jan. 1875.

[148] Ironside, 'Political Organization', *NW*, 9 Nov. 1878, 4; [la.], 'The New Liberal Organization', *NW*, 4 Apr. 1874, p. 4.

Weekly Times defended it energetically against Tory attacks.[149] Other undoubtedly working-class organs, like *Reynolds's Newspaper*, also expressed firm support and encouragement.[150]

In the 1870s critics were to be found in less radical circles. *Lloyd's Weekly* opposed the NLF from its foundation,[151] and defended the local autonomy of working-class associations against the alleged 'Chamberlain Parliament'.[152] However, since in those years *Lloyd's* was militantly hostile to Gladstone, it is possible that the real basis of its hatred for the caucus was expressed more sincerely by one of the paper's correspondents, who, describing those who wanted to set up a caucus in his constituency, wrote:

Some of them are teetotal spouters; others, tools employed to work the Gottenburg [sic.] system, for jobbing the public houses by the vestries; others are for locking out everybody on Sunday; some are for hiring our armies to Russia to please Mr. Gladstone, and others for cutting them down to nothing, to please Mr. Bright.[153]

However, there is no doubt that popular Liberalism could be militantly anti-caucus. The very model of direct democracy of the Athenian *agorà* was somehow irreconcilable with this sort of 'intermediate body' between the citizens and the political magistracy: in the direct democracy of the *ekklesia* or the Swiss *Landesgemeinde* there were no parties, and citizens voted at the end of a free discussion where rhetoric was supposed to be the midwife of truth and public interest.[154] Moreover, recent studies have shown that in some contexts working-class liberalism was a specifically 'anti-party' creed, looking back to the tradition of town meetings and the 'direct democracy' of 'free' and 'unorganized' nominations.[155] The very expression 'party' – in the caucus sense – was alien to the language of plebeian liberalism, and as late as 1867 expressions like 'the great Liberal Party of England' were still used with an indefinite sense, meaning 'all those who were committed to reform

---

[149] Littlejohn, 'Electioneering in America and England', *WT*, 23 Dec. 1877, p. 6.
[150] [L.a.], 'The Bill, the Whole Bill, and Nothing but the Bill', *RN*, 15 Jun. 1884, p. 1; [l.a.], 'The Day in South-East Durham', *Northern Echo*, 12 Jun. 1886, pp. 2–3.
[151] [L.a.], 'Mr. Forster and the Bradford Caucus', *LW*, 18 Aug. 1878, p. 6; [l.a.], 'The Caucus in Belgium', *LW*, 15 Sept. 1878, p. 6.
[152] [L.a.], 'Liberal Prospects', *LW*, 18 Nov. 1877, p. 1.
[153] 'A Finsbury Elector', 'The Birmingham Model', *LW*, 25 Feb. 1877, p. 6; the author defined himself 'an old radical' desirous to defend individual freedom at elections.
[154] See Hansen, *Athenian Ecclesia*, pp. 220–1.
[155] Lawrence, 'Wolverhampton', in Biagini and Reid (eds.). *Currents of Radicalism*, pp. 65–85.

the electoral system and enlarge the franchise'.[156] Howell in the 1870s and Cowen in the 1880s advocated the classical viewpoint of Henry Hunt[157] that candidates and MPs were to be independent of organizations and responsible only to the electors: though belonging to an extremely democratic current of liberalism, they were decidedly hostile to any concept of mandatory representation.[158] Howell defined caucus 'interference' as 'a violation of all constitutional rights and personal freedom in electoral matters';[159] writing in 1878, he objected to the caucus on five counts:

(1) That it is a mechanical contrivance intended to produce uniformity in the Liberal ranks, which is impossible. –
(2) That it does not or cannot command the confidence of the majority of the electoral body in the constituency.
(3) That it tends to encourage professional politicians and throws into their hands the power to manipulate the elections.
(4) That it assumes dictatorial powers in trying to enforce its authority.
(5) That it arrogates to itself the right which belongs only to the great body of the electors, namely of deciding who shall, or shall not, stand as a candidate . . .[160]

His remarks were probably widely representative of the unease felt by artisan radicals in regions like London, where trade unionism was weak and dispersed, unable to bring any significant influence to bear on the official Liberal party organizations, and nostalgic for the old-style popular politics based on open-air demonstrations. The caucus seemed to them an anti-democratic institution controlled by middle-class notables. Interestingly enough, these artisan radicals often criticized those who controlled the machine, rather than the machine itself, and in fact in London they set up their own 'party organization', the Metropolitan Radical Federation. Davis has shown the way in which this association differed from the caucus, especially as far as political strategy was concerned, since the former still tried to organize working men for 'monster meetings', while the caucus tried to organize electors for

---

[156] See e.g. G. Howell to Lord Russell, 14 Mar. 1867, in *G. Howell Coll., Lett. Bk*, 348.
[157] Belchem, *'Orator' Hunt*, p. 25.
[158] G. Howell, 'The Birmingham Scheme of Organization', in *G. Howell Coll., Lett. Bk*, 220ff., and especially 223.
[159] G. Howell, 'The Peterborough Election – To the Editors of the Economist', (Oct. 1878), in *G. Howell Coll., Lett. Bk*, 310.
[160] Howell, 'The Caucus System', (1878), in *G. Howell Coll., Lett. Bk*, see Howell, 'The Caucus System and the Liberal Party', in *ibid.*, 579–90.

the ballot box. But it is unquestionable that the caucus' strategy was bound to be the most effective after the 1883–85 reforms;[161] and it is also clear that the case of London itself confirms the crucial importance of the unions in the rise of a working-class party.[162]

In the specific case of Howell, his hostility to the caucus had much to do with the fact that as a 'labour' candidate without trade union backing, he had frequently to fight single-handed against local Liberal associations unwilling to sponsor a pennyless candidate. In this hopeless situation, his philippics begin to sound like consolatory rhetoric.[163] Even Cowen's hatred of the Newcastle caucus was based not only on principle, but also on personal motivation, since it is clear that it was greatly stimulated – if not produced – by Cowen's isolation in Liberal circles: his irredeemable independence and unorthodox views on foreign policy forced him to look for electoral support in areas different from those of Gladstonian radicalism, which dominated the Newcastle Liberal Association.[164] But in 1882 the organized labour movement and the most active plebeian radicals in Newcastle began to abandon him, some attracted by salaried positions within the caucus machine, others by a seat on the School Board or the Town Council.[165] However, most of them acted – as we shall see – under pressure from the pro-caucus stance of the trade union leadership, and the fear of breaking up the Liberal front on issues which looked increasingly futile. As a consequence, after his return in 1886, Cowen decided to withdraw from his seat.[166]

'DIRECT' REPRESENTATION

We therefore have different models of 'caucus' and different attitudes to the official Liberal organizations. It is difficult and possibly pointless to try to define which of the various models or

---

[161] Davis, 'Radical Clubs', in Feldman and Stedman Jones, *Metropolis*, pp. 106ff.

[162] *Ibid.*, p. 123.

[163] A parallel is provided by Arch's attitude towards the Primrose League in 1887, when his trade union lay in ruins and was not able to counteract effectively the influence of this Conservative organization: see Arch's speech in [rep.], 'Enthusiastic Liberal Meeting at Bradford', *English Labourers' Chronicle*, 8 Jan. 1887, p. 4.

[164] For a criticism of Cowen by an orthodox Newcastle radical, see *A Plain Letter to Joseph Cowen, Esq., M.P., by a Gladstonian Radical*, London and Newcastle, 1882. Cf. Todd, *Cowen*, pp. 120–2, 153.

[165] 'Caucustown', 5 Aug. 1882, in *J. Cowen Coll.*, B 255.

[166] Item dated 30 Oct. 1886, *ibid.*, B341.

cases was the most 'representative'. This can only be assessed by focusing on the specific problems of working-class representation.

As Shepherd has shown in his recent study,[167] the movement for 'direct' representation was not conceived in a 'class' spirit, but rather as an expression of the old radical struggle *against* 'class exclusion'.[168] Especially in the first decades, what was desired was not a new 'labour' party, but rather the parliamentary representation of a pressure group hitherto voiceless. As the *Bee-Hive* declared,

Providing a careful selection of working class representatives be made, there is no reason why they should stand isolated as a class in Parliament any more than the special representatives of many other interests now sitting there. We have the railway interest, the banking interest, the manufacturing interest, the landed interest, &c., all represented by men especially ... returned for that purpose; but those interests being attended to, we do not find these representatives incapable or unwilling to take part in the general business of the legislature. So would it be with the representatives of the labour interest ... they would ... blend with the other members in performing the usual duties expected from members of the House.[169]

In varying degrees, this platform found support among both radical[170] and moderate Liberals[171], including the party leader and the chief whip.[172] However, when the elections came, it appeared that 'direct representation' was less feasible than most had anticipated. The real problem was not Howell's 'corruption',[173] but rather general lack of precise plans and real commitment: as late as July 1868 the labour leaders had not yet advanced any candidature,[174] and this in itself was a serious handicap at a time when

---

[167] Shepherd, 'Labour and Parliament', in Biagini and Reid (eds.), *Currents of Radicalism*, pp. 187–212.

[168] 'The Labour Representation League ... to the Working-Class Voters of the United Kingdom', *TI*, 29 Jan. 1874, p. 7; See T. Burt, 'Working Men and Reform', *NW*, 26 Jan. 1867, p. 4.

[169] [L.a.], 'The Representation of Labour', *BH*, 19 Oct. 1867, p. 4.

[170] Like Mill, Morrison, Dilke and Fawcett: see Packe, *Mill* pp. 473, 476; [letter by] J. S. Mill, 'Aylesbury', *BH*, 31 Oct. 1868, p. 1; Evans, *Randall Cremer* (1909), 51; Soutter, *Recollections of a Labour Pioneer* (1923), pp. 49–50; Holt, *Life of Henry Fawcett* (1915), p. 121.

[171] See the report of the meeting of Broadhurst and Troup with Goschen and Layard, *BH*, 9 Nov. 1867, p. 1; [l.a., n.t.], *LM*, 26 Oct. 1867, p. 5.

[172] Thompson, 'Gladstone's Whips', p. 199.

[173] Harrison, *Before the Socialists*, pp. 190, 202.

[174] [L.a.], *BH*, 4 Jul. 1868, 4; though there had been some discussions: [rep.], 'Lambeth and Its Representation', *BH*, 23 May 1868, p. 5. See Harrison, *Before the Socialists*, pp. 141–2, 180.

constituencies liked to be 'fed'. Eight or nine trade unionists eventually put themselves forward as candidates when it was too late for all practical purposes, to the dismay of the chief whip:[175] in these circumstances, and without adequate financial support, the fight was desperate, to the extent that some withdrew before the contest, while Cremer, Howell, Jones and Bradlaugh were defeated. Afterwards, with the decline of popular mobilization and the disbanding of the Reform League, the chance of labour candidates being elected did not increase, though some of them stood at by-elections in 1869[176] and 1871.[177]

Those who tried to analyse these failures at the time stressed working-class disorganization,[178] corrupt practices, the cost of elections, and the absence of a secret ballot, and the payment of MPs.[179] This criticism was well-founded, but while it explained why labour MPs could not enter Westminster *en masse* without a democratization of the system, it did not explain why not even one or two had been elected. Though the *Bee-Hive* placed the responsibility on the Liberal party,[180] the basic reason was rather that working-class interest in 'direct representation' was still very limited even in radical constituencies.[181] All sections of the electorate seemed to agree that it was not 'social standing', but 'locality' which an MP ought to represent,[182] and none of the first labour

---

[175] Leventhal, *Howell* (1971), p. 121; Harrison, *Before the Socialists*, pp. 175, 182–3. The working-class candidates were: W. R. Cremer (Warwick); G. Howell, (Aylesbury); E. O. Greening (Halifax); E. Jones (Manchester); R. Hartwell (Lambeth and Stoke); A. McDonald (Kilmanrock); G. J. Holyoake (Birmingham); G. Odger (Chelsea): Cole, *British Working-Class Politics*, pp. 45–7; moreover, W. Newton stood for Tower Hamlets (Leventhal, *Howell*, p. 117); C. Bradlaugh (Northampton) should also be included in the list.

[176] G. Odger (Stafford); G. Potter (Nottingham); and then Odger for Southwark; see Cole, *British Working-Class Politics*, p. 56.

[177] G. Howell for Norwich (*ibid.*, p. 57).

[178] Plain Dealer, *BH*, 9 Jan. 1869, p. 4.

[179] J. W. Mayhew, *BH*, 4 Feb. 1871, p. 12; Lloyd Jones, 'The House of Commons Estinguishing Working Men's Candidates', *BH*, 5 Aug. 1871, p. 1; [l.a.], 'The Opening Session', *WT*, 20 Dec. 1868, p. 1; [l.a.]. 'The Contest for Southwark', *WT*, 19 Dec. 1869, p. 1; Goldwin Smith, *BH*, 2 Jan. 1869, p. 1. For payment of members cf. [rep.], 'Newcastle Election . . . Mr. Cowen's Speeches . . . Shieldfield', *NW*, 17 Nov. 1874, p. 2.

[180] [L.a.], 'Working-Men Candidates', *BH*, 14 Sept. 1872, p. 9.

[181] See the unsuccessful 'independent Labour' campaign of R. Hartwell in the Potteries: [rep.], 'The Potteries Election', *BH*, 17 Oct. 1868, p. 1; [rep.], 'Stoke-on-Trent Election', *BH*, 31 Oct. 1868, p. 1.

[182] See [l.a., n.t.], *LM*, 19 Nov. 1868, p. 2. See letter from Blackburn declaring that a 'labour' candidate could be easily elected 'provided he is a local man': *Labour Representation League Papers*, Meeting of Business Committee, 4 Apr. 1873. Even later to be a 'local man' could be a determining factor: Pelling, *Social Geography*, p. 324.

candidates had a close relationship with the local constituencies for which they stood. Unable to relate effectively to this reality, and unwilling to stir up class struggle,[183] their main appeal was not as working men, but as ordinary 'advanced Liberals':[184] but constituencies had no inclination to choose a *poor* Liberal candidate in place of one who was equally Liberal, but *wealthy*.

Though a Labour Representation League was set up to provide an organizational framework, its apparatus was very weak and quite ineffective. The problem was that the LRL did not exercise any effective influence on trade unions, and labour leaders sat on its executive only as individuals and not as delegates of their respective organizations.[185] Thus, while Howell's call for a general mobilization of popular liberalism remained largely unanswered,[186] the 'labour' rhetoric of those who asked for an independent working-class party[187] was shipwrecked on the cultural and political divisions of the labour movement.[188]

The 1874 election was a turning point in several respects, not

---

[183] As maintained by many, including A. A. Walton: see his article in *BH*, 13 Nov. 1869, p. 7.

[184] Davies, *Political Change and Continuity* p. 208. Even their programme was hardly distinguishable from that of a typical middle-class radical one: see for some examples: G. Howell, 'To the Electors of the Borough and Hundreds of Aylesbury' (1868), in *G. Howell Coll., Lett. Bk*, 744; cf. Howell, 'Worst for the Future', a Lecture to the Pimlico Branch of the Reform League, March 28th, 1868', *ibid.*, 379; Howell, 'To the Electors of the City of Norwich', *ibid.*, 27; G. Odger, *BH*, 8 Jan. 1870, p. 4.

[185] Cole, *British Working-Class Politics*, p. 52. These leaders were: Daniel Guile, Secretary of the Ironfounders; John Kane, Secretary of the Ironfounders Association; G. Howell, Secretary of the Trades Union Parliamentary Committee; Alexander McDonald, President of the Miners' National Association; Thomas Halliday, President of the Amalgamated Association of Miners; Thomas Ashton, Secretary of the National Ropemakers and Twine Spinners' Association; J. P. D. Prior, Secretary of the Amalgamated Association of Carpenters & Joiners; R. Applegarth, G. Potter and Lloyd Jones; J. Ryan of the Compositors, A. Wadkinsons of the Boilermakers, L. Hearn, Secretary of the Westminster Working Men's Association, and the 'labour' lawyer F. W. Campin. The League's President was the lawyer R. M. Latham, and its Secretary was H. Broadhurst ('The Labour Representation League – To the Trades Unionists of the United Kingdom and Working Men Generally', printed leaflet *Labour Representation League Papers*, pp. 18–19).

[186] G. Howell, 'Working Men in Parliament', an address to the Birmingham Labour Representation League Meeting, 1872, in *G. Howell Coll., Letter Book*, 144.

[187] [L.a.], 'The Direct Representation of Labour', *RN*, 15 Dec. 1872, 1; speech by R. M. Latham (mentioning the hoped for foundation of a 'Labour Party'), *Meeting of Business C.ttee*, 26 Feb. 1873, p. 20 and *Meeting of the General Council*, 15 Mar. 1873, pp. 13–14 (speech by R. M. Latham), both in *Labour Repres. League Papers*.

[188] Which union leaders knew too well to commit their organizations to political action: debates between Liberals and Conservatives were frequent at TUCs: e.g. *Nineteenth T.U.C., Hull, &-11 Sept. 1886, Report*, p. 34, speeches by Kirman (Bolton), Hughes (Liverpool) and Shipton (Bradford).

least because it demonstrated the fragility of the alliance of reformers and the new potential of the Conservative party. At the same time, the mobilization of the north-eastern miners for the election of their leader – an operation in which the LRL did not take part[189] – provided a new model for labour politics. Burt's electoral base was a regional organization, completely independent of London, with strong community roots and close links with a locally-dominant trade union. While the LRL was a relatively centralized body with the appearance of a party embryo, almost a forerunner of the Labour Representation Committee (LRC), the associations which supported Burt had no ambition for independence at a national level.

The differences between the two models and their respective philosophies became apparent when the issue of financing working-class candidates was brought up at the TUC. The lack of an adequate electoral fund was probably the greatest single handicap of the LRL.[190] For a long time there were talks of setting up a special national fund, to which all the TUC unions would subscribe. Some thought from a purely economic point of view that this would be easy.[191] According to the computation that G. Shipton submitted to the 1882 TUC, one extra penny per week per individual trade unionist would provide an annual fund of £25,000, enough to pay for the cost of returning and maintaining twenty-five working-class MPs.[192] However, it is significant that Shipton's proposal was immediately curtailed by an amendment supported by both Wight and Trotter, delegates of the Northumberland and Durham miners, whose unions were the most politically aware and effective. They were spokesmen for the 'second model', and feared the formation of a central committee which might control and

---

[189] Broadhurst, *The Story* (1901), p. 67.

[190] Leventhal, *Howell* (1971), p. 141. Desperate lack of funds was lamented in the 'Seventh Annual Report', 30 Apr. 1875, in *Labour Representation League Minutes*, pp. 129–30.

[191] E. Garbett to T. Dixon, 20 Oct. 1876, in Dixon Papers. But many did not agree, either in 1882 or later: see speech by Blackie (Edinburgh), at the 1885 TUC (*Eighteenth TUC Report, Southport*, 7–12 September 1885, p. 34): '. . . it was all very well to say that if they were to have labour representatives they must pay them. In the association he represented the members paid over 1s. 6d. a week for the protection of trade and for other purposes, and if he asked them to pay more for the support of members of Parliament, he knew very well what the answer would be.' Blackie also declared that even if 'they agreed to pay a candidate's expenses, and he did not do every little thing that some of them might want, they would withdraw their subscriptions.' For lack of interest in direct representation among Scottish workers, see also Hutchison, *Scotland*, p. 113.

[192] *Fifteenth TUC Manchester 18–23 September 1882, Report*, p. 28.

repress the autonomy and aspirations of the various regions.[193] In 1884 the leaders of the Miners' National Union defined as 'visionary and impracticable' the idea of centralizing finance, stressing that it would be very easy for any union numbering even only 10,000 members to elect and maintain an MP. They especially emphasized that the candidate ought not to be a 'stranger', but a man 'selected by the trade to which he belongs, [who] must have their confidence, and remain, altho' sent to Parliament, a paid official of such trades organization'.[194] Two years later, at the 1886 TUC, a proposal for centralizing finances and the direction of labour candidates was submitted again by Shaftoe, who pointed to Parnell's Irish party as an example;[195] but he was answered that 'it was unnecessary to form a costly central organization',[196] and Benjamin Pickard cut short the discussion by forcefully stating that 'so far as he was concerned he was a Radical, Liberal, or Whig, before he thought of becoming a labour representative'.[197] Again, it was Pickard who spoke on behalf of the politically strong sections of organized labour, for which it was axiomatic 'that labour is best served by the Liberal party, and that the Liberal programme is a working man's programme'.[198]

In this situation, the LRL's model could only reveal its short-comings and inadequacy. The League met with a major electoral failure at the 1870 London School Board elections, when it selected about twenty candidates, but brought only nine to the poll, of whom only one was returned.[199] The general election of 1874 confirmed its weakness. The working-class candidates were thir-teen in all[200] – fourteen if Bradlaugh is included – but only two

---

[193] *Ibid.*, pp. 28–9, W. Wight (Northumberland), Trotter (Durham), and Knight (Newcastle). Wight declared: 'The Northumberland miners had sent Mr. Burt to Parliament – (applause) – and not only had they no difficulty in raising the requisite funds, but would have no difficulty in obtaining much more, if required, for a like purpose.'

[194] *Miners National Union – Working Men's Representatives in the House of Commons*, 1884, p. 3, in DMA, *Minutes*.

[195] *Nineteenth TUC . . . 1886*, p. 33, Shaftoe (Bradford).

[196] *Ibid.*, p. 34, Mr Marks (London).

[197] *Ibid.*, p. 33, B. Pickard, MP. Though the TUC proceeded to establish the LEA, the latter became increasingly identified with the Liberal Party.

[198] J. Wilson: newspaper cutting from the *Northern Echo*, 5 Jul. 1890, in *J. Wilson Papers*, D/X 188/12, issue 138.

[199] Cole, *British Working-Class Politics*, p. 54.

[200] Namely: A. A. Walton (Stoke-on-Trent); G. Potter (Peterborough); W. Pickard (Wigan); T. Halliday (Merthyr); G. Odger (Southwark); B. Lucraft (Finsbury); G. Howell (Aylesbury); J. Kane (Middlesborough); T. Mottershead (Preston); W. R. Cremer (Warwick); H. Broadhurst (Wycombe); A. Macdonald (Stafford); T. Burt (Morpeth): (Cole, *British Working-Class Politics*, pp. 67–9).

were elected, both miners: and of those elected, only Alexander McDonald received any support form the LRL.[201] But McDonald's case was exceptional, because, as well as being a trade union leader he was also a small employer and thus economically independent; moreover his electoral expenses were completely paid by the Durham Miners' Association, which allocated £1,000 for this purpose.[202] As a consequence, the role of the LRL was limited to the organization of the working-class vote at Stafford: not a difficult operation because, even if it was a constituency without miners, a large section of the electorate was made up of radical shoemakers.[203]

Without the special advantages enjoyed by McDonald, the other two miners' candidates supported by the LRL – William Pickard at Wigan, and Thomas Halliday at Merthyr Tydfil – were defeated: the former by working-class Toryism and sectarian strife,[204] the latter by middle-class Liberal candidates with a strong Welsh identity.[205] In other cases defeat for the LRL candidates was easier to forecast. In fact in the radical borough of Stoke-on-Trent, at the announcement of A. A. Walton's candidature[206] popular participation was lamentably small:[207] the public had not been attracted even by the fact that Henry Broadhurst and William Owen (editor of the local *Potteries Examiner* and enthusiastic advocate of trade union rights) chaired the meeting and supported Walton's candidature. In his speech Owen thought it useful to remark that it would not be necessary to pay a salary to Walton if he was returned, because he had a sufficient personal income, and deplored the fact that 'working men were not educated enough . . . to realize the fact that they would gain something by *even* paying

---

[201] Broadhurst, *The Story* (1901), p. 67.

[202] [Rep.], 'The Representation of Labour. Speech of Mr. MacDonald', *Potteries Examiner*, 28 Jun. 1873, p. 6.

[203] Pelling, *Social Geography*, p. 191. On shoemakers' radicalism, see Hobsbawm-Scott, 'Political Shoemakers', in Hobsbawm, *Worlds of Labour*, pp. 103–30.

[204] Pelling, *Social Geography*, pp. 266–7.

[205] The successful candidates were H. Richard (7,606 votes) and S. Fothergill (6,908 votes); Halliday got 4,912 votes: Morgan, *Wales in British Politics*, p. 39.

[206] A well-known 'labour' journalist who had been a stonemason in his early years; he had already been a candidate for Stoke in 1874: see 'Alfred A. Walton, Liberal Candidate for Stoke-upon-Trent', *BH*, 30 Jan. 1875, pp. 1–2.

[207] [Rep.], 'Labour Representation in Stoke-upon-Trent', *Potteries Examiner*, 4 Oct. 1873, p. 6; one of the speakers indignantly pointed out that there were 'a few empty benches' in the hall.

one of their representatives to go to the House of Commons'.[208] Walton's programme was the typical radical one, including a strong stress on retrenchment in government expenditure (apparently the cause cherished most by the leader of the local miners).[209] Walton was a 'stranger' in Stoke; but the local labour leaders did not have 'one of themselves' for a candidate, and in fact had previously offered the candidature to another 'stranger', G. M. W. Reynolds of *Reynolds's Newspaper*.[210] Successive meetings were much more successful[211] and Walton paraded a great self-confidence (at the 1873 TUC he had boasted that the working classes could elect forty or fifty MPs in the new Parliament).[212] But in spite of the personal intervention of Broadhurst and Howell, secretaries of the LRL and the TUC respectively,[213] and the passionate support of the main local working-class weekly, the *Potteries Examiner*, Walton was defeated.[214] Broadhurst and Howell themselves had no better luck in their own constituencies: this provides further evidence that their prestige as national leaders could not compensate for the lack of any basis in the local trade union movement.

The LRL blamed its defeat on the Liberal party, which had allegedly eliminated working-class candidatures.[215] That this was little more than consolatory rhetoric was further shown by the 1875 Stoke by-election, at which the 'labour' candidate William Owen, the local journalist, received a humiliating defeat at the hands of a 'stranger' of dubious reputation, Dr E. Kenealy. At the time the latter was famous for his role in the 'Tichborne case', and had a strong appeal to anti-aristocratic, anti-Catholic plebeian radicalism. Kenealy's election provoked great indignation among

---

[208] *Ibid.*; my italics.

[209] *Ibid.*, speech by James Hand, Secretary of the North Staffordshire District Miners' Association.

[210] Who declined on account of health problems: [rep.], 'Stoke-on-Trent Labour Representation League', *Potteries Examiner*, 29 Mar. 1873, p. 6.

[211] [Rep.], 'Mr. Walton's Candidature: Great demonstration at the People's Music Hall, Hanley', *Potteries Examiner*, 7 Feb. 1874, p. 7.

[212] A. A. Walton, 'Representation of Labour in Parliament . . .', cit. in *Potteries Examiner*, 22 Feb. 1873, p. 3.

[213] *Ibid.*

[214] For the strength of the workers see [rep.], 'Labour Representation in Stoke-upon-Trent', *Potteries Examiner*, 4 Oct. 1873, p. 6, speech of W. Owen: 'he computed that there were in this borough no less a number than ten or twelve thousand working men – many of them heads of families and householders – and to his mind their success was irresistible'.

[215] 'The Labour Representation League and the Late Election', *BH*, 14 Mar. 1874, p. 9.

the most austere of the popular Liberals,[216] but showed that, of condescending 'labour' and the 'good old platform', working-class electors still preferred the latter.[217]

After 1875 it was quite clear to sympathetic Liberal observers that the cause of 'direct representation' was not strongly supported by the majority of the working classes; in spite of the indignant recriminations of the *Bee-Hive*,[218] even many labour leaders eventually admitted that the explanation for their continuing defeats was that 'the working men as a body were not anxious to be represented in Parliament by their own class'.[219]

All these problems had already come to light at the 1875 TUC. The delegate of the host city, moving a resolution in favour of 'labour representation', said that if the working men had been united and organized throughout the country it would have been easy to return twenty-two labour MPs[220]: while this figure was lower than in previous forecasts, the real problem was – of course – that the working men were *not* united, not even on the preliminary question of whether it was useful to have working class MPs at all.[221] Moreover, as Taylor, Leamington delegate for the NALU,

---

[216] E.g. [l.a.], 'The Stoke Election', *NW*, 9 Jan. 1875, p. 4. Kenealy's election was the fruit of irrational reactions against imaginary injustice allegedly suffered by 'the Doctor' and his client at the hands of 'Government oppression, legal corruption, and Romish machinations': [l.a.], 'The Startling Elections', *NW*, 20 Feb. 1875, p. 4). A few months later 'Ironside' wrote that Kenealy's election had brought discredit to the cause of all the miners, and would delay the achievement of county franchise ('The Northumberland Miners', *NW*, 29 May 1875, p. 4). As late as 1877 *Lloyd's Weekly* savaged Kenealy for discrediting the House of Commons [l.a.], 'Mr. Whalley's Tea Party', 22 Apr. 1877, p. 6). On the incident see also Anderton, *Thesis*, pp. 180–9; on Kenealy, see McWilliam, 'The Tichborne Agitation', in Biagini and Reid (eds.), *Currents of Radicalism*, pp. 44–64.

[217] The anti-clerical *Reynolds's Newspaper* and *Labourers' Union Chronicle* did not have the scruples of their more respectable contemporaries. This passage is significant:

> for Dr. Kenealy goes the 'whole hog' in politics, and is a root and branch reformer of the most decisive and thorough going school. Talk of the grievances of the agricultural labourers, of land reform, of State Church abolition, of reconstitution of our legal system, of rational Sabbath observance, of the absurd pretensions of priestism, of the destruction of privilege, or of any of the numerous evils, obsoletisms, and anomalies which fetter the liberty of the people and obstruct the national growth; and Dr. Kenealy is the man to reduce your talk into a form of practical action . . .
> ([L.a.], 'The Election of Dr. Kenealy', *Labourers' Union Chronicle*, 20 Feb. 1875, p. 1).

[218] [L.a.], 'The Liberal Party and the Working Men', *BH*, 9 Jan. 1875, p. 10.

[219] *Fifteenth TUC . . . 1882*, Coote (London), p. 29: Coote declared that he was not keen on labour MPs, and pointed out that his view was likely to be shared by a majority of the trade unionists since the resolutions of the previous congresses had never been applied; he concluded that labour representatives could be elected only in some regions, to be considered as special cases.

[220] *Seventh Trade Union Congress, Report, Liverpool, 18–23 Jan, 1875*, Clark (Liverpool), p. 19.

[221] *Ibid.*, Johnston (Glasgow), p. 21.

appropriately pointed out, it was rash to talk of 'direct' representation of labour when millions of workers were still unenfranchised.[222] There was agreement with Broadhurst's defence of the
general principle of attempting to return working-class MPs, but
the morale of the supporters of 'independent labour' fell to its
lowest point when Banks, the delegate from Boston, and G. Potter
pointed out that there were

> thousands and thousands of voters who would not vote unless they were
> paid to do so, and working men candidates could not find the money
> which the present corrupt system rendered necessary to fight the battle
> successfully . . . At the last election he [Potter] stood for a burgh in which
> there was a sufficient number of [working] men to have returned him had
> they not been bribed to vote for a richer man. They should . . . try to
> teach working men to renounce a temporary pleasure or a temporary
> advantage for a permanent good.[223]

This was the real situation: in spite of the secret ballot, many
electors of the subaltern classes still preferred to accept bribes
rather than voting for 'labour' candidates. Kane, who had unsuccessfully tried to conquer Middlesborough, added another element
to this discouraging picture, saying that a labour candidate had to
bribe not only the electors whom he particularly wanted to
represent, but also the local press, charities and other associations,
and that at the same time he had to show no scruples in flattering
local vanities and prejudices. In short, a candidate ought to be
ready to become 'a sort of political chameleon – he must hold all
sorts of opinions, he must promise to be all things to all men, he
must be full of deception',[224] and only at the price of this 'little
harlequinade' could he hope to have a chance of being elected,
whether or not he was a 'working-class candidate'.

THE LIB-LABS AND THEIR CONSTITUENTS

It should be noted that the leaders who related these frustrating
experiences had contested boroughs where they were more or less
outsiders, and certainly none of them could claim to be anything
like a local 'notable'. But this was not necessarily the situation of

---

[222] *Ibid.*, p. 19.
[223] *Ibid.*, p. 20.
[224] *Ibid.*

all working-class candidates, as demonstrated by Burt's experience at Morpeth.

The previous chapter has shown with what care and on what scale the first candidature of the leader of the Northumberland miners was prepared. Not only was he a 'local' man standing for a constituency in which the majority of the electors were members of the trade union which he led, but his electors also felt that the reasons for returning him were more concrete than the usual rhetoric about the 'vindication' of labour. As an artisan declared during a meeting,

> They had received nothing like justice at the hands of the House of Commons as yet . . . There was no one in the House of Commons to defend the workmen's rights . . . They wanted . . . better regulations of the mines, and to have someone made responsible for the sacrifice of life which was frequently occurring. They would no longer have the lives of their fellow-workmen muffed out like a half-penny candle, and with better representation they would soon have better protection . . . [225]

Kane had complained of pressure from the local lobbies, but Burt's case gives the impression that he at least was not subject to anything of that sort: in fact, he presented a straightforward radical programme, argued in a clear and resolute way, and including (in 1873) explicit support for Home Rule for Ireland.[226] Burt's style was simple and concise, with a clear syntax and a linear logic: he always went to the heart of an issue and never supported a thesis without detailed documentation. He did not parade his learning, though it was remarkably wide ranging, nor did he try to provoke applause and acclamation, though he was continually cheered and his public appearances were accompanied by scenes of great enthusiasm and authentic mass elation. The polling day in 1874 was particularly spectacular. According to 'Ironside', the scenes were even more impressive than the annual festivals at the miners' 'pic-nics':

> Business of all kinds, except that connected with the refreshment of hungry and thirsty souls, was entirely suspended. Indeed, from Blyth to Morpeth and from Cambois to Bedlington, the whole district observed a general holiday . . . All the pits in the borough were idle for the day. Even

---

[225] [Rep.], 'The Great Demonstration in Favour of Manhood Suffrage on the Town Moor', *NW*, 14 Apr. 1873, p. 6, speech by T. Wilson, joiner, of Newcastle.

[226] [Rep.], 'Representation of Morpeth – Mr. Thomas Burt at Blyth', *NC*, 14 Nov. 1873, p. 3.

some of the pits beyond the boundaries were partially denuded of the usual complement of the workpeople. Every man was not only dressed in his best but placed himself on his best behaviour. The chief centres of interest – Blyth, Bedlington, and Morpeth – presented the gayest and happiest aspect from the number of lads and lasses who congregated around the polling booths.[227]

But this atmosphere of village celebration had a strongly political colour, even in a literal sense. At Blyth

The colours of the popular candidate were hung from hundreds of windows . . . Even the public houses had caught the infection of radical-ism. Almost every man, woman, and child, wore green and white favours. The only bit of blue I saw was that worn by Captain Duncan himself [the Tory candidate]. Thousands of people thronged the streets and congre-gated in the open space in front of the Central Hall. Of course the enthusiasm was immense. When Mr. Burt drove up to his committee rooms at the Central Hall, he was hoisted shoulder-high, carried to a waggon near at hand, and required to make a speech to the vast audience intoxicated with enthusiasm.[228]

Burt's journey from Blyth to Morpeth was accompanied by further scenes of popular excitement:

Along the route – a distance of about ten miles – the cheering was almost continuous. Farm labourers, whose horses were decked with green and white, left their ploughs and their harrows to wave their caps for the Radical candidate. Flags flaunted from nearly every cottage on the way. Stone breakers on the roadside, candymen tramping from village to village with their wares, wore upon their breasts rosettes of the favourite colour. Belside was almost deserted: the whole male population, excepting the children, had gone to Blyth to record their votes.[229]

There then followed a traditional electoral scene: the enthusiastic crowd unharnessed the horses of Burt's coach and pulled it by hand through the streets of Bedlington. In the main square Burt was persuaded to give a speech to 'Many thousands of sober well-conducted miners . . . all wearing favours, all listening intently to the candidate, all animated by one political sentiment.' At the end of his speech the applause became deafening and 'Mr. Burt's arm was almost dislocated by the vigorous hand-shaking he had to endure'.[230] At Morpeth the horses were unharnessed again and the

---

[227] Ironside, 'What I saw in Morpeth', *NW*, 31 Jan. 1874, p. 3.
[228] *Ibid.*
[229] *Ibid.*
[230] *Ibid.*

crowd wanted to honour Burt with a reception 'such as might have gratified even a Roman hero'. But in spite of the enthusiasm the poll took place with great order and discipline, with an unusual respect shown even to the Tory candidate – possibly because his position was clearly hopeless and he accepted his fate with a sportsman's good humour. It is worth noting that some sections of the miners' union went to the poll in properly officered columns:

One of the most impressive events of the day was the march of the men of Cambois, seven hundred strong, headed by a band of music, nearly four miles to the polling place at Bedlington. It was the first time that most of these men had ever given a vote at a Parliamentary election. The manner in which they gave it conveyed the impression that every one of them felt that he was engaged in performing a solemn and yet agreeable duty.[231]

Once Burt's election had been proclaimed, Robert Elliot read his famous poem, 'The Pitman gan te Parliament',[232] specifically written with a view to Burt's certain triumph. Then the huge throng dispersed peacefully.

The contrast with the scenes of Walton's contemporary contest at Stoke is striking, and in itself explains the different outcome in each case. Of course, Burt had the advantage of being supported by Cowen personally[233] and by his newspaper[234] – the most influential in the region, and much more important than the *Potteries Examiner* which so unsuccessfully supported Walton. However it is doubtful whether this support, useful as it was, was really determinant in the way suggested by Aaron Watson.[235] In fact, Watson himself offers much evidence that Burt's popularity in his district was in any case altogether extraordinary. Before Burt's candidature was officially announced, and indeed before the miners had even obtained the franchise, some of the citizens of Morpeth showed hostility to the possibility of having him, a despised 'Howky', as a prospective candidate for Parliament. In an atmos-

---

[231] *Ibid.* see also [rep.], 'Morpeth', *ibid.*

[232] Cit. in J. Dyson (ed.), *Tommy Burt. A Howky in Parliament*, Metropolitan Borough of North Tyneside n.d., pp. 30–3.

[233] Cowen himself had moved Burt's candidature at a meeting at Morpeth: see 'Representation of Morpeth. Requisition to Mr. Thos. Burt. Saturday, October 18, 1873', TS, *J. Cowen Coll.*, B154.

[234] Which sponsored Burt's candidature as early as 1872: see [l.a., n.t.], *NW*, 13 Jul. 1872, p. 4.

[235] Watson, *Burt* (1925), p. 96.

phere of rising tension a satirical poem was circulated, violently attacking Burt, and proclaiming, among other things,

> Nine groans for Burt the Howky;
> And if he ventures here,
> His dry teetotal carcase
> We'll soak in Robberts' beer.[236]

As Watson relates, the pamphlet stirred up the district's mining population, who immediately boycotted all the pubs where 'Robberts' beer' was sold. The scale of this boycotting increased over the following days and soon involved all the trades of Morpeth: even the miners' wives co-operated by refusing to buy anything from Morpeth pedlars. The situation soon became very serious. James Trotter, the pitmen's doctor, wrote:

The whole district is in a blaze. The tradesmen of Morpeth are likely to be ruined ... A reward of £150 is offered by the tradesmen for the publishers and authors of the squibs which are setting the miners in so desperate a state of excitement. All the inns and beer shops in the district have orders to receive no more ale or spirits from Morpeth on pain of instant extinction, and all have complied with the demand. The pitmen made an entrance into every public house, took down all the Morpeth spirit advertisements framed on the walls, trampled them underfoot, and sent the fragments to the owners carefully packed and labelled.[237]

To render their action more effective the miners transformed the boycot into a real siege: all the mineowners selling coal to Morpeth were threatened with a strike to the bitter end, and eventually the town was left in the cold after having been deprived of its business. Since Burt had been refused permission to address a meeting in Morpeth, the miners prepared plans to 'invade' the town with a demonstration in which 10,000 of them were to take part, and deliberately spread the rumour that this operation was imminent: 'if the men get determined', Trotter concluded, 'the devil himself will hardly be able to prevent them making an inroad . . . Besides, Mr. Burt will . . . surely be MP for the borough of Morpeth . . .'.[238]

Under such tremendous pressure the Morpeth townsfolk surrendered: after disowning the 'Hubbubboo', they invited Burt to hold a meeting in the town. Only after victory was achieved was it

---

[236] From the 'Morpeth Hubbubboo', cit. in *ibid.*, p. 128. Roberts (this being the correct spelling of his name) was an eminent citizen of Morpeth and owner of a local brewery.

[237] *Ibid.*

[238] *Ibid.*

revealed that the infamous pamphlet had been written not by one of Burt's enemies, but by one of his friends – possibly James Trotter[239] or Robert Elliott[240] – to provoke the miners into using their indignation to crush completely, from the outset, any hostility to Burt's candidature. The result was a complete success, and showed both Burt's standing in the local community and the unity and strength of the miners.

Since this was the situation, it is quite unlikely that Cowen's support was decisive: in fact Burt was continually re-elected during the 1880s – when Cowen was attacking him because of his loyal support for Gladstone; Burt's standing also survived a later crisis[241], and eventually he retired as 'Father of the House' in 1918. Moreover, while the importance of Cowen's support in Burt's election is debatable, the support of Burt's union for Cowen's election was possibly crucial: in January 1874 the pitmen set up an electoral committee presided over by Burt himself and John Dixon, with the specific purpose of ensuring Cowen's return.[242] Given the organization of the miners and their concentration in the district, there is no doubt that their unanimous support was very important for Cowen, if not decisive: and it is unlikely that Cowen would have obtained such support had he opposed Burt, as is also shown by the events of 1883–6, which we examined in the previous section.

As far as block community support is concerned, it is possible to find parallels to Burt's case in those of several Lib-lab MPs returned from 1885.[243] In the preceding section I have already mentioned Benjamin Pickard, the 'dictator' of South Yorkshire, as well as the leaders of the DMA – Charles Fenwick, John Wilson and William Crawford – who were generally safe in their respective constituencies. But possibly the most spectacular case is that of William Abraham – 'Mabon', who in South Wales enjoyed a popularity similar to, or even greater than that of Burt in Northumberland.[244] 'Mabon's' hold on the Rhondda was also strengthened by

[239] *Ibid.*, p. 129.
[240] Dyson (ed.), *Tommy Burt*, p. 19.
[241] See Satre, 'Thomas Burt', pp. 174–93.
[242] [Rep.], 'The Miners and the Election', *NW*, 3 Jan. 1874, p. 3.
[243] Shepherd, 'Labour and Parliament', in Biagini and Reid (eds.), *Currents of Radicalism*, pp. 187–213.
[244] It is significant that Burt was apparently also very popular in the Rhondda: when he visited it in 1883 he was welcomed as a hero:

the fact that – with his Calvinist theology and command of the Welsh language – he was completely identified with Welsh nationalism. Deacon of Capel Nazareth (Pentre), poet and bard, 'Mabon' spoke for 'his' people and for 'his' miners at one and the same time.[245] His grip on his men is well illustrated by an incident reported by Smillie:

> If any friction arose and pandemonium threatened – so easy to rouse, so difficult to quell – 'Mabon' never tried to restore order in any usual way. He promptly struck up a Welsh hymn, as that magical melody, 'Land of My Fathers' . . . Hardly had he reached the second line when, with uplifted arms, as though drawing the whole multitude into the circle of his influence, he had the vast audience dropping into their respective 'parts' and accompanying him like a great trained choir. It was wonderful, almost magical, and the effect was thrilling. When the hymn or song was finished he raised a hand, and instantly perfect silence fell. The storm had passed. This is not an isolated case. I have seen many such.[246]

In this way, appealing to both his supporters' nationalism and their religion, 'Mabon' made the most of his charismatic personality and of the potential offered by his peculiar position in the rural and mining community of South Wales. In his case we again find a strong emphasis on the theme of village democracy, which was of great importance in Wales.[247] The *Cymru Fydd* developed in this Arcadian and Dissenter atmosphere:

> The very ideal of *Cymru Fidd* was a small-scale, familiar rural world, in contrast to the twentieth century . . . Legend had much to do with building up this ideal. So too did the strength of indigeneous rural institutions such as the chapels, when pulpit oratory so often identified the simple values of the Old Testament with realities of the Welsh countryside. Preachers and poets (or perhaps preacher-poets such as Elfed) sang the virtues of the rural existence, and of closeness to nature and the sustaining force of mother earth.[248]

From early morn . . . hundreds of thousands of workmen from the two Rhonddas, the Ogmore, the Taff, and even the remote Garw Valley, wended their way across the mountains, and Mr. Burt's reception at the station and along the route may be described as a triumphal march . . . ([Rep.], 'Great Demonstration of Miners in the Rhondda Valley – Speeches by Mr. Burt, M.P., Mr. Walter Morgan, Mr. Halliday, Mabon, Lewys Afan, & Others', *The Miners' National Gazette*, 14 Jul. 1883, p. 142)

[245] Morgan, *Wales 1880–1980*, 49; and *Wales in British Politics*, pp. 66 and 203.
[246] Smillie, *My Life for Labour* (1924), pp. 62–3.
[247] Morgan, *Wales, 1880–1980*, p. 86.
[248] *Ibid.*, p. 237.

Wales and Northumberland shared many features, like the strength of trade unions and Nonconformity, the village mining communities, and the pastoral nature of the rural economy accompanied by the comparative local weakness of the landed aristocracy.[249] In view of these similarities the affinities between the position of the miners' leaders in the two cases are perhaps not surprising. But quite different is the case of another great Lib-lab who enjoyed a similar prestige and an analogous, almost magic of appeal to 'his' people: Joseph Arch.[250]

Like 'Mabon', 'Joe' Arch too was a famous Methodist lay preacher[251] when he became the 'Moses of the agricultural labourers'.[252] The labourers represented a group so oppressed and badly paid that, even though they did not form 'a people' in the same sense as the Welsh, they often compared themselves to 'a people of slaves' and looked up to Arch as the heaven-sent leader who guided them through the 'Red Sea' of disorganization and political non-existence into the 'promised land' of trade unionism and the electoral franchise. Many labourers described him as a man of extraordinary gifts and virtues, a messianic figure who spoke 'of the misery of his fellows . . . the workhouse of the future, the denial of manhood to labourers, the downthrusting of their children . . .';[253] the nickname 'prophet' became almost his second name.[254] One of Arch's staunch followers, Josiah Sage, commenting on the beginning of the 'prophet's' work, namely the founding of the union under the famous 'Wellesbourne tree', wrote:

I cannot help thinking that when Arch stood beneath that Wellesbourne tree on that memorable night of 1872, that he did not stand alone, but behind him was the Unseen. I think there was one thing about Arch that proved that he was called to the work, for where the enemies of the Union came like a flood, he was always ready for them . . . [255]

That was a turning point in the history of hundreds of thousands of labourers' lives and was celebrated in epic verses:

---

[249] Pelling, *Social Geography*, p. 343.

[250] The only common trait between East Anglia and the mining districts seem to be the strong Nonconformist tradition and the 'open' character of the villages (*ibid.*, pp. 104–5).

[251] Sage, *Memoirs*, (1951), p. 9.

[252] Often defined in this way both by his constituency and by himself: Arch, *The Story*, p. 225.

[253] Ashby, *Joseph Ashby*, (1961), p. 60.

[254] *Ibid.*, p. 59: 'it was late July before the prophet visited Tysoe'.

[255] Sage, *Memoirs*, 1951, p. 49. Notice that personal success is once again taken as an indication of the divine call: a typical trait of Weberian charismatic leadership.

> When Arch beneath the Wellesbourne tree,
> His mighty work began,
> A thrill of hope and energy, all through the country ran,
> The farmer, parson, lord and squire, looked on with evil eye.
> Some looked with scorn and some with ire,
> And some in dumb surprise.[256]

While the oppressors were dumbfounded, the oppressed welcomed the liberator:

> The night is past, the day has dawned –
> The day we have longed to see;
> When high o'er Norfolk county waves
> The flag of liberty.[257]

Arch was a powerful preacher, whose rhetoric was simple but effective, and left an indelible mark on conscience and memory:

Arch had no poetry, no rhetoric, but his voice was full and clear, reaching far beyond the limits of the crowd, thrown back now and then from the houses and even from the hills behind in a fine echo. Joseph [Ashby], more or less on the edge of the crowd, was completely lost, absorbing every fact, every note. When a horse or gig came up the road, forcing the people to press forward on to the green, it seemed an outrage that anyone should have any purpose but to listen.[258]

Men and women, old and young flocked to hear the good news of their liberation.[259] Recollecting the first meeting in which he participated as a boy, Sage wrote:

Young as I was, I was simply captivated by Arch's personality, for Arch's was a personality that, once he was seen or heard, you never could forget him. When I grew older and began to understand the position of the labourers, and how the union did so much for them, and with them my own people, including myself – I was more captivated with him than ever. Arch became my hero and my ideal in life . . . [260]

---

[256] Cit. in Howkins, *Poor Labouring Men*, p. 57.

[257] 'A Union Man', 'The Liberal Lads and the Tory Blue', *English Labourers' Chronicle*, 4 Apr. 1885, p. 5.

[258] *Ibid.*, p. 61.

[259] 'The name of Joseph Arch became very familiar to me when I was very young, and so did his personality, for I could not have been more than six or seven years old when I was taken to hear Arch speak. And I heard him a good many times after, as my father was very interested in the Union. So, indeed, were all the family . . .' (Sage, *Memoirs* (1951), p. 48).

[260] *Ibid.*; see also pp. 50–1, where Arch's great moral heritage is described. Even young Tom Mann felt Arch's appeal and influence: Mann, *Memoirs*, p. 18.

In addition the practical effects of his speeches on the audience were extraordinary, comparable to those of the preachers of the Revival: in fact, they sometimes led to an immediate 'conversion' to unionism, as in the case of Joseph Ashby, whose 'deep excitement about Arch kept him *and* his mother from their beds a long time that evening';[261] before the two went to sleep their decision to join the trade union had been taken in a solemn way.[262]

Part of this myth derived from the enormous difficulties which had to be overcome in order to set up an agricultural labourers' union in the face of the intimidation and active hostility of the rural elites. In this long conflict Arch appealed to the imagination of even the most humble 'primitive rebels'. One of these – a Norfolk poacher – recollected Arch's work almost as if the leader of the labourers had been a Robin Hood figure: 'At last, when things were as bad as they could be, Joseph Arch came along to be the Champion for Labour . . . He stood up in Norfolk and gathered the men round him . . .'.[263] The Norfolk poacher wrote how Arch – just like the heroes of certain sagas – was eventually forsaken by his own people, once they had obtained the initial benefits: but they soon met with the just retribution of their sin, in the form of a decline in the level of wages. At that stage, with typical generosity, 'Arch came again to there resque [sic]'.[264]

The Liberals had always actively supported Arch,[265] and in 1885 his candidature for North-West Norfolk was endorsed by the local Liberal association.[266] However, success was by no means easy because the Tories, whose candidate was Lord Henry Bentinck, exercised a strong influence in that district,[267] to the extent that the Liberals had invariably been beaten in every election for the last sixty or seventy years.[268] But in 1885 the registers were flooded by the new proletarian electors, and Arch's 'tremendous support in the highlands of Norfolk', where farms were large and labourers

---

[261] Ashby, *Joseph Ashby* (1961), p. 62, my italics; notice the woman's participation in this important decision.

[262] *Ibid.*, p. 63.

[263] *King of Norfolk Poachers* (1935), pp. 101–2.

[264] *Ibid.*, p. 102; see also Hawker *A Victorian Poacher* (1961), p. 71.

[265] See for two examples *J. Cowen Coll.*, C1839 J. Arch to Sir Charles Dilke, 7 Mar. 1873, *Dilke Papers*, 43309, f.315.

[266] Horn, *Joseph Arch*, p. 234.

[267] Pelling, *Social Geography*, pp. 97–8.

[268] Arch, *The Story* (1898), p. 356.

more independent,[269] was decisive for the election's outcome. The same prestige and appeal allowed Arch's return in 1892 and 1895, in spite of an intensified campaign of intimidation by the local gentry.[270] In particular, the 1892 victory – reversing the outcome of 1886 – was celebrated with scenes of collective elation similar to those which accompanied Burt's election at Morpeth in 1874: the enthusiasm of the rural crowds being embodied in one of the electoral songs:

> Shout a loud hurrah! boys,
> Raise your voices high,
> Arch is going to Parliament
> With a grand majority.
> Shout hurrah! boys.[271]

All this suggests that the rash judgement passed on Arch by Clegg, Fox and Thompson – that 'Arch did nothing whatsoever except symbolize Liberal exploitation of the growing discontent of argicultural labour'[272] – is hardly fair. If Arch was not a brilliant parliamentarian, his constituents thought him a worthy representative, and demonstrated their trust by returning him several times: and it must be remembered that these results were achieved without the support of any strong 'trade union caucus', since by then the NALU had collapsed under the strain of strikes and lockouts. Indeed, Arch's degree of popularity and continued electoral support is remarkable even when compared with the extremely high standards of the north-east miners.[273]

Certainly, in many other regions working-class MPs had a more precarious success, which exposed the limited nature of their representation. For instance, the difficult election of Sam Woods at Ince (Lancashire) in 1892 was possibly due more to his influence as a leading Baptist, than as a miners' leader,[274] but this was not a safe situation for a labour MP, as was shown by Woods' defeat in 1895. In 1897 he managed to return to Westminster, but for

---

[269] Pelling, *Social Geography*, p. 98.

[270] *Ibid.*, pp. 386–7; see Edwards, *Crow-Scaring* (1922), p. 50, about the persecutions he had to endure in 1886 because of his passionate attachment to the Liberal party; and Horn, *Joseph Arch*, p. 183.

[271] Arch, *The Story* (1898), p. 388.

[272] Clegg, et al., *A History of British Trade Unions*, p. 284.

[273] Even John Wilson of the DMA was defeated in 1886 in a constituency where the miners represented 55 per cent of the electors (*ibid.*, p. 278).

[274] Shepherd, *Thesis*, pp. 220–1; cf. H. O. Taylor to H. Broadhurst, 22 Apr. 1880, in Broadhurst Papers.

another borough, Walthamstow (Essex), a working-class suburb without miners but with a strong Nonconformist presence.[275] Comparable to this was the case of Henry Broadhurst. Though he was one of the outstanding personalities in the British labour movement, it did not prove easy for him to be returned, though he did succeed in 1880. In 1886 he was forced to give up his Birmingham seat when his working-class electors turned Unionist. Broadhurst moved to Nottingham, but since he did not support the Eight-Hour Bill, in 1892 he was again abandoned by the electorate, and lost his seat in spite of Gladstone's personal intervention.[276] The workers followed the instructions of their local leaders, and voted for a Unionist mine-owner sympathetic to the eight-hour platform.[277]

On the basis of what we have seen, it is possible to divide the Lib-labs elected from 1874 to the 1890s into three categories.[278] First, there were those – like Thomas Burt and William Abraham – who were strongly identified with the local working-class community: in such cases success was almost virtually guaranteed by the fact that the candidate was perceived to be 'one of ours',[279] and so supported at any cost against his opponent – whether 'one of them', a 'stranger' or an enemy pure and simple. Second, there were Lib-labs like Broadhurst and Howell, who had illustrious careers in the central organizations of the labour movement (like the Reform League, the LRL, the TUC, etc.), but without any committed trade union support or community identification with their constituents.[280] Third, there were those like Sam Woods, who, though local trades union leaders, did not have a solid basis of consensus because the workers in their constituencies were politically and culturally fragmented. In the second and third cases the

---

[275] Clegg et al., *A History of British Trade Unions*, p. 278; for the social composition of the electorate, see Pelling, *Social Geography*, p. 65.

[276] See 'An Appeal to the Nottingham Miners from Mr. Gladstone', in *Gladstone Papers*, 44515, f.86. The letter, printed on yellow paper, was to be used as a leaflet. See also Gladstone's autograph letter, in *ibid.*, and Broadhurst's reply, *ibid.*, f.85.

[277] Pelling, *Social Geography*, p. 208.

[278] For a comprehensive list of the Lib-lab MPs, see Shepherd, 'Labour and Parliament', in Biagini and Reid (eds.), *Currents of Radicalism*, pp. 211–2.

[279] 'Was not Charlie Fenwick one of ourselves? – wondered the miners of Wansbeck (Northumberland) – And was not he going straight from pit to Parliament? This was to the miners an issue of much greater importance than the fate of Ireland' (Armstrong, *Pilgrimage* (1938), p. 68).

[280] Clegg et al., *A History of Trade Unionism*, p. 277.

electoral success of a Lib-lab candidate was uncertain, and essentially depended on the support which they managed to win in each case: they were thus very vulnerable to changes in the mood of the local electors, lobbies and caucuses. Broadhurst was forced to leave Birmingham for Nottingham in 1886, and then Nottingham for Leicester in 1894: in each case he chose constituencies which were famous for their established radical (but not necessarily labour) traditions. Curiously, even Broadhurst's famous adversary, Keir Hardie, found himself in a similar situation: in 1888 he suffered a humiliating defeat in Mid-Lanark, where he obtained only 617 votes against 3,847 for the official Liberal candidate and 2,917 for the Conservatives.[281] This was a failure which – taking place in a Scottish constituency dominated by miners – was more serious than any rout previously suffered by men like Howell, and which cannot be explained by reference to some 'bourgeois-ridden caucus conspiracy'. It is significant that Hardie, just like Howell, was eventually returned for a radical London constituency with which he had no trade union or community links.

Clearly it was not enough to be a 'labour candidate' – however radical or even socialist – to obtain working-class support: the 'labour' MPs, in spite of their name and social background, were never popular as class representatives, and exercised no special appeal to any working-class constituency which was not at the same time a radical one. In other words, if the working men were not culturally and politically united, they were unlikely to show any coherent electoral behaviour along class lines.

From the point of view of organized labour the Lib-labs's work in Parliament was extremely useful and indeed increasingly essential: but one of the reasons why workers were not so unanimous about labour MPs was that there were many middle-class radicals who were just as active and useful, and less difficult to return: men like Bradlaugh, Cowen, Dilke,[282] Mundella – appropriately defined by his biographer 'the pre-eminent Lib-lab of his generation'[283] – Sydeny Buxton,[284] L. A. Atherley Jones, and others. Bradlaugh

---

[281] Pelling, *Origins of the Labour Party*, p. 68.

[282] Who enjoyed massive working class support – as a radical-republican even more than as a 'social' Liberal – in the mining constituency of the Forest of Dean: Pelling, *Social Geography*, pp. 149, 155–7.

[283] Armytage, *Mundella*, p. 335.

[284] Who was regularly returned to parliament for the working-class constituency of Poplar from 1885 to the World War (Pelling, *Social Geography*, pp. 46–7).

and Cowen in particular occupied an outstanding position in working-class radicalism. A well-informed observer wrote that Bradlaugh was – in spite of his atheism (which in any case was never paraded on his political platform) – 'almost an idol of the Northumbrian miners in his later years',[285] and it is significant that between 1874 and 1888 he was invited to be an official speaker at nine of the fifteen annual DMA Galas.[286] His popularity was so great that, like Gladstone and Burt, he became an inspiring motif of local commercial advertising.[287] His charismatic power was also impressive: on his arrival at a 30,000 strong meeting in 1883,

the crowd surged and swayed in a very dangerous fashion that overpowered everything . . . Mr. Bradlaugh, who is gifted with an extraordinary faculty of controlling a mob, lifted his stick high above his head, and called on his supporters to be 'steady' and this shortly had the desired effect . . . The appearance of Mr. Bradlaugh, who, as one of his delighted supporters declared, looked like 'a real Tribune of the People', was hailed with hearty applause. At once bringing his powerful lungs into play, at a moment when the linked area keepers were being somewhat severely tested he shouted, 'I am strong enough to lock any one up who disturbs, and I will do it, upon my honor.'[288]

Cowen's case was different. A wealthy manufacturer and model employer (who even set up an advanced social security system for his own workers),[289] he was the 'tribune of the plebs' of Newcastle and district.[290] He identified himself with his supporters to such an extent that he used to dress in a miner's Sunday clothes, and spoke with a strong Northumberland accent – almost incomprehensible in London, but very effective with his Newcastle audiences.[291] Typically, when talking to his workers he used the Biblical 'thou'.[292] The extent to which the workers trusted him is suggestively indicated by the famous episode of a pitman who – travelling

---

[285] Watson, *Burt* (1908), p. 166.

[286] See 'List of the Gala Dates and Speakers', *Durham Miners' Association 101st Annual Gala, Racecourse, Durham, Saturday July 13th, 1985*, Durham 1985, pp. 44–5. It must be remembered that speakers at the Galas were (and still are nowadays) not appointed by the union leaders, but elected by the lodges.

[287] [Advert.], 'Thorough. A FIRST CLASS RAZOR, made especially to mark the great event of MR. CHARLES BRADLAUGH's election . . .', *NR*, 16 Jan. 1881, p. 48.

[288] [Rep.], 'Trafalgar Square', *NR*, 25 Feb. 1883, 116; for another example, see [rep.], 'Great Meeting at Northampton', *NR*, *Special Extra Number*, 11 Aug. 1881, pp. 177–9.

[289] DLB, I, pp. 82–4.

[290] Adams, *Memoirs* (1903), p. 495.

[291] *Ibid.*, p. 497.

[292] Holyoake, *Bygones* (1905), II, p. 41.

on a train – was forced to give up his seat to a more 'respectable' passenger: the furious miner, 'swearing and gesticulating at large' said that 'Joe Cowen shall hear of this . . . [he] winnot see a working man wranged'.[293]

There cannot be any doubt that Cowen was much more than a provincial demagogue: it would be more appropriate to define him as a sort of wealthy precursor to Keir Hardie, with whom indeed he shared some personality traits, such as an exasperating spirit of independence which brought him into collision first with the parliamentary leadership of the Liberal party,[294] then with the Newcastle caucus, and finally with the whole of the party. At a local level this escalation became even more dramatic when Cowen began to support working-class candidates with a view to dismantling the power of the caucus, both at local and national levels: ironically, in the process he himself resorted to a sort of 'anti-caucus caucus', the Democratic Federation, which in 1882 was made up of radical workers firmly hostile to Gladstone's Irish policy, but on other issues essentially indistinguishable from the Liberal 'stupid hundreds'.[295]

When in 1883 the junior radical MP for Newcastle, Ashton Dilke, resigned on account of health problems, the local caucus chose John Morley as its candidate. The relationship between the Liberal Association and Cowen was so bad that Morley had been contacted even before Dilke's resignation, with a view to his standing in direct competition with Cowen: but Morley had declined, and only the vacancy left by Dilke convinced him that he should accept a candidature for the second seat.[296] He seemed an ideal candidate for a radical, working-class, home ruler seat like Newcastle: indeed his programme was very similar to Cowen's, and his left-wing credentials were so strong that – though in 1903 he would be considered a die-hard Cobdenite – in 1883 he was

[293] Adams, *Memoirs* (1903), pp. 411–12.

[294] From 1874, when he was elected on a purely Gladstonian platform: but Cowen was not prepared to co-operate with the other Liberal candidate and as a consequence a Tory came second. See Waitt, *Thesis*, pp. vi, viii; and DLB, I, p. 84.

[295] See Pelling, *Origins of the Labour Party*, pp. 15–17. The Democratic Federation stressed old radical ideas, like hostility to party discipline and the 'cloture' in parliamentary debates, and support for the greatest individual freedom. See [rep.], 'Democratic Federation . . . – Address by Mr. Lloyd Jones', *NC*, 9 Nov. 1882, p. 3.

[296] [Rep.], 'Liberal Meeting at Elswick – Speech by Mr. John Morley', *NC*, 13 Feb. 1883, p. 3; see also Waitt, *Thesis*, p. viii.

accused of being a communist.[297] The only charge that he received from the 'left' was that he had plotted against Cowen to deprive him of his seat,[298] though this was false and in any case quite irrelevant since he stood for Dilke's seat. But Morley's candidature had been prompted in some haste and secrecy, rather than in the usual open way.[299] As a consequence, he was disparaged as the nominee of the 'clique' of 'lawyers and broken-down merchants'[300] which allegedly made up the caucus – [301] though in fact this organization was composed of two-thirds manual workers, including such great labour leaders as Charles Fenwick, MP, Robert Knight,[302] and the young Arthur Henderson.[303]

The atmosphere was becoming very tense. In quite a sectarian spirit about fifty manual workers decided to present an independent working-class candidature, and chose the artisan Elijah Copland: he was committed to being an 'independent radical' in Cowen's sense of the word, that is one who 'would abandon his party' whenever he felt that it was going against the 'true principles' of liberalism.[304] But his candidature was unpromising, not only because the meeting which proposed it was small, but also because Thomas Burt – who declined an invitation to participate – had sent a letter recommending that he desist from this project and loyally support Morley instead.[305] Burt's advice was rejected with scorn, and the miners' leader dismissed as 'a Liberal Association man'.[306] In his speech Copland said that he was sure that Newcastle workers were certainly no less 'patriotic' than those of Morpeth and that therefore it would be easy to collect the money

---

[297] [Rep.], 'Mr. Bruce's Candidature', *NC*, 21 Feb. 1883, p. 3.

[298] [Rep.], *NC*, 13 Feb. 1883, p. 3, amendment by R. Middleton to the resolution moved by W. H. Henzell.

[299] Hamer, *Morley*, p. 128.

[300] [Rep.], 'Meeting of Working Men – A Labour Candidate', *NC*, 13 Feb. 1883, p. 3, speeches by the chairman (John Hall, joiner) and R. Heslop, bricklayer.

[301] *Ibid.*

[302] Waitt, *Thesis*, Appendix B; 600 out of 994 members were working class; Waitt stresses that 'only' 460 of these 600 were 'workmen', while the others were 'craftsmen': but 'craftsmen' were also a majority of those who took part in the meeting of the 'fifty' who nominated the independent labour candidate.

[303] Purdue, 'Arthur Henderson', p. 199. Henderson was on excellent terms with Morley and the local Liberal leadership.

[304] [Rep.], *NC*, 13 Mar. 1883, p. 3, speech by E. Copland. Cf. Todd, *Cowen*, pp. 150–1.

[305] See the letter in *ibid.* Burt in fact chaired the meeting for Morley's candidature: [rep.], 'Liberal Meeting in the Circus – Mr. Morley's Candidature', *NC*, 12 Feb. 1883, p. 3.

[306] [Rep.], *NC*, 13 Feb. 1883, p. 3.

necessary to pay the electoral expenses and provide a salary for him once he was returned: however this did not give enough weight to the fact that not only the workers of Morpeth, but many of those in Newcastle itself were members of Burt's trade union, whose funds would not be available for financing a candidate disowned by it.

In spite of all the odds, a second meeting, where Copland's candidature was officially presented, was much better attended: thousands of people thronged the outside of the town Lecture Hall once it had been filled to overflowing half-an-hour before the proceedings began. The audience, however, contained many of Copland's opponents in addition to his supporters. A *Chronicle* reporter assessed the former at no more than a hundred[307] – 'manifestly an organized opposition': but it appears that they were strong enough to successfully resist all attempts to eject them, and that they continuously interrupted the proceedings with whistles, roars and noises. Every mention of Burt's name was greeted with enthusiastic cheers, and when one of the speakers said that J. C. Laird of the Trades Council 'was now the pet of the Caucus: he had sold his birthright for a mess of pottage',[308] he was almost silenced by 'Loud cheering and continuous interruptions'. The chairman addressed Copland's opponents several times, ordering them to keep quiet and charging them with being caucus agents; but this was of no avail. Indeed the audience as a whole seemed seriously divided on Copland's candidature, and the meeting ended in total confusion when general uproar rendered the speakers completely inaudible.

There were rumours that Copland was financed by the Tories,[309] but though they were likely to gain from this situation, Copland's actual support came rather from the *Chronicle*, which was strongly behind him and relentlessly attacked the caucus.[310] However, it is significant that it did not criticize Morley for his programme –

---

[307] [Rep.], *NC*, 16 Feb. 1883, p. 3.

[308] *Ibid.*, speech by G. Hill.

[309] [Rep.], 'Liberal Meeting in the Town Hall – Speech by Mr. Morley', *NC*, 17 Feb. 1883, p. 3, question from the floor, read to Morley by the chairman.

[310] [L.a.], 'The Labour Movement', *NC*, 17 Feb. 1883, p. 2. For the change in the *Chronicle*'s attitude to the caucus, see also [l.a.], 'The Despotism of Party', *NC*, 29 Aug. 1884, p. 2, which declares the paper's total rejection of 'a few Yankee phrases and smart methods'.

which was evidently considered to be unobjectionable[311] – but only for the procedure by which his candidature had been advanced in a 'rash' and 'oligarchic' way, without 'consulting' the people of Newcastle in a series of traditional open meetings. Since the proper procedure had been followed for Copland, his candidature was considered more representative.

But in spite of the *Chronicle*'s rhetoric, Copland soon met with bitter disillusionment: the Irish electors, on whose support he had pinned his greatest hope, declared that they were going to vote for the Conservative candidate instead, as a means of retaliation against the policy of the Liberal government.[312] A second and inevitable blow came from the trade unions, who, at a public meeting, emphatically disowned Copland and declared themselves in favour of Morley: it is significant that this resolution was approved 'with only one or two dissentions'.[313] The immediate consequence was that Copland decided to withdraw. His official explanation was that he had not been able to collect the £750 necessary for the deposit,[314] which, if true, would only confirm that his support was very circumscribed and his organization non-existent; otherwise it would have been easy for him to collect such a sum from the 16,000 working men who were on the electoral registers as well as the many thousands who were not.

In the meantime Morley continued his campaign, being especially successful among the workers,[315] and eventually was elected with a large majority, which enabled him to begin his career as MP for Newcastle with confidence. This career was to

---

[311] As admitted by T. Beckwith, a firm opponent of the caucus, in a letter entitled 'The Labour Candidate', in *NC*, 19 Feb. 1883, p. 3. Copland's programme focussed on Home Rule, the repeal of Irish coercion laws, and a strictly pacifist policy: 'Peace, Retrenchment, and Reform' was his motto (see [rep.], 'Mr. Copland's Candidature', *NC*, 3, and also his programme in *ibid.*, p. 2 ('To the Electors and Non-Electors of Newcastle-upon-Tyne').

[312] [Rep.], 'Irish Electors' Meeting – Decision to Support Mr. Bruce', *ibid.* This incident suggests that Parnell possibly acted in response to popular pressure when in 1885 he asked the Irish electors to vote Conservative to spite the Liberals.

[313] [Rep.], 'Mr. Morley's Candidature – Meeting in the Circus', *ibid.*

[314] See [rep.], 'The Labour Candidate – Retirement of Mr. Copland', *ibid.*, 20 Feb. 1883, p. 3. Later Copland admitted that it had not been only because of the deposit, but also because of the declaration of the Irish electors in favour of the Tory candidate: [rep.], 'Proposed Labour Representation League for Newcastle', *NC*, 21 Feb. 1883, p. 3.

[315] For Morley's popularity among the workers, see the reports of the two meetings of 20 February: 'Mr. Morley's Candidature – Address to Quayside Workmen', *NC*, 21 Feb. 1883, p. 3; and 'Speech at Messrs. Atkinson and Philipson's Works', *ibid.*

continue, in spite of Copland's repeated candidatures,[316] until 1895, when, in the general Liberal rout, he lost his seat to a Conservative.[317]

An analogous incident took place in 1885 in Durham. After the Third Reform Act the DMA intended to have some of its men elected to the new mining constituencies. With a procedure which shows the strength and self-confidence of the pitmen's union, and the way in which this sort of 'bloc vote' worked, the Federation Board began by agreeing a salary of £500 for each of its prospective MPs, and autonomously deciding to 'reserve' three constituencies for them; it was only later that 'They further decided to inform the North and South Durham Liberal Associations about what had been done, and asked them if they would co-operate with the Board'.[318] The Liberal Associations readily accepted, and indeed agreed to set up mixed electoral committees made up of the representatives of the caucus, of the Federation Board, and of the miners' Franchise Association.[319] The 'reserved' constituencies were: Mid-Durham for W. Crawford; Houghton-le-Spring for J. Wilson; and Bishop Auckland for J. Trotter. The agreement was that no other Liberal candidate would stand for these constituencies, and the miners would accept Liberal candidates for the other constituencies.[320] However in the district of Chester-le-Street – which had been assigned to the Liberal Associations, and for which the official candidate was a mineowner popular with the DMA, J. Joicey – the old journalist Lloyd Jones decided to stand as an unofficial Lib-lab candidate. A former contributor to the *Bee-Hive* and still active as a labour writer, Lloyd Jones was very popular among the Durham miners – who eleven times invited him to their Galas between 1873 and 1885[321] – and his thinking had deeply influenced many DMA leaders, including William Crawford.[322] It

---

[316] At the 1885 general elections Copland's candidature was presented at a controversial workers' meeting, during which many from the floor shouted their support for Cowen and Morley as the representatives in whom the working class could put its trust. After a resolution which split the audience evenly, the resolution in favour of Copland was re-worded as a general resolution in favour of 'a labour candidate', and only then was approved ([rep.], 'Newcastle election of a Labour candidate', *NC*, 20 Aug. 1885, p. 3.

[317] Hamer, *Morley*, p. 305.

[318] Wilson, *A History* (1910), p. 194.

[319] *Ibid.*, p. 195.

[320] *Ibid.*, p. 196.

[321] See *DMA, 101st Annual Gala*, pp. 44–5.

[322] Clegg et al., *A History of British Trade Unions*, I, p. 437.

was therefore probably a mistake not to offer him a constituency,[323] not least because Lloyd Jones was also an intimate friend of Cowen's, who no doubt desired to see him as a candidate, and would have been particularly keen to support him against the nominations of the Liberal Associations.

If Cowen did try to create problems for the Chester-le-Street caucus by getting it into conflict with the electors, he was completely successful: the only weak point in his plan was that in this case the caucus also included delegates from the pitmen's union and Franchise Association. The miners' leaders found themselves having to choose whether to break the previous agreement with the Liberal Associations, or deprive an old and trusted friend of their electoral support. In the meantime Lloyd Jones, who was a great orator, raged throughout the Chester-le-Street constituency with a series of very successful meetings,[324] actively publicized by the *Newcastle Chronicle*, during an electoral campaign which went on for months[325] and which increasingly assumed an anti-caucus tone.[326] By August rank-and-file miners everywhere were in revolt against their union and proclaimed their support for Lloyd Jones rather than for Joicey.[327]

The situation was becoming untenable, but relief came at the end of October when Trotter – one of the Lib-lab candidates for Bishop Auckland, a DMA constituency – decided to withdraw for reasons which allegedly had nothing to do with the conflict at Chester-le-Street.[328] In any case, the Federation Board immediately sent a deputation – consisting of some of its most representative and authoritative members – to Lloyd Jones, to offer him the

---

[323] Metcalfe, *A History*, I, p. 437.

[324] See [rep.], 'Lloyd Jones at Winlaton', *NC*, 16 Mar. 1885, p. 3; [rep.], 'Mr. Lloyd Jones at Gateshead', *NC*, 19 Mar. 1885, p. 3; [rep.] 'Mr. Lloyd Jones at Birtley', *NC*, 20 Mar. 1885, p. 3.

[325] [Rep.], 'Mr. Lloyd Jones at Kibbleworth – Unanimous Vote of Confidence', *NC*, 19 Jun. 1885, p. 3; [rep.], 'Enthusiastic Meeting at Swalwell', *ibid.*

[326] [Rep.], 'The Chester-le-Street Division – Mr. Lloyd Jones' Address', *NC*, 8 Aug. 1885, p. 3.

[327] Cf. the speeches at the above quoted meeting and the following letters to the press: 'Inquiry', 'Capital v. Labour', *NC*, 16 Mar. 1885, p. 3; J. Tweddle, 'The Selection of Candidates', *ibid.* (stressing that a good point about Joicey was that he was a 'local man'); G. S. Scott, *NC*, 20 Mar. 1885, p. 3; C. Simpson, 'The Durham Miners and Mr. Lloyd Jones', *NC*, 30 Mar. 1885, p. 3 (accusing Crawford of having ignored the requests of the rank-and-file by excluding Lloyd Jones).

[328] Wilson, *A History* (1910), p. 196.

candidature.[329] But Lloyd Jones declined, probably because he thought that it was too late to start a new campaign even for what the miners promised would be 'a safe seat';[330] but surely also because he had committed himself to the anti-caucus crusade at Chester, and being – as John Wilson remarked – 'Cowen's nominee', 'It was felt that he was not free . . .'.[331]

The outcome of the election was that Crawford and Wilson were both returned to their 'reserved' constituencies, while Lloyd Jones was defeated at Chester-le-Street, which went to the official Liberal candidate, Joicey. Bishop Auckland – the third DMA seat which had been offered to Lloyd Jones – went to a Liberal candidate selected by the local Liberal Association at the eleventh hour, once they had obtained the DMA's authorization to proceed. Thus the attempt by Cowen and Lloyd Jones to ignore the caucus even when this was made up of delegates of trade unions and labour associations not only wreaked havoc among working-class electors and endangered the prestige, authority, and organization of one of the most important trade unions in the United Kingdom; but also caused a net loss for the cause of labour representation.

The traditional approach to electioneering had undoubted moral value and constitutional legitimacy, but it was increasingly out of tune with the reality of politics. The old model was not applicable to labour representation because – as demonstrated by the repeated failures of able and intelligent politicians like Howell, Broadhurst, Odger, and others – working-class candidates on their own had no resources to counterbalance the wealth and influence of middle- and upper-class opponents: in fact, the poorer the candidate was, the more important party organization became. The most effective formula was the mixture of trade union-chapel-party which stood behind the north-eastern Lib-labs: as a Miners' Federation Board circular stated in 1884, this meant the formation of strong 'caucuses', or 'Political Associations, to be worked in close alliance with the Labour Associations' (namely the trade unions), having as 'their special work both to give political information, watch political events, and when the time came utilize the dual power thus possessed', to ensure the return of labour candidates. 'The establishment of such Political Associations' – the circular con-

[329] Metcalfe, *A History*, pp. 437–8.
[330] Wilson, *A History* (1910), p. 197.
[331] *Ibid.*

cluded – 'is in keeping with the progressive spirit of the age.'[332] Even in other parts of the country those who intended to make 'direct representation' workable followed this method, either by setting up radical organizations (as John Burns did at Battersea in 1892),[333] or through the 'permeation' of the official Liberal caucuses (as in the case of J. Havelock Wilson at Middlesborough).[334] And it is interesting to observe that, wherever this manoeuvre was successful, popular Liberalism retained an extraordinary strength, and independent Labour politics spread only with difficulty and at a later stage than elsewhere.[335]

In conclusion, Cowen's struggle against the very principle of the caucus was the futile last battle of a romantic supporter of the old, 'direct' style of popular politics. He could afford the luxury of indulging in this nostalgia because of his personal wealth and charisma: but his principles could not have been carried out by labour candidates, who – in contrast – were then successfully extending trade union discipline and organization into politics. In this respect, Cowen's stress on 'free elections' might be considered as a political parallel to the 'free labour', eulogized by some Liberals, but totally at odds with the real needs of the working classes. Therefore it is no surprise that Cowen's persistence in his anti-party mood eventually caused the break-up of his relationship with the DMA,[336] just as previously it had spoiled his long and close friendship with Thomas Burt,[337] and led to a crisis in Newcastle popular Liberalism.

---

[332] Circular signed by all the main leaders of the miners of Northumberland, Durham and Yorkshire (T. Burt, B. Pickard, J. Nixon, J. Wilson, E. Cowey, D. Reid, T. Toyne, W. Wight, W. Crawford), describing the Manchester conference of 24 Apr. 1884, *DMA, Minutes and Balance Sheets from July to September 1884*, Durham 1884, p. 4, in D/DMA8.

[333] Clegg et al., *A History of British Trade Unions*, p. 277.

[334] Wilson, *Life*, I, pp. 246–50.

[335] Such a 'delay' did not take place only in Durham, but also, e.g., in London, where as late as 1906 the ILP managed to conquer only two peripheral constituencies, Deptford and Woolwich, in contrast to a phalanx of Liberal radicals returned by other working class constituencies (Pelling, *Social Geography*, p. 58; Thane, 'Labour and Local Politics', in Biagini and Reid (eds.), *Currents of Radicalism*, pp. 244–70).

[336] See J. Cowen to W. Crawford, 10 Aug. 1886, *DMA, Minutes and Balance Sheets, 1886*, p. 85: Cowen resigned as a Trustee of the DMA arguing that he was going to leave on a journey and was uncertain about his future; see also *J. Cowen Coll.*, B393, newspaper cutting dated 21 Mar. 1893, about the bad relations between the DMA and Cowen.

[337] From 1881; see Burt's reply to Howell, who had asked the miners' leader to intercede for him with Cowen for a candidature:

Private

Mr. Cowen and I are strict friends but from the way he and his paper are treating me over the

Irish question I am sure he will not say a word in your favour unless you are prepared to follow Mr. Parnell and his party, blindfold, and surrender your own judgement. But I know that will not do. The Newcastle Chronicle (Mr. Cowen's paper) has for long been doing its foremost to discredit & devalue the Liberal Party in the North & to help the Tories. I need say no more on that point. Of course I cannot ask him to help you in any way. (T. Burt to George Howell, 12 Nov. 1881, in *G. Howell Coll.*, Ind.).

It is interesting to note that this great labour leader was here applying back to Cowen Cowen's own charge against the caucus, that of exercising despotic pressure and imposing unconditional adhesion to sectarian policies.

CHAPTER 7

The charismatic leader

In our hearts, GARIBALDI! thy place hath been given
Near Liberty's martyr, our WALLACE, in Heaven:
Like valour, like virtues, unselfish and pure
Thou conqer'd, hast suffer'd, hast learned to endure.
[. . .]
Reformers, we urge on the tide of Reform
With the shock of earthquake, the roar of storm
Advancing, progressive, majestic and grand,
Till sweeping resistless, it rolls o'er the land.[1]

It may be said of Mr Gladstone that he found the
people who live in cottages hostile to political parties,
and that he had succeeded in uniting them with the rest
of his countrymen. Those who are old enough to remember the sentiments of the working classes thirty or forty
[years] ago will not need to be told that they were a
nation apart, that they had nothing in common with the
political parties of the day, that they were, in fact, at
war with every government which came into existence.
Well, Mr Gladstone has remedied this unhappy state of
things. Politics now, at all events to a large extent, are of
no class. Working men, instead of being a party of
themselves, are honourably associated with the great
party of progress. That this revolution – for it is a
revolution – has been brought about by Mr Gladstone
is, I think, the grandest and most gratifying feature of
his career. If England is more a nation and less an
aggregation of classes than she was a generation ago, we
ought not to forget to whom we owe the beneficient
change.[2]

---

[1] Hamilton, *Poems and Ballads* (1868), p. 88.
[2] Ironside, 'Mr. Gladstone', *NW*, 7 Aug. 1880, p. 4.

THE NEED FOR A CHARISMATIC LEADER

The contrast between the vicissitudes of some Lib-labs, such as Broadhurst and Howell, and the unwavering popularity of others, such as Burt and 'Mabon', shows that within the framework of community politics there were two factors which were most important for a successful leader and representative of working men's liberalism: namely, personal charisma and 'party' organization (whether the latter took the form of the caucus, trade union, or both). However, we have already seen that charisma alone, without – or even against – party organization could be insufficient, as suggested by the 1885 defeat of Lloyd Jones. On the other hand, party organization could hardly be effective without a charismatic leader providing a focus for rank-and-file attention, as suggested by the growing difficulties of Newcastle Liberalism once Cowen and the caucus were openly and irreconcilably set against each other. That not only miners' leaders in strongly-unionized areas, but also men like Joseph Arch – whose 'party' backup was comparatively slight – could make successful candidates, relying on the fact that their stirring rhetoric and ability as mass communicators would attract 'party' support for them, suggests that of the two afore-mentioned elements charisma was ultimately the most important.

Similar was the situation at the level of national politics. Especially before 1886 the NLF was a decentralized and heterogeneous body for the representation and discussion of internal opinion, rather than for the imposition of programmes on the parliamentary party, and was far from being fully institutionalized.[3] There lacked a precise definition of the authority of the leader and his relationship with the constituency associations and the parliamentary party – a fluid situation which, in various ways, has for a long time remained typical of the Liberal party.[4] In this 'absence of formal party structure', charismatic leaders and 'the policies developed in their rhetoric' could become 'the unifying and determining element which made up the Liberal party in the late nineteenth century'.[5] In a system in which bureaucratic control played a marginal role, the authority of the leader could impose

---

[3] McGill, 'Schnadhorst and Liberal Party Organization', pp. 19–39.
[4] See Cook, *History of the Liberal Party*, p. 123.
[5] Matthew, 'Rhetoric and Politics in Great Britain', p. 53.

itself only as something 'foreign to all rules',[6] through the art of persuasion, the 'charisma of rhetoric',[7] 'the force of the demagogic speech'.[8]

Max Weber wrote that the development of 'demagogy' – intended in a purely descriptive, value-free sense, as popular and populist rhetoric – and the cult of the democratic leader are both functions of the enlargement of the franchise.[9] This is well illustrated in the case of Britain, as we have seen in the previous chapter. It is true that here 'demagogy' is much older than democracy, going back to the eighteenth century,[10] and already important during the first half of the nineteenth century, when the major radical tribunes were able to unify popular radicalism under some sort of national leadership.[11] However, these 'demagogues' exercised mainly 'pressure from without': it was only with the enlargement of the franchise that popular rhetoric acquired any direct influence within the representative system. This development was emphasized by technological changes which transformed the style and effectiveness of political communications,[12] made it much easier to set up and sustain a national debate, and conferred on the 'demagogues' a definite capacity for influencing and unifying 'party' opinion.[13]

In chapter 5 we have seen that popular mobilization for Reform in 1864–67 was articulated in three phases: 1) a state of agitation was generated by the impact of a series of 'great events' with or without an immediate connection with the franchise question; 2) anti-reform reaction produced popular indignation and provided the radicals with mass support; finally, 3) outstanding leaders emerged to exercise a unifying influence on all sections of the extra-

---

[6] Weber, *Theory*, p. 361.
[7] Weber, *Selections*, p. 244.
[8] Weber, *Politics as a Vocation*, p. 32.
[9] Weber, *Theory*, p. 421. Weber had in mind especially the cases of Britain and the United States, though subsequent scholars have applied this or similar models rather to Germany, Italy, the Soviet Union, and third-world countries (see Willner and Willner, 'The Rise and Role of Charismatic Leaders', p. 358; Lindholm, *Charisma*, pp. 93–116). In the process they have placed much emphasis on the dictatorial aspects of charismatic leadership. As a consequence there is now the risk of linking it exclusively to forms of totalitarianism, though the context in which it was first elaborated was that of prosperous liberal democracies.
[10] E.g. Rude, *Wilkes*, pp. 26–7, 39–42, 68–71.
[11] Belchem, *'Orator' Hunt*.
[12] Vincent, *The Formation*, p. 96.
[13] Matthew, 'Rhetoric and Politics', pp. 41ff.

parliamentary movement. This scheme is also useful for understanding the years between 1853 and 1865, when popular radicalism was reorganized around a post-Chartist platform and
'nationalized',[14] as it gradually switched its focus from local to
national issues. This process began as a result of the impact of
international events which for twelve years – between 1853 and
1865 – produced a state of almost continuous uproar throughout
the country, and provided the impetus for the new mass press to
take off.[15]

The first of these events, the Crimean War, was initially
perceived as an exciting military adventure, with the ideological
spur of liberal and democratic hatred for autocratic Russia, which
was seen as the driving force behind the Leviathan of Continental
despotism. Later, the war revealed the inefficiency of the British
army and civil service, thus exposing the aristocratic system on
which they were based, and further exciting radical reformers.

However, the decisive turning point came in the decade following the Paris Treaty, with the Italian Risorgimento and the
American Civil War. For about eight years – from Orsini's attempt
at Napoleon III in 1858 to the assassination of Lincoln in 1865 –
these events provided popular journalism with a supply of sensational news which could easily be interpreted in a radical way,
but which did not reproduce the atmosphere of social antagonism
typical of the Chartist unrest. The cumulative effect of these great
events was to revive working-class interest in politics.

The Risorgimento had all the prerequisites for exciting both the
inveterate Protestant hatred for popery, and the popular Whig
sympathy for peoples fighting for national independence and
constitutional liberty. Moreover, the Risorgimento leaders also
provided the symbolic focus which plebeian radicalism needed to
translate ideals from the realm of abstraction into that of political
reality. In the first chapter we saw that Mazzini had passionate
admirers in Britain: however, it was Giuseppe Garibaldi who best
personified the reasons for the British love of the Risorgimento.

Garibaldi's popularity had become evident during his 1854 visit
to Newcastle, and was confirmed in 1860, when a volunteer British

[14] Vincent, *The Formation*, pp. 15, 19–20.
[15] Catling, *My Life* (1911), pp. 42–3. See Lee, *Origins of the Popular Press*, pp. 67–9.

Legion joined his army in southern Italy.[16] Two years later, after
the Aspromonte incident, the English fought again for 'the General', this time in Hyde Park, during the famous riots.[17] But the
full extent of Garibaldi's popularity was realised only during his
1864 tour. The whole country – from London to Scotland –
celebrated the event, and popular sentimental verse became the
most expressive interpreter of the general feeling.[18] Janet Hamilton
– the radical bard of the Glasgow workers – sang:

> The warm bluid's swallin' like the tide
> Through my auld heart; the ran tears glide
> Adown my cheek, for joy and pride,
> To shake yer haun', and, side by side,
> Staun' wi' my Garibaldi!
>
> I ca' ye mine, for ye're the brither
> O' my ain Wallace; twa sic ither
> Ne'ever leeved upon the yirth thegither,
> Blest among women was the mither
> That bore thee, Garibaldi![19]

She saw Garibaldi as a liberator, a sort of Italian Moses or Joshua,
simple and sublime at one and the same time, the 'eagle' of Liberty
which put to flight the 'vultures' of Tyranny and threw open the
filthy prisons of slavery to let in the atoning light of Heaven. A
staunch Evangelical, Janet Hamilton often invited 'the General' to
go straight to the heart of the evils of Italy: to strike at popery
more effectively he should become 'Soldier of the Cross, a victor /
In the battles of the Lord.'[20]

In fact not only in Scotland, but all over the country Protestants
and Radicals set up welcoming committees for the man who had
cracked the Temporal power of 'Babylon'. Liberal activists who
had long tried in vain to arouse enthusiasm for franchise reform,

---

[16] See Trevelyan, *Garibaldi and the Making of Italy*, pp. 98, 259–60, 279; McIntire, *England against the Papacy*; Holyoake, *Bygones Worth Remembering*, I, pp. 243–59; MacAdam, *Autobiography*, pp. 130ff. See also Todd, *Cowen*, pp. 17–22.

[17] See Gilley, 'The Garibaldi Riots of 1862', pp. 697–732.

[18] For some examples, see Marian Richardson, 'A Welcome to Garibaldi', *BH*, 2 Apr. 1864, p. 1; T. Butler, 'Garibaldi', *BH*, 16 Apr. 1864, p. 4; M. Richardson, 'Farewell to Garibaldi', *BH*, 30 Apr. 1864, p. 1; M. F. Tupper, 'Garibaldi', *BH*, 21 May 1864, p. 4.

[19] Hamilton., 'Auld Scotland's Welcome to Garibaldi', in *Poems, Essays, and Sketches* (1870), p. 164.

[20] Hamilton, 'Garibaldi's Mission', in *Poems and Ballads* (1868), p. 90.

suddenly found themselves at the centre of a mass movement such as had not been seen for years.

It was with a view to welcoming Garibaldi that for the first time the London trades unions took up an official position on an issue with clear political undertones: if we consider that the fear of breaking up the labour movement had previously prevented the trade union leadership from even commenting on politics,[21] it appears that 'the General's' visit was the real turning point which quickened the radical revival. Proclamations exalting Garibaldi and his work as a democratic leader were printed by the trade union leaders and circularized among members.[22] Even the *Bee-Hive* – which for a long time had been unable to take a consistent position on the issue of the American Civil War[23] – acclaimed Garibaldi as the 'Friend of the Working Man', 'a man of the people' and 'the Man of the People', 'a modern Cincinnatus';[24] 'Joseph Garibaldi has, indeed, lived and struggled, not for himself, not alone for his country's freedom, but for freedom in all parts of the world.'[25]

When eventually 'the General' arrived in London, huge crowds were waiting to welcome him, thronging the streets from Nine Elms station to Stafford House, where he was to stay. Preceded and followed by a trade union procession with bands and banners, Garibaldi's coach moved on 'amid vast continuous multitudes, blocking roadways, filling windows, lining every parapet and roof with eager gazers. For five hours Garibaldi passed on amid tumultuous waves of passionate curiosity, delight, enthusiasm.'[26]

[21] See [rep.], 'London Trades' Council', *BH*, 26 Mar. 1864, p. 5: 'The Council has been appealed to to take part in many political questions; such as the American, the Polish, and the Suffrage question; on each of these subjects we have felt to be our duty as Council to take no action, leaving the members as individual Unionists to do as they please in such matters.'

[22] [Rep.], 'Garibaldi in England', *BH*, 26 Mar. 1864, p. 1; see [rep.], 'Garibaldi's Visit to England – Meeting of the Reception Committee' *BH*, 2 Apr. 1864, p. 1; [rep.], 'The Arrival of Garibaldi', *BH*, 9 Apr. 1864, p. 1.

[23] See Harrison, *Before the Socialists*, pp. 42–50.

[24] [L.a.], 'The Arrival of Garibaldi', *BH*, 26 Mar. 1864, p. 4.

[25] *Ibid* . . . Howell wrote:

Garibaldi is on his way to England . . . Every lover of liberty is expected to meet and receive this great, good and honest patriot, and give him a working man's welcome. The name of Garibaldi, his deeds, his sufferings have been a household word in our homes; his sword has ever been drawn on the side of right and defence of public liberty – then, as free men, meet him and prove your faithful gratitude for his honesty and patriotism by giving him a honest and sincere welcome.' (*The Operative Bricklayers' Trade Circular*, 1 Apr. 1864, p. 263).

[26] Morley, *Gladstone*, II, p. 109; see Mack Smith, *Garibaldi*, pp. 133–47; Beales, 'Garibaldi in England', pp. 184–216.

The very fact that it took five hours to travel three miles is in itself
an indication of the density of the crowd. Amidst continuous
cheering, acclamation, waving of handkerchiefs, and the music of
the bands, enraptured men and women thronged the coach trying
to shake 'the General's' hand, or at least to touch his clothes. He –
always smiling and available – seemed to personify the ideals with
which he was popularly identified. When, in responding to the
address by the Working Men's Committee, Garibaldi said that he
was honoured to belong to the 'working class', popular enthusiasm
reached a climax: loud and sustained acclamations[27] showed that
with these words he had expressed one of the reasons why the
crowd idolized him – 'In honouring such a man . . . we but honour
ourselves'.[28]

It was on this sense of identification that Garibaldi's charisma
was based. His appeal was important because it involved not only
the radical activists, but also huge numbers of non-political people,
the crowds of 'indifferents'. The latter could be brought into the
arena of political commitment only occasionally, whenever they
were affected by any extraordinarily intense emotional stimulus,
which affected prejudices and convictions deeply rooted in the
collective subconscious.

Between 1861 and 1865, and especially from 1863, the American
Civil War generated a similar excitement and mobilization on a
larger scale. Like the Italian Risorgimento, it offered to British
popular radicalism a platform which was democratic but not
socially threatening, and leaders who personified and popularized
it. In this way it stabilized a sort of 'Garibaldian' political platform,
giving it an increased ideological articulacy and feasibility, and a
focus on a national leader, John Bright.

In the early 1860s Bright's popular appeal and prestige increased
considerably. The repeal of the 'bread tax' and the growing mid-
Victorian prosperity brought credit both to him and to Cobden;
but, in contrast to Cobden, Bright could also claim an almost
uninterrupted commitment to the enfranchisement of the working
classes. Bright's style and ability as an orator, and his simple but
effective language, were the gifts which enabled him to exercise the
kind of moralistic appeal to which the subaltern classes were

---

[27] [Rep.], 'Garibaldi's Entry in London', *BH*, 16 Apr. 1864, p. 1; the report (6 columns)
occupied the first page completely.
[28] [L.a.], 'The Arrival of Garibaldi', *BH*, 26 Mar. 1864, p. 4.

receptive.[29] In the late 1850s he lacked only some great political event to excite popular feeling and to stir the apathy of the town workers and middle-class radicals alike. As perceived in Britain, the American Civil War became exactly that sort of event, and enabled Bright to combine all the currents of plebeian radicalism, both in London and in the 'provinces', in a great national popular liberal upheaval.

From at least as early as 1860 Bright had publicly prophesied that an armed conflict on the issue of slavery in the United States would force the British working classes to resume political activity.[30] When the hostilities ended, he did not hesitate to take the leadership of the supporters of the Federal States. Asa Briggs has written that Bright used the American Civil War as Palmerston did the Crimean War:[31] he seized on its universal dimension and linked it to the passions, hopes, and fears of the British people; he was also able, through the press,[32] to turn popular excitement into political support for his platform. As we saw in chapter 1, Bright displayed his usual firm judgement and moral sensitivity in identifying the issue at stake not as one of a 'civil' war, but as one of conflict between different models of civilization in which the working classes of the entire world had a vital interest: it was a war for or against democracy, liberty, and the dignity of labour.[33]

But Bright's argument did not rest solely on an appeal to international co-operation between workers and democrats; in fact this was subordinated to another appeal, of a logically higher order and purely moral character. Working men were presented as upholders of true political morality, in contrast with the aristocracy to whom were ascribed Pharisaic and hypocritical attitudes. With a style anticipating Gladstone's Midlothian speeches, Bright appealed to the 'people' to denounce the meanness of the wealthy and powerful, invoking against the latter the inexorable verdict of God, History, and the Nation.[34] His critics disparaged Bright's passionate rhetoric as 'the half-poetical rant and the wild perver-

[29] See Beales, 'Garibaldi in England', pp. 000.
[30] [Rep.], 'Parliamentary Reform Demonstration', *LM*, 13 Dec. 1860, at Leeds, when a Liberal Working Men's Association was established: see the first and second speech by Bright.
[31] Briggs, *Victorian People*, p. 223
[32] Vincent, *The Formation*, p. 212.
[33] Cit. in Trevelyan, *Bright*, p. 307.
[34] See for a good example Bright, *Speeches*, 1, pp. 252–53 (26 Mar. 1863).

sion of fact',[35] but the multitude of his admirers exalted it as 'true eloquence . . . [which was] none but the serious and hearty love of truth'.[36] Biblically stressing the moral superiority of 'Lazarus' over 'Dives' and the corruption which affects those who trust in material wealth, Bright clothed the cause of the working classes – the issue of Negro emancipation, but also that of the enfranchisement of British artisans – with a character of absolute sacrality. It was not the cause of one class against another, but the cause of humanity against barbarity and despotism. In Bright's words the 'people' became what 'the working class' was to Marx, and what the Third Estate had been to Sieyès: 'the Nation', the class which abolishes all classes not at a future moment, through a revolution, but by its political practice and forms of organization in the present. But Bright knew how to articulate this metamorphosis or sublimation into a language that – in contrast to the language of either Siéyés or Marx – was familiar to the great bulk of the British common people: a language in which the peroration of their rights seemed founded, as Trevelyan has written, on the joint authority of the Old and New Testaments, upon justice and humanity blended together.[37]

In this way Bright managed to consolidate a remarkable consensus throughout the country, especially after the Proclaim of Emancipation of October 1862. At that stage the names of Bright and Lincoln were closely linked in the popular mind:[38] the triumph of Lincoln reverberated on Bright, who was now exalted as 'a free, outspoken lover of freedom'.[39] The assassination of the President following the achievement of victory had the effect of emphasizing this phenomenon: 'good and great Abraham Lincoln',[40] 'a man of the people',[41] was the martyr, but the triumphant hero was 'Lincoln's friend', John Bright, who, 'above all others, [. . .] upheld

[35] 'Mr. Bright and His Audience', *BH*, 14 Feb. 1863, p. 2, quoting from the *Saturday Review*.
[36] [L.a.], 'The Presidential Election', *NW*, 5 Nov. 1868, p. 4, applying a quotation from John Milton to Bright.
[37] Trevelyan, *Bright*, pp. 2–3.
[38] Harrison, *Before the Socialists*, p. 55.
[39] *Ibid.*
[40] [Rep.], 'Assassination of President Lincoln – Great Meeting of Working Men', *BH*, 6 May 1865, pp. 5–6. See in [rep.], 'The Assassination of President Lincoln – Meetings of Sympathy', *NW*, 6 May 1865, p. 7, the meetings held in Newcastle, Gateshead and North Shields.
[41] *Ibid.*

the cause of freedom in this country'.[42] This sensation of deeply-felt gratitude lasted a long time, and was renewed by the vicissitudes of the agitation for the second Reform Bill. As a Glasgow Liberal worker – W. Freer[43] – wrote in his memoirs, in those months 'Bright was the idol of the workers':[44]

In 1866, just after the American Civil War, in which Bright had, against the general view, sided with Abraham Lincoln, the assassination of the great President and the almost sacramental nature of his obsequies had changed him [Bright] in the minds of the British. John Bright's popularity was tremendous . . . When he came to Glasgow . . . we young craftsmen organised an immense procession in his honour . . . Some of us desired to make a presentation to him. The most appropriate gift was a Bible. But we couldn't get near him. The friends at the hotel point-blank refused us entry . . . not to be outdone we strung a stout string across Argyle Street and folded the Bible over the string . . . When the carriage was approaching we lowered the string so that the Bible dropped gently in the carriage beside the great reformer. Then we rushed round to the City Hall to hear the speech.[45]

Such episodes were not frequent, but the least that happened at public meetings was that the crowds addressed by Bright accompanied his words with continuous cheering from the beginning to the end.[46] It is certain that Bright's popularity among the subaltern classes was unequalled in Britain. Many young artisans probably acquired the nickname given to Will Crooks – then an apprentice cooper in the Thames dockyards – who was such a fervent admirer of the Quaker tribune that his fellow-workers called him 'Young John Bright'.[47] Not surprisingly Freer concluded his recollections of the 1866 Glasgow demonstration with this interesting reflection:

We were all hero-worshippers in those days. Thomas Carlyle was spreading the cult of the heroic man, Joseph Mazzini had for years been hammering at thrones and systems and at the same time inspired thousands with his religious political theories, while Kossuth in Hungary and Garibaldi in Italy were doing what Kosciusko had previously attempted in Poland.[48]

---

[42] *Ibid.*
[43] It is worth noting that this staunch Gladstonian (b. 1846) was the son of a 'committed Chartist and a vitriol thrower' (Freer, *My Life* [1929], pp. 11–12).
[44] *Ibid.*, p. 125.
[45] *Ibid.*
[46] See for instance [rep.], 'Working-Class Meeting', *MG*, 6 Nov. 1868, p. 3.
[47] 'How I Got On – Life Stories by Labour M.P.'s – V. Mr. Will Crooks, M.P.', *Pearson's Weekly*, 22 Feb. 1906, p. 1.
[48] Freer, *My Life* (1929), p. 125.

THE 'PEOPLE'S WILLIAM', 1862–1876

Bright had something in common with Lincoln and Garibaldi,[49] being able to claim to be 'one of the people' whose strength rested in his wisdom and honesty. Part of this capacity was derived from his education in his Quaker meeting house, and from his earliest experiences of life in his father's factory in Rochdale: Bright had grown up in contact with simple workers, who had called him and his brother by their Christian names, and their father 'owd Jacob'.[50] Young John had his first political discussions with some of the survivors of Peterloo, who shared with him their bitterness and their hopes. Given this background, Bright could convincingly stand before his artisan electors as 'a working man as much as you'.[51] He, more than any other national politician of his day was, and remained, a 'Tribune of the People', intrinsically different from the governing elite.

It is less obvious how Bright's heritage could be passed on to, and greatly extended by a man who in many respects stood at the opposite end of the spectrum in terms both of biography and political career – namely, W. E. Gladstone.[52] Because of his social background and religious convictions Bright was a radical and tended to identify himself, and to be identified with, the mass of discontented middle- and working-class people. But for the same reasons Gladstone – son of a wealthy Liverpool merchant and slaveowner, High-Churchman educated at Eton and Oxford, then a Tory MP for a rotten borough – should have identified with the ruling class. At the beginning of his career he seemed 'predestined' to be the 'rising hope of those stern and unbending Tories', and even later, when he had settled into the Liberal party, Gladstone was by no means a 'demagogue', but almost antonomastically 'the' Chancellor of the Exchequer, an 'executive politician' born to rule.[53]

Yet, in the early 1860s something unusual began to happen. While Bright remained the last representative of the dynasty of the great 'demagogues' – the dynasty of 'Orator Hunt' – Gladstone

---

[49] Perhaps it is significant that the greatest biographer of Bright has been also the greatest biographer of Garibaldi – G. M. Trevelyan.
[50] Trevelyan, *Bright*, pp. 16–7.
[51] *Ibid.*, p. 113.
[52] Vincent, *The Formation*, p. 261; Pelling, *Popular Politics*, p. 17.
[53] Matthew, *Gladstone 1809–1874*, p. 106.

was becoming the first 'People's Chancellor' and indeed the first prospective 'Premier of the working classes': a 'demagogue-states-man', 'Sir Robert Peel and Feargus O'Connor rolled into one – an explosive combination'.[54] The first foreshadowing of this phenom-enon was his visit to Newcastle in 1862, recalled by Holyoake in 1865:

When Mr. Gladstone visited the North, you well remember when word passed from the newspaper to the workman that it circulated through mines and mills, factories and workshops, and they came out to greet the only English minister who ever gave the English people a right because it was just they should have it . . . and when he went down the Tyne, all the country heard how twenty miles of banks were lined with people who came to greet him. Men stood in the blaze of chimneys; the roofs of factories were crowded; colliers came up from the mines; women held up their children on the banks that it might be said in after life that they had seen the Chancellor of the People go by. The river was covered like the land. Every man who could ply an oar pulled up to give Mr. Gladstone a cheer . . . he heard cheers that no other English minister ever heard . . . the people were grateful to him, and rough pitmen who never approached a public man before, pressed round his carriage by thousands . . . and thousands of arms were stretched out at once, to shake hands with Mr. Gladstone as one of themselves.[55]

In 1862 Gladstone and working-class radicals were entering into an alliance that perhaps began as 'a parallel movement of fairly distinct forces',[56] but soon became a full symbiosis. This relation-ship is too complex and important to be simplistically dismissed as a product of the 'political imagination' of the working classes.[57] Gladstone, with his rich and multi-faceted personality and *Weltan-schauung*, reacted in a peculiar way to the contrasting tensions to which he was subjected from the 1860s. He had developed a specifically Christian, some would say 'Episcopalian',[58] interpreta-tion of the idea of the moral obligations of the aristocracy towards the poor, and at the same time shared the Evangelical conviction that the latter, in their humility and simplicity, were closer to God

---

[54] Taylor, *Trouble Makers*, p. 69.
[55] G. J. Holyoake, 'The Liberal Situation, or the Parliamentary Treatment of the People, II.', *NW*, 18 Mar. 1865, p. 4. H. Fraser (*Trade Unions and Society*, p. 155) maintains that the cult of Gladstone began in 1864, but an earlier date seems to be suggested by episodes like this, which was not isolated one.
[56] Feuchtwanger, *Gladstone*, p. 116.
[57] As suggested by Vincent, *The Formation*, p. 265.
[58] *Ibid.*, pp. 245–6.

than the wealthy. However, he gradually came to realize that the landed gentry no longer exercised their privileges with Peelite self-denial, and had therefore forfeited their moral justification. While disappointment pushed Gladstone towards a more critical assessment of the aristocracy – culminating in the famous 1894 attack on the Lords – he concentrated his hopes on the common people, whom he admired for their (real or supposed) puritanism and sensitivity to moral appeal.

In the early 1860s, after the frustrations suffered within the Palmerstonian alliance, Gladstone found in the subaltern classes the necessary encouragement to overcome – politically and psychologically – this impasse in his career.[59] If, politically, he needed the votes of the artisans, psychologically Gladstone needed the support of the masses to acquire that extraordinary self-confidence that enabled him to go his own way – once this had been chosen carefully – like a 'high-pressured engine'[60] on the rails. As Hammond has pointed out, other statesmen were pleased when they received expressions of popular support, but they did not feel that their own resolve grew because of the acclaim of the common people: on the contrary Gladstone came out of popular meetings 'with a confidence and a spirit immensely strengthened and encouraged by the friendship of a thousand unknown faces'.[61] In this respect he was quite unique among party leaders: indeed not even John Bright held the people in such esteem, and at times would look almost annoyed while witnessing scenes of wild popular enthusiasm which would have impressed Gladstone.[62]

---

[59] Magnus, *Gladstone*, pp. 164–65; see Shannon, 'Midlothian 100 Years After', in Jagger (ed.), *Politics and Religion*, pp. 94–6.

[60] [L.a.], 'The Premier's Industry', *NW*, 10 Jul. 1869, p. 4.

[61] Hammond, *Gladstone and the Irish Nation*, p. 709. Lady Frederick Cavendish wrote at the end of the Midlothian 1879 campaign: 'For the first time, I deliberately believe, in my recollection, he seemed a little personally elated' (cit. in Jenkins, 'Leadership of the Liberal Party', p. 344).

[62] See [rep.], 'Mr. Bright's Triumph', *LM*, 23 Oct. 1873, p. 5:

Not for a single minute, but for several, did that mighty roar of human voices continue to be heard, whilst the acres of faces in the area of the hall were hidden beneath the waving cloud of hats and handkerchiefs. Mr. Bright dressed in the familiar black coat and velvet waistcoat, and looking touchingly like his former self, stood beside the Mayor without taking any open notice of the wonderful demonstration. True, his lips quivered, his cheek flourished, and his eyes grew suddenly dim, but not even by the slightest bow did he acknowledge the enthusiasm of the greeting he received. Presently he sat down, as though anxious to bring the impressive and moving scene to an end. But still cheer after cheer went up, each seemingly louder than the last, and it was not until after repeated appeals had been made by the Mayor, that the tumult of cheer at last was stilled into comparative silence.

The mass of Gladstone's admirers were attracted not only by the comparative novelty of a statesman who openly and directly expounded great national questions to the electors,[63] but also by the reciprocal respect and moral affinity that he was able to establish with them. With Bright he shared the ethical-religious rhetorical style, and the capacity to convey the conviction that he was 'passionately in earnest, sincere not only in his opinions, but in his treatment of their [the common people's] right to be asked their opinion'; it was his 'sensibility for the self-respect of others [. . .] [which] gained for him their intuitive sympathy'.[64] His working-class audience – who thought they had an instinctive capacity for recognizing their real friends[65] – saw in Gladstone traits which brought to mind the familiar image of an Old Testament prophet. Their excitement was further increased by the impression that the very qualities which endeared him to them, made him hateful to the ruling classes:

It is Mr. Gladstone's moral position, as the embodiment of the collective wisdom of the people, and representing the collective opinions and feelings of the people, which marks him out as a target at which to discharge the poisoned arrows of Conservative abuse and malignity.[66]

In spite of his aristocratic upbringing, Gladstone's popularity was partly due to the fact that – like Bright, Lincoln and Garibaldi – he did *not* belong to the nobility, and could be seen as standing for the 'subversive' principle of promotion through merit and capacity, rather than privilege. In this sense it was the traditional hostility to 'squirearchy' which dominated popular perceptions both of Gladstone, and of his achievements: typically, a letter to *Reynolds's Newspaper* recapitulating the reforms introduced by the 1868–74 government presented almost all of his most important legislative measures as either explicitly anti-aristocratic (4 out of 9), or implicitly so (3 out of 9),[67] If the Liberal government disappointed the people, it was not Gladstone's fault, but only that

---

[63] The novelty was pointed out by *The Times* with some concern in the early 1860s: [l.a., n.t.], *TI*, 20 Oct. 1864, p. 6.
[64] Hammond, *Gladstone and the Irish Nation*, p. 707.
[65] [L.a.], 'The Greatest Working Man in England' (i.e. Gladstone), *LW*, 15 Apr. 1866, p. 1.
[66] [Lett. by] R Bulgin, 'Mr. Gladstone's Position', *BH*, 10 Oct. 1868, p. 7.
[67] [Lett. by] A. Mackenzie, 'Justice to England', *RN*, 8 Mar. 1874.

of his aristocratic ministers and 'treacherous' majority;[68] in contrast, Gladstone alone had stood up against the 'social tyranny' embodied in the system of 'Old Corruption'.[69]

The anti-aristocratic component makes it easier to understand why Gladstone and Bright were given all the credit for the 1867 electoral reform, which, after all, had been passed as a result of the efforts of Disraeli. Just as in the case of Garibaldi's triumph in 1864, by exalting Gladstone and Bright the radical common people celebrated their own victory, the victory of those who recognized themselves in what men like Gladstone and Bright stood for. In this way, despite the intricate manoeuvring which led to the 1867 Reform Act, Gladstone managed to remain, in the eyes of working-class radicals, the man in whose honesty 'Our faith is not shaken'.[70]

Gladstone's high moral standards and style, together with his puritan respect for the 'man who earns his livelihood' were also elements of his success, especially with the Nonconformists,[71] who became his staunchest supporters and his strategic reserve among the subaltern classes. To them, the Biblical overtones of his rhetoric were easily linked to the 'golden age' of popular liberalism and Dissent, the period of Cromwell's Commonwealth:

> The Cause for which our Milton wrote, for which our Eliot died,
> The Cause that charged with Cromwell on Marston's bloody Moor,
> [. . .]
> Hurrah! for *that*, the Good Old Cause, again we strike today;
> Again the Tories bar our path, again deny us right,
> But do we doubt we'll win our way with Gladstone and with Bright![72]

On the eve of the general elections of 1868 his popularity reached a first zenith: Walter Bagehot wrote that during the electoral

---

[68] [L.a.], 'The Dissolution of Parliament', *RN*, 1 Feb. 1874, p. 1:

Mr. Disraeli's Parliament of 1868–1873 is no more. Mr. Gladstone could do nothing with it that was good . . . By a kind of "happy dispatch" Mr. Gladstone resolved to appeal – over the heads of the Opposition, of his own party, and of his own colleagues – to the people. Mr. Gladstone has had enough of it, and he seems to have suddenly conceived an idea that the virtue which was not to be found in parliament was to be found in the ranks of the people . . . Mr. Gladstone wisely resolved to appeal to Caesar, for the only Caesar is the people.

[69] Gracchus, 'Social Tyranny', *RN*, 15 Nov. 1876, p. 3.

[70] [L.a.], 'Are We to Have an Honest Reform Bill?', *BH*, 2 Mar. 1867, p. 4; cf. [l.a., n.t.], *LM*, 20 Dec. 1867, p. 2.

[71] Machin, *Politics and the Churches in Great Britain, 1832–1868*, pp. 327–8.

[72] 'With Gladstone and with Bright. A Song for the People' in G. Howell Coll., 'Poems, Songs'. See G. Howell to T. W. White, York Branch [of the Reform League], 15 May 1867, in *G. Howell Coll., Lett. Bk*, 626: 'at present the House itself is so rotten that many of our efforts are wasted. We want Gladstone to firmly plant his foot on some ground simple principle and call all the reformers to him': almost a call for a Lord Protector!

campaign the very mention of Gladstone's name at Liberal meetings was sufficient to excite waves of cheers and applause.[73] Like
Garibaldi, Gladstone too was the theme of popular poems. One of
them read:

> 'Who's the Liberal Leader, who?'
> Hark to all their fuss;
> Tory-Whigs would settle that, Never asking us.
> We the People have a voice
> In that question still;
> Yes, and Gladstone is our choice,
> Choose they who they will;
> At the hustings he would need us
> He shall know that Gladstone leads us.
>
> Who's the Liberal Leader? he
> Who for us has stood, Stood through triumph and defeat
> For the People's good;
> We the People have a mind
> Well, it shall be known,
> Gladstone, he shall lead us still,
> He and he alone.
> We have votes and let them need us
> Gladstone, he alone shall lead us.
> Why? Because our wrongs he feels
> And our right would win;
> Why? Because for us he fights
> Out of power and in. [. . .]
> Voters, tell them, they who'll need us
> Gladstone, he alone shall lead us.[74]

In another song 'the man of the People' was celebrated as:

> Hope of the Nation! England's man to be,
> Gladstone – vanguard of liberty . . .
> In faith go forth! And round their cause on thee
> The people in their million's strength shall throng . . .[75]

The 'People' claimed to have a right to nominate him Premier,
independent of the Queen's personal preferences.[76] When eventually he was appointed, popular enthusiasm was such that the event
was almost seen as the beginning of the Millennium: 'To myself,

[73] Bagehot, *English Constitution*, p. 274.
[74] W. J. Bennet, 'Gladstone, He Alone Shall Lead Us', *BH*, 4 Apr. 1868, p. 5.
[75] A. G. Murdoch, 'Gladstone', *The Reformer*, 29 Sept. 1868.
[76] Plain Dealer, 'Gladstone and His Party', *BH*, 28 Nov. 1868, p. 4.

and to many thousands' – the ex-Chartist T. Frost wrote – 'the assumption by Mr. Gladstone of the leadership of the Liberal party in the House of Commons seemed to promise the inauguration of a new era'.[77] The euphoric atmosphere of those days is testified in a political song composed to the tune of a famous hymn:

> 'See the conquering hero comes!' . . .
> His golden chariot brings him. Hale, the guns
> Of liberty speak forth upon the gale.
> Gladstone! Gladstone! on the electric runs
> The chief of England new, o'er hill and dale.
> Like household words are welcomed: freedom reigns.
> The franchise to the world its needs proclaims.[78]

THE BULGARIAN AGITATION AND THE ORIGINS OF THE 'DEMAGOGUE'

Even if Gladstone was a Premier imposed by public opinion on the parliamentary majority and the Queen herself,[79] even if during his five years in power he managed to preserve the support of the working classes to a greater extent than often alleged,[80] his transformation into a 'demagogue-statesman' had not yet been completed by the time he resigned the party's leadership in 1875. In reality, his resignation was the turning point in his career, anticipating the great change which took place between 1876 and 1879.

---

[77] Frost, *Recollections* (1880), 291.

[78] A. Innes, 'The Result', *BH*, 12 Dec. 1868, p. 6.

[79] Vincent, *The Formation*, p. 260.

[80] Though already very critical towards Gladstone, *Lloyd's Weekly* declared in 1871:

> Were we casting up an estimate of Mr. Gladstone's claims on the gratitude of his contemporaries and of posterity, we should find no words of praise too strong – no tribute of veneration and thankfulness overmuch. Mr. Gladstone has done more than any living statesman for the welfare of the people in England. His life is at once an example to his countrymen and an honour to the fame of our race abroad. He is a mighty worker, a man of deep and passionate thought for common good. ([l.a.], 'Mr. Gladstone at Greenwich', *LW*, 29 Oct. 1871, p. 6)

See [l.a.], 'Mr. Gladstone and His Critics', *WT*, 6 Aug. 1871, p. 1; [l.a.], 'Mr. Gladstone and the People', *RN*, 30 Mar. 1873, p. 1). In the north support for Gladstone was more deeply rooted: for instance G. Julian Harney wrote in March 1874: 'Take Gladstone with all his mistakes, his faults, his weakness, who will deny that he is a man of sincerity, a man of honour, a man whose brilliant capacities Englishmen, even the humblest, may feel a natural and national pride? Doesn't one insult common sense by comparing such a man with the leader of the Conservatives?' (G. J. Harney, 'Mr. George Julian Harney on the General Elections', *NW*, 28 Mar. 1874, p. 5). See also the discussion of the 1874 Liberal defeat above, pp. 112–9, 162–4.

Plebeian Liberal activists perceived and reacted to this transformation in different ways in different regions. Gladstone's popularity declined in London after the early 1870s, to such an extent that in 1875 he decided to give up his Greenwich seat.[81] By contrast, in Wales and the Nonconformist north,[82] his support did not suffer in the same way. In Wales, when he presided over the 1873 Eisteddfod, 'His reception was most enthusiastic, and the large concourse of people listened to his rounded periods with delight'.[83] In 1874, in the north of England both the old Nonconformist radicalism of the *Leeds Mercury*,[84] and the new working-class radicalism of Cowen and Thomas Burt[85] were aligned behind Gladstone, while from Manchester the *Guardian* provided its readers with electrifying descriptions of Gladstone's campaign:

The scene at Blackheath yesterday was typical. A dense mist, a drizzling rain, a rude platform hastily put up, in the midst Mr. Gladstone with his hat off, regardless of weather and intent only on the work in hand; round about a multitude of men equally regardless of discomfort, applauding with enthusiasm. This is the Liberal party and their chief. There have been discouragements, but they are now forgotten; there have been defections, but there will be defections no longer. The party is united round a statesman whom it admires and trusts. It is resolute to succeed, and by that very resolution almost assures success.[86]

The outcome of the election was a surprise, as we have seen,[87] but it did not diminish popular Liberal loyalty to Gladstone. On the contrary, as time went on, the ex-premier's semi-retirement had the effect of eradicating the memories of disappointments that

---

[81] Matthew, 'Introduction' to *Diaries*, IX, p. liv; see Crossick, *An Artisan Elite*, pp. 225–26.

[82] In spite of Gladstone's education policy and his hostility to disestablishment, which he stressed just before the general election [rep.], 'The Nonconformists and the General Elections', *LM*, 28 Jan. 1874, p. 8.

[83] [L.a.], 'The Welsh Festival', *LW*, 24 Aug. 1873, p. 6. A popularity which must have been reinforced by Gladstone's decision to appoint to the see of St Asaph Joshua Hughes, as the first Welsh-speaking bishop for over a century: K. O. Morgan, 'Gladstone and Wales', p. 67–8.

[84] [L.a., n.t.], *LM*, 26 Jan. 1874, p. 2.

[85] Cf. [rep.], 'Great Meeting of Mr. Cowen's Supporters in the Town Hall – Enthusiastic Proceedings', *NW*, 10 Jan. 1874, p. 3, [Cowen's speech]: 'Gentlemen, if I go to Parliament, I will recognise as my trusted leaders Mr. Gladstone and Mr. Bright – (great cheers) – two men to whom we are more indebted for our enlarged political freedom and extended commercial prosperity than to any other two men now living within the confines of this kingdom. (Hear, hear, and renewed cheering). See also [rep.], 'Local Elections', *NW*, 31 Jan. 1874, p. 3.

[86] [L.a., n.t.], *MG*, 29 Jan. 1874, p. 5.

[87] See above, chapter 2, pp. 188–9.

working-class radicals had suffered, and of enhancing those of the triumphs obtained under his leadership.

In the meantime, a new generation was coming of age: it was to know Gladstone only in his post-1876 version, and represented the majority of those who stuck to him with blind passion and unconditional loyalty until 1894. To some extent, therefore, the transformation in Gladstone's political personality was accompanied by a generational change in his support.

It is significant that – in the aftermath of 1874 – the renewal of popular support for Liberalism took the form almost of a personal devotion to Gladstone, rather than to his party or government.[88] In 1875, when Gladstone resigned the leadership, though *Lloyd's Weekly* was further entrenched in its anti-Gladstonian mood,[89] the great majority of commentators adamantly stressed that no statesman could be compared with 'Mr. Gladstone', who 'has been a giant among pigmies'.[90] Prominent labour leaders like Thomas Burt,[91] William Newton,[92] and the executive committee of the Labour Representation League,[93] expressed their deep-felt gratitude and admiration for the 'People's William'. They respected his need for some rest after many battles, but wished that he would resume the party leadership in the near future, since he was irreplaceable.[94]

Such a wish could not have been more completely fulfilled. What *Lloyd's Weekly* wrote of Bright in January 1876 – that the position he held in the Liberal heart 'is equalled by no living statesman'[95] – was soon to be disproved. It was not simply that Gladstone's position was equal to Bright's; but rather that he also had decisive advantages over Bright in the late 1870s, when popular politics was increasingly characterized by a need for charismatic leadership which was not satisfied by any of the party leaders, and which

---

[88] See e.g.: A. Mackenzie, cit. in *RN*, 8 Mar. 1874, p. 1; [l.a.], 'The Agricultural Lock-Out', *NW*, 2 May 1874, p. 4; in June Gladstone was portrayed as the pilot of the 'Durham County Franchise Association's Ship Progress', on the association's banner ([rep.], 'Great Franchise Demonstration at Bishop Auckland', *NW*, 20 Jun. 1874, p. 5).

[89] [L.a], 'Stray Liberal Sheep', *LW*, 24 Jan. 1875, p. 1; [l.a.], 'A Liberal Victory and Defeat', *LW*, 20 Jun. 1875, p. 6.

[90] Ironside, 'Mr. Gladstone and the Liberal Party', *NW*, 16 Jan. 1875, p. 4.

[91] [Rep.], 'Mr. Burt on Mr. Gladstone's Retirement', *NW*, 30 Jan. 1875, p. 5.

[92] *East London Observer*, 6 Feb. 1875, cit. in DLB, ii, p. 274.

[93] General Council Meeting 29 Jan. 1875, *Labour Representation League Papers*, p. 116.

[94] Cf. letter by 'A Warwickshire Labourer', *RN*, 17 Dec. 1875, p. 3.

[95] [L.a.], 'Mr. Bright at Birmingham', *LW*, 23 Jan. 1876, p. 6.

indeed could occasionally be focused on foreign statesmen.[96] While the Quaker tribune was either unable,[97] or possibly unwilling because of lack of Evangelical 'enthusiasm',[98] to take the leadership of a great popular upheaval such as the Bulgarian agitation, Gladstone was then at the height of his energies and in the right mood to be involved in that wave of collective moral indignation.[99]

Gladstone had long developed his critique of the British approach to the Eastern Question,[100] but had never found sufficient political support to translate it into practical politics. The new fact in 1876 was the realization that 'he and a great mass movement were in a state, or potential state, of moral rapport':[101] 'the people' voiced Heaven's indignation.[102] If the wealthy were hardened and unrepentant in their materialism, the 'masses', thanks to the comparative absence of temptation in their simple life,[103] showed moral discernment and integrity. The fact that the 'masses' were affected by that 'virtuous passion' without which 'good ends can rarely be attained in politics',[104] clearly showed that the time for action had come. It was this awareness which gave Gladstone that sense of moral justification, indeed authentic moral 'investiture', which he needed to resume a central role in national politics. Gladstone, like Joseph Arch,[105] believed that this investiture resided in God's call to a special mission.[106]

As is well-known, Gladstone's intervention had immediate success. While his pamphlet *The Bulgarian Horrors and the Question of the East* – designed for a working-class audience[107] – sold 40,000 copies within three or four days of its publication,[108] the Nonconformists,

---

[96] See Brewster, 'Ulysses Grant and Newcastle upon Tyne', pp. 119–24, which contains remarkable illustrations of the charismatic power of the 'conqueror' of the 'slaveholding rebels'.

[97] J. Bright to W. T. Stead, 21 Apr. 1878, in Stead Papers, Trevelyan, *Bright*, p. 419.

[98] Parry, *Democracy and Religion*, p. 227.

[99] Shannon, *Bulgarian Agitation*, pp. 45ff.

[100] Parry, *Democracy and Religion*, pp. 174–6.

[101] Shannon, *Bulgarian Agitation*, p. 110.

[102] Puritans expected that power corrupted those who held it (see Bendix, *Max Weber*, pp. 312–13). Gladstone shared this point of view (see Parry, *Democracy and Religion*, p. 150).

[103] Shannon, *Bulgarian Agitation*, p. 164; Taylor, *Trouble Makers*, pp. 69–70.

[104] W. E. Gladstone, cit. in Shannon, *Bulgarian Agitation*, pp. 106–7.

[105] See chapter 1, p. 35.

[106] Matthew, 'Introduction' to *Diaries*, IX, p. xlix.

[107] Matthew, 'Vaticanism and the East', p. 439. Cf. W. Lake to W. E. Gladstone, 24 Sept. 1876, in Gladstone-Glynne Papers, 702.

[108] Morley, *Gladstone*, II, p. 552; 200,000 copies were sold within the first month: Jenkins, *Whiggery and the Liberal Party*, p. 56.

who were amongst the most active supporters of the anti-Turkish agitation, greeted him as 'a prophet of the most high God . . . called to the side of truth, righteousness & humanity',[109] the one who had 'expressed in words of sustained eloquence, which have much of the terrible earnestness of the Hebrew Seer, the Anathema of Humanity upon the Devastators of Bulgaria'.[110]

The most significant episode of the new relationship which was then being forged between Gladstone and the crowd was the great meeting held at Blackheath on 9 September. Like the pamphlet (which had just been published) his speech was a vigorous invective against Turkish misgovernment in the Bulgarian provinces, against genocide as an instrument of repression, and finally against the complicity to which the Tory government had acceded by its withholding of information from the British public, and by its offering of substantial support to the Sultan. The constructive part of the speech was moderate: Gladstone asked for administrative and political autonomy for the Bulgarians, but within the Turkish suzerainty.[111] The 10–15,000 people,[112] who had come together to listen to Gladstone's speech, followed his exposition with an extraordinary enthusiasm which even the bad weather was unable to quench. A reporter wrote that while Gladstone spoke it was as if the crowd was holding their breath for fear 'of "missing their joy"': but every pause in the speech became an occasion for voicing their sentiments with shouts of 'Long life to you' and 'We want you'.[113] Another witness wrote that it was as if 'the tremendous energy of the speaker was reflected by his audience' when 'a roar went up from the whole of the great throng – a roar which might justly be regarded as the inarticulate condemnation which Democracy was pronoucing upon the Ottomans'.[114] Morley acutely pointed out that

it was not words that made the power of the orator, it was the relation in purpose, feeling and conviction between him and his audience. He forced them in unity with himself by the vivid strength of his resolution and

---

[109] Shannon, *Bulgarian Agitation*, p. 165. Cf. 'Resolution dopted by the Newport Road Baptist Church, Middlesborough, 11 Jan. 1878, in Glynne-Gladstone Papers, 715.

[110] [L.a.], 'Gladstone to the Front!', *Northern Echo*, 7 Sept. 1876, p. 2. On Nonconformist attitudes see Bebbington, 'A Religious Affinity in Politics'.

[111] [Rep.], 'The Turkish Atrocities in Bulgaria – Great Meeting at Greenwich', *DN*, 11 Sept. 1876, p. 2.

[112] *Ibid.*   [113] *Ibid.*

[114] Stead, *1809–1898*, p. 14.

imagination; he could not believe that his own power of emotion was not theirs too . . . [115]

W. T. Stead has written one of the most significant accounts of the way in which Gladstone exercised his rhetorical magnetism, a picture whose importance has never been fully appreciated by historians. Neither physically imposing nor tall in stature, Gladstone's charisma was based on the musicality of his powerful voice, on the use of the rhythmic prepositions, on the eloquence of gesticulation and the movement of his whole chest, when from time to time 'the whole energy of the man concentrated into a single act'[116] – and especially on his extraordinarily expressive face and eyes. 'His whole body debates in every part of it, from head to foot, his mobile features, vibrating and pointing finger, threatening arm, restless figure, turning now this way, now that . . .'.[117] These gifts made his philippics more immediately and universally effective than mere words would have allowed. The public did not focus on his modest physical appearance, but was completely absorbed by the materialization of concepts and moral imperatives in which the orator seemed to transfigure himself. 'Mr. Gladstone's personality was more or less suffused among his hearers. It was a kind of hypnotism to which an audience temporarily succumbed',[118] 'only those who have been under the spell of the magician can rightly understand the hold which he exercised over his audience'.[119] This was the well-attested phenomenon of 'being Gladstonized',[120] that a Victorian artisan still recalled vividly after thirty years:

Without an effort – so it seemed to me – the great orator held his audience for nearly two hours. I stood so far off that the features were indistinct, but was spellbound by the music and magnetism of the wonderful voice . . . I was only conscious of the presence of a great human personality under whose spell I was, and from whom I could in no way escape . . . If the things he said were unintelligible to me, the voice brought with it something of an inspiration and of uplifting power . . . I felt lifted into a

---

[115] Morley, *Gladstone*, II, p. 554.
[116] Stead, *1809–1898* (1898), pp. 14–15. See the charisma ascribed to Gabriele D'Annunzio during the occupation of Fiume (Mosse, *Masses and Man*, pp. 96–8); obviously the rhetoric of the two men had completely different aims.
[117] Furnniss, *Victorian Men* (1924), p. 229.
[118] Stead, *1809–1898* (1898), p. 15.
[119] *Ibid.*, pp. 13–14.
[120] See *Gladstone Diaries*, IX, p. 491, n.8. See for another example Lloyd, *1880*, p. 153.

holy region of politics, where Tories cannot corrupt or Jingoes break through and yell.[121]

At Gladstonian meetings, as Mosse has observed about a very different kind of leader, 'The audience . . . experienced the logic in the speeches emotionally; they felt only the militancy and the faith, without grasping the real content or reflecting on its meaning. The crowd was captured by the prose itself, they "lived" the speeches rather than examining the content',[122] and, as if hypnotized, submitted to the 'head', whose leadership they invoked: at the end of the Blackheath meeting many shouted continuously 'Lead us!', 'Lead us!'[123]

But even though the impact of Gladstone's rhetoric was overwhelmingly emotional and did not – at the time – allow any possibility of the listeners analysing the content, the latter was not unrelated to the effect. In this respect, it is Lassalle, among the great European 'demagogues', who seems closest to the Gladstonian model: at Lassalle's meetings both the speech content and the oratory were essential components in a sort of drama[124] which took place in an atmosphere of sacrality and prophetic revelation.[125] Even more deeply religious connotations were present in the 1876 Gladstonian meetings, which have been compared to those of the Evangelical revivals.[126] Since the orator – just like the great revivalistic preachers – aimed at obtaining acceptance of the 'faith' by the public, the articles of this 'faith' were an integral part of the 'evangelistic' message: therefore the content contributed towards creating the charisma, while the very language and style of expression defined – in part – the content. Gladstone's audience, especially those who belonged to the subaltern classes and who were frequent victims of injustice, loved 'the respectful intimacy with the Almighty which Mr. Gladstone was in the habit of affecting' and which recommended him as 'the blessed man who walketh not in the counsels of the ungodly, but whose delight is in the law of the Lord, and in his law doth he meditate day and night'.[127] He was 'the idol of the popular heart' because – just like

---

[121] Rogers, *Labour*, pp. 25–6.
[122] Mosse, *The Nationalization of the Masses*, p. 227.
[123] Stead, *1809–1898* (1898), p. 15.
[124] Mosse, *The Nationalization of the Masses*, p. 162.
[125] *Ibid.*, 162–3; see Stead, *1809–1898* (1898), p. 13.
[126] Shannon, *Bulgarian Agitation*, pp. 115–16.
[127] Ostrogorski, *Democracy*, I, p. 180; the reference is to Psalm 1:1–2.

Arch in East Anglia and 'Mabon' in the Rhondda[128] – he convincingly presented himself as 'the Heaven-sent leader of Englishmen',[129] one who 'was animated by a supreme regard for the welfare of the common people, and an all-constraining conviction of his obligation to God'.[130] The audience perceived these meetings as religious occasions, to the extent that in working-class autobiographies participation in Gladstonian Liberalism is often recalled as if it had been a religious experience: 'for years I worshipped at the political shrine of Mr. Gladstone',[131] Lansbury wrote from London: 'Gladstone was the political god and Jenkins was one of his prophets',[132] Barnes remarked, speaking of the Liberal candidate for Dundee.

Thus Gladstone's hold on the crowd seems to have had an even more markedly charismatic character than Weber thought.[133] It was accompanied by all the usual features, such as the capacity for creating an emotional form of communitarian relationship,[134] and the salvationist-messianic aspects which according to Weber specifically characterize charismatic leadership.[135] Gladstone's magnetism seems comparable with the kind of control exercised by the greatest twentieth-century leaders: to judge by the reactions of the audience, it shows impressive affinities with that exercised by Lenin, as analysed by Tucker.[136] Moreover Gladstone's tendency to appeal to the country over the heads both of parliament and the party – that is, in Weberian terms, to speak to the 'layfolk' ignoring the 'clerics' – offers an interesting scholarly support to certain popular descriptions then current, because it assimilates him to the Weberian ideal-type of the 'prophet',[137] even more than to the simple charismatic political leader.

In spite of the presence and strength of all these 'irrational' components,[138] Matthew is right in stressing that the peculiarity of

[128] See above, chapter 6, pp. 351–6.
[129] Stead, *1809–1898* (1898), p. 15.
[130] *Ibid.*, p. 27.
[131] Lansbury, *My Life* (1928), 86.
[132] Barnes, *Workshop to the War Cabinet* (1924), p. 18.
[133] Weber, *Politics as a Vocation*, pp. 31–2.
[134] Weber, *The Theory*, p. 360.
[135] Tucker, 'The Theory of Charismatic Leadership', pp. 742–3.
[136] *Ibid.*, p. 747.
[137] Bendix, *Weber*, pp. 90, 299–301.
[138] In a Weberian sense: Weber, *The Theory*, p. 361.

Gladstone's case was that he managed to square the circle of reconciling mass democracy with the values of the traditional liberal ethos of a politically conscious and actively critical citizenry, in no way prone to the will of the leader, and that he formulated a political system which was at the same time charismatic and rational.[139] Matthew has acutely shifted attention from the delivery of Gladstone's speeches, to their national diffusion through the press.[140] The conclusions he has reached for the general public can be applied to the specific case of the working classes: veneration for the charismatic leader and close attention to and study of the content of his speeches went together. The latter was a matter of real study, which took place *after* the meetings, in the workers' homes or in other social centres, where the printed version of the speeches became the subject of long conversations and discussions. There are many examples. For instance, in North Oxfordshire agricultural labourers meeting in the village pub, used to listen to Gladstone's speeches read aloud from the recent newspapers by one of their members, while the others solemnly punctuated the declamation with a fervent 'Hear, hear'.[141] Another example is recounted by George Ratcliffe in his autobiography. He wrote that, at some stage during the second half of the 1870s, his grandfather called him aside one day, and told him:

George, my lad, as you grow up, watch Gladstone. It has nothing to do with it, but your birthday and his are on the twenty-ninth of December. To me he is the greatest living statesman. Read and study what he says, like I do.[142]

This plebeian Liberal admired Gladstone to such an extent that he celebrated his birthday, but at the same time he also 'read and studied' his speeches. It is important to stress that he was neither a labour leader nor in any other way an 'exceptional' or 'atypical' individual, but an ordinary man who remained completely anonymous, and who, but for this single incident, would have been lost in the mass of his contemporaries. The case of Jack Lawson's father was analogous: he was a poor, anonymous working man – earning his living working either as a mariner or a miner – who periodically 'inflicted' upon his wife and children his meditations

---

[139] Matthew, 'Introduction' to *Diaries*, ix, p. lxix.
[140] *Ibid.*, pp. lxiii–lxix; and 'Rhetoric and Politics', p. 41ff.
[141] Horn, *Joseph Arch* (1898), p. 164.
[142] Ratcliffe, *Sixty Years of It* (n.d.), p. 28.

on Gladstone's latest speech.[143] Lansbury's mother too, used to speak to her children about her favourite heroes – Gladstone, Bright and Cobden.[144] The case of Joseph Arch is also well known, who as a young man used to buy old newspapers to read the speeches of Gladstone and Bright.[145]

But finally, there is the evidence offered by the structure and content of the popular periodical press. In fact it was not only for the great London and 'provincial' dailies that Gladstone's speeches represented important events, but also for the more popular weeklies which reported them in several columns, so that even those who read a newspaper only on Sundays could have at least a partial insight into this aspect of national political life.[146] The case of the *Newcastle Weekly Chronicle* is especially interesting, because it laid quite an extraordinary emphasis – even by Victorian standards – on reports of political speeches. One of its typical features was that of publishing special editions with a 'free supplement' which doubled the number of pages of the ordinary newspaper, and consisted almost entirely of political reports. Cowen was obviously the most frequently reported orator: and – though he had considerable charismatic powers – his speeches provide an example of didactic rationalism applied to popular political rhetoric, an approach which well suited the Puritan 'mass intellectualism' of the northern counties. For instance, they often illustrate the general tendency to present long historical surveys of the successes achieved by the Liberals in the past, including long discussions of eighteenth-century history,[147] but also examinations of the *loci classici* of popular radicalism (like 'Saxon democracy' and the Magna Charta): excursions which had both a didactic and an emotional function.[148] What is especially interesting is that both Cowen and the newspaper editors attributed great importance to the publication of printed versions of his speeches. The *Weekly Chronicle* declared in 1874:

---

[143] Lawson, *A Man's Life* (1932), p. 49.

[144] DLB, ii, p. 214.

[145] Arch, *The Story* (1898), p. 49.

[146] See *WT*, 1 Dec. 1878, which published – on the first page – a verbatim edition of Gladstone's speech.

[147] See e.g. [rep.], 'Great Meeting of Mr. Cowen's Supporters', *NW*, 10 Jan. 1874, p. 3, containing a long discussion of the 'taxes upon knowledge' and their repeal by Gladstone.

[148] Lloyd, *1880*, p. 42.

Taken together these speeches form an educational treatise of no mean value to citizens of a composite Commonwealth like that of England . . . The permanent value of such electioneering addresses . . . is to be measured not so much by the success they have absolutely secured for the speaker, as by their influence in commending political study . . . Whoever will read, mark and digest the whole series must of necessity become an intelligent politician . . . a true and faithful citizen of a glorious commonwealth.[149]

These observations can be generalized and applied to the great national speakers; 'Thousands have heard and millions have read', wrote *Reynolds's Newspaper*, commenting upon Gladstone's speeches during the first Midlothian campaign.[150] These orations – like other series of important speeches – were also collected in volumes or sold in cheap editions as pamphlets. The Midlothian speeches were not difficult to edit, because they had an expository order which provided a systematic commentary on the conditions of Britain and the Empire. Judging from the number of these editions and from the incredibly cheap price at which they were sold, these collections must have been a very popular literary genre in the Victorian age.[151]

THE CULT OF THE LEADER

During the Midlothian campaigns both the rationalistic and the charismatic components attained their maximum development: an extraordinary blend of an electrifying style with 'the demagogy of popular rationalism'.[152] Gladstone's achievements as a popular leader were accompanied and completed by the foundation of a real 'cult of the leader', which has not yet been systematically studied.[153] This 'cult' was formally analogous to – though ideologically very different from – that which developed in France with

---

[149] [L.a.], 'Political Instruction', *NW*, 10 Jan. 1874.
[150] [L.a.], 'Mr. Gladstone's Progress', *RN*, 7 Dec. 1879, p. 1.
[151] The speeches of the 1884 campaign were for sale at 1 penny (see advertisement in *DN*, 2 Mar. 1884, p. 1).
[152] Matthew, 'Introduction' to *Diaries*, IX, p. lxiii.
[153] The only specific work on this subject is Hamer, 'Gladstone: The Making of a Political Myth', pp. 29–50, based only on popular biographies, a source heavily conditioned by apologetic or polemic aims which make it difficult to assess the real dimensions of the question.

Boulanger, in Germany with Lassalle, and in Austria with Karl Lueger.[154]

The figure and even the name of Gladstone had begun to be clothed with strong symbolic connotations in the period of the campaign for the second Reform Bill: it was then that the mottoes of 'Gladstone and Liberty', 'Gladstone for ever', 'Gladstone and Reform' became popular, and were paraded together with the effigy of the Liberal leader,[155] while the production of knick-knacks inspired by Gladstone spread immediately afterwards.[156] However Hamer's thesis that it was in the years after the Bulgarian agitation that the cult of Gladstone took off seems well corroborated. Besides the chronology and content of popular biographies,[157] there is the politicization of Gladstone's private life. The 'Hawarden cult', which represented one of the most remarkable aspects of the Gladstone myth, began to manifest itself after his resignation from the Liberal leadership in 1875, and was fostered less by popular biographies than by the mass press.

It was normal for newspapers to take some interest in the recreational activities of the great political leaders. However it was not frequent for a statesman to have Gladstone's hobby – chopping down trees with an axe. The very fact that an ex-prime minister devoted himself to this rustic pastime in the bucolic atmosphere of Hawarden, after his partial but sudden political eclipse, gave him the appearance of a modern Cincinnatus, a British Garibaldi in his Welsh Caprera. Even *Lloyd's Weekly* – which was then hostile to Gladstone – could not but be fascinated by the vision of the ex-premier

in his shirt sleeves, his braces thrown off, and his arms bare, lustily at work upon a giant tree at Hawarden. Two days' hard labour were necessary to overcome the stubborn trunk, but at length it yielded, and the woodcutter, casting his axe over his shoulder, strode homewards.[158]

---

[154] Mosse, *The Nationalization of the Masses*, pp. 118–19.

[155] Vincent, *The Formation*, pp. 30–1.

[156] Like the sugar bowls and the small glass plates made by Henry Green & Co., Wear Flint Glass Works, in 1869 (Sunderland Museum, Fine and Applied Arts).

[157] Which show the different degree of 'market' interest in different periods of Gladstone's life: the *Life of Gladstone, D.C.L., Etc., A Popular Biography* (London 1898) out of a total of 200 pages, devoted only 105 to the 69 years between 1809 and 1875, and as many as 96 to the 22 years between 1876 and 1898.

[158] [L.a.], 'Mr. Gladstone at Hawarden', *LW*, 19 Jun. 1875, p. 6.

Here the working-class readers found a great statesman and popular leader in the plain clothes of the labourer: a most suggestive vision for democratic fantasy, pregnant with precise moral and political values and as eloquent as a long speech. Besides, it had been Gladstone himself who had first applied the woodsman language to politics: in his 1868 electoral campaign he had spoken of the Liberal axe which was going to chop down the 'upas tree' of Anglican ascendancy and the landlords' Establishment in Ireland.[159] Also very popular was the often-quoted anecdote that the Queen's summons reached him at Hawarden just while he was enjoying his hobby: Gladstone, leaning on his axe, listened to the telegram, then pronounced the historical phrase – 'My mission is to pacify Ireland' – before resuming his work with great energy and without uttering a single word until the tree had fallen under his vigorous blows.[160]

But the imagery of the axe and the woodsman chopping down 'evil' trees had a long tradition in British radicalism. Its origins can be found in well-known Bible passages,[161] to which the metaphor was occasionally explicitly referred. Moreover, in the nineteenth century there was an established iconographic tradition, no longer explicitly Biblical, which likened the resolute reformer to the axeman attacking grotesque trees which provided a shelter for snakes, scorpions and all sorts of wicked creatures symbolizing 'evils' to be amended.[162] It is also remarkable that – contrary to what both Victorian and modern critics have maintained[163] – this symbolism was not symptomatic of a *laissez-faire*, 'negative' Liberalism, but rather was shared even by Marxist socialist movements in other European countries.[164]

Given the extent of the woodsman imagery it is not surprising that it enjoyed a wide appeal for a long time in the contemporary press. *Punch* was only one among many periodicals which used it

---

[159] Hamer, 'Gladstone: The Making of a Political Myth', pp. 39–40.
[160] Morley, *Gladstone*, II, p. 252.
[161] Especially Matthew 3:10 and Luke 3:9.
[162] See the splendid 1832 broadsheet entitled 'The Reformers' Attack on the Old Rotten Tree: Foul Nests of Cormorants in Danger', *John Johnson Coll.*, Box Political General 1.
[163] Hamer, 'Gladstone: The Making of a Political Myth', p. 38.
[164] The Italian Socialists, for instance: see 'Il male è nella radice', cartoon in *L'Asino*, a.V, n.48, 29 Nov. 1896 (cit. in Andreucci, *Il marxismo collettivo*, p. 192). This cartoon is remarkably similar to one showing Gladstone chopping down the upas tree of the Turkish Empire (*Punch*, 15 May 1877).

to comment on Gladstone's political initiatives,[165] while anecdotes with a 'woodsman' background were common in popular biographies.[166]

When Hawarden became a pilgrimage centre for the members of Liberal and Radical clubs, the greatest aspiration of the excursionists was to see 'Mr' Gladstone felling a tree, and to be able to pick up a few chips as a souvenir or relic. Hostile observers made a great deal of this kind of story, which was supposed to be repeated frequently. But in reality the press – which kept a close eye on Gladstone's activities at Hawarden – reported only one occurrence, in August 1877: and it is clear that Gladstone did not appreciate the incident, and instead of exploiting the occasion to project himself, was quite restive about satisfying his fans' expectations.[167] This episode remained an isolated one: three other groups visited the castle that summer, but had to be content with speeches from a balcony.[168] The following year Gladstone presided at the testing of a steam saw, but did not try to exploit the occasion politically, though his arrival was greeted with 'loud cheers from the workmen round about'.[169] Finally, in March 1878 Gladstone declined the request of a group of Leeds admirers who wished to meet him at Hawarden, because, he said, 'experience has shown that an essentially public character inevitably attaches to excursions so received', transforming every meeting into 'an exhibition of domestic life to the world at large such as does not, and . . . ought not, meet with general approval'.[170]

But this reserve did nothing to dampen popular enthusiasm.

---

[165] See also the cartoon in *Punch*, 21 Nov. 1874, commenting on the publication of *Vaticanism*. For other examples, see Stead, *Gladstone in Contemporary Caricature*; and W. E. Gladstone, *Political Life . . . Illustrated from 'Punch'*.

[166] For two picturesque examples, see *The Life of the Right Hon. W. E. Gladstone, M.P., D.C.L.. Etc., A Popular Biography*, p. 191; and Jerrold, *W. E. Gladstone, England's Great Commoner*, pp. 145–7.

[167] *Diaries*, IX, entry for 4 Aug. 1877, p. 240: 'A party of 1400 from Bolton! We were nearly killed with kindness. I began with W.[illiam] the cutting of a tree; and had to speak to them, but not on politics'; see [re[.], 'Mr. Gladstone at Home', *TI*, 6 Jun. 1877, p. 8.

[168] See [rep.], 'Vacation Speeches. – Mr. Gladstone and the Eastern Question', *TI*, 20 Aug. 1877, p. 12; [rep.], 'Mr. Gladstone and the Liberal Party', *TI*, 21 Aug. 1877, p. 4; [rep.], 'Mr. Gladstone at Home', *TI*, 3 Sept. 1877.

[169] [Rep.], 'Mr. Gladstone on Tree Felling', *TI*, 4 Feb. 1878, p. 6.

[170] [Lett. by] W. E. Gladstone, 'Mr. Gladstone at Hawarden', *TI*, 27 Mar. 1878, p. 11. Even the following year Gladstone did not receive personally the members of the Halifax Liberal Club who visited Hawarden: it was up to his son Stephen to play the host (Wilson, *The Struggles of an Old Chartist* [n.d.], p. 239; the episode took place on 24 Jun. 1879).

The 1877 meetings with the 'excursionists' received enormous publicity in the popular press. Even anti-Gladstonian newspapers contributed,[171] while sympathetic observers interpreted these events as a further confirmation that 'the people' could find in Gladstone a never-failing paladin, 'ready, at any moment, to speak the nation's sentiments and proclaim the people's will'.[172] Not surprisingly, the symbolism of the axe became very common, especially during the following years.

All sorts of axes began to be presented to Gladstone by his working class admirers as well as by others. One of the most symbolic was perhaps the axe that he received – together with an inkstand – from the workers building the bridge over the Firth of Forth, in Scotland: the blade (as well as the inkstand) had been cast from the steel used for the piers of the bridge, and the handle made out of the wood of an oak felled by Gladstone himself in 1879.[173] In this case the axe and the pen, symbols of Gladstone's tribuneship, were made from the people's working materials, and Gladstone's own past labour.

In 1884 the symbolism of the axe was almost a constant theme at the demonstrations against the House of Lords: at Hyde Park, during the July mass meeting, the Battersea contingent paraded a banner showing an axe in the vigorous hands of a Gladstone-labourer,[174] at the Birmingham demonstration, in August, there was displayed 'a model supposed to represent the House of Lords, with a figure of Mr. Gladstone and his axe, standing in front of the building and the inscription beneath "cut it down, why it cumbereth the ground" ';[175] at Edinburgh, in September, one of the large banners showed Gladstone with his axe on his shoulders marching at the head of an army of working men, each bearing the tool typical of their respective trades. The motto was 'The People's Bill Will Clear the Way', and was accompanied by another illustration: a fallen tree ('Obstruction') and a large dog ('The House of Lords')

[171] [L.a.], 'The Woodman at Hawarden (A Comedy)', *LW*, 12 Aug. 1877, p. 1.
[172] [L.a.], 'Mr. Gladstone and the Excursionists', *WT*, 20 Aug. 1877, p. 1.
[173] [Rep.], 'Mr. Gladstone in Edinburgh – Third Meeting Last Night – Address to Working Men – An Audience of 15,000', *NC*, 3 Sept. 1884, p. 3.
[174] [Rep.], 'The Great Reform Demonstration', *DN*, 22 Jul. 1884, p. 5.
[175] [Rep.], 'The Monster Anti-Aristocratic Demonstration at Birmingham', *RN*, 10 Aug. 1884, p. 1. The inscription is a Biblical quotation (Luke 13:7).

upon which an axeman stood in triumph.[176] A few months later, at the time of the general elections of 1885, a new Liberal symbol was made available for sale and widely advertised: 'The Gladstone Axe Scarf Pin & Souvenir', as a non-official badge of the Liberal party, in various forms, for men and women, produced in different metals at different prices.[177]

Closely akin to the symbol of the Gladstone-axeman there was that other rural and romantic symbolism of the Gladstone-swordsman, a Highland chief; this too became common from 1879 because of the statesman's link with Midlothian. After the triumph of 1880 this theme found many enthusiastic popular bards, who celebrated the Liberal victory as if it were the advance of the warriors of the 'Gladstone clan':

> The Gladstones are coming from mountain and glen! –
> From town, from country – from green land and fen –
>
> All Titanic Knights of the lance or the pen
> With the resolute footsteps of Highland Men!
>
> Joy o'er it! Ye, down trodden serfs of the soil;
> Joy o'er it ye, martyrs of trouble and toil . . . [178]

Another little poem celebrated a Gladstone-Highlander adorned with thistles, triumphant over the Duke of Buccleuch, the Tory candidate's father and a symbol of the aristocracy.[179] It was inevitable that this imagery would become successful among the Highland crofters, whose banner proclaimed in 1886:

> Gladstone will back you
> If needs be with swords,

---

[176] [Rep.], 'Mr. Gladstone in Edinburgh . . . Address to Working Men', *NC*, 3 Dept. 1884, p. 3. The imagery of the dog as a symbol of reaction was also common in other European countries: for an Italian example see the Socialist cartoon published in Andreucci, *Il marxismo collettivo*, p. 179.

[177] THE GLADSTONE AXE SCARF PIN & SOUVENIR, Election Motto TRIED! TRUSTED! TRUE! The Gladstone Axe motto being the official badge of the Liberal Party should be worn by every admirer of Mr. Gladstone and all professing Liberal principles throughout the country. These can be supplied either in metal, silver, bright, gold or coloured gold, in the form of Bracelets, Brooches, Lockets. (Advertisement, *DN*, 21 Nov. 1885, p. 7)

[178] G. L. Banks, 'Gladstone and Good Cheer!', *LW*, 18 Apr. 1880, p. 5.

[179] 'To the Right Honourable W. E. Gladstone, M.P.', ibid.: 'With thistle-garland com'st thou crowned, [. . .] Triumphant over the renowned / Fierce-foe defying "bold Buccleuch!"'

To give crofters their right
And abolish the Lords.[180]

In addition to giving rise to the stereotypes of the 'woodsman' and the 'Highland warrior', Gladstone frequently inspired both plebeian artists and orators who were looking for symbols. The veteran Chartist W. H. Chadwick – who in 1879 was venerated as a Liberal martyr while speaking to Gladstonian crowds – used prophetic-apocalyptic language and proclaimed to 'see' 'glorious Gladstone' as the 'good old pilot' of the 'grand old ship' which on the bow bore the motto 'Peace, retrenchment and reform', and on whose flag there were the words 'Free land, free church and a free people for old England'.[181]

At the level of popular visual art, two splendid standards of the Durham Miners' Association ought to be mentioned: painted on silk and interwoven with golden threads, they were paraded for the first time at the Gala of 1884: one of these banners showed Gladstone receiving a petition from the miners' leaders (significantly both Gladstone and the miners sat around a table, on a level of equality); the other represented Gladstone holding the 1884 Reform Bill.[182] Other artistic objects were prepared to celebrate his visit to Birmingham in 1888: the artisans of each of the trades of that city prepared special gifts for the Liberal leaders – 'all sorts of things bearing Gladstone's effigy. Gladstone's household arms, etc.'.[183] This was a significant indication that Gladstone's personal appeal survived even in Chamberlain's Unionist stronghold. A similar initiative had been taken in 1885 by the workers of Manchester, who – 'apart from politics' – intended to honour Gladstone as the man who ' has never toadied to "sovereigns and statesmen", but has identified his illustrious career with the well-being of the masses'.[184]

The latter element – the identification of Gladstone with 'the

---

[180] Cit. in Dunbabin, 'Ideas and Arguments – Crofters', in Dunbabin (ed.), *Rural Discontent*, p. 280.
[181] [Rep.], 'Chartist Lecture', *English Labourers' Chronicle*, 18 Jan. 1879, p. 7; in the final part there are clear overtones of Revelation 1:12–3 and 10:1. 'The Good Old Pilot' was also the title of a popular song on Gladstone (Clarke, *Lancashire*, p. 136).
[182] [Rep.], 'Durham Miners' Annual Gala', *DC*, 11 Jul. 1884, p. 6; a photograph of the latter is published in Moyes, *Banner Book*, p. 113.
[183] [L.a.], 'The Birmingham Meetings – The Artizans and Mr. Gladstone', *English Labourers' Chronicle*, 27 Oct. 1888, p. 4.
[184] [Rep.], 'Workmen's Tribute to Mr. Gladstone', *MG*, 5 Oct. 1885, p. 5.

people' and the appreciation for his alleged rejection of privilege – was always strongly emphasized: it was not forgotten that – in contrast to Disraeli, Lord Beaconsfield – he had preferred to remain simply 'Mr.' Gladstone', the commoner, twice declining a peerage.[185] Consequently there was ascribed to 'Mr.' Gladstone a 'natural homely nature lying behind his outward uncosciousness of greatness and power'.[186] This was seen on a number of occasions, for example when he was invited for lunch in a working-class tavern in Glasgow: 'Seeing the working men sitting at their tables ... [he] took a vacant seat among the ordinary workaday customers', instead of sitting at the special table which had been reserved for him and his retinue; and wanted to eat an ordinary 4s ½d meal, rather than the sumptuous luncheon they had prepared for him.[187] Another instance is recalled by Henry Broadhurst, that once when he had visited Gladstone at Hawarden:

Dressed in tweed of old time well worn, trousers a little short, and slightly frayed at the bottom, he presented a totally different appearance to his House of Commons costume. It was only on his approaching me that I noticed his clothes, which on an ordinary man would have been thought untidy.[188]

This 'homely nature' could also be shown on public occasions. Once, at the end of a speech in Glasgow, while 'the audience went wild with enthusiasm', the statesman's wife got up from her chair on the platform next to him, and began to moisten 'the great man's face, ears and neck, while he sat back like a young child'. The effect of this unexpected scene on the audience was immediate and powerful:

Their complete forgetfulness of the enthusiastic audience touched everyone, and the whole place was overcome with emotion. The cheering died

---

[185] Amidst the exultation of plebeian radicals: [l.a.], 'Mr. Gladstone and the People', *LW*, 21 Jun. 1885, p. 6.

[186] Freer, *My Life* (1929), p. 46.

[187] *Ibid.*, p. 50.

[188] Broadhurst, *The Story* (1898), p. 165. Broadhurst went on to say:

After the commencement of his conversation one did not see his covering, one only saw and heard his mind. To a greater degree than any other person I ever met he could, and did adapt his talk and his subject to the person he was addressing ... Mr. Gladstone played the host to perfection, pointing out all the views of interest in the park and the village, not omitting the fine old church. (*Ibid.*, pp. 165–6).

away, and in all parts of the hall one could see handkerchiefs as the members of the audience wiped their tear-filled eyes.[189]

Such was the extent of the empathy between Gladstone and popular Liberals that veneration and familiarity were closely intertwined. Perhaps few went as far as walking more than ten miles to present home-made butter and eggs to 'dear Mr. Gladstone' as an old countrywoman did at the 1876 Blackheath meeting[190]; but cases like that of James Hawker, the Leicestershire poacher, who kept in his diary a photograph of the 'People's William'[191] must have been quite common. While in some regions on the Continent it was usual for workers to choose names like 'Lassallo' and 'Marxina'[192] for their children, in Great Britain there was a proliferation of 'William Ewarts'[193] And of course both veneration and familiarity were equally implicit in the appellative 'Grand Old Man'.

It is not clear when this sobriquet was applied to Gladstone for the first time: according to Donald Read it was in 1879 when somebody, perhaps Harcourt, inaugurated the expression.[194] However, Read does not quote his evidence, while Gardiner mentions 1880, rather than 1879, as the date when Harcourt first used the sobriquet 'in one of his first addresses to his constituents in Derby':[195] however, as before, the evidence is not specified, and *The Times* reports of Harcourt's speeches do not contain any reference to the nickname. Another similar claim about Bradlaugh – who allegedly 'invented' the expression in 1881 – is likewise unsubstantiated by an analysis of his main speeches: we can conclude that if he used the sobriquet, few people realized it. But

---

[189] Freer, *My Life* (1929), pp. 53–4. On the importance of women in building up the myth of the 'People's William' see Jalland, 'Mr. Gladstone's Daughters', in Kinzer (ed.), *The Gladstonian Turn of Mind*, pp. 97–122; and Matthew, 'Rhetoric and Politics', p. 42.

[190] *Gladstone Papers*, Add. MSS. 44451, f.200, [newspaper cutting], 'An Admirer of Mr. Gladstone'; the old woman's attempt was unsuccessful when she was stopped by a bad-tempered navvy who did not appreciate her resolute way of cutting her way through the crowd. The old lady sat down on a stone and wept. Some kindred heart tried to satisfy her wish to reach the Liberal leader, but to no avail and 'dear Mr. Gladstone' was left without butter and eggs.

[191] Christians, 'Introduction' to Hawker, *Journal* (n.d.), p. xi; the diary also contained other photographs, including those of Charles Bradlaugh, Augustine Birrell, 'Tom Sayers, the Boxer', and Gladys Cooper, an actress.

[192] In central Italy: Michels, *Political Parties*, p. 73.

[193] Bradley, *Optimists*, p. 9.

[194] Read, *England 1868–1914*, p. 168.

[195] Gardiner, *Harcourt*, I, p. 457n; see Lucy, *Diary of the Salisbury Parliament*, p. 229.

apart from the lack of evidence, there are other reasons to be perplexed: in 1879 Beaconsfield, who was older than Gladstone, was still alive, and was certainly reputed 'great', especially after his success at the Berlin Congress and before the defeat of 1880.[196] Moreover, *Punch*, which is likely to have been quick to pick up any new nicknames of statesmen, did not use the expression before 1882.[197] By then Beacsonsfield had been dead over a year, while Gladstone was premier and Chancellor of the Exchequer at the same time: this would have been quite a task for anybody, but was absolutely prodigious for a seventy-three-year-old man. In such a context he was undoubtedly entitled to the appellation of 'Grand Old Man', whether the phrase was meant to express respect or derision. These considerations add credibility to Henry Labouchere's claim that he was the first to use the expression, in the summer of 1881.[198] As far as the subaltern classes are concerned, there are no traces of the nickname before 1883,[199] when it began to be used in the popular press with loving admiration. In 1884 it was so common that it was printed on the workers' banners at demonstrations for the Reform Bill, both in London[200] and elsewhere,[201] while the mass press celebrated the fact that ' "the grand old man", as the immense majority of his fellow-subjects affectionately and the apes and asses of "Society" derisively, designate the Premier, spoke over the heads of the Commons, and addressed himself to the people!'.[202]

---

196 Read's hypothesis seems even less convincing when we consider that in an anti-Gladstonian ballad published in 1880 the Liberal statesman was referred to by various nicknames (including 'People's William'), but not that of 'Grand Old Man' (*Gladstone's Garland*, in Catalogue of Supplementary Materials, Cambridge University Library).

197 See 'The Nice Old Ladies', *Punch*, 1 Jul. 1882, p. 302; ' "The Grand Old Man" as "Paul Pry" in Ireland Visits Captain Moonlight after Sunset', *ibid.*, 304; 'The Royal Academy of Sculpture – The Grand Old Man Going On Ahead', *Punch*, 8 Jul. 1882; and 'St Stephen's Music Hall', *Punch*, 29 Jul. 1882, p. 39.

198 Thorold, *Labouchere*, p. 144; this claim has been accepted by H. C. G. Matthew ('Introduction' to *Diaries*, x, p. clxxvii).

199 [Rep.], 'Great Demonstration of Miners in the Rhondda Valley', *The Miners' National Gazette*, 21 Jul. 1883, p. 143: Rymer concluded his speech 'by a pathetic appeal for support to trade unionism, the "Grand Old Man" and Mr. Bright.'

200 [Rep.], *DN*, 22 Jul. 1884, p. 5: the name 'Grand Old Man' appeared on the banner of the Battersea contingent.

201 [Rep.], 'Great Franchise Demonstration' (in Stoke-on-Trent), *Staffordshire Knot*, 11 Oct. 1884, p. 2; one of the Longton miners' banners bore the motto: 'The sons of Longton will do what they can / For the Franchise Bill and the Grand Old Man'. See [l.a.], 'Mr. Woodall and Woman's Suffrage', *Staffordshire Knot*, 14 Jun. 1884, p. 1; and [rep.], 'Great Demonstrations of Agricultural Labourers', *English Labourers' Chronicle*, 7 Jun. 1884, p. 7.

202 Gracchus, 'Political Rascality', *RN*, 20 Apr. 1884, p. 3.

More than any other, the nickname of 'Grand Old Man' expressed the 'charismatic-familiar' dimension of the Liberal leader's appeal. To 'Gracchus', 'Grand Old Man' was in fact something like the Weberian 'prophet', the one who 'rises among the crowd . . . his strength and authority only coming from a mysterious, divine "irruption of grace" which forces him to make a stand',[203] and therefore bypasses the institutions and appeals directly and personally to the people, as a 'tribune of the plebs' in a sense close to that of the original Roman magistracy. He was greeted as 'the deliverer of nations, the inspired leader of peoples . . . a giant of unsurpassed strength wrestling with and conquering the powers of injustice and oppression',[204] the inexorable executor of the will of the people, 'the agent of progressive ideas'.[205] The frequency with which the expression was used grew in proportion to the tireless activity of the premier, who, besides his government, parliamentary, and party commitments, between 1884 and 1886 led another three 'crusades' in Midlothian. After 1886 the nickname was also commonly used in the shortened version, GOM.[206] By then it had become what a *Daily News* reporter defined as a 'historic cry',[207] which provided the title to several party songs[208] – some of which remained popular until the 1910s[209] – and even inspired commercial advertising.[210]

THE EPIC OF MIDLOTHIAN

These manifestations of charismatic power reached their zenith during the Midlothian campaigns, between 1879 and 1892, when Europe was witness to political scenes which were as yet unknown on the eastern shores of the Atlantic. Contemporary reports of

---

[203] Ferrarotti, *Max Weber*, p. 73.

[204] Broadhurst, *The Story* (1898), p. 88, on the Nonconformists' point of view.

[205] So defined in a 'Spiritualist' conference of 1890: Barrow, *Independent Spirits*, p. 242.

[206] See [rep.], 'Mid-Durham Division – Mr. Crawford at Low Spennymoor', *DC*, 6 Nov. 1885, p. 6; [rep], 'Mr. Gladstone at Liverpool – Imposing Meeting', *DN*, 29 Jun. 1886, p. 5; [rep.], 'Mr. Gladstone at Hawarden – The G.O.M. Interviewed', *English Labourers' Chronicle*, 1 Dec. 1889, p. 1.

[207] [Rep.], 'Mr. Gladstone's Journey to Scotland – Enthusiastic Receptions', *DN*, 18 Jun. 1886, p. 5.

[208] E. King, 'The Grand Old Man', *English Labourers' Chronicle*, 5 May 1888, p. 2.

[209] Like 'God Bless the Grand Old Man' (1888: cit. in Clarke, *Lancashire*, p. 2).

[210] See advertisement, *NR*, 26 May 1885, p. 52: 'THE "GRAND OLD MAN" CIGARS are so named because, like the "Grand Old Man" himself, they are unequalled. All Liberal and Radical Clubs should try them.'

those extraordinary days show not only the widespread extent of Gladstone's popularity, but also his capacity for spreading enthusiasm throughout the variety of regions along the route of his electoral travels. Typically, the collective euphoria always erupted even before he began to speak, as soon as he appeared in front of the audience, or even in anticipation of his appearance, while the audience was waiting for him.

The 'Midlothian style' had developed slowly, but its perfection from November 1879 was – to a large extent – imposed by popular reactions. On the 24th of that month Gladstone left on an ordinary train from Liverpool to Edinburgh, to inaugurate his candidature for the county of Midlothian. It was a very unusual journey. Though the train left at 8:45 am, it did not arrive until the evening: 'and the delay was occasioned by the insistence of the populace at the halting places from Liverpool to see and cheer the great Liberal statesman'.[211] Not only great numbers of people crowded the main stations along the line in order to present the 'People's William' with addresses; but 'even at the wayside stations, through which the train passed at a speed of forty miles an hour, the people had assembled in hundreds to see it go by with its illustrious passenger'.[212]

This welcome was all the more spectacular and impressive because it had been neither organized nor even expected by the statesman's electoral committee,[213] but took place spontaneously. Gladstone himself was surprised and embarrassed at first: at Preston, where the train had its first stop, he thanked the public for the welcome, but invited them to disperse in order to avoid the danger of accidents, since the station looked dangerously overcrowded. Embarrassment and surprise faded as similar demonstrations were repeated: at Hawick Gladstone spoke to 3,000 people from the railway bridge; at Galashiels the band of the Volunteers welcomed the train playing 'See the Conquering Hero Comes', and Gladstone and his wife received from local workers a present of tweed and plaids woven specifically for them. At Edinburgh some workers had woven a special carpet with the inscription 'Welcome'; their intention was to lay it 'at the feet of the workmen's friend

[211] [Rep.], 'Mr. Gladstone's Visit to Midlothian – Receptions at Carlisle, Hawick, Galashiels, and Edinburgh', *DN*, 25 Nov. 1879, p. 5.
[212] *Ibid.*
[213] *Ibid.*

when he alighted on Scottish soil'.[214] Others had planned to unharness the horses from his coach and to haul it themselves through the streets of the city: this was one of the honours usually reserved for victorious candidates, but in this case was to be celebrated not only before the election, but also with unusual pomp, 2,000 men having volunteered to organize the necessary relays. Eventually they were persuaded to abandon their project when they realized that the 'People's William' was completely exhausted.

Gladstone himself was so impressed that for once he abandoned his telegraphic diary style, and wrote:

the journey from Liverpool was really more like a triumphal procession. I had to make short speeches at Carlisle Hawick & Galashiels: very large numbers were assembled & at Edinburgh ... the scene ... was extraordinary, both for the numbers and the enthusiasm ... We drove off to Dalmeny with Ld Rosebery and were received with fireworks & torches. I have never gone through a more extraordinary day.[215]

The following days were characterized by similarly exciting scenes, but Gladstone had recovered his laconic style: 'Much enthusiasm along the road';[216] 'The enthusiasm, great along the road, was at the centre positively overwhelming'.[217] On 27 November at West Calder Gladstone passed under half a dozen triumphal arches covered with evergreens and framed with the flags of Britain and several other countries. His wife and daughter were presented with great bunches of flowers.[218] On the 29th at Waverley Market Gladstone spoke to more than 17,000 workers ('a wonderful meeting of 20,000')[219]. Sixty addresses were presented to him, signed by about 100,000 workers; moreover, a special illuminated address was put into his hands in a coffer of solid silver.[220] When he arrived, the ovations lasted for 'a considerable time': responding to this overwhelming welcome Gladstone said – among other

---

[214] *Ibid.*; apparently the plan failed because the station was overcrowded to the extent that the worker entrusted with the mission could not reach the carriage's door.

[215] *Diaries*, IX, entry for 24 Nov. 1879, p. 461.

[216] *Ibid.*, entry for 25 Nov. 1879, p. 461.

[217] *Ibid.*, entry for 27 Nov. 1879, p. 462.

[218] [Rep.], 'Mr. Gladstone in Mid-Lothian – Address at West Calder', *DN*, 28 Nov. 1879, p. 5.

[219] *Diaries*, IX, entry for 29 Nov. 1879, p. 463.

[220] [Rep.], 'Address to Working Men', *DN*, 1 Dec. 1879, p. 4.

things – 'Your gathering to-day, in almost countless thousands, I regard as a festival of freedom'.[221]

Similar 'festivals of freedom' accompanied him regularly in his triumphal return from Edinburgh to Glasgow, via Perth. Remembering the inconvenience of the outward journey, Gladstone used a special train so that he was able to stop for longer at each of the stations along the line, a whistle-stop tour reminiscent of the American style of 'stumping the country', but which had been imposed upon him by popular request.[222] Though accustomed to large crowds, Gladstone was deeply impressed: 'Fervid crowds at every station. The torchlight process at Glasgow was a subject for Turner'.[223] The pace of speeches was by then almost frantic:

At 12 delivered the inaugural address to 5000 [at the University] . . . Then went to the Academical luncheon, where I spoke. Away at 4. At 5.15 off to St Andrew's Hall. Spoke 1 1/2 hour to 6500 or 7000. Finally at 9 to the City Hall: spoke again to 3000. Did not God in His mercy wonderfully bear me through?[224]

The triumphal scenes accompanying his outward journey were repeated on his return: at Carlisle the station was so crowded that Gladstone was unable to get off the train, and had to speak from the window of his compartment;[225] at Preston the station was in total chaos and huge crowds surrounded the special train. But the final triumph was celebrated in Chester, where huge throngs had convened to greet him and accompany his coach towards Hawarden.

When Mr. Gladstone appeared outside the station, a scene of indescribable enthusiasm took place. As far as the eye could reach, the streets were crowded with people, and thousands of upturned faces shone in the glare of the torches. The cheers were again and again renewed, and it was some time before the carriage could be started. Mr. Gladstone repeatedly bowed in acknowledgement.[226]

When eventually the procession began to move, it was possible to appreciate its magnitude:

[221] *Ibid.*
[222] [Rep.], 'Mr. Gladstone in Scotland – The Journey to Perth – Presentation of the Freedom of the City', *DN*, 2 Dec. 1879, p. 5.
[223] *Diaries*, IX, entry for 4 Dec. 1879, p. 404.
[224] *Ibid.*, entry for 5 Dec. 1879, p. 404.
[225] [Rep.], 'Mr. Gladstone's Return from Scotland', *DN*, 9 Dec. 1879, p. 3.
[226] [Rep.], 'Reception at Chester', *ibid.*

The whole city had turned out to do honour to Mr. Gladstone, and the scene as the procession passed through the quaint and narrow streets of Chester, lit up by hundreds of flambeaux, the people cheering from every coign of vantage and handkerchiefs waving from every window, was one to be remembered. In Eastgate-street a countryman elbowed his way through the crowd, and grasping Mr. Gladstone's hand, cried 'God bless thee, owd mon'; and another shouted 'You'll be Premier again after this'.[227]

The result of the campaign seemed to reflect its enthusiasm. Wherever Gladstone passed he stirred the Liberals' blood. 'Ironside' could write:

The reception of Mr. Gladstone in Scotland is the greatest political event in these islands for many years past . . . It is more than a royal progress that has been seen in Scotland – it is a veritable uprising of the populace. To find anything like it we must go back to the period when Kossuth and Garibaldi, the representatives of European freedom, were the idols of the British people.[228]

'An uprising of the populace' was a curious definition, but not a totally inappropriate one if one considers that the campaign and succeeding elections have been seen by one historian as 'a phenomenon to puzzle anyone who argues that social influence, often assisted by corruption and intimidation, remained determinant in nineteenth-century elections'.[229] In fourteen days Gladstone had delivered thirty speeches in front of audiences totalling more than 86,000,[230] according to his own computation, in various places along the north-western route of Chester-Liverpool-Glasgow-Edinburgh. However, the elections were still far away and sceptics wondered how it would be possible 'to keep this pot of enthusiasm boiling' for several months.[231] Gladstone's reply was very simple: in March 1880, after the dissolution of Parliament, he repeated the 'Midlothian operation', this time moving along the strategic route of the north-east, from London to Grantham-York-Newcastle-upon-Tyne-Edinburgh.[232] By all accounts the success of the previous years recurred: 'At Edinburgh the wonderful scene of Nov.

---

[227] *Ibid.*

[228] Ironside, 'Mr. Gladstone's Visit to Scotland', *NW*, 6 Dec. 1879.

[229] Lloyd, *Election of 1880*, pp. 2, 29.

[230] More precisely 86,950: *Diaries*, IX, cit., p. 466.

[231] Cit. in Jenkins, 'Leadership of the Liberal Party', p. 340.

[232] See *Diaries*, IX, entry for 16 Mar. 1880, p. 492. See also Morley, *Gladstone*, II, p. 608.

was exactly repeated',[233] 'Great & most enthusiastic meeting',[234] 'Great & enthusiastic meeting',[235] were Gladstone's diary entries in those days. Activity was unremitting, just as in 1879: 'Travelled forty miles & delivered three speeches of 45 or 50 min. each at Juniper Green, Colington . . . and Mid-Calder . . . Enthusiasm unabated'.[236] The *Daily News* commented: 'there is no centre of population within the county that the Liberal candidate has not visited, and the smallest places whither he has not gone have poured forth their population to greet him at the nearest halting-place'.[237] And of the reception granted to Gladstone it added:

It is physically impossible that any greater crowds can meet than have hitherto gathered wherever Mr. Gladstone has been announced to speak. Nor can [there] be any louder cheering or more frantic waving of hats and handkerchiefs than follows upon a sight of the face and figure that is now so familiar in the capital county.[238]

As Morley recollected, 'people came from the Hebrides to hear Mr. Gladstone speak. When there were six thousand seats, the applications were forty or fifty thousand. The weather was bitter and the hills were covered with snow, but this made no difference in cavalcades, processions, and the rest of the outdoor demonstrations'.[239] Between November-December 1879 and March-April 1880 hundreds of thousands of people listened to at least one of Gladstone's speeches, and were directly influenced by him, as also suggested by the fact that the Liberals 'gained a seat at every stop where he had spoken'.[240] But his fascination reached out well beyond the regions that he visited. For instance, at Leeds, where Gladstone had a second candidature and was elected with a huge majority without even appearing, the *Mercury* observed: 'We see here what was seen on Tuesday in every town at which Mr. GLADSTONE stopped in the course of his journey to Edinburgh, a burning eagerness to render homage to his genius and his words'.[241] Mundella observed:

[233] *Diaries*, IX, entry for 16 Mar. 1880, p. 492.
[234] *Ibid.*, entry for 17 Mar. 1880, pp. 492–3.
[235] *Ibid.*, entry for 19 Mar. 1880, p. 493.
[236] *Ibid.*, entry for 20 Mar. 1880, p. 493.
[237] [Rep.], 'The General Election – The Campaign in Mid-Lothian', *DN*, 3 Apr. 1880, p. 5.
[238] *Ibid.*
[239] Morley, *Gladstone*, II, p. 588.
[240] Lloyd, *1880*, p. 25.
[241] [L.a., n.t.], *LM*, 18 Mar. 1880, p. 6.

The reaction for *Gladstone* is very remarkable. As I passed a Stationer's shop in Queen Victoria Street, in the city (this morning) the window was crowded with Gladstone's photographs, and there was printed up in large letters 'The man for England'. This would have been impossible a year and a half ago. In Portsmouth people went almost mad at the mention of his name. I have some capital Liberal songs sung in the Portsmouth demonstration. The effect was almost inspiriting.[242]

Daily throughout the country millions of people followed his precise, hammering rhetoric in the reports published by all newspapers – both Liberal and Conservative – with regularity and completeness, though with very different comments. In this way the propaganda effect was considerably magnified, and Gladstone could reach out, not only to dissatisfied Conservatives, but also the mass of those who were either politically unaware or who had not yet made up their minds.[243] 'Like the holy HERMIT PETER by millions I'm adored',[244] wrote a Tory cartoonist with unconscious propriety, though his words were true in a sociological, Weberian, sense, rather than in a psychological one.[245]

As far as popular Liberalism was concerned, the effects of the campaigns were even more overwhelming than it has traditionally been accepted.[246] While Gladstone received the expression of the most complete devotion of Broadhurst's National Liberal League,[247] 'Ironside' proclaimed him 'the real though no longer the nominal leader of the Opposition'.[248] Even *Lloyd's Weekly* – discerning that the public mood had changed – abandoned Hartington and Granville and proclaimed that 'The People expects

---

[242] Cit. in Armytage, *Mundella*, p. 197.

[243] Matthew, 'Introduction' to *Diaries*, IX, pp. lxi–lxiii; and 'Rhetoric and Politics', pp. 47–8.

[244] Anon., *Gladstone's Garland. Materials Collected by an Elector*, London, 1880, (pamphlet in Cambridge University Library).

[245] The arrogance that this pamphlet ascribed to Gladstone did not correspond to the Liberal leader's attitude. On 30 April 1880, coming back from an hour and a half speech to 4,000 people (successful as always: 'High tide of enthusiasm'), Gladstone wrote in his diary: 'The beginning of the elections. May God from heaven guide every one of them; and prosper or abase and baffle us for His glory; lift us up, or trample us down, according as we are promoting or opposing what He knows to be the cause of Truth, Liberty, and Justice' (*Diaries*, IX, p. 496). When the final victory appeared certain, Gladstone commented: 'The triumph grows and grows: to God be the praise!' (Magnus, *Gladstone*, p. 270).

[246] Ensor, *England 1870–1914*, p. 66.

[247] W. E. Gladstone to H. Broadhurst, 27 Dec. 1879, in *H. Broadhurst Papers*, I, item 62, pp. 89–91.

[248] Ironside, 'Lord Hartington's Visit', *NW*, 20 Sept. 1879, p. 4.

him to lead and will be content with no less illustrious captain'.[249]
Just as in the days of the Bulgarian agitation, it reserved whole
pages to *verbatim* reports of the 'People's William's' speeches,[250]
and Thomas Catling's leading articles were as staunchly Gladstonian as those of W. T. Stead and 'Ironside': 'His was a holy wrath;
and he spoke as a tribune of the people'.[251] Disraeli's appeal had
vanished: now *Lloyd's* rejoiced that Beaconsfieldism's 'evil days'
were 'numbered',[252] while the Liberal leader's rhetoric was
described as 'the mighty sword flaming through the North, like
lightening in the storm, of the "Paladin of Humanity", as a learned
Jew has styled him – William Ewart Gladstone!'.[253] *Reynolds's* was
even more passionately Gladstonian:

We, sir, say to the Reform Club, 'Give us Gladstone'. As the first and
more important section of the Liberal party, we decline to worship rank
and incapacity in Granville. Equally we decline to accept the heir of the
Devonshires, because he was nominated liutenant at a time when timidity
was the badge of a beaten cause. If our demand is rejected the inevitable
must follow, and both Radical, Whig, and Liberal will be involved in a
disastrous defeat, which the selection of the Premier we nominate would
prevent.[254]

Thus the working-class press campaigned for 'Gladstone for
Premier' from at least November 1879 – some from July 1878[255] –
though the issue became topical only in April 1880. Since Gladstone 'saw himself as representing the rightness of "popular
judgement" expressed through the Liberal movement (as distinct
from the parliamentary Liberal party)',[256] it was not inappropriate
that popular enthusiasm was the steadfast factor working on his
behalf throughout the 'campaign' for his appointment.[257] However,
it soon became generally accepted that only 'the magic of [the
People's William's] genius had given victory to his followers', and

[249] [L.a.], 'Mr. Gladstone in Midlothian', *LW*, 30 Nov. 1879, p. 1.
[250] See e.g. [rep.], 'Mr. Gladstone's Visit to Scotland', *LW*, 30 Nov. 1879, p. 3.
[251] [L.a.], *LW*, 30 Nov. 1879, p. 1; see Ironside, 'The Liberal Triumph', *NW*, 10 Apr. 1880,
p. 4.
[252] [L.a.], 'The Liberal Victory', *LW*, 4 Apr. 1880, p. 6.
[253] [L.a.], 'The Liberal Outlook', *LW*, 28 Dec. 1879, p. 1.
[254] Northumbrian, 'The Radical Demand', *RN*, 16 Nov. 1879, p. 3.
[255] Leading labour figures had spoken in favour of Gladstone's 'reinstatement' even earlier:
see W. Patterson's speech in [rep.], 'Annual Demonstration of Durham Miners', *DC*, 12
Jul. 1878, p. 6.
[256] Matthew, 'Introduction' to *Diaries*, ix, p. lxxi.
[257] Jenkins, *Whiggery and the Liberal Party*, p. 133.

that 'the people had [. . .] strongly expressed their determination
to confide their destinies' only to his hands.[258]

As is well-known, however, the parliamentary leaders did not
see the situation in the same light: yet, just as Beaconsfield had
'provoked' Midlothian by his mistakes,[259] Hartington and Granville, by failing to provide effective leadership within the Opposition in the country, prepared the ground for Gladstone's
intervention. Gladstone's 'presidential style'[260] and capacity for
breaking traditional patterns could not have been imposed so
easily in different circumstances. No doubt, a section of the
electorate appreciated the moderation of Hartington and feared
the emotionalism and moralism of Gladstone;[261] it is also likely
that the party would have accepted the former had he been
recommended by the latter – and that even some of the radical
chiefs would have preferred such a solution[262]. But Nonconformists
and working-class radicals could be stirred up only by the sort of
arguments used by the 'People's William' himself,[263] and without
his intervention they would have remained substantially
apathetic[264]. The 1874 elections had already demonstrated that the
apathy and absenteeism of the electors was a factor which operated
against the Liberals,[265] and there is no evidence that in 1880, had
the Liberal leaders gone to the polls without Midlothian, the
general but inarticulated dissatisfaction with the national economy

---

[258] [L.a.], 'The People's Premier', *LW*, 25 Apr. 1880, p. 6; the *Daily News* took this view not
from 12 April, as Jenkins writes (*Whiggery and the Liberal Party*, p. 134), but from the very
time when the Liberal majority became 'practically assured': 'there can be no doubt that
the country has now . . . declared, not only in favour of a Liberal Government, but of
Mr. GLADSTONE as the chief of the Government' ([l.a., n.t.], *DN*, 9 Apr. 1880, p. 4).

[259] Shannon, 'Midlothian: 100 Years After', in Jagger (ed.), *Politics and Religion*, pp. 101–2.

[260] Hanham, *Elections and Party Management*, pp. 202–4.

[261] Jenkins, 'Leadership of the Liberal Party', pp. 340, 346, and 348–9.

[262] *Ibid.*, p. 349.

[263] Especially in the north, where a vigorous denunciation of 'Beaconsfieldism' was what
plebeian radicals wanted to hear. See Bradlaugh's speech in [rep.], 'Annual Demonstration of Durham Miners', *DC*, 12 Jul. 1878, p. 6: 'He strongly denounced what he
characterized as the trickery and juggling of Lord Beaconsfield, and held that the people
had nothing to expect from the present Government. Its whole policy was imperialism
and aristocracy, and what had been got from it had been wrung out of it. (Hear, hear,
and applause).' It is remarkable that this statement was made at just the time of
Beaconsfield's Berlin triumph. Cf. T. Burt to W. T. Stead, 14 Jan. 1879, in Stead Papers.

[264] Brooks, 'Gladstone and Midlothian', p. 53.

[265] Cornford, 'The Transformation of Conservatism', p. 54) has pointed out the existence of
an inverse correlation between Tory success and electoral turn out: 'the smaller the poll,
the larger the Conservative share of it, and this was most true in constituencies where
Conservatives were most successful.'

would have provided a majority for them: in fact many forecast a hung parliament, or even a renewal of the Conservative majority.[266] Gladstone's campaigns had the effect of providing what had characterized the 1868 election, and had been lacking in 1874:[267] the opportunity of starting and fostering for several months a national debate on a series of questions which the majority of electors considered of great importance. The aim of Midlothian was clearly to 'stir up the country', not in a vulgarly demagogic sense, but – as Matthew has written – by 'encouraging a new and high standard of political awareness, discussion, and citizenship'.[268]

The events which followed the elections simply reflected the importance of Gladstone's action, and his assumption of the *nominal* leadership of the Liberal party was the logical outcome of the fact that he had *actually* provided it with an effective leadership.[269] A government without Gladstone was not possible. Neither was one with him in a subordinate position, not because of his ambition or pride, but because it would have been quite foolish of him to accept an appointment in a government led by Hartington, whose leadership of the party Gladstone had found so unsatisfactory that he had twice felt compelled to resume an active role in politics over the past five years. Especially in foreign policy, the disagreement between the two statesmen had been clear from 1876,[270] though it had later been officially reconciled;[271] and of course the reversal of

---

[266] Ironside, 'Prospect of Parties', *NW*, 21 Feb. 1880, p. 4. See Jenkins, *Whiggery and the Liberal Party*, pp. 118–19; Blake, *Disraeli*, p. 716.

[267] Brooks, 'Gladstone and Midlothian', p. 52.

[268] Matthew, 'Introduction', *Diaries*, ix, p. lxix.

[269] Brooks, 'Gladstone and Midlothian', p. 65. To stress the 'highly developed faculty for self-deception' which allegedly characterized Gladstone in order to explain the fact that he was convinced 'that his conduct was motivated by something more than a base desire for a renewed lease of personal power' (Jenkins, 'Leadership of the Liberal Party', pp. 343–4), can be misleading. Jenkins argues effectively each passage of his article. But the whole of it can stand only if his initial hypothesis – that is, that the traditional interpretation stressing the importance of the Midlothian campaigns is untenable – is demonstrated: but the author simply formulates this hypothesis (pp. 337–8) without providing any evidence. At the end of the article he suggests that the opinion that Gladstone was the main architect of the victory is 'possibly inaccurate' (p. 359), and adds a concluding footnote (p. 360), without any reference – suggesting that it was the agricultural depression which decided the outcome of the election against the Tories. The impact of the depression is discussed *infra*, p. 415.

[270] Leach, *Devonshire*, pp. 173, 175–6; Jenkins, 'Leadership of the Liberal Party', p. 347.

[271] But perhaps only officially: after the elections, when the choice of a premier came under review, Gladstone insisted on the candidature of the 'little-Englander' Granville, rather than that of the quite Palmerstonian Hartington:

Beaconsfield's foreign policy had been one of the main themes in the electoral campaign.

The negative trade cycle and the agricultural depression certainly had an important role. But – at a time when labourers were still excluded from the franchise – it was not clear to what extent this crisis would affect the election.[272] In this context, effective propaganda and an ability to appeal to those who had no strong commitment to either party was of special importance: and it was Gladstone's intervention which transformed the 'discontent factor' from an ill-defined, a-political, and non-party subconscious feeling, into conscious and determined support for the Liberals.[273] He effectively touched the imagination of those who usually did not vote 'for', but 'against' a party, by giving them convincing reasons why they ought to vote 'against' Beaconsfield. By focussing the nation's attention on the government's aggressive foreign policy and mismanagement of the Exchequer as the causes of the national and international economic confusion, Gladstone showed – once more – his political intuition and his famous capacity for 'letting the facts speak for themselves'.

This important factor – which *usually* determines the outcome of an election – may perhaps be assessed as the 'ability to provide a moral framework for more materialistic feelings of discontent':[274] but the fact is that 'moral' frameworks are as real as material ones. The framework of Gladstone's rhetoric served its purpose. In this sense,

---

I could not find that she [the Queen] expressed clearly the reason for appealing to him as a responsible leader, and yet going past the leader of the party, namely Granville . . . She however indicated to him her confidence in his moderation, the phrase under which he is daily commended in the D.[aily] Telegraph, at the moment I think Beaconsfield's personal organ & recipient of his inspirations. By this moderation the Queen intimated that Hartington was distinguished from Granville as well as from me. (*Diaries*, IX, 'Secret, April 22, 1880', p. 504.)

Gladstone also wrote that he 'felt a *tolerable* degree of confidence' in promising a *conditional* support to a Hartington government because he did not see 'any *substantive* divergence of ideas between us' (*ibid.*, my italics). There is no doubt that, from the point of view of the Queen and Beaconsfield, Hartington was a 'good' candidate especially because of his divergences from Gladstone and Granville, the latter being 'too much devoted to Gladstone' (Magnus, *Gladstone*, p. 271; Blake, *Disraeli*, pp. 716–17).

[272] There was a Liberal improvement in the counties (Jenkins, 'Leadership of the Liberal Party', p. 260), though it was mainly the recovery of Liberal seats lost in 1874: in England the Liberal position improved on 1868 only by 8 seats. On the whole the Conservatives preserved the great majority of the counties (116:54, see Hanham, *Elections and Party Management*, p. 25).

[273] T. Burt to W. T. Stead, 8 Feb. 1879, in Stead Papers. Cf. Lloyd, *1880*, pp. 27–9, 152–60; McGill, 'Francis Schnadhorst and Liberal Party Organization', p. 22.

[274] Jenkins, 'Leadership of the Liberal Party', p. 360 n.

he was the 'architect' of the electoral victory of 1880 – though he did not provide its 'building materials'; but this, of course, is not the role of architects. Equally, it can be said that the strategy of the Conservatives failed completely, to the extent that they were defeated even in their strongholds, losing twenty-seven of their faithful English counties: this was the final seal on a series of political mistakes, not the inevitable result of a negative economic trend.

THE GOM IN THE 1880s

From the point of view of his capacity for preserving popular support, Gladstone's second premiership was much more successful than his first. Even the controversial invasion of Egypt in 1882 – which directly contradicted the Midlothian programme – found many advocates among plebeian radicals, and had the benefit of a substantial silent complicity even from the most inflexible anti-imperialists, like Joseph Arch and his men.[275] Paraphrasing a common expression, it could be said that the accepted opinion among the radical common people was that Gladstone was, 'our William, right or wrong'. The long campaign for the 1884 Reform Bill came at the right time to re-invigorate rank-and-file Liberalism and to renew the cult of the GOM, as the man who 'has ever been ready to advance the interests of all those who lived by labour'.[276] In those months many other statesmen received enthusiastic receptions at Liberal meetings, particularly John Bright, who again lived through triumphal days like those of 1866–7.[277] But nobody, not even Bright, was able to maintain a relationship with the masses similar to the one firmly established by Gladstone.

It is a striking fact that the intimacy between the GOM and the workers had apparently increased, though he was now premier and had been in power for four long and difficult years. Not only were the usual frantic scenes and continuous celebrations repeated during his third Midlothian campaign, but the press also reported a number of short dialogues between Gladstone and his admirers. For instance, once, when waiting for the train in Edinburgh, Gladstone began talking to the railwaymen: 'Why don't you come oftener?', one of them asked the premier, and he answered,

[275] Horn, *Arch*, p. 360 n.
[276] [Rep.], 'The Workmen's Address to Mr. Gladstone', *DN*, 10 Nov. 1884, p. 3.
[277] See [rep.], 'Great Demonstration at Manchester', *DN*, 28 Jul. 1884, p. 5.

laughing, 'I would, but I am an old fellow now'; then another worker said 'You have got the nation at your back and you can't be beaten'.[278] A similar, but even more significant, scene took place during the campaign of 1886, when one evening at a meeting,

... one of the villagers [of Penicuick] stepped forward and told Mr. Gladstone, in his homely Doric, that they had only come a mile or so to see him, but they would have come fifty miles to see the man that had fought for them and given them the vote to fight for themselves – a speech which evidently gave the Prime Minister much gratification.[279]

'Mr. Gladstone responded to this expression of feeling by very warmly shaking hands with Mr. Black', who led the Penicuick group.[280] On other occasions the dialogue assumed choral form: 'Give us a speech, if only a sentence', 8,000 shouted at the Aberdeen station; from the compartment window Gladstone answered, 'Well, gentlemen, if you want one sentence from me, that sentence ought to be to say that I am one of yourselves. (Cheers.)'.[281] And soon after, referring to the Third Reform Act he said: 'I have done my duty pretty well so far. (A Voice "And we will do ours") Now you have got to do your duty. (Cheers and cries "We will.")'.[282]

However, in 1884 as in 1880 and 1879, the fulcrum of the campaign was not these short speeches with more or less choral dialogues, but the great mass meetings and long and elaborate speeches addressed as much to the local audience as to the newspaper readership. On these occasions Gladstoneian rhetoric remained faithful to the model of 'popular rationalism': He neither provided room for any dialogue with the public, nor did he try to excite choral replies – though his meetings were regularly opened, concluded, and occasionally interrupted by long ovations. But at the meeting in Waverley Market – where 15,000 workers congregated, and several thousand more crowded the adjoining streets[283] – there took place a different kind of 'dialogue' between audience and speaker, indeed a typical expression of the rationalism char-

---

278 [Rep.], 'Mr. Gladstone's Journey to Invercauld – Enthusiastic Receptions', *DN*, 4 Sept. 1884, p. 5.
279 [Rep.], 'Mr. Gladstone in Edinburgh – Extraordinary Scenes', *DN*, 21 Jun. 1886, p. 5.
280 [Rep.], 'Mr. Gladstone in Mid-Lothian. – Popular Enthusiasm. – Extraordinary Scenes', *LM*, 21 Jun. 1886, p. 8.
281 [Rep.], cit., *DN*, 4 Sept. 1884, p. 5.
282 *Ibid.* See for another example, Lloyd, *1880*, p. 152.
283 [Rep.], 'Great Meeting in the Waverly Market Hall', *DN*, 3 Sept. 1884, p. 5.

acterizing the liberalism of the subaltern classes. On this occasion, before Gladstone spoke, an address was read aloud to him by a spokesman for the public.[284] The address contained not only the workers' welcome, but also a political programme which went far beyond the immediate question of the franchise reform. And it is interesting to note that Gladstone explicitly articulated his speech as a reply to this message.

The Waverley Market meeting is also interesting for another reason, which concerns its 'choreography'. Among the decorations in the hall there was a remarkable use of elements which would have been familiar to a reporter of Lassalle's meetings in Germany, items such as the flags of the local trade unions hanging from the ceiling together with portraits of Gladstone and Bright. On the whole the scene symbolized well the 'fusion' between organized labour movement and charismatic leader, and – through the latter – the integration of the trade unions into the Liberal party.[285] A hypothetical German observer would also have been struck by other similarities to Lassallian gatherings, and especially by the fact that the 'entrance of the leader' had become the celebrative moment of highest collective exaltation. As in the Rhineland, so in Midlothian, the leader's entrance provided impressive evidence 'of the unity of a movement'[286] and of the extent to which it was personified:

It is impossible to describe the scene. Myriads of handkerchiefs were fluttering in the hands of the ladies upon the galleries, and the still greater number of hats waving upon the heads of the dense throng in the area, was a sufficiently impressive scene to the eye to be for ever remembered by anyone who witnessed it. But when to this was added the universal roar of welcome which proceeded forth from countless throats, the intensity was immensely deepened.[287]

The previous day, at a meeting in the Corn Exchange, upon the entrance of the Premier 'Instantly the great audience rose, and old men as well as young men mounted their seats in order to obtain a

---

[284] *Ibid.* There are many examples of a similar procedure: see [rep.], 'Election Meetings and Speeches – Mr. Gladstone in Scotland – Important Speech at West Calder', *DN*, 18 Nov. 1885, p. 2.

[285] [Rep.], 'Mr. Gladstone in Edinburgh . . .', cit., *NC*, 3 Sept. 1884, p. 3.

[286] Mosse, *The Nationalization of the Masses*, p. 163.

[287] [Rep.], 'Mr. Gladstone in Edinburgh . . .', *NC*, 3 Sept. 1884, p. 3.

good view of the Dalmany party [Gladstone and his suite]. Tremendous cheering resounded through the large hall . . .'.[288]

It is noteworthy that the length of the initial cheers apparently increased year by year: in 1884 a record was established by an audience at Old Meldrum, where the GOM 'was cheered for nearly five minutes'[289] before he was able to begin his speech, and at the 1887 meeting of the NLF he was applauded 'for many minutes'.[290] On other occasions the welcoming ovations assumed a more elaborate character and were interposed with songs struck up by the audience, either spontaneously or encouraged by the local organizers. An impressive example is provided by the welcome that Gladstone received at the Manchester Free Trade Hall during the fifth Midlothian campaign, in 1886:

The interval of waiting for Mr. Gladstone was excellently employed. A pink programme of music was sown broadcast among the audience, its colour contributing a singular effect to the scene, the organ was played and the vast audience whiled away the time in singing right vigorously a series of songs, mostly in praise of the Premier. One of these, it was announced, had been composed by a farm labourer living near Middleton. The verses were sung with much vigour. . . . 'Gladstone shall be our leader' was the burden of another song, and words were even set to the National Anthem in his honour:

> Not of patrician blood,
> Thwarted, misunderstood,
> He seeks the public good,
> And holds the field.

A solo was sung entitled 'The Pilot of the State', the chorus of which was vigorously taken up by the whole audience.[291]

But, the reporter went on,

. . . at Mr. Gladstone's appearance the enthusiasm was unbounded; flags, handkerchiefs – red and white and green – hats and programmes were frantically waved, and the cheering was sustained for fully two minutes. Then the people started 'Should auld acquaintance be forgot' . . . the chairman . . . after this interposed a few words of introduction, and Mr.

---

[288] [Rep.], 'Mr. Gladstone in Mid-Lothian – Important Vindication of Government Policy', *DN*, 2 Sept. 1884, p. 5.

[289] [Rep.], 'Mr. Gladstone in Scotland. – The Journey from Mar Lodge to Haddo House', *NC*, 16 Sept. 1884, p. 3.

[290] Watson, *The National Liberal Federation*, p. 80.

[291] [Rep.], 'Mr. Gladstone at Manchester. – Stirring Scenes of Welcome', *DN*, 26 Jun. 1886, p. 5. Cf. Coffey, *Thesis*, pp. 14–6.

Gladstone rose to speak. Nearly two minutes more of cheering, then 'He's a jolly good fellow' with the 'hip, hip, hurrah!' most energetically delivered, and Mr. Gladstone standing all the while smiling, but evidently eager to commence.[292]

At Glasgow that same year, to increase the spectacular effect of the 'entrance of the leader' into the meeting hall – Hengler's Circle, 'crowded from floor to ceiling' – 'special effects' were produced with gas lights, which stressed the theatrical side of the 'demagogic' occasion and would have provided a scholar of modern political leadership like Robert Michels with more conclusive evidence than that which he collected at Socialist meetings on the Continent. As in Manchester, the crowd, 'full of eager expectation', was waiting for Gladstone's arrival by singing with great gusto popular songs such as 'Auld Lang Syne' and 'Scots wha hae wi' Wallace Bled'.

But in the way of stirring emotions nothing in this grand meeting equalled the strikingly dramatic scene which occurred right in the middle of this song and put an abrupt end to the chorus. The lights suddenly went up, and in the brilliant illumination of the great assembly the Prime Minister and his friends were seen advancing to the front of a small railed enclosure left in one portion of the amphitheatre to serve for a platform. The music spontaneously died on the lips of the thousands who were singing, and there broke forth from all those hearty voices a deafening cheer. At the same moment the whole house rose, and . . . wild waving of handkerchiefs by the whole mass of the people. Whether by accident or desire, the majority of the handkerchiefs were red, and the effect produced was extremely striking and gay in brilliant light . . . The Premier repeatedly smiled and bowed his acknowledgement. The audience were however in no hurry to stop; the cheers continued to resound through, the cold wind of the whirling handkerchiefs continued to blow, and when at last the cheers died away it was only to be followed up by the chorus, 'For he's a jolly good fellow', sung with the most fervent accent.[293]

It is safe to say that by 1886 the style of Gladstone's electoral campaigns – as far as their effectiveness in bringing a political message to the masses was concerned – had overtaken any Continental model, whether republican, socialist or Bonapartist. As we have seen, choral singing – which so deeply struck both

---

[292] [Rep.], 'Mr. Gladstone at Manchester', *DN*, 26 Jun. 1886, p. 5.

[293] [Rep.], 'Mr. Gladstone – Brilliant Reception', *DN*, 23 Jun. 1886, p. 5. Comparable techniques were used later at American Democratic Conventions: Bell, 'Authoritarian and Democratic Leaders', in Gouldner (ed.), *Studies in Leadership*, pp. 401–2.

Michels and Mosse when they studied Lassallian demonstrations[294] – was the normal routine in the Midlothian campaigns. In contrast to Lassalle, Gladstone did not even need to bother about the organization of these details, nor about writing hymns in honour of himself.[295] The habit of presenting the ladies of the retinue with flowers – a bunch at each station for Catherine Gladstone, the 'Grand Old Lady'[296] – together with special presents for both the leader and his wife, were as common in Midlothian and in northern England,[297] as they were in the Rhineland; and the same can be said of floral decorations along the route – garlands across the streets, triumphal arches, and flags all over the place.[298] Lassalle was met by special committees at the stations; but Gladstone was welcomed by whole towns in large cities like Manchester: thousands upon thousands of people who occupied all the best positions for four or five hours in advance, and lined the streets an hour before the expected time of the train's arrival at the station – multitudes more than once described as 'beyond calculation'.[299] Besides travelling by train hundreds of miles, pronouncing five or six speeches in different places, Gladstone's electoral day could include shaking dozens of hands, kissing children, congratulating enthusiastic, energetic old men who had walked forty miles or more to see 'the grandest man of the age', and also facing fanatical working men who, while the train was still in motion, would jump into his compartment to shake frantically the GOM's hand.[300] A 'typical Gladstone action' at one of the Scottish meetings were so described by W. Freer: 'The Old Man spotted three wee boys wedged in among the crowd. Stop-

---

294 Michels, *Political Parties*, p. 70; Mosse, *The Nationalization of the Masses*, pp. 161–2. Choral singing – indeed, trained choirs – were used also by other minor English charismatic leaders, like Charles Bradlaugh: see the role of the London Secular Choir Union in [rep.], 'Land Law Reform', *NR*, 22 Feb. 1880, p. 113. In the same period the use of choirs was developed to an unprecedented scale in evangelistic campaigns, to reach out to the indifferent: Kent, *Holding the Fort*, p. 35; Coffey, *Thesis*, p. 14..

295 Mosse, *The Nationalization of the Masses*, p. 162.

296 [Rep.], 'Mr. Gladstone's Journey . . .', *DN*, 18 Jun. 1886, p. 5.

297 See for other instances: [Rep.], 'Derbyshire. – The Working Men's Gift to Mr Gladstone', *WT*, 23 Dec. 1883, p. 6; Feuchtwanger, *Gladstone*, pp. 256–7.

298 See for instance [rep.], 'Mr. Gladstone at Dalkeith. – Local Government and the Local Question', *DN*, 23 Nov. 1885, p. 5.

299 [Rep.], 'Mr. Gladstone at Manchester', *DN*, 26 Jun. 1886, 26 Jun. 1886, p. 5.

300 All these things took place on 15 September 1884, in Scotland: see [rep.], *NC*, 16 Sept. 1884.

ping, he patted the youngsters on the head, while he and Mrs. Gladstone spoke to them – to the frantic envy of everyone else'.[301]

If Lassalle's aim was 'above all . . . the winning of those who are indifferent and to involve the greatest possible numbers',[302] he would have been greatly impressed by the success of Gladstone, at whose passage through Yorkshire railway stations even 'women and children mingled with the excited crowds who struggled to shake the hand of the PRIME MINISTER',[303] while boys and railway-men left their jobs and climbed onto the roofs of the carriages (including the one in which Gladstone was travelling).[304] On some occasions even the gas lamps had to accommodate athletic fans of the Liberal statesman.[305] When the train travelled in the open countryside the miners left their pits, the labourers their fields and the workers the ironworks to line up along the rails and greet the train on which they knew that Gladstone was travelling – though, because of its speed, it was not possible for them to see the GOM.[306] And the fact that similar scenes took place not only during the summer, but also in the cold that must have character-ized Chester at midnight on 29 November 1885 – when thousands of people celebrating the return of the GOM from the fourth Midlothian campaign swarmed over every surface on which it was possible to stand, sit or climb[307] – shows that Gladstone reached peaks of popularity that few other political leaders have achieved, either before or since. As one plebeian admirer wrote,

There has been nothing, I'm sure, since Gladstone's time to correspond to the hero-worship he excited. His was a personality that attracted everybody – even those who were not of the same political faith.[308]

This 'hero worship' stimulated a trend, also shared by Continen-tal labour movements,[309] towards identifying the party with its

---

[301] Freer, *My Life* (1929), p. 52.

[302] Mosse, *The Nationalization of the Masses*, p. 161.

[303] [L.a.], 'A Triumphal Progress', *DN*, 18 Jun. 1886, p. 4.

[304] [Rep.], 'Mr. Gladstone's Journey . . .', *DN*, 18 Jun. 1886, p. 5.

[305] [Rep.], 'Mr. Gladstone's Midlothian Campaign', *DN*, 10 Nov. 1885, p. 5.

[306] [Rep.], 'Mr. Gladstone's Journey . . .', *DN*, 18 Jun. 1886, p. 5.

[307] [Rep.], 'Mr. Gladstone's Journey to Hawarden', *DN*, 30 Nov. 1885, p. 2.

[308] Freer, *My Life* (1929), p. 52.

[309] Michels, *Political Parties*, p. 69, recollects the cases of the Broussists, Allemanists, Blanquistes, Guesdistes, Jauresists, Lassallians, and Marxists; to this list the Mazzinians and the Garibaldians could be added. Michels also suggested an interesting analogy between labour parties based on a charismatic personality and religious sects or monastic orders: an analogy that could be further developed by a comparative study and application of Weberian concepts.

leader. This phenomenon became prevalent after the secession of the Unionists, but at least as early as 1884–85 the most popular sections of the Liberal electorate (and non-electorate) identified the party with Gladstone. For instance, Joseph Arch organized mock elections to 'drill' his men in the secret ballot: they used a ballot paper on which Gladstone's name was printed in place of the local Liberal candidate's one, while Northcote's name stood for the name of the Conservative candidate.[310] Similarly, in 1886 the *Northern Echo* published an 'Elector's Guide' which included a ballot paper with two names printed on it and a big 'X' printed against the 'right' name: the two names were Gladstone and Salisbury (who was chosen to symbolize the Tories, though he was not, obviously, a candidate for the House of Commons).[311]

Of Gladstone's first six Midlothian campaigns, that of 1886 was the only one which was not followed by national success for the Liberal party. However, at a regional level the success of the GOM was quite extraordinary even in 1886: while in many parts of the United Kingdom the Liberal party fell apart, in eastern Scotland the labour movement remained intact behind Gladstone,[312] and the Gladstonians conquered thirty-two seats, while the Unionists were left with only nine (and only one of these went to the Tories).[313] 'Supposing for the sake of argument that Gladstone had stood for all the English marginal seats in the way he came forward to crush a supposed Liberal dissident by standing at Leith, the elections could have taken a very different aspect'.[314] And it is well-known that in many cases the Liberals, wary of the complexity of the pros and cons of the Home Rule proposals, decided to 'trust only Gladstone in this doubtful business',[315] and 'come what may, . . . [to] stand by the Grand Old Man'.[316]

Even if his Home Rule Bills never overcame the opposition of the Lords, by 1892 Gladstone managed to make Irish government an electoral question on which the Liberal party could obtain a

---

[310] Horn, *Arch*, p. 164; in the instance mentioned by Horn, out of 26 electors, 25 voted for Gladstone and one ballot paper was void.

[311] Poster contained in the *Northern Echo*, June 1886.

[312] Hutchison, *Scotland*, pp. 181, 263.

[313] Cooke and Vincent, *Governing Passion*, p. 435.

[314] *Ibid.*, p. 436. See Cooke, 'Gladstone's Election for the Leith District'.

[315] Morgan, *Wales in British Politics*, p. 71.

[316] Parry, *Democracy and Religion*, pp. 439–40. See Goodlad, 'Gladstone and his Rivals', in Biagini and Reid (eds.), *Currents of Radicalism*, pp. 163–84.

majority of the popular vote, confirming his character of a great popular leader and his relationship with the radicals of the subaltern classes. In 1887 his denunciation of the repression of the workers' demonstrations on 'Bloody Sunday' as an importation of Irish military rule, and as illustrating the coercion and unconstitutional procedures were contagious,[317] strengthened his appeal to the workers and provided further arguments in favour of his thesis that there was a close link between the liberties of Britons and Home Rule for the Irish. His determined stand in favour of the successful London dock strike of 1889 as a 'satisfactory, as a real social advance [that] tends to a fair principle of division of the fruits of industry',[318] has no parallel in the rest of Europe except in the rhetoric of the toughest socialist leaders, and earned him charges of being a 'seditious agitator', a dangerous revolutionary and a threat to property and the Crown.[319] But these and other similar stands of his gave the GOM an unparalleled prestige among the labour movement: according to Atherley Jones, at the end of the century it was commonly believed 'that Gladstonianism is the natural creed of the working man', while the Liberals had become a party 'almost exclusively identified with the particular interest of the working class'.[320] It is significant that Labour leaders like Ramsay MacDonald imitated his rhetoric,[321] while for a long time men like Keir Hardie kept alive the moral pathos which characterized Gladstonianism. It is impossible to predict what the outcome of a general election against the Lords' veto in 1894 would have been, had the Liberal government dissolved Parliament as Gladstone advised, and accepted the GOM's lead in this last crusade: but there can be no doubt that it would not have been so disastrous as the outcome of the election which Rosebery fought in desperate conditions a year later.

The old statesman retired from Parliament without really disappearing from the political scene or being forgotten; indeed his influence remained strong for a long time, especially in popular

---

[317] Barker, *Gladstone and Radicalism*, pp. 90–1.
[318] *Ibid.*, p. 92.
[319] Churchill, *My Early Life* (1930), pp. 21–2. Similar charges had been voiced as early as 1879: see the *Standard* as quoted by Ironside, 'Political Prospects', 25 Jan. 1879, p. 4.
[320] L. A. Atherley Jones in 1889, cit. in Wald, *Crosses on the Ballot*, pp. 29–30, see also p. 21ff; and H. Pelling, *Popular Politics*, p. 17.
[321] Matthew, 'Rhetoric and Politics', p. 54; DLB, 1, *sub voce*.

politics.[322] Some of the most heart-felt – and surely the most sincere – messages that the GOM received upon his retirement, came from labour associations and leaders, who wanted once more to honour the one who had not 'sought for honours conferred by monarchs, but the higher honour, that inward consciousness that results from right doing', and reassure him 'that a grateful people will hold you in kind and lasting remembrance'.[323] Uncertain whether to regret his retirement or congratulate him on his long and glorious career, Thomas Burt wrote to Gladstone:

Your life has been grand – the noblest and best I have ever known. It has been an inspiration and a triumph; fruitful in untold benefits to millions of men and women. And indeed I feel that the fitting word is neither condolence nor congratulation, but gratitude; – devout thankfulness that such a man has been given to us, and that he knew so well how to direct and use his gifts to the highest service of humanity.[324]

Though some historians maintain that Gladstone's political longevity was a tragedy for the Liberal party, it is well-known to scholars of the labour movement that to the very end of his life he remained the unparalleled leader of the British working classes, and even had some influence on Continental labour movements.[325] Gladstone equipped Victorian Liberalism for mass democracy in an age when charismatic leadership was the only effective means of reaching out to the new mass electorate and effectively mobilizing popular radicalism.[326] His success – extraordinary and almost unique in length and extent – prevented the development of a bureaucratic party system.[327] The fact that charisma and Liberal rationalism were so closely intermixed in Gladstone protected the country against any development of the authority of the leader towards authoritarianism, and brought the Liberal creed – as people said in those days – 'to the millions'.

---

[322] E.g., John Wilson's declaration in *Aldergate Magazine*, June 1902, *John Wilson Papers*, D/X 188/16, p. 46.

[323] Address of the DMA, 1894, cit. in Wilson, *Memories*, p. 254.

[324] Thomas Burt to W. E. Gladstone, 6 Mar. 1894, *Gladstone Papers* 44518, ff.82, 83, 84.

[325] Andreucci, *Socialdemocrazia e imperialismo*, p. 161.

[326] Stedman Jones, *Languages of Class*, p. 181.

[327] Cf. Matthew, 'Introduction' to *Gladstone Diaries*, IX, p. lvii.

Bibliography

The bibliography is divided into the following sections:

1. REFERENCE WORKS

Baylen, J. O., and Gossman N. J. (eds.), *Biographical Dictionary of Modern British Radicals*, vol. 2, *1830–1870*, Brighton, 1984

Bellamy, J., and Saville J. (eds.), *Dictionary of Labour Biography*, London, 1972–

Burnett, J., Vincent, D., and Myall, D., *The Autobiography of the Working Class. An Annotated, Critical Bibliography*, vol. 1, *1790–1900*, Brighton, 1984

Craig, F. W. S. (compiler and ed.), *British Electoral Facts 1832–1980*, Aldershot, 1989

Dictionary of National Biography and *Supplements*, Oxford, 1917–

Gallino, L. (a cura di), *Dizionario di sociologia*, Turin, 1978

Harrison, R., Wolven, G. B., and Duncan R. (eds.), *Warwick Guide to British Labour Periodicals 1790–1970*, Hassocks, 1977

Houghton, W.E. (ed.), *The Wellesley Index to Victorian Periodicals 1824–1900*, Toronto and London, 1966

Le Roy Malchov, H., *Agitators and Promoters in the Age of Gladstone and Disraeli. A Biographical Dictionary of the Leaders of British Pressure Groups founded between 1865 and 1886.* New York and London, 1985

Madden, L., and Dixon, D., *The Nineteenth Century Periodical Press in Britain. A Bibliography of Modern Studies*, New York and London, 1976

Matthews, W. (compiler), *British Diaries: An Annotated Bibliography of British Diaries Written between 1442 and 1942*, Berkeley, Cal., 1950

British Biographies: An Annotated Bibliography of British Autobiographies Published or Written before 1951, Berkeley, Cal., 1955

Mitchell, B. R., and Deane, P., *Abstract of British Historical Statistics*, Cambridge, 1971

Newspaper Press Directory, London, 1860–1886

Woolf, R., North J., and Deering, D. (eds.), *Waterloo Directory to Victorian Periodicals*, 3 vols., Waterloo, 1976

2. MANUSCRIPTS

Bradlaugh Papers, Bishopsgate Institute, London

Broadhurst Papers, British Library of Political and Economic Science, London

Bryce Papers, Bodleian Library, Oxford

J. Chamberlain Papers, Birmingham University Library

Richard Congreve Papers, British Library of Political and Economic Science, London

Joseph Cowen Papers, Tyne-and-Wear Archives, Newcastle upon Tyne

C. Dilke Papers, British Library, London

Thomas Dixon Papers, Tyne-and-Wear Archives, Newcastle upon Tyne

Gladstone Papers, British Library, London

Glynne-Gladstone Papers, St. Deiniol's Library, Hawarden

Frederick Harrison Papers, British Library of Political and Economic Science, London

George J. Holyoake Papers, microfilm copy in the Seeley Library, Cambridge

George J. Holyoake Papers, Bishopsgate Institute, London

George Howell Papers, Bishopsgate Institute, London

Alfred Marshall Papers, Marshall Library, Cambridge

J. S. Mill–H. Taylor Collection, British Library of Political and Economic Science, London

Henry Solly Collection, British Library of Political and Economic Science, London

W. T. Stead Papers, Churchill College, Cambridge

John Wilson Papers, Durham County Record Office

3. PAPERS OF TRADE UNIONS AND OTHER WORKING-CLASS AND RADICAL ORGANIZATIONS; OTHER COLLECTIONS OF EPHEMERA

Amalgamated Society of Carpenters and Joiners, Annual Reports, 1866–87, Bishopsgate Institute, London

Amalgamated Society of Carpenters and Joiners, Monthly Reports, 1867–1876, Bishopsgate Institute, London

Annual Reports of the Amalgamated Engeneers, 1871–86, Bishopsgate Institute, London

Boiler Makers' Annual Reports, 1877–85, Bishopsgate Institute, London

Co-operative Congresses, Proceedings, 1869–85, Bishopsgate Institute, London

Co-operative Wholesale Society Ltd., Annual Reports, 1883–5, Bishopsgate Institute, London

Cowen Collection, Tyne and Wear Archives, Newcastle upon Tyne.

The Debater [paper of the Newcastle Debating Society], 1877–8, Tyne and Wear Archives, Newcastle upon Tyne.

Durham Miners' Association Records, 1880–90, Durham County Record Office

Durham Miners' Association Records, 1886–1900, Durham Miners Association, Redhill, Durham City

Financial Reform Union, Papers on Taxation and Expenditure, Bishopsgate Institute, London

Howell Collection, Bishopsgate Institute, London

John Johnson Collection, Bodleian Library, Oxford

Labour Representation League Papers, British Library of Political and Economic Science, London

National Liberal Federation, Annual Reports and Council Proceedings, 1877–86, Harvester Press Microfilm Edition

National Secular Society Papers, Bishopsgate Institute, London

Newcastle-upon-Tyne Liberal Club, Records, 1879–92, Tyne and Wear Archives, Newcastle upon Tyne

Nuffield Collection of Electoral Materials, 1880–86, Nuffield College, Oxford

Operative Bricklayers' Trade Circular, 1870, 1876, Bishopsgate Institute, London

TUC Papers:
>   *Annual Congress of Trades Unions, Birmingham, 23–28th August 1869*, Minutes, Bishopsgate Institute, London
>
>   *TUC 1871, Minutes of the Business Committee*, in G. Howell Collection, Bishopsgate Institute, London
>
>   *The Third Annual Trade Union Congress, London, March 6th to 11th Inclusive, 1871*, London 1871
>
>   *Minutes of Trades' Union Congress 1872, Nottingham*, London 1872
>
>   *Reports of the Annual Trades Union Congresses*, 1875–86, Minutes, London

Vigilance Association for the Defence of Personal Rights, Annual Reports, 1871, 1872, Cambridge University Library

4. PARLIAMENTARY DEBATES AND
PARLIAMENTARY PAPERS

Hansard Parliamentary Debates, 3rd Series, 1871–1886.
Proceedings of the Select Committee on the Education of Destitute Children, PP 1861, VII.
Report from Borough Authorities in England and Wales relating to the Licensing Act, 1872, PP 1874, LIV
Report of the Select Committee on the Present Mode of Assessing and Collecting the Income and Property Tax, PP 1861, VII
Reports of the Select Committee of the House of Lords on Intemperance, PP 1877, XI; 1878, XIV; 1878–79, X
Report of the Select Committee on School Board Election (Voting); together with the Proceedings of the Committee, Minutes of Evidence and Appendix, PP 1884–5, XI, 389–728
Royal Commission on Friendly and Benefit Building Societies, PP 1872, XXVI
Royal Commission on Labour 1891–4, PP 1892, XXVI; 1893–94, XXXIV; 1893–94, XXXIX
Royal Commission on the Working of the Criminal Law Amendment Act, PP 1874, XXIV
Royal Commission on Liquor Licensing Laws, PP 1899, XXXIV
Royal Commission on Local Taxation, PP 1898, XLI
Royal Commission Reports on the Trades Unions, PP 1867, XXXII; 1867–68, XXXIX; 1868–69, XXXI
Royal Commission Reports on the Working of the Master and Servant Act, 1867, and the Criminal Law Amendment Act, 1871, PP 1874, XXIV; 1875, XXX
Select Committee Reports on Local Government and Local Taxation of the Metropolis, PP 1866, XIII
Second Report of the Royal Commission appointed to Inquire into the Working of the Elementary Education Acts, England and Wales, PP 1887, XXIX, and 1887, XXX

5. AUTOBIOGRAPHIES AND BIOGRAPHIES OF
POPULAR RADICALS

[Anon], *Scenes from My Life, by A Working Man* London, 1858
Abraham E. W. Evans, *Mabon William Abraham 1842–1922,* Cardiff, 1959
Adams, A. C. *The History of a Village Shopkeeper,* Edinburgh, 1878
Adams, W. E. *Memoirs of a Social Atom,* 2 vols., London, 1903
    O. R. Ashton, *W. E. Adams: Chartist, Radical and Journalist 1832–1906,* Whitley Bay (Tyne and Weir), 1991

Andrews *The Diary of William Andrews*, in V. E. Chancellor (ed.), *Master and Artisan in Victorian England*, New York, 1969

Applegarth A. W. Humphrey, *Robert Applegarth: Trade Unionist, Educationist, Reformer*, London, n.d. [but 1914]

Arch *Joseph Arch, the Story of His Life*, London, 1898
P. Horn, *Joseph Arch (1826–1919). The Farm Workers' Leader*, Kineaton, 1971

Armstrong *Pilgrimage from Nenthead. An Autobiography*, London, 1938

Ashby M. K. Ashby, *Joseph Ashby of Tysoe 1859–1919*, London, 1974 [1st ed. 1961]

Bamford, S. *Passages in the Life of a Radical*, Oxford, 1984 [1st ed. 1844]

Barnes, G. *From Workshop to the War Cabinet*, London, 1924

Bell, R. 'How I Got On', *Pearson's Weekly*, 19 Apr. 1906

Bradlaugh G. W. Foote, *Reminiscences of Charles Bradlaugh*, London, 1891
H. Bradlaugh, *Charles Bradlaugh*, 2 vols., London, 1895
A. S. Headingly, *The Biography of C. Bradlaugh*, London, 1880
W. Irving, *C. Bradlaugh as a Politician . . .*, London, 1887
G. Standring, *Biography of Charles Bradlaugh*, London, 1888
C. R. McKay, *The Life of C. Bradlaugh, M.P.*, London, 1891
C. C. Cattell, *Recollections of the Late Mr. Bradlaugh*, London, 1891

Broadhurst *Henry Broadhurst, M.P., The Story of His Life . . .*, London, 1901

Buckmaster *A Village Politician. The Life-story of John Buckley* [alias John Buckmaster], London, 1982 [1st ed. 1897]

Burns W. Kent, *John Burns: Labour's Lost Leader*, London, 1950
K. D. Brown, *John Burns*, London, 1977
J. Burgess, *John Burns: Rise and Progress of a Labour Leader*, Glasgow, 1911

Burt *Thomas Burt, M.P., D.C.L., Pitman and Privy Councillor, An Autobiography*, London, 1924
A. Watson, *A Great Labour Leader. The Life of Thomas Burt, M.P.*, London, 1908
T. C. Meach, *From Mine to Ministry. The Life and Times of Thomas Burt, M.P.*, London, n.d.
J. Dyson (ed.), *Tommy Burt. A Howky in Parliament*, Newcastle upon Tyne, Tyneside, n.d.

Carnegie, A. *Autobiography*, New York, 1920

Catling, T. T. *My Life's Pilgrimage*, London, 1911

Christie, A. V. *Brass Tracks and Fiddle*, Kilmanrock, 1943

Cobbett *The Autobiography of William Cobbett*, ed. by W. Reitzel, London, 1933

Cooper *The Life of Thomas Cooper*, Leicester, 1971 [1st ed. 1872]

Cowen E. R. Jones, *Life and Speeches of Joseph Cowen, M.P.*, Newcastle, 1885
D. William, *The Life of J. Cowen*, London, 1904

N. Todd, *The Militant Democracy: Joseph Cowen and Victorian Radicalism*, Whitley Bay (Tyne and Wear) 1991

Cremer H. Evans, *Sir Randal Cremer, His Life and Work*, London, 1909

Crooks G. Haw, *From Workhouse to Westminster. The Life Story of Will Crooks*, *M.P.*, London, n.d.

Dunning *The Reminiscences of Thomas Dunning*, in D. Vincent (ed.), *Testaments of Radicalism. Memoirs of Working Class Politicians 1790–1885*, London, 1977

Dunning, T. J., [biographical art. in] *Bee Hive*, 8 Nov. 1873, pp. 1–2

Edwards, G. *From Crow Scaring to Westminster*, London, 1922

Elliott *J. Watkins, Life, Poetry and Letters of Ebenezer Elliott, the Corn Law Rhymer*, London, 1850

Evans, H. *Radical Fights for Forty Years*, London, n.d. [but 1913]

Freer, W. *My Life's Memories*, Glasgow, 1929

Frost, T. *Forty Years Recollections: Literary and Political*, London 1880

Gammage, R. *Reminiscences of an Old Chartist*, ed. by W. H. Maehl, Aids to Research No. 4, Manchester, *Society for the Study of Labour History Bulletin Supplement 1983*.

Gaskell, E. *Norfolk Leaders Social and Political*, London, 1910

Gill, M. A. 'Made by Self-Help', in 'How I Got On', *Pearson's Weekly*, 22 Mar. 1906, p. 675

Gould, F. J. *The Life Story of a Humanist*, London, 1923

Greenwood, J. 'Reminiscences of Sixty Years Ago', *Copartnership*, N.S., xv(1909) and xvi(1910)

Gutteridge *Lights and Shadows in the Life of an Artisan, by Joseph Gutteridge, Ribbon Weaver*, in V. E. Chancellor (ed.), *Master and Artisan in Victorian England*, New York, 1969

Haggard, H. R. *The Days of My Life*, London, 1926

Hardie K. O. Morgan, *Keir Hardie, Radical and Socialist*, London, 1984

Harney A. R. Schoyen, *The Chartist Challenge: A Portrait of George Julian Harney*, London, 1958

Hawker, J. *A Victorian Poacher. James Hawker's Journal*, ed. C. Christian, Oxford, 1979 [1st ed. 1961]

Henderson, A. 'How I Got On. From Errand Boy to M.P.', *Pearson's Weekly*, 8 Mar. 1906

M. A. Hamilton, *Arthur Henderson, A Biography*, London, 1938

F. M. Leventhal, *Arthur Henderson*, Manchester, 1989

Hodge, J. *Workman's Cottage to Windsor Castle*, London, 1931

Holyoake, G. J. *Sixty Years of an Agitator's Life*, London, 1893

Bygones Worth Remembering, 2 vols., London, 1905

Hopkinson *Victorian Cabinet Maker. The Memoirs of James Hokinson 1819–1894*, New York, 1968

Howell, G. 'The Autobiography of a Toiler . . .', MS, Bishopsgate Institute, London

F. M. Leventhal, *Respectable Radical: George Howell and Victorian Working Class Politics*, London, 1971

Hudson, W. 'How I Got On', *Pearson's Weekly* 5 Apr. 1906

Jones, H. *Old Memories*, London, 1922

Key, R. *The Gospel Among the Masses*, London, 1872

'THE KING OF NORFOLK POACHERS' *I Walked by Night. Being the Life and Story of the King of Norfolk Poachers, Written by Himself*, ed. by L. R. Haggard, Oxford, 1982 [1st ed. 1935]

Knee, F. *The Diary of Fred Knee*, ed. by D. Englander, Aids to Research No. 3, Manchester, *Society for the Study of Labour History, Bulletin Supplement*, 1977

Lansbury, G. *My Life*, London, 1928

Looking Backwards and Forwards, London, 1935

Lawson, J. J. *A Man's Life*, London, 1932

P. Lee, *Jack Lawson*, London, 1936

Leno, J. B. *The Aftermath, with an Autobiography of the Author*, London, 1892

Linton, W. J. *Memories*, London, 1895

F. B. Smith, *Radical Artisan William James Linton 1812–1897*, Manchester, 1973

Lovekin, E. 'Some Notes of My Life', in J. Burnett (ed.), *Useful Toil. Autobiographies of Working People from the 1820s to the 1920s*, London, 1974

Lovett, W. *Life and Struggles of William Lovett*, London, 1967 (1st ed. 1876)

J. Wiener, *William Lovett*, Manchester, 1989

Lowery, R. 'Passages in the Life of a Temperance Lecturer . . .', in B. Harrison and P. Hollis (eds.) *Robert Lowery, Radical and Chartist*, London, 1979

MacAdam *Autobiography of John MacAdam*, ed. by J. Fyfe, Edinburgh, Scottish Historical Society, 1983

MacDonald G. M. Wilson, *Alexander MacDonald, Leader of the Miners*, Aberdeen, 1982

Mann, *Tom Mann's Memoirs*, London, 1923

Meek, G. *George Meek, Bath Chair-Man. By Himself*, London, 1910

Norfolk and Suffolk in East Anglia: Contemporary Biographies, ed. by W. T. Pike, Brighton, 1911

Parry J. R. Williams, *Quarryman's Champion. The Life and Activities of William John Parry of Coetmor*, Denbigh (Wales), 1978

Place *The Autobiography of Francis Place*, ed. by M. Thale, Cambridge, 1972

D. J. Rowe (ed.), *London Radicalism 1830–43. A Selection from the Papers of Francis Place*, London, 1970

Ratcliffe, G. *Sixty Years of It. Being the Story of My Life and Public Career*, London & Hull, n.d.

Rogers, F. *Labour, Life and Literature. Some Memoirs of Sixty Years*, Hassocks 1973 (1st ed. 1913)

Rymer, E. 'The Martyrdom of the Mine. A Sixty Years' Struggle for Life', introd. by R. G. Neville, *History Workshop*, No.1 (1976), pp. 220–44, and No.2 (1976), pp. 148–170 [1st edn Middlesborough, 1898]

Sage *The Memoirs of Joseph Sage*, London, 1951

Shaw, C. *When I Was I Child, by an Old Potter*, London, 1903

Shaw, S. *Guttersnipe*, London, 1946

Smillie, R. *My Life for Labour*, London, 1924

Snowden, J. [Autobiograhical speeches delivered at the King Cross Liberal Club, Oct. 1876, and at Queensbury Liberal Club, Nov. 1881], in *Halifax Courier*, 6 Sept. 1884

Snowden, *An Autobiography of Philip Viscount Snowden*, 2 vols., London, 1934

Solly, H. *These Eighty Years*, 2 vols., London, 1893.

Somerville, A. *Free Trade and the League. A Biographic History of the Pioneers of Freedom of Opinion, Commercial Enterprise, and Civilization in Britain . . .*, 2 vols., Manchester, 1853
The Autobiography of a Working Man, London, 1851

Soutter, F. W. *Recollections of a Labour Pioneer*, London, 1923
Fights for Freedom: the Story of My Life., London, 1925

Spencer, F. H. *An Inspector's Testament*, London, 1938

Stead, W. T. E. W. Stead, *My Father, Personal and Spiritual Reminiscences*, London, 1913
F. Whyte, *The Life of W. T. Stead*, 2 vols., London, 1925
E. K. Harper, *Stead: the Man, Personal Reminiscences*, London, 1914

Summersell, T. 'How I Got On, From Barber's Shop to Parliament', *Pearson's Weekly*, 22 Mar. 1906

Swan 'The Journal of William Swan', in *The Journals of Two Poor Dissenters, 1786–1880*, ed. by G. Swan and J. Holliday, London, 1970

Taylor, J. W. 'How I Got On', *Pearson's Weekly*, 22 Mar. 1906

Taylor, S. *Records of an Active Life*, London, 1886

Terry, J. *Recollections of My Life*, in J. Burnett (ed.), *Destiny Obscure. Autobiographies of Childhood, Education and Family from the 1820s to the 1920s*, London, 1982

Thomas, J. H. *My Story*, London, 1937

Ward 'The Diary of John Ward of Clitheroe, Weaver 1860–64', ed. R. S. France, *Transactions of the Historic Society of Lancashire and Cheshire* vol. 105 (1953), pp. 137–86

Watson, A. *A Newspaper Man's Memoirs*, London, 1925

Williams, H. W. *Some Reminiscences*, Penzance, 1918

Wilson, B. *The Struggles of a Chartist*, in D. Vincent (ed.), *Testaments of Radicalism. Memoirs of Working Class Politicians 1790–1885*, London, 1977

Wilson, J. *Memories of a Labour Leader: The Autobiography of John Wilson, J.P., M.P.*, Firle (Sussex), 1980 [1st edn London, 1910]

Wilson, Jo. *Joseph Wilson, His Life and Work*, London, n.d.
Wilson, J. H. *My Stormy Voyage Through Life*, Newcastle, 1925
Wright, T. *Some Habits and Customs of the Working Classes*, New York, 1970
    [1st edn London, 1867]
    The Great Unwashed, New York, 1970 [1st edn London, 1868]
    Our New Masters, New York, 1970 [1st edn London, 1873]

6. POLITICAL WRITINGS BY POPULAR RADICALS

[Anon.], 'Mid-Durham Election: or the Capitalist's Rout' [1900], in *John Wilson Papers*, Durham County Record Office
Arch, J., *A Word of Counsel to the New Electors of Warwickshire*, London, 1885
Broadhurst, H., 'The Ideas of the New Voters. I,' *Fortnightly Review*, N.S. CCXVIII (1885), pp. 149–55
Broadhurst, H., and Reid T., *Leasehold Enfranchisement*, London, Imperial Parliament, 1885
Burns, J., *Labour and Free Trade*, London, n.d.
Burt, T., 'Working Men and the Political Situation', *Nineteenth Century*, IX (April 1881), pp. 611–22.
    'Labour in Parliament', *Contemporary Review*, LV (May 1889), pp. 678–91
Davis, W. J. ('A Trade Union Official'), 'The Ideas of the New Voters, No. II', *Fortnightly Review*, vol. 43 os, 37 ns (Feb 1885), pp. 149–55.
Evans, H., *The Price of Priestcraft. A Book for the People*, London, 1904
    Songs for Singing at Agricultural Labourers' Meetings, London, 1875
Fynes, R., *The Miners of Northumberland and Durham. A History of Their Social and Political Progress*, Sunderland, 1971 (1st edn 1873)
Gammage, R. G., *History of the Chartist Movement, 1837–1854*, London, 1976 (1st edn 1854)
Hamilton, J., *Poems and Ballads*, Glasgow, 1868
    Poems, Essays, and Sketches, Glasgow, 1870
Henderson, A., 'Christianity and Democracy', in E. T. Whittaker (ed.), *Man's Place in Creation* . . . , London, 1905
Holyoake, G. J., *Self-Help a Hundred Years Ago*, London, 1891 (1st edn 1888)
    The History of Co-operation in England, 2 vols., London, 1906 (1st edn 1875)
    The History of the Rochadale Pioneers 1844–92, London, 1893
    English Secularism, A Confession of Belief, Chicago, 1896
    'A Dead Movement which has Learned to Live Again', *Contemporary Review*, XXVIII (1876), pp. 444–62
    'The Beginning of the Co-operative Trouble', *Contemporary Review*, XXVI (1875), pp. 269–81
    'Gambling in Politics', *Contemporary Review*, XXIII (1874), pp. 638–57
Howell, G., *The Conflicts of Capital and Labour Historically and Economically Considered*, London, 1878

'Intimidation and Picketing: Two Phases of Trade Unionism', *Fortnightly Review*, vol. xxx, ns (June–Nov. 1877), pp. 598–625

'Trades Unions, Apprentices, and Technical Education', *Contemporary Review*, xxx (1877), pp. 833–57

'The History of the International Association', *Nineteenth Century*, IV (July 1878), pp. 19–39

'Are the Working Classes Improvident?', *Contemporary Review*, XXXII (1878), pp. 501–19

A History of the Working Men's Association from 1836 to 1850, introd. by D. J. Rowe, Newcastle, n.d. [but 1971, 1st edn 1900]

Trade Unionism New and Old, ed. by F. M. Leventhal, Brighton, 1973 [1st edn 1891]

A Handy Book of the Labour Laws, London, 1895

[no title, on retrenchment in public expenditure], in W. Leigh Bernard and A. Reid (eds.), *Bold Retrenchment, or the Liberal Policy which will Save One-Half of the National Expenditure*, London, 1888

'Liberty for Labour', in T. MacKay (ed.), *A Plea for Liberty. An Argument against Socialism and Socialist Legislation*, London, 1891

Howell, G., and Mundella, A. J., 'Industrial Associations', in T. H. Ward (ed.), *The Reign of Queen Victoria*, II, London, 1887, pp. 43–82

Leno, J. B., *Muscular Poetry, or Songs for the People*, London, 1864

The Reformers' Book of Songs and Recitations, London, Office of the *Commonwealth* [newspaper], n.d. [but 1866–67]

Linton, W. J., *The English Republic*, London, 1851

The Plaint of Freedom, Newcastle upon Tyne, 1852

Lloyd Jones, P., *Progress of the Working Class, 1832–1867*, London, 1867

Lovett, W., *Social and Political Morality*, London, 1853

Woman's Mission, London, 1853

Odger, G., 'The Land Question', *Contemporary Review*, XVIII (1871), pp. 23–42

'The Working Man in Parliament', *Contemporary Review*, XVI (1870), pp. 102–23

Potter, G., 'The Church of England and the People', *Fortnightly Review*, N.S. XI (Jan. to June 1872), pp. 176–90

'The Workman's View of "Fair trade"', *Nineteenth Century*, x (Sept. 1881), pp. 430–47

'The Trade Societies of England', *Contemporary Review*, XVI (1870), pp. 386–404

'Strikes and Lock-Outs', *Contemporary Review*, xv (Aug–Nov. 1870), pp. 32–54

'The First Point of the New Charter. Improved Dwellings for the People', *Contemporary Review*, XVIII (Nov. 1871), pp. 547–58

'Conciliation and Arbitration', *Contemporary Review*, xv (1870)

Wright, T., 'The Composition of the Working Classes', *Contemporary Review*, XVII (Apr.–July 1871), pp. 515–26

7. PERIODICALS

JOURNALS

Contemporary Review 1868–86
Fortnightly Review 1865–86
Nineteenth Century 1877–80
Primitive Methodist Quarterly 1880, 1885–86
Westminster Review 1866–86

NEWSPAPERS

Bee Hive 1864–76
The Commonwealth, 1866
Co-operative News, 1871–3, 1879–81, 1885
The Co-operator, 1860–70
The Co-operator and Anti-Vaccinator, 1871
The Daily News, 1868–86
The Debater. A Weekly Record of the Newcastle Parliamentary Debating Society,
    1877
English Labourer 1877–94
The Financial Reformer. A Monthly Periodical, 1867–1876
Forest of Dean Examiner 1873–77
Glasgow Sentinel and Scottish Banner, 1868
The Halifax Courier 1884
Industrial Review 1877–78
Labour Standard 1881–82
Labourer's Press and Workman's Examiner 1875–76
Labourers' Union Chronicle 1873–75
The Leeds Evening Express 1871
The Leeds Mercury 1865–86
Leeds Weekly Express 1871
Lloyd's Weekly 1866–86
The Manchester Guardian 1859–68, 1871, 1874–76, 1880, 1885–86
The Miner 1877–78
The Miners' National Gazette, 1883
National Agricultural Labourers' Chronicle 1875–77
The National Reformer 1866–86
The Newcastle Daily Chronicle 1868, 1873–74, 1880, 1886
The Newcastle Weekly Chronicle 1865–86
The Nonconformist 1869–71, 1874, 1876
The Northern Echo 1871, 1876, 1886
Pearson's Weekly 1906
Potteries Examiner 1873–80
The Reformer, 1868
The Republican, 1870, 1871

Reynolds's Newspaper 1865–86, 1891–92, 1898–99, 1902
Sheffield & Rotherham Independent 1868, 1874, 1880, 1885, 1886
Staffordshire & Potteries Examiner 1881–86
The Times 1865, 1868, 1871–75, 1879–80, 1885–86
Weekly Times 1866–86
The Workman's Advocate, 1866

8. ESSAYS, SPEECHES, OTHER PRINTED SOURCES

[Anon.], 'The Government and the Education Act', *Westminster Review,* 97 os, 41 ns (Jan. 1872), pp. 164–83
Adams, F., *History of the Elementary School Contest* ed. A. Briggs, Brighton, 1972 [1st edn 1873]
 The Free Schools of the United States, London, 1875
 The Elementary Education Act, 1870, London, n.d. [but 1870]
Amberley, Lord, 'Liberals, Conservatives, and the Church', *Fortnightly Review,* II (1865), pp. 161–8
Apjohn, L., *Richard Cobden and the Free Traders,* London, n.d. [but 1878]
Bagehot, W., *The English Constitution,* Glasgow, 1974 (first edn. 1867)
Becker, L. E., 'Female Suffrage', *Contemporary Review,* IV (1867), pp. 307–16
Beesly, E. S., 'The Social Future of the Working Classes', *Fortnightly Review,* N.S. V (Jan.–June 1869), pp. 344–63
 'The Amalgamated Society of Carpenters', *Fornightly Review,* N.S. I (Jan.–June 1867), pp. 320–31
 'The Trades' Union Commission', *Fortnightly Review,* N.S. II (1867), pp. 1–18
 'The International Working Men's Association', *Fortnightly Review,* N.S. VIII (July–Dec. 1870), pp. 517–35
 'The Game Laws and the Committee of 1872', *Fornightly Review,* N.S. XIII (Jan.–June 1873), pp. 352–72
Besant, A., *Free Trade versus 'Fair Trade', being the substance of Five Lectures delivered at the Hall of Science, London, in October, 1881, with Appendix,* London, 1881
Brassey, T., 'The Advance Note. What It Is and Why It Should be Abolished', *Contemporary Review,* vol. XXVI ns (June–Nov. 1875), pp. 404–11
 'Co-operative Production', *Contemporary Review,* XXIV (June–Nov. 1874), pp. 212–34
Briggs, T., *Poverty, Taxation, and the Remedy: Free Trade, Free Labour, or Direct Taxation the True Principle of Political Economy, Universal Free Trade the First Condition of Universal Peace,* London, n.d. [but 1883]
Bright, John, *The Work of the Liberal Party during the Last Fifty Years. A Letter from the Right Honourable John Bright, M.P.,* London, 1885
 Speeches, ed. J. Thorold Rogers, London, 1868

Buxton, S., *Finance and Politics; and Historical Study 1783–1887*, II, London, 1888

Mr Gladstone as Chancellor of the Exchequer. A Study, London, 1901

Chalmers, M. D., *Local Government*, London, 1883

Chamberlain, J., 'Free Schools', *Fortnightly Review*, XXI, (Jan. 1877), pp. 54–72

'A New Political Organization', *Fortnightly Review*, N.S. xxii (1877), pp. 126–34

The Radical Platform. Speeches by the Right Hon. Joseph Chamberlain, M.P., Edinburgh and London, 1886

Chapman, S. J., *Local Government and State Aid*, London 1899

Churchill, W. S., *My Early Life*, London, 1930

Cobbett, W., *Rural Rides*, Harmondsworth, 1987 [1st edn 1830]

Cottage Economy, Oxford, 1979 [1st edn 1822]

Cobden, Unwin. J. (ed.), *The Hungry Forties. Life under the Bread Tax*, Shannon, 1971 (1st edn 1904)

Cobden, R., *Speeches by Richard Cobden*, ed. J. Bright and J. Thorold Rogers, 2 vols., London, 1870

[Anon], *Cobden, the Friend of the People. The Story of His Life Told for Popular Reading*, London, 1886

Constant, B., *De la liberté des Anciens comparée a celle des Modernes* (1819), in *De la liberté chez les Modernes*, Paris, 1980, pp. 491–518.

Crompton, H., *Industrial Conciliation*, London, 1876

Dale, R. W., 'The Nonconformists and the Educational Policy of the Government', *Contemporary Review*, XXII (June–Nov. 1873), pp. 643–62

Desmoulines, A., 'The Paris Workmen and the Commune', *Fortnightly Review*, N.S. x (July–Dec. 1871), pp. 308–20

Dilke, Sir C., 'Free Schools', *Fortnightly Review*, N.S. xiv (July–Dec. 1873), pp. 789–95

Dorricott, I., 'Disestablishment in Wales and Monmouthshire', *The Primitive Methodist Quarterly Review*, 9 April 1887

Eversley, Lord (Shaw Lefevre), *Commons, Forests and Footpaths. The Story of the Battle during the Last Forty-two Years for Public Rights over the Commons, Forests and Footpaths of England and Wales*, London, 1910

Fawcett, H., *Labour and Wages*, London, 1881

Manual of Political Economy, London, 1876 (1st edn 1863)

The Economic Position of the British Labourer, Cambridge and London, 1865

'The Nationalization of the Land', *Fortnightly Review*, N.S. xii (July–Dec. 1872), pp. 627–43

Furniss, H., *Some Victorian Men*, London, 1924

George, H., *Progress and Poverty*, London, 1953 [1st edn 1881]

Protection of Free Trade, London, 1886

Gladstone, W. E., *Speeches*, ed. A. Tinley, Bassett, 1916

Midlothian Speeches, 1879, ed. M. D. R. Foot, Leicester, 1971 (1st edn 1879)

Gladstone Diaries, ed. H. C. G. Matthew, v, vi, Oxford 1978

Gladstone Diaries, ed. H. C. G. Matthew, vii and viii, Oxford, 1982

Gladstone Diaries, ed. H. C. G. Matthew, ix, Oxford, 1986.

Gladstone Diaries, ed. H. C. G. Matthew, vols. x and xi, Oxford, 1990

[Anon.], *Gladstone's Garland, the Materials Collected by an Elector,* s.d. [but 1880]

[Anon.], *Life of Gladstone, D.C.L., Etc., A Popular Biography,* London, 1898

Godkin, J., 'Ireland without a Church Disestablishment', *Fortnightly Review,* ii (1865), pp. 280–98

'Fenianism and the Irish Church', *Fortnightly Review,* N.S. iii (Jan.–June 1868), pp. 191–205

Goschen, G. J., *Reports and Speeches on Local Taxation,* London, 1872

Godwin, W., *Enquiry Concerning Political Justice,* Harmondsworth, 1985 (1st edn 1793)

Graham, J. C., *Taxation Local and Imperial and Local Government,* London, 1899

Grant, J., *The Metropolitan Weekly and Provincial Press,* London, 1872

Hare, T., 'An Electoral Reform', *Fortnightly Review,* ii (1865), pp. 438–42

Harrison, F., 'Industrial Co-operation', *Fortnightly Review,* iii (1865–66), pp. 489–90

'The Trades Union Bill', *Fortnightly Review,* N.S. vi (July-Dec. 1869), pp. 30–45

'The Revolution of the Commune', *Fortnightly Review,* N.S. ix (Jan.–June 1871), pp. 556–79

'The Fall of the Commune', *Fortnightly Review,* N.S. x (July–Dec. 1871), pp. 129–55

Hodder, E., *Life of Samuel Morley,* London, 1887

Holt, W., *A Beacon for the Blind, Being a Life of Henry Fawcett, the Blind Postmaster-General,* London, 1926 (1st edn 1915)

Hyndman, H. M., *Record of an Adventurous Life,* London, 1911

Jevons, W. S., *Methods of Social Reform,* London, 1883

The Match Tax: A Problem in Finance, London, Stanford, 1871

The State in Its Relations to Labour, London, 1882

Leslie, T. E. Cliffe, 'The Incidence of Imperial and Local Taxation on the Working Classes', *Fortnightly Review,* N.S. xv (1874), pp. 248–65

'Ireland in 1868', *Fortnightly Review,* N.S. iii (Jan–June 1868), pp. 131–44

Levi, L., *Estimate of the Amount of Taxation Falling on the Working Classes of the United Kingdom,* London, 1873

Ludlow, J. M., 'Mr Hare's Scheme of Parliamentary Representation', *Contemporary Review,* ix (1868), pp. 80–97

Maine, H. J. S., *Village Communities in the East and West,* London, 1871

Marshall, A., *Principles of Economics,* London, 1890

'The Future of the Working Classes', in *Memories of Alfred Marshall*, ed. A. C. Pigou, London, 1925, pp. 101–18

Maurice, F. D., *The Suffrage Considered in Reference to the Working Classes*, London, 1860

Maxse, Capt. F., 'Our Uncultivated Lands', *Fortnightly Review*, N.S. VIII (July–Dec. 1870), pp. 198–215

Mazzini, G., 'The Commune in Paris', *Contemporary Review*, XVII (Apr.–July 1871), pp. 307–18

'Letter to the Members of the Oecumenical Council', *Fortnightly Review*, N.S. VII (Jan.–June 1870), pp. 725–51

The Duties of Man and Other Essays, London, 1961 (1st edn 1894)

Miall, A., *Life of Edward Miall*, London, 1884

Michelet, J., *Histoire de la Revolution Francaise*, Vol.I, Paris, 1961 (1st edn 1847–50)

Mill, J. S., 'Maine on Village Communities', *Fortnightly Review*, N.S. I (Jan.–June 1871), pp. 543–56

'Professor Leslie on the Land Question', *Fortnightly Review*, N.S. VII (Jan.–June 1870), pp. 641–54

Collected Works, vol.I, *Autobiography and Literary Essays*, ed. J. M. Robson and J. Stillinger, Toronto and London, 1981

Collected Works, vols.II, III, *Principles of Political Economy*, ed. J. M. Robson, introd. V. W. Bladen, Toronto and London, 1965

Collected Works, vols.IV, v, *Essays on Economics and Society*, ed. J. M. Robson, introd. Lord Robbins, Toronto and London, 1975

Collected Works, vols.XIV, XV, XVI, XVII, *Later Letters 1849–1873*, ed. F. E. Mineka and D. N. Lindley, Toronto and London, 1972

Collected Works, vol.XVIII, *Essays on Politics and Society*, ed. J. M. Robson, Toronto and London, 1977

Collected Works, vols.XXII–XXV, *Newspaper Articles*, ed. A. R. Robson and J. M. Robson, Toronto and London, 1986

Morley, J., *The Struggle for National Education*, in F. Adams, *History of the Elementary School Contest in England*, and J. Morley, *The Struggle for National Education*, ed. A. Briggs, Brighton, 1972 (1st edn 1873)

The Life of Richard Cobden, London, 1879

Life of Gladstone, 3 vols., London, 1903

Noble, J., *Fiscal Reform: Suggestions for Further Remissions of Taxation*, London, 1865

Local Taxation: A Criticism of Fallacies and a Summary of Facts, London, 1876

Fiscal Legislation 1842–1865. A Review of the Financial Changes of that Period and their Effects upon Revenue, Trades, Manufactures and Employment, London, 1867

National Finance: A Review of the Policy of the Last Two Parliaments and the Result of Modern Fiscal Legislation, London, 1875

Northcote, Sir S., *Twenty Years of Financial Politics*, London, 1862

Owen, H., *The Elementary Education Act 1870 (33 and 34 Vict., c.75), with Introduction, Notes and Index*, London, 1871 (1st edn 1870)

Paine, T., *Rights of Man*, Harmondsworth, 1984 (1st edn 1791)

Reid, A. (ed.), *Bold Retrenchment, or the Liberal policy which will save one-half of the National Expenditure*, London, 1888

Reid, A. (ed.), *Why I am a Liberal*, London n.d. [but 1885]

Reid, T. W., *Life of the Rt Hon. W. E. Forster*, intro. V. Chancellor, New York, 1970 [1st edn 1888]

Report on Taxation: Direct and Indirect, Adopted by the Financial reform Association, Liverpool, and Presented at the Annual Meeting of the National Association for the Promotion of Social Sciences, at Bradford, October 1859, Liverpool, 1859

Reynolds, S., and Woolley, B. and T., *Seems so! A Working-Class View of Politics*, London, 1911

Row-Fogo, J., *An Essay on the Reform of Local Taxation in England*, London, 1902

Sidgwick, H., *The Principles of Political Economy*, London, 1901

Stead, W. T., *1809–1898. Gladstone. A Character Sketch*, London n.d. (but 1898)

Stephen, L., *The Life of Henry Fawcett*, London, 1885

Taylor, R. W. Cooke, 'The Factory and Workshops Acts', *Westminster Review*, LI (Jan.–April 1877), pp. 36–58, 462–93

Thornton, W. T., *A Plea for Peasant Proprietors with the Outlines of a Plan for their Establishment in Ireland*, London, 1848

'England and Ireland, by J. S. Mill', *Fortnightly Review*, N.S. III (Jan.–June 1868), pp. 471–4

Tocqueville, A. De, *De la democratie en Amerique*, 2 vols., Paris, 1951 (1st edn 1835–1842)

Trollope, A., 'The Irish Church', *Fortnightly Review*, II (1865), pp. 82–90

Watson, R., *The National Liberal Federation from the Commencement to the General Election of 1906*, London, 1907

Wemyss Reid, T., *Life of the Rt Hon. W. E. Forster*, intr. V. Chancellor, New York, 1970 (1st edn 1888)

Whitehurst, E. C., 'The Disestablishment and Disendowment of the Church of England', *Westminster Review*, XLV (January 1874), pp. 1–31

9. MODERN WORKS

Addison, W. G., *Religious Equality in Modern England 1714–1914*, London, 1944

Agulhon, M. A., *The Republican Experiment 1848–1852*, Cambridge, 1985

Anderson, O., 'Gladstone's Abolition of Compulsory Church Rates: A Minor Political Myth and its Historiographical Career', *Journal of Ecclesiastical History*, XXV, 2, (April 1974), pp. 192–5

'Wage-earners and Income Tax: A Mid-Nineteenth Century Discussion', *Public Administration*, XLI (1963), pp. 189–92

'Women Preachers in Mid-Victorian Britain: Some Reflections on Feminism, Popular Religion and Social Change', *Historical Journal*, XII (1969), pp. 467–84

Anderton, P., 'The Liberal Party of Stoke-on-Trent and Parliamentary Elections 1860–1880. A Case Study in Liberal-Labour Relations', MA thesis, University of Keele, 1974

Andreucci, F., *Il marxismo collettivo*, Milan, 1986

Socialdemocrazia e imperialismo, Rome 1988

Aquarone, A., *Alla ricerca dell'Italia liberale*, Naples, 1972

Armytage, W. H. G., 'The 1870 Education Act', *British Journal of Educational Studies*, XVIII, 2, (June 1970), pp. 121–33

A. J. Mundella, 1825-1897. The Liberal Background to the Labour Movement, London, 1951

Arnstein, W. L., *The Bradlaugh Case. A Study in Late Victorian Opinion and Politics*, Oxford, 1977

'The Survival of the Victorian Aristocracy', in F. C. Jaher (ed.), *The Rich, the Well-Born, and the Powerful*, Urbana, Ill., 1973

Ashplant, T. G., 'London Working Men's Clubs, 1874–1914', in S. and E. Yeo (eds.), *Popular Culture and Class Conflict 1590–1914*, Brighton, 1981, pp. 241–70

Balls, F. E., 'The Endowed Schools Act 1869 and the Development of English Grammar Schools in the Nineteenth Century', *Durham Research Review*, No. 19, September 1967, pp. 207–16

'The Endowed Schools Act 1869 and the Development of English Grammar Schools in the Nineteenth Century. II. The Operation of the Act', *Durham Research Review*, No. 20, April 1968, pp. 219–29

Barker, M., *Gladstone and Radicalism. The Reconstruction of Liberal Politicy in Britain 1885-94*, Brighton, 1975

Barnes, D. G., *A History of the English Corn Laws*, London, 1930

Barrington Moore, *Social Origins of Dictatorship and Democracy*, Boston, 1966

Barrow, L., *Independent Spirits, Spiritualism and English Plebeians, 1850-1910*, London, 1986

Baysinger, B., and Tollison, R., 'Chaining the Leviathan: The Case of Gladstonian Finance', *History of Political Economy*, XII (1980), pp. 206–13

Beales, D. E. D., 'Victorian Politics Observed', *Historical Journal*, XXI, 3 (1978), pp. 697–707

'Garibaldi in England: The Politics of Italian Enthusiasm', in J. Davis and P. Ginsborg, *Society and Politics in the Age of the Risorgimento. Essays in Honour of Denis Mack Smith*, Cambridge, 1991

England and Italy 1859-1860, London, 1961

'Parliamentary Parties and the 'Independent' Member, 1810–1860', in
R. Robson (ed.), *Ideas and Institutions of Victorian Britain*, London, 1967
'Gladstone and his Diary: "Myself, the worst of all interlocutors"'.
Historical Journal, xxv, 2 (1982), pp. 463–69
'Gladstone and his First Ministry', *Historical Journal*, xxvi, 4 (1983),
pp. 987–98
Beard, C. A., *Economic Origins of Jeffersonian Democracy*, New York, 1936
Bebbington, D. W., *The Nonconformist Conscience*, London, 1982
Gladstone and the Nonconformists: A Religious Affinity in Politics', in
D. Baker (ed.), *Church, Society and Politics* (Papers of the Ecclesiastical
History Society), Oxford, 1975
Bell, D., 'Authoritarian and Democratic Leaders', in A. W. Gouldner
(ed.), *Studies in Leadership. Leadership and Democratic Action*, New York,
1965
Bendix, R., *Max Weber, An Intellectual Portrait*, Berkeley, 1977
Bentley, M., *Politics without Democracy. Great Britain 1815–1914*, Oxford,
1984
The Liberal Mind 1914–1929, Cambridge, 1977
Berridge, V., 'Popular Journalism and Working-Class Attitudes. A Study
of *Reynolds's Newspaper*, *Lloyd's Weekly Newspaper*, and *Weekly Times*,
1854–1886', 3 vols., PhD thesis, University of London, 1976
'Popular Sunday Papers and Mid-Victorian Society', in G. Boyce, J.
Curran, P. Wingate (eds.), *Newspaper History: From the Seventeenth
Century to the Present Day*, London, 1978
Best, G. F. A., *Temporal Pillars. Queen Anne's Bounty, the Ecclesiastical
Commissioners, and the Church of England*, Cambridge, 1964
Biagini, E. F., 'Rappresentanza virtuale e democrazia di massa: i
paradossi della Gran Bretagna vittoriana', *Quaderni storici*, 69, 3
(1988), pp. 809–38
'Popular Liberals, Gladstonian Finance, and the Debate on Taxation,
1860–1874', in E. F. Biagini and A. J. Reid (eds.), *Currents of
Radicalism. Popular Radicalism, Organized Labour, and Party Politics in
Britain, 1850–1914*, Cambridge, 1991
'British Trade Unions and Popular Political Economy, 1860–1880',
Historical Journal, xxx, 4 (1987), pp. 811–40
'Per uno studio del liberalismo popolare nell'eta' di Gladstone', *Movi-
mento operaio e socialista*, v, 2, (1982), pp. 209–38
'Liberalismo e cultura popolare in Inghilterra: un dibattito aperto',
Passato e presente, vi (1984), pp. 149–64
'"La liberta' degli antichi paragonata alla liberta' dei moderni", John
Stuart Mill e la democrazia ateniese 1832–1861', *Critica storica*, xxii,
4 (1985), 4, pp. 469–501
Blewett, N., 'The Franchise in the United Kingdom, 1885–1918', *Past &
Present*, xxxii (Dec. 1965), pp. 27–56
Blickle, P., *Die Revolution von 1525*, München, 1981

Block, P., 'Polish Democrats and English Radicals, 1832–1862', *Journal of Modern History*, xxv, 2 (June 1953), pp. 139–56

Bolton King, H., *Mazzini*, London 1902

Bonner, A., *British Co-operation*, Manchester, 1961

Bowen, I., *Cobden*, London, 1935

Brailsford, N., *The Levellers and English Revolution*, ed. by C. Hill, Nottingham, 1976

Bradley, I., *The Optimists. Themes and Personalities in Victorian Liberalism*, London, 1980

Bravo, G. M., *Storia del socialismo 1789–1848*, Rome 1976

Brebner, J. B., 'Laissez-faire and State Intervention in Nineteenth-Century Britain', *Journal of Economic History*, 8 (1948), pp. 59–73

Brent, R., *Liberal Anglican Politics, Whiggery, Religion, and Reform, 1830–1841*, Oxford, 1987

'The Whigs and Protestant Dissent in the Decade of Reform. The Case of the Church Rates, 1833–1841', *English Historical Review*, CII (1987), pp. 887–910

Breuilly, J., 'Artisan Economy, Artisan Politics, Artisan ideology: The Artisan Contribution to Nineteenth-Century European Labour Movement', in C. Emsley and J. Walvin (eds.), *Artisans, Peasants and Proletarians, 1760–1860*, London, 1985

'Liberalism and Social Democracy: A Comparison of British and German Labour Politics, c.1850–75', in *European History Quarterly*, 15, 1 (Jan. 1985), pp. 26–31

Briggs, A., *Victorian Cities*, Harmondsworth, 1968

History of Birmingham, London, 1952, vol.2

The Age of Improvement, London, 1978 [1st edn 1959]

Brewster, D., 'Ulysses Grant and Newcastle upon Tyne', *Durham University Journal*, ns. vol. 30, no. 3 (1969), pp. 119–28

Brooks, D., 'Gladstone and Midlothian: The Background to the First Campaign', *Scottish Historical Review*, 64, 177 (April 1985), pp. 42–67

Brown, K., 'The Lodges of the Durham Miners' Association, 1869–1926', *Northern History*, xxxii (1987), pp. 138–52

Brown, K. D., *Labour and Unemployment 1900–1914*, Newton Abbot, 1971

A Social History of the Nonconformist Ministry in England and Wales 1800–1930, Oxford 1988

'Conflict in Early British Welfare Policy: The Case of the Unemployed Workmen's Bill of 1905', *Journal of Modern History*, 43, 4 (Dec. 1971), pp. 615–30

'Nonconformity and the British Labour Movement: A Case Study', *Journal of Social History*, Winter 1975, pp. 113–20

'Nonconformity and Trade Unionists: the Sheffield Outrages of 1866', in E. F. Biagini and A. J. Reid (eds.), *Currents of Radicalism*, Cambridge 1991, pp. 86–105

Brown, S., 'One Last Campaign of the GOM: Gladstone and the House of Lords in 1894', in B. L. Kinzer (ed.), *The Gladstonian Turn of Mind*, Toronto, Buffalo and London, 1985

Brunello, P., 'Agenti di emigrazione, contadini e immagini dell'America nella provincia di Venezia', *Rivista di storia contemporanea*, fasc.1, xi (gennaio 1982), pp. 95–122

Burrow, J. W., *Whigs and Liberals. Continuity and Change in English Political Thought*, Oxford, 1988
'The "Village Community" and the Uses of History in Late Nineteenth-Century England', in N. McKendrick (ed.), *Historical Perspectives. Studies in English Thought and Society*, London, 1984

Bush, W. C., 'Population and Mill's Peasant-Proprietor Economy', *History of Political Economy*, v (Spring 1973), pp. 110–21

Calhoun, C., *The Question of Class Struggle*, Oxford, 1983

Calkins, W. N., 'A Victorian Free Trade Lobby', *Economic History Review*, 2nd Series, xiii (1960–1), pp. 90–104

Camaiani, P. G., 'Valori religiosi e polemica anticlericale della sinistra democratica e del primo socialismo', *Rivista di storia e letteratura religiosa*, 2 (1984), pp. 232–41

Candeloro, G., *Storia dell'Italia Moderna*, vol.iii, Milano, 1960

Chabod, F., *Storia della politica estera italiana dal 1870 al 1896*, Bari, 1976 [1st edn 1951]

Chadwick, M. E. J., 'The Role of Redistribution in the Making of the Third Reform Act', *Historical Journal*, xix (1976), pp. 665–84

Charlesworth, A. (ed.), *An Atlas of Rural Protest in Britain 1548–1900*, London, 1983

Chester, N., *The English Administrative System*, Oxford, 1981

Clapham, J. H., *An Economic History of Modern Britain, Vol.ii, Free Trade and Steel*, Cambridge, 1926

Clarke, P. F., 'Electoral Sociology of Modern Britain', *History*, vii, 1 (1972), pp. 31–55
Lancashire and the New Liberalism, Cambridge, 1971
'The End of *laisser-faire* and the Politics of Cotton', *Historical Journal*, xv, 3 (1972), pp. 493–512

Clayes, G., 'Mazzini, Kossuth and British Radicalism 1848–1854', *Journal of British Studies*, 28, 3, (July 1989), pp. 225–62

Clegg, H. A., Fox, A., Thompson, A. F., *A History of British Trade Unions since 1889, Vol. 1, 1889–1910*, Oxford, 1977 (1st edn 1964)

Clements, R. V., 'British Trade Unions and Popular Political Economy 1850–1875', *Economic History Review*, NS 14, 1 (1961–62), pp. 93–104

Cobb, R., *Les armées revolutionaires*, Paris, 1961–3

Coffey, J., 'Intellectuals, Revivalism, and Mass Communication: Moody and Sankey's Mission to Britain 1873–5', BA dissertation, Cambridge University, 1991

Cohen, I. J., 'Toward a Theory of State Intervention: The Nationalization of the Telegraphs', *Social Science History*, IV, 2 (Spring 1980), pp. 155–206

Cole, G. D. H., *History of Socialist Thought*, vol.I, London, 1959

British Working Class Politics, 1832–1914, London, 1950

A Century of Co-operation, Manchester n.d. [but 1944–45]

Collier, C., 'Henry George's System of Political Economy', *History of Political Economy*, 11, 1 (1979), pp. 64–91

Colls, R., *The Pitmen of the Northern Coalfields: Work, Culture, and Protest 1790–1850*, Manchester, 1987

Coltham, S., 'George Potter, the Junta and the "Bee Hive"', *International Review of Social History*, IX (1964), pp. 390–432, and X (1965), pp. 23–65

Cook, C., *A Short History of the Liberal Party 1900–88*, London, 1989

Cooke, A. B., 'Gladstone's Election for the Leith District of Burghs, June 1886', *Scottish Historical Review*, XLIX (1970), pp. 172–94

Cook, A. B., and Vincent, J. R., *The Governing Passion*, Brighton, 1974

Cornford, J., 'The Transformation of Conservatism in the Late Nineteenth Century', *Victorian Studies*, vol.7 (Sept. 1963), pp. 37–66

Cowherd, R. G., *The Politics of English Dissent*, London, 1956

Cowling, M., *1867. Disraeli, Gladstone and Revolution*, Cambridge,1967

Religion and Public Doctrine in Modern England, Cambridge, 1980

Cox, J., *The English Churches in a Secular Society: Lambeth 1870–1930*, Oxford, 1982

Crossick, G., *An Artisan Elite in Victorian Society*, London, 1978

Crossick and Haupt, H.-G. (eds.), *Shopkeepers and Master Artisans in Nineteenth-Century Europe*, London, 1984

Crouch, R. L., 'Laissez-faire in Nineteenth Century Britain: Myth or Reality?', *Manchester School*, XXXV (1967), pp. 199–216

Crowley, D. W., 'The "Crofters" Party, 1885–1892', *Scottish Historical Review*, XXXV (1956), pp. 110–26

Crowther, M. A., *The Workhouse System 1834–1929*, London, 1983

Cruickshank, M., *Church and State in English Education 1870 to the Present Day*, London, 1963

Curthoys, M. C., 'Trade Union Legislation, 1871–6; Government Responses to the Development of Organized Labour', DPhil thesis, Oxford University, 1988

Dahrendorf, R., *Class and Class Conflict in Industrial Society*, London, 1959

Davies, R. D., *Political Change and Continuity 1760–1885: A Buckinghamshire Study*, Newton Abbot, Devon, 1972

Davis, J., *Reforming London. The London Government Problem 1855–1900*, Oxford, 1988

'Radical Clubs and London Politics 1870–1900', in D. Feldman and G. Stedman Jones (eds.), *Metropolis – London: Histories and Representations since 1800*, London, 1990, pp. 103–28

Della Peruta, F., *Democrazia e socialismo nel Risorgimento*, Rome, 1965

I democratici e la rivoluzione italiana, Milan, 1981 (1st edn 1958)

De Marchi, N. B., 'The Success of Mill's Principles of Political Economy', *History of Political Economy*, 6 (1974), pp. 119–57

Derrington, A. P., 'Education and the Disestablishment Movement', PhD thesis, Manchester University, 1979

Dewey, C. J., 'The Rehabilitation of the Peasant Proprietor in Nine-teenth-Century Economic Thought', *History of Political Economy*, 6 (1974), pp. 17–47

Dickinson, H. T., *Radical Politics in the Northeast of England in the Late Eighteenth Century*, Durham County Local History Society, 1979

Dingle, A. E., 'Drink and Working-Class Living Standards in Britain, 1870–1914', *Economic History Review*, 2nd Series xxv, 4 (Nov. 1972), pp. 608–22

Drummond, A., and Bulloch, J., *The Church in Late Victorian Scotland*, Edinburgh, 1978

Dunbabin, J. P. D., 'The "Revolt of the Field": The Agricultural Labourers' Movement in the 1870s', *Past & Present*, 26 (November 1963), pp. 68–97

'British Local Government Reform: The Ninteenth Century and After', *English Historical Review*, xcii (1977), pp. 777–805

'Expectations of the New County Councils and Their Realization', *Historical Journal*, viii, 3 (1965), pp. 353–79

Dunbabin, J. P. D. (ed.), *Rural Discontent in Nineteenth-Century Britain*, London, 1974

Ellegård, A., 'The Readership of the Periodical Press in Mid-Victorian Britain', *Acta Universitatis Gothoburgensis-Göteborgs Universitets Arsskrift*, LXIII (1957), pp. 1–41

'Darwin and the General Reader. The Reception of Darwin's Theory of Evolution in the British Periodical Press', *Acta Universitatis Gothob-urgensis-Göteborgs Universitets Arsskrift*, LXIV (1958), pp. 7–394

Emy, H. V., *Liberals, Radicals and Social Politics 1892–1914*, Cambridge, 1973

Ensor, R. C. K., *England 1870–1914*, Oxford, 1980 [1st edn 1936]

Epstein, J., *The Lion of Freedom. Feargus O'Connor and the Chartist Movement, 1832–42*, London, 1982

'Some Organizational and Cultural Aspects of the Chartist Movement in Nottingham', in D. Thompson and J. Epstein, *The Chartist Experience*, London, 1982

Erickson, C., *English Women Immigrants in America in the Late Nineteenth Century. Expectation and Reality*, London, 1983 [Fawcett Library papers, No.7]

Evans, E. J., 'The Church in Danger? Anticlericalism in Nineteenth-Century England', *European Studies Review*, 13, 2 (April 1983), pp. 201–24

'Some Reasons for Growth of English Rural Anti-clericialism, *c*.1750–*c*.1830', *Past & Present*, 66 (1975), pp. 84–109

The Contentious Tithe. The Tithe Problem and English Agriculture, 1750–1850, London, 1976

Evans, E. W., *The Miners of South Wales*, Cardiff, 1961

Faulkner, H. V., *Chartism and the Churches. A Study in Democracy*, London, 1970 (1st edn 1916)

Ferrarotti, F., *L'orfano di Bismarck. Max Weber e il suo tempo*, Rome 1982

Feuchtwanger, E. J., *Gladstone*, London, 1975

Finlay, M. I., *Democracy Ancient and Modern*, London, 1973

Fisher, C., *Custom, Work, and Market Capitalism: the Forest of Dean Colliers*, London, 1981

Fisher, C., and Smethurst, J., ' "War on the Law of Supply and Demand": the Amalgamated Association of Miners and the Forest of Dean Colliers, 1869–1875', in R. Harrison (ed.), *Independent Collier*, Brighton, 1978

Fisher, C., and Spaven, P., 'Edward Rymer and the "Moral Workman" – The Dilemma of the Radical Miner under "McDonaldism" ', in R. Harrison (ed.), *Independent Collier*, Brighton, 1978

Fisher, H. A. L., *The Republican Tradition in Europe*, London, 1911

Fletcher, R. A., 'Cobden as Educator: The Free Trade Internationalism of Eduard Berstein, 1899–1914', *American Historical Review*, 88, 3 (June 1983), pp. 561–78

Fletcher, S., *Feminists and Bureaucrats. A Study in the Development of Girls' Education in the Nineteenth Century*, Cambridge, 1980

Floud, R., Watcher, K., Gregory, A., *Height, Health and History: Nutritional Status in the United Kingdom, 1750–1980*, Cambridge, 1990

Foner, E., *Thomas Paine and Revolutionary America*, New York, 1976

Free Men, Free Soil Free Land. The Ideology of the Republican Party on the Eve of the Civil War, New York, 1970

Foshee, A. W., 'Jeffersonian Political Economy and the Classical Republican Tradition: Jefferson, Taylor and the Agrarian Republic, *History of Political Economy*, 17, 4 (1950), pp. 523–50

Foster, J., *Class Struggle and the Industrial Revolution*, London, 1974

Fraser, D., *Urban Politics in Victorian England*, London, 1976

The Evolution of the British Welfare State, London, 1973

Fraser, D. (ed.), *A History of Modern Leeds*, Manchester, 1980

Fraser, W. H., *Trade Unions and Society, the Struggle for Acceptance, 1851–80*, London, 1974

Freeze, G. L., 'A Case of Stunted Anti-clericalism: Clergy and Society in Imperial Russia', *European Studies Review*, 13, 2 (April 1983), pp. 177–200

Frith, S., 'Socialization and Rational Schooling: Elementary Education in Leeds before 1870', in P. McCann (ed.), *Popular Education and Socialization in the Nineteenth Century*, London, 1977

Gadille, J., 'On French Anti-clericalism: Some Reflections', *European Studies Review*, 13, 2 (April 1983), pp. 127–44

Gardner, P., *The Lost Elementary Schools of Victorian England. The People's Education*, London, 1984

Garrard, J., *Leadership and Politics in Victorian Industrial Towns*, Manchester, 1983

Gash, N., *Sir Robert Peel*, London, 1972
Pillars of Government and Other Essays on State and Society, c.1770–1880, London, 1986

Gilbert, B. B., *The Evolution of National Insurance in Great Britain*, London, 1966

Gillespie, F. E., *Labor and Politics in England 1850–1870*, Durham, North Carolina, 1927

Gilley, S., 'The Garibaldi Riots of 1862', *Historical Journal*, XVI, 4 (1973), pp. 697–732

Ginzburg, C., *The Cheese and the Worms, The Cosmos of a Sixteenth-Century Miller*, London, 1980

Goldman, L., 'The Social Science Association, 1857–1886: A Context for Mid-Victorian Liberalism', *English Historical Review*, CI (1986), pp. 95–134

Goodlad, G., 'Gladstone and His Rivals: Popular Liberal Perceptions of the Party Leadership in the Political Crisis of 1885–86', in E. F. Biagini and A. J. Reid (eds.), *Currents of Radicalism, Popular Radicalism, Organized Labour, and Party Politics in Britain, 1850–1914*, Cambridge, 1991

Gosden, P. H. J., *The Friendly Societies in England 1815–75*, Manchester, 1961
Self-Help: Voluntary Associations in the Nineteenth Century, London, 1974

Gosh, P., 'Disraelian Conservatism: A Financial Approach', *English Historical Review*, XCIX (1984), pp. 268–96

Gray, R. Q., *The Labour Aristocracy in Victorian Edinburgh*, Oxford, 1976
The Aristocracy of Labour in Nineteenth Century Britain, London, 1981

Gregory, R., *The Miners and British Politics*, Oxford, 1968

Griggs, C., *The Trades Unions Congress and the Struggle for Education 1868–1925*, Lewes, Sussex, 1983

Groves, R. *Sharpen the Sickle!*, London 1949

Guérin, D., *La lutte de classe sus la première Republique*, vol.I, Paris, 1968

Gulley, E. E., *Joseph Chamberlain and English Social Politics*, New York, 1923
'Labour and Education', in K. D. Brown (ed.), *The First Labour Party 1906–1914*, London, 1985

Gwynn, S., and Tuckwell, G. M., *The Life of the Right Hon. Sir Charles W. Dilke, Bart., M.P.*, 2 vols., London, 1917

Halliday, R. J., *John Stuart Mill*, London, 1976

Hamer, D. A., *Liberal Politics in the Age of Gladstone and Rosebery*, Oxford, 1972

The Politics of Electoral Pressure, Hassocks, Sussex, 1977

'Gladstone: The Making of a Political Myth', *Victorian Studies*, XXII, 4 (1978), pp. 29–50

John Morley. Liberal Intellectual in Politics, Oxford, 1968

Hammond, J. L., *Gladstone and the Irish Nation*, London, 1964

Hanham, H. J., *Elections and Party Management. Politics in the Time of Disraeli and Gladstone*, Hassocks, Sussex, 1978 (1st edn 1959)

'Tra l'individuo e lo Stato', in P. Pombeni (a cura di), *La trasformazione politica nell'Europa liberale*, Bologna, 1986, pp. 93–102

The Nineteenth-Century Constitution, Cambridge, 1969

Hansen, M. H., *The Athenian Ecclesia*, Copenhagen, 1983

Harrison, B., 'Teetotal Chartism', *History*, LVIII (1973), pp. 193–217

Drink and the Victorians. The Temperance Question in England 1815–1872, London, 1971

'State Intervention and Moral Reform in Nineteenth-Century England', in P. Hollis (ed.), *Pressure from Without in Early Victorian England*, London, 1974

Harrison, R., *Before the Socialists*, London, 1965

Harrison (ed.), *Independent Collier*, Brighton, 1978

Hart, J., 'Nineteenth-Century Social Reform: A Tory Interpretation of History', *Past & Present*, no. 31 (1965), pp. 39–61

Harvie, C., *The Lights of Liberalism*, London, 1976

'Revolutions and the Rule of Law', in K. O. Morgan (ed), *The Oxford Illustrated History of Britain*, Oxford, 1984

The Lights of Liberalism, London, 1976

'Gladstonianism, the Provinces and Popular Political Culture 1860–1906', in R. Bellamy (ed.), *Victorian Liberalism*, London, 1990, pp. 152–74

Haupt, G., *Aspects of International Socialism 1871–1914*, Cambridge, 1986

Hay, D., 'Property, Authority and the Criminal Law', in E. P. Thompson et. al., *Albion's Fatal Tree*, London, 1975

Hay, J. R., *The Origins of the Liberal Welfare Reforms 1906–1914*, London, 1983

Hayes, W. A., *The Background and Passage of the Third Reform Act*, New York and London, 1982

Henderson, W., *Victorian Street Ballads. A Selection of Popular Ballads sold in the Streets in the Nineteenth Century*, London, 1937

Henderson, W. O., *The Lancashire Cotton Famine 1861–5*, Manchester 1934

Hennock, E. P., 'The Role of Religious Dissent in the Reform of Municipal Government in Birmingham', PhD thesis, Cambridge University 1956

'Finance and Politics in Urban Local Government in England, 1835–1900', *Historical Journal*, II, 6 (1963), pp. 212–25

Hill, C., *A Turbulent, Seditious and Factious People. John Bunyan and his Church*, Oxford, 1982

Hilton, B., 'Gladstone's Theological Politics', in M. Bentley and J. Stevenson (eds.), *High and Low Politics in Modern Britain*, Oxford, 1983, pp. 28–57

The Age of Atonement, Oxford, 1987

Hilton, R. H., 'The Origins of Robin Hood', *Past & Present*, 14 (Nov. 1958), pp. 30–54

Hinde, W., *Richard Cobden*, London, 1987

Hirst, F. W., *Gladstone as a Financier and an Economist*, London, 1931

Hobsbawm, E. J., *The Age of Capital*, London, 1975

Worlds of Labour. Further Studies in the History of Labour, London, 1984

Labouring Men, London, 1964

Industry and Empire, Harmondsworth, 1968

The Age of Empire, London, 1987

Hollenweger, W. J., *The Pentecostals*, London, 1972

Hollis, P., *Ladies Elect. Women in Local Government 1865–1914*, Oxford, 1987

Horn, P. (ed.), *Agricultural Trade Unionism in Oxfordshire, 1872–1881*, Banbury, Oxfords., 1974

Howarth, J., 'The French Socialists and Anti-clericalism: The Position of Eduard Vaillant and the Parti Socialiste Revolutionnaire', *International Review of Social History*, xxii (1977), pp. 165–83

Howell, R., 'Cromwell and the Imagery of Nineteenth Century Radicalism: the Example of Joseph Cowen', *Archaeologia Aeliana*, 5th Series, vol. 10, 1982, pp. 193–9

Howkins, A., *Poor Labouring Men, Rural Radicalism in Norfolk 1870–1923*, London, 1985

'"The Great Momentous Time": Radicalism and the Norfolk Farm Labourer, 1872–1923', PhD thesis, University of Essex, 1983

Hughes, J. Stuart, *Consciousness and Society*, Brighton, 1979

Hugins, W., *Jacksonian Democracy and the Working Class*, Stanford, 1960

Humphreys, A., 'G. W. M. Reynolds: Popular Literature and Popular Politics', *Victorian Periodical Review*, vol. 16, part 3/4. Fall 1983, pp. 79–89

Hurst, M., 'Liberal versus Liberal: The General Election of 1874 in Bradford and Sheffield', *Historical Journal*, xv, 4 (1972), pp. 669–713

Hurt, J. S., 'Drill, Discipline, and the Elementary School Ethos', in P. McCann (ed.), *Popular Education and Socialization in the Nineteenth Century*, London, 1977

Elementary Schooling and the Working Classes 1860–1918, London, 1979

Hutchins, B. L., and Harrison, A., *A History of Factory Legislation*, London, 1926

Hutchison, I. G. C., *A Political History of Scotland 1832–1824*, Edinburgh, 1986

Ingham, S. M., 'The Disestablishment Movement in England, 1868–1874', *Journal of Religious History*, III, (1964–65), pp. 38–60

Jalland, P., 'Mr Gladstone's Daughters', in B. L. Kinzer (ed.), *The Gladstonian Turn of Mind*, Toronto, London, Buffalo, 1986, pp. 97–122

Jenkins, T. A., 'Gladstone, the Whigs and the Leadership of the Liberal Party', *Historical Journal*, XXVII, 2 (1984), pp. 337–60
Gladstone, Whiggery, and the Liberal Party 1874–1886, Oxford, 1988

Johnson, R., ' "Really Useful Knowledge": Radical Education and Working-Class Culture 1790–1848', in J. Clarke, C. Critcher, R. Johnson (eds.), *Working Class Culture*, London, 1979

Jones, Aled, 'Workmen's Advocates: Ideology and Class in a Mid-Victorian Labour Newspaper System', in J. Shattock and M. Woolf (eds.), *The Victorian Periodical Press: Samplings and Soundings*, Leicester, 1982, pp. 297–316

Jones, A., *The Politics of Reform 1884*, Cambridge, 1972

Jones, B., and Keating, M., *Labour and the British State*, Oxford, 1985

Jones, D. K., 'Socialization and Social Science: Manchester Model Secular School 1854–1861', in P. McCann (ed.), *Popular Education and Socialization in the Nineteenth Century*, London, 1977
The Making of the English Education System 1851–81, London, 1977

Joyce, P., *Work, Society & Politics*, Brighton, 1980
Visions of the People. Industrial England and the Question of Class 1848–1914, Cambridge, 1991

Judd, D., *Radical Joe. A Life of Joseph Chamberlain*, London, 1977

Kent, J., *Holding the Fort*, London, 1978

Kent, S. K., *Sex and Suffrage in Britain, 1860–1914*, Princeton, 1987

Keynes, J. M., *The End of Laissez-Faire*, London, 1926

Kirk, N., 'The Growth of Working Class Reformism in Mid-Victorian England, London, 1985

Kitson Clarke, G. S. R., 'The Electorate and the Repeal of the Corn Laws', *Transactions of the Royal Historical Society*, 5th Series, I (1951)

Knox, W. W., 'Religion and the Scottish Labour Movement 1900–39', *Journal of Contemporary History*, 23 (Oct. 1988), pp. 609–30

Koss, S., *The Rise and Fall of the Political Press in Britain*, London, 1981

Kox, K., 'Geography, Social Context and Voting Behaviour in Wales, 1861–1951', in E. Allardt and S. Rokkan (eds.), *Mass Politics, Studies in Political Sociology*, New York and London, 1970

Lambert, R., 'Central and Local Relations in Mid-Victorian England: The Local Government Act Office, 1858–1871', *Victorian Studies*, VI, 2 (Dec. 1962), pp. 121–50

Lambert, R. J., 'A Victorian National Health Service: State Vaccination 1855–71', *Historical Journal*, V (1962), pp. 1–18

Lambert, W. R., *Drink and Sobriety in Victorian Wales, c.1820–c.1895*, Cardiff, 1983
'Some Working-Class Attitudes towards Organized Religion in Nine-

teenth Century Wales', in G. Parsons (ed.), *Religion in Victorian Britain*, IV *Interpretations*, Manchester, 1988, pp. 96–114

Lancaster, B., *Radicalism, Co-operation and Socialism: Leicester Working Class Politics 1860–1906*, Leicester, 1987

Laqueur, T. W., *Religion and Respectability. Sunday Schools and Working-Class Culture 1780–1850*, New Haven and London, 1976

Lawrence, E. P., *Henry George in the British Isles*, East Lansing, Michigan, 1957

Lawrence, J., 'Popular Politics and the Limitations of Party: Wolverhampton 1867–1900', in E. F. Biagini and A. J. Reid (eds.), *Currents of Radicalism*, Cambridge 1991, pp. 65–85

Layburn, K., and Reynolds, J., *Liberalism and the Rise of Labour 1890–1918*, London, 1984

Leach, H., *The Duke of Devonshire*, London, 1904

Leathers, C. G., 'Gladstonian Finance and the Virginian School of Public Finance: Comment', *History of Political Economy*, 18, 3 (1986)

Lindholm, C., *Charisma*, Oxford, 1990

Lloyd, T., *The General Election of 1880*, Oxford, 1968

Lovegrove, D. W., *Established Church, Sectarian People, Itinerancy and the Transformation of English Dissent 1780–1830*, Cambridge, 1988

Lubenow, W. C., *The Politics of Government Growth. Early Victorian Attitudes towards State Intervention, 1833–1848*, Newton Abbot, Devon, 1971

Lyttelton, A., 'An Old Church and a New State: Italian Anti-clericalism 1876–1915', *European Studies Review*, 13, 2 (April 1983), pp. 225–48

McCann, W. P., 'Popular Education, Socialization and Social Control: Spitafield 1812–1824', in *Popular Education and Socialization in the Nineteenth Century*, London, 1977

'Trade Unionists, Artisans and the 1870 Education Act', *British Journal of Educational Studies*, XVIII (1970), pp. 138–41

'Trade Unionist, Co-operative and Socialist Organizations in Relation to Popular Education 1870–1902', PhD thesis, Manchester University, 1960

Maccoby, S., *English Radicalism 1832–1852*, London, 1935

McCord, N., 'Ratepayers and Social Policy', in P. Thane (ed.), *The Origins of British Social Policy*, London, 1978

The Anti-Corn Law League 1838–46, London, 1968

Machin, G. I. T., *Politics and the Churches in Great Britain, 1832–1868*, Oxford, 1977

Politics and the Churches in Great Britain 1869 to 1921, Oxford, 1987

McClelland, K., 'Patrick Joyce, Work, Society and Politics', *History Workshop*, 11 (1981), pp. 169–73

McCready, H. W., 'British Labour and the Royal Commission on Trades' Unions, 1867–69', *University of Toronto Quarterly*, XXIV (1955), pp. 390–410

'The British Labour Lobby, 1867–1875', *Canadian Journal of Economic and Political Science*, XXII (1956), pp. 141–60

McGill, B., 'Francis Schnadhurst and Liberal Party Organization', *Journal of Modern History*, vol.34 no. 1 (1962), pp. 19–39

McHugh, P., *Prostitution and Victorian Social Reform*, London, 1980

McIntire, C. T., *England against the Papacy, 1858–61*, Cambridge, 1983

MacIntosh, W. H., 'The Agitation for the Disestablishment of the Church of England in the Nineteenth Century (Excluding Wales) with Special Reference to the Minutes and Papers of the Liberation Society', DPhil thesis, Oxford University, 1956

McKay, D., 'Joseph Cowen e il Risorgimento', *Rassegna storica del Risorgimento*, 51 (1964), pp. 5–26

McKibbin, R., 'Why was there no Marxism in Great Britain?', *English Historical Review*, XCIX (1984), pp. 297–331

The Evolution of the Labour Party 1910–1924, Oxford, 1986 [1st edn 1974]

MacKintosh, W. H., *Disestablishment and the Labour Movement*, London, 1972

MacDonagh, O., *Early Victorian Government, 1830–1870*, London, 1977

McLeod, H., *Religion and the People in Western Europe 1789–1970*, Oxford, 1981

Religion and the Working Class in Nineteenth-Century Britain, London, 1984

Class and Religion in the Late Victorian City, London, 1974

MacPherson, C. B., *The Political Theory of Possessive Individualism: Hobbes to Locke*, Oxford, 1962

McWilliam, R., 'Radicalism and Popular Culture: the Tichborne Case and the Politics of Fair Play, 1876–86', in E. F. Biagini and A. J. Reid (eds.), *Currents of Radicalism*, Cambridge 1991, pp. 44–64

Maehl, W. H. jr., 'The Northeastern Miners' Struggle for the Franchise, 1872–74', *International Review of Social History*, XX (1975), Part 2, pp. 198–219

'Gladstone, the Liberals and the Election of 1874', *Bulletin of the Institute of Historical Research*, XXXVI (1963), pp. 53–69

Magnus, P., *Gladstone. A Biography*, London, 1978 (1st edn 1954)

Magraw, R., *France 1815–1914 The Bourgeois Century*, Oxford, 1983

Mallinson, V., *Power and Politics in Belgian Education 1815–1961*, London, 1963

Manson, B. J., 'The Part Played in British Social and Political Life by the Protestant Nonconformists between the Years 1832 and 1859, with Special Reference to the Disestablishment of the Church of England', MA thesis, Southampton University, 1956

Marsh, P., *The Discipline of Popular Government*, Brighton, 1978

Marx, L., *The Machine in the Garden. Technology and the Pastoral Ideal in America*, New York, Oxford, 1964

Mason, B. J., 'The Rise of Combative Dissent 1832–1859', MA thesis, Southampton University, 1958

Mason, J. W., 'Thomas MacKay: The Anti-socialist Philosophy of the Charity Organization Society', in K. D. Brown (ed.), *Essays in Anti-Labour History*, London, 1974

Mather, F. C., 'The Government and the Chartists', in A. Briggs (ed.), *Chartist Studies*, London, 1978 (1st edn 1959), pp. 372–406

Mather, F. C. (ed.), *Chartism and Society*, London, 1980

Mathews, H. F., *Methodism and the Education of the People 1791–1851*, London n.d. [but 1949]

Matsumura, T., *The Labour Aristocracy Revisited*, Manchester, 1983

Matthew, H. C. G., McKibbin, R. I., Kay, J., 'The Franchise Factor in the Rise of the Labour Party', *English Historical Review*, XCI (1976), pp. 723–52

Matthew, H. C. G., *Gladstone 1809–1874*, Oxford, 1986

'Rhetoric and Politics in Great Britain, 1860–1950', in P. J. Waller (Ed.), *Politics and Social Change. Essays Presented to A. F. Thompson*, Oxford, 1987, pp. 34–58

'Disraeli, Gladstone, and the Policy of Mid-Victorian Budgets', *Historical Journal*, XXII, 3 (1979), pp. 615–43

'Gladstone, Vaticanism, and the Question of the East', in D. Baker (ed.), *Religious Motivation: Biographical and Sociological Problems for the Church Historian*, Oxford, 1978

Mayor, S., *The Churches and the Labour Movement*, London, 1967

Medick, H., 'Plebeian Culture in the Transition to Capitalism', in R. Samuel and G. Stedman Jones (eds.), *Culture, Ideology and Politics*, London, 1982

Michels, R., *Political Parties: A Sociological Study of the Oligarchical Tendency of Modern Democracy*, London, 1915

Milne, M., *The Newspapers of Northumberland and Durham*, Newcastle-on-Tyne, s.d. [but 1977]

Moltman, J., *Experiment Hope*, London, 1975

Money, J., 'Taverns, Coffee Houses and Clubs: Local Policy and Popular Articulacy in the Birmingham Area, in the Age of the American Revolution', *Historical Journal*, XIV 1 (1971), pp. 15–47

Morgan, K. O., 'Gladstone and Wales', *Welsh History Review*, I, 1 (1960), pp. 65–82

Wales in British Politics 1868–1922, Cardiff, 1963

Wales 1880–1980, Rebirth of a Nation, Oxford, 1982

Moore, D. C., *The Politics of Deference*, Brighton, 1976

Moore, R., *Pitmen, Preachers and Politics*, Cambridge, 1974

Morris, R. J., 'Samuel Smiles and the Genesis of Self-Help: the Retreat to a Petit Bourgeois Utopia', *Historical Journal*, XXIV, 1 (1981), pp. 89–109

Mosse, G. L., *Masses and Man: Nationalist and Fascist Perceptions of Reality*, New York, 1980

The Nationalization of the Masses, New York, 1975

Moyes, W. A., *The Banner Book*, Newcastle, 1974

Munson, J. E. B., 'The London School Board Election of 1894: A Study in Victorian Religious Controversy', *British Journal of Educational Studies*, XXIII, 1 (1975)

Muris, C., 'The Northern Reform Union, 1858–1862', MA thesis, University of Durham, 1959

Murray, B. K., 'The Politics of the "People's Budget"', *Historical Journal*, XVI, 3 (1973), pp. 555–70

The People's Budget 1909–10, Oxford, 1980

Murray, M., 'Child Labour in the Northumberland and Durham Coalfield during the Early Nineteenth Century', BA dissertation, Cambridge University, 1987

Musson, A. E., *The Congress of 1868. The Origins and Establishment of the Trades Union Congress*, London, 1982 (1st edn 1955)

Neale, R. S., *Writing Marxist History*, Oxford, 1985

Neuburg, V. E., *Popular Literature. A History and Guide, from the Beginning of Printing to the Year 1897*, London, 1977

Newton, J. S., 'Edward Miall and the Diocese of Durham: The Disestablishment Question in the North-East in the Nineteenth Century', *Durham University Journal*, 72 (June 1980), pp. 164–65

Nossiter, T. J., *Influence, Opinion, and Political Idioms in Reformed England*, Brighton, 1975

Obelkevich, J., *Religion and Rural Society: South Lindsey 1825–1875*, Oxford, 1976

O'Leary, C., *The Elimination of Corrupt Practices in British Elections 1868–1911*, Oxford, 1962

Ostrogorski, M., *Democracy and the Organization of Political Parties*, vol.1, London, 1902

Palmer, R. R., 'Popular Democracy in the French Revolution', *French Historical Studies*, 1 (1958–60), pp. 445–469

Parris, H., *Government and the Railways in Nineteenth Century Britain*, London, 1965

Parry, J. P., *Democracy and Religion, Gladstone and the Liberal Party 1867–1875*, Cambridge, 1986

'Religion and the Collapse of Gladstone's First Government, 1870–1874', *Historical Journal*, XXV, 1 (1982), pp. 71–101

Parsons, F. D., 'Thomas Hare and the Victorian Proportional Representation Movement, 1857–1888', PhD thesis, Cambridge University, 1990

Passerin d'Entreves, E., 'Le "religioni del progresso" nell'eta' romantica e il vangelo politico-religioso di Giuseppe Mazzini (1830–6)', *Vita e pensiero*, LII (1965), pp. 248–68, 354–68

Pearsall, L., *The Worm in the Bud*, London, 1969

Pelling, H., *Popular Politics and Society in Late Victorian Britain*, London, 1968

Social Geography of British Elections, London, 1967

Origins of the Labour Party, Oxford, 1983 [1st edn 1954]

Popular Politics and Society in Late Victorian Britain, London, 1968

Peterson, M. D., *The Jefferson Mind in the American Image*, New York, 1960

Petrella, F., 'Individual, Group or Government? Smith, Mill and Sidgwick', *History of Political Economy*, 2, 1, pp. 152–76

Pickering, P. A., 'Class without words: symbolic communication in the Chartist movement', *Past & Present*, 112, (August 1986), pp. 144–62

Pigou, A. C. (ed.), *Memorials of Alfred Marshall*, London 1925

Pirenne, H., *Histoire du Belgique*, vol.7, Brussels, 1932

Pitkin, H. F., *The Concept of Representation*, Berkeley and Los Angeles, 1967

Plumb, J. H., 'The Growth of the Electorate in England from 1600 to 1715', *Past & Present*, XLV (1969), pp. 90–116

Pollard, S., 'Introduction' to *The Sheffield Outrages*, London, 1971

Pombeni, P., 'Ritorno a Birmingham. La "nuova organizzazione" politica di Joseph Chamberlain e l'origine della forma partito contemporanea', *Ricerche di storia politica*, III (1988), pp. 37–62

Powell, D., 'The Liberal Ministers and Labour, 1892–1895', *History*, LXVIII (1983), pp. 408–26

Prothero, I., *Artisans and Politics in Nineteenth-Century London. John Gast and His Times*, London, 1979

Pugh, M., *The Making of Modern British Politics 1867–1939*, Oxford, 1982

Purdue, A. W., 'Arthur Henderson and Liberal, Liberal–Labour and Labour Politics in the North-East of England, 1892–1903', *Northern History*, XI (1976 for 1975), pp. 195–217

Read, D., *England 1868–1914*, London, 1979

Reid, A. J., 'Intelligent Artisans and Aristocrats of Labour: The Essays of Thomas Wright', in J. Winter (ed.), *The Working Class in Modern British History*, Cambridge, 1983

'Old Unionism Reconsidered: the Radicalism of Robert Knight 1870–1900', in E. F. Biagini and A. J. Reid (eds.) *Currents of Radicalism*, Cambridge 1991, pp. 214–43

Restaino, F., *J. S. Mill e la cultura filosofica britannica*, Florence, 1968

Richards, N. J., 'Religious Controversy and the School Boards 1870–1902', *British Journal of Educational Studies*, XVIII, 2, (June 1970), pp. 180–96

Robbins, K., *Nineteenth-Century Britain, Integration and Diversity*, Oxford, 1988

John Bright, London, 1979

Robbins, L., *The Theory of Economic Policy in English Classical Political Economy*, London, 1952

Roberts, B. C., *The Trades Union Congress 1868–1921*, London, 1958

Roberts, D., 'Tory Paternalism and Social Reform in Early Victorian England', *American Historical Review*, 63, 2 (1957–8), pp. 323–37

Roland, D., 'The Struggle for the Elementary Education Act and Its Implementation 1870–1873', B.Litt thesis, Oxford University, 1957

Roe, M., *Kenealy and the Tichborne Case. A Study in Mid-Victorian Populism*, Carlton, Victoria 1974

Romanelli, R., 'Autogoverno, funzioni pubbliche, classi dirigenti locali: un'indagine del 1869', *Passato e presente*, 4 (1983), pp. 35–83

Romano, A., *Storia del movimento socialista in Italia*, vol.ii, *L'egemonia borghese e la rivolta libertaria 1871–1882*, Bari, 1966

Roper, H., 'W. E. Forster's Memorandum of 21 October, 1869: A Re-examination', *British Journal of Educational Studies*, xxi, 1 (Feb. 1973), pp. 64–75

Roth, G., *The Social-Democrats in Imperial Germany*, Totowa, NJ, 1963

Royle, E., *Victorian Infidels*, Manchester, 1974

Radicals, Republicans and Secularists, Manchester, 1980

'Mechanics Institutes and the Working Classes, 1840–1860', *Historical Journal*, xiv, 2 (1971), pp. 305–22

Rubinstein, D., 'Socialization and the London School Board 1870–1904: Aims, Methods, and Public Opinion', in P. McCann (ed.), *Popular Education and Socialization in the Nineteenth Century*, London, 1977

'The Independent Labour Party and the Yorkshire Miners: the Barnsley By-election of 1897', *International Review of Social History*, xxiii (1978), Part 1, pp. 102–176

Rubinstein, W. D., 'The End of "Old Corruption" in Britain 1780–1855', *Past & Present*, 101 (1983), pp. 55–86

'New Men of Wealth and the Purchase of Land in Nineteenth-Century Britain', *Past & Present*, 92 (1981), pp. 125–47

Rudé, G., *Wilkes and Liberty*, London, 1983 (1st edn 1962)

Ruthven, M., *The Divine Supermarket. Travels in Search of the Soul of America*, London, 1989

Salvemini, G., *Mazzini*, London, 1956

Samuel, R., 'Liberalism', *History Workshop*, 17 (1984), pp. 1–2

St John Packe, M., *The Life of John Stuart Mill*, London, 1954

Sanderson, M., 'Education and Factory in Industrial Lancashire', *Economic History Review*, 2nd Series xx (1967), pp. 266–79

Sarti, R., *Long Live the Strong. A History of Rural Society in the Appennine Mountains*, Amherst, Conn. 1985

Satre, J. L., 'Thomas Burt and the Crisis of Late-Victorian Liberalism in the North East', *Northern History*, 22 (1987), pp. 174–93

Saville, J., *1848. The British State and the Chartist Movement*, Cambridge, 1987

Schumpeter, J. A., *History of Economic Analysis*, London, 1954

Schwartz, P., *The New Political Economy of J. S. Mill*, London, 1972

Scotland, N., *Methodism and the Revolt of the Fields*, Gloucester, 1981

Semmel, B., *Imperialism and Social Reform. English Social Imperial Thought, 1895–1914*, London, 1960

The Governor Eyre Controversy, London, 1962

Shannon, R. T., *Gladstone and the Bulgarian Agitation 1876*, Hassocks, Sussex, 1975 (1st edn 1963)

Gladstone, vol.1, 1809–65, London, 1982

'Gladstone, la Chiesa cattolico romana e l'Italia', in R. Gherardi and N. Matteucci (eds.), *Marco Minghetti statista e pensatore politico*, Bologna, 1988, pp. 161–87

'Midlothian 100 Years After', in P. J. Jagger, (ed.), *Gladstone, Politics and Religion*, London, 1985

Shepherd, J. S., 'The Lib-Labs and English Working-Class Politics, 1874–1906', PhD thesis, University of London, 1980

'James Bryce and the Recruitment of Working-Class Magistrates in Lancashire, 1892–94', *Bulletin of the Institute of Historical Research*, LII 126 (Nov. 1979), pp. 155–69

'Labour and Parliament: the Lib-Labs as First Working-Class MPs, 1885–1906', in E. F. Biagini and A. J. Reid (eds.), *Currents of Radicalism, Popular Radicalism, Organized Labour and Party Politics in Britain 1850–1914*, Cambridge, 1991, pp. 187–213

Shiman, L. L., *Crusade against Drink in Victorian England*, London, 1988

Silver, H., *The Concept of Popular Education. A Study of Ideals and Social Movements in the Early Nineteenth Century*, London, 1965

English Education and the Radicals 1780–1850, London, 1975

Silver, P. and H., *The Education of the Poor. The History of a National School 1824–1974*, London, 1974

Simon, A., 'Church Disestablishment as a Factor in the General Election of 1885', *Historical Journal*, XVIII, 4 (1975), pp. 791–820

Skidelski, R., *Politicians and the Slump. The Labour Government of 1929–1931*, London, 1967

Smith, D., *Conflict and Compromise. Class Formation in English Society 1830–1914. A Comparative Study of Birmingham and Sheffield*, London, 1982

Smith, D. M., *Garibaldi*, London, 1957

Smith, F., *A History of English Elementary Education 1760–1902*, London, 1931

Smith, F. B., *The Making of the Second Reform Bill*, Cambridge, 1966

Smith, J., 'Labour Tradition in Glasgow and Liverpool', *History Workshop*, 9, 17 (1984), pp. 32–56

Smith, P., *Disraelian Conservatism and Social Reform*, London, 1967

Smout, T. C., *A Century of the Scottish People 1830–1950*, London, 1987

Soboul, A., *Movimento popolare e rivoluzione borghese. I sanculotti parigini nell'anno II*, Bari, 1959

Les sansculottes parisiens en l'An II, Paris, 1962

Soldani, S., 'Contadini, operai e "popolo" nella revoluzione del 1848–49 in Italia', *Studi storici*, XIV, 3 (July–Sept. 1973), pp. 557–613

Spain, J., 'Trade Unionists, Gladstonian Liberals, and the Labour Law Reforms of 1875', in E. F. Biagini and A. J. Reid (eds.), *Currents of Radicalism*, Cambridge 1991, pp. 109–33

Spriano, P., 'Introduzione' to L. Einaudi, *Le lotte del lavoro*, Turin, 1972

Springall, L. M. (ed.), *Labouring Life in Norfolk Villages 1834–1914*, London, 1934

Stedman Jones, G., *Outcast London*, London, 1984 (1st edn 1971)

Languages of Class, Cambridge, 1983

Steele, E. D., 'John Stuart Mill, and the Irish Question: Reform and the Integrity of the Empire, 1865–1870', *Historical Journal*, XIII, 3 (1970), pp. 419–50

Stephens, W. R., *Education, Literacy and Society 1830–1870: the Geography of Diversity in Provincial England*, Manchester, 1987

Stigant, P., 'Wesleyan Methodism and Working-Class Radicalism in the North, 1722–1821', *Northern History*, VI (1971), pp. 98–117

Stokes, E. T., 'Bureaucracy and Ideology: Britain and India in the Nineteenth Century', *Transactions of the Royal Historical Society*, XXX (1980), pp. 131–56

Sutherland, G., *Policy-Making in Elementary Education 1870–1895*, Oxford, 1973

Tanner, D., 'The Parliamentary Electoral System the "Fourth" Reform Act and the Rise of Labour in England and Wales', *Bulletin of the Institute of Historical Research*, LVI, 134 (1983), pp. 205–19

Taylor, A. J., *Laissez-faire and State Intervention in Nineteenth Century Britain*, London, 1972

Taylor, A. J. P., *The Trouble Makers*, Harmondsworth, 1985

Taylor, M., 'Radicalism and Patriotism, 1848–1859, Cambridge Ph.D. Thesis, 1989

Temmel, M. R., 'Liberal Versus Liberal, 1874: W. E. Forster, Bradford, and Education', *Historical Journal*, XVIII, 3 (1975), pp. 611–22

Thane, P., 'The Working Class and State "Welfare" in Britain, 1880–1914', *Historical Journal*, XXVII, 4 (1984), pp. 877–900

Tholfsen, T., *Working-Class Radicalism in Mid-Victorian England*, London, 1976

'The Origins of the Birmingham Caucus', *Historical Journal*, 2(1951), pp. 161–84

Thompson, A. F., 'Gladstone's Whips and the General Election of 1868', *English Historical Review*, 63 (1948), pp. 189–200

Thompson, D. M., 'The Liberation Society, 1844–1868', in P. Hollis (ed.), *Pressure from Without in Early Victorian England*, London, 1974

Thompson, D. M. (ed.), *Nonconformity in the Nineteenth Century*, London, 1972

Thompson, D., *The Chartists*, London, 1984

Thompson, D. and Epstein, J., *The Chartist Experience*, London, 1982

Thompson, D. F., *John Stuart Mill and Representative Government*, Princeton, 1976

Thompson, E. P., *Whigs & Hunters*, London, 1975

'Introduction', Ashby, M. K., *Joseph Ashby of Tysoe 1859–1919*, London, 1974

The Making of the English Working Class, Harmondsworth, 1981 [1st edn 1963]

Thompson, F., *Lark Rise to Candleford*, Oxford, 1945

Thompson, F. M. L., *English Landed Society in the Nineteenth Century*, London 1963

Thompson, N. W., *The People's Science. The Popular Political Economy of Exploitation and Crisis, 1816–1834*, Cambridge, 1984

Thompson, P., *Socialists, Liberals and Labour. The Struggle for London 1885–1914*, London, 1967

Thorold, A. L., *The Life of Henry Labouchere*, London, 1913

Tiller, K., 'Late Chartism in Halifax 1847–58', in J. Epstein and D. Thompson, *The Chartist Experience*, London, 1982, pp. 311–44

Tilly, C., *GBS+GLC=?, Evidence on British Contention, 1828–1834*, New York, New School for Social Research, The Working Papers Series, No. 18, July 1985

Trevelyan, G. M., *Garibaldi and the Making of Italy*, London, 1912

The Life of John Bright, London, 1925

Tucker, R. C., 'The Theory of Charismatic Leadership', *Daedalus*, Summer 1968, pp. 731–56

Ullman, J. C., 'The Warp and Woof of Parliamentary Politics in Spain, 1808–1939: Anti-clericalism Versus "Neo-Catholicism"', *European Studies Review*, 13, 2 (April 1983), pp. 154–65

Vicinus, M., *Broadsides of the Industrial North*, Newcastle upon Tyne, 1975

Vincent, D., *Bread, Knowledge and Freedom. A Study of Nineteenth-Century Working-Class Autobiography*, London, 1982

Vincent, J. R., *The Formation of the British Liberal Party 1857–68*, Harmondsworth, 1972 (1st edn 1966)

Viola, P., *Il trono vuoto*, Turin, 1989

Vivarelli, R., *Il fallimento del liberalismo*, Bologna, 1981

Vogel, U., 'The Land Question: A Liberal Theory of Communal Property', *History Workshop*, 27 (Spring 1979), pp. 106–36

Waitt, E. I., 'John Morley, Joseph Cowen and Robert Spence Watson. Liberal Divisions in Newcastle Politics 1873–1895', PhD thesis, Manchester University, 1972

Wald, K. D., *Crosses on the Ballot: Pattern of British Voters Alignement since 1885*, Princeton, 1983

Walkowitz, J. R., *Prostitution and Victorian Society*, Cambridge, 1980

Waller, P. J., *Democracy and Sectarianism*, Liverpool, 1981

Ward, W. R., 'The Tithe Question in England in the Early Nineteenth Century', *Journal of Ecclesiastical History*, XXVI, 1 (1965), pp. 67–81

Wardle, D., *Education and Society in Nineteenth Century Nottingham*, Cambridge, 1971

Wearmouth, R. F., *Methodism and the Working-Class Movement of England 1800–1880*, London, 1937

Methodism and the Struggle of the Working Classes 1850–1900, Leicester, 1954

Weaver, S. A., *John Fielden and the Politics of Popular Radicalism 1832–1847*, Oxford, 1987

Webb, B., *Our Partnership*, ed. B. Drake and M. I. Cole, London, 1948

Webb, R. K., *The British Working-Class Reader 1790–1848. Literary and Social Tensions*, London, 1955

Webb, S and B., *English Local Government*, vol.i, *The Parish and the County*, London, 1963

History of Trade Unionism, London, 1920

Weber, M., *The Theory of Social and Economic Organization*, New York, 1964

Max Weber. Selections in Translation, ed. W. G. Runciman and E. Matthews, Cambridge, 1978

Politics as a Vocation, Philadelphia, 1965

The Protestant Ethic and the Spirit of Capitalism, London, 1965

'Die protestantischen Sekten und der Geist des Kapitalismus', in *Gesammelte Aufsatze zur Religionsociologie*, Tübingen, 1934

West, E. G., 'The Role of Education in Nineteenth-Century Doctrines of Political Economy', *British Journal of Educational Studies*, xii, 2 (May 1964), pp. 161–65

Education and the State, A Study in Political Economy, London, 1965

Education and the Industrial Revolution, London, 1975

Wiener, M. J., *English Culture and the Decline of the Industrial Spirit 1850–1980*, Cambridge, 1981

Williams, G. A., *Artisans and Sans-culottes. Popular Movements in France and Britain during the French Revolution*, London, 1973

'Druids and Democrats: Organic Intellectuals and the First Welsh Radicalism', in R. Samuel and G. Stedman Jones (eds.), *Culture, Ideology and Politics*, London, 1982

Williamson, B., *Class, Culture and Community. A Biographical Study of Social Change in Mining*, London, 1982

Willner, A. R., and Willner, D., 'The Rise and Role of Charismatic Leaders', in *The Annals of the American Academy of Political and Social Science*, 358 (March 1965), pp. 77–88

Winter, J., *Robert Lowe*, Toronto, 1976

Wohl, A. S., *The Eternal Slum*, London, 1977

Wolfe, D. M. (ed.), *Levellers Manifestoes of the Puritan Revolution*, London, 1967

Wright, D. G., 'Leeds Politics and the American Civil War', *Northern History*, ix (1974), pp. 96–122

Yeo, E., 'Christianity and Chartist Struggle 1838–42', *Past & Present*, No. 91 (1981) pp. 109–39

Young, G. M., and Handcock, W. D. (eds.), *English Historical Documents*, vol.xii, 1, London, 1956

Zahler, H. S., *Eastern Working Men and the National Land Policy 1829–62*, New York, 1941

Index

Abraham, W. ('Mabon') (1842–1922), 332–3, 351–2, 357, 370, 392
Adams, W. E (1832–1906) *see* 'Ironside'
Afghan War, 124–5
agricultural labourers, 13, 32, 52, 59–60, 90, 186; and disestablishment, 248–51; and the franchise, 268 and n.71, 269–70, 274, 278; and the Liberal party, 293; and local government, 325–8
Annand, J., 24,
America *see* United States
American Civil War, 17, 69–81, 372, 374 and n.21, 375, 376, 378; and democracy, 258; and Emancipation Proclaim (1863), 70, 377; and the rights of labour, 70 and n.235, 72 and n.251, 77, 78, 80, 82; *see also* United States
American Revolution, 10, 72
Annuities Bill (1864), 85
anti-clericalism, 6, 18, 54, 176, 213–14, 217–22, 249–51, 345 n.217; and liberty, 253; and the Roman Catholic Church, 217–28, 233, 345 n.217; *see also* church rates, tithe, education
Anti-Corn Law League, 32, 38, 98 and n.85
Applegarth, R. (1834–1924), 71, 193, 198 n.48, 202, 205, 340 n.184
Arch, J. (1826–1919), 9, 14, 35, 56, 59–60, 87 n.19, 188, 250, 280, 288 and n.168, 291, 292, 298–9, 299 n.223, 306, 324, 325–6, 333, 394, 416; and charismatic politics, 353–6, 369, 388, 392, 423; and labour representation, 353–6, 354 n.259, 370
aristocracy, hostility to, 1, 18, 45, 52–5, 57, 74 n.270, 77, 133, 186; and emigration, 90 n.40, 91; and 'feudalism', 53–4; and Ireland, 53; and temperance, 176
Arminianism, 35

Armstrong, Chester, 49
army, 1, 424
army, citizens' *see* volunteer army
artisans, 11, 116; and education, 193, 201 n.67; and peasant farmers, 88 n.21
Artizans Dwellings Act (1875), 180
Artizans' and Labourers' Dwelling Company, 180 n.245
Ashby, J., 355
Ashton, T., 340 n.184
Ashton under Lyme, 262
Aspromonte, 223, 373
Athens, 69 and n.228, 314, 335
Australia, 90
Austria, 95, 222, 396
Avanti, l', 21

Bagehot, W. (1826–77), 383–4
Baines, E. (1800–90), 208
ballot, 271 n.89, 294–5; Ballot Act (1872), 294
Bamford, S., 83, 263–4, 271
banks, popular hostility to, 108 n.157
Baptists, 15 and n.93, 31, 79, 207, 251
Barnes, G. (1859–1940), 80, 392
Barnsley, 321, 332
Barrow, L., 219
Battersea, 367
Beaconsfield, Lord *see* Disraeli
Beales, D. E. D., 5
Beales, Edmund, 236–7, 238–9, 273–6
Beckwith, T., 286–7
Bedlington, 281, 347–9
Beesly, E. S., 64, 76, 228
Bee-Hive, 22, 25, 64, 76, 85, 86, 101, 102, 110, 114, 162, 163, 176, 190, 191, 199–200, 207, 239, 242 n.308, 268, 273, 275, 290 n.182, 308, 338, 339, 345, 364, 374

463

Hampshire, 37

Hampden, J., 90, 313

Harcourt, Sir W. G. V. (1827–1904), 155–6, 237, 403

Hardie, J. Keir (1856–1915), 41, 233, 358, 360, 424

Hardenberg, K. von (1750–1822), 190

Hare, T., and CLAA, 151 n.74, 315, 316 n.18

Harney, G. J. (1817–97), 42, 72, 76, 81, 385 n.80

Harrison, B., 10, 177

Harrison, F. (1831–1923), 63–4, 149, 209, 249, 268 n.71

Harrison, R., 63, 70, 71, 150 n.62, 191, 268

Hartington, Lord (1833–1908), 22, 129, 412, 413, 414 and n.271

Hartwell, R., 73, 78, 237, 238, 339 n.175

Hawarden, 396, 398 and n.170, 402, 408

Hawick, 406–7

Hawker, J., 217, 403

Hearn, L., 340 n.184

Hebrides, 410

Henderson, A. (1863–1935), 361

Hepburn, T., 38 n.42

Highlands, 332, 400

Hill, C., 37

Hobhouse, Sir J. C., 325

Hobsbawm, E. J., 7, 8,

Holborn, 237

Hollis, P., 10

Holyoake, G. J. (1817–1906), 62, 141 n.15, 231, 339 n.175, 380; and co-operation, 140; and Paris Commune, 65

'home colonization' *see* land reform

Home Rule, 304, 305, 347, 363 nn.311–12, 423–4

Hornby *v.* Close judgement, 149

household franchise *see* franchise

House of Commons, 118, 121, 125, 138, 156, 221, 230, 239, 300, 307, 331, 344, 347, 385, 402, 404, 423

House of Lords, 105, 113, 156, 241, 299–303, 401, 423

Howell, G. (1833–1910), 48, 49, 71, 72 n.254, 94, 102 n.112, 109–10, 112, 116, 150, 177, 202, 298 n.225, 316, 317, 374 n.25; and the 'caucus', 333–4, 336, 337; and disestablishment, 243, 247; and factory laws, 171, 173; and franchise reform, 273, 275 and n.104, 276–7, 280, 290 n.177, 305–6 and n.278, 308–9; and labour laws, 151 n.71, 153, 156–8, 162 n.137, 163; and labour representation, 338–40, 339

n.175, 340 n.184, 342 n.200, 344, 357–8, 366, 367–8, n.337, 370; and land reform, 189–90; and reform of local goverment, 183 and n.262

Howkins, A., 6

Huddersfield, 240

Hughes, J., Bishop of St. Asaph, 386 n.83

Hughes, T. (1822–96), 76, 149

Hull, 332

Hungary, 378

Hunt, H., 272, 336, 379

Hurt, J. S., 199, 216

Hyde Park, 221, 261, 301 and n.248, 373

income tax *see* taxation

'independence', popular value of, 6, 14, 59–60, 84–93, 96, 194–5, 252, 272, 293–4 and nn.196, 198; and co-operation, 84, 85 n.10, 139–44; and the franchise, 270–5, 279, 304 n.266; and friendly societies, 144–7; and trade unions, 84; *see also* peasant farmers, yeoman, Jeffersonians, Mill

Independent Labour Party (ILP), 13, 38

India, 121, 126, 227

International, First, 60–2, 73, 121, 225

International Democratic Association, 64 n.196

Ireland, 1, 16, 20, 53, 56, 58, 167, 187, 190, 233, 235, 240, 250, 357, 397; *see also* Irish, Roman Catholics

Irish, 116, 219, 223, 363 and n.312 and 314, 423–4; tenant farmers, 58

Irish Reform League, 237, 238

'Ironside' (W. E. Adams, 1832–1906), 24, 44, 65, 72, 119, 216, 221, 345 n.216, 347–8, 411, 412

ironworkers, 29

Israel, 79–80

Issachar, 13 n.79

Italy, 2, 12, 16, 47 n.97, 218 n.172, 223, 224–5, 226–7, 286, 320–1, 371 n.9, 378, 400 n.176

Jacksonians, 11, 17, 91 and n.45, 96, 108 n.157

Jacobins, 34, 50, 268, 303

Jefferson, T. (1743–1826), 86 and n.17

Jeffersonians, 11, 17, 93, 252, 314

Jenkins, T., 413 n.258, 414 n.269

Jerrold, Blanchard (1826–84), 22

Jesuits and clerical conspiracies, 222, 225–6, 225 n.214

Jesus Christ, 32, 33, 36, 38, 40, 240

Jews, 37, 123, 227 n.226, 236 n.276